BIRMINGHAM BYZANTINE AND OTTOMAN MONOGRAPHS

About the series

Birmingham Byzantine and Ottoman Monographs is a new series of studies devoted to all aspects of the history, culture and archaeology of the Byzantine and Ottoman worlds of the East Mediterranean region from the fifth to the twentieth century. It aims to provide a forum for the publication of work carried out by scholars while at the Centre for Byzantine, Ottoman and Modern Greek Studies at the University of Birmingham, or who are connected with the Centre and its research programmes.

About the volume

Few works exist in any language on Byzantine literature as literature and still fewer full-length studies of individual texts. This reading of the letter-collection (c.1090-c.1100) of Theophylact of Ochrid employs a variety of approaches in order to characterise a work which is both a literary artefact in a long Greek tradition and the only trace of a complex network of friends, colleagues, patrons and clients within Byzantine Bulgaria and and also within the empire as a whole. These letters are acknowledged to be of great importance for local economic and ecclesiastical history, relations with the Slavs and the arrival of the First Crusade, but have not hitherto been studied as an example of Byzantine letter-writing. This volume is a first attempt to place an epistolary text in a succession of literary and historical contexts which allow it to reveal insights into the mentality of the Byzantine elite, the function of literature in Byzantine society and the status of utterances in rhetorical and autobiographical texts at the time of the revival of fiction in Byzantium.

About the author

Margaret Mullett graduated in Medieval History and Medieval Latin at the University of Bimingham in 1970 and then studied for her doctorate there with Anthony Bryer. She has written on literacy, patronage, genre and friendship in Byzantine society and has edited books on the classical tradition, Alexios I Komnenos, the Forty Martyrs and two on eleventh-century monasticism; she is currently working on the processes of Byzantine letter-exchange and on eleventh- and twelfth-century literary society. From 1989 to 1996 she was Secretary of the Society for Promotion of Byzantine Studies. She was appointed to the Queen's University of Belfast in 1974, and is now Senior Lecturer in Byzantine Studies, Director of the Evergetis Project and General Editor of Belfast Byzantine Texts and Translations. She is currently a British Academy Research Reader.

For Michael

THEOPHYLACT OF OCHRID

THEOPHYLACT OF OCHRID

READING THE LETTERS OF A BYZANTINE ARCHBISHOP

Margaret Mullett

VARIORUM
1997

BIRMINGHAM BYZANTINE AND OTTOMAN MONOGRAPHS

Volume 2

General Editors

Anthony Bryer
John Haldon

Centre for Byzantine, Ottoman and Modern Greek Studies
University of Birmingham

This edition © 1997 by Margaret Mullett.

Published by   VARIORUM
                    Ashgate Publishing Limited
                    Gower House, Croft Road
                    Aldershot, Hampshire GU11 3HR

                    Ashgate Publishing Limited
                    Old Post Road
                    Brookfield, Vermont 05036
                    USA

ISBN 0 86078 549 1

The quotation on page 11 is from THE DIALOGIC IMAGINATION: FOUR ESSAYS by M.M. Bakhtin, edited by Michael Holquist, translated by Caryl Emerson and Michael Holquist, Copyright ©1981

Margaret Mullett has asserted her right under the Copyright, Designs and Patents Act 1988 to be identified as the author of this work

British Library Cataloguing-in-Publication Data
Mullett, Margaret
  Theophylact of Ochrid: reading the letters of a Byzantine Archbishop
  1. Theophylact of Ochrid - correspondence. 2. Byzantine letters - history and criticism.
  3. Byzantine literature - criticism, textual. I. Title.
  886'.02

US Library of Congress Cataloging-in-Publication Data
Mullett, Margaret
  Theophylact of Ochrid: reading the letters of a Byzantine Archbishop
  Margaret Mullett.
  p. cm. Includes bibliographical references and index. (Cloth.)
  1. Theophylactus, of Ochrida, Archbishop of Ochrida, c.1050-c.1130 - correspondence - History and criticism. 2. Orthodox Eastern Church - Balkan Peninsula - Bishops - Correspondence - History and criticism. 3. Byzantine Letters - History and criticism. I. Title.
  BX395.T48M85 1996   5-5063
  281.9'092-dc20   CIP

Printed in Great Britain by Galliard (Printers) Ltd, Great Yarmouth

Birmingham Byzantine and Ottoman Monographs
Volume 2

CHRONOLOGY

1088, 6 January	Theophylact's last known speech in Constantinople
1088-89	Appointment and enthronement at Ochrid
1091, Lent	Melissenos recruiting before the Pecheneg war
1091, 29 April	Battle of Lebounion
1092, spring	John Doukas replaced at Dyrrachion by John Komnenos
1093	Komnenian family dispute
1093-94	Cuman invasions
1094, 29 June	Diogenes plot
1094-95	Synod of Blachernai
1095	Alexios campaigning at Nicomedia
1095	Cuman invasions
1096-97	First Crusade crosses Macedonia
1097	First reference to Nikephoros Bryennios as *panhypersebastos*
1097, 10 June	Capture of Nicaea
1098, 3 June	Capture of Antioch
1099, 15 July	Capture of Jerusalem
1100	Capture of Bohemond
1101	Death of Anna Dalassene
1102-04	Death of *sebastokrator* Isaac
1103, 15 May	Theophylact attends *panegyris* of Achilleios at Prespa
1103, summer	Campaigns of Gregory Taronites in Pontos
1104, 19 April	Death of Adrian, Grand Domestic
1105, September-	Emperor and *augousta* based at Thessalonike
1106, February	Comet; emperor in Thessalonike from November
1106	Theophylact at Ekklesiai; Demetrios ill
1107	Death of Demetrios
1107	Edict on the reform of the clergy
1107, 9 October	Invasion of Bohemond
1108	Theophylact visits Constantinople, returns via Thessalonike (last datable letter)
1108, September	Treaty of Diabolis (Devol)
1109	Campaigns of Eumathios Philokales in Asia Minor
1110	Death of Cyril Phileotes
1111	Death of patriarch Nicholas
1112, Easter	Illness of the emperor
1112, before Sept.	Conversations with Grossolano
1112-13, winter	Emperor at Chersonesos
1113	Summer Turkish campaign: winter at Mt Papikion
1114	Conversations at Philippopolis
1115	Nikephoros Bryennios in charge of government
1116	Alexios's last campaign in Asia Minor
1117	Condemnation of Eustratios of Nicaea
1118, 15 August	Death of Alexios I Komnenos
1125/26	Poems on Symeon the New Theologian

There is a sharp and categorical boundary line between the actual world as source of representation and the world represented in the work. We must never forget this, we must never confuse—as has been done up to now and as is still often done—the *represented* world with the world outside the text (naive realism); nor must we confuse the author-creator of a work with the author as a human being (naive biographism), nor confuse the listener or reader of multiple and varied periods, recreating and renewing the text, with the passive listener or reader of one's own time (which leads to dogmatism in interpretation and evaluation). All such confusions are methodologically impermissible. But it is also impermissible to take this categorical boundary line as something absolute and impermeable (which leads to an oversimplified, dogmatic splitting of hairs). However forcefully the real and the represented world resist fusion, however immutable the presence of that categorical boundary line between them, they are nevertheless indissolubly tied up with each other and find themselves in continual mutual interaction; uninterrupted exchange goes on between them, similar to the uninterrupted exchange of matter between living organisms and the environment that surrounds them. As long as the organism lives, it resists a fusion with the environment, but if it is torn out of its environment, it dies. The work and the world represented in it enter the real world and enrich it, and the real world enters the work and its world as part of the process of its creation, as well as part of its subsequent life in a continual renewing of the work through the creative perception of listeners and readers.

Bakhtin, *The Dialogic Imagination*

CONTENTS

A note on using this book   ix
List of illustrations   x
Abbreviations   xi
Preface   xiv
Map of Theophylact's Letter-Network   xvi
Map of Theophylact's Bulgaria   xvii

1 Text and Context   1

2 Genre and Milieu
Issues of genre
  1 Epistolarity   11
  2 Evaluation   23
  3 Reception   31

Theophylact's milieux
  4 Eleventh-century Constantinople   43
  5 Byzantine Bulgaria   53
  6 Alexian Literature   69

3 Collection and Network (I)
Portrait of a collection
  1 Dating and Ordering   79
  2 Preoccupations and Concerns   98
  3 Rhetoric   133

4 Collection and Network (II)
Portrait of a network
  1 Detecting Theophylact's Network   163
  2 Theophylact's First Order Zone   178
  3 The Uses of Network   201

5 Author and Man
Theophylact the author
  1 Theophylact as *Auctor*   223
  2 Letters in the Oeuvre   230
  3 Other People's Letters   247

Theophylact the man
  4 The Constantinopolitan   261
  5 The Bulgarian   266
  6 The Exile   274

6 Context and Text   279

The Collection   291
The Network   347

Tables   383
I   Concordance of Numbers   385
II   Lost Letters   387
III   Letters referred to   390
IV   Silence referred to   391
V   Communication Problems   391
VI   Documents requested   392
VII   Letters received   394
VIII   Bearers of the Letters   398
IX   Gifts in the Letters   401
X   Journeys in the Letters   403

Bibliography   409
Index   425

A NOTE ON USING THIS BOOK

The titles of (only) works which cited more than once in any chapter in the text, or are given in 'The Collection' or 'The Network' by short title may be found in full in the Bibliography, 409-424. References to people (including Theophylact), places and concepts are listed in the 'Index', 425-441. References to discussions throughout the book of individual letters of Theophylact are gathered in 'The Collection,' 291-346, under Gautier's numbers. A concordance of numbering of the letters may be found as Table I, 385-386. Members of Theophylact's network are identified by a bracketed number in bold; chapters 4.2 and 4.3, 178-222, with figs. 1-7, explain and illustrate the network; 'The Network', 347-381, lists the members. When referring to a letter of Theophylact, I have made it my normal practice as a point of principle (Demetrios, *Peri Hermeneias*, 124) to follow Gautier's number with the name of the recipient. Space has not allowed me to do the same for other letter-collections, except where absolutely necessary. Place-names are transliterated in their most familiar form, or, where more than one form is familiar, in the form closest to Theophylact's usage.

LIST OF ILLUSTRATIONS

Figures

1. Theophylact's first order zone (Ben Willmore)   180
2. First order zone of Theophylact's personal cell (Ben Willmore)   192
3. Theophylact and Nicholas Kallikles (Ben Willmore)   195
4. Analysis by age, gender, residence and taxis (Ben Willmore)   198
5. Theophylact's network in action: requests (Ben Willmore)   202
6. Theophylact's network in action: cases (Ben Willmore)   206
7. Theophylact's network in action: instrumental and non-instrumental (Ben Willmore)   216

Plates

1. Seal of Theophylact of Ochrid
(© 1997 Dumbarton Oaks, acc.55.1.4714)   xv
2. Theophylact's see: Lake Ochrid and Hagia Sophia, Ochrid
(A.A.M. Bryer)   xviii
3. Theophylact's synod-church: Hagios Achilleios, Prespa from the west
(R.K. Loverance)   162
4. Theophylact's patronage? Hagios Achilleios, Prespa: wall-painting of
the second period   278

ABBREVIATIONS

ABME	*Archeion ton Byzantinon mnemeion tes Hellados*
AcadRoumBullSectHist	*Académie roumaine: bulletin de la section historique*
AIPHOS	*Annuaire de l'Institut de Philologie et d' Histoire Orientales et Slaves*
AK	*Logos eis ton autokratora kyrin Alexion ton Komnenon*
AmHR	*American Historical Review*
AmJPhil	*American Journal of Philology*
AnalBol	*Analecta Bollandiana*
Annales ESC	*Annales: économies, sociétés, civilisations*
ANRW	*Aufstieg und Niedergang der römischen Welt*
AOC	Archives de l'orient chrétien
AOO	*Anselmi opera omnia*, ed. F. S. Schmitt, III (Edinburgh, 1943)
ArtBull	*Art Bulletin*
BARIntSer	British Archaeological Reports, International Series
BB	*Byzantinobulgarica*
BBOMS	Birmingham Byzantine and Ottoman Monograph Series
BBS	Birmingham Byzantine Series
BBTT	Belfast Byzantine Texts and Translations
BCH	*Bulletin de correspondance hellenique*
BJRL	*Bulletin of the John Rylands Library*
BMGS	*Byzantine and Modern Greek Studies*
BNJ	*Byzantinisch-neugriechische Jahrbücher*
BollGrott	*Bollettino della Badia Greca di Grottaferrata*
BS	*Byzantinoslavica*
BSA SupplVols	*Annual of the British School at Athens, Supplementary volumes*
BS-EB	*Byzantine Studies-Études Byzantines*
BTT	Byzantine Texts in Translation
Byz	*Byzantion*
ByzAus	Byzantina Australiensia
ByzetNeohellNap	Byzantina et Neohellenica Neapolitana
ByzForsch	*Byzantinische Forschungen*
ByzSorb	Byzantina Sorbonensia
ByzVind	Byzantina Vindobonensia
BZ	*Byzantinische Zeitschrift*
CA	*Cahiers archéologiques*
CAG	Commentaria in Aristotelem graeca
CCCM	Corpus christianorum continuatio medievalis
CF	Cistercian Fathers
CFHB	Corpus fontium historiae Byzantinae
CHCL	*Cambridge History of Classical Literature*
Class et Med	*Classica et medievalia*
ClPhil	*Classical Philology*
CS	Cistercian Studies
CSEL	Corpus scriptorum ecclesiasticorum latinorum

CSHB	Corpus scriptorum historiae Byzantinae
DHGE	*Dictionnaire d'histoire et de géographie ecclésiastique*
DMA	*Dictionary of the Middle Ages*
DOP	*Dumbarton Oaks Papers*
DOS	Dumbarton Oaks Studies
DOT	Dumbarton Oaks Texts
DTC	*Dictionnaire de théologie catholique*
EA	*Ekklesiastike aletheia*
EEBS	*Epeteris tes hetaireias Byzantinon spoudon*
EEPS	*Epistemonike Epeteris tes Polytechnikes Scholes tou Aristoteleiou Panepistemiou Thessalonikes*
EEPT	*Epistemonike Epeteris tes Philosophikes Scholes tou Aristoteleiou Panepistemiou Thessalonikes*
EncCatt	*Enciclopedia cattolica*
EO	*Échos d'Orient*
GOThR	*Greek Orthodox Theological Review*
GBL	K. Krumbacher, *Geschichte der byzantinischen Literatur* (Munich, 1897)
GRBS	*Greek, Roman and Byzantine Studies*
HetMakSp	Hetaireia Makedonikon Spoudon
IntCong	*Congrès internationale d'études byzantines*
IRAIK	*Isvestija Russkogo Arkheologicheskogo Instituta v Konstantinopole*
JHS	*Journal of Hellenic Studies*
JÖB	*Jahrbuch der österreichischen Byzantinistik*
JRA	*Journal of Roman Archaeology*
JRS	*Journal of Roman Studies*
JThS	*Journal of Theological Studies*
KCL	Centre for Hellenic Studies, King's College London
LMA	*Lexikon des Mittelalters*
LRB	*London Review of Books*
Med et Hum	*Medievalia et humanistica*
MedHistRev	*Mediterranean Historical Review*
MiscByzMonac	Miscellanea Byzantina Monacensia
MiscMercati	*Miscellanea Giovanni Mercati* III (Studi e Testi, 193, Vatican City, 1946)
MLJ	*Mittellateinisches Jahrbuch*
MLN	*Modern Language Notes*
MM	F. Miklosich and J. Müller, *Acta et diplomata graeca medii aevi sacra et profana*, 6 vols (Vienna, 1860-90)
NE	*Neos Hellenomnemon*
NLH	*New Literary History*
OC	*Orientalia christiana*
OCA	Orientalia christiana analecta
OCP	*Orientalia christiana periodica*
ODB	*Oxford Dictionary of Byzantium*
Par.Gr.	*Corpus paroemiographorum graecorum*, ed. E. Leutsch and F. Schneidewin, 2 vols (Göttingen, 1839)

PB	*Logos eis ton Porphyrogenneton kyr Konstantinon (Paideia Basilike)*
PCPS	*Proceedings of the Cambridge Philological Society*
PG (Paris,	Patrologiae cursus completus, series graeca, ed. J.P. Migne, 161 vols 1857-66)
PL (Paris,	Patrologiae cursus completus, series latina, ed. J.P. Migne, 221 vols 1844-90)
PLP	*Prosopographisches Lexikon der Palaiologenzeit*
PMLA	*Proceedings of the Modern Language Association*
P&P	*Past & Present*
P&PP	Past & Present Publications
RE	A.F. von Pauly and G. Wissowa, *Real-Encyclopaedie der classischen Altertumswissenschaft* (Stuttgart, 1893--)
REB	*Revue des études byzantines*
RESEE	*Revue des études sud-est européennes*
RevBen	*Revue bénédictine*
ROL	*Revue de l'orient latin*
RSBS	*Rivista di studi bizantini e slavi*
SBN	*Studi bizantini e neoellenici*
SC	Sources chrétiennes
SicGymn	*Siculorum Gymnasium*
SPBS	Publications of the Society for Promotion of Byzantine Studies
StudClass	Studi classici
SubsHag	Subsidia Hagiographica
TLS	*Times Literary Supplement*
TM	*Travaux et mémoires*
TRHS	*Transactions of the Royal Historical Society*
VClem	*Vita Clementis*
VV	*Vizantiiski Vremennik*
WByzSt	Wiener Byzantinistische Studien
XV	*Historia martyrii XV martyrum*
YFS	Yale French Studies
ZRVI	*Zbornik Radova Vizantološkog Instituta*
Z&V	G. Zacos and A. Veglery, *Byzantine Lead Seals*, I (Basel, 1972)

PREFACE

This book has been many books (a lyrical first draft, a ponderous thesis, a theoretical sketch) and each one has incurred many debts which cannot be counted here or ever repaid. It began as a Birmingham thesis and I am very proud that it now appears in a Birmingham series, yet another of the national Byzantine institutions that we owe to Anthony Bryer. Dumbarton Oaks awarded me a summer fellowship to turn it into a book; this gave me a blissful bookful summer in Irene Vaslef's wonderful library and all that Washington friendship can provide: Marlene Chazan has followed Julia Warner's example in making a point of turning fellows into friends. Nikos Oikonomides and John Nesbitt guided me through the labyrinth of seals and Susan Boyd and Stephen Zwirn did their best with a photograph of Theophylact's. My family (Betty and Maurice, Michael and Leo) sacrificed two more summers to give me time with Theophylact, only one example of their constant generosity and consideration. For over twenty years the Queen's University of Belfast has offered me a challenging post and constant distraction from my research, with compensating stimulus from generations of undergraduates, research students and teaching assistants, all of whom have taught me an enormous amount, and made me feel it was all worthwhile: Earl Collins and Damian Leeson, Dion Smythe and Anthony Kirby, Shaun Tougher and Barbara Hill, Liz James, Barbara Zeitler and Tony Eastmond, as well as the current Byzantine community, with friends who travel year after year (Lyn Rodley) or week after week (Sarah Ekdawi) to teach with us, and my colleague Bob Jordan who makes everything come right. I owe a great deal also to the medievalists at Queen's (Judith Green, Evelyn Mullally, Tom McNeill, Bruce Campbell, Nicole Mezey, John Thompson and Marie-Thérèse Flanagan) who have maintained my morale and set high standards, and to the wider circle of Hibernian Hellenists (George Huxley, John Dillon, Gerry Watson), who have always made room for Byzantium. Most of all I must thank my friends, the scattered Byzantinists in Manchester and St Andrews, London and Cambridge, Newcastle and Warwick, Minnesota and Melbourne, in particular Rosemary Morris (my oldest and ablest ally), Paul Magdalino and Ruth Macrides; they prove Momigliano wrong in his assertion that Byzantinists do not all read the same texts: these friends always know the text and passage I am talking about. I have learned so much from so many people: Peter Brown, Alexander Kazhdan, Peter Megaw, but Bryer is my only inspiration, Robin Cormack my inscribed reader, and Michael Angold an ingenious devil's advocate. Averil Cameron made me finish. John Smedley bullied and nursed the final text along, with his famous patience, and Ruth Peters was always there with extra rulings and encouragement, to which the providential patronage of the British Academy hastened my response. Marie Taylor Davis and Tony Sheehan computerised me; Bryer and Rowena Loverance provided photographs; Diana (and Ken) Wardle organised illustrations (and saved me from many errors); Ben Willmore drew with skill and tact. Ruth Webb lent me her Bakhtin which provided a way of explaining (after the event) what I was trying to do; I am grateful to the University of Texas Press for permission to reproduce the passage. In the last stages Judith Waring, Peter Hatlie and (especially) Pamela Armstrong were generous with their library time, and Elizabeth Mullett and Ellen Russell held out inducements for finishing. Estelle Sheehan's sharp eyes and cheerful professionalism rescued and reassured. Leo's company in our study and his assumption that writing books is the most normal of activities sustained me to the end. But I owe most of all to Michael, my husband who did not compile the index, but has read and improved more of this book, more times, in more ways, than I can remember. He is my most rigorous critic and the best of my friends, and this book is for him.

Belfast, 31.xii.96

Seal of Theophylact of Ochrid

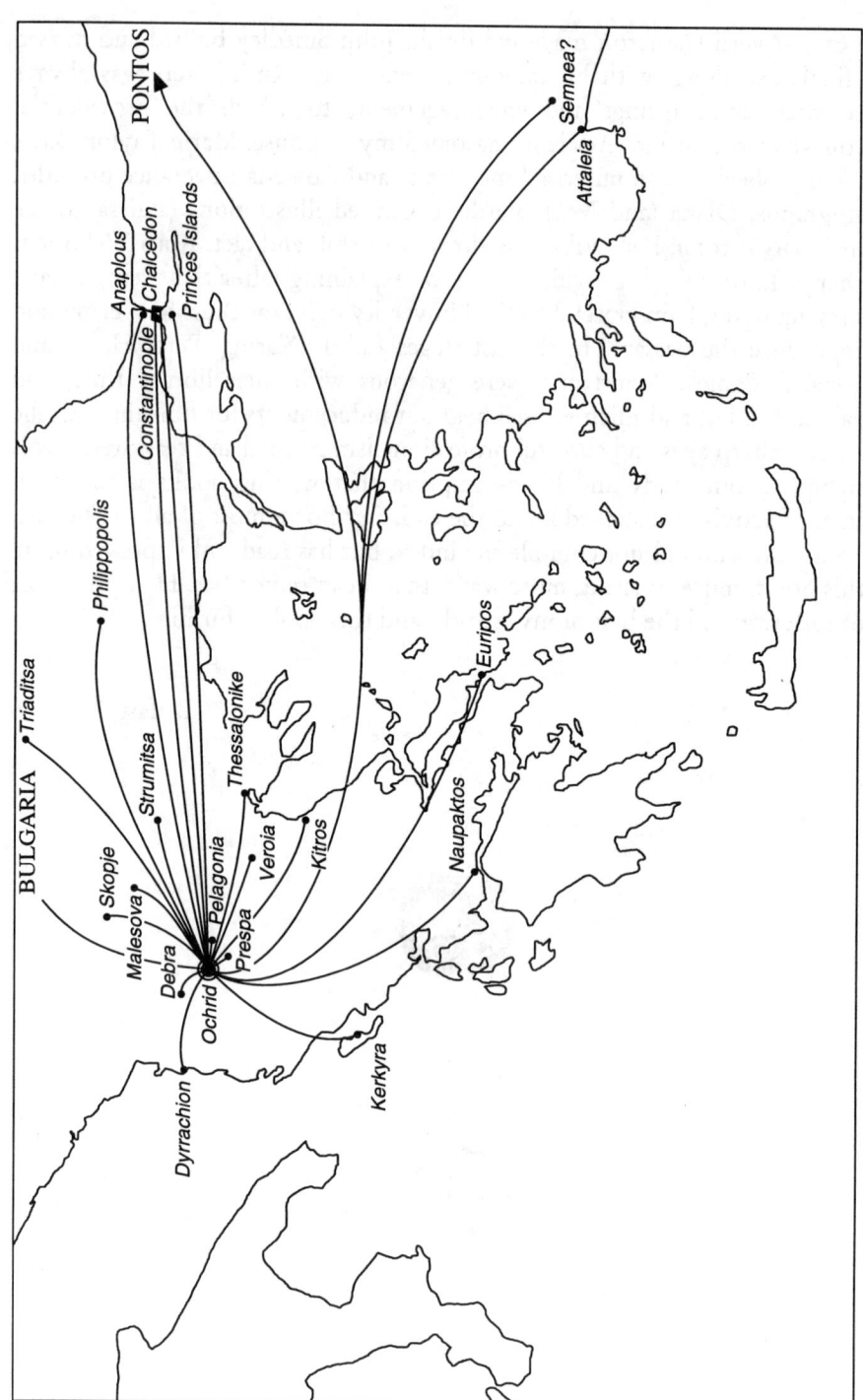

Map of Theophylact's Letter-Network

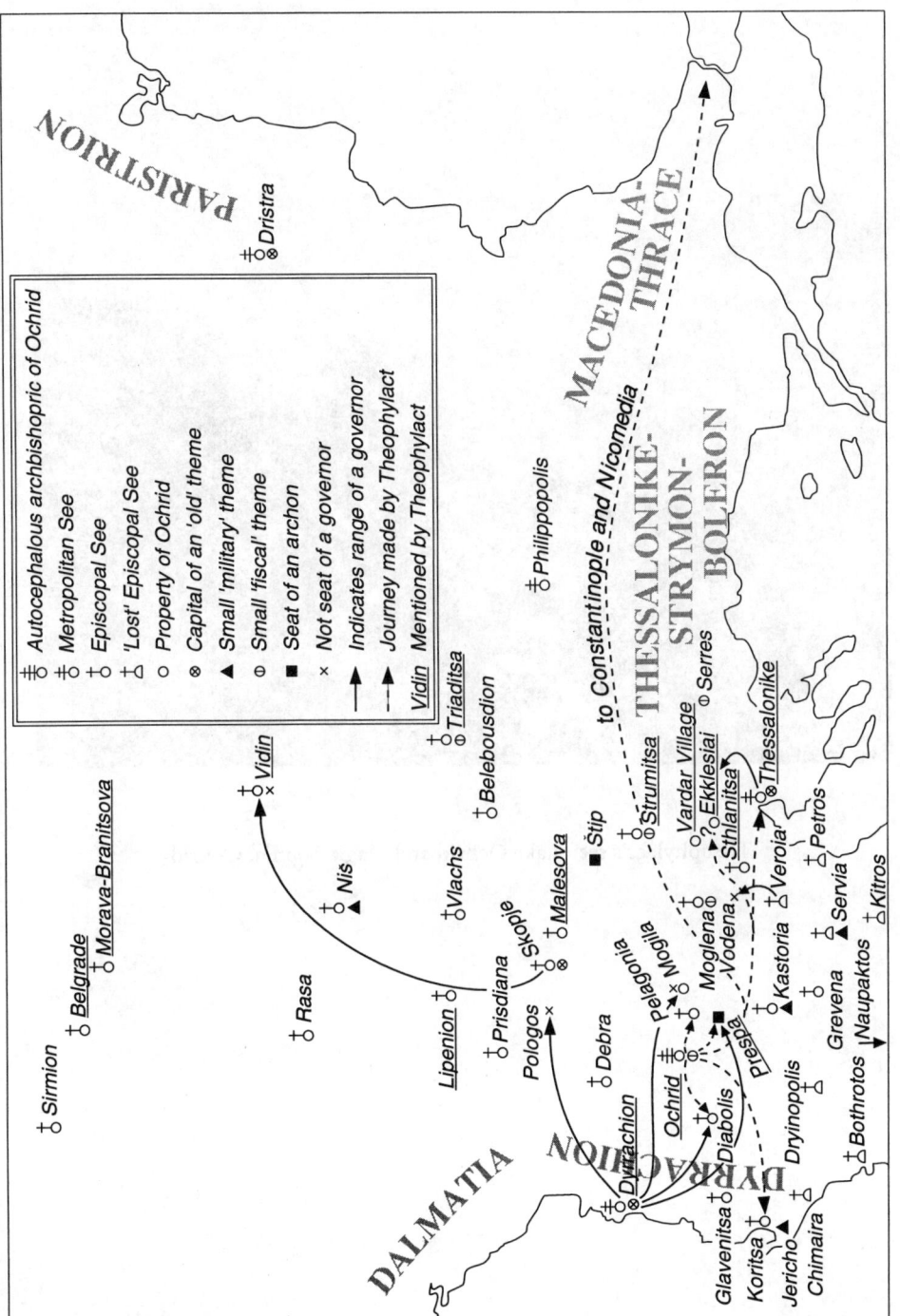

Map of Theophylact's Bulgaria

Legend:

☩ Autocephalous archbishopric of Ochrid
☦ Metropolitan See
† Episcopal See
☩ 'Lost' Episcopal See
○ Property of Ochrid
⊗ Capital of an 'old' theme
◀ Small 'military' theme
⊖ Small 'fiscal' theme
■ Seat of an archon
× Not seat of a governor
↑ Indicates range of a governor
↑ Journey made by Theophylact
Vidin Mentioned by Theophylact

PARISTRION

☩○⊗ Dristra

DALMATIA

† Sirmion
† Belgrade
† Morava-Branitsova
☩○× Vidin
☦ Triaditsa
☩⊖ Belebousdion

† Rasa
† Prisdiana
† Nis ◀
† Vlachs
Lipenion ☩
Pologos ×
Skopje ○⊗
† Debra
Malesova ○
■ Štip
Strumitsa ○○
Vardar Village ○

MACEDONIA-THRACE

† Philippopolis

to Constantinople and Nicomedia

THESSALONIKE-STRYMON-BOLERON

⊖ Serres
Ekklesiai ☩
Sthlanitsa ☦
☩⊗ Thessalonike

DYRRACHION

☩⊗ Durrachion
Ochrid ☩○
Diabolis ○
Prespa ■
Pelagonia ☩
Mogila ×
Moglena ⊖
Vodena ⊖
☦× Veroia
◀ Kastoria
† Petros
Dryinopolis ○
◀ Servia
☩ Grevena
Naupaktos ○
† Bothrotos
Glavenitsa ○
◀ Jericho
Koritsa
Chimaira
◀ Kitros

Theophylact's see: Lake Ochrid and Hagia Sophia, Ochrid

CHAPTER ONE

TEXT AND CONTEXT

This is a book about a text. And it is about reading that text. The text belongs to what used to be regarded as the unproblematic and privileged category of 'literature'.[1] But Byzantine literature should be regarded as anything but unproblematic. It has never had a good press, least of all from its own students. The inferior nature of Byzantine literature[2] was for Gibbon an essential plank of his thesis of decline and fall, which has gone unquestioned until very recently. And it has been *de rigueur* for professors of Byzantine language and literature to echo Gibbon's harsh judgment. Romilly Jenkins put it best:

> The Byzantine empire remains almost the unique example of a highly civilised state lasting for more than a millennium, which produced hardly any educated writing which can be read with pleasure for its literary merit alone.[3]

This prevailing view has had the effect of ensuring that Byzantine literature is not only marginalised,[4] and so not viewed as part of any 'great tradition' of European literature,[5] but also that it has never been regarded as a literature in

---

[1] On definitions of literature see A. Fowler, *Kinds of Literature. An Introduction to the Theory of Genres and Modes* (Oxford, 1982), 1-19; *NLH* 5 (1973); for the question of Byzantine concepts of literature see below chapter 6, esp. 288-289.

[2] E. Gibbon, *The History of the Decline and Fall of the Roman Empire,* ch. 53, ed. J.B. Bury, 3rd edn (London, 1907), VI, 107-8: 'not a single composition of history, philosophy or literature has been saved from oblivion by the intrinsic beauties of style or sentiment, of original fancy or even of successful imitation. Their prose is soaring to the vicious affectation of poetry, their poetry is sinking below the flatness and insipidity of prose.' The poet Cavafy deserves recognition for his early and direct refutation of this passage, both in his reading notes and in his 1892 article 'Hoi Byzantinoi Poietai,' *Anekdota Peza Keimena,* ed. tr. M. Peridis (Athens, 1963), 43-50.

[3] R.J.H. Jenkins, *Dionysius Solomos* (Cambridge, 1940), 57; see C. Mango, *Byzantine Literature as a Distorting Mirror* (Inaugural Lecture, University of Oxford, 1975), 4: 'I do not wish to dispute this harsh verdict'.

[4] The application of Edward Said's *Orientalism* (New York, 1978) to Byzantium has been made most pertinently by Averil Cameron, *The Use and Abuse of Byzantium* (Inaugural Lecture, King's College, London, 1993).

[5] E.W. Said, *The World, the Text and the Critic* (London, 1984), 5-9 on Auerbach, western literature and Istanbul. Compare on a more political level the assumption of the

its own right: it is virgin territory for the criticism of the twenty-first century. This might be thought by some to have a liberating effect, allowing the future critic to be uncluttered by Romantic views and false evaluations; that may be, but the predominant result has been rather one of invisibility. An excellent study of Byzantine scholarship can use the term 'Greek literature' to *exclude* Byzantine authors.[6]

This position has changed recently; denigration of Byzantine literature can no longer go unquestioned, but the handful of literary studies of Byzantine literature is still pitifully tiny.[7] This also means that the level of criticism of Byzantine literature has been extremely low, largely unaided as it has been, in contrast to other literatures, by advances in theory. Here also the picture has changed,[8] but there is a long way to go before Byzantine literary studies inhabit the same universe as contemporary literary criticism and theory.

This book will not alter that picture. It is not primarily a work of criticism or theory but of cultural history. But in that it attempts to consider how a text may or should be read, it is unusual[9] in studies of Byzantine texts. An unselfconsciousness about modes of reading is another result of the invisibility of Byzantine literature: if it is not worthy of study we do not need to evolve reading strategies to cope with it. But once we decide upon re-evaluation (or on no evaluation) innocent reading is no longer possible.

But precisely inasmuch as my reading of this text is not primarily literary, it becomes all the more problematic. It looks at the text and at the intertextual dimension; at other texts like this one, at other texts by the same author, at texts emulated and quoted in the text. But it also looks at the relationship of the text with what is beyond the text, with the world, with the milieu (or milieux) in which the text was generated, with the interpretative

---

European Science Foundation network on the classical tradition that the link from the classical world to the renaissance runs though the Latin, western, line.

[6] N. Wilson, *Scholars of Byzantium* (London, 1983), 1: 'This book is intended to give an account of what happened to Greek literature from the end of the ancient world until the time of its reappearance in Western Europe during the Renaissance.'

[7] On the change in attitudes to literature see E. Hanawalt, 'Dancing with Rhetoricians in the Gardens of the Muses,' *BS-EB* 13 (1986), 1-23.

[8] See my 'Dancing with Deconstructionists in the Gardens of the Muses: New Literary History vs ?' *BMGS* 14 (1990), 258-275.

[9] A shining exception is Averil Cameron, *Procopius and the Sixth Century* (London, 1985).

communities[10] which first (and later) received the text, with the effect of the text on politics and the world. This is viewed as problematic by both the interpretative communities I have invoked so far, Byzantinists and literary critics. Byzantinists have been alerted to the dangers of using literary sources as historical evidence by the more recent of the inaugural lectures of Cyril Mango, which characterised Byzantine literature as a distorting mirror, the effect of which is to mislead the unwary reader.[11] The timelessness and placelessness of Byzantine literature for scholars like Mango mean that we cannot ever be certain of the relationship between a text and its context.[12] In fact this perception had little effect on the way texts were read, because of the nature of Byzantine texts—and because they were read in isolation from literatures whose students were more alive to these issues. However much Byzantinists accepted Mango's view, they could not carry through its logic and eschew literary sources, because the vast majority of texts which have survived to us from the Byzantine empire appear to be privileged, 'literary'. Legal texts,[13] foundation charters,[14] inscriptions[15] have an undeniable literary dimension (though it remains to be discovered what that is). Ancient historians may choose (though it is a questionable practice) between 'literary' sources and 'hard' evidence;[16] Byzantinists do not have that luxury. Only material evidence appears to offer the illusion of evidence free from the taint of literariness.[17] And in the analysis of material evidence Byzantinists have clearsightedly turned away from empiricism.[18] But as far as literary sources are

---

[10]   The concept is central to the thinking of S. Fish, *Is there a Text in this Class? The Authority of Interpretive Communities* (Cambridge, Mass. and London, 1980) and to reader-response criticism.

[11]   Mango, *Distorting Mirror*.

[12]   At a very basic level see the pair of papers by Morris and Mullett in *The Theotokos Evergetis and Byzantine Monasticism*, ed. M.E. Mullett and A.J. Kirby (BBTT, 6.1, Belfast, 1994), 348-361, 362-370.

[13]   See H. Hunger, *Prooimion. Elemente der byzantinischen Kaiseridee in den Arengen der Urkunden* (WByzSt, 1, Vienna, 1964).

[14]   See M.J. Angold, 'Were Byzantine Monastic *Typika* Literature?' *The Making of Byzantine History*, ed. R. Beaton and C. Roueché (KCL, 1, Aldershot, 1994), 46-70.

[15]   See for example the Porphyrius inscriptions, Alan Cameron, *Porphyrius the Charioteer* (Oxford, 1973).

[16]   See Averil Cameron, *History as Text: The Writing of Ancient History* (London, 1989), 3.

[17]   For an excellent attempt to write history entirely from 'hard' evidence see A. Harvey, *Economic Expansion in the Byzantine Empire, 850-1250* (Cambridge, 1990); for an object-based introduction to Byzantium, see R. Loverance, *Byzantium* (London, 1990).

[18]   E.g. R. Cormack, *Writing in Gold* (London, 1985) and the intellectual odyssey of *The Byzantine Eye. Studies in Art and Patronage* (Aldershot, 1989), 1-3.

concerned invisibility appears to serve as a protective device saving
Byzantinists from having to glance into the abyss. If we once accept that
Byzantine literature is a distorting mirror we must try to understand (even if
we cannot correct) that distortion, because (apart from a handful of
documentary texts) we have no alternative.

But it is not immediately apparent to those who habitually read
privileged text that this is an option at all. The divorce of text from context
has been an accepted principle of literary criticism from the early years of this
century. Russian Formalism preceded New Criticism[19] by some considerable
time in removing critical emphasis from the author and placing it on the text.
New Criticism by identifying an intentionalist[20] and an affective[21] fallacy
concentrated attention entirely on the text, a verbal icon, which was typically
a short piece of verse, the very type of text which might exhibit the New
Critical virtues of organicism, complexity and ambiguity[22] and its
characteristic strategy of close reading. There was no room for broader sweeps
of text or intertext. The eclipse of New Criticism by structuralism did
nothing for literary history; Saussure's apparent privileging of the synchronic
over the diachronic saw to that.[23] And although poststructuralism has offered
the possibility of reintegrating the diachronic, it still encompasses in the
concept of indeterminacy a determination not to be trammelled by
referentiality; Derrida's much-quoted dictum, 'il n'y a pas de hors-texte' found
its most thorough-going practice in de Man's deconstruction, and was seen by
its critics as 'a sealed echo-chamber in which meanings are reduced to a
ceaseless echolalia...bombinating in a void.'[24] Foucault, though focusing on the
surely contextual issue of power, arrived at a means of defusing historicism by
denying the possibility of a generalised cultural history, through his emphasis
on discontinuous fields of discourse.[25] For these theorists, all now

---

[19]   For a comparative treatment of the two movements see E.M. Thompson, *Russian
Formalism and Anglo-American New Criticism* (The Hague, 1971).

[20]   W. Wimsatt and M. Beardsley, 'The Intentional Fallacy', in W. Wimsatt, *The Verbal
Icon* (Lexington, 1954), 3-18.

[21]   W. Wimsatt and M. Beardsley, 'The Affective Fallacy', ibid., 21-39.

[22]   Classically, though not centrally, W. Empson, *Seven Types of Ambiguity* (London,
1930); *Some Versions of Pastoral* (London, 1935); *The Structure of Complex Words* (London,
1952).

[23]   See J. Culler, *Structuralist Poetics* (London, 1975), 12 ff.

[24]   J. Derrida, 'Il n'y a pas de hors-texte,' *On Grammatology*, tr. G.C. Spivak (Baltimore,
1976), 158; on de Man see *Reading de Man Reading*, ed. L. Waters and W. Goodrich
(Minneapolis, 1989); for the echo-chamber see M.H. Abrams, 'The Deconstructive Angel,'
Critical Inquiry 3 (1977), 430.

[25]   On Foucault see helpfully V.B. Leitch, *Deconstructive Criticism: An Advanced
Introduction* (London, 1983), 143-163.

tarred with the same brush of formalism by New Historicists, referentiality is the fundamental vice.

But this is an extreme picture, and a place for context is often found in all but the most stringent boa-deconstructors.[26] New Critical reading practice assumed a canon; attacks on the affective fallacy restored to a text the context of reception.[27] Eco conceded that 'no text is read independently of the reader's experience of other texts.'[28] Marxists have until recently stood outside this tendency, with the originating conditions of a text's production their major concern.[29] Of late there has been a discernible dissatisfaction with decontextual strategies.[30] As early as 1970 the foundation of the journal *New Literary History* signalled a sense that history needed to be restored to criticism.[31] The New Historicists of renaissance English literature saw a way which allowed the marking of the intertextuality of their texts with discursive, non-literary, texts without leaving themselves open to the charge of simply returning to the world-view approach of a Tillyard.[32] The politically engaged American poststructuralists Lentricchia and Said insist on the importance of 'the events and circumstances entailed by and expressed in the texts themselves',[33] as against the 'repeated and often extremely subtle denial of history by a variety of contemporary theorists.'[34] For them American poststructuralists have, under the influence of New Critical preconceptions, denied what is contextual in European poststructuralism. Derrida's use of margins may be seen either to

---

[26] For this description of de Man, Derrida and Hillis Miller see G. Hartman in H. Bloom et al., *Deconstruction and Criticism* (New York, 1979), ix.

[27] S. Fish, *Is there a Text in This Class?* 21-67.

[28] U. Eco, *The Role of the Reader: Explorations in the Semiotics of Texts* (London, 1981), 21.

[29] The standard introduction to Marxist criticism is T. Eagleton, *Marxism and Literary Criticism* (London, 1976), but for a new pluralist perspective, see *Poststructuralism and the Question of History*, ed. D. Attridge, G. Bennington and R. Young (Cambridge, 1987).

[30] See for example C. Porter, 'History and Literature: "After the New Historicism" ,' *NLH* 21 (1990), 253-272.

[31] The first issue offered itself to 'all engaged or interested in a reconsideration of literary history'; the second included the influential R. Jauss, 'Literary History as a Challenge to Literary Theory,' *NLH* 2 (1971), 7-38 and H. White, 'Literary History: the Point of It All,' 173-185.

[32] See for example the work of Jonathan Goldberg, Louis Montrose and Stephen Greenblatt, but cf. R. Levin, 'Unthinkable Thoughts in the New Historicising of a Renaissance Drama,' *NLH* 21 (1990), 433-448; E. Pechter, 'The New Historicism and its Discontents: Politicising Renaissance Drama,' *PMLA* 102 (1987), 292-303; *The New Historicism*, ed. H. Aram Veeser (New York and London, 1989) and *The New Historicism Reader*, ed. H. Aram Veeser (New York and London, 1994).

[33] Said, 'Secular Criticism,' *The World, the Text and the Critic*, 4.

[34] F. Lentricchia, *After the New Criticism* (London, 1980), xiii.

elide or to make concrete the difference between the text and the hors-texte, but not to ignore the latter;[35] Foucault's 'archaeology' may fragment history but his system of epistemes and discourses is essentially cultural rather than textual.[36] Hayden White denies the reality of reality, but by textualising context welcomes it into the fold of critical discourse.[37] To take a remark out of context, 'Context matters, whatever the book.'[38]

So when Brian Stock says that 'there is at the present time more opportunity of a rapprochement between history and literature,'[39] he may well be right, and Byzantine studies must surely benefit. The applicability of techniques of literary criticism and of the concerns of literary theory to literary texts would seem self-evident, but it is not—even to Byzantinists who are otherwise open to theory.[40] The exploitation of literary texts by historians has hitherto looked rather more like rape. My own text is a case in point. The letters of Theophylact of Ochrid have been plundered for evidence of the use of the classics in Byzantium,[41] for the history of Macedonia[42] and Bulgaria in the Middle Ages,[43] for provincial economic and ecclesiastical history,[44] for

---

[35] J. Derrida, 'Living On/Borderlines,' *Deconstruction and Criticism*, ed. H. Bloom et al. (London, 1979), 75-176. On Derrida and margins see Leitch, *Deconstructive Criticism*, 121.

[36] On the contrast between Foucault's early 'archaeological' period of the 1960s and his later work in which 'practices and discourses intertwine' see P. Rabinow, *The Foucault Reader* (Harmondsworth, 1984), 27.

[37] H. White, *Metahistory* (Baltimore, 1973); *Tropics of Discourse* (Baltimore, 1978).

[38] Marilyn Butler reviewing Jerome McGann in *TLS*, 20 August 1994, 34.

[39] B. Stock, 'History, Literature and Medieval Textuality,' *Images of Power. Medieval History/Discourse/Literature*, ed. K. Brownlee and S.G. Nichols (YFS, 70, New Haven, Conn., 1986), 7.

[40] Even J. Haldon's classic 'Jargon vs "the Facts",' *BMGS* 9 (1984-85), 95-132 carries no implication that a double level of theory is necessary.

[41] K. Praechter, 'Antike Quellen des Theophylaktos von Bulgarien,' *BZ* 1 (1892), 399-414.

[42] E.g. B. Panov, *Teofilakt Ohridski kako izvor za srednovekovnata istorija na Makedonskiot narod* (Skopje, 1971).

[43] V.G. Vasilevskii, 'Vizantiia i Pechenegi', *Trudy*, I (St Petersburg, 1908), 1-175, esp. appendix III, 'Feofilakt Bulgarskii i ego sochineniia', 134-49; V. Zlatarsky, *Istoriia na Bulgarskata durzhava prez sriednitie viekove*, II (Sofia, 1934), 352-366.

[44] D. Xanalatos, *Beiträge zur Wirtschafts- und Sozialgeschichte Makedoniens im Mittelalter, hauptsächlich auf Grund der Briefe Theophylakts von Achrida* (Munich, 1937); now much more sympathetically, E.S. Papayanni, 'Phorologikes plerophories apo epistoles tou megalou Basileiou (329/31-379) kai tou Theophylaktou (1050/55-1125/6),' *He kathemerine zoe sto Byzantio* (Athens, 1989), 391-407; and analytically, A. Harvey, 'The Land and Taxation in the Reign of Alexios I Komnenos: the Evidence of Theophylakt of Ochrid,' *REB* 51 (1993), 139-154.

patterns of heresy,[45] for Byzantine feudalism.[46] It has never been looked at as a text in its own right. Stock's optimistic viewpoint is based—in a somewhat limited way—on the openness to texts of Annales-school history[47] with its concern for mentalities. Here, unless the literary dimension is uppermost, there is a new danger: before, historians charged through literary texts looking for peasants; now they charge through looking for mentalities. Here Mango's warning should be heard, and every possible weapon in the arsenal of contemporary theory be used to fend off the rapists and arrive at as sophisticated a reading of literary text as is possible. Whether texts are read as literature or as history is in a sense immaterial in the aftermath of twentieth-century movements whose achievement is to break down the boundaries between kinds of discourse; the lesson for the Byzantinist is that there is nothing that is not text.

This said, it must also be acknowledged that my concern is ultimately with cultural history, and that no historian can be totally unconcerned with referentiality. However committed we are to the enclosed world of our text, that text reflects and affects a world outside, equally composed, from our point of view, of texts but still outside our text. Texts are of course not innocent. It was a letter of Theophylact which caused the first visible split in the family government of the Komnenoi. In delating on John Komnenos, son of the *sebastokrator*, to the emperor in 1093 this letter caused a major family dispute which was patched up with great difficulty by Alexios.[48] Historians must by the nature of their calling deal with the world as well as the text and the critic.

In what follows I maintain some distinctions between text and context. I look at Theophylact's letter-collection (and it is a collection rather than a correspondence) as a collection of letters and as the material evidence for a nexus of relationships; I look at the collection in terms of other people's letters and of other works of Theophylact; I also look at Theophylact as author and as man. I look at the historical conditions which created reading formations for this text and on which the text itself acted. In each case I

---

[45] D. Obolensky, *The Bogomils. A Study in Balkan Neomanichaeism* (Cambridge, 1948), 171-2.

[46] B.A. Nikolaev, *Feodalni otnoshenie v pokorenata ot Byzantiia Bulgariia otrazeni v pismata na Teofilakt Okhridski Archiepiskop Bulgarski* (Sofia, 1951); I.A. Božilov, 'Pismata na Teofilakt Ochridski kato istoricheski izvor', *Izvestiia na Durzhavnite Archivi* 14 (1967), 60-100.

[47] The classic article by E. Patlagean, 'Ancienne hagiographie byzantine et histoire sociale,' *Annales ESC* 23 (1968), 106-124 is an early example.

[48] Anna Komnene, *Alexiad*, VIII.vii.3-8, ed. B. Leib, 3 vols (Paris, 1937-45), II, (Paris, 1943), 147-151.

distinguish between the referential and the non-referential by means of the structure of the book, marked by a fault-line down the middle along which text and context interact: genre and milieu, collection and network, author and man.[49]

The text is the letters[50] of Theophylact Hephaistos,[51] fifth of the Byzantine archbishops of Ochrid[52] and before that *maistor ton rhetoron* in Constantinople.[53] He appears to have been born some time around the middle of the eleventh century,[54] brought up in Euboia[55] and educated in Constantinople in the 1070s.[56] He taught during the 1080s[57] and was appointed to his bishopric after 6 January 1088.[58]

Those letters which can be dated belong to the 1090s and 1100s,[59] though other works may be dated to the 1110s and 1120s.[60] His writings are numerous;[61] commentaries on the Gospels, the Epistles, the Minor Prophets,

---

[49] For this purpose chapters 3 and 4 form a single unit comparable with chapter 2 and with chapter 5.

[50] I use the new edition, sadly posthumous, of P. Gautier, *Théophylacte d'Achrida*, II *Lettres* (CFHB, 16/2, Thessalonike, 1986). For the old numbering according to the editions of Meursius, Lamius and Finetti see Table I below, which corrects errors noted in my review in *BS* 52 (1991), 157-162.

[51] On Theophylact's surname see Gautier, 'L'épiscopat,' *REB* 21 (1963), 165-168; *Théophylacte d'Achrida*, I, *Discours, Traités, Poésies* (CFHB, 16/1, Thessalonike, 1980), 13-14.

[52] H. Gelzer, *Das Patriarchat von Achrida* (AbhLeip, phil-hist. Kl., 20, Leipzig, 1907).

[53] The primary evidence is the superscription of a manuscript of the *Vita Clementis*, PG, 126, 194; for discussion see below, 233, n. 50.

[54] See Gautier, *Théophylacte*, I, 12, n. 3; D. Obolensky, *Six Byzantine Portraits* (Oxford, 1988), 36, suggests between 1050 and 1060; R. Katičić, 'Biographika peri Theophylaktou archiepiskopou Achridos,' *EEBS* 30 (1960-61), 364-385 at 365 suggests before 1055. These solutions can only be estimated from his activity in the 1080s.

[55] The evidence for his Euboian origins is two letters, G8 and G17, *Théophylacte*, II, 155, 188, an epigram prefaced to a manuscript of his commentaries, Cod. Laur. gr. VI. 26, fol. 243, ed. Gautier, *REB* 32 (1963), 170 and the ἐξ Εὐρίπου in the bishop list, Paris. gr. 880, fol. 407v, see Gelzer, *Patriarchat*, 7.

[56] He fell under the influence of Michael Psellos, though it would be rash to say that he was actually his pupil, G132, II, 589 and G27, II, 219.6: πολλὰ γὰρ οἶδα τῆς μούσης τοῦ ἀνδρὸς ἀπονάμενος.

[57] G1, 2, 3, II, 131-175.

[58] His appointment is dated from the *basilikos logos* to Alexios, 6 January 1088, see Gautier, 'L'épiscopat,' *REB* 21 (1963), 159-178 at 159-164.

[59] For the dating of the letters see below chapter 3.1, 82-85.

[60] The treatise on the Latins may have been written for the visit of Peter Grossolano in 1112; G136 may have been written for the disputations at Philippopolis, 1114-15; the poem on the hymns of Symeon the New Theologian is dated in the manuscript to 1125/26; for a cautious interpretation see Gautier, *Théophylacte*, I, 37.

[61] See PG 123-126.

the Psalms, the Acts of the Apostles,[62] saints' lives,[63] speeches to the emperor, discourses on the liturgy, on the Latins, and on eunuchs, his poems[64] and letters.[65] So much for text, oeuvre and author.

Other works which are read in relation to the letter-collection both span the Byzantine centuries[66] and focus on the reign of Alexios I Komnenos.[67] The present study is a companion piece also to two other projects: my study of the processes of Byzantine letter-writing and a Belfast project on Alexios.[68] Full treatments of parallels and more complete bibliography will be found in those works: here I concentrate on what is essential to Theophylact.

But why should I have chosen this text? Historiography might have seemed a more obvious genre on which to begin a text-centred analysis. Yet historiography has already been worked over by generations of scholars determined to winnow rhetorical chaff from historical wheat.[69] Hagiography has the advantage (or disadvantage) of the Bollandist tradition, which before Mango's warning represented the height of sophistication in the use of privileged text.[70] Epistolography on the other hand forms a body of material which is comparatively untouched by critics or historians,[71] while holding out the promise of allowing us to hear the conversation of the Byzantine elite.[72]

---

[62] Ibid.

[63] See PG 126, 151-222; 1193-1240; A. Milev, *Grutskite zhitiia na Kliment Okhridski* (Sofia, 1966); P. Gautier, *Deux oeuvres hagiographiques du pseudo-Théophylacte* (Diss., Paris, 1968).

[64] Gautier, *Théophylacte*, I.

[65] Gautier, *Théophylacte*, II.

[66] A table of Byzantine letter-collections, fig. I, may be found in my thesis, *Theophylact through his Letters: the Two Worlds of an Exile Bishop* (PhD Diss., Birmingham, 1981), II, 794-824. For discussion see my 'The Classical Tradition in the Byzantine Letter', *Byzantium and the Classical Tradition*, ed. M. Mullett and R. Scott (Birmingham, 1981), 75-93 at 75.

[67] For the range of contemporary works which need to be read with the letters see Gautier's annual articles in *REB* from 1962 until his death in 1983, *REB* 42 (1984), 371-373.

[68] The first is in progress; the second may be read as *Alexios I Komnenos*, I: *Papers of the Second Belfast Byzantine International Colloquium*, ed. M.E. Mullett and D.C. Smythe (BBTT, 4.1, Belfast, 1996); *Alexios I Komnenos*, II: *Works attributed to Alexios I Komnenos*, ed. M.E. Mullett (BBTT, 4.2, Belfast, forthcoming).

[69] See Cameron, *History as Text*, 1-2.

[70] See F. Van Ommeslaeghe, 'The Acta Sanctorum and Bollandist Methodology,' *The Byzantine Saint* (Studies Supplementary to Sobornost, 5, London, 1981), 155-163.

[71] See below, 2.2, 11-13.

[72] On the inappropriateness of regarding letters as written conversation see below, 148; for literary—and other—elites see my 'Aristocracy and Patronage in the Literary Circles of Comnenian Constantinople,' *The Byzantine Aristocracy, IX-XIII Centuries*, ed. M.J. Angold

Some scholars are inclined to make the wildest of claims for the usefulness of letters;[73] others to despair of ever being able to use them.[74] This contrast cannot but be illuminating. And why Theophylact's collection? The letters are not numerous compared with those of a Libanios or a Psellos, or as accessible as those of Basil the Great or Manuel II, but Theophylact's collection was hailed by no less an authority than Ostrogorsky as of considerable concern to historians. If we are interested in how to read Byzantine texts as history, as literature, as text, this text looks promising.

This book is itself a text, and though I make no claims of authorial authority, I avoid other claims also. Despite the (muted) trumpet-calls earlier in this introduction, it is not a work of poststructuralist criticism, nor of historiography or metahistory. It depends heavily on the magnificent positivist tradition of the Assumptionists, the order which has done so much for Byzantine texts, and in particular the work of Paul Gautier on the letters of Theophylact. As for its theoretical debts, interactionists are foremost, both in literature and in social anthropology. In general I am more concerned with the reception than the generation of text, and with the diachronic than with the synchronic, but all these concerns are represented. It is otherwise completely eclectic, and like Tzetzes on history[75] I hope it will persuade.[76]

(BAR IntSer, 221, Oxford, 1984), 173-201 and my forthcoming network study of literary society in the twelfth century.

[73] G. Ostrogorsky, *History of the Byzantine State*, tr. J. Hussey (London, 1968), 314.

[74] G. Dennis, *The Letters of Manuel II Palaeologus* (DOT, 4=CFHB, 8, Washington, DC, 1977), xviii-xx.

[75] J. Tzetzes, ed. W. B. Stanford, 'Tzetzes' Farewell to Thucydides,' *Greece and Rome* 11 (1941-42), 40-41, quoted by R. Scott, 'The Classical Tradition in Byzantine Historiography', *Classical Tradition*, 61.

[76] On persuasion rather than proof: M. Beard and M. Crawford, *Rome in the Late Republic* (London, 1985), 3-4; Fish, *Is there a Text in This Class?*, 338-371.

CHAPTER TWO

GENRE AND MILIEU

Before examining Theophylact's letter-collection in detail this chapter will consider two kinds of backdrop to the text. The first is the horizon of expectations of its receivers,[1] which for the purposes of this study I shall take to be determined by genre, by the letter. I shall examine it from the points of view of epistolarity, of evaluation and of reception. The second backdrop to the collection is the originating conditions[2] of our text, which I take to be eleventh-century Constantinople, Byzantine Bulgaria and Alexian literature.

2.1 The epistolarity of the Byzantine letter

Theophylact's letter-collection is one of 150 major collections; the total of extant letters could number somewhere around 15,000.[3] No exhaustive survey of the Byzantine letter exists; there is no corpus of Byzantine letters or even a checklist. The general studies of Tomadakes and Smetanin are not exhaustive and Hunger's treatment in his *Handbuch* makes no attempt at quantification or even at a chronological survey.[4] In 1962 Gustav Karlsson noted that 'la

---

[1] H. R. Jauss, 'Literary History as a Challenge to Literary Theory,' *NLH* 2 (1970), 14; *Towards an Aesthetic of Reception*, tr. T. Bahti (History and Theory of Literature, 2, Minnesota, 1982), 3-45 at 22-24.

[2] For a reconstructed understanding of this term see T. Bennett, 'Texts in History,' *Poststructuralism and the Question of History*, ed. D. Attridge, G. Bennington and R. Young (Cambridge, 1987), 69-77.

[3] This was my estimate in 1981, 'The Classical Tradition in the Byzantine Letter,' *Byzantium and the Classical Tradition*, eds M. Mullett and R. Scott (Birmingham, 1981), 75-93 at 75 on the basis of my doctoral thesis, *Theophylact through his Letters* (Birmingham, 1981), fig. I, Byzantine Letter-collections, 793-813. If 'Byzantine' is defined to exclude the fourth and fifth centuries the number drops sharply.

[4] N. Tomadakes, *Byzantine epistolographia* (Athens, 1955) and see also his three-volume *Eisagoge eis ten Byzantinen philologian* (Athens, 1952). V.A. Smetanin, *Epistolografiia* (Sverdlovsk, 1970) and *Vizantijskoe obschestvo XIII-XV vekov po dannym epistologafii* (Sverdlovsk, 1987) largely deal with Byzantine letters after 1261. See also H. Hunger, *Hochsprachliche profane Literatur der Byzantiner*, I (Munich, 1978), 214-239, and for a sensitive approach to the Byzantine letter I. Ševčenko, 'Nicolaus Kabasilas' Correspondence and the Treatment of Late Byzantine Literary Texts,' *BZ* 47 (1954), 49-59.

littérature épistolaire byzantine est dans une large mesure un domaine resté inexploré', but he was only echoing the call of J. Sykutres to the delegates of the Third International Congress of Byzantine Studies in 1930 and Monica Wagner's comment in 1948: 'From time to time there appear signs of dissatisfaction with the literary history of the letter.'[5] The position has changed very little since these strictures. The tenth century is a period of comparative light: Jean Darrouzès identified and painstakingly attributed the epistolary contents of manuscripts in the libraries of Patmos, the Lavra and the Bodleian and then assembled these findings into first an inventory and then a collection and study of the letters of the period; Gustav Karlsson has analysed these tenth-century letters and by isolating various literary topoi which recur throughout the collections has sketched the chains of influence from ancient Greek writers through the fathers and early Byzantine letter-writers to the tenth century.[6]

The one area of considerable progress is in the editing of texts: since Monica Wagner wrote and Tomadakes's book appeared, editions of the letters of Nicholas Mystikos, Arethas, Niketas Magistros, Michael Gabras, the Tornikai, Michael Italikos, John Tzetzes and Niketas Choniates were published. After Hunger's *Handbuch* came Manuel II, Athanasios the patriarch, Theodore Daphnopates, Gregory Akindynos, Eirene Eulogia Choumnaina Palaiologina, Leo of Synada among others.[7] New letter-writers

---

For a searching critique of current work on the Byzantine letter see P. Hatlie, 'Redeeming Byzantine Epistolography,' *BMGS* 20 (1996), 213-248.

[5] G. Karlsson, *Idéologie et cérémonial dans l'épistolographie byzantine*, 2nd edn (Uppsala, 1962), 3; J. Sykutres, 'Probleme der byzantinischen Epistolographie,' *III IntCong* (Athens, 1932), *Actes*, 295-310; M. Wagner, 'A Chapter in Byzantine Epistolography: The Letters of Theodoret of Cyrus,' *DOP* 4 (1948), 121.

[6] J. Darrouzès, 'Un recueil épistolaire byzantin: le manuscript de Patmos 706,' *REB* 14 (1956), 87-121; 'Inventaire des épistoliers byzantins du Xe siècle,' *REB* 18 (1960), 109-135; *Épistoliers byzantins du Xe siècle* (AOC, 6, Paris, 1960); G. Karlsson, 'Formelhaftes im Paulusbriefen,' *Eranos* 54 (1956), 138-141; *Idéologie et cérémonial*, passim.

[7] L.G. Westerink, *Arethae scripta minora*, 2 vols (Leipzig, 1968-72); J. Darrouzès, *Georges et Démétrios Tornikès, Lettres et discours* (Le monde byzantin, Paris, 1970); P. Gautier, *Michel Italikos, Lettres et discours* (AOC, 14, Paris, 1972); P.A.M. Leone, *Johannes Tzetzae epistolae* (Leipzig, 1972); I.A. van Dieten, *Nicetae Choniatae orationes et epistulae* (Berlin and New York, 1973); R. Jenkins and L.G. Westerink, *Nicholas I Patriarch of Constantinople, Letters* (DOT, 2, CFHB, 6, Washington, DC, 1973); G. Dennis, *The Letters of Manuel II Palaeologos* (DOT, 4, CFHB, 8, Washington, DC, 1977); A.M. Maffry-Talbot, *The Correspondence of Athanasios I Patriarch of Constantinople* (DOT, 3, CFHB, 7, Washington, DC, 1975); J. Darrouzès and L. Westerink, *Theodoros Daphnopates, correspondance* (Le monde byzantin, Paris, 1978); A. Garzya, *Synesii Cyrenensis epistolae* (Rome, 1979); A.C. Hero, *The Letters of Gregory Akindynos* (DOT, 7, CFHB, 21, Washington, DC, 1983); B. Laourdas and L.G. Westerink, *Photii epistolae et Amphilochia*, I

have joined the old ones re-edited and it begins to be possible to take an overview. We are still however considerably behind the work which has been done in the medieval west: we have no equivalent, for example, to Giles Constable's *Letters and Letter-collections*,[8] and studies of individual letter-collections are thin on the ground. In looking at the epistolarity of the Byzantine letter in this book we seem to be asking new questions.

We are not however totally without assistance and I propose to take advantage of very useful work done recently on the epistolary novel. In that the elements of narrative and indeed fictionality are far stronger than in a letter-collection like Theophylact's, not all our concerns are common, but the kind of questions asked by Janet Altman in her recent study[9] can only illuminate a collection like Theophylact's. To what extent is it as it is because of the process of letter-exchange? What is special about a letter? How are the letter's formal properties used to create meaning?

An obvious way in is what Altman calls the polarity between letter as bridge and letter as barrier; I prefer with the Byzantines to see this contrast in terms of separation, a prerequisite for epistolary communication. 'I have just set foot in Ochrid and I long for the city that holds you'.[10] This is not a novel sentiment. Behind Theophylact stretch six centuries at least of loneliness. The impression of isolation one receives from reading almost any medieval letter-collection is overwhelming. Separation is firmly embedded in the Byzantine letter; the classic statement is Synesios's letter 138 to Herkoulanios: 'the letter has the power to be a solace for unhappy lovers, affording as it does in bodily

---

(Leipzig, 1983); II (Leipzig, 1984); III (Leipzig, 1985); M.P. Vinson, *The Correspondence of Leo Metropolitan of Synada and Syncellus* (DOT, 8, Washington, DC, 1985); Eirene Eulogia Choumnaina Palaiologina, ed. A.C. Hero, *A Woman's Quest for Spiritual Guidance* (Archbishop Iakovos Library of Ecclesiastical and Historical Sources, 11, Brookline, Mass., 1986); P. Maraval, *Grégoire de Nysse, Lettres* (SC, 363, Paris, 1990); G. Fatouros, *Theodori Studitae epistolae*, 2 vols (CFHB, 31.1-2, Berlin and New York, 1992).

[8] G. Constable, *Letters and Letter-collections* (Typologie des sources du moyen age occidental, 17, Turnhout, 1976); 'Dictators and Diplomats in the Eleventh and Twelfth Centuries: Medieval Epistolography and the Birth of Modern Bureaucracy,' *Homo Byzantinus. Papers in Honor of Alexander Kazhdan*, ed. A. Cutler and S. Franklin = DOP 46 (1992), 37-46.

[9] J. Altman, *Epistolarity: Approaches to a Form* (Columbus, Ohio, 1982). *Writing the Female Voice, Essays on Epistolary Literature*, ed. E.C. Goldsmith (London and Boston, 1989) has important insights for epistolary texts though its main focus is elsewhere, cf. E. Grubgeld, *George Moore and the Autogenous Self* (New York and London, 1994), esp. ch. 6, 174-199; B. Redford, *The Converse of the Pen. Acts of Intimacy in the Eighteenth-Century Familiar Letter* (Chicago and London, 1986) and L.S. Kauffman, *Discourses of Desire. Gender, Genre and Epistolary Fiction* (Ithaca and London, 1986).

[10] G6, II, 147.2-3.

absence the illusion of actual presence.' By the time of Psellos this had become a 'law': 'I approve the law of letters, most honoured Lord and equal-souled brother, and the purpose of speaking through letters from those who are away from home.' [11]

With Synesios's definition more complicated concepts were intertwined, like the letter as consolation, the insufficiency of the letter, the letter as second best and the *unio mystica*.[12] Byzantines (as well as modern literary scholars) describe separation in a series of antitheses as if to embody the paradox provided by Synesios's definition. The first of these is presence/absence. Gregory of Nazianzos describes his own inconsistency caused by his *askesis*:

> It is an odd state of affairs that has happened to me. When you were here you were silent; now you have gone away I long to see you to communicate my words to you and to see yours in return.[13]

Euthymios Tornikes describes the effect of a common acquaintance to Michael Choniates: 'present here he charmed me; absent he comforted me' and John Mauropous talks of the ancient habit of presence formed in words.[14]

Another antithesis is of far/near. St Basil while writing to the bishops of Italy and Gaul says that 'even if we are separated very far from each other by habitation, yet by reason at least of our union we are near each other.' Distance strikes many letter-writers as crucial: Gregory of Nazianzos notes 'What distance there is between Iberia and us! The way is more than a matter of a few days. But friendship joins those who are far apart.' John Mauropous begins a letter, 'From afar (*makrothen*) I extend you this letter as a pledge of friendship.'[15] The third antithesis is of soul/body which has ramifications far

---

[11] Synesios, ep. 138, ed. Garzya, 240-241.

[12] See Karlsson, *Idéologie et cérémonial*, 23-33; 34-56; For the letter as consolation see also below, 141; for the 'second best', see Libanios, ep. 83, ed. R. Foerster (Leipzig, 1921) X, 84; Michael Choniates, ep. 65, ed. S.P. Lampros, *Michaelis Acominati opera*, II (Athens, 1880), 105; for the shortened form *to deuteron* see Nicholas Mystikos, ep. 135, ed. Jenkins and Westerink, 436; on the *unio mystica* see below, 113.

[13] Gregory of Nazianzos, ep. 117, ed. P. Gallay, *Saint Grégoire de Nazianze, Lettres*, 2 vols (Paris, 1967), II, 10-11.

[14] For Euthymios Tornikes see J. Darrouzès, 'Un recueil épistolaire du XIIe siècle: Acad. roum. cod. gr. 508,' *REB* 30 (1972), 209; John Mauropous, ep. 29, ed. A. Karpozilos, *The Letters of John Mauropous, Metropolitan of Euchaita* (CFHB, 34, Thessalonike, 1990), 117.

[15] John Mauropous, ep. 16, ed. Karpozilos, 69; Basil, ep. 243, ed. R.J. Deferrari, *Saint Basil, the Letters*, 4 vols (London and Cambridge, Mass., 1930), III, 434; Gregory of Nazianzos, ep. 229, ed. Gallay, II, 120: ἀλλ' ἡ φιλία καὶ τὰ διεστῶτα ποιεῖ πλησίον.

beyond the Byzantine letter and yet regularly appears in it. Gregory of Nazianzos writes to Peter: 'I am cheered because the distance between us is of our bodies, not of the spirit'.[16]

Last there is the antithesis of separation/unity. It is expressed by Basil in a letter to Festus and Magnus:

> We though so much separated from you in body are always united in thought and converse easily with you, since teaching is not hindered by land or sea if you have any concern at all for your own souls.[17]

Invitations to stay are common in Byzantine letters, sometimes commuted into a desire to be 'visited by letter', a distant cousin of Karlsson's 'winged visit'. Hierotheos says 'a time difficult to evaluate has separated us and left us open to forgetfulness. Let us know where you are and visit us by letter.'[18] The effects of separation are also noted, the cooling of love and the danger of calumny.

A final result of the consciousness of distance as separation is the way in which voyages, real and imaginary, find their way into the Byzantine letter. Since the Hellenistic letters of fishermen,[19] Greek letters had a recurring connection with the sea. Recipients were more grateful for letter and bearer coming by sea and value their correspondents the more. Journeys were a consequence of separation and it is not surprising that they should have become an expected part of the Byzantine letter.

Voyage imagery is quite common, in the letter as elsewhere. Psellos uses an extended account of his wanderings in a desert, lame and without directions, to represent to John Mauropous his rhetorical meanderings in the letter;[20] real journeys also appear. Gregory of Nazianzos writes to Gregory of Nyssa:

> You are distressed by your journey, and you have the impression of being tossed like pieces of wood carried on the waters. No, admirable friends, do not think like that; your voyage was ordained by God.[21]

---

[16] Gregory of Nazianzos, ep. 242, ed. Gallay, II, 132.

[17] Basil, ep. 294, ed. Deferrari, IV, 204.

[18] Hierotheos, ep. 39, see Darrouzès, 212.

[19] E.g. Alkiphron, *Epistolai alieutikai*, ed. A.R. Benner and F.H. Fobes, *Alciphron, Aelian, Philostratus, The Letters* (London and Cambridge, Mass., 1962); on letters in the Second Sophistic see B. Reardon, *Courants littéraires grecs des IIe et IIIe siècles après J.C.* (Paris, 1971), 180-4; 187.

[20] Michael Psellos, ep. 45, ed. E. Kurtz and F. Drexl, *Scripta minora*, II (Milan, 1941), 76.

[21] Gregory of Nazianzos, ep. 81, ed. Gallay, I, 104.

Basil impresses on his correspondents the difficulties of travel:

> We have had great difficulty in obtaining a carrier for our letter to your
> reverence because in our land people shudder so at the winter that they
> cannot bring themselves even to put their heads out of their rooms for a
> moment. [22]

Euthymios Tornikes writes to Michael Choniates:

> I should like to travel to Keos, but fearful by nature, I content myself with
> hungry eyes in that direction. I am a land creature; I fear the sea and the
> hands of pirates who lurk around there.[23]

It is not surprising that set piece travel descriptions are among the most
elaborated scenes in Byzantine letters. Synesios's shipwreck and the
Palaiologan globetrotters are cases in point,[24] but there are also two brilliant
descriptions in Theophylact's collection. One, possibly dating from 1095,
describes how a storm prevented him from visiting Maria the ex-*basilissa* on
the Princes' Islands on his way back from Nicomedia to Constantinople.
Another, probably from 1108, describes in graphic detail his seasickness on
the boat from Constantinople to Thessalonike and his plans for returning on
horseback to Ochrid.[25] Letters are both bridge and barrier, and separation is
inscribed in the Byzantine letter.

   Another polarity which impresses students of epistolary literature is the
idea of confidentiality and mistrust. For Byzantine letters the polarity might
be put better in terms of public/private, for it is a commonplace that
Byzantine letters like western medieval ones were 'intimate and confidential
and intended for publication'.[26] They convey a very strong charge of intimacy,
yet Byzantines assumed that their letters would be seen by others.
Theophylact's G7 is a case in point:

> We wanted to pass our time in writing many words to your holiness and to
> show your eyes of affection the scene of many tragedies. But since we are

---

   [22] Basil, ep. 48, ed. Deferrari, I, 314; cf. Nicholas Mystikos, ep. 106, ed. Jenkins and
Westerink, 388.
   [23] Euthymios Tornikes, no.23, see Darrouzès, 'Un recueil,' 210.
   [24] Synesios, ep. 5, ed. Garzya, 11-26; Palaiologan letter-writers give an impression of
always being ahead of the mail, see Mullett, 'Classical Tradition,' 87-88.
   [25] G4, II, 137-141; G120, II, 553.14-28.
   [26] A. Morey and C.N.L. Brooke, *Gilbert Foliot and his Letters* (Cambridge, 1965), 13.

unfortunate in this, learn of it from our letter to our common acquaintance the Grand Domestic...[27]

The atmosphere of mistrust which coexists with the sense of confession and revelation in letters is clear in Theophylact's collection. Calumny is a constant worry for him. He berates the bishop of Triaditsa for bearing false witness about him to Constantinople, warns Michael Pantechnes of the dangers of becoming the emperor's doctor, and lives through a prolonged bout of calumny during which he begins to fear all his friends will be turned against him, and urges them to 'dispel the clouds of deceit'. He reports to the *chartophylax* Nikephoros that he had heard some very unattractive rumours about him.[28] But it was not a personal or hysterical worry peculiar to Theophylact: Basil explains the distress calumny can cause:

> Wherefore we have locked within the depth of our heart the pain which rises within us from calumny. For truly calumny humbles a man and calumny troubles a poor man.[29]

And Byzantine letter-writers are constantly alive to the possibility of calumny. John Mauropous write 'so some idle rumour has troubled you...I have not heard a single rumour against you.'[30]

One result is the formality of Byzantine letters which coexists with the intimacy; it is a public intimacy. As Julian wrote

> With regard to the letters which he asserts you made public after receiving them from me, it seems ridiculous to bring them into court. For I call the gods to witness I have never written to you or any other man a word which I am not willing to publish for all to see. I have always expressed myself with more dignity and reserve than one observed even on a sacred subject. I call the gods and goddesses to witness that I should have not resented it even if someone had published abroad all that I ever wrote to my wife, so temperate was it in every respect. [31]

This vaunted restraint did not stop Julian referring to the beginnings of his campaign against Constantius in ep. 6. Very often, as the Madrid Skylitzes records, writing a letter was a political act. But if restraint is one result of the

---

[27] G7, II, 151.2-6.

[28] G45, 57, 61, 87, 89, II, 281-287, 323-325, 351-353, 445-451, 457-459, 465-467.

[29] Basil, ep. 223, ed. Deferrari, III, 289.

[30] John Mauropous, ep. 3, ed. Karpozilos, 47.3-8.

[31] Julian, ep. 29, ed. W.C. Wright, *The Works of the Emperor Julian*, III (London and Cambridge, Mass., 1923), 100, 102.

lack of privacy of letters, allusiveness is another: Julian referred to that campaign as 'hunting small deer'.[32] Theophylact masks his enemies; they are ὁ καστροκτίστης καὶ ὁ κατεπάνος, or a nickname like Beliar, Briareus, Typhon, Charybdis.[33] Sometimes calumny is mentioned but not a calumniator.[34] Better still the problem is reduced to generalities. In a letter to the metropolitan of Kerkyra he tells us why, in terms of the trust/mistrust polarity:

> But all this, though I very much long to spew it all out, to get some small consolation, I will bear with endurance and without feebleness, and I will place a guard upon my tongue, as if the sinner were standing in front of me, so that I do not shame the great name and reality of the archiepiscopate. For it is the function of the letter to chatter, not to be discreet...[35]

This leads us to another polarity observed by students of the epistolary novel: the writer and the reader. Byzantine composition and reception were more complicated than this, but the relationship between writer and recipient is central. Every letter must be interpreted in terms of what is known of the recipient as well as the writer;[36] the letter is an interactive form and any collection is only half of the whole. Mention of third persons distracts attention from the central relationship, which is nurtured and portrayed by the letter. This is why the names of third persons, external events and direct speech are rare in the letter;[37] all appear in Theophylact's collection, but they

---

[32] Julian, ep. 6, ed. Wright, 18; for political letters in the Madrid Skylitzes, including the case of Patriarch Tryphon, see my 'Writing in Early Mediaeval Byzantium,' *The Uses of Literacy in Early Mediaeval Europe*, ed. R. McKitterick (Cambridge, 1989), 156-185 at 170-171. For illustrations of the manuscript see J.C. Estopañan, *Skylitzes Matritensis, I: Reproducciones y miniaturas* (Barcelona and Madrid, 1965); A. Grabar and M. Manoussacas, *L'Illustration du manuscrit de Skylitzes de la Bibliothèque nationale de Madrid* (Bibliothèque de l'Institut hellénique d'études byzantines et post-byzantines de Venise, 10, Venice, 1979). For rebellions (of Leo Phokas in 919, John Tzimiskes in 969 and Leo Tornikios in 1046-47) see fol. 125v, E fig. 306, p. 133, GM299; fol. 157vb, E fig. 415, GM408 and fig. 204; fol. 230b, E fig. 569, p. 212; GM562. The most furtively conspiratorial case is that of Joseph Bringas in 963, fol. 144a, E fig. 378, p. 152, GM363.

[33] G32, 55, 61, 96, 31, II, 237.18-19, 317.21, 351.12, 483.23, 233.18.

[34] See n. 26 above.

[35] G75, to the bishop of Kerkyra, II, 401.35-36, quoting from Synesios.

[36] Demetrios, *Peri Hermeneias*, 124, ed. R. Roberts, *Demetrius on Style* (Cambridge, 1902), 177: 'it is right to have regard to the person to whom the letter is addressed'.

[37] Third persons: Lazaros in G96, 98; Iasites in G88; the 'good young governor' in G79; the eunuch cantor Gregory in G66. External events: the First Crusade in G52; the Reconquest in G8; Gregory Taronites' campaigns in Pontos; the war with Bohemond,

are exceptions. Letter G21 shows us the changeover of local officials in detail; a total of five other persons are mentioned in what appears to be an urgent briefing. One is the outgoing *strategos*, another Eumathios, who has been put in to inspect his administration, a third is the new *strategos*, Michael son of Polyeuktos. In this situation Theophylact asks the bishop to look after Demetrios Kritopoulos and his brother, who has many enemies, and to see that the interests of Eumathios are his own. Presumably on this occasion names had to be named if the bishop was to react correctly. In G23 he also reveals names; those of the litigious Nicholas *ho tou Boutou* and his victim Michael Beses Lampenos, together with a Makrembolites whom he accuses of being expert in removing other people's property.[38] But the most remarkable is the long letter to Gregory Taronites, G127, in which after mentioning the Cyclops, Beliar and Polyphemos, possibly local enemies, he expounds upon the extraordinary abilities and charms of one Theodore Chryselios. The tone of the letter is light, gossipy and secure in the central relationship of Gregory and Theophylact, but the concentration on the satiric characterisation of Theodore is extraordinary; one might almost have assumed that it (God's gift, the golden boy) was not his real name.[39] This letter has the sense of a shared joke which will always elude the modern scholar.[40] A tax-collector Iasites is mentioned twice in the correspondence, a peasant Lazaros memorably, and various officials drift into Theophylact's range or out of it,[41] but nothing quite so extraordinary as G127.

A final polarity which is worth considering is the relationship between letter and letter-collection.[42] We rarely know in Byzantium how the collection came into being, and we can never be certain of its original arrangement. But a problematic letter can frequently be explained by others in the collection, though there is a danger of allowing context (in the sense of surrounding

---

G130. Direct speech: Demetrios in G123; the archontes at the synod in G58; the desired speech of Melissenos in G9.

[38]   G21, II, 199; G23, II, 207.3-5.

[39]   But see J.C. Cheynet, *Pouvoir et contestations à Byzance, 963-1210* (ByzSorb, 9, Paris, 1986), 234, 342, on members of the Dyrrachion family of Chryselios.

[40]   G127, II, 571-579; cf. the punchline of 'a certain priest and Aelfgyva,' F.M. Stenton, *The Bayeux Tapestry: a Comprehensive Survey* (London, 1957); 19; see J.B. McNulty, 'The Lady Aelfgyva in the Bayeux Tapestry,' *Speculum* 55 (1980), 659-668 and a letter to the *Times* by E.L. Harrison, 22 January 1981.

[41]   Iasites: G11, II, 163.19, 165.26; G88, II, 461.13; Lazaros: G96, II, 485.27, 32, 493.143, G98, II, 501.31, 503.70.

[42]   On the relationship of part and whole (though in epistolary novels) see Altman, *Epistolarity*, ch. 6, 'The Epistolary Mosaic,' 167-184. A similar study is needed of letters in collections in the Byzantine world.

letters) to create meaning. An example is Meursius's reading of G123, which he assumed to have the same subject-matter as the two preceding it. In fact there appears to be a disturbance in the collection at that point and in any case G123 does not appear to be connected to G121 and G122, the accounts of the death of Theophylact's brother Demetrios.[43] But our text is the collection and we must look at its articulation, checking all the time where individual letters may fit.

Sir Walter Scott described the letter as a slow moving form, but it can accelerate, as we see in the letters of Theophylact's collection during the Lazaros crisis. What appears to be an occasional grumble speeds up into feverish activity and winter letter-bearing. A more cinematic image is perhaps better, of a series of stills jerkily spliced together. In the uncertainty over the dating of Theophylact's collection and the homogeneity of much of his discourse, it is a considerable challenge to reconstruct the narrative of his letter-collection.

A final note about the term 'genre', which I have used so far to describe the letter. It is probably a misnomer; Janet Altman for example talks about 'approaches to a form'. Could it be a mode? a type?[44] Discussions of genre sometimes imply that there is a single immutable genre-system; few theorists now would agree.[45] It is for us to identify the Byzantine genre-system.[46] Everyone agrees that the Byzantines were very genre-conscious although there

---

[43] G123, II, 563, cf. PG 126, 488 where M LXVIII has the heading *de eadem* (i.e. de fratris morte). The effect of this reading is to take the χωρίζω of line 2 to mean death and probably to read the σεβαστός of 563.9 as God. For an alternative reading see below, 22 and 342.

[44] For definitions of 'mode' see A. Fowler, *Kinds of Literature: an Introduction to the Theory of Genres and Modes* (Oxford, 1982), 106-111; H. Dubrow, *Genre* (The Critical Idiom, 42, London and New York, 1982) on Northrop Frye's modes and myths, 99-100; F. Cairns, *Generic Composition in Greek and Roman Poetry* (Edinburgh, 1972), ch. 3, 'The Categories of Genres,' 70-85. For 'kind' see Fowler, 56-74, for 'type', see 126-128. Cairns distinguishes 'rhetorical' from 'non-rhetorical'. I use 'form' to indicate mode of communication (speech, letter, poem) and 'type' to represent the occasional element or subject matter generally. In general see R. Champigny, 'Semantic Modes and Literary Genres,' *Theories of Literary Genres*, ed. S. Strelka (University Park, PA and London, 1978), 94-111.

[45] On this see Fowler, *Kinds*, 37; P. Hernadi, *Beyond Genre: New Directions in Literary Classification* (Cornell, 1972).

[46] Recording how texts are identified in the works themselves and in inventories and library collections is of vital importance but only a first step. It would be very disappointing to rely on these identifications without further analysis (as well as abdicating the duty of the literary historian); it seems to be emerging (from the doctoral research of Judith Waring) that inventories and catalogues are remarkably unconcerned with genre, while writers are very genre-conscious.

is no Byzantine treatise on the systems of genres. Even if there were one it is questionable whether it would be applicable over the whole period of the Byzantine empire. But the *Souda* is frequently concerned to fit a work into the right category, and Photios is usually aware of the kind of work he is reviewing.[47] Theophylact on several occasions makes it clear by a kind of Foucault-like exclusion[48] that he knows what a letter is not. In G53 he says it is time to speak τὸ προφητικόν; in G95 he offers his correspondent the opportunity of listening to *tragedies*; in G76 he opposes *iambics* and *elegies*; in G47 he recalls a line from the *Frogs* as '*comic*'; the frogs jumping on the back of the rhetorical eagle sing an *epinician paean*; Theophylact in G55 *lamented his fate*.[49] So it seems reasonable to arrive at some view of where letters fit with other kinds of writing in Byzantium. The examples from Theophylact show that the Byzantines thought in terms of external forms as well as content, and that to use only Menander's types, which are based on content and occasion,[50] would be unsatisfactory.

We need, I believe, classification both in terms of form—epic, epigram and so on—and also in terms of types, of occasional content—*epibaterion*, *basilikos logos* and so on. Where these two coordinates meet is a genre. The form provides an element of performance or reception: is it oral or written? prose or verse? in what metre? reciprocal or not? long or short? (i.e. performed at a single sitting or more?) It also determines the nature of the discourse. The type provides the occasion, the function and the status and

---

[47] Photios to Tarasios: 'The works will be arranged in the order in which our memory recalled each of them; it is not difficult if one wishes to separate all the historical works on one hand and on the other books of various different types', ed. R. Henry, *Photius, Bibliothèque*, 6 vols (Paris, 1959-), I, 1-2; tr. N. Wilson, *The Bibliotheca of Photius* (London, 1994), 1-2. And see the *Souda*, for example on Procopius, *Anekdota*, ed. A. Adler (Leipzig, 1935), IV, 211: ψόγους καὶ κωμῳδίαν.

[48] M. Foucault, 'The Discourse on Language,' tr. R. Sawyer, appendix to *The Archaeology of Knowledge*, tr. A.M. Sheridan-Smith (New York, 1972), 216-219.

[49] G53, to Gregory Kamateros, II, 307.2 (quotations from Joel, Jeremiah, Jonah, Lamentations, Micah, Hagar, Isaiah and the Psalms follow; G95, to Smyrnaios, II, 481.2; G76, to Mermentoulos, II, 405.24-25; G47 to Mermentoulos, II, 293.2: τὸ κωμικόν, εὖ οἶδα, κομμάτιον; G6, to Smyrnaios, for the frogsong, II, 147.19; G55, to Pakourianos, II, 317.2: πάλαι τὴν ἐμαυτοῦ θρηνῶν τύχην. They are not all to literary producers, but note how characteristically they come at the beginning of a letter, signalling its literary pretensions for the reader/listener at the start.

[50] There may be many levels of classification working in Byzantine minds, by Muse, by occasion, by progymnasmatic technique, by style, by metre, which by themselves do not add up to a genre-system. For a suggestion of ways forward in determining the genre-system of the Byzantines see my 'Madness of Genre,' *Homo Byzantinus*, 233-243.

transactional relationships between the implied speaker and the implied recipient. It too can determine discourse. So Theophylact's G4 to Maria is in form a letter, written, reciprocal, performed at a sitting but part of a collection which is not, and is characterised by intimacy, restraint, a lack of third persons and a slow-motion or jerky narrative structure. In type it is an apologetic *hodoiporikon*, addressed to a patroness in place of a personal visit. Together the type and the form define the kind of letter G4 is. It could have been a hexameter poem, or a speech, but it is a letter. It could have been a letter sending Maria off to the Princes' Islands or consoling her for her fate; it would then have been a propemptic letter or a *paramythetike*.

Sometimes the generic pattern is not simple. An included genre or modulations of genre are also possible;[51] let us look at the puzzling G123, odd in so many ways. It has no forms of address, it is quite short, it uses direct speech and it describes an incident involving a third person, Theophylact's brother. In it Theophylact describes how his brother looked at the moment of leaving Theophylact, transfused with a radiance which makes Theophylact ask him why. 'Because I hope to see the *sebastos*', he replied, 'and the hope passed by way of my veins to my face.' Theophylact bit his lips at this reminder and reflected how blessed his brother was to enjoy that sight and to regale himself with the ambrosia and nectar of the other's character. 'Do not cease', says Theophylact, 'to continue drawing everyone to you by the golden chain of goodness'. Certainly this letter does not admit of complete explanation, but considerable elements of it suggest another genre, hagiography, in vision scenes especially close to the death of the saint.[52] Demetrios then is saintly, but the *sebastos* is God-like. Like art,[53] genre can say the unsayable.

So inclusion of another genre within epistolography contributes tacitly to its message: hagiography here, *basilikos logos* in G81 and G8. We may not reconstruct the eleventh-century genre-system in all its complexity. But

---

[51] On inclusion see Cairns, *Generic Composition*, 158-176; on modulation, Fowler, *Kinds*, 191-212.

[52] Cf. in particular Niketas Stethatos, *Bios kai politeia tou en hagiois patros hemon Symeon tou neou theologou, presbyterou, hegoumenou mones tou hagiou Mamantos tes Xenokerkiou*, ed. I. Hausherr, *Un grand mystique byzantin. Vie de Syméon le nouveau théologien* (OC, 12, Rome, 1928), 126, where again the watcher and his reactions are in the foreground.

[53] R. Cormack, *Writing in Gold. Byzantine Society and its Icons* (London, 1985), 242.

understanding the form and the conventions of the type are prerequisites to understanding Theophylact's letter-collection.

2.2 The evaluation of the Byzantine letter

What value should we place on the Byzantine letter? Recent scholars have been unsure. In 1963 Jenkins wrote:

> To us a letter is a message accompanied by an expression of personal regard; a Byzantine letter is an impersonal rhetorical flourish which either contains no message at all, or if it does, the message is couched in so obscure and allusive a fashion as to be nearly unintelligible.[54]

Schubart had gone further in denying the epistolarity of the Byzantine letter:

> Mit dem ausgebildeten Byzantinismus der Sprache im 6.Jh. geht der griechische Brief unter, denn den Privatbriefen dieser Zeit fehlen so gut wie alle seine wesentliche Merkmale.[55]

Dennis agreed:

> The average Byzantine letter is about as concrete, informative and personal as the modern mass-produced greetings card.[56]

echoing the judgment of Sir Samuel Dill on the letters of Symmachus:

> Indeed it is hard to see why a great many of these letters should have been written at all. They are about as interesting as a visiting card, and seem to have had no more significance than a polite attention.[57]

Dennis then took a moral stance:

> Manuel's letters are primarily of a rhetorical nature...As such they reflect the worst characteristics of the rhetoric employed by the Byzantines. There is a

---

[54] R.J.H. Jenkins, 'The Hellenistic Origins of Byzantine Literature,' *DOP* 17 (1963), 45.
[55] W. Schubart, *Einführung in die Papyruskunde* (Berlin, 1918), 212.
[56] Dennis, *The Letters of Manuel II*, xix.
[57] S. Dill, *Roman Society in the Last Century of the Western Empire* (London, 1899); cf. J. Matthews, 'The Letters of Symmachus,' *Latin Literature of the Fourth Century*, ed. J.W. Binns (London, 1974), 62: 'we have nothing but a stack of visiting cards, a series of polite attentions; to put it otherwise, a museum of late Roman amicitia in all its complacency, with its affected rules of etiquette, its repetitive trivialities.'

fundamental dishonesty; while living in one world they speak from another.
It is unimportant whether or not what they say is related to reality; how
they say it is what matters.[58]

Even the most experienced editors of Byzantine letters are unsure of their
value once they are edited. In Gautier's most useful edition of the letters of
Michael Italikos he warns the reader that 'la coutume solidement établie qui
impose à un épistolier byzantin de s'abstenir de détails personnels...a pour
effet constant de placer dans le plus grand embarras celui qui se propose
d'esquisser sa biographie, et avec Michel Italikos nous n'y echappons pas.' He
adds, rather despondently, 'Le resultat n'a pas...répondu à nos espérances',
and, almost apologetically, 'le lecteur, tenté de critiquer l'incompétence de
l'éditeur, voudra donc bien aussi s'en prendre aux silences de l'auteur.'[59] In his
edition of the letters of Gregory, abbot of Oxeia, he even poses the question:
'L'édition de ces lettres était-elle justifiée?' and answers it in a way that seems
less than confident: 'Nous le croyons, en depit de leur apparente vacuité, car il
est déjà arrivé que la découverte de nouveaux textes ou une meilleure édition
de textes connus attirât l'attention sur les documents jusqu'alors jugés
insignifiants et en facilitât la compréhension.' He explains elsewhere what has
been so dispiriting: 'Le contenu des lettres est decevant, au moins pour les
historiens. Grégoire se maintient dans la droite ligne des épistoliers byzantins:
ils ne s'abandonne jamais, sauf une ou deux fois, au moindre détail concret, à
la moindre allusion à des événements contemporains.'[60]

This would immediately damn them with Darrouzès as well. In 1970 he
laid down his ground-lines: 'Les lettres sont d'autant plus utiles pour
l'historien que leur insertion dans le contexte historique est precisé par la date,
par des noms connus, pars des allusions claires.'[61]

Where do the letters of Theophylact rate on this exacting scale which
makes no allowance for literary value or the study of unidentified personal
relations? Curiously Theophylact has done well, and appears to stand out
from other collections:

---

[58] Dennis, *The Letters of Manuel II*, xix-xx. But note the 'conversion' of Fr Dennis, 'The
Byzantines revealed in their letters', *Gonimos: Neoplatonic and Byzantine Studies presented to
Leendert G. Westerink at 75=Arethusa* (Buffalo, 1988), 159, where he generously refers to
the passages quoted above as 'my unkind words'.

[59] P. Gautier, *Michel Italikos, Lettres et discours* (AOC, 14, Paris, 1972), 14, 5, 14.

[60] P. Gautier, 'Les lettres de Grégoire, higoumène d'Oxia,' *REB* 31 (1973), 203-227 at
204.

[61] J. Darrouzès, *Georges et Dèmètrios Tornikès, Lettres et discours* (Le monde byzantin,
Paris, 1970), 5.

A ses diverses sources il faut ajouter les écrits de Théophylacte, archevêque de Bulgarie sous le règne d'Alexis, qui nous ont fourni quantité de renseignements précieux.

So Chalandon; Ostrogorsky agrees:

The occasional writings and letters of Byzantine authors of this period form an important supplement to historical works. The correspondence of Archbishop Theophylact of Ochrid is of the greatest value in throwing light on the conditions in Macedonia under Byzantine rule in Alexius's reign.[62]

It sounds like a different genre. But with the new Assumptionist edition Theophylact is put back in his place:

La correspondance de Théophylacte obéit aux lois de l'épistolographie byzantine, dont le but est plus littéraire qu'utilitaire, plus théorique que pratique...Mais abondance de paroles n'implique pas richesse d'informations...Souhaitons que, pour l'essentiel, il ait su y faire apparaître, sous la paille foissonnante des mots, le grain epars des realités.[63]

It is perhaps more useful to ask what value Byzantines placed on their letters. Rarely are we told directly. The emperor Julian said

There is a tradition that Alexander of Macedon used to sleep with Homer's poems under his pillow...but I sleep with your letters as though they were healing drugs of some sort, and I do not cease to read them constantly as though they were newly written and were only just come into hand.[64]

More often we need to examine how they are described. For St Basil the letter was an opportunity for good deeds.[65] Most of his contemporaries and successors saw it in much more romantic terms; it is essentially something very precious, rare and longed for. Theophylact uses the image of dew in a desert.[66] Music is often evoked: Gregory of Nazianzos decribed Amphilochios's letters as a lyre set within his soul, and the monk Hierotheos in the twelfth century told his correspondent that letters had the same power

---

[62] F. Chalandon, *Les Comnène,* I, *Essai sur le règne d'Alexis Ier Comnène* (Paris, 1900), I, xxiii; G. Ostrogorsky, *History of the Byzantine State,* tr. J.M. Hussey (London, 1968), 314.

[63] A. Failler, 'Introduction,' Gautier, *Théophylacte,* II.

[64] Julian, ep. 12, ed. Wright, 30.

[65] Basil, ep. 306, ed. Deferrari, IV, 238.

[66] G73, II, 389.2; G75, II, 399.13.

as the music of Orpheus.[67] Birdsong, especially that of nightingales or
swallows, is extremely common.[68]

A conceit popular with Hierotheos in the twelfth century is the idea of
a mirror which shows not the features of the recipient but of the sender:

> I have received the golden letter, emanation of your spirit, your hand's
> writing, as if in a mirror I saw all the qualities of my holy lord.

'Do not cease,' he exhorts a correspondent elsewhere, 'to see us through the
mirror of letters.'[69]

This is clearly connected to the most prevalent and precious of images
used of letters in the Byzantine period, that of an icon of the soul. The image
has a long pedigree, being found first in the *Peri Hermeneias* of 'Demetrios'
and appearing frequently in Julian, Gregory of Nyssa, John Chrysostom,
Theodoret and in later writers.[70] Symeon Metaphrastes speaks of his desire to
see the prototype of the icon, that is his correspondent, an image which is
rather more elevated than others of the tenth century which usually speak of
images of honey, fragrant flowers or the bewitching song of the Sirens.[71] A
higher note is struck by Gregory of Nazianzos, who in an Easter letter says,
'Your letter also is a feast.' Michael Psellos found the letter was a truer

---

[67] Gregory of Nazianzos, ep. 171, ed. Gallay, II, 60; Hierotheos see Darrouzès, 224.

[68] For nightingales and swallows see John Mauropous, ep. 1, ed. Karpozilos, 43-45;
Michael Psellos, ep. 199, ed. Kurtz-Drexl, II, 227; Procopius, ep. 69, ed. R. Hercher,
Epistolographi graeci (Paris, 1873), 558; see Karlsson, *Idéologie et cérémonial*, 106-111; M.
Herzfeld, *The Chelidonisma: a Study in Textual and Ritual Variation* (unpublished MA
thesis, Birmingham 1972).

[69] Hierotheos, ep. 186, see Darrouzès, 326.

[70] Demetrios, *Peri Hermeneias*, 227, ed. Roberts, 174. For examples see Julian, epp. 12,
16, 67, ed. Wright, 30, 36, 223-224; Gregory of Nyssa, ep. 18, ed. Maraval, 232-234; John
Chrysostom, ep. 68, PG 52, 646; Theodoret, ep. 50, ed. Y. Azéma, *Theodoret de Cyr,
Correspondance*, II (SC, 98, Paris, 1964), 126. A. Littlewood, 'An Ikon of the Soul: the
Byzantine Letter', *Visible Language* 10 (1976), 197-226.

[71] Symeon Magistros, epp. 85, 89, ed. Darrouzès, *Épistoliers byzantins*, 147, 151; for
honey see Symeon Magistros again, epp. 84, 91, ed. Darrouzès, 147, 152; Theodore of
Kyzikos, epp. 4, 6, 16, ed. Darrouzès, 321, 323, 331; Nikephoros Ouranos, epp. 4,5,16, ed.
Darrouzès, 218, 219, 225; for flowers see Symeon Magistros, epp. 23, 91, ed. Darrouzès,
114, 152. For sirens see Symeon Magistros, ep. 23; Nikephoros Ouranos, ep. 19, ed.
Darrouzès, 114, 226. On all this, A.R. Littlewood, 'Byzantine Letterwriting in the Tenth
Century,' *Aufstieg und Niedergang der römischen Welt*, alas still (twenty years later) in press,
is essential.

distillation of friendship than physical presence but the finest sentiment of all, found in several twelfth-century writers, 'letters are a gift from God.'[72]

Failure in communication is also worth observing. Demands for letters range in Byzantine letters from the simple request to desperation and threats. Silence (*sige* or *siope* or *agraphia*) was castigated or apologised for. Gregory of Nazianzos appeared to believe that letter-writing was possible during a vow of complete silence, a mean between speech and silence, a positive shared silence. But by the tenth century *siope* means 'failure to write letters', a synonym of *agraphia,* and Symeon Magistros complains to a friend who has just entered a monastery that he is practising Pythagorean silence. For George Tornikes the opposite of *siope* was *lalia* or *polyphonia*, profoundly to be hoped for. *Agraphia* was to be avoided and was a matter for reproach or shame.[73]

What has Theophylact to say about letters? His simplest definition is this: 'Letters are a gift from God, through which friends address friends and slaves greet their masters from afar',[74] an admirably functional view. But elsewhere he puts it more emotively:

> As I returned from my wearisome journey of many days, most honoured Lord, the letter of your holiness fell into my hands, and it appeared sweeter to me than a following wind to sailors after they have toiled at rowing, or (if you prefer) than a fountain to a thirsty deer. May you never rob me of your beautiful speech, and for ever and ever may you make me hear your voice, which is the same as saying your rejoicing. But in these pitiless parts of the world, the workshop of all evil, if you do not spoonfeed us with these sweet pages, what else is there for us, but to descend into hell or to float away towards evil?[75]

Elsewhere he reverses the order: in a letter written in early May, 1103, he describes first the effect on him: 'Nothing of my misfortune remains to me, for I have received an address from the sweetest of all men in voice and mind, and not for a moment like a stroke of lightning, which comes and goes at once, but steady and continuous.' Then we are told that this happened 'while seizing the letter'; the image of Medea's love-charm is added, and finally the actual physical receipt of the letter is again described, 'for while we were on

---

[72] Gregory of Nazianzos, ep. 115, ed. Gallay, II, 9-10; Michael Psellos, ep. 11, ed. K.N. Sathas, *Mesaionike Bibliotheke*, V (Venice and Paris, 1876), 242-244; e.g. Hierotheos, ep. 84, see Darrouzès, 216.

[73] Gregory of Nazianzos, epp. 107-119, ed. Gallay, II, 5-11, letters dating to the Lent of 382 and Gregory's vow of complete silence; Symeon Magistros, ep. 11, ed. Darrouzès, 105. George Tornikes, epp. 6, 16, ed. Darrouzès, 117, 140.

[74] G10, II, 161.2-4.

[75] G30, II, 229.2-15.

the road to Great Achilleios, whose feast we will celebrate, your letter was put in our hands.'[76]

G75 celebrates a letter received by Theophylact:

> What is there to say...? I received your letter with great pleasure, most honoured lord, and everything is beautiful at the right time, but especially the word, and especially the word born of such thought and delivered by such a tongue.

That tongue he says is 'seasoned with the charm and salt of brotherly love.'[77] He frequently recounts the effect letters have on him:

> It was very sweet to receive your letter. In my present depression you offer me a medicine banishing care and to a thirsty man the sweetest liquid out of the rock...The dew around you is become a medicine to us.

> The hand of your letter saved me from faintheartedness and led me back from the hurricane and the abyss and drew me out of the mud of pollution.[78]

He claims he gains therapeutic value also from writing letters. He writes to the patriarch: 'I do not give more joy than I receive from these letters written to your holy lordship...It is enough to look at the desired even through a mirror or in a riddle, and to listen out to the uttermost despite the distance.'[79]

But letters are the symbol of reciprocity and must be a two-way traffic. 'It is a real feast for me to write to you, you who outshine anything which characterises a man. But when I receive a letter in return, then that is for me the supreme feast and a real crown of graces.' He requests letters in fourteen of his own letters,[80] once, unselfishly not for himself, and once pretends (unconvincingly) that he is glad not to have had a letter.[81] He excuses his own sige, caused by worry or illness or a lack of schole.[82] But this is a temporary

---

[76] G78, II, 415.2-18.

[77] G75, II, 399.2-4.

[78] G75, to the bishop of Kerkyra, II, 399.5-6; 12-13; G54, to the patriarch, II, 313.8-10, quoting Ps 54.9 (55.8) and 70 (71).20.

[79] G64, to the patriarch, II, 361.1-2; 13-15.

[80] G25, to Mermentoulos, II, 213.2-4. Letters requested: G12, 25, 33, 42, 44, 49, 76, 104, 109, 115, 130, 131. G67, to Gregory Kamateros, asks for letters for the 'good young governor'. See below, Table VI.

[81] G130, to Michael Pantechnes, II, 585.2-3.

[82] Worry: G52, to the bishop of Kitros, II, 303; illness: G103, to the Bulgarians taught by him, II, 517.2-4; lack of leisure: G62, to the maistor John, II, 355.2-3.

condition, for *sige* for Theophylact was a crime against λόγοι and against φιλία. Letters are 'the spring of the year and the music of the Olympian gods,'[83] like 'medicine to a sick man and allies to a man worn down by war,' 'the dew of consolation,' (after a period of *sige*) 'the phoenix of Helioupolis', or quite simply 'pearl-like'.[84] We might suspect that what he values so greatly is not the letter but what lies behind it, the message, except that he sometimes explicitly praises the transaction of letter-exchange.

One of the great effects of a letter, he tells the bishop of Pelagonia, is that one is able to be in two places at once; the letter in this way performs miracles. 'With God's grace of letters,' he tells the bishop of Kerkyra, 'the clever tricks of the envious are utterly foiled.' 'Praise be to God for all the examples of his outpouring goodness, and especially for letters.'[85] But the central conviction of his belief in letters is expressed in a letter to Machetares, G44: 'If God is love, as the disciple beloved in Christ declared, I believe that letters of love are not a descent from God, but an ascent to Him, and that they are Jacob's ladder, having words which unite instead of angels, and that at the top, and before all is God.' A whole heavenly dimension is elaborated here; letters between friends emanate from God in the first place, but are judged worthy to lead the soul back to God.[86] Later in this letter he adds another heavenly image:

> Write to us for this reason, and make us a present of your letters like a golden chain suspended from the heaven, to quote an ancient author, carrying with it those who climb upon it.[87]

---

[83] (not as Gautier says the Olympic games): G33, to Mermentoulos, II, 241.5-6.

[84] Medicine and allies; G33, to Mermentoulos, II, 241.7-9; dew of consolation: G73 to the caesar Melissenos, II, 389.2-3; the phoenix, G76, to Mermentoulos, II, 403.4; pearly: G127, to Gregory Kamateros, II, 573.26.

[85] For bilocation: G36, to the bishop of Pelagonia, II, 249.2-5; for the tricks of the envious G77, to the bishop of Kerkyra, II, 407.10-13; especially for letters: G10, to the son of the sebastokrator, II, 161.2-3.

[86] G44, to Machetares, II, 277.2-6. Theophylact uses the image of Jacob's ladder elsewhere, G43, probably not to Theophylact Romaios but to Tarchaneiotes, II, 275.4 but in the sense of spiritual progress, cf. the *Ladder of Divine Ascent* of St John Klimax.

[87] G44, II, 277.10. quoting Homer, *Il.*, 8.19, cf. Symeon the New Theologian, *Kephalaia praktika kai theologika*, no 4, ed. J. Darrouzès, *Chapitres théologiques, gnostiques et pratiques* (SC, 51, Paris, 1957), 81; the long chain of reminiscences of this passage include Milton, Spenser, Blake and Tennyson. We have seen the golden chain used in another sense, a kind of golden net (ἐπιπλέκων) to draw other people to the *sebastos*, G123, to Constantine Komnenos, II, 563.15-16: 'see how you draw everyone to you by the golden chain of your goodness'.

Letters as ladder and chain connect their writers with the Judaeo-Christian and the pagan heavens; they are 'a visit from on high'. But they have a more mundane function, especially for bishops. 'If,' Theophylact says, 'today's clergy experience pressure like a swimmer immersed, why deprive us of the consolation that we draw from your letters? It would be like depriving a sick man of his medication or a general of auxiliary troops.'[88]

This attempt to understand the value of letters to Byzantines may point the way to readers struggling with the vacuity or obscurity of letter-collections. For all kinds of reasons letters are not easily legible to us; Jenkins, with his concept of the wrapping-up of the message, noted an important point here. So did Dennis with his concept of two worlds. It was for Theophylact the function of letters to carry him into a different world, whether the centres of power in the capital or circles of likeminded scholar-administrators—or to God.

Failler's point about the status of letters is also a good one. But in suggesting that Byzantine letters are literary rather than utilitarian, he goes too far; we have seen enough to grasp that letters were regarded as valuable and precious, *inter alia* because they were functional. Theophylact brackets λόγοι with φιλία. Letters were evaluated by recipients on literary grounds, but those literary criteria verged frequently on the social.

Historians may benefit greatly from Byzantine letter-collections, and often in a straightforward positivist way. Without Gautier's painstaking prosopography our knowledge of the literary and ecclesiastical world at the turn of the eleventh and twelfth centuries would be very much less. Nor is it true that Byzantine letters do not deal with everyday reality;[89] they do, that is their function. But it was also their function to withdraw correspondents from that world and allow them to transcend it. If we read letters carefully we may learn a great deal about the shared aspirations and values of an enclosed group, which was responsible both for the administration of the empire and for what we know of it.

Failler would seem to hand letters over to the literary scholar. What is she to do with them? It is clear that letters were a valued form in Byzantium, more central than in many cultures. Literary scholars have still to analyse the techniques of production, but still more the expectations of reception. Evaluation is perhaps not the best way to approach the problem (and certainly not in the pejorative manner beloved of Byzantinists until recently). Literary scholars in other literatures have shrunk from evaluation in recent years

---

[88] G33, to Mermentoulos, II, 241.7-9.

[89] P. Magdalino, 'The Literary Perception of Everyday Life in Byzantium: Some General Considerations and the Case of John Apokaukos,' *BS* 47 (1987), 28-38.

(though some are nostalgic);[90] the study of Byzantine literature is so young that it seems more urgent to examine its nature and its first evaluative community than to offer evaluation itself. To discover the horizons of expectation of the various stages of reception of the Byzantine letter would seem to be desirable, and in this the literary scholar and the historian are not very far apart.

2.3 The reception of Byzantine letters

Twenty illustrations in the Madrid manuscript of the eleventh-century chronicle of Skylitzes show the process of letter-exchange, epitomised in the transaction of delivery.[91] The bearer, the *komistes*, hands over a scroll to the recipient.[92] In some cases the whole process is shown, like a communication diagram.[93] But unlike that diagram the scene in the manuscript should be read from right to left: the handing over of the letter to the bearer by the sender, then the carrying of the letter and then the delivery of the letter to the recipient. In three cases the swift horses of the bearer are shown;[94] in two cases the recipient waits patiently for his aide de camp to receive the letter and either hand it to him or read it aloud.[95] The emphasis is on ceremony, on the

---

[90] For a straightforward account of a concept of 'literature' freed from aesthetics or 'literariness' see T. Bennett, *Formalism and Marxism* (London, 1979); cf. S. Fish, *Is there a Text in this Class? The Authority of Interpretive Communities* (Cambridge, Mass. and London, 1980) 10-11 on literature as a conventional category. But for a nostalgic attachment to evaluation see Fish, 37.

[91] On the manuscript see N.G. Wilson, 'The Madrid Skylitzes,' *Scrittura e civiltà*, 2 (1978), 209; I. Ševčenko, 'The Madrid ms of the Chronicle of Skylitzes in the Light of its New Dating,' *Byzanz und der Westen. Studien der Kunst des europäischen Mittelalters*, ed. I. Hutter (Oesterreichische Akademie der Wissenschaften, Phil.hist. Kl., Sitzungsberichte, 432, Vienna, 1984), 117-130; C. Walter, *Art and Ritual in the Byzantine Church* (BBS, 1, London, 1982), 41-45. On using the manuscript see my 'Writing,' 169-170. A Belfast project will examine narrative in text, captions and illustrations.

[92] On an iconography of 'the sending of a letter' see G. Galavaris, *The Illustrations of the Prefaces in Byzantine Gospels* (ByzVind, 11, Vienna, 1979), 54.

[93] E.g. fol. 75v=E191=GM185, fig. 76. The fundamental communication diagram reads as follows:

information source→transmitter→channel→receiver→destination

For more sophisticated refinements see U. Eco, *The Role of the Reader. Explanations in the Semiotics of Texts* (London, 1981), fig. 0.2 and 0.1; Altman, *Epistolarity*, 134-135.

[94] Fol.19va=E35=GM29; fol.19vb=E36=GM30; fol.230rb=E569=GM562, fig. 270.

[95] Fol. 230rb=E569=GM562, fig. 270; fol. 78a=E197=GM191.

transaction, on the public nature of letter-exchange, on the social and political importance of communication.[96]

The reality must have been rather different. Few letters can have been a single leaf of rolled parchment,[97] and the whole process must have been far more unwieldy: not only must the infrequent opportunity to send letters have meant that more than one letter was carried at once; but also it is clear that a large proportion of the letters we know of, and Theophylact's are not exceptional, were accompanied by gifts, whether poems, books, works of art, lettuces or fish.[98] The variety of objects sent with letters has frequently been noted,[99] but usually no satisfactory explanation is offered. Why should the elegant compression of literary art be marred by the banality of cabbages or sheepskins? One reason is that the letter was itself regarded as a gift; another is that letter-exchange was not viewed as a totally literary experience.

Gifts were associated with letters from the time of the Second Sophistic, particularly gifts of flowers and produce including spring figs and honeycombs; it was a pastoral genre at this period.[100] It is justified in terms of

---

[96] On all this see my 'Writing,' 156-185 and 'The Language of Diplomacy,' *Byzantine Diplomacy, Papers from the Twenty-fourth Spring Symposium of Byzantine Studies, Cambridge, March 1990*, ed. J. Shepard and S. Franklin (SPBS, 1, Aldershot, 1992), 203-216.

[97] I know of no work on the physical letter in the middle ages to match A.K. Bowman, *Life and Letters on the Roman Frontier: Vindolanda and its People* (London, 1994) for Roman letters.

[98] John Geometres made a present of six apples and three encomia, see A.R. Littlewood, *The Progymnasmata of Joannes Geometres* (Amsterdam, 1972); Symeon Magistros received butter and sent bread and wine, epp. 72, 99, ed. Darrouzès, *Epistoliers byzantins*, 141, 157; Michael Italikos sent sheepskins and cheese from Philippopolis, ep. 42, ed. Gautier, 237-238. The correspondence of Theodore of Kyzikos and Constantine Porphyrogennetos is rich in gifts; lettuce from Olympos, wine, cake, fish and incense, and an Arab goblet, Theodore of Kyzikos, epp. 7, 10, 11 and 12, 1 and 3, 1, 6, 12, ed. Darrouzès, *Epistoliers byzantins*, 324, 327 and 328, 320 and 322, 318, 323, 329. Whether the imperial status of Constantine made this necessary is unclear. Diplomatic gifts also seem to have gone in fashions, the sundials and clocks of Theodoric to the Burgundians, the vogue for eunuchs and elephants in the seventh to ninth centuries, the mummy sent from the Arab world to Byzantium and the heraldic beasts exchanged by Edward I and the Ilkhan Argun. See *Byzantine Diplomacy* and in particular R. Cormack, 'But is it Art?' 219-236. A new study is needed of medieval gift-exchange and particularly the relationship between letter-exchange and diplomatic gift-giving.

[99] For example by L. Robert, 'Les kordakia de Nicée, le combustible de Synnade et les poisson-scies. Sur les lettres d'un métropolite de Phrygie au Xe siècle. Philologie et réalités,' *Journal des savants* (July-Dec 1961), 97-106 (Jan-June 1962), 5-74; A. Karpozilos, 'Realia in Byzantine Epistolography, X-XII c.,' *BZ* 77 (1984), 20-37.

[100] See Alkiphron and Aelian and B. Reardon, *Courants littéraires grecs des IIe et IIIe siècles après J.C.* (Paris, 1971), 180-184, 187, emphasising for Alkiphron the world of comedy

κοινὰ τὰ τῶν φίλων, still a justification for letter- and gift-exchange in Synesios and Gregory of Nazianzos.[101] Part of the force of the exchange of gifts is the sense of obligation which their receipt incurs; gifts are not immediately dispatched in return, but the relationship is maintained and intensified. The nature of the gift is of secondary importance. Basil says; 'I was very much pleased by the gifts sent me by your charity, *which even by their nature* were indeed very pleasing.'[102]

Theophylact appears mostly to have sent fish, presumably salmon trout from the lake at Ochrid and usually to officials in the vicinity. To Constantine Doukas he sends 'this little gift of fishes', to John, son of the *sebastokrator* one hundred salt fish, to Bryennios, *doux* of Dyrrachion, probably one hundred fish (the number symbolism used means that we have to calculate the sum). Melissenos the Caesar twice receives fish, once 200 when he was in Macedonia recruiting and then 50 or 500 more, some recently salted, some baked into rolls (there is a play here on ἄρτι, just, and ἄρτος, bread).[103] Theophylact rarely risks the fate of John Tzetzes' fish, which arrived at Dristra stinking.[104] In each case he justifies the gift in terms of the perfection of the numbers and an association with the Theotokos.[105] The second gift to

---

and for Philostratos the imperatives of rhetoric. The pastoral element in the letter disappeared after the sixth and seventh centuries apart from the topos of the locus amoenus or the occasional ekphrasis.

[101] Synesios, epp. 8, 19, ed. Garzya, 29, 38; Gregory of Nazianzos, ep. 31, ed. Gallay, I, 38. See references in C. White, *Christian Friendship in the Fourth Century* (Cambridge, 1992) under the index, 273.

[102] Basil, ep. 291, ed. Deferrari, IV, 196. For the seminal anthropological treatment of gift-exchange see M. Mauss, *Essai sur le don. Forme archaique de l'échange* (Paris, 1925), tr. I. Cunnison, *The Gift, Forms and Functions of Exchange in Archaic Societies* (London, 1954).

[103] Constantine Doukas: G119, II, 551-2; John Komnenos, G12, II, 169.32-33; Bryennios, G105, II, 521.2-4; Melissenos: G13, II, 171.17-173.24; G73, II, 391.48-393.56. The suggestion by S. Maslev, 'Les lettres de Théophylacte de Bulgarie à Nicéphore Mélissénos,' *REB* 30 (1972), 179-186 that these letters should in fact be addressed to the emperor Alexios, despite the comment of H.G. Beck, *BZ* 66 (1973), 150: 'Maslev macht es so gut wie zweifelfrei' is not convincing. See my 'Patronage in Action: the Problems of an Eleventh-century Archbishop,' *Church and People in Byzantium*, ed. R. Morris (Birmingham, 1990) for the gifts in their social setting, and below, Table IX.

[104] See J. Shepard, 'Tzetzes' letters to Leo at Dristra,' *ByzForsch* 6 (1979), 191-239 on Tzetzes, ep. 39, ed. Leone, 57.

[105] Pythagorean number symbolism in Byzantium has been less studied than in the medieval west, but was the concern of writers like Clement of Alexandria and John Lydos. See F.E. Robbins, 'The Traditions of Greek Arithmology,' *ClPhil* 16 (1929), 97-123. E. Reiss, 'Number Symbolism and Medieval Literature,' *Med et Hum* n.s.1 (1970), 161-174; U. Grossmann, 'Studien zur Zahlensymbolik des Frühmittelalters,' *Zeitschrift für katholische Theologie* 6 (1954), 19-54. The connection with the Theotokos may be explained either by

Melissenos is part of his *consolatio* and is intended to tempt his appetite. Theophylact also received gifts, two flasks of rose essence and four sticks of cinnamon from the bishop of Kitros, and four sticks of cinnamon again with twenty-four flasks of perfumed oil from the patriarch.[106] He asked for medical books from Nicholas Kallikles, and two poems suggest they arrived; he sent a Chrysostom to Anemas and appears to have exchanged a Symeon the New Theologian with Nicholas of Kerkyra.[107]

Letters were suited to the gifts they accompanied, or rather one may suspect that certain imagery suggested the gift accompanying a letter: perfume or incense to the fragrant Maria in G4, oil to Anemas, honey to Mermentoulos, flowers to Makrembolites.[108] Often the gift was a poem, like those to Bryennios and Pantechnes.[109] But the letter in itself was quite present enough: ἡ δὲ γράφεται καὶ δῶρον πέμπεται τρόπον τίνα.[110] And the present, like any example of the Byzantine minor arts, should be small and perfect and richly ornate.

It would then be a mistake to regard the reception of a letter as a totally literary experience; it was something more complex. Just as the Madrid Skylitzes uses the gesture of the bearer as a shorthand indication of the transaction, so Byzantine letters often focus on the *komistes*—and not only recommendatory letters where the purpose of the letter is to validate the bearer.[111] Other letters cue the bearer to expand or confirm the message of the letter.[112] Occasionally he conveys a message desired by the recipient but not articulated in the letter by the sender.[113] But a great deal depended on the quality of the bearer. In his commentary on the Epistle to the Colossians

---

an association of the archdiocese of Ochrid with her, see V. Zlatarsky, 'Namestnitsi-upraviteli na Bulgariia prez tsaruvaneto na Aleksiia I Komnin,' *BS* 4 (1932), 145 or by the occasion of the gift, possibly a feast-day (or associated fast?) of the Virgin.

[106] G14, to the bishop of Kitros: rosewater and cinnamon sticks; G54 to the patriarch: phials of ointment and four cinnamon sticks. See Table IX below.

[107] G112, to Nicholas Kallikles, II, 537.6; Poem 3 on a book of Galen, I, 351-352; Chrysostom: G34, to Anemas, II, 243.21; poem 4, on a volume of Symeon the New Theologian, I, 353.

[108] To Maria, G4, II, 141.74-77; to Anemas, G32, II, 237.7-11; Mermentoulos, G25, II, 213.13; Makrembolites, G108, II, 527.16.

[109] Poem 1, to Bryennios, I, 347-9; Poem 2 to Michael the doctor, I, 349-351.

[110] Demetrios, *Peri Hermeneias*, 224, ed. Roberts, 173: 'The letter is written and (in a way) sent as a gift.'

[111] On the recommendatory letter see Demetrios, *Typoi epistolikoi*, ed. V. Weichert,, *Demetrii et Libanii qui feruntur typoi epistolikoi et epistolimaioi charakteres* (Leipzig, 1910), 3-4; Libanios, *Epistolimaioi charakteres*, ibid., 10, 22, 58.

[112] E.g. Basil, epp. 203 and 245, ed. Deferrari, II, 152, 474.

[113] E.g. Nicholas Mystikos, ep. 182, ed. Jenkins and Westerink, 512.

Theophylact comments that in leaving it to his bearer to deliver personal information about himself Paul indicates his feelings towards the bearer and his confidence in him. Many things, for security reasons, cannot be put in a letter.[114]

Theophylact complains of the difficulty of getting good bearers.[115] Once found, he expects them to be vocal.[116] Theophylact often used his brother, who was party to Theophylact's most secret thoughts. 'If you have difficulty in grasping my thoughts, ask your pupil, my brother and you will find in him a teacher who will inform you of our troubles.'[117] In G61 he is to give specific information about Theophylact's difficulties concerning his rights over the lake at Ochrid. In G116 he begins with the suggestion that his brother can inform the recipient of his present situation. In G7 it is suggested that Theophylact's brother can arrange for his teacher to read letters addressed to other people.[118] But others were also trusted. G86 explains that the bearer will explain better than his letter since he is one of Theophylact's own people who lives with him and so is informed about what he is recounting, as well as sharing Theophylact's feelings; since his memory preserves what he has heard, he will now if he is invited to speak instruct Bryennios on Theophylact's misfortunes.[119] On other occasions he uses a bearer who has brought him a letter, G37 (and G52?)[120] the monk of Anaplous, G87 (and possibly G65)[121] the servant of the bishop of Triaditsa. Or the bearer may be the subject of the letter (G58), or someone in need of a job (G27) or of a rest (G40). Or someone who solicited letters (G114 and G117).[122] Occasionally it may be possible to

---

[114]   Theophylact, *Comm. Coloss.* 4.5, PG 124, 1272.

[115]   G52, to the bishop of Kitros, II, 303.13-15.

[116]   G86, to John Bryennios, II, 453.22-27.

[117]   G7, to Niketas *ho tou Serron*, II, 151.9.

[118]   G61, to ?John Komnenos, II, 353.25-27; G116, to ?Michael Pantechnes, II, 545.2; G7, to Niketas *ho tou Serron*, II, 151.

[119]   G86, to John Bryennios, II, 453.22-27.

[120]   Certainly both bearers are associated with a Symeon *hegoumenos*, G37 with the *hegoumenos* of Anaplous. There is a problem with dates however: it looks as if G37 is some time prior to the synod of Blachernai at which Symeon turns up as a recluse (on the practice of the double hegoumenate at Kyr Philotheos see M.J. Angold, 'Monastic Satire and the Evergetine Monastic Tradition in the Twelfth Century,' *The Theotokos Evergetis and Eleventh-century Monasticism,* ed. M. Mullett and A. Kirby [BBTT, 6.1, Belfast, 1994], 86-102 at 90-91), but G52 is by all agreement dated to 1096.

[121]   Only the conjunction of time suggests this; it is unlikely that the bishop's servant could be diverted to Pontos. G87, to the bishop of Triaditsa, II, 451.40.

[122]   G58, to the bishop of Triaditsa, ὁ παρὼν γέρων, II, 327.2; G27, to Kamateropoulos for the relative of Psellos, II, 219.8-10; G40, to Niketas Polites, on the exhaustion of the

see letters carried together, though this is rarely certain: G5, 6 and 7; G96, 98 and possibly 94; G112 and 114, G121 and 122. Gautier believed that G88-95 were all carried at one time; G90, G93 and possibly G91 may well have been.[123] Sometimes the mechanics of the letter-exchange are puzzling. Did the bishop of Side carry G104?[124] Presumably Constantine Choirosphaktes of G32 did not.[125] Is Demetrios in G4 to benefit from Theophylact's absence because he carried it, or just because he was closer to Maria?[126] When in G123 Theophylact describes his brother's reactions on setting out for Veroia, had he kept him back so that Theophylact could send that letter?[127] When in G127 he says he is glad that Gregory has taken pleasure in both his letter and Demetrios, are we to believe that Demetrios made the return journey between that pleasure and G127?[128] What is clear is that Theophylact did not undervalue the importance of letter-bearing. He detested journeys and was astonished at his brother's intrepid travels; he was concerned about his winter journey with G90 and G93: 'The very fact that I send my brother in the middle of winter on this long and grievous journey is the proof of the necessity which grips us, holy father and lord.' 'Seeing him undertaking such a long journey at such a season will persuade you of the great necessity which made him leave here.' And Theophylact was also aware of what could go wrong. In G18 an official *pittakion* from Skopje had failed to turn up and the official had assumed that Theophylact had simply ignored it, causing much confusion and distress.[129]

But it is possible also to overvalue the bearer: when John Mauropous writes, 'Letters are as useless as a lantern at midday or well water in midwinter when you have a talkative and many-voiced bearer',[130] he does not mean, as

---

bishop of Glavenica, II, 267; G114, to Pantechnes (bearer is a relative of Theodore Smyrnaios), II, 541.

[123] It is all a matter of weighing the incompleteness of our knowledge (and so the unlikelihood of these matches) against the clear advantage for the letter-writer of sending as many letters as possible when he had the opportunity.

[124] G104, to the *doux* of Attaleia, John Attaleiates, II, 519.7-8: ἐν τῷ τοῦ ἱεροτάτου μητροπολίτου Σίδης ἀντιλαμβάνεσθαι.

[125] G32, to Anemas, II, 239.25-26: ὁ δὲ παρ'ἡμῶν προληφθεὶς Κωνσταντῖνος ὁ Χοιροσφάκτης.

[126] G4, to the ex-*basilissa* Maria, II, 141.53-54.

[127] G123, to the *sebastos* Constantine Komnenos, *doux* of Veroia, II, 563.

[128] G127, to Gregory Kamateros, II, 571.2: εἴ σε διά τε τἀδελφοῦ καὶ τῆς ἐπιστολῆς εὐηργέτησα τὸν δύο λαχόντα μακαριότητας.

[129] G90, to the *chartophylax*, II, 469.2-4; G93, to the *archiatros* Nicholas Kallikles, II, 477.8-10; G18, to John Taronites, *doux* of Skopje, II, 191.10-13.

[130] John Mauropous, ep. 2, ed. Karpozilos, 42.1-3. The point of the device is to flatter and recommend the bearer.

some have assumed, that as a general rule the letter carried no message and should be seen as mere wrapping paper for the message of the bearer. Most often it would seem that the letter and the oral report were meant to supplement each other, both bearing the same message.[131] Basil says that the bearer can supply what is missing in the letter and act as 'a living epistle'.[132] What is missing, of course, is ultimately to be defined by the recipient; in this way the letter is more interactive, more responsive to its reception. Synesios saw letters as double, the living and the lifeless.[133] And this is probably the way we should see Theophylact's letters, as comprising two parts, the written letter and the oral report, each validating the other, and the whole, with all its paraphernalia of fish and perfume and books and poems, validated by his lead seal.[134] Two exemplars[135] of this seal have survived; compared with contemporary seals it is small and unpretentious, but it served its purpose, which was communication.

It would be a mistake then to see the reception of Byzantine letters as purely literary. In fact we must distinguish different stages of reception. The first, the delivery of the letter by bearer to recipient, was clearly a multi-media experience, and governed by considerable ceremonial.[136] Theophylact describes how his eyes and ears and tongue participate in the receipt of a letter from the patriarch; he also sees letters as a means of furthering relationships defined by *taxis* (social order).[137] 'Blessed be God, who among other marks of his generosity, has given us letters through which friends may greet their friends

---

[131] Nicholas Mystikos, ep. 6, ed. Jenkins and Westerink, 38, suggests that the letter and the bearer carried the same message but concentrated on different aspects of it. See also ep. 19, ibid., 126. Sometimes the bearer was used as a safety-net in case more detailed letters failed to arrive, ep. 77, ibid., 330.

[132] Basil, ep. 205, ed. Deferrari, III, 174. He does also, ep. 200, ibid., 135, describe a favourite bearer as a man capable even of taking the place of a letter, but the letter in question is particularly long and complex. For value added, see Michael Italikos, ep. 1, ed. P. Gautier, 64.7-9, with the satiric suggestion that the Boiotian delivery of his *komistes* lends charm to his letter.

[133] Synesios, ep. 85, ed. Garzya, 149.

[134] N. Oikonomides, 'The Usual Lead Seal,' *DOP* 37 (1981), 147-157.

[135] Vienna no. 193=DO 55.1.4714; Laurent no. 1493, ed. V. Laurent, *Le corpus des sceaux de l'empire byzantin*, V.2, *L'église* (Paris, 1965), 321-322.

[136] For thoughts and cautions on the ceremony of letter-delivery see my 'Writing', 184 and 'Diplomacy,' 204-206, 216.

[137] On *taxis*, see the tenth-century *taktika*, ed. N. Oikonomides, *Listes de préséance*, where imperial officials are ranked for seating at table; for a nuanced study see P. Magdalino, 'Byzantine Snobbery,' *Aristocracy*, 58-78. In Theophylact's letter the distinction made is one of symmetry, see below, 164-165.

and slaves address their masters from afar.'[138] He talks of *proskynesis* by letter and *synkatabasis* by letter,[139] but what actually happened in the first reception of a Byzantine letter?

The Madrid Skylitzes points us to the first stage, arrival of the *komistes* at the residence of the recipient, his reception, entertainment, ushering into the presence of the recipient and the handing over of the parchment and the gifts.[140] Byzantine letter-writers tended to concentrate on the next stage, the holding in the hand, the loosing of the seal, the unrolling of the letter. John Mauropous describes this moment:

> I thought that the season was already autumn and not spring. Where then did this nightingale of spring come from to visit me now? Its voice did not resound from some distant wood or grove, but—wonderful to tell—it flew into my very hands. and here it sings to me of spring. And listening to the liquid notes here close at hand, I stand spellbound. Yet if I must speak the truth, it seems to me that though the voice of this most beautiful bird is that of a nightingale, its form is that of a swallow. Its song is clear and melodious like the nightingale's; but on its body two contrasting colours are wonderfully blended together like the swallow's. The black words stand out on the white paper, like a rich purple embroidery on a shining and translucent material. But whether a nightingale or a swallow, this marvellous letter filled me with complete joy.[141]

Symeon Metaphrastes unrolls his own:

> When your letter reached me these worries were dissipated like the shadows of dreams after waking. When I got it into my hands, I loosed the fastening and immediately looked at its length, just as the thirsty gaze at the size of the cup before drinking...[142]

Theophylact dwells on the placing of the letter in his hand, 'when I got the letter in my hand', and on the circumstances of arrival; on the way to Hagios Achilleios, on his return from a journey. It is public: he records in G37 the raillery of his entourage at his reaction to the news of the death of the ex-

---

[138]   G10, to John Komnenos, II, 161.2-4.

[139]   G118, to Constantine Doukas, II, 549.6-7; G64, to the patriarch Nicholas, II, 361.15-16.

[140]   See my analysis in 'Writing,' 172.

[141]   John Mauropous, ep. 1, ed. Karpozilos, 43.2-13, tr. J.M. Hussey.

[142]   Symeon Magistros, ep. 94, ed. Darrouzès, 154.

abbot of Anaplous; all the bishops at the synod read the letter of the bishop of Triaditsa.[143]

But what happened next is clear neither from the Madrid Skylitzes illustrations nor from letter-writers' accounts. Whether a member of the household read it to him, or whether the bearer read it to him before he offered his oral contribution, or whether the recipient read the letter himself is not clear. Symeon Metaphrastes goes on: 'then slowly dwelling on each syllable, I read it, prolonging for myself the pleasure and desiring not to stop its cause until I was sated.'[144]

Theophylact's emphasis in G54 on his tongue as well as his brain, his eyes and ears may suggest not totally silent reading.[145] But private reading must surely have followed the public ceremony; however sophisticated aural comprehension was and however well the letter was performed, the complex layers of Theophylact's letters could not have been unpeeled at one hearing. A quotation at the beginning might have been placed by the end; one missed half way through might have impeded the flow of comprehension. A reference to some classical monster might have to be compared with an earlier letter. Communication theory which makes use of the concept of decoding may be helpful here to explain this unpacking of the letter.[146] But as we shall see, Theophylact believed in active reading[147] and that is what is suggested in Byzantine letters themselves.

But the first delivery of a single letter is only the first stage in the process of reception. It is becoming increasingly clear that many letters were written for performance, and that literary judgements were then applied. In

---

[143] G37, II, 255.26-27; καὶ ὅτι γεγόναμεν μυκτηρισμὸς καὶ χλευασμὸς τοῖς κύκλῳ ἡμῶν; G59, II, 337.2-4.

[144] Symeon Magistros, ep. 89, ed. Darrouzès, 150.

[145] G54, II, 313.4: συνέντες, διελθόντες, ἀκηκοότες may refer to different processes—or to the same. The issue of silent reading emerges in nearly all recent treatments of literacy in the ancient and medieval worlds, e.g. W.V. Harris, *Ancient Literacy* (Cambridge, Mass., 1989); McKitterick, *The Uses of Literacy*; M. Beard et al., *Literacy in the Roman World* (JRA, suppl. 3, Ann Arbor, 1991); A.K. Bowman and G. Woolf, *Literacy and Power in the Ancient World* (Cambridge, 1994). M. Carruthers, *The Book of Memory. A Study of Memory in Medieval Culture* (Cambridge Studies in Medieval Literature, 10, Cambridge, 1990), 170-173 is interesting on the parallel status of the two kinds of reading, though only from a western perspective.

[146] A. Silverstein, *Human Communication: Theoretical Explanations* (Hillsdale, Erlbaum, New York, London, 1974); W. Weaver, 'The Mathematics of Communication,' *Scientific American* 181 (1949), 11-15; A.G. Smith, *Communication and Culture. Readings in the Code of Human Interaction* (New York, 1966).

[147] E.g. G56, to the bishop of Semnea, II, 321.9-10; G36, to the bishop of Pelagonia, 250.22-251.30.

the absence of a formal secular theatre in Byzantium,[148] circles of friends and intellectuals met to hear read out to all the letter of an absent friend and to evaluate together its subtleties and intricacies of style. In the early period Libanios, Synesios and Procopius of Gaza indicate this practice; later, Michael Psellos, Nikephoros Gregoras, John VI Kantakouzenos (who records the amount of applause given to a particular offering), Demetrios Kydones and John Chortasmenos and Manuel II (whose circle listened to speeches, poems and letters).[149]

The evidence for the Komnenian period is slighter but suggests that *theatra* did exist. Michael Italikos in letter 17 to Nikephoros Bryennios the historian sends greetings from Constantinople to somewhere in the provinces and describes the effect the other's letter had had on his 'theatre of speech':

> When your letter was brought into the *logikon theatron* it gave forth your voice and your song, with such literary grace, such a gift of the Muses, such rhetoric that I cannot describe. How it sang, how it filled us with joy!....Were it not for the form, the regularity of rhythm and the appropriateness of the language we should all have been carried away with enthusiasm, both the reader of the letter and the audience.[150]

From other references we can begin to see the membership of these *theatra*, and connect them to groupings of litterati, and perhaps to other, less literary, gatherings, often, though not always, associated with imperial ladies such as Eirene Doukaina, Anna Dalassene, Anna Komnene, the *sebastokratorissa* Eirene.[151] We lack direct evidence in Theophylact's letters, though they are

---

[148] See V. Cottas, *Le théâtre à Byzance* (Paris, 1939); see also K. Mitsakes, *Byzantine Hymnography*, I, *From the New Testament to the Iconoclastic Controversy* (Patriarchal Institute for Patristic Studies in Christian Literature, 1, Thessalonike, 1971), 330-353 on the lack of a religious theatre.

[149] See my 'Aristocracy and Patronage in the Literary Circles of Comnenian Constantinople,' *Aristocracy*, 173-201; H. Hunger, *Reich der neuen Mitte* (Graz, Vienna and Cologne, 1965), 341.

[150] Michael Italikos, ep. 17, to Nikephoros Bryennios, ed. Gautier, 154.

[151] For Eirene Doukaina, Michael Italikos, no. 15, ed. Gautier, 146-7; no. 11, ed. Gautier, 86; George Tornikes, no. 14, ed. Darrouzès, 255. For Anna Dalassene, see Anna Komnene, *Alexiad*, III.viii.3, ed. B. Leib, *Anne Comnène, Alexiade. Règne de l'empereur Alexis I Comnène (1081-1118)*, 3 vols (Paris, 1937-45), I, 126; S. Runciman, 'The End of Anna Dalassena,' *AIPHOS* 9 (1949), 517-524; for Anna Komnene, see George Tornikes, no. 14, ed. Darrouzès, *Tornikai*, 221-323; R. Browning, 'An Unpublished Funeral Oration on Anna Comnena,' *PCPS* 188 (1962), 7. For Eirene *sebastokratorissa* see E.M. Jeffreys, 'The Sebastokratorissa Eirene as Literary Patroness: the monk Jakobos,' *JÖB* 32/1 (1982), 63-71, and M. and E. Jeffreys, 'Who was Eirene the Sebastokratorissa?' *Byz* 64 (1994), 40-68. On all this see my 'Literary Circles' and for a feminist view-point, B.N. Hill, *Patriarchy and*

suffused with a sense of orality,[152] and we must not rule out too quickly the possibility of performance in the *theatra* of Constantinople.[153]

And there is the final stage of the reception of a letter. The formation of a letter-collection is in a sense also the final stage in the generation of the text. We know very little about the keeping and gathering of letters in Byzantium. Most of the letter-writers of Late Antiquity kept copies of their letters and assumed that their correspondents did too. Augustine writes to Evodius, 'Of the two letters from you containing many extensive queries, one indeed has gone astray and after a long search eludes discovery.' Julian writes to the people of Alexandria, 'Now compare this letter of mine with the one I wrote to you a short time ago and mark the difference well.'[154] In the medieval west there are certain indications that the practice was not universal among writers of personal letters and that its gradual reintroduction may owe something to the keeping of papal registers; Gerbert of Rheims only began to keep regular copies of his letters when he found that the emperor Otto II's replies to his letters did not tally with the questions he had actually asked. Herbert de Losinga excuses himself for his negligence in a letter and we can observe Anselm in the process of building up his register.[155]

Evidence for Theophylact's Byzantium is much sparser. Far more letters are preserved in collections than separately,[156] and it is from the nature

---

Power: Imperial women from Maria of Alania to Maria of Antioch (PhD Diss., Belfast, 1994), ch. 4, 'Power through Patronage,' 127-172.

[152] In G8 he discusses the performance element, the λογικὴ χορεία, II, 153.7—see below, 233-234 for its similarities with a *basilikos logos*—and in G69 he promises to celebrate the achievements of Opheomachos with *epinikia* better than any of Bacchylides or Simonides, and perhaps even up to Pindar, but on a much more majestic stage.

[153] W. Hörandner, 'Zur kommunikativen Funktion byzantinischer Gedichte,' *XVIII IntCong* (Moscow, 1991), *Rapports pleniers*, 415-432 is a rare example of concern for oral reception. For orality in Modern Greek literature see the colloquium ed. P. Mackridge in *BMGS* 14 (1990), 123-239, papers by P. Mackridge, R. Finnegan, M. Herzfeld, R. Beaton, D. Holton, S. Ekdawi and C. Robinson.

[154] Augustine, ep. 159, ed. A. Goldbacher, *S. Aureli Augustini Hipponiensis episcopi epistulae* (CSEL, 44, Leipzig, 1904), 498; Julian, ep. 21, ed. Wright, 64.

[155] H. Platt Lattin, *The Letters of Gerbert with his Papal Privileges as Sylvester II* (New York, 1961), 20; Herbert of Losinga, ep. 1, ed. R. Anstruther, *Epistolae Herbert de Losingae, primi episcopi Norwiciensis, Osberti de Clara et Emeri prioris Cantuariensis* (Brussels and London, 1846, repr. London, 1948), 1; Anselm, ep. 147, ed. F.S. Schmitt, *AOO*, III (Edinburgh, 1946), 294: mittite mihi.

[156] To take the eleventh and twelfth centuries, a tiny number (1-5) of letters has been preserved for each of the following writers: Leo archbishop of Bulgaria, Peter patriarch of Antioch, Michael Keroullarios, Symeon metropolitan of Euchaita, Basil of Reggio, Nikephoros the *chartophylax*, Maximos the recluse of Corinth, Leo of Chalcedon, Nicholas metropolitan of Adrianople, Basil metropolitan of Euchaita, Athanasios *hegoumenos* of

of these collections and from inference about purpose that we must argue. Letters were not systematised with model letters organised under subject, though some manuscripts may have served as models for composition, possibly Acad. roum. cod. gr. 508; Patmos 706, Lavra Ω 136.[157] Some letters were preserved in their entirety, others with their occasional detail left out.[158] Some were preserved because of their subject matter, others as the integral work of a great writer.[159] If a collection was made it is likely to be arranged in a roughly chronological way rather than arranged by theme or subject or type.[160] A surprisingly large number may never have been collected at all.[161]

We know that letters were borrowed, like the letters of Synesios asked for by a tenth-century schoolmaster.[162] Letters became models for composition. Photios points us to models of rhetoric; to the old canon of ten Athenian orators had been added first Dio, Herodes, Philostratos and Aristides, but also Basil, Gregory and Isidore, all letter-writers. In the later Byzantine period in the rhetorical handbook of Joseph Rhakendytes the model epistolographers were the Cappadocians, Synesios, Libanios and

---

Panagiou, Niketas deacon of the Great Church, Niketas *synkellos* and *chartophylax*, Symeon patriarch of Jerusalem, John the Oxite, Nicholas Grammatikos, Nicholas Kataskepenos, the *hegoumenos* of St George in the Mangana, Gregory *hegoumenos* of Oxeia, Eustathios Makrembolites, Theorianos, Michael *ho tou Anchialou*, Manuel Karentenos, John Mesarites, Leo Balianites, Constantine Stilbes, Nikephoros Chrysoberges, Basil Pediadites. For a survey of the full span of the empire, see *Theophylact*, fig. I.

[157] See Darrouzès, 'Un recueil;' Darrouzès, 'Patmos 706,' 87-121. On Lavra Ω 136 see Darrouzès, *Épistoliers byzantins*, 20-27.

[158] Some letters (184-196) of Nicholas Mystikos; the letters of John Mauropous, see Karpozilos, *The Letters*, 29 on his selection and arrangement.

[159] For content: the diplomatic letters of Nicholas Mystikos, the letters of Theodore of Stoudios. For 'Variorum reprints', collected editions of an individual's work, see Mauropous's Vat. gr. 676, Nikephoros Basilakes, prooimion, see A. Garzya, 'Intorno al prologo di Nicefore Basilace,' *JÖB* 8 (1969), 57-73, more complicatedly John Tzetzes, see P. Leone, ix-xxii.

[160] But note that Laur. acquisti 39 included G133, the letter to Demetrios while sick, with the title τοῦ Βουλγαρίας παραμυθητικὴ ἐν θλίψεσι διαφόροις καὶ ἀσθενείαις; G39 and G132 consolatory letters are also preserved with it, as are consolatory letters of other writers. It is not clear however whether these are the traces of a medieval generic collection or the achievement of a group of humanists.

[161] See Gautier, *Michel Italikos*, 13.

[162] Anon. Londiniensis, ep. 105, ed. R. Browning and B. Laourdas, 'To keimenon ton epistolon kodikos BM 36749,' *EEBS* 27 (1957), 206.

Psellos.[163] These were used for educational purposes as well as private reading; letters were particularly useful for *ethopoiia*, an exercise practised in Byzantine schools, and some are preserved among the grammatical texts and schoolmasters' notes of the twelfth century.[164] Contemporary letters also were used in education; the anonymous schoolmaster read out one correspondent's letters to the senior pupils.[165] These are indications but a great deal of work remains to be done on the nature of Byzantine letter-collections.[166]

Theophylact clearly did not regard epistolography as an ephemeral art, and saw St Paul's letters as comparable with contemporary ones. He refers back to earlier letters and assumes that the bishop of Triaditsa has kept his letter and could show it to anyone else to assure him of its mild tone.[167] But of how his collection came to be put together we have very little idea. This I discuss below in 3.1, but turn now to non-generic questions of context.

2.4 Eleventh-century Constantinople

Theophylact arrived in Constantinople to complete his education some time in the 1070s and stayed there, teaching in the same school where he had studied,[168] before taking on the responsibility of *maistor ton rhetoron*.[169] He appears to have left for Bulgaria some time around 1090.[170] These two decades were looked back upon from the crisis winter of 1090-91 as disastrous for

---

[163] Photios, ep. 207, ed. Lourdas and Westerink, I, 107: Basil, Gregory and Isidore. Photios says of the letters of Basil, cod. 143, ed. Henry, II, 110, tr. Wilson, 137: 'from these one can not only gauge the character of this admirable man but also find a model, should no other one be available for the epistolary style'; Joseph Rhakendytes, *Synopsis rhetorikes*, XIV, *peri epistolon*, ed. C. Walz, *Rhetores graeci*, III (Stuttgart and Tübingen), 55-59. On Joseph see R. Webb, 'A Slavish Art? Language and Grammar in Late Byzantine Education and Society,' *Dialogos* 1 (1994), 81-103.

[164] Particularly those preserved in Marc. gr. 11.31 and Laur. conv. soppr. 2, see R. Browning, 'The Patriarchal School at Constantinople,' *Byz* 32-33 (1962-63), 167-201; 11-40.

[165] Anon. Lond., ep. 105, ed. Browning and Laordas, 206.

[166] I am addressing these problems in a study of the processes of Byzantine letter-exchange.

[167] G60, to the bishop of Triaditsa, II, 343.12-14.

[168] G1, to his unruly pupils, ed. Gautier, *Théophylacte*, I, 131.14-15.

[169] See below, 233, n 50.

[170] See Gautier, *Théophylacte*, I, 33. The terminus post quem is provided by the date of the *basilikos logos* to Alexios of 6 January 1088; the terminus ante quem by the first clearly datable event of his archiepiscopate, the departure of John Doukas as *megadoux* in the spring of 1092.

the empire:[171] the loss of Bari and the defeat at Manzikiert combined to contract the empire more radically than at any time since the seventh century.[172] Yet it is unlikely that this would have occurred to the young Theophylact. The prosperity of the eleventh century may have been more manifest in the provinces, particularly the European provinces, with urban and also agrarian growth, than in the City, but Constantinople was without doubt the place to be.[173]

> Why do you not set about choosing the most apt life? At least you have as a home the great, the beautiful, the Queen of Cities, with which not even Envy himself could find fault for failing to keep the seasons in due proportion or to luxuriate in the blissful harmony of its climate. Here winter does not rebel, nor does he rush the frontiers and fall upon us in Scythian fashion, freezing the blood of living creatures and laying crystalline fetters upon the rivers. Summer also does not dissolve or destroy all men's strength by rousing Sirius to snarl angrily at their healthy bodies. Winter is able to support our strength and to hold together the arrangement of the

---

[171] See John the Oxite, *Logos eis ton basilea kyr Alexion ton Komnenon*, ed. P. Gautier, 'Diatribes de Jean l'Oxite contre Alexios Ier Comnène,' *REB* 28 (1970), 15-55 at 27.

[172] See J. Cheynet, 'Manzikert: un désastre militaire?' *Byz* 50 (1980), 410-438. On the state of the empire in the eleventh century there is an impressive bibliography. J.M. Hussey, 'The Byzantine Empire in the Eleventh Century: Some Different Interpretations,' *TRHS* 32 (1950), 71-85 first posed the problem. S. Vryonis, 'Byzantium: the Social Basis of Decline in the Eleventh Century,' *GRBS* 2 (1959), 159-175 represents the strongest expression of the idea of the period as a trough between the peaks of Basil I and the Komnenoi; the French reassessment in *TM* 6 (1976) and P. Lemerle, *Cinq études sur le XIe siècle byzantin* (Le monde byzantin, Paris, 1977) represent a persuasive revisionism, followed by Kazhdan with the addition of an urban perspective. For a useful reconsideration of the eleventh and twelfth centuries in association see P. Magdalino, *The Empire of Manuel I Komnenos, 1143-1180* (Cambridge, 1993), Epilogue, 489-493. The thesis of rival civil and military aristocracies has taken longer to nail since it was endorsed by A. Kazhdan, *Sotsial'nyi sostav gospodstvuishchego klassa Vizantii XI-XII vv.* (Moscow, 1974) but see now J.C. Cheynet, *Pouvoir et contestations à Byzance 963-1250* (ByzSorb, 9, Paris, 1990), 191-198 and S. Kamer, *Emperors and Aristocrats in Byzantium, 976-1081* (PhD Diss., Harvard, 1987).

[173] On the prosperity of the provinces see A. Kazhdan and A. Epstein, *Change in Byzantine culture in the eleventh and twelfth centuries* (The Transformation of the Classical Heritage, 7, Berkeley and Los Angeles, 1985), esp. ch. 2; A. Harvey, *Economic Expansion in the Byzantine Empire, 800-1200* (Cambridge, 1990); on Constantinople, Magdalino, *Manuel I Komnenos*, 109-123 looks forward to his next book, *Constantinople médiévale: études sur le mutation des structures urbaines* (Travaux et mémoires, série de monographies, Paris, 1996). The need for it is signalled in C. Mango, 'The Development of Constantinople as an Urban Centre', *XVIII IntCong* (New Rochelle, NY, 1986), 131: 'I have no doubt that Constantinople continued to expand in the eleventh and twelfth centuries, while also becoming more cosmopolitan.'

elements, not allowing it to be completely scattered and dispersed, and summer is able to warm the body while ventilating the City's rubbish. And the rest of the seasons take their shape in harmony with the form of their sisters. Do you not see also the fruit of our trees upon which we dwellers in the blessed city indulge ourselves?[174]

This is how Theophylact congratulated the young co-emperor in his *basilikos logos* some time in the early 1080s. It is a formal piece of rhetoric, conforming to Menander's advice on the praise of the subject's native land, and it stands in a long line of praises of Constantinople which continued when the death of the great cities of antiquity made urban praises otherwise redundant.[175] Michael Psellos had emphasised the significance of Constantinople's position, and incidentally its splendid night-life; John Mauropous had identified its spiritual focus with his speeches in honour of the Virgin of Constantinople after the Tornikes crisis of 1047. Theodore Prodromos would summon the personification of the city of Constantinople to address John Komnenos on the occasion of his *adventus* and triumph in 1134 after the capture of Kastamon, thus underlining the intimate relationship of the emperor, his city and his panegyrist in the rhetorical and cultural *anakainesis* of the Komnenoi; Constantine Manasses would praise the city in his travelogue, the *Hodoiporikon*, and Eustathios would find room for praises of the city in his monastic satire *De emendanda vita monachica*.[176] Yet it is important not to see these praises only as a formal exercise in a developing rhetoric. Fenster's reading of Theophylact's praise is suggestive: 'Klima ist für Theophylaktos ein pars pro toto; was er sagen will, ist: in dieser Stadt mit ihrem angenehmen "Klima" lässt es sich am besten leben.'[177]

Many would have agreed with him in the eleventh century. Kekaumenos's well known dictum that the emperor in Constantinople always

---

[174] Theophylact, *PB*, I, 181.2-15. On the date see Gautier, I, 67.

[175] E. Fenster, *Laudes Constantinopolitanae* (MiscByzMonac, 9, Munich, 1968). See Menander, *Peri epideiktikon*, ed. D.A Russell and N.G. Wilson, *Menander Rhetor* (Oxford, 1981), 78.

[176] Michael Psellos, e.g. the encomium on John Xiphilinos, ed. K.N. Sathas, *Mesaionike Bibliotheke*, IV (Paris and Athens, 1874); ep. 97, ed. Kurtz and Drexl, *Scripta minora*, II, 125. John Mauropous, speeches, ed. Lagarde, 140; see J. Lefort, 'Rhétorique et politique; trois discours de Jean Mauropous en 1047,' *TM* 6 (1976), 265-303. Theodore Prodromos, no. 5, ed. W. Hörandner, *Theodoros Prodromos, Historische Gedichte* (WByzSt, 11, Vienna, 1974), 214-217; Constantine Manasses, *Hodoiporikon*, ed. K. Horna, 'Das Hodoiporikon des Konstantinos Manasses,' *BZ* 13 (1904), 328; Eustathios, *De emendanda vita monachica*, ed. T.L.F. Tafel, *Eustathii metropolitae Thessalonicensis opuscula* (Frankfurt, 1832), 234-5; and on these last two, Fenster, *Laudes*, 151-159.

[177] Fenster, *Laudes*, 140.

wins could speak also for other classes of the population.[178] For the first time since late antiquity it is possible to isolate a group of families who provided a constant stream of officials in both patriarchal and palace administration. There was increasing consciousness of a civil way of life, a *politikos bios*, a *politikon genos*.[179] Aristocratic families moved into the capital, particularly after Basil II began to make a policy of posting Anatolia-based individuals to Western official commands. Even the most provincial and military families of the state began to keep a pied-à-terre in town, and a mythology grew up of ancestral homes standing deserted in the provincial countryside.[180]

Constantinople was filling up also with Armenian immigrants, occupying important posts in civil and military administration,[181] and other foreigners, even English.[182] Ambassadors came and went; foreign princesses came to stay.[183] (It was a period of unprecedented female visibility.[184]) Both sides hoped to see a solution to the difficulties between the Roman church and

---

[178] Kekaumenos, *Strategikon*, 196, ed. B. Wassilewsky and V. Jernstedt (St Petersburg, 1896, repr. Amsterdam, 1965), 74. Charlotte Roueché reminds me that Kekaumenos also talks of people going on pilgrimage to Constantinople. See H. Ahrweiler, 'La société byzantine au XIe siècle: nouvelles hierarchies et nouvelles solidarités,' *TM* 6 (1976), 99-124.

[179] On the Beamtenfamilien see G. Weiss, *Oströmische Beamte im Spiegel der Schriften des Michael Psellos* (MiscByzMonac, 16, Munich, 1973), 20-23, cf., for a much earlier period, P. Heather, 'New Men for New Constantines? Creating an Imperial Elite in the Eastern Mediterranean,' *New Constantines. The Rhythm of Imperial Renewal in Byzantium, 4th to 13th Centuries*, ed. P. Magdalino (SPBS, 2, Aldershot, 1994), 11-33. On the *politikon genos* see Ahrweiler, 'Nouvelles hiérarchies,' 113-115.

[180] On the town bases of military families, see Weiss, *Beamten*, 20-23; Ahrweiler, 103; references to deserted country houses, Psellos, ep. 50, ed. Kurtz-Drexl, II, 82 (Alopos) and Nikephoros Bryennios, *Hyle Historias*, II.26, ed. P. Gautier (CFHB, 9, Brussels, 1976), 197 (Komnenos).

[181] G. Dédéyan, 'L'immigration en Cappadoce du XIe siècle,' *Byz* 45 (1975), 41-116; G. Dagron, 'Minorités ethniques et religieuses dans l'Orient byzantin à la fin du Xe et XIe siècle: immigration syrienne,' *TM* 6 (1976), 117-216; P. Charanis, *The Armenians in the Byzantine Empire* (Lisbon, 1963), 35-48.

[182] J. Shepard, 'The English and Byzantium: a Study of their Role in the Byzantine Army in the later XIth Century,' *Traditio*, 29 (1973), 53-92.

[183] H. Bibicou, 'Une page d'histoire diplomatique de Byzance au XIe siècle: Michel VII Doukas, Robert Guiscard et la pension des dignitaires,' *Byz* 29/30 (1959/60), 43-75. On the surfeit of foreign visits to Constantinople in the mid-eleventh century see J. Shepard, 'Byzantine Diplomacy AD 800-1204: Means and Ends,' *Byzantine Diplomacy*, 41-72 at 54-55. For brides, from Georgia and Bulgaria, and a Norman fiancée, see R. Macrides, 'Dynastic Marriages and Political Kinship,' ibid., 263-280 at 270-271.

[184] See B. Hill, L. James and D. Smythe, 'Zoe: the Rhythm Method of Imperial Renewal,' *New Constantines*, 215-229; N. Oikonomides, 'Le serment de l'impératrice Eudocie (1067): une épisode de l'histoire dynastique de Byzance,' *REB* 21 (1963), 101-128.

Constantinople.[185] Clerics arrived displaced from their sees by Turkish and Norman invasion and regrouped around the patriarchal offices.[186] This was an indicator of the far-reaching changes of the period in Anatolia: the decade after Manzikiert saw Turks established throughout Anatolia.[187] Civil war, separatist movements by Normans and Armenians and the attempts of the Doukas government in Constantinople to use Turkish assistance in domestic disputes turned Anatolia into a kind of adventure playground reminiscent of *Digenes Akrites*.[188] Anatolia at this date was also the setting for the rise of the Komnenoi, if not for the boy-meets-girl romance of Nikephoros Bryennios's *Hyle Historias* which reflects far more the dynastic politics of the capital.[189]

---

[185]   S. Runciman, *The Eastern Schism. A Study of the Papacy and the Eastern Churches during the XIth and XIIth Centuries* (Cambridge, 1955); W. Holtzmann, 'Die Unionsverhandlungen zwischen Kaiser Alexios I. und Papst Urban II. im Jahre 1089,' *BZ* 28 (1928), 38-67.

[186]   The displacement is dated to 1071-78 by J. Darrouzès, 'L'éloge de Nicolas III par Nicolas Mouzalon,' *REB* 46 (1988), 5-53 at 13; S. Vryonis, *The Decline of Medieval Hellenism in Asia Minor and the Process of Islamization from the Eleventh through the Fifteenth Century* (Berkeley, Los Angeles and London, 1971), 169-216; J. Darrouzès, 'Le mouvement des fondations monastiques au XIe siècle,' *TM* 6 (1976), 160-176. For the Italian exiles see Holtzmann, 'Die Unionsverhandlungen'; D. Stiernon, 'Basile de Reggio,' *Rivista di storia della chiesa in Italia* 38 (1964), 214-226; V. Tiftixoglu, 'Gruppenbildungen innerhalb des konstantinopolitanischen Klerus während der Komnenenzeit,' *BZ* 72 (1969), 25-72; J. Darrouzès, *Documents inédits d'ecclésiologie byzantine* (AOC, 10, Paris, 1966), 3-53, 66-74.

[187]   C. Cahen, *Pre-Ottoman Turkey. A General Survey of the Material and Spiritual Culture and History c. 1071-1330* (London, 1968); Vryonis, *Decline*, 69-142; W.C. Brice, 'The Turkish colonisation of Anatolia,' *BJRL* 38 (1955), 18-44.

[188]   Bryennios, II-III, ed. Gautier, 142-255; Angold, *The Byzantine Empire, 1025-1204; A Political History* (London, 1984), 94-98; Cheynet, *Pouvoir et contestations*, 345-347. For Armenian independence T.S.R. Boase, *The Cilician Kingdom of Armenia* (Edinburgh and London, 1978), 1-4; on Digenes remember Magdalino's description: 'a man's man who lived on the frontier and dedicated his life to sex and violence' in 'Byzantine Snobbery,' *Aristocracy*, 69; on Digenes see *Digenes Akrites, New Approaches to Byzantine Heroic Poetry*, ed. R. Beaton and D. Ricks (KCL, 2, Aldershot, 1993); R. Beaton, 'Cappadocians at Court,' *Alexios I Komnenos*, I, *Papers of the Second Belfast Byzantine International Colloquium*, eds. M.E. Mullett and D.C. Smythe (BBTT, 4.1, Belfast, 1996), 329-338.

[189]   On the rise of the Komnenoi, see K. Barzos, *H Genealogia ton Komnenon* (Byz. keim. kai meletai, 20, Thessalonike, 1984), I, 25-32; J. Crow, 'Alexios Komnenos and Kastamon: Castles and Settlement in Middle Byzantine Paphlagonia,' *Alexios I Komnenos*, I, 12-36. On Nikephoros Bryennios as protoromance see Kazhdan and Epstein, *Change*, 202 and C. Roueché, 'Byzantine Writers and Readers: Story-telling in the Eleventh Century,' *The Greek Novel, AD 1-1985*, ed. R. Beaton (London, New York and Sydney, 1988), 123-133.

There is little evidence that the Anatolian situation caused concern for the capital in the 1070s, though a lively interest was taken in questions of military strategy.[190] Though the stage-management of John Caesar Doukas[191] was becoming more and more obvious, the reign of Michael VII saw a final flowering of the 'gouvernement des philosophes', of an empire open to the talents.[192] The opening of the senate to foreigners and merchants is a feature of Attaleiates's portrait of the reign of Nikephoros Bryennios.[193] Urban groupings also reach the sources; Michael VII seems to have been particularly conscious of the populace of the City. Nikephoritzes, 'the last reformer', and, like John of Side, one of the last eunuchs in power, is notorious for his attempt to nationalise the corn supply in the interests of the City as well as himself.[194] Social mobility appears to have been at its height, and the great generation of Constantine Monomachos's scholar-courtiers was still heard.[195]

In the 1070s John Xiphilinos was still alive, as was John Mauropous, although by now retired.[196] Michael Psellos was still teaching, or at least

---

[190] Cheynet, 'Manzikiert,' 410-438.

[191] B. Leib, 'Jean Doucas, césar et moine: son jeu politique à Byzance de 1067 à 1081,' *AnalBoll* 68 (1958), 163-180.

[192] See Angold, *Byzantine Empire*, 73-74; Lemerle, *Cinq études*, 309-312; Ahrweiler, 'Nouvelles hiérarchies,' 108-109.

[193] A. Kazhdan, 'The Social Views of Michael Attaleiates,' *Studies on Byzantine Literature of the Eleventh and Twelfth Centuries* (P&PP, Cambridge, 1984), which shows that he is not particularly biased towards the senate; H.G. Beck, *Senat und Volk von Konstantinopel* (Munich, 1966), 56; A. Christophilopoulou, *He synkletos eis to Byzantinon kratos* (Athens, 1949), 140.

[194] For favourable views see Lemerle, 'Le dernier réformateur' in *Cinq études*, ch. 5, 'Byzance au tournant de son destin'; P. Karlin-Hayter, 'Not in the Strict Sense of the Word an Emperor,' *Alexios I Komnenos*, I, 138.

[195] For social mobility see Ahrweiler, 'Nouvelles hiérarchies' and my 'Byzantium, a Friendly Society?' *P&P* 118 (1988), 3-24; Weiss's case studies of the rising stars of Attaleiates and Psellos are instructive: *Beamte*, 128-152.

[196] On the end of the career of John Xiphilinos, see A. Kazhdan, *ODB*, III, 2211; on the end of the career of John Mauropous, see A. Karpozelos, *The Letters of John Mauropous, Metropolitan of Euchaita* (CFHB, 34, Thessalonike, 1990), 26-27; A. Kazhdan, 'Some Problems in the Biography of John Mauropous,' *JÖB* 43 (1993), 87-111. On the puzzle of the date of the death of Psellos see D. Polemis, 'When did Psellos die?' *BZ* 58 (1965), 73-75 who raises the 1078 date to 1081; P. Gautier, 'Monodie inédite de Michel Psellos,' *REB* 24 (1966), 159-164 disposes of his arguments but in *Théophylacte*, II, 115-116 is rather less certain, perhaps because of the intervention of Ia.N. Ljubarskii, *Mikhail Psell. Lichnost' i tvorchestvo k istorii vizantiiskogo predgumanizma* (Moscow, 1978), 33-35, followed by A. Kazhdan, 'Social Views,' *Studies On*, 54-55 who both argue that he lived on into the reign of Alexios Komnenos. This had already appeared possible in 1897 with A. Sonny, 'Das Todesjahr des Psellos und die Abfassungszeit der Dioptra,' *BZ* 3 (1897), 602-603 which noted that he is credited with the introduction to the *Dioptra*, dated to 1097, as V. Grumel

inspiring, the young, and it is likely that what Lemerle called his 'singular vanity' and Theophylact his 'unrivalled eloquence', celebrating at once his poetry and his friendship, outshadowed other luminaries.[197] Certainly Theophylact's early letters to his pupils and the grand *oikonomos* are not unlike some of Psellos's, and it is likely that some of Theophylact's interests, like medicine for example, have a great deal to do with the society of Psellos.[198]

The revival of rhetoric in the eleventh century[199] and the proximity to power of Psellos himself must have been a prime factor in the institutionalisation of that art, which an early twelfth-century text clearly believed was a mark of the period.[200] The teaching and study of law must be seen to be at the heart of eleventh-century metropolitan culture, as being the prime training for officials.[201] Philosophy was also in vogue: the creation of a post of consul of the philosophers saw that the reception of Plato and Aristotle was very much in progress, as was the speculative philosophy of Psellos and his pupil Italos.[202] Other figures active in the 1070s and 1080s were the historians Attaleiates and Skylitzes, Niketas Stethatos, pupil of Symeon the New Theologian but active in theology generally, Symeon Seth.[203] Niketas

---

made clear in 'Recherches sur le Dioptra de Philippe le solitaire,' *BZ* 44 (1951), 198-211. So far no overwhelmingly convincing arguments point to a death either in 1078 or after 1097.

[197] G27, II, 219.4.

[198] Compare for example the early letters of Theophylact G1 and G2 with Psellos's letters to his pupils. For medicine, see below, 3.2, 102-111.

[199] G.L. Kustas, *Studies in Byzantine Rhetoric* (Analecta Vlatadon, 13, Thessalonike, 1973) sees what is missed by G.L. Kennedy, *Greek Rhetoric under Christian Emperors* (A History of Rhetoric, 3, Princeton, 1983).

[200] *Timarion*, 619-620, ed. R. Romano, *Timarione* (ByzetNeohellNap, 2, Naples, 1974), 72.

[201] See G. Weiss, *Oströmische Beamte*, esp. 28-37; see though P. Magdalino, 'Die Jurisprudenz als Komponente der byzantinischen Gelehrtenkultur des 12. Jahrhunderts,' *Cupido Legum*, ed. L. Burgmann, M.-T. Fögen and A. Schmink (Frankfurt-am-Main, 1985), 169-177 at 175.

[202] On philosophy in the period see P. Joannou, *Die Illuminationslehre des Michael Psellos und Joannes Italos* (Ettal, 1956), 9-31; P. Stephanou, *Jean Italos, philosophe et humaniste* (Rome, 1949); J. Gouillard, 'La religion des philosophes,' *TM* 6 (1976), 305-316; B. Tatakis, *La philosophie byzantine* in L. Bréhier, *Histoire de la philosophie*, 2, suppl. fasc. (Paris, 1959).

[203] On Attaleiates see Kazhdan, 'Social views'; on Skylitzes, W. Seibt, 'Joannes Skylitzes. Zur Person des Chronisten,' *JÖB* 25 (1976), 81-85; A. Laiou, 'Imperial Marriages and their Critics in the Eleventh Century: the Case of Skylitzes,' *Homo Byzantinus*, 165-176. On Niketas Stethatos, see J. Darrouzès, *Nicétas Stéthatos, opuscules et lettres* (SC, 81, Paris, 1961), 7-39; on Symeon Seth see Kazhdan and Epstein, *Change*, 154-156, 207, 211 (reflecting his versatility); M. Brunet, *Simeon Seth, médecin de l'empereur Michel Doukas. Sa vie, son oeuvre* (Bordeaux, 1939). A new monograph is much needed.

ho tou Serron was teaching at the Chalkoprateia, and Theodore of Smyrna *magistros* and judge, not yet dominant in education.[204]

Much of Theophylact's Constantinople would have been recognisable earlier in the century. It was still a very rural city with meadows and pastures as well as the famous orchards, but its articulation was changing. The great imperial monastic foundations, like Basil II's St Mokios, Romanos III's Peribleptos, Michael IV's Kosmidion and the magnificent St George of the Mangana of Constantine Monomachos were not always within the city,[205] but they set a pattern for major complexes, complete with hospital and bath, which looked forward to Ottoman town planning.[206] Aristocratic founders followed suit,[207] and there was a growth of interest in the Princes' Islands as monastic, as well as exile, settlements.[208] The schools operating in the 1070s appear to be still those of the mid-century, St Paul, St Peter, the Forty Martyrs, St Theodore *tou Sphorakiou*, all in the Chalkoprateia district or at least on the Mese.[209] Nor had the syllabus changed, though the new participatory teaching method of schedography appeared now to be well

---

[204] On Niketas *ho tou Serron* and on Theodore Smyrnaios see below, 205.

[205] Indeed the suburbs were thought by some to be an extremely suitable place for monasteries, cf. the Theotokos Evergetis; see M. Kaplan, 'L'hinterland religieux de Constantinople: moines et saints de banlieu d'après l'hagiographie,' *Constantinople and its Hinterland*, ed. C. Mango and G. Dagron with G. Greatrex (SPBS, 3, Aldershot, 1995), 191-205.

[206] For St Mokios, see R. Janin, *La géographie ecclésiastique de l'empire byzantin*, I, *La siège de Constantinople et le patriarchat oecuménique*, III, *Les églises et les monastères de l'empire byzantin* (Paris, 1969), 354-358; W. Müller-Wiener, *Bildlexikon zur Topographie Istanbuls* (Tübingen, 1977), 172, 297; for the Peribleptos, see Janin, 218-222; Müller-Wiener, 200; for the Kosmidion, Janin, 286-289; for the Mangana, Janin, 69-76, Müller-Wiener, 136-138. For the idea of the imperial abbeys see Mango, 'Development,' 131.

[207] On aristocratic monastic foundations, see R. Morris, 'The Byzantine Aristocracy and the Monasteries,' *Aristocracy*, 112-137 and 'Monasteries and their Patrons in the Tenth and Eleventh Centuries,' *ByzForsch* 10 (1985), 185-231; for the domestic model for aristocratic foundations see P. Magdalino, 'The Byzantine Aristocratic Oikos,' and L.-A. Hunt, 'Comnenian Aristocratic Palace Decoration: Description and Islamic Connections,' *Aristocracy*, 92-111, 138-157. There is still work to be done on the categorisation of the foundations after C. Galatariotou, 'Byzantine Ktetorika Typika: a Comparative Study,' *REB* 45 (1987), 77-138 and J. Klentos, 'The typology of the typikon as liturgical document,' *Theotokos Evergetis*, 294-305.

[208] Theophylact, *PB*, I, 191.4-6 for Maria the ex-*basilissa*'s efforts there. See R. Janin, 'Les îles des princes,' *EO* 23 (1924), 326-327; E. Evert-Kappesowa, 'L'archipel de Marmara comme lieu d'éxile,' *ByzForsch*, 5 (1977), 23-34.

[209] W. Wolska-Conus, 'Les écoles de Psellos et de Xiphilin sous Constantin Monomaque,' *TM* 6 (1976), 223-243; Lemerle, *Cinq études*, 193-248, esp. 227-235; Kazhdan and Epstein, *Change*, 121-126.

established, with interschool debates and processions.[210] Pupil demand was not always answered; Psellos records how his pupils clamoured for him to teach law and medicine; Theophylact, like Psellos, refused to teach Hermogenes.[211]

But these two decades did see major shifts in the power structures and mentality of the empire. Komnenian family government impresses the twentieth-century scholar,[212] but the Doukai anticipated them. The Komnenoi simply drew the conclusions for government and for the system of titles. New respect for military values brought Kekaumenos, Digenes Akrites and the soldier saints Demetrios, Theodore and George back into the public eye.[213] A new piety allied to dynastic politics made maternity powerful; Maria the ex-*basilissa* is the prototype for Anna Dalassene.[214] The Blachernai quarter, after a disastrous fire at the church of the Theotokos, saw a revived cult of Constantinople's Virgin with the 'habitual miracle' there and increased

---

[210] On schedography see R. Browning, 'Il codice Marciano gr. XI.31 e la schedografia bizantina,' *Medioevo e Umanesimo* 24 (1976), 21-34; G. Schiro, 'La schedografia a Bisanzio nei secoli XI-XIII e la Scuola dei SS XL Martiri,' *BollGrott* 3 (1949), 11-29; Lemerle, *Cinq études*, 235-241.

[211] Compare Michael Psellos, *Eis ten metera autou*, ed. Sathas, *Mesaionike Bibliotheke*, V, 61.7-18 with Theophylact, G2, to his pupils, I, 147.23-149.16. On the new rhetoric see P. Gautier, 'Michel Psellos et la rhétorique de Longin,' *Prometheus, Rivista quadrimestale di studi classici* 3 (1977), 193-203.

[212] On Komnenian family government, A. Hohlweg, *Beiträge zur Verwaltungsgeschichte des oströmischen Reiches unter den Komnenen* (MiscByzMonac, 1, Munich, 1965); N. Oikonomides, 'L'évolution de l'organisation administrative de l'empire byzantin au XIe siècle 1025-1118,' *TM* 6 (1976), 125-152; P. Magdalino, 'Innovations in Government,' *Alexios I Komnenos*, I, 147-149; Hill, *Patriarchy and Power*, ch. 3, 'The Method of Marriage,' 88-126.' See also Oikonomides, 'Le serment.' All this is predicated upon the brilliant series of five articles by L. Stiernon, 'Notes de prosopographie et de titulature byzantines, 1-5,' *REB* 19 (1961), 273-283; 21 (1963), 178-198; 22 (1964), 184-198; 23 (1965), 222-243; 24 (1966), 89-96.

[213] On the Doukai and the family politics of John Caesar Doukas, see D.I. Polemis, *The Doukai, A Contribution to Byzantine Prosopography* (London, 1968), 34-41. On military values preeminently A. Kazhdan, 'The Aristocracy and the Imperial Ideal,' *Aristocracy*, 43-57 (though he neglects to point out that he is dealing with a shift within rhetorical bounds); Kazhdan and Epstein, *Change*, 104-110. On Alexios's use of St Demetrios on his coinage, and John's use of George and Manuel's Theodore see P. Grierson, *Byzantine Coins* (London, 1982), 217-218 (also Isaac II's St Michael); note however both that Alexios's St Demetrios was struck at Thessalonike, and that other types exist, like the Virgin on the hyperperon and Christ Emmanuel for Manuel. For Alexios see my 'Imperial Vocabulary,' 395-396.

[214] For the praise of maternity see *PB*, 23, I, 191. See my 'The "disgrace" of the ex-basilissa Maria,' *BS* 45 (1984), 202-211; 'Alexios I Komnenos and Imperial Renewal,' *New Constantines*, 259-267.

occupation of the Blachernai palace by the Komnenoi.[215] The Komnenian court resembled a monastery, and holy men were visited, taken on campaign and seen in visions.[216]

The Komnenian revolution did not go unopposed, although the trial of John Italos appears to have cut off one obvious source of criticism.[217] Alexios's very piety was hard to maintain in the face of the difficulties of running a successful military coup and of equipping an army.[218] A senatorial attempted coup was quietly put down, as were apparently twelve others during the reign. But effective protest came from the church, from Leo of Chalcedon, from the permanent synod and from John the Oxite.[219] Alexios could deal with their separate demands, but on issues where they were united he was essentially in sympathy with them, and they with him: all the supernatural forces he could

---

[215] On the Blachernai miracle see Psellos, *Logos epi toi en Blachernais gegonoti thaumati*, ed. J. Bidez, *Catalogue des manuscrits alchimiques grecs*, VI (Brussels, 1928), 195. Cyril Mango spoke of the Blachernai as a downtown Kastamon, where the Komnenoi felt at home; for its military nature see his *Byzantine Architecture* (London, 1979), 130 and for the suggestion that Alexios was not interested in ceremony S. Runciman, 'Blachernae Palace and its Decoration,' *Studies in Memory of David Talbot Rice*, ed. G. Robertson and G. Henderson (Edinburgh, 1975), 278: 'no great liking for ritual' and again 'it must have had the character of a castle'; on the relationship of the Great Palace and the Blachernai see P. Magdalino, 'Manuel Komnenos and the Great Palace,' *BMGS* 4 (1978), 101-114.

[216] *Al.*, III.viii.2, L, I, 125.20-31. Visits to holy men, see Nicholas Kataskepenos, *Bios kai politeia kai merike thaumaton diegesis tou hosiou patros hemon Kyrillou tou Phileotou*, ch. 36, 46, 47, ed. E. Sargologos, *La vie de saint Cyrille le Philéote, moine byzantin (+1110)* (SubsHag, 39, Brussels, 1964), 154, 211, 225-235; for Alexios's three spiritual fathers whom he took on campaign with him, Ignatios, Joannikios, Symeon, see *VCyril*, ch. 47, ed. Sargologos, 234; Bryennios, IV.21, ed. Gautier, 289 and *Al*, I.viii.2, L, I, 32; Bryennios, IV.27, ed. Gautier, 295. For George Palaiologos's vision of Leo of Chalcedon see *Al.*, VI.iv.1, L, II, 101-102.

[217] The trial of Italos should not however be seen as simple Doukas-bashing, nor as the beginning of an attempt to put down the intellectuals, see below, 2.6, 72, n. 302.

[218] *Al.*, III.v.2-3, L, I, 117; V.i.5-11-ii.1-4, L, II, 9-12. For the *Orphanotropheion* as Alexios's self-imposed penance see P. Magdalino, 'Innovations in government,' *Alexios I Komnenos*, I, 158.

[219] For opposition to Alexios see B. Leib, 'Complots à Byzance contre Alexios I Comnène (1081-1118),' *BS* 23 (1962), 250-275 and Cheynet, *Pouvoirs et contestations*, case studies 114-133. On ecclesiastical opposition see J. Thomas, *Private Religious Foundations in the Byzantine Empire* (DOS, 24, Washington, DC, 1987), 186-207, whose over-homogenised interpretation of an ecclesiastical reform party only slightly vitiates an excellent study. On Leo of Chalcedon see below, 2.6, 72, n. 305; for the synods see Darrouzès, *Documents inédits*, 37-53; Tiftixoglou, 'Gruppenbildungen.'

raise, all the saintly support for victory,[220] were needed to protect the empire of the 1080s and 1090s.

Theophylact adjusted to the new circumstances apparently without trouble, and we see him setting the tone for the new imperial ideology of the new dynasty.[221] His network, as we shall see, comprised much of the old order as well as the new, and he appears not to regret that he cannot take on the role of a Psellos as intellectual at court, except by advising his pupils and protegés.

Constantinople remained at the centre of his *oikoumene* because it was where decisions were made, but also because of the formative relationships and studies, the learned and friendly companionship of the schools and *theatra*. His Constantinople was human.

2.5 Byzantine Bulgaria

Theophylact was appointed to the autocephalous archbishopric of Ochrid[222] by the emperor between the *basilikos logos* of 1088 and those letters (G8, G17) which bear on the reconquest expedition of John Doukas in 1092,[223] so around

---

[220] Note how Meletios of Myoupolis and Christodoulos of Patmos converge on Euboia for John Doukas's *profectio bellica* in 1092/93; see also how in *Al.*, XV.xi.9, L, III, 234, 'all hermits living in caves or leading their lives in solitude elsewhere' were urged to make long supplications, this time for Alexios in terminal illness.

[221] For the two *basilikoi logoi* of the 1080s see below, 5.2, 232-233; my 'Maria,' and 'The Imperial Vocabulary of Alexios I Komnenos,' *Alexios I Komnenos*, I, 359-397, esp. 363-364; Magdalino, *Manuel I Komnenos*, 426-427. There is no justification with Gautier, *Michel Italikos*, 29 in assuming that Theophylact was not accepted in the ambience of the Komnenoi, or that he 'fréquenta presque exclusivement la famille des Doukas;' there are more Komnenoi than Doukai in his network, and recent scholarship has emphasised the complicity rather than the rivalry of the two families; indeed by the mid-twelfth century a certain amount of cachet attached to Doukas ancestry, see Stiernon, 'Notes de prosopographie,' *REB* 22 (1964), 184. But there seems no justification either for Angold's description of Theophylact, *Church and Society*, 62, as 'one of the emperor's New Men.'

[222] H. Gelzer, *Das Patriarchat von Achrida: Geschichte und Urkunde* (Abh. der phil.-hist. Kl. der Kön. Sächsische Gesellschaft der Wissenschaften, Leipzig, 1903), 201; I. Snegarov, *Istoriia na Okhridskata arkhiepiskopiia*, I (Sofia, 1924), 222-224; A.A.M. Bryer, 'Ochrida: Holy City of Bulgaria,' *History Today* 11 (1961), 418-428; G.J. Konidares, 'Zur Frage der Entstehung der Diöcese des Erzbistums von Achrida und des Notitia III bei Parthey,' *Theologia* 21 (1959), 1-14.

[223] For the dating of the two expeditions, against Tzachas and against Crete and Cyprus, see P. Gautier, 'Défection et soumission de la Crète sous Alexis I Comnène,' *REB* 35 (1977), 215-227; 'La date de la mort de Christodule de Patmos (mercredi 16 Mars 1093),' *REB* 25 (1967), 235-238.

1090. He appears in the bishop list of Ochrid, compiled in the mid-twelfth century, as sixth in line of the Byzantine archbishops of Bulgaria.[224] From his archiepiscopal church, surrounded by painted representations of prelates of all patriarchates and by local bishops, by reminders of the world-wide liturgy and by local cults,[225] he controlled a vast archdiocese. It represented very largely the same area as the Bulgaria ceded in 1018 when Basil Boulgaroktonos received the major fortresses of his newly conquered territory.[226] It was described as the archiepiscopate of all Bulgaria.[227]

The term Bulgaria is used in various senses in Byzantine writers. It can mean the area of Tsar Samuel's kingdom, or the archdiocese of Ochrid, or simply the vast area inhabited by Bulgars. It can also mean the extent of the theme or duchy of Bulgaria. Occasionally a writer will give an indication of the general limitations of the term: Kekaumenos describes Servia as being on the borders of Bulgaria: according to Skylitzes Samuel escapes back into Bulgaria after his foray into Hellas by reaching the Pindos mountains; Theophylact describes Mt Bagora as the division between Bulgars and 'Dyrrachians' and Anna twice refers to the Zygon as the frontier between Bulgaria and Dalmatia.[228] In practice, geographically rather than administratively speaking, it was bounded by the Adriatic in the west, the Danube in the north, the Strymon in the east, and in the south by the routes over the Pindos which connect Ioannina with Larissa.[229]

---

[224] Paris. gr. 880, fol. 407v, and Mosq. synod., 286, fol. 5v, see Gelzer, *Patriarchat*, 6-7.

[225] On the painted decoration of Hagia Sophia Ochrid see A. Grabar, 'Les peintures murales dans le choeur de Sainte Sophie d'Ochride,' *CA* 15 (1965), 257-265; C. Walter, *Art and Ritual of the Byzantine Church* (BBS, 1, London, 1982), 193-198, correcting Ann Wharton Epstein, 'The Political Content of the Paintings of Saint Sophia at Ohrid,' *JÖB* 29 (1980), 315-329.

[226] John Skylitzes, *Synopsis historion*, ed. H. Thurn, *Synopsis historiarum, editio princeps* (CFHB, 5, Berlin and New York, 1973), 351; Gelzer, *Der Patriarchat*, 4; idem, 'Ungedruckte und wenig bekannte Bistümerverzeichnisse der orientalischen Kirche,' *BZ* 2 (1893), 22-72.

[227] On titles see G. Prinzing, 'Zur Entstehung und Rezeption der Ohrider Justiniana-Prima-Theorie im Mittelalter,' *BB* 5 (1978), 269-287. See Skylitzes *Interpolatus*, ed. Thurn, 365.

[228] Kekaumenos, ed. Wassilewsky and Jernstedt, 28-29; Skylitzes, ed. Thurn, 342; Theophylact, G120, II, 555.31; *Al.*, IX.i.1; IX.iv.3, L, II, 157.1-5; 167.11-13. On the definition of Bulgaria see H. Ahrweiler, 'Recherches sur l'administration de l'empire byzantin aux IXe siècle-XIe siècle,' *BCH* 84 (1960), 85, n. 13; E. Stanescu, 'Byzantinovlachia: 1. Les Vlaques à la fin du Xe siècle-début du XIe siècle et la restauration de la domination byzantine dans la péninsule balkanique,' *RESEE* 6 (1968), 429.

[229] On these routes see A. Ducellier, *La façade maritime de l'Albanie au moyen âge. Durazzo et Valona du XIe au XVe siècle* (HetMakSp, 177, Thessalonike, 1981), 3-8, 684.

Theophylact's Bulgaria was rather a different entity. Michael Italikos while metropolitan of Philippopolis sent Theodore Prodromos an *ekphrasis* of the Rhodope mountains:[230] we look in vain for anything similar in the collection on the passes of Albania, or Lake Ochrid, or the mountain areas of Prespa or Moglena, or the peninsula of Kastoria, which had caught Procopius's imagination.[231] For Theophylact the lake was an oppressive image or a source of fish; the mountains which enclose Macedonia were the lairs of the enemies of the empire and the Vardar was a barrier between him and his correspondent.[232] He was not concerned to give a clear picture of the extent and resources of Bulgaria. The area presented in the letters is very largely the area of Macedonia in its widest sense[233] with the addition of Albania; Theophylact does not seem to have known intimately the great extent of his clerical dominions. Yet even within the restricted area familiar to him (Pelagonia, Diabolis, a military camp, Kanina, Ekklesiai)[234] there was great geographical variety.

In the West was the coastal strip bordering on the Adriatic, occupied by Byzantine administrators, and under constant threat of invasion during Theophylact's archiepiscopate.[235] From the plain led various routes over the mountains along the valleys of the various rivers which drained into the Adriatic and served to connect Bulgaria proper with Albania. A traveller who

---

[230] For Prodromos's reply, see R. Browning, 'Unpublished correspondence between Michael Italikos, archbishop of Philippopolis and Theodore Prodromos,' *BB* 1 (1962), 287.

[231] Procopius, *De aed.*, IV.iii.1, ed. H.B. Dewing and G. Downey, *Procopius*, VII (London and Cambridge, Mass., 1940), 240.

[232] For the lake as an oppressive image see G6, to Theodore Smyrnaios, II, 149.32-34; for the mountains harbouring enemies G120, to John Pantechnes, II, 555.29-33; the Vardar as barrier, G110, to Niketas the doctor of the emperor, II, 531.8-15.

[233] In the definition of N.G.L. Hammond, *A History of Macedonia,* I, *Historical Geography and Prehistory* (Oxford, 1972), 3: 'as a geographical entity, Macedonia is best defined as the territory which is drained by the two great rivers, the Haliacmon and the Vardar and their tributaries.'

[234] He visited Pelagonia, fled there from the fisc, G94, 479.6 and was ill there, G96, II, 487.55; he saw the terrible state of Diabolis with his own eyes, G22, II, 203.22. He intended to visit Kanina, G35, II, 245.20. He went to Prespa for a *panegyris* G78, II, 415.17 and a synod, G108, 527.7 and G31, 235.35. He stored things in a little house on Thessalonike, G111, II, 535.11 and spent a considerable time at Ekklesiai which is probably Asprai Ekklesiai = Eccliso on the Vardar. His visit(s) to a military camp, G77, II.411.68ff; G30, II, 229.2-4 cannot be located with any certainty. See below, Table X.

[235] See A. Ducellier, 'L'Arbanon et les albanais au XIe siècle,' *TM* 3 (1968), 353-368; 'L'Albanie entre Orient et Occident aux XIe et XIIe siècles,' *Cahiers de civilisation médiévale* 19 (1976), 1-7.

followed one of these vital strategic routes[236] would find himself climbing steadily from the foothills until he reached the high Macedonian lakeland cupped by the Candavian chain, the Šar Planina and the foothills of the Pindos. This was archbishop Theophylact's heartland: the mountain lakes of Ochrid, and the two Prespas, Megale and Mikre, with the area of Poloske to the south and the other Macedonian lake at Kastoria, seat of Theophylact's *protothronos*. This area, although nowadays remote, was a nerve-centre of Balkan communications in the Middle Ages.[237] The pass of the Gryke e Ujkut connected the region with the Poloske plain and the Devol valley, which commanded the major route to the coast, and which is the probable site of Diabolis, Alexios's forward base in both Norman wars. Communications to the south relied on the routes from Koritsa, which became important in the later Middle Ages and the Tourkokratia. Access to the north of the lakeland was easy along the Drin valley, and above all the area was linked to Italy in the west and to Constantinople in the east by one of the two Balkan arteries, the Via Egnatia, which passed through Ochrid itself, on the shores of the lake, with its litter of streets and churches dominated by Samuel's castle on the hill above.[238]

To the east of this important lakeland area, source of the fish with which Theophylact flattered his local officials, was the plain of Pelagonia, with its city of great antiquity, in which Theophylact appears to have spent some time, and which was a crossroads of communications: from Pelagonia roads led north to both Niš and Triaditsa, which linked up with the other major artery of Balkan communications, the Royal Road. Beyond Pelagonia to the east along the Via Egnatia was another mountain area, Moglena, which was an ethnic and religious microcosm of the Byzantine empire at the time: Vlachs, Cumans, Pechenegs, Paulicians, Bogomils and Armenians are all

---

[236] On the strategic importance of the Albanian passes see Ducellier, 'Orient et Occident', 1-2.

[237] On the centrality of the Prespa area to ancient communication, see N.G.L. Hammond, 'Alexander's Campaign in Illyria,' *JHS* 94 (1974), 66-77.

[238] On the city and buildings of Ochrid at this date see D. Bosković and K. Tomovski, 'Architecture médiévale d'Ochrid,' *Musée nationale d'Ochrid, Recueil de travaux. Edition spéciale publiée à l'occasion du Xe anniversaire de la fondation de la musée et dédiée au XII Congrès internationale des études byzantines* (Ochrid, 1961), 71-100; V. Kravari, *Villes et villages de Macédoine occidentale* (Réalités byzantines, Paris, 1989), 357-361. The dictionary articles of B. Krekić, 'Ochrid,' *DMA*, 9 (1987) and especially G. Prinzing, 'Ohrid,' *LMA*, 6 (1993) contain further bibliography. B. Nerantze-Barmaze, 'Ho Theophylaktos Achridas kai ho dutikomakedonikos choros,' *Praktika tou 8. Panhelleniou istorikou synedriou* (Thessalonike, 1987) has not yet reached me.

attested during the eleventh and twelfth centuries.[239] Beyond the Vardar was territory only loosely to be included within the boundaries of Bulgaria, but just as Albania was strategically important for Theophylact and his neighbours, so the Vardar valley had economic importance for them; Theophylact held estates there and occasionally spent time in a house at Ekklesiai.[240] His most distant suffragans to the east were to be found on the Strymon; we may suspect that Theophylact's own horizons did not lie as far to the east. To the north Theophylact's interest may well have ended with the Vardar route up to Skopje: although he was in correspondence with his bishops on the Danube, his letter to the bishop of Vidin shows, perhaps in spite of itself, that their problems were different,[241] and it is unlikely that Theophylact, who so hated travelling, would have penetrated the Silva Bulgarorum through which the Crusaders emerged into his recognisable Bulgaria in 1096-97.

To what extent was this Bulgaria Byzantine? A local administration of some complexity had been imposed upon it; Byzantines like Theophylact were appointed to Bulgarian sees, and Byzantines came to hold lands and estates. Bulgaria was also Byzantine in the most characteristic way of all: in paying taxes. But Basil II had taken the precaution of allowing taxes to be paid in kind and in preserving the archdiocese of Ochrid very much in the form of Samuel's patriarchate. These arrangements appeared to hold the reconquered territory together.[242] But when in the 1030s the tax privileges were revoked

---

[239] For Moglena see the *Life* of St Hilarion by Euthymios of Trnovo, ed. E. Kałużniacki (Vienna, 1900, repr. London, 1971), Lavra, nos 60, 66, 69, ed. P. Lemerle, A. Guillou, and N. Svoronos, *Actes de Lavra* (Archives de l'Athos, 5, Paris, 1970), 313, 344, 345, 360; Zonaras, ed. Büttner-Wobst, III, 740; D. Zakythinos, 'Meletai peri tes dioiketikes diaireseos kai tes eparchiakes dioikeseos en to byzantino kratei,' *EEBS* 17 (1941), 234-6; C. Jireček rev. G. Weigand, *Vlacho-Meglen: Eine ethnographisch-philologische Untersuchung* (Leipzig, 1892) in *Archiv für slavische Philologie* 15 (1893), 97-102.

[240] The Ekklesiai of G31, G90 and G111 if it is the Vardar village of G88 and G118 could well be Anna's Asprai Ekklesiai, *Al.*, V.v.1, L, II, 22.23-24, where Bohemond spent three months in 1082. Its position was clearly near to Moglena (the route was Veroia-Servia-Edessa-Moglena-Asprai Ekklesiai) on the Vardar. Leib, loc. cit., refers to C. Lebeau, *Histoire du Bas Empire* (Paris, 1824-26), XV, 154, who identifies it with Eccliso.

[241] G57, II, 323.21-29.

[242] Skylitzes, ed. Thurn, 412; see N. Oikonomides, 'Tax Exemptions for the Secular Clergy under Basil II,' *Kathegetria, Essays presented to Joan Hussey for her 80th Birthday*, ed. J. Chrysostomides (Camberley, 1988), 317-326; J.V.A. Fine, *The Early Medieval Balkans: A Cultural Survey from the Sixth to the Late Twelfth Century* (Ann Arbor, 1960), 199-200; G. Litavrin, *Bolgariia i Vizantiia v XI-XII vv* (Moscow, 1960), 73-77. Doubt was (unconvincingly) cast on the authenticity of these sigillia, see S. Antoljak, *Samuilovata dr ava* (Skopje, 1969), 72ff; M. Loos, 'Symposium historique: l'insurrection des

and a Byzantine *chartophylax* of Hagia Sophia in Constantinople was appointed to Ochrid, rebellion broke out in the north and was taken over by Peter Deljan, who was crowned in 1040 in Belgrade. He pushed south, taking Niš and Skopje and, connecting with a second rebellion around Dyrrachion and a third around Nikopolis, added Prespa and some of northern Greece to the rebellion. Only when Alousianos, a descendant of Samuel's brother Aaron, attempted to take over the revolt and had Deljan blinded did the Byzantines regain control.[243]

The 1040s saw a war against Diokleia during which some territory of the *doux* of Dyrrachion was lost, and George Maniakes's revolt, which drew support from inhabitants of Macedonia.[244] The first Pecheneg war in northern Bulgaria lasted from 1047 to 1050, and raids continued through the 1060s, involving the Hungarians, who took Belgrade from the empire in 1071 or 1072.[245] In 1066 a serious revolt in Thessaly among Bulgarians and Vlachs spread into Bulgarian territory from Larissa.[246] Another rebellion broke out against the Byzantines in Macedonia in 1072, based on Skopje and under George Vojteh but with military assistance from Diokleia under Constantine Bodin, who was crowned tsar of the Bulgarians at Prizren in 1072, and his commander-in-chief Petrilo.[247] After the revolt was put down, Bodin was held

---

Comitopoules et la création de l'état de Samuel,' *BS* 31 (1970), 292; B. Granić, 'Kirchenrechtliche Glossen zu den von Kaiser Basileios II. dem autokephalen Erzbistum von Achrida verliehenen Privilegien,' *Byz* 12 (1937), 395-415.

[243]   Skylitzes, ed. Thurn, 409-415; J. Ferluga, 'Les insurrections de Slaves de la Macédoine au XIe siècle,' *La Macédoine et les Macédoniens dans le passé* (Skopje, 1970), 71-84 = *Byzantium on the Balkans. Studies on the Byzantine Administration and the Southern Slavs from the VIIth to the XIIth Centuries* (Amsterdam, 1976), 379-399 at 384-390.

[244] Skylitzes, ed. Thurn, 425-428; Ferluga, *Byzantium on the Balkans*, 390-391; Fine, *Early Medieval Balkans*, 206-207; J. Ferluga, 'Die Chronik des Priesters Diokleia als Quelle für die Byzantinisches Geschichte,' *Byzantina* 10 (1980), 431-460 at 447-450.

[245] Fine, *Early Medieval Balkans*, 208-211; P. Diaconu, *Les Pechénègues au Bas-Danube* (Bucharest, 1970), 73-109; Angold, *Byzantine Empire*, 14-17.

[246]   On the Vlach war see Kekaumenos, *Strategikon*, 172-187, ed. Wassilewsky and Jernstedt, 66-75; Ferluga, *Byzantium on the Balkans*, 391-393; Skylitzes, ed. Thurn, 364; Fine, *Early Medieval Balkans*, 216-217; M. Gyoni, 'Skylitzes et les Vlaques,' *Revue d'histoire comparée* 25 (1947), 155-173.

[247]   Petrilo took Ochrid though he was stopped at Kastoria; a defeat at Skopje dealt with Bodin. Skylitzes Continuatus, ed. E. T. Tsolakes, *He synecheia tes chronographias tou Ioannou Skylitze* (HetMakSp, 105, Thessalonike, 1968), 715.21-719.8; Fine, *Early Medieval Balkans*, 211-216; 220-223; Ferluga, *Byzantium on the Balkans*, 393-397. On the First Norman War, Chalandon, *Les Comnène*, I, 51-94; Ducellier, 'L'Arbanon et l'Albanais'; *La façade maritime*, 3-112; H. and H. Buschhausen, *Die Marienkirche von Apollonia in Albanien, Byzantiner, Normannen und Serben im Kampf um die Via Egnatia* (ByzVind, 8, Vienna, 1976), 19-41.

captive in Constantinople until 1078. The revolts of the Byzantine aristocrats Bryennios and Basilakes at the end of the 1070s drew on support in Thessaly and Macedonia as well as Thrace.[248] When Michael of Diokleia died in 1081 or 1082, Bodin succeeded and played a vital role in the loss of Dyrrachion to Guiscard in the first Norman war.[249] Alexios seeing the weakness of his position, and troubled by raiding from Raška, personally saw to the fortification of the Zygon and launched an offensive against the Serbs of Diokleia in 1093/94, after the Pecheneg victory. His difficulties were solved by the submission of Bolkan, just in time for the Cuman invasion.[250] But the Serbs were a continuing problem as were the Hungarians; even the Pechenegs outlived the massacre of Lebounion, and any of these peoples could provide an opportunity for revolt in Bulgaria. It has often been assumed that Bulgarian revolt frequently took the form of Bogomilism, and that the cradle of that heresy was in the Macedonian highlands: this view has recently looked more dubious.[251] But even without the heretical connection, the history of Bulgaria after the Byzantine conquest is one of uneasy loyalty, punctuated by bids for independence assisted by Balkan neighbours, or revolts against the tax-machine, which were eventually in 1187 to lead to a Second Bulgarian Empire.[252]

This may go some way towards explaining the complications of the local administration of Bulgaria in Theophylact's period. All accounts of it

---

[248] Bryennios, III, 4-25, ed. Gautier, 215-255.

[249] *Al.*, IV.iv-vi, L, I, 150-163.

[250] *Al.*, ix.i.1, L, II, 157. The Zygon included Lipenion and Sphentzanion in its foothills, *Al.*, IX.iv.2 and 3, L, II, 167.4 and 11. Alexios built fortifications of three kinds to prevent easy access of Dalmatians, Serbs and Pechenegs into the empire. We are told that he put up ξυλίνους πύργους; where the land allowed it he added πολίχνια of brick or stone, taking care about their διαστήματα and μέγεθος; third he blocked the valleys with tree-trunks. This is a rare account of a programme of fortification and offers some clue to what the castles may have looked like. See however R. Browning, 'An Anonymous *basilikos logos* addressed to Alexius I Comnenus', *Byz* 28 (1958), 45 who locates the Zygon as 'the vernacular name of a pass somewhere in Thrace'.

[251] For the traditional view see D. Obolensky, 'Bogomilism in the Byzantine Empire,' *VII IntCong* (Paris, 1950), 289-297; D. Angelov, 'Le mouvement bogomile dans les pays balkaniques et son influence en Europe occidentale,' *Actes du colloque internationale de civilisations balkaniques* (Bucharest, 1963), 171-182. On the 'political interpretation' see D. Obolensky, *The Byzantine Commonwealth. Eastern Europe, 500-1453* (London, 1971), 282; on the geographical argument P. Koledarov, 'On the Initial Hearth and Centre of the Bogomil Teaching,' *Hommage à Dimitar Angelov = BB* 6 (1980), 237-242.

[252] See G. Cankova-Petkova, 'La libération de la Bulgarie de la domination byzantine,' *BB* 5 (1978), 95-121.

have so far erred on the side of simplicity: Zlatarsky's integral Bulgaria,[253] Banescu's two themes,[254] Kyriakides's hierarchy,[255] even Ahrweiler's complex development,[256] all assume that the Byzantines found a single solution for the problems of Bulgaria.

---

[253] Zlatarsky, *Izvestija Bulgarsko Istor. Druzhestvo* 9 (1929), 25-50; 'Byzantinische stellvertretende Verwalter in Bulgarien während der Regierung des Alexios I Komnenos,' *BS* 4 (1932), 139-158, 371-398; 'Der staatliche Aufbau Bulgariens und die Lage des bulgarischen Volkes unmittelbar nach der Eroberung des Landes durch den Kaiser Basileios II.,' *Seminarium Kondokovianum* 4 (1931), 49-67.

[254] N. Banescu, *Les duchés byzantins de Paristrion (Paradounavon) et de Bulgarie* (Bucharest, 1946), argues strongly for the existence only of the theme of Bulgaria and of Paristrion/Paradounavon during the period between 1018 and the end of the reign of Alexios Komnenos in the case of the latter and the late twelfth century in the case of Bulgaria; he recognises only a frontier governor-voevodat at Sirmion and refuses to admit into his scheme the many examples of towns with a *strategos*-governor known from both narrative sources and seals; he does not explain though how his two themes were different in organisation, though he deals elsewhere with officials other than the *katepano-doux*, see 'La signification des titres de πραίτωρ et de προνοητής à Byzance aux XIe et XIIe siècles,' *Misc. Giovanni Mercati*, III = *Studi e Testi*, 193 (Rome, 1946), 381-398; he lays no stress on the existence or not of civil officials in a theme. For more detailed arguments of his thesis see *BNJ* 3 (1922), 287-310; *AcadRoumBullSectHist* 10 (1923) 49-72; *BZ* 30 (1930), 439-444; *Byz* 8 (1933), 277-304; *AcadRoumBullSectHist* 11 (1924), 26-36.

[255] See S.P. Kyriakides, 'Byzantinai Meletai, IV, Boleron,' *EEPT* 3.1 (1939), 267-596, which is essentially a study of the theme of Boleron and its relation to the secular administration in the rest of Macedonia. He argues that Boleron-Strymon-Thessalonike was subdivided into smaller themes under a *strategos*, a system originating in the toparchs of Samuel's Bulgaria. He attributes the unification of Boleron-Strymon-Thessalonike to Basil II; he is followed by D. Zakythinos, 'Meletai peri tes dioiketikes diareseos kai tes eparchiakes dioikeseos en to byzantino kratei,' *EEBS* 19 (1949), 3-25 at 24, in a short section of argument in which he states that the disintegration of the theme system was not a twelfth-century phenomenon but probably to be attributed to Basil II. The map of Kyriakides, op. cit., 593, which represents the administrative pattern of Alexios I is identical to that of Basil II except that the thema of Ochrid has been separated from that of Prespa and that a theme of the Vardar has been substituted for that of Zagoria. The boundaries marked except that of Thessalonike-Veroia (*Al.*, I.vii.3, L, I, 30) are speculative.

[256] H. Ahrweiler, 'Recherches sur l'administration de l'empire byzantin aux IXe-XIe siècles,' *BCH* 84 (1960), 1-111, accepted to some extent the 'little theme' idea of Kyriakides, called by Banescu 'une curieuse interprétation des sources', but built it into a much wider study of changes in local administration from the 'classical' system of the ninth century to the reformed theme system of Manuel I. The only period left unclear is that of Alexios's provincial reforms in which, 63, she describes as 'une nouvelle étape transitoire et de courte durée'. Otherwise she sees change as development, whereas in the threatening security position of the eleventh century, military administration as revealed by literary sources may have been temporary in each place described; permanence is only required with the

In fact Bulgaria was not a simple problem for the Byzantines. It seems most likely in the first place, as Zlatarsky and Banescu suggest, that an attempt was made to create a large theme of Bulgaria, which would correspond to the archdiocese and also to the nearby 'old' themes of Hellas-Peloponnese, Boleron-Strymon-Thessalonike and Macedonia-Thrace, but the shortage of references to a theme of Bulgaria suggest that the attempt was a failure.[257] One reason may be that it already appeared essential to provide separately for Paristrion and Dyrrachion and subsequently for Sirmion-Serbia. In addition the underlying local loyalties of the huge area known as Bulgaria may have reasserted themselves. It was Kyriakides[258] who first pointed out the remarkable similarity between the tour of Basil II in 1017-18 around the *kastra* of his newly-conquered territory, the dioceses of the archdiocese of Ochrid and the administrative picture of the Alexios III chrysobull of 1198 with its 'little fiscal' themes of the Komnenian reform. Kyriakides argued for a continuity of the old local pattern of Samuel's Bulgaria, with a hierarchy of minor themes under the overlordship of Thessalonike-Strymon-Boleron. No-one now supports this view, but there is much more evidence for continuity than has been in general realised. Thus the 'little military' themes postulated by Ahrweiler in the Balkans in the eleventh century closely coincide with the pattern of fortresses already clear at the end of Samuel's reign. And the 'little fiscal' themes of the twelfth century had made an appearance already in Bulgaria at the end of the eleventh century.[259] This is partly a consequence of the survival of the Athos archives,[260] yet the Athos documents do not point to

---

installation of local fiscal units. Seals, which might argue for permanence, are not easily or so precisely datable.

[257] On the old themes see Ahrweiler, 'Administration,' 83-86; for the organisation of one of these, Hellas-Peloponnese in the twelfth century, see J. Herrin, 'Realities of Byzantine Provincial Government, Hellas and Peloponnesos, 1180-1205,' *DOP* 29 (1975), 255-284. The impressive deposit of seals at Veliki Preslav announced by I. Yordanov, 'Établissement administratif byzantin à Preslav aux Xe-XIe siècles,' *XVII IntCong* (Vienna, 1983), 35-44 tells us much about Preslav and nothing about the administration of Bulgaria.

[258] Kyriakides, 'Byzantinai meletai,' 415-424.

[259] For the dating of these 'little themes' see *Theophylact*, 869-871. Ahrweiler's list of these is somewhat misleading, for she relies greatly upon the evidence of Demetrios Chomatianos.

[260] And of the existence of the *typika* of the Petritziotissa at Bačkovo and the Eleousa at Strumitsa, see respectively *To typikon to ekethen para tou megalou domestikou tes duseos kyrou Gregoriou tou Pakourianou pros ten par'autou ktistheisan monen tes hyperagias Theotokou tes Petritziotisses*, ed. P. Gautier, 'Le typikon du sébaste Grégoire Pakourianos,' *REB* 42 (1984), 5-145 and *To ison tes diataxeos tou hosiotatou patrosemon Manouel monachou kai ktetoros tes hyperagias Theotokou tes Eleouses tes en to themati men Stoumitzes en to chorio de Anopalaiokastro legomeno idrumenes*, ed. L. Petit, 'Le monastère de Notre-Dame de Pitié

the fiscal machine of the theme of Skopje-Bulgaria; they point instead to the
activity of both 'little fiscal' and the large 'old' themes, a pattern which was to
be universal in the twelfth-century empire. It might have been Bulgaria, like
the reconquered eastern frontier a century before, which set the pattern for
the empire.[261]

To this pattern there are exceptions. Although the castles must have
been kept up more or less throughout the eleventh century, they were not in
constant use: the advantage of a system of *strategoi/doukes* based on a *kastron*
and its surrounding territory was that it could be used when necessary—at
least until the provision of each of these centres with financial officials, which
does not seem to have been general until the reign of Alexios. Even then, as
Theophylact's letters show us, the real fiscal power was still exerted by the big
'old' themes and especially by Dyrrachion. First attested as a mere border
duchy, it rose during the eleventh century to its supreme status under Alexios
because of its position as a jumping-off place for usurpers and the growth of
the Norman danger; it was to Dyrrachion that close relatives of the emperor
were often posted.[262] In fiscal matters Theophylact did not write to Servia or
Veroia or Strumitsa or Diabolis; he called upon the officials in either
Dyrrachion or Thessalonike.[263] In military matters it was clearly Dyrrachion
which was of greatest importance on both Serbian and Norman fronts;
Diabolis and Lipenion were forward bases; Thessalonike and Ochrid were
recruiting and resting points. Yet in day-to-day matters of administration and
justice, these great themes must have left matters largely in the hands of the
strategoi or *doukes* or *archontes* of the new 'little themes'.[264]

So of the large 'old' themes Theophylact turned to the *doux* of Boleron-
Strymon-Thessalonike on the issue of his village on the Vardar, to the *doux* of
Bulgaria at Skopje only over the election to the see of Vidin, and frequently,

---

en Macedoine,' *IRAIK* 6 (1900), 1-153 and the use made of them by e.g. Cankova-Petkova,
'La population agraire dans les terres Bulgares sous la domination Byzantine, XIe-XIIIe
siècles,' *BB* 1 (1962), 299-311.

[261] For the tenth-century reconquest see Oikonomides, *Listes de préséance*, 340-363 and
map 1; on the Komnenian reconquest, H. Ahrweiler, 'Les forteresses construites en Asie
Mineure face à l'invasion seljoucide,' *XI IntCong* (Munich, 1958), 182-189, which relates
public opinion in the form of the *basilikos logos* so neatly to castle renovation and renewed
administration.

[262] See Hohlweg, *Verwaltungsgeschichte*, 17, n. 5.

[263] When he did not appeal direct to his contacts in Constantinople, see below, 4.3 at
205, 212.

[264] These are not the οἰκτρότατα θέματα of G24, to John Komnenos, II, 209.10-11;
Theophylact is not here recording size of local government units but bewailing (probably
mendaciously and certainly conventionally, see 209.4-6) the poverty of his own area.

on issues involving Pologos, Mogila, Diabolis and Prespa, to the *doux* at Dyrrachion.[265] He has in the collection no relations with Paristrion, or with Sirmion-Serbia (Western Paristrion) and Dalmatia had ceased to exist at this date. Of eight possible 'small military' themes, Theophylact has dealings with only one, Ochrid; of the nine possible 'small fiscal' themes, he dealt with possibly three, Ochrid, Pelagonia and possibly Triaditsa; he dealt also with the *archon* of Prespa but not the *archon* of Štip or the *krites ton Drougoubiton,* or other smaller units known from the sources.[266]

---

[265] The strategos of Thessalonike is mentioned in the *Taktikon Uspenskij,* see Oikonomides, *Listes de préséance,* 49, and *doukes* until 1081, whereas civil officials had belonged to all three from much earlier. Boleron-Strymon-Thessalonike was still listed as one theme in 1198, see Zakythinos, 'Meletai,' *EEBS* 17 (1941), 242. For tax purposes it seems that Thessalonike was grouped with Serres and Strymon with Boleron, see Lavra I, no. 39; *Schatzkammer,* no. 65; that the three units separated again in keeping with the growth of little fiscal themes, but the examples that she quotes are of a theme used for descriptive purposes and not for indication of separate officials. The amalgamation of the theme with Thrace and Macedonia, Dölger, *Regesten,* no. 117, is unique and points to the pluralism of John Taronites rather than to administrative organisation. See Kyriakides, 'Byzantinai Meletai,' 331. The theme of Bulgaria was created after the conquest of Basil II with a military head *(doux-katepano)* and civil officials *(pronoetes* and *krites).* No *anagrapheus* has yet been recorded. It appears that the administration was based on Skopje, Skylitzes, ed. Thurn, 409. Officials though are more often towards the end of the eleventh century entitled *doux* of Skopje and it may be that as other cities and *kastra* received an administration the organisation at Skopje shrank to just another of these. The theory that the seat rotated with the commander is unsatisfactory, see Banescu, *Les duchés,* 121-2. Dyrrachion was a creation of the ninth century and a *strategos* is listed in the Taktikon Uspenskij, see Oikonomides, *Listes de préséance,* 49, and marched with Dalmatia to the north at the time of the *De administrando imperii.* On the history of the theme, see Zakythinos, 'Meletai,' 210-218. For officials of all these themes see Mullett, *Theophylact,* fig. III. On Theophylact's dealings with successive officials, Constantine Doukas of Thessalonike, John Taronites of Bulgaria, John Doukas, John Komnenos, John Bryennios of Dyrrachion, Constantine Komnenos of Veroia, Makrembolites of Prespa and the officials with unidentified sees, Gregory Pakourianos, John Opheomachos and Nicholas Anemas see my 'Patronage,' 125-147 and 187 and 204-205 below.

[266] Paristrion was created by John Tzimiskes and revived after Basil's conquest of Bulgaria, see E. Condurachi, I. Barnea and P. Diaconu, 'Nouvelles recherches sur le *limes* byzantin du Bas-Danube aux Xe-XIe siècles,' *XIII IntCong* (Oxford, 1967), 179-193; Sirmion-Serbia, sometimes called Western Paristrion, has caused more dispute than any other administrative area. All are agreed that whatever land was captured by Basil II, and however it was administered later, the Western Patristrian towns and Serbia were lost in the rising of 1072. For Dalmatia see J. Ferluga, *L'Administration byzantine en Dalmatie* (Belgrade, 1971), 160. For the category of 'small fiscal' see Ahrweiler, 'Recherches,' 87ff. Veroia is given by Ahrweiler, 63, as a military theme on the evidence of G123 but it may very well be fiscal, since the official who is mentioned in G49 was dealing with a civil matter. Ochrid is cited as a theme in G24 as the poorest of all to be compared unfavourably

The administration of the archdiocese of Ochrid appears to be somewhat simpler than the civil administration, though it is seen by many commentators as holding equal importance in the Byzantinisation of Bulgaria. We cannot see any organisational structure beyond the bishops; but we can see, in the three charters of Basil II, the provision for the archdiocese after the reconquest.[267] All the bishoprics which were part of Samuel's patriarchate were to be retained; numbers of *paroikoi* and *klerikoi* in each of the *kastra*, diocese by diocese, on which *exkousseia* was granted were recorded. The two further *sigillia*, dated to May 1020 and shortly after, indicate the difficulties of reconciling this wisely generous settlement with the rights of the neighbouring metropolitans at Thessalonike, Larissa and Dyrrachion; we can trace the development of the archdiocese through bishop-list evidence.[268] Seventeen bishoprics were mentioned in the first *sigillion* and were still suffragans of Theophylact.[269]

---

with the size and richness of Pelagonia—but wordplay πέλαγος/Pelagonia may be at stake here. There is no independent evidence for a theme of Pelagonia. For Prespa see G108; for Štip and Drougoubiton see *To ison tes diataxeos tou hosiotatou patrosemon Manouel monachou kai ktetoros tes hyperagias Theotokou tes Eleouses tes en to themati men Stroumitzes en to chorio de Anopalaiokastro legomeno idrumenes*, ed. L. Petit, 'Le monastère de Notre-Dame de Pitié en Macédoine,' *IRAIK* 5 (1900), 1-153 at 122; Michael Psellos, ep. 90, ed. Kurtz-Drexl, 118-119.

[267] F. Dölger, *Regesten*, nos 806, 807, 808, ed. Gelzer, 'Ungedruckte und wenig bekannte Bistümerverzichnisse der orientalischen Kirche II,' *BZ* 2 (1893), 42-46 and J. Ivanov and V. Tapkova-Zaimova, *Izvori za Bulgarskata istoriia*, II (Sofia, 1965), 40-47; B. Granić, 'Kirchenrechtliche Glossen.'

[268] *Sigillion*, I, ed. Gelzer, 'Ungedruckte Bistümerverzeichnisse,' 42-44; *Sigillion* II, 44-46; III, 46. For material evidence and a discussion of Gelzer 'B' and 'C' see my 'The Monumental Bishop-list at Prespa,' *A Mosaic of Byzantine and Cypriot Studies for A.H.S. Megaw*, ed. J. Herrin, M.E. Mullett and C. Otten-Froux (forthcoming).

[269] Gelzer, 'Ungedruckte Bistümerverzeichnisse,' 46: 1) *Kastoria*, of which we are told that Theophylact's suffragan was a scholar, appears as *protothronos* in all but the Prespa list; the bishopric had been moved by Justinian from Diocletianopolis. 2) *Skopje* was also of ancient foundation and held its position as second suffragan right through the lists. 3) *Belebousdion* (Köstendil) improved its position from fifth on the Prespa list to second under Manuel. 4) *Triaditsa* (Sofia) was called Sardike in the Prespa list, although the Slav name was in use from the tenth century; the city was of increasing importance in the later middle ages. 5) *Malesova* was not discernible in the Prespa list, but at fifth place in both Gelzer B and C. Laurent argues that in the course of the eleventh century the seat of the diocese moved from Morobisdos to Malesova, and it is certainly described as such by Theophylact. It is curious that Gelzer C lists it under the former name only, for it is more characteristic of that Notitia to sum up all previous and possible alternatives, however archaic; its position is also unknown. 6) *Moglena*, currently under excavation by the Greek archaeological service, is the successsor to Edessa, which appears in the Prespa list but not in the *sigillia* or Gelzer B. Possibly the strategic importance of the mountain area and its

The second and third *sigillia* allow us to see the disadvantages of Basil's policy: the neighbouring metropolitans had complained, and with the single exceptional case of Glavenitsa, they clearly won. Twelve dioceses are listed in sigillion II[270] or III[271] but were not part of Theophylact's archdiocese. The lost

---

castles together with the increasing missionary role of its bishop in the Komnenian period with the settlement of Cumans and Pechenegs after Lebounion caused the move. 7) *Pelagonia*, Theophylact's neighbour and refuge has seventh position in the Prespa list under its Roman name of Herakleia. The name Bouteles (Bitola) is used in the *sigillia* only; usually at this date Pelagonia signifies both the plain and the city. 8) *Prisdiana* keeps its position through our period. 9) *Strumitsa* is the ancient Tiberioupolis, first attested under its modern name in the *sigillia*, and the home of the both the cult of the XV Martyrs and of the Eleousa monastery, founded by bishop Manuel in 1080. 10) *Niš* is the ancient Naissos and held tenth place; its secular importance was not matched with ecclesiastical weight. 11) *Glavenitsa* (?Ballsh) is the diocese most affected by the problems of dating Parthey III. It had possibly been a see of Dyrrachion at the time of its expansion, but was in Samuel's control by the end of the tenth century. Its position is uncertain. 12) *Morava/Branitsova* (Branicevo) was the ancient Viminacium, a second Danube see for Theophylact with which he was in epistolary contact. 13) *Belgrade* is not Berat in Albania, because of its bracketing in *sigillion* I with Branitsa and Thramos, both on the Danube, and because of its alternate Sigidon (Singidunum) in Gelzer C. 14) *Bidene* (Vidin is not Vodhena/Edessa despite the spelling 'Bodine' in *Sigillion* II). It was thirteenth suffragan in the Prespa list, fourteenth in B and C. 15) *Sirmion* was like Belgrade, a church which coexisted with its western counterpart; it was hardly within easy reach of Theophylact. 16) *Rasos* was another border diocese which appears for the first time in the *sigillia*. 17) *Lipainion* (Lipenion, Lipljan) is possibly listed in the Prespa Notitia; it varies between fifteenth and sixteenth position in the late lists.

[270] In *Sigillion* II, ed. Gelzer, 44-46: 1) *Servia* was first mentioned in the Notitia of Leo VI as a suffragan of Thessalonike and held that position in the *Nea Taktika* also. The claim of the archbishop of Ochrid seems never to have been a strong one, despite the strong geographical connections of Servia to the rest of Macedonia. The fact that it is mentioned again in the third *sigillion* surely points to the failure of Ochrid to get it securely back, and it was listed under Thessalonike in both Parthey III and Parthey II (1080s). 2) *Dristra* was raised to a metropolis by the 1080s and could never have been a happy suffragan of Ochrid; it was impossibly distant. It went from no suffragans under Manuel to hypertimos and exarch of 'all Paradanube'. 3) *Oraia* is unknown, unless it is the suffragan of Athens and later Euripos. 4) *Tzernikos* is also unknown. 5) *Chimaira* was founded in the tenth century and claimed in *Sigillion* II. In Parthey II it appears as a suffragan of Naupaktos, and by the time of Gelzer B was no longer among the sees of Ochrid. 6) *Dryinopolis* was a suffragan of Naupaktos in Parthey III; it was again a short-lived claim on the part of Ochrid lost by Gelzer B and certainly by the chrysobull of Alexios. 7) *Bothrotos* has a similar pattern of dependence first from Nikopolis then from Naupaktos and then from Ioannina; it was lost to Ochrid by Gelzer B. 8) *Ioannina* was another of the Naupaktos sees, listed as such in the *Nea Taktika*. 9) *Kozile* is unknown. 10) *Petros/Petrai* was listed as seventh suffragan of Thessalonike by Parthey III, regained by Thessalonike certainly by Parthey II.

[271] Gelzer, 'Ungedruckte Bistümerverzeichnisse,' 46: 1) *Stagoi* (Kalambaka), the ninth

dioceses were compensated for by creating daughters from existing sees. Six were not attested in the *sigillia* but were in existence by the time of Theophylact.[272]

Despite the *sigillia* we do not know a great deal about properties of the archdiocese. We do not even know where Theophylact lived; no bishop's palace has been identified in Ochrid.[273] He talks about an *archaia aule* at Mogila which may be the same village in which he held an *aule* and an *hospition*. In Thessalonike there was an *oikidion* where Theophylact stayed and stored things; the church held a village on the Vardar which is probably the same as Ekklesiai, Anna's Asprai Ekklesiai.[274] It is not clear where the airy high-rise residence was which in the criticisms of his *paroikos* Lazaros

---

suffragan of Larissa in Parthey III having risen from tenth in the Taktikon of Leo the Wise. Astruc suggests that it returned to the allegiance of Larissa soon after Basil's death in 1025. 2) *Veroia* was a Pauline foundation, second suffragan of Thessalonike from the Taktikon of Leo and had returned to that position in Parthey II.

[272] *Deabolis* (Diabolis, Devol) had already evolved from Kastoria by the 1070s, perhaps as a result of its military importance. In the Prespa Notitia it appeared in first place as Selasphoros (Zvevdze) but it is generally held that the medieval archbishop had his seat elsewhere, possibly in the *kastron* of the same name. Gelzer found no difficulty in 1893 in placing it at Eski-Devol, but it has since become a puzzle; the three houses which Boris gave to Clement and the 'most splendid of the Bulgarian churches' have not been found. 2) *Sthlanitsa* (Giannitsa) is mentioned by Theophylact in passing; it was already in existence by Gelzer B. 3) *Grevena* was a daughter diocese of Kastoria, and was in existence by the compilation of Gelzer B; Laurent places its foundation well before 1130. 4) *Kanina* was a *kastron* of Glavenitsa in 1020 and divided, presumably to rival the firmly Dyrrachian see of Avlona although it could be proposed as a meeting place with the metropolitan of Naupaktos under Theophylact. The see was in existence by Gelzer B. 5) *Debrai* was possibly a *kastron* in 1018-20; it was certainly subdivided from Ochrid by 1107, but it appears already in Gelzer B. 6) The bishop of the *Vlachs/Breanotes* is attested first in Gelzer B, but Popescu has attempted to push the foundation back to 1050; the alternative listed in Gelzer C has been identified variously, including the possibility of Branje, which has the advantage of being a possible Vlach area at the time, but the disadvantage of another form, Branea, which frequently appears.

[273] On Ochrid see Kravari, *Villes et villages*, 357-361; for the architectural structure of Hagia Sophia see B.M. Schellewald, *Die Architektur der Sophienkirche in Ohrid* (Bonn, 1986).

[274] G17, to John Doukas, II, 187.21; G26, to ?the son of the Sebastokrator, II, 215.17-18; G111, to Nicholas Kallikles, II, 535.11; for the Vardar village, G88, to John *grammatikos* of Palaiologos, II, 461.11; G118, to Constantine Doukas, II, 549. 13-14. For Ekklesiai, G31, to Kamateros, II, 233.16; G90, to the *chartophylax* Peter, II, 469.10; G111, to Nicholas Kallikles, II, 535.15. For the location, see above, 55, n.234; for the dating see below, 3.1, 95-96; for the case, 4.3, 213-214 and fig. 6.

outclassed the palaces of Susa and Ekbatana.[275] We hear of course only about the problem cases.

Theophylact was at great pains to present the archdiocese as poor, and not just because of the fisc. He talks of the thin wine of Ochrid and the fantasies of tax-collectors ('they do not believe that the bishop is poor and think that crops grow for him from untilled and unsown lands, and that rivers yield up gold for him without fire and that dogs give birth to asses and mules') and of *paroikoi* ('they think my roads are flowing with cheese and my mountains with milk').[276] Against this politic poor mouth must be set the general prosperity of Bulgaria in the eleventh and twelfth centuries.[277] Quite a number of aristocratic and Athonite estates are attested in the region of Macedonia, and anecdotal as well as archaeological evidence builds up a picture of urban and rural economic expansion.[278] Mango may have contrasted the *archiespiskope* at Ochrid with more glamorous and sizeable monastic foundations:[279] the historic church was newly decorated however, and Leo's successor had built an upper church for the archdiocese as well.[280] Big basilicas had gone up at Veroia and Servia, fully decorated, and the major monastic foundation at Bačkovo complete with its ossuary, decorated 1074-83, and the remarkable Eleousa monastery at Veljusa with its mosaic floor and frescoes, as well as the *protostrator* Alexios's church at Manastir-Prilep, show money brought into the archdiocese.[281] At Kastoria, the *protothronos*, surely a prosperous small

---

[275] G96, II, 487.65-69.

[276] G113, to the bishop of Kitros, II, 539.9-11; G24, to John Komnenos, II, 209.9-11; G129, to Pantechnes the doctor of the emperor, II, 583.7-11; G45, to the patriarch, II, 285.56-62; G96, to Nikephoros Bryennios, II, 487.63-64, quoting Job, 29.6.

[277] It is taken for granted by Kazhdan and Epstein, *Change*, 31-39; see P. Magdalino, *Manuel I Komnenos*, 135-136; E. Papayanni, 'Oi Boulgaroi stis epistoles tou Theophylaktou Achridas,' *I' Panellenio Istoriko Synedrio. Praktika* (Thessalonike, 1989), 63-72.

[278] See for example A. Harvey, *Economic Expansion in the Byzantine Empire, 900-1200* (Cambridge, 1989), 244-268; M. Hendy, *Studies in the Byzantine Monetary Economy*, 85-90; Magdalino, *Manuel I Komnenos*, 150-171.

[279] C. Mango, 'Les monuments de l'architecture du XIe siècle et leur signification historique et sociale,' *TM* 6 (1976), 351-365.

[280] Gelzer, *Patriarchat*, 6: Θεοδούλος ἡγούμενος τοῦ ἁγίου Μωκίου, ὁ κτίσας τὴν ἄνωθεν μεγάλην ἐκκλησίαν διὰ συνδρομῆς Ἰωάννου τοῦ Ἀντζᾶ.

[281] On the big basilicas see D. Stričević, 'La renovation du type basilical dans l'architecture ecclésiastique des pays orientales des Balkans aux IXe-Xe siècles,' *XII IntCong*, I (Belgrade, 1963), 155-211. For Servia, A. Xyngopoulos, *Ta mnemeia ton Serbion* (Athens, 1957), 29-75; Bačkovo, S. Grishin, 'Literary Evidence for the Dating of the Bačkovo Ossuary Frescoes,' *Byzantine Papers* (ByzAus, 1, Sydney, 1981), 90-100 and bibliography; for the Eleousa, V.D. Djurić, 'Fresques du monastère de Veljusa,' *XI IntCong* (Munich, 1960), 113-121; P. Miljović-Pepek, 'Les données sur la chronologie des fresques de Veljusa entre les ans 1085 et 1094,' *XV IntCong, Actes*, II (Athens, 1981), 499-510; for Manastir-

town, the church of the Mauriotissa was decorated during Theophylact's archiepiscopate.[282] At Vodoča, at Boiana, at Prespa, at Strumitsa, even in Theophylact's own church at Ochrid, paintings above the *diakonikon* of the late eleventh and early twelfth centuries suggest money to spend.[283] We should wonder again about the 'refreshing' of G22: Theophylact may appear to have had no visual sense, but the combination of bishop and local official was a classic patronage pattern in the Balkans at the time.[284] So Ochrid may not have been an impossible place to live a life with a *kyklos* (G37) and a devoted brother, with the chance always of a stimulating new governor or of an imperial expedition bringing friends. Monasticism flourished in northern Macedonia, not only at the sites of the life and death of Clement and Naum and the foundations of Tsar Peter round Ochrid, Skopje and Bitola, but also a second wave of foundations in the upper valleys of the Strymon and Rila.[285]

Veljusa entre les ans 1085 et 1094,' *XV IntCong, Actes*, II (Athens, 1981), 499-510; for Manastir-Prilep, F. Barišić, 'Dva grutka natpisa iz Manastira i Struge,' *ZR VI* 8.ii (1964), 28-31; D. Koco and P. Milković, 'La basilique de S. Nicolas,' *XI IntCong* (Istanbul, 1957), 138-140.

[282] For the Mauriotissa see N. Moutsopoulos, *Kastoria: Panagia e Mauriotissa* (Athens, 1967); A. Epstein, 'Middle Byzantine Churches of Kastoria: Dates and Implications,' *ArtBull* 62 (1980), 191-207, esp. appendix, 202-207; 'Frescoes of the Mauriotissa monastery near Kastoria: Evidence of Millenarianism and Anti-Semitism in the Wake of the First Crusade,' *Gesta* 21 (1982), 21-29. The source of wealth of Kastoria (exiles? fur?) is much disputed, see Chatzidakes and Pelekanides in *Kastoria* (Byzantine Art in Greece, Athens, 1985), 50.

[283] See G. Babić, *Les chapelles annexes des églises byzantines. Fonction liturgique et programmes iconographiques* (Bibliothèque des Cahiers archéologiques, 3, Paris, 1969), 110-117 for Hagia Sophia Ochrid; 95-105 for Veljusa; N. Okunev, 'Fragments de peintures,' *Mélanges C. Diehl*, II (Paris, 1930), 117-131; J. Djurić, *Byzantinische Fresken in Jugoslavien* (Munich, 1956), 9-31 for Macedonian painting in the period. Boiana: A. Grabar, *L'église de Boiana* (Sofia, 1978), for fragments of early twelfth-century decoration. For Hagios Germanos at Prespa, S.M. Pelekanides, *Byzantina kai metabyzantina mnemeia tes Prespas* (HetMakSp, 35, Thessalonike, 1960), 7-53; N. Moutsopoulos, *The Churches of the Prefecture of Florina* (HetMakSp, 88, Thessalonike, 1966), 10-11 for the eleventh-century layer.

[284] G22, II, 203.2-5: καὶ Πρέσπαν ἅμα καὶ Διάβολιν ἀναψύξας. I have elsewhere been sceptical about this passage as clear indication of artistic activity, and the action proposed of the *doux* is hardly in terms of paint, but this may at least explain one of the paint layers at Prespa. For the patronage pattern see D. Mouriki, 'Stylistic Trends in Monumental Painting of Greece during the Eleventh and Twelfth Century,' *DOP* 34-35 (1980-1), 77-124.

[285] Clement (d. 916) and Naum (d. 910) were both buried in the monasteries they founded, see D. Koco, 'Klimentoviot manastir "Sv. Pantelejmon": raskopkata pri "Imaret" vo Ohrid,' *Godišen Zbornik* 1 (1948), 129-180. On Tsar Peter's foundations, the 'monastic reign,' see Obolensky, *Bogomils*, 102-103; on St John of Rila, I. Ivanov, *Godishnik na Sofiiskiia Universitet*, ist-fil.fak. 32-22 (1931), 28-37. There is no evidence of contact beween

Ochrid itself had hermit caves.[286] But it also had a scriptorium and a local history to research, and the year was punctuated by the *panegyreis* of local cults, of the Virgin and of the Forty as well as of the Fifteen Martyrs, and of St Achilleios and St Germanos of Prespa.[287] And every spring brought letters.

2.6 Alexian literature

Despite Theophylact's life-sentence in the archdiocese of Ochrid,[288] through his responsiveness to commissions from Constantinople and through his choice of the one genre which not only allowed but demanded distance from the *omphalos*, he remained part of the literary scene. The last letter we can date securely belongs to 1108,[289] but two other works have been placed

---

Theophylact and the following of north Macedonian hermits like Gabriel of Lesnovo, see Obolensky, *Commonwealth*, 296-297.

[286] At Kalista, Rododza, Pestani and Treja; the paintings are thirteenth-century at the earliest, but the caves may well have been used before by anchorites, see Bošković and Tomovski, *L'architecture médiévale d'Ochride: recueil et travaux* (Ochrid, 1961), 99.

[287] On the scriptorium of Ochrid, see A. Dostál, 'Les relations entre Byzance et les slaves (en particulier les Bulgares) aux XIe et XIIe siècles du point de vue culturel,' *XIII IntCong* (Oxford, 1966), 173-174. On the cult of Clement see D. Obolensky, *Six Byzantine Portraits* (Oxford, 1988), 8-33; I.G. Iliev, 'La mission de Clément d'Ochride dans les terres sud-ouest de la Bulgarie médiévale,' *Études historiques*, *Acad.Bulg.Sc.Inst.Hist*.13 (1985), 63-64; *Kliment Okhridski*, eds B.S. Angelov et al. (Sofia, 1966), 21; on the cult of the Virgin at Ochrid, see V.N. Zlatarsky, 'Namestnitsi-upraviteli na Bulgariia prez tsaruvaneto na Aleksiia I Komnin,' *BS* 4 (1932), 139-145; on the cult of the Forty Martyrs in the period and present-day customs in the region, Z. Gavrilović, 'The cult of the Forty Martyrs of Sebasteia in Macedonia and Serbia,' *The Forty Martyrs of Sebasteia*, I, *Papers*, ed. M. Mullett and A. Wilson (BBTT, 2.1, Belfast, 1997), forthcoming. On the cult of the Fifteen Martyrs of Strumitsa (Tiberioupolis), see Obolensky, *Portraits*, 71-76; for the discovery of a martyrium in Strumitsa with a painting of the XV see D. Koco and P. Miljković-Pepek, 'Rezultatite od arheoloshkite iskopuvanija vo 1973 g. vo crkvata "Sv. Tivriopolski mačenici"—Strumica,' *Arheolshki Muzej na Makdonija* 8.9 (Skopje, 1978), 93-97, esp. plates 3 and 4; on the Prespa saints Germanos and Achilleios see L.A. Mellios, 'Thrulos kai paradoseis tes perioches Prespas,' *Aristoteles* 29 (1961), 23.

[288] G4, II, 141.63 and see below, 4.6.

[289] G120, to John Pantechnes, II, 553-557 if the δοῦλος καὶ ἀποστάτης of 30-31 is Bohemond. The reference to Michael the *protostrator* dates it to 1107-08, according to Gautier, *Théophylacte*, II, 92, referring to a non-existent 'notice de Michel Doukas'. The Bohemond suggestion is infinitely better than any of the alternative suggestions, Bolkan, Lazaros, Iasites etc. The consolatio to Michael Pantechnes (G39) must then be later than G120.

possibly in 1112 and in 1114.[290] The subscription to the poems on Symeon the New Theologian in Paris. suppl. gr. 103, fol. 16 dates them to 1125/26.[291] Born at about the same date as Alexios, Theophylact may have outlasted him.[292]

But was there any literary society for him to belong to?[293] Even if twelfth-century literature has gradually shaken off its characterisation as 'uncreative erudition, of sterile good taste',[294] the literature of Alexios's reign has not. And Alexios himself has been portrayed as inherently opposed to letters, an ignorant backwoodsman who knew what he liked and who disapproved of long-haired philosophers.[295] He has been saddled with the full blame for the Italos trial and its supposed consequences, the repression of litterati. He is seen in contrast to his womenfolk, all of whom encouraged learning and literature. Maria the ex-*basilissa* read hard books, the fathers and ascetic works; Eirene Doukaina read Maximos Confessor at mealtimes,[296] and collected around her an important circle of litterati including Michael Italikos, commissioning Nikephoros Bryennios's *Hyle Historias*; Anna the first woman historian also organised a collaborative research team on Aristotle; Alexios's grandson's wife Eirene the *sebastokratorissa* has been credited with perhaps more than she deserves.[297] The picture in Anna is of course more flattering to Alexios:

---

[290] The treatise *On the Errors of the Latins* has been dated 'comme une simple hypothèse' by Gautier, *Théophylacte*, I, 114 to 1112. The fragment *To Tibanios the Armenian*, G135, is dated (cautiously) by Gautier, *Théophylacte*, II, 130 to 1114.

[291] Ed. J. Koder and J. Paramelle, *Syméon le nouveau théologien, Hymnes*, I (SC, 156, Paris, 1969), 64-67. See Gautier, I, 121 for a more cautious approach to the dating than his 'L'épiscopat', 169-170. It is not clear what implications for absolute dating lie in the proposal by Anastasi that the two poems on Symeon represent an earlier poem incorporated into a later diptych, see R. Anastasi, 'Teofilatto di Bulgaria e Simeone il Teologo,' *SicGymn* 34 (1981), 279-283.

[292] Gautier, *Théophylacte*, I, 63, n. 67. Alexios died on 15 August 1118, see Barzos, *Genealogia*, I, 103.

[293] H. Hunger, *Das literarische Schaffen der Byzantiner: Wege zu einem Verständnis* (Vienna, 1974); H-G. Beck, *Das byzantinische Jahrtausend* (Munich, 1978), 123ff; Kazhdan, *People and Power*, 100-102.

[294] R. Browning, 'Enlightenment and Repression in Byzantium in the Eleventh and Twelfth Centuries,' *P&P* 69 (1975), 5.

[295] L. Clucas, *The Trial of John Italos* (MiscByzMonac, 26, Munich, 1981), esp. 3-8.

[296] This is the literary equivalent of Anna Dalassene's custom of never sitting down to eat without holy men present.

[297] For Maria, see Theophylact, *PB*, I, 191.15-22; Anna Dalassene, φιλομόναχος, see the encomium in John the Oxite, ed. Gautier, 'Les diatribes,' *REB* 22 (1964), 156-157; Anna, *Al*, III.ii.7, L, I, 109.25-110.16. Eirene Doukaina: *Al.*, V.ix.3, L, II, 37-38. For Anna, see George Tornikes, op. 14, ed. Darrouzès, *Tornikai*, 221-323. For Eirene *sebastokratorissa* we await the final work of Elizabeth Jeffreys but see 'The Sebastokratorissa Eirene as a

It was natural that men of culture should attend the palace when the devoted pair (my parents I mean) were themselves labouring so hard night and day in searching the Holy Scriptures.[298]

She contrasts (in a perfectly conventional way) the state of letters before and after his accession:

In fact from the reign of Basil the Porphyrogennetos until that of Monomachos, letters although treated with scant regard by most folk at least did not die out, and once again they shone in bright revival when under Alexios they became the object of serious attention to those who loved philosophical argument. Before then the majority had lived a life of luxury and pleasure; because of their wanton habits they concerned themselves with quail-catching and other more disreputable pastimes, but all scientific culture and literature were to them of secondary importance.[299]

She even makes this contrast her explanation of how Italos fell into bad ways. There is a new seriousness about learning: Alexios like Kekaumenos believed that one could learn from history, whether classical or biblical.[300]

Besides, the interests of literary society at the turn of the century are different from those of the mid-eleventh century, though there is continuity—in medicine, in astronomy, in certain kinds of philosophy. There does seem to be a turning away from the concerns of Psellos and Italos and a concentration more on theology than on philosophy. Theodore of Smyrna, who succeeded them as *hypatos ton philosophon*, has left largely theological works; so have Eustratios of Nicaea, Italos's pupil, Niketas Seides, Niketas *ho tou Serron*, John Phournes, the *chartophylax* Nikephoros, Niketas Stethatos.[301] It may be partly

---

Literary Patroness: the Letters of the Monk Iakovos,' *JÖB* 32/1 (1982), 63-71 and M. and E. Jeffreys, 'Who was Eirene the Sebastokratorissa?' *Byz* 64 (1994), 40-68.

[298] *Al.*, V.ix.3, L, II, 37.29-38.1.

[299] *Al.*, V.viii.2, L, II, 33.19-30; cf Psellos, *Chronographia, Constantine IX*, xxxvii-xliii, ed. E. Renauld, *Michel Psellos, Chronographie*, I (Paris, 1967), 135.4-138.14.

[300] *Al.*, XV.iii.6, L, III, 198.2-9, esp. 6-7: ἦν γὰρ οὐδὲ τῆς Αἰλιάνου τακτικῆς ἀδαής on Alexios's preparation for battle; Kekaumenos on what, how and why to read: the Old Testament and the *strategika* of the ancients, 54, ed. Wassilewsky and Jernstedt, 19; on reading a book several times, 113, ed. Wassilewsky and Jernstedt, 47; on reading when alone, 160, ed. Wassilewsky and Jernstedt, 64.

[301] On Theodore Smyrnaios see the list of works in Gautier, *Théophylacte*, II, 118-119. On Eustratios of Nicaea, P. Joannou, 'Eustrate de Nicée: trois pièces inédites de son procès,' *REB* 10 (1952), 24-34; on Niketas Seides, Browning, 'Patriarchal School,' *Byz* 33 (1963), 25; O. Schissel, 'Niketas Seidos, eine Handschriftenstudie,' *Divus Thomas* 15 (1937), 78-90; on Niketas *ho tou Serron*, J. Darrouzès, 'Notes de littérature et de critique: I, Nicétas d'Heraclea *ho tou Serron*,' *REB* 18 (1960), 179-184; on John Phournes, protos of Ganos, J. Darrouzès, 'Documents byzantines du XIIe siècle sur la primauté romaine,' *REB* 23 (1965),

a matter of survival, in that we have lost the major part of the imperial rhetoric of the period; it was certainly not a matter of playing safe after the Italos trial, since several theologians fell from grace under Alexios—apparently for inadequate polemic.[302]

Religious polemic certainly appears to have been in vogue. Anna Komnene presents her father as thirteenth apostle, heroically combating heretics, whether Manichaean rebels or Paulicians in Philippopolis or intellectuals in the capital. Four long sections in the *Alexiad* are devoted to the question of heresy, and additions to the *Synodikon of Orthodoxy* show that for the first time since Iconoclasm heresy appeared to be a problem.[303] The cases of John Italos,[304] Leo of Chalcedon,[305] Neilos of Calabria, Gerontios of Lampe,

---

52-59; on the *chartophylax* Nikephoros, see P. Gautier, 'Le chartophylax Nicéphore. Oeuvre canonique et notice bibliographique,' *REB* 27 (1969), 159-195; on Niketas Stethatos, J. Darrouzès, *Nicétas Stéthatos, opuscules et letters* (SC, 81, Paris, 1961), 7-24. On the period, S. Salaville, 'Philosophie et théologie ou épisodes scolastiques à Byzance,' *EO* 29 (1938), 132-156.

[302] On the fall of the theologians see Browning, 'Enlightenment and Repression.' His picture of academic repression works only for John Italos—if there, see the good arguments of D.F.J. Leeson, *Imperial Orthodoxy. Heresy and Politics during the Reign of Alexios I Komnenos (1081-1118)* (MA Diss., Belfast, 1987), ch. 1, 5-35. Of the Alexian heretics, Neilos the Calabrian was notoriously unintellectual; Leo of Chalcedon was famous not as a scholar but as a holy man (see the vision of George Palaiologos in *Al.*,VII.iv,1, L, II, 101-2) and Alexios did his best to get Eustratios off the charge, or at least to have him reinstated. It is the small political issues at both ends of the reign—the shadow of the Doukai and the Normans in the Italos affair and the succession in the Eustratios case—which impinged on heresy trials rather than any great Komnenian conspiracy against academics and free speech. Neilos failed to convince the Armenians in his debates and Eustratios put a foot wrong in the disputations at Philippopolis.

[303] Alexios as Thirteenth Apostle: *Al.*, XIV.viii.8, L, 181.2-5; for the *Synodikon*, see J. Gouillard, 'Le synodikon de l'Orthodoxie: édition et commentaire,' *TM* 2 (1967), 183-237. The four passages are: *Al*, V.vii.1, L, II, 32-40 (Italos); X.i.1-6, L, II, 187-189 (Neilos and Blachernites); XIV.viii.1-ix.5, L, III, 177-185 (Philippopolis); XV.viii.1-x.5, L, III, 218-228.

[304] On John Italos, see P.E. Stephanou, *Jean Italos, philosophe et humaniste* (Rome, 1949); P. Joannou, *Christliche Metaphysik in Byzanz: Die Illuminationslehre des Michael Psellos und Johannes Italos* (Ettal, 1959), and for the trial, F.I. Uspenskii, 'Deloproizvodstvo po obvineniyu Ioan Itala v eresi,' *IRAIK* 2 (1897), 1-66; see now J. Gouillard, 'Le procès officiel de Jean l'Italien: les actes et leurs sous-entendus,' *TM* 9 (1985), 133-180.

[305] The case is not yet totally understood, see P. Gautier, 'Le synode,' *REB* 29 (1971), 213-215; 280-284; V. Grumel, 'Les documents athonites concernant l'affaire de Léon de Chalcédoine,' *MiscMercati*, III=*Studi e Testi* 193 (1946), 12; 'L'affaire de Léon de Chalcédoine: le chrysobulle d'Alexis,' *EB* 11 (1944), 127; 'Le décret ou séméioma d'Alexis Ier Comnène (1086),' *EO* 39 (1941-42), 333-341; P. Stephanou, 'Le procès de Léon de Chalcédoine,' *OCP* 9 (1943), 26-27; 'La doctrine de Léon de Chalcédoine et de ses

Theodore Blachernites,[306] Basil the Bogomil[307] and Eustratios of Nicaea[308] break suddenly on the calm of Orthodoxy.

Various interpretations of this phenomenon have been offered, but the question remains open. We have seen that it cannot be answered by positing anti-intellectualism for the new regime: the opposite, in demanding more rigorous standards in debate,[309] might be the case. Nor is the explanation of a growing rationalism convincing. There may be an element of political expediency: although Alexios was probably not responsible for the Italos trial, heresy was a useful way of dealing with political opponents, or keeping rowdy metropolitans busy; Alexios's own political demise was clear when opponents could beat him at his own game.[310] And the heroic heresy-hunter may be partly a creation of Anna's filial pen. But there is enough evidence to believe that Alexios was actually interested in heresy[311] and that that interest is reflected in an impressive body of religious polemic at the time directed against both the Armenians and the Latins.[312] Formal disputations were organised in Constantinople for the visit of Peter Grossolano in 1112,[313] and in

---

adversaires sur les images,' *OCP* 12 (1946), 177-179; A.A. Glabinas, *Epi Alexiou Komnenou (1081-1118) peri hieron skeuon, keimelion kai hagion eikonon eris* (Thessalonike, 1972).

[306] On these figures see Gouillard, 'Le synodikon,' 186-188, 202-206.

[307] On the Bogomil case see D. Gress-Wright, 'Bogomilism in Constantinople,' *Byz* 47 (1977), 163-185; for the date see D. Papachryssanthou, 'La mort du Sebastokrator Isaac, frère d'Alexis I, et de quelques événements contemporains,' *REB* 21 (1963), 255, although one need not accept Gautier's date of 'vers 1098' in 'Le synode,' 225, the trial must predate the death of Isaac in 1102-04. Anna is notoriously cavalier in her arrangement of material and it is arguable that she moved the Bogomil trial to the last available position in her work to compensate for that other heresy trial at the end of the reign, that of Eustratios of Nicaea, in which Alexios did not live up to Anna's idealised picture of him.

[308] For the trial of Eustratios see Joannou, 'Trois pièces;' 'Der Nominalismus und die menschliche Psychologie Christ. Das Semeioma gegen Eustratios von Nikaia (1117),' *BZ* 47 (1954), 358-378; 'Le sort des évêques hérétiques reconciliés: un discours inédit de Nicétas de Serres contre Eustrate de Nicée,' *Byz* 28 (1958), 1-30.

[309] Note Alexios's reaction ('conquerendo') to the performance of his team in the Grossolano debates, A. Amelli, 'Due sermoni inediti di Pietro Grosolano, arcivescovo di Milano,' *Fontes Ambrosiani* 4 (1933), 35.

[310] As in the Eustratios case.

[311] Cf. W. Hörandner, 'Poésie profane et auteurs anciens,' *TM* 6 (1976), 253: 'Les Comnènes s'intéressent beaucoup plus aux lettres que leurs prédécesseurs.'

[312] More works of religious polemic have survived from the eleventh and twelfth centuries than any other literary genre.

[313] See H. Bloch, 'Monte Cassino, Byzantium and the West in the Earlier Middle Ages,' *DOP* 3 (1946), 163-214; V. Grumel, 'Autour du voyage de Pierre Grossolano, archevêque de Milan à Constantinople en 1112,' *EO* 32 (1933), 22-33; J. Darrouzès, 'Les conférences de 1112,' *REB* 23 (1965), 51-59.

Philippopolis in 1114; people who look almost like court theologians appear
to join the court doctors.[314] Alexios was responsible for the birth of one genre,
the panoply of heresies, invented at his commission by Euthymios Zigabenos
and emulated later by Andronikos Kamateros and Niketas Choniates.
Euthymios was known to Maria the Bulgarian and had excellent credentials:
'He had a great reputation as a grammarian, was not unversed in rhetoric and
had an unrivalled knowledge of dogma. Zigabenos was commanded to publish
a list of all heresies, to deal with each separately and to append in each case the
refutation of it in the texts of the holy fathers.'[315] The twenty-eight *titloi*
contain various statements of the Orthodox faith, following a prologue which
is an encomium of Alexios and an attack on Epicurean atheism and pagan
polytheism. The first seven *titloi* deal with Christological problems, then
Euthymios goes on to the ancient heresies: Judaism, Simon of Samaria, the
Sabellarii, Arius and Athanasius, Apollinarius, Nestorius and the
Monophysites with special reference to Eutyches; aphthartodocetism, Origen
and the Monothelites bring the list up to iconoclasm. The final part of the
work deals with the heresies of his own day: Armenians, Paulicians,
Massalians, Bogomils and Islam.

   Two splendid copies of the presentation volume exist[316] showing Alexios
receiving the work from an assembled band of saintly doctors. We cannot be
sure of the date of the work nor of its purpose: as an encyclopaedia of heresies
it was surely too elementary to be a working guide for the patriarch's resident
synod, the *synodos endemousa*; it may have been for Alexios's and perhaps
Isaac's private reading. Other works of compilation of the period are
Theodore Bestes's revision of the *nomokanon* and John Xiphilinos II's
hagiographical collection.[317]

---

   [314]   Necessity may have brought forth fruit; see the observations of G. Dagron,
'Minorités ethniques,' 214, n. 185 and 213, n. 181 that a) anti-Armenian polemic sets the
agenda for anti-Roman polemic and b) that in Skylitzes Continuatus, ed. Tsolakes, 140-141
and Attaleiates, ed. Bonn, 96-97 heresy is seen as an historical event, something which
happened. The concept of 'court' writers, doctors, theologians is overdue for revision. I
hope to return to it in my work on twelfth-century literary society.
   [315]   *Al.,* XV.ix. 1, L, 223.18-224.1; Euthymios Zigabenos, *Panoplia Dogmatike,* PG 130;
M. Jugie, 'La vie et l'oeuvre d'Euthyme Zigabène,' *EO* 15 (1912), 215-225. On the new
genre of the panoply see H.G. Beck, *Kirche und theologische Literatur im byzantinischen
Reich* (Munich, 1959), 614, 626-627, 663-664.
   [316]   Vat. gr. 666, and Mosquens. gr. 387, see Walter, *Art and Ritual,* 40; Spatharakis, *The
Portrait in Byzantine Illuminated Manuscripts* (Leiden, 1976), 122-129. See my 'Imperial
Vocabulary,' 374-375.
   [317]   On Theodore Bestes see R. Macrides, 'Nomos and Kanon on Paper and in Court,'
Church and People in Byzantium, ed. R. Morris (Birmingham, 1990), 61-85 at 67; for John
Xiphilinos II see A. Kazhdan, *ODB,* III, 2211.

It has been observed for some time that hagiography was on the way out by the end of the eleventh century,[318] but we are fortunate in having a sparkling hagiography by Nicholas Kataskepenos of Cyril Phileotes. Kazhdan's dismissive judgement—'every fact in the biography is presented amid numerous patristic quotations: schematization squeezed all the life out of the essay'[319]—is uncharacteristic, and unfair. The ambience of the court is very clear (we have a letter from Nicholas to Eirene Doukaina); there are descriptions of Alexios setting out with his household, πανοικί, to visit the aged ascetic near Derkos. Other luminaries of the court, the *protostrator* Michael, Eumathios Philokales, Constantine Choirosphaktes, visited on their own account, and on one occasion see something like court gossip fermenting in the suburban calm of Derkos: John Komnenos, son of the *sebastokrator*, is seen by the saint celebrating a black mass in his cell. In view of the part often played by demonology in Byzantine Kaiserkritik and psogos generally it is tempting to read this together with the story of Theophylact's denunciation as a pointer to John's dubious loyalty.[320] Other lives of Alexian holy men, Meletios of Myoupolis and Christodoulos of Patmos, belong to a later period, though Christodoulos has left autobiographical writings.[321]

It is unfortunate that we do not have much imperial rhetoric for the period.[322] Theophylact's 1088 speech is the only epiphany *basilikos logos* for the reign. We have a speech of Manuel Straboromanos (and Alexios's reply), an alphabetical poem of Stephen Physopalamites, the (far from panegyric) speeches of John the Oxite, after which he was encouraged to take up his see in Antioch, and some of the occasional verse of Nicholas Kallikles.[323] His

---

[318] P. Magdalino, 'The Byzantine Holy Man in the Twelfth Century,' *The Byzantine Saint*, 51-66.

[319] *VCyril*, ed. Sargologos; Kazhdan and Epstein, *Change*, 201.

[320] *VCyril*, ch. 47, 46, 35, 34, 53.2-5, ed. Sargologos, 451, 146-153, 213-225, 370-372, 476.

[321] For Meletios see V. Vasilievskii, 'Nikolaou episkopou Methones kai Theodorou Prodromou bioi Meletiou tou Neou,' *Pravoslavnyi Palestinskii Sbornik* 17 (1886); S.K. Orlandos, 'He mone tou hosiou Meletiou kai ta paralavria autes,' *ABME* 5 (1939-40), 34-118; P. Armstrong, *The Lives of Meletios of Myoupolis. Introduction, translation and commentary* (MA Diss., Belfast, 1988) and her forthcoming new edition and translation as BBTT, 3; for Christodoulos, E. Vranoussi, *Ta hagiologika keimena tou hosiou Christodoulou* (Athens, 1966); R. Morris, 'Divine Diplomacy in the Late Eleventh Century,' *BMGS* 16 (1992) 147-156; A.J. Kirby, *The Archaeology of Christodoulos. Monastic Practice and Monastic Building in Eleventh-Century Byzantium* (MA Diss., Belfast, 1993).

[322] But see my 'Imperial Vocabulary' for a more positive view.

[323] For the 1088 speech see Gautier, I, 215-243; for Manuel Straboromanos, Gautier, 'Le dossier de Manuel Straboromanos,' *REB* 23 (1965), 168-204; Stephen Physopalamites, ed. K. Welz, *Analecta Byzantina. Carmina inedita Theodori Prodromi et Stephani Physopalamitae* (Diss., Leipzig, 1890), 54 and 58-59; John the Oxite, Gautier, 'Les Diatribes de Jean

poems appear to date from the very end of Alexios's reign although Theophylact's letters to him start around the turn of the century. The poems are largely commissioned epigrams for inscription on works of art: crosses for the *porphyrogennete* Eudokia and the empress, a crucifix, a St George, John Arbantenos's *peplon* for the church of the Hodegetria, an icon of the Saviour for John's foundation of the Pantokrator, and funerary poetry, for Andronikos Doukas, Gregory Kamateros, Dokeiane, Eirene Doukaina, and to Theodore Smyrnaios on his speech on the death of the *protostrator*'s son. Much seems clearly rooted in the reign of John although poems on the Second Coming and the Golden Kouboukleion have been associated with Alexios. Much work remains to be done.[324]

Another major interest of Alexian literature appears to continue the genre of *parainesis* popular from slightly earlier: advice to emperors was fairly well established in Byzantium, though its frequent classification as 'mirror for princes' is unfortunate: another type, of general advice, became more and more important. Kekaumenos had practised both, interspersed with his after-dinner stories, his memoirs of the Vlach wars and his personal eccentricities; Theophylact combined *parainesis* in his *basilikos logos* to the boy-emperor Constantine, but the *Spaneas* and Philip the Solitary's *Dioptra* offer it straight. With Symeon Seth's translation from the Arabic of *Stephanites and Ichnelates*, advice on personal relations at court, we are over the boundaries of *parainesis* and into fiction.[325]

The revival of fiction has lately been scrutinised carefully[326] and it is clear that the reign of Alexios is crucial. The novelettish tendencies of Nikephoros Bryennios, the story-telling of Kekaumenos, the author-in-the-text of Psellos, the translation of *Syntipas* all point in that direction. Certainly a penchant for autobiography can be documented under Alexios: the resignation poems of Nicholas of Kerkyra (possibly in 1094) and of Nicholas Mouzalon (disputed),[327] particularly the outspokenness of the latter, appear to

---

l'Oxite,' *REB* 28 (1970), 5-17. Nicholas Kallikles, ed. R. Romano (ByzetNeohellNeap, 8, Naples, 1980). See my 'Imperial Vocabulary,' 363-374.

[324] Poems 27, 6, 3, 1, 2, 10, 18 and 21, 22, 28, 30. Second coming: poem 24; golden cubiculum: poem 25. See R. Nelson and P. Magdalino, 'The Emperor in Byzantine Art of the Twelfth Century,' *ByzForsch* 8 (1982), 123-183.

[325] See C. Roueché in *Alexios I Komnenos*, II (BBTT, 4.2, Belfast, 1997), forthcoming.

[326] Notably in *The Greek Novel, AD 1-1985*, ed. R. Beaton (London, 1988), and in R. Beaton, *The Medieval Greek Romance* (Cambridge, 1989).

[327] See J. Darrouzès, 'L'éloge de Nicolas III par Nicolas Mouzalon,' *REB* 46 (1988), 5-53.

belong to this category.[328] But it has also become clear that to this period belong two most interesting literary experiments, the Grottaferrata Digenes and the *Timarion*. Both have been assigned to a single milieu, of the exile communities in Constantinople after the loss of Anatolia;[329] both need to be viewed in terms of the literature of Alexios. The *Digenes* is important for aristocratic attitudes and entertainment and has been compared recently with Kekaumenos's *Advice*, both from a social anthropological and from a psychological viewpoint.[330]

The *Timarion*, which looks forward to the circle of Nicholas Kallikles and Michael Italikos as well as to the satire boom of the twelfth century, cannot be dated too far from the memory of the emperor Romanos Diogenes and Psellos.[331] It might be thought that a picture of Alexian literary society could be deduced from a reading of the *Timarion*, but the delight of the Hades episode is in its synchronicity, reminiscent of progymnasmata on what Aristotle would have said to the emperor Theophilos; John Italos gets no better a rating from Academy and Stoa than he did from Anna Komnene. *Timarion's* Theodore Smyrnaios gives us some hints towards real-life literary society, though we constantly run the danger of naiveté: are we to believe that Theodore was carried in on a litter to perform in front of the emperor? But when he says 'in the life above it was all verbal dexterity and popular prettification that counted. Down here, it is all philosophy and true culture with less demagogic display,' we may get some flavour of Alexian priorities.

---

[328] Nicholas of Kerkyra, ed. S. Lampros, *Kerkyraika anekdota* (Athens, 1882), 27-41; Nicholas Mouzalon, ed. S.I. Doanidou, 'He paraitesis Nikolaou tou Mouzalonos apo tes archiepiskopes Kyprou. Anekdoton apologetikon poiema,' *Hellenika* 7 (1934), 109-150.

[329] For the exile community theory see R. Beaton, 'Cappadocians at Court,' *Alexios I Komnenos,* I, 329-338; on Digenes see *Digenes Akrites. New Approaches to Byzantine Heroic Poetry,* ed. R. Beaton and D. Ricks (KCL, 2, Aldershot, 1993). A new edition and commentary of the Grottaferrata Digenes are expected from Elizabeth Jeffreys. For *Timarion,* ed. R. Romano, tr. B. Baldwin, and the best study, though not sufficiently rhetorically aware, M. Alexiou, 'Literary Subversion and the Aristocracy in Twelfth-century Byzantium: a Stylistic Analysis of the *Timarion* (ch 6-10),' *BMGS* 8 (1982-83), 29-45.

[330] P. Magdalino, 'Honour among Rhomaioi: the Framework of Social Values in the World of Digenes Akrites and Kekaumenos,' *BMGS* 13 (1989), 183-218; C. Galatariotou, 'Open Space and Closed Space, the Perceived Worlds of Kekaumenos and Digenes Akrites,' *Alexios I Komnenos,* I, 303-328.

[331] On the dating see Beaton, 'Cappadocians at Court'; B. Baldwin, *Timarion* (Detroit, 1984): by the death of John Komnenos on the analogy of the trial of Brutus and Cassius in line 777 see Romano, *Timarione,* 141, Baldwin, 22, 28-32; his interpretation of βασιλεῖς to mean sequentially Alexios I Komnenos and John II Komnenos is unnecessary, see my 'Imperial Vocabulary,' 377-379; an earlier date close to 1100 is preferable.

And when Theodore is himself described, his voice and the brilliant lectures and the resonant delivery and the 'impressive size', we may believe it as much or as little as we believe in his gout, or indeed in anything addressed to a living recipient: the biggest joke would surely be if Theodore were still alive.[332]

Redating these works and anchoring them in an Alexian milieu forces a reconsideration of the period as experimental and innovative. Together with the adoption of the *politikos stichos*, well under way by now, the author-in-the-text, and the use of the vernacular, it is the revival of romance and satire[333] which has been most hailed in twelfth-century literature and this should be accepted as Alexian.

It is interesting to note how well those works which have been attributed to Alexios conform to the preferences of the period observed in works other than his own. The new piety in a prayer attributed to him in a Bodleian manuscript; the taste for polemic in the speech 'to an Armenian'; the autobiography, eschatology and *parainesis* mingled in the *Mousai*; all these show that even if he had a great deal of help in composing them, or even if the *Mousai* belongs to the reign of John, as it may well, they are all in tune with genuine literary concerns of the turn of the century. The author of the *Mousai*, while no great philosopher, is certainly neither nervous of neoplatonism, nor credible as an anti-intellectual soldier with no time for λόγοι.[334] Theophylact was unusual (more than he would have been in the middle of the twelfth century) in writing outside the capital but he was in touch with the concerns and the interests of those who were there. And these were not negligible.

---

[332] *Timarion*, 1095-1116, 589-599, 619-622, ed. Romano, 89, 70-71, 72.

[333] On *politikos stichos* see M.J. Jeffreys, 'The Nature and Origins of the Political Verse,' *DOP* 28 (1963), 39-52; on the vernacular see R. Beaton, 'De vulgari eloquentia,' *Byzantium and the West c. 850-c.1200* (Amsterdam, 1988), 261-268; on satire, R. Beaton, 'Oi satires tou Theodorou Prodromou kai oi aparches tes neollenikes grammateias,' *Ariadne* 5 (1989), 207-214.

[334] All these works will be published with translation and commentary in *Alexios Komnenos*, II. For the *Mousai* and the Bodleian prayer see also P. Maas, 'Die Musen des Kaisers Alexios I.,' *BZ* 22 (1913), 348-359; for the *logos* against the Armenians, see A. Papadopoulos-Kerameus, *Analekta Hierosolymitikes Stachylogias* (St Petersburg, 1891) I, 116-123.

CHAPTER THREE

COLLECTION AND NETWORK (I)

The next two chapters seek to describe our text as a whole, something which has not yet been attempted. It has been studied by historians with special interests,[1] especially those concerned with the local history of Macedonia and the economic history of Byzantium. But a description which takes into account all the letters, the apparently vacuous as well as the immediately informative, is still needed. Chapter 3 looks at the collection as a bundle of letters, how they are organised, what they are concerned with, how they are written. Chapter 4 will look at the letters as the only surviving traces of a parallel network of personal relationships, at how these may be discerned, what can be said about them, and how they were used by Theophylact.

3.1 The dating and the ordering of the collection

In one sense the collection of Theophylact's letters has existed only since 1986 when Gautier's edition was published, bringing together letters which survive only in scattered manuscripts,[2] sometimes, but not always, in association with other works of Theophylact,[3] and integrating them with the letters already known from the 1754-63 Venice collected edition.[4] This combined letters edited and published by Johannes Meursius in 1617 from Laur. gr. 59.12, those edited and published by Jean Lami in 1746 from Laur. gr. 10.13 and those transcribed by Assemani from Vat. gr. 432 and inserted by Finetti in the collected edition in 1754. This edition was reprinted in the *Patrologia Graeca* of 1862-64. Simeon, metropolitan of Varna, published his Bulgarian translation of this text in 1931. Individual letters have been reedited and published separately; the complete edition promised by Alice Leroy-Molinghen in 1938[5] did not appear.

---

[1] See above, ch. 1, 6-7.

[2] For a list of manuscripts see Gautier, *Théophylacte*, II, 13-27.

[3] For the manuscripts of other works of Theophylact, see Gautier, *Théophylacte*, I, 417-418 and for their relationship with the C group of manuscripts, *Théophylacte*, II, 25-27.

[4] For this and other editions see below, Bibliography.

[5] A. Leroy-Molinghen, 'Prolégomènes à une édition critique des lettres de Théophylacte de Bulgarie,' *Byz* 13 (1938), 253-262.

In another sense of course Theophylact's letters existed from an early stage as part of a larger unit, the letter-collection, or, certainly from the fourteenth century,[6] two letter-collections. Gautier's patient study of the manuscript tradition has made a certain amount clear; unfortunately he died before solving completely the problem of how the letters came to be collected in the form in which we find them.

He distinguished three groups of manuscripts. One (C) is of letters preserved piecemeal, often though not always associated with other works of Theophylact. These are early letters (G1, G2, G3, G132, G134) or late letters (G135) or possibly not letters at all (G134, G135). There is one case of group C preserving a letter (G100) also belonging to one of the other groups. G133 remains a puzzle. A second group (A) consists only of Laur. gr. 59-12 from which Meursius made his edition of 1617 and Paris. Suppl. gr. 1200, copied from Meursius's edition. There are seventy-six letters and the manuscript also contains the early letters (C), separated from the collection of seventy-six, and the two *basilikoi logoi*, as well as the works of Michael Choniates. It belonged to Isaac Mesopotamites[7] who also owned Petrop. gr. 250, a companion volume of late twelfth- and early thirteenth-century episcopal writers. One letter (G100) is copied twice at 45 and 68. Gautier believes that four folios are missing between G62 and G63 and there has been some disturbance in the region of G123. The third group (B) he traces back through a Spanish ambassador to the Vatican and before that to Venice[8] to an 'antiquissimus' Patmos manuscript, unfortunately not in the 1201 catalogue or in the 1355 summary. This group contains sixty-four letters, always in the same order, and as part of a two-volume collection of mainly ascetic works.[9] Thirty-seven

---

[6] The main ms of the 'A' group (of 75), Laur. gr. 54-12, see Gautier, *Théophylacte*, I, 39-40, dates to the end of the thirteenth century or the fourteenth century; Gautier traces the 'B' group (of 64) to a Patmos ms, 'ex antiquissimo codice descriptae allato nuper ex Patmo insula', Conrad Gesner, *Bibliotheca universalis*, I (Zurich, 1545) in C. Graux, *Essai sur les origines du fonds grecs de l'Escurial* (Paris, 1880), 399. But both Vat. gr. 509 (dated 1313) and Vat. gr. 432 are fourteenth-century.

[7] On Isaac Mesopotamites see *Théophylacte*, I, 39-40; *PLP*, 92105, I/1-8Add, 166-177.

[8] On Don Diego Hurtado de Mendoza (b. Granada 1503, ambassador to Venice 1538-47; ambassador to the Vatican from 1547) and on the arrival of his books in the Escorial see Graux, *Origines*, 153-195.

[9] In the first part: Gregory of Nyssa, the letter of Photios to tsar Michael, Maximos Confessor, Chrysostom on parables, more Maximos Confessor, Neilos on Prayer, Stephen of Nicomedia, Anastasios of Sinai, Severian of Gabala, Athanasios, John Klimax, Dorotheos of Gaza, more Chrysostom. In the second part: Basil's ascetic works, Theodore of Rhaithou, Anastasios of Sinai, Psellos, *De omnifaria doctrina*, Maximos Confessor, Wisdom of Sirach, astronomical works, Basil on Baptism, an incomplete world chronicle, the synaxarion for September.

letters of this group, including three which had already been published by Meursius, were published by Lami from Laur. gr. 10-13 in 1746. A further nineteen (including two of Lami's) together with G135 were transcribed by Assemani from Vat. gr. 432 and sent on by Finetti for the Venice edition of 1754. Thirteen letters are in common between groups A and B.[10]

What is the relationship between the two groups? Gautier, wisely, nowhere commits himself to an answer to this question, but it is implicitly clear that he regards the two groups as two parts of a single collection which had become separated by the early fourteenth century. He certainly[11] considers our stock of the letters of Theophylact as by no means complete, which the hypothesis of the missing four folios in Laur. gr. 59-12 may tend to support. By continuing the sequence from the end of the B group 64 to the beginning of the A group 74, framing them in the C group, Gautier maintains (more or less) the integrity of the groups while indicating their chronological relationship. The B group contains letters from the beginnings of Theophylact's archiepiscopate while the A group contains letters from the period of the second Bohemond war, fifteen years later, and there is nothing to suggest that the two collections were put together on any other basis than chronology. To take the obvious alternatives, neither is more 'literary' than the other:[12] the two great voyage set-piece letters, G4 and G126,[13] are at opposite ends of the collections; practical details are omitted in neither;[14] there is no sense of organisation by sub-genre.[15] Nor is there a thematic selection in keeping with any presumed interests of the patrons or owners of the manuscripts;[16] there is nothing particularly ascetic or spiritual about the B set, and if

---

[10] G14, G27, G28, G29, G32, G34, G71, G72, G74, G75, G79, G80, G81.

[11] *Théophylacte*, I, 119.

[12] I am addressing the theoretical issues raised here in a work on the processes of Byzantine letter-exchange.

[13] G4 is addressed to Maria the ex-*basilissa* and appears out of chronological sequence, perhaps as a dedication piece? G126 has been taken by a majority of commentators to refer to the Bohemond war early in 1108.

[14] As in for example the letters of John Mauropous, see above, 42, n.158.

[15] As in for example Cicero's letters. The titulus to G133 in Laur. acquisti 39, fol. 108, Τοῦ Βουλγαρίας παραμυθητικὴ ἐν θλίψεσι διαφόροις καὶ ἀσθενείαις, and the presence in the manuscript of two of Theophylact's three (or four?)*consolationes*, see below, 3.3, 143-144, as well as *consolationes* of other writers suggest that the consolatory letters had been specially selected in this manuscript.

[16] The postulated 'antiquissimus codex' of Patmos contained, as well as the sixty-four letters of Theophylact, devotional and theological works plus the monastic classics of the Ladder and Anastasios of Sinai; it is unlikely to have been made for Patmos which in 1201 already owned these works, but nothing more may be deduced; Isaac Mesopotamites from the books he owned appears to have been interested in episcopal letter-collections of the

the patron wanted information on ecclesiastical administration he might have done better with letters from the other group, for example G96, G98. Similarly if the patron of the A set wanted a full picture of the problems of a twelfth-century bishop, it was a pity to omit letters from the correspondence with the son of the *sebastokrator*. So a hypothesis of a single collection, which became separated before the late thirteenth to fourteenth century, is quite a serious option. Here the thirteen letters which appear in both groups are of vital importance and it is possible that clever codicology may reveal something of the relationship between the groups. Gautier's table[17] shows that the order of the common letters goes in groups of letters, one of three (G10, G11, G13 in A; G54, G55, G58 in B) changing place with one of seven (G14, G15, G16, G17, G18, G19, G21 in A; G11, G24, G25, G26, G27, G30, G32 in B); in both groups, but particularly in B, other letters are interspersed within the 'double' letters. Nor does the overlap come at the very beginning of the 'second' collection though it does involve the last letters of the 'first'. It is not a problem which will instantly be solved.

i. *Dating*

But what are the implications for the dating of the letters? Can a historian give any credence to the dates proposed in Gautier's edition? His methodology of dating is clear, although nowhere set out: he dates where possible (36 letters) from external sources, e.g. the Bohemond war, then from internal evidence, e.g. early in the episcopate, after letter G20. The run of a case, the pattern of all the letters addressed to a particular addressee, the practicalities of letter-exchange are brought into play. Twenty-nine letters fall into this category. Only when these fail (and they do for 71) does he turn to the order of the letters in the manuscripts, and proposes dates for 23 more. He assigns no dates to 39 others: 9 appear to have dates but their basis is unclear. It would be convenient if the order of the manuscripts could be relied upon. A first look at the letters dated by external evidence is discouraging. As we might have suspected from the effort and attention Gautier paid to the question of the reconquest expedition of 1092,[18] the letters, G8, 9, 12, 17, 26, which touch on the departure of John Doukas are very confused. G57, dated by Gautier to the

---

eleven to twelfth centuries; on the theoretical and methodological drawbacks to deducing patrons from product see R. Cormack, 'Patronage and New Programs of Byzantine Iconography,' *XVII IntCong* (New Rochelle, NY, 1986), repr. in *The Byzantine Eye. Studies in Art and Patronage* (London, 1989), 609-638.

[17] *Théophylacte*, II, 24.

[18] P. Gautier, 'La date de la mort de Christodoule de Patmos (mercredi 16 mars 1093),' *REB* 25 (1967), 235-238; 'Défection et soumission de la Crète sous Alexis I Comnène,' *REB* 35 (1977), 215-227.

Cuman crisis of 1094-95,[19] comes in the correspondence after G52, which all agree refers to the First Crusade.[20] The juxtaposition in the manuscripts of G29 (after May 1092 on the basis of the career of Mermentoulos)[21] with G12 (after the Komnenos family row of 1093 according to Roth)[22] seems only to justify Gautier's doubts about this reference. Other considerations are more encouraging. The watershed of the 1094-95 synod, so well exploited by Gautier,[23] certainly produces 'before synod' letters numbered from 18 to 77 and 'after synod' letters G82 and G84.

When we look at letters dated from internal evidence there are more grounds for optimism. Letters clearly written at the same time are close in the numbering (G88, G118, G127 form a troublesome exception)[24] and it is possible to follow whole sequences of letters to a single correspondent (e.g. Anemas)[25] without disturbance. Readers will differ on how many letters may be dated this way: Gautier, mindful of the difficulties of medieval letter-

---

[19] Gautier, *Théophylacte*, II, 67-68.

[20] G52, II, 303.4. See S. Runciman, 'The First Crusaders' Journey across the Balkan Peninsula,' *Byz* 19 (1949), 208; F. Chalandon, *Les Comnène*, I (Paris, 1900), 160; J. Nesbitt, 'The Rate of March of Crusading Armies in Europe: a Study and Computation,' *Traditio* 19 (1963), 167-181.

[21] He appears to be already Grand *droungarios* of the Watch, II, 235.4-5 and John Thrakesios was still in that post in May 1092, Grumel, *Regestes*, no. 963.

[22] K. Roth, *Studie zu den Briefen des Theophylaktos Bulgarus* (Ludwigshafen am Rhein, 1900), 10-11; the family row of Anna Komnene, *Alexiad*, VIII.viii.1-4, ed. B. Leib, 3 vols (Paris, 1937-45), II, 149-151; see B. Leib, 'Complots à Byzance contre Alexis I Comnène (1081-1118),' *BS* 23 (1962), 250-275; A. Hohlweg, *Beiträge zur Verwaltungsgeschichte des oströmischen Reiches unter den Komnenen* (MiscByzMonac, 1, Munich, 1965), 18 on the implications of the affair.

[23] P. Gautier, 'Le synode des Blachernes (fin 1094): étude prosopographique,' *REB* 29 (1971), 213-284. 'Before synod' letters: G28 has Theodore Smyrnaios as *proedros* (*protoproedros* at the synod); G37 has Symeon *hegoumenos* of Anaplous not apparently a recluse (Symeon *hegoumenos* recluse of Kyr Philotheos at the synod); G51 to the *chartophylax* Nikephoros, also G30, G66, ?G83 (ex-*chartophylax* at the synod); G75 and G77 are to Nicholas of Kerkyra who resigned at the synod, see poem, ed. S. P. Lampros, *Kerkyraika anekdota ek cheirographon Hagiou Orous, Kantabrigias, Monachou kai Kerkyras, nun to proton demosieuomena* (Athens, 1882), 27-41; conceivably G70 (someone else was *didaskalos* at the synod). G65, to the nephew of Taronites, suggests a date before the Diogenes crash of 1094.

[24] G88, to John, *grammatikos* of Palaiologos, talks about the appointment to the 'rule of the Vardar' of the son of our *pansebastos authentes* and the problems of a village there; G127, to Gregory Kamateros, refers to the appointment of the *pansebastos* son of the *protostrator;* G118 is an *adventus* letter to Constantine Doukas which also refers to a Vardar village.

[25] See below, 4.2, 183 for the letters to Anemas.

exchange,[26] tends to fling into a single post-bag anything he can possibly squeeze in, so G88-95, G94-99, G111-118, where there is convincing evidence only for G90 and G93, G96 and G98, G112 and G114.[27] But a sensitive reading might allow a hypothesis of a basically chronological collection with some obviously displaced letters: G4? G17? G88? G30?[28] and a band of disturbance around the overlap of the collections B and A. Letters numbered in the 50s and in the 70s may appear to be contemporary and to predate the synod of 1094;[29] but note and beware that G73, G78, G81 appear to establish us firmly in the early 1110s with the death of the *sebastokrator* and Gregory Taronites' campaigns in Pontos.[30] A batch of letters may well have dropped out here.

So what can be done about the seventy-one letters which can be dated neither from external nor from internal evidence? Gautier, perhaps because of

---

[26] See above, 35-37. Theophylact complains several times of communication difficulties: in G18 the *pittakion* never arrived; in G52 no good bearer came along, and in G117 the bearer rushed him, being in too great a hurry to depart. See below, Table V.

[27] G90 to the *chartophylax* and G93 to Nicholas Kallikles both draw attention to the fact that Theophylact has sent his brother in winter as an indication of the severity of the crisis (Ekklesiai and calumny); G96 and G98 have an almost identical and very explicit subject-matter, clearly referring to exactly the same phase of the affair; G112 and G114 both refer to a relative of Theodore Smyrnaios who carried the letters. G112 seems a follow-up to G111; the ἐνταῦθα of G113 echoes the αὐτόθι of G112, but could have been sent with either. G5, G6, G7 appear to be written shortly after arrival in Ochrid and to be carried by Theophylact's brother, but Gautier's reattribution of G6 so that it can be one of the letters referred to in G7 does not convince. See below, Table VIII.

[28] G4 is certainly later than the 'arrival letters' G5, G6, G7. G17 hangs on the chronology of the John Doukas expeditions but is most likely the spring of 1092 while G8 is the second half of 1092. (G17 could however be in spring 1093.) Two of G88, G118, G127 must be misplaced, see above, 83, n. 23. G127 certainly is since Demetrios is alive and well and is already dead in G121 and G122. If the journeys to the army camp are the same, as Zlatarsky argued, V.N. Zlatarsky, *Istoriia na Bulgarskata durzhava prez sriednitie viekove*, 3 vols (Sofia, 1918-40), II, 511-515, G30 should come after G77. In addition, G39 (consolatio on John Pantechnes) must postdate G120 (alive and well); G132 (death of Psellos) should precede G27 (recommendatory for his grand-son).

[29] E.g. G58, G59, G60 to the bishop of Triaditsa may be referred to in G77 as a recent problem.

[30] G73 is a consolatio to Melissenos on the death of the sebastokrator Isaac, pinpointed to 1102 by D. Papachryssanthou, 'La date de la mort du Sebastokrator Isaac Comnène, frère d'Alexis Ier, et de quelques événements contemporains,' *REB* 21 (1963), 250-255; for the dating of Taronites' activities in Pontos see H. Hagenmeyer, 'Chronologie du royaume de Jérusalem,' *ROL* 12 (1908), 73; (with care) N. Adontz. 'L'archevêque Théophylacte et le Taronite,' *Byz* 11 (1936), 577-588; M.E. Mullett, 'The Madness of Genre,' *Homo Byzantinus, Papers in Honor of Alexander Kazhdan*, ed. A. Cutler and S. Franklin = *DOP* 46 (1992), 233-243.

his distaste for Laur. gr. 59-12,[31] is noticeably less willing the later he gets in the collection to date in relation to neighbours. Caution urges us to apply this rule throughout, and to look carefully before accepting any date argued simply from the position of the letter in the manuscripts.

ii. *Events, sequences and cases*

Among the blurred and persistent *symphoriai* and *epereiai* of Theophylact's archiepiscopate, events are atypical, and certainly events which appear in history books. Yet Theophylact lived in exciting times, in an exciting place, in one of the major theatres of war, on the major artery of the empire. It is not surprising that scholars looked to Theophylact's letters as vital supplementary evidence to histories of the period. They were disappointed. Even the famous reference to the passing of the First Crusade occurs in only one letter;[32] it is characteristic of Theophylact that it is mentioned only as an excuse for not writing earlier. That the letter is not longer or clearer is easily explained; his correspondent was the bishop of Kitros whose see was also along the route of the First Crusade, and must himself have experienced a Φραγγικὴ διάβασις. It is a reminder to us that epistolary discourse is reciprocal and involves an inscribed narratee.

It is not however correct to assume with Failler[33] that events have no place in letters, for Theophylact was affected by the vicissitudes of the empire and these find a place in the correspondence, not perhaps where we should expect to find them but they are there. The problem is often to identify events known to us from narrative sources in references made from Theophylact's personal viewpoint and in his elaborate and allusive style: the very epistolary emphasis on correspondent and addressee means that third persons rarely appear, or are wrapped up in a mist of metaphor; it can be an indicator of difficulty for Theophylact when he is forced to identify a third person clearly.[34]

But it is possible for example to observe in his letters the beginnings of the Byzantine reconquest in the departure from Dyrrachion of John Doukas, the *gambros* of the emperor, on the campaigns which won back the Aegean islands and then Crete and Cyprus for the empire in 1092 and 1093. Typically we see this major turning-point of Alexios's reign, which Ahrweiler regarded as the revival of the Byzantine navy and the beginnings of Alexios as

---

[31] *Théophylacte*, II, 14.

[32] G52, see above, 82, n. 18.

[33] A. Failler, 'Introduction' to Gautier, *Théophylacte*, II, 7.

[34] As in the Lazaros group, G96 and G98, and the letters to the bishop of Triaditsa, G58, G59, G60, where his letters are longer and more explicit.

providential saviour, in a rather different light. For Theophylact its importance is the crisis of the change of governor at Dyrrachion and an opportunity for himself to ask a favour on behalf of his relatives in Euboia. The letters which touch on these events are clearly out of chronological order. The sequence and dating of John Doukas's expedition are debated, but it is clear that if G26 is to him it must predate the campaign, that G17 is to him after he had left Macedonia but had not been replaced as *doux*, while G8 belongs to the second half of 1092 on his return to Euboia in triumph.[35] G10 is an 'adventus letter' to John Doukas's successor, John Komnenos, the son of the *sebastokrator*, and in G23, to John Komnenos, Theophylact appeals on the basis of a decision made by his predecessor.

Other events of the reign appear even more tangentially: the arrival of Caesar Melissenos on a recruiting mission in 1091; Theophylact's plea to John Komnenos to stop depopulating his area (only the word πεζῶν points to the Serbo-Dalmatian wars of 1093-94).[36] An event which earlier commentators considered pivotal to the collection is the great Komnenos family dispute of 1093 (or 1094?) caused by a letter from the archbishop of Bulgaria, delating upon the *doux* of Dyrrachion, son of Isaac the *sebastokrator*. The problem is that not only is that letter not preserved in the correspondence, hardly surprisingly, since in the end the emperor ignored the warning and restored John to his post, but that there is no evidence that relations between Theophylact and the *doux* deteriorated. Roth claimed that when in G12 Theophylact admits to have been somewhat rough with the other's reputation he is referring to this event. In context the proposal is less convincing.[37]

---

[35] On John Doukas and the reconquest see H. Ahrweiler, *Byzance et la mer. La marine de guerre, la politique et les institutions maritimes de Byzance au VIIe -XVe siècles* (Paris, 1966), 182-189.

[36] On these wars see J.V.A. Fine, *The Early Medieval Balkans. A Cultural Survey from the Sixth to the Late Twelfth Century* (Ann Arbor, 1983), 225-230; J. Ferluga, *Byzantium on the Balkans. Studies on the Administration and the Southern Slavs from the VIIth to the XIIth Centuries* (Amsterdam, 1976), 182-189; G13, to Melissenos, II, 171-173 appears to date from 1091 as a first appearance rather than April 1093 in the Dalmatian campaign. G24, to John Komnenos, II, 209.11: τῶν πεζῶν ἐκβολῇ is as evidence hardly open and shut.

[37] See above, n.20. On the dating of the family row, 'sans doute en 1093', *Théophylacte*, II, 45, see Gautier, 'Le synode,' *REB* 19 (1971), 281, n.3: early 1094. This redating (the account in Anna seems to fall in 1091) creates difficulties in the spring and summer of 1094, including a fairly hot pace for the emperor. Alexios must leave Constantinople for Philippopolis, sort out the John crisis, move on to the Zygon and supervise much fort-building, return to Constantinople and then leave on the direct route for Dalmatia (=the Via Egnatia?), stay in Serres, stay at Pentegostes, again at Serres and solve the problems arising from the Diogenes conspiracy by June 29! (Before Stephanou corrected the date

Balkan campaigns of these years[38] may have provided opportunities for Theophylact to have visited an army camp and to see Gregory Kamateros. Other events of the mid-1090s impinge even more slightly. The Diogenes crash of the summer of 1094 may have very slightly affected his acquaintance.[39] He was not himself present at the synod of Blachernai in 1094-95 although many of his correspondents were. The suffragan bishop of Vidin apparently complained about the Cuman invasions threatened in 1093-94 and begun in 1095;[40] we have Theophylact's acerbic reply (G57) pointing out that his own problems were worse. Theophylact was in Nicomedia at one time during the correspondence: could it have been to see the emperor there in 1095?[41]

The campaigns of Gregory Taronites in Pontos in 1103 (though a tangled issue for the modern scholar) were for Theophylact a straightforward matter for amazement and praise. A single victory—the engagement which defeated Danishmend and freed Bohemond and Richard of the Principate—broke the arrogance of two peoples. Three letters celebrate the campaign of that year, ending with the return to Constantinople of Gregory.[42]

The second Norman war, during much of which Theophylact appears to have been living on his Vardar estate, provided more opportunities for Theophylact to (fail to) visit his doctor friends in the emperor's camp and just possibly for the empress to visit him. He elsewhere (G127) tells us that the emperor's constant campaigning (shunning the capital, the palace and all the other delights for the discomforts of campaign) inspires fear in the enemies of the state. By the time of Bohemond's arrival and the final stage of the war

---

from February 8, 'Le procès de Léon de Chalcédoine', 56 it would have been even worse.) This merits further consideration, but 1093 looks most likely.

[38] According to Anna, Alexios was in the Zygon fortifying mountain passes, in 1093 Alexios got as far as Skopje when Bolkan burnt Lipenion; in 1094 Alexios went via Serres and Pentegostes to Lipenion when Bolkan surrendered and again around Anchialos and Adrianople in the Cuman war of 1094.

[39] See *Al.*, IX.v-ix, L, II, 169-184; B. Leib, 'Les complots à Byzance contre Alexis I Comnène,' *BS* 23 (1962), 250-275; see my 'The "Disgrace" of the Ex-basilissa Maria,' *BS* 45 (1984), 202-210 at 206; J.C. Cheynet, *Pouvoir et contestations à Byzance 963-1250* (ByzSorb, 9, Paris, 1990), case-study no. 128, pp. 98-99.

[40] See Gautier, II, 67 for an excellent summary; P. Diaconu, *Les Coumanes au Bas-Danube aux XIe et XIIe siècles* (Bucharest, 1978), 41-58.

[41] G4 to the ex-*basilissa* Maria, II, 137.19: ὡς ἀπὸ Νικομηδείας ἐπανερχόμενος; 141.56 ἐν τῇ πόλει ταύτῃ is not clear. Constantinople? Nicomedia? or Ochrid? Alexios was seeing to the defence of Nicomedia *Al.*, X.v.2, L, II, 205.10-25. The account comes after the end of the Cuman war and before the news of the Crusading armies—but a close study of the narrative technique of the *Alexiad* and its implications for chronology is well overdue.

[42] On the problems of these letters, G81, G78, G92, see my 'Madness of Genre.'

Theophylact was in Constantinople, but in G120 he has returned to Thessalonike and reported to his correspondent that the whole region of Ochrid was in fear and that Bohemond had ravaged Mokros and now held the Bagora. The *protostrator* Michael is recruiting and Theophylact is confident that the lizard who had warmed himself in the rays of the emperor's sun would find no escape. Theophylact has hired horses and is about to set out for Ochrid.[43]

A final event which may be marked in the correspondence is the disputations at Philippopolis in 1114; we know that Alexios was accompanied by Eustratios, bishop of Nicaea, Nikephoros Bryennios and the archbishop of Philippopolis; Theophylact's G135 may have been written for that occasion.[44]

But in general the correspondence has its own rhythm, unmarked by external events. Apart from the three early letters, which must date from the 1080s, when Theophylact was teaching in Constantinople, and the letter on the death of Michael Psellos, probably in 1078, the letters fall into the period of the archiepiscopate. We have three 'arrival-in-see' letters;[45] the letters are articulated in other ways by internal developments. Some relationships can be traced, some problems followed through, Theophylact's movements around his archdiocese tracked, and his illnesses compared. But although certain sequences of events become clear, the history of his archiepiscopate will not be written. The order of letters in the manuscripts is simply not reliable enough,

---

[43] Theophylact is probably near the Vardar in G110, G111, G112, G113, G114. G127, II, 579.118-126 mentions the emperor on campaign in the context of a μάκρα ἀποδημία of which Gregory is tiring. It is impossible to narrow down the possibilities, see above, n. 38 for the range of possibilities. During the Bohemond war Alexios left Constantinople after a visit to Cyril Phileotes in September 1105 with the *augousta* and went to Thessalonike. In February 1106 he went via Strumitsa (and probably the Eleousa) and Slopimos to fortify the frontiers of the empire, then from the autumn to January was in Thessalonike and returned to Constantinople 25 January 1107. On 1 November he went again with the *augousta*, via Geranios, Choirovachi, Mestos to Psyllos and then to winter in Thessalonike, after which he set out for Pelagonia and Diabolis where he stayed until the Treaty of Diabolis in September 1108. G120, to John Pantechnes, 555.29-44. If the *despoina* of G107 is Eirene Doukaina rather than Anna Dalassene or Maria the ex-*basilissa* this would seem to be the nearest she got to Theophylact. F. Chalandon, *Les Comnène*, 2 vols (Paris, 1900), I, *Essai sur le règne d'Alexis I Comnène*, 217-253; R.J. Lilie, *Byzanz und die Kreuzfahrerstaaten* (Poikila Byzantina, 1, Munich, 1981), 54-88.

[44] *Al.*, XIV.viii.9, L, III, 181.25-182.23; John Zonaras, *Epitome Historion*, XVIII.26.10, ed. T. Büttner-Wobst (CFHB, Bonn, 1897), III, 753.15-755.19. Cf. Eustratios of Nicaea, *Elenchos kai anatrope*, ed. A. Demetrakopoulos, *Ekklesiastike Bibliotheke*, I (Leipzig, 1866), 160-198; Alexios I Komnenos, *Ekdotheis par' autou pros Armenious doxazontas kakos mian physin epi Christo*, ed. A. Papadopoulos-Kerameus, *Analekta Hierosolymitika*, I (St Petersburg, 1891), 116-123. On Eustratios, see above, 2.6, 73, n.308.

[45] G5, G6, G7, see below, 3.3, 144-146.

and the jerky succession of photographic stills to which we have compared epistolographic narrative leaves out too much for us to be certain of the plot.

An event which appears to stand out from among the letters is the synod of Prespa.[46] In G108 Theophylact announces that he has recovered from an illness which had kept him in bed, and calls upon the archon of Prespa, Makrembolites, to assist an ecclesiastic in making preparations for a synod. In G31 he tells Gregory Kamateros that he will be with him, God willing, after the synod held at St Achilleios, but until that synod is over it is impossible to come to him however much he wants to.[47] Four (or possibly five or six)[48] other letters in the collection deal with a synod and its aftermath and it is not impossible that they refer to the same event. They tell the story of the bishop of Triaditsa (known from G18 as a bishop appointed for his monastic achievements) and his failure to attend the synod to answer accusations against him by one (or two) Bulgarian monks and to justify his accusations against the bishop of Lipenion.[49] The first letter, G58, begins dramatically with the arrival of the *geron*, just as Theophylact was going into church with a large number of ecclesiastics and lay notables, and proceeds with the monk's accusations. From the month of July the bishop had mistreated him, so he had complained to Theophylact on a previous occasion when the bishop was with Theophylact, who had instructed the bishop to treat him well; the bishop had not so the *geron* went to the emperor for help and succeeded. But he was then expelled from the region of Triaditsa and so came back to Theophylact. Theophylact reported the views of the archontes at the synod, instructed the bishop to restore the monk to his monastery and ordered him to turn up at the synod to explain the charges against him. The next two letters, G59 and G60, are written from the synod, one from Theophylact himself, the other

---

[46] See my 'The monumental bishop-list at Prespa,' *A Mosaic of Cypriot and Byzantine Studies presented to A.H.S. Megaw*, ed. J. Herrin, M.E. Mullett and C. Otten-Froux, forthcoming.

[47] G108, II, 527.7; G31, II, 235.34.

[48] G58, G59, G60, G87. G75 and G77 to the bishop of Kerkyra seem to refer to the trouble with the bishop, who appears to have been known to Nicholas, G77, 409.47-411.67; φιλάδελφος is the word used at 411.57. If G75 and G77 belong it is likely that the synod took place before 1094-95, the date of the synod of Blachernai at which Nicholas of Kerkyra is thought to have resigned. For the resignation poem see Nicholas of Kerkyra, ed. S. Lampros, *Kerkyraika anekdota* (Athens, 1882), 30-41 and on the dating Gautier, *Théophylacte*, II, 88 and P. Gautier, 'Le synode de Blachernes (fin 1094), Etude prosopographique,' *REB* 29 (1971), 280-284.

[49] On this case see now M.D. Spadaro, '*Archontes* a confronto nella periferia dell'impero sotto la basileia di Alessio I Comneno,' *Syndesmos, Studi in onore di Rosario Anastasi* (Catania, 1991), 83-114 and R. Morris, *Monks and Laymen in Byzantium 843-1118* (Cambridge, 1995), 151.

from the members of the synod, deploring the response of the bishop of Triaditsa that he could not attend because he was taking some converted Armenians to Constantinople to show the emperor. A second accusation had been made against him, and the synod decided to give him a fortnight to chrismate all the converts, after which time he was to be suspended. It appears that the bishop proceeded to Constantinople with the converts and spread malicious rumours about Theophylact. It is possible that the harsh and difficult bishop to whom Theophylact alludes in G75 and G77, both addressed to the metropolitan of Kerkyra, was this bishop; in G87 Theophylact replies to a letter from him apologising and asking for restoration.[50]

These letters are scattered through the collection, and it must be asked whether they refer to the same event. Their interest would seem to be that it is remarkable that Theophylact should have held a local synod at all at this date. At some time before 1084 the emperor had delivered a speech to the metropolitans reproaching them for holding their annual reunions in Constantinople rather than in their provinces. Reactions seems to have been fairly swift and a speech is preserved by Niketas bishop of Ankyra who felt constrained to reply on behalf of bishops like himself, who had been forced by the Seljuk invasion to linger, σχολάζοντες, in the capital. I know of only two twelfth-century local synods, one in Euboia and one in Cyprus.[51] The canon Theophylact insists upon is 5 Nicaea calling for two meetings a year in every diocese but the council in Troullo modified this to once a year in times of barbarian invasion. By 1175 Balsamon refused to comment on the canon in question, as not in force (ὡς μὴ ἐνεργοῦντα), and added a bibliography of references to provincial councils in general.[52] It may be that provincial synods continued in hardworking annual anonymity, but there is a strong sense that they had been superseded by the *synodos endemousa* in Constantinople.[53] So Theophylact's may be a rare survival.

---

[50] G87, II, 457-459.

[51] Niketas of Ankyra, *Hos ou dei ton Konstantinoupoleos cheirotonein eis tas heterois hypokeimenas*, ed. J. Darrouzès, *Documents inédits d'ecclésiologie byzantine* (AOC, 10, Paris, 1966), 44-48, 208-237. For the other synods, see Michael Choniates, ep. 20, ed. S. Lampros, II (Athens, 1879), 180-186 and the commentary in J. Herrin, *The Social and Economic Structure of Central Greece in the Late Twelfth Century* (PhD Diss., Birmingham, 1972), 265, n. 58.

[52] Canon 5 Nicaea, G.A. Rhalles and M. Potles, *Syntagma ton theion kanonon*, II (Athens, 1852), 124-125; Canon 37 In Trullo, ibid., II, 388; Balsamon, *Kanones*, PG 137, 240; 545. He underlines canonical strictness in his summing-up. Allowance must be made for his own non-residence as patriarch of Antioch.

[53] On the *synodos endemousa* see M. Hajjar, *Le synode permanent dans l'église byzantine* (OCA, 164, Rome, 1962); J. Darrouzès, *Recherches sur les ὀφφίκια de l'église byzantine*

But it is equally arguable that if Theophylact held one synod he may well have held them annually. If so, the case of the bishop of Triaditsa may not have anything to do with the synod of Prespa, or indeed with any synod of Prespa. Gautier had a great deal of difficulty in dating this (or these) events; he began by associating G108 with the May 1103 visit of Theophylact to the *panegyris* of Achilleios,[54] proceeded to separate the Triaditsa letters from the Prespa ones,[55] but in both cases ended up with a date in 1093 or 1094.[56] None of his arguments is totally convincing. The assumption that the synod described in the letter to Makrembolites took place at the time of the *panegyris* rests on a literal reading of fanciful imagery;[57] the dating and placing of G58 and G31 are very uncertain; the choice of a campaign to bring Gregory Kamateros within reach of Prespa is quite arbitrary,[58] and dating by G75 and G77 is of course shaky.[59] Unless three different synods are under discussion there is considerable disturbance in the manuscripts. It is unlikely that on the basis of this evidence more progress can be made.

The only other event which stands out with similar prominence in the letters is a personal one; the death of his brother Demetrios. Two letters and

---

(Paris, 1971), 13-18, 132-134; S. Vailhé, 'Le droit d'appel en Orient et le synode permanent de Constantinople,' *EO* 20 (1921), 129-146. The effect of barbarian invasion is hard to assess, see S. Vryonis, *The Decline of Hellenism in Asia Minor and the Process of Islamization from the Eleventh through the Fifteenth Century* (Berkeley, LA and London, 1971), 201. On the normal running of the *synodos topike* see J. Zhishman, *Die Synoden und die Episcopalämte in der morgenländischen Kirche* (Vienna, 1897), 57-86, although the evidence is scarce, see E. Herman, 'Appunti sul diritto metropolitano nella chiesa orientale,' *OCP* 13 (1947), 522-535.

[54] G78, to Gregory Taronites, II, 415, 17-18: ἀπίοντι γὰρ πρὸς τὸν μέγαν ᾿Αχίλλειον ὡς ἂν τῇ πανηγύρει συνεορτάσαιμι... The feast-day of Achilleios is 15 May; the 1103 date is provided by the career of Gregory Taronites in Pontos.

[55] So G108 as against G58, G59, G60, G87.

[56] 1103 (début mai) and 1093/94 as against 1093/94?(in all), Gautier, *Théophylacte*, II, 526, 258, 326, 344, 456.

[57] G108, II, 527.11: τοὺς τὰ τῆς ἑορτῆς ᾄσοντας τέττιγας ἀτεχνῶς ἀποδείξητε καὶ ἐν πανηγύρει μεθυόντων αὐτοὶ λιμώξωμεν; the letter starts with the image of Theophylact in bed, roused by the voice of the canons, proceeds to explain the purpose to the archon and then builds on the idea of grasshoppers living on song alone to show the archon how not to victual the synod. For parallels to the grasshopper conceit, Aristophanes, *Clouds*, 1360; Plato, *Phaedrus*, 262D; Simonides, frag. 173; the fable of the grasshopper and the ants, Aesop, 401, ed. C. Halm, *Aisopeion Mython Synagoge* (Leipzig, 1854), 193.

[58] See again 86, n.37 for the options. Gautier, II, 75 suggests either the first half of 1093 or June 1094 during the campaign against the Serbs and Dalmatians. In fact Skopje in 1093 may be the nearest the emperor's entourage was to Ochrid before the Diabolis campaign of 1108.

[59] See 89, n.47 above.

two poems deal with this event; three letters about a brother's illness seems to prepare for them. The first appears to be G133, edited for the first time by Gautier, which records Theophylact's distress at learning that his brother has fallen ill and wishing to hear of his speedy recovery. It is not clear where Theophylact was writing from, or where Demetrios was at the time. But in a letter to the bishop of Kitros he explained Demetrios's serious symptoms: an inability to eat, a longstanding headache and a stomach full of fluid. He blamed the move from Ochrid to Ekklesiai, the absence of the light wine of Ochrid and other nourishing food. Theophylact had tried *oxysacchari*, to no avail; Demetrios had a distaste for all medicinal food. In G111, he sends his brother's greetings to Nicholas Kallikles, 'from Tainaros, from which he descends to Hades, escorted by consumption.' Two letters are preserved relating the death, one to the bishop of Debra, which Simeon associated with the Bohemond war, since the bishop is absent from his see and Theophylact urges him to return. The other, to the bishop of Kitros, is reminiscent of the letter about the First Crusade; the first mention of the death is a third of the way into the letter and is only introduced then as the latest of his burdens. He then enlarges: '...the brother on whom my breath depended, who was really everything to me, who would throw himself in the path of fire and swords so that I could live relaxed and free from pain.' Theophylact then describes his own physical condition: he feels his body slipping away into a complete collapse. Taken with the two poems published by Gautier in 1963 which detail the help Demetrios gave him in his dealings with the fisc, it is clear that the death of this brother, called Demetrios in Paris. gr. 1277, was an event no less important for Theophylact and the church in Ochrid than any invasion or synod.[60]

Manuscripts and commentators are agreed in placing the death late in the collection, and in general to the period of the second Norman war. The proximity of Nicholas Kallikles in G111 can be explained by his presence with the emperor on campaign in Thessalonike and environs in September 1105 - February 1106, September 1106 - January 1107 and January and February 1108.[61] Some discussion has been devoted to the placing of G120: if this refers

---

[60] G133, II, 591; G111, II, 535; G113, II, 539; G121, II, 559; G122, II, 561, poems 14 and 15, I, 369-377. See D. Obolensky, *Six Byzantine Portraits* (Oxford, 1988), 55-57; the discussion in Gautier, I, 15-22, is vitiated by the invention of a healthy brother John.

[61] *Al.*, XII.iii-XIII.xii.28, L, III, 59-139. There is some scope for fine-tuning, e.g. XII.iv.4, L, III,66.8: ἐπὶ ἐνιαυτὸν (where? Strumitsa and Slopimos? surely not?) ἕνα καὶ μῆνας δύο. We can be sure he was at the Eleousa shortly before the chrysobull of August 1106, *To ison tes diataxeos tou hosiotatou patros hemon Manouel monachou kai ktetoros tes hyperagias Theotokou tes Eleouses tes en to themati men Stroumitzes en to chorio de*

to the last stage of the war is it before or after the death? A reference in the first poem to Demetrios's assistance in maintaining morale at a time when 'Beliar' was terrorising all around has been taken to mean that he was still alive in 1108; other commentators have taken the *doulos kai apostates,* the lizard who basked in the emperor's favour, of G120 to be Bolkan in the 1090s rather than Bohemond in the 1100s.[62]

The major difficulty lies in making sense of all the letters in the collection which mention a brother. No solution can allow the order in the manuscripts to remain unchanged, for G127 has a brother named Demetrios, very much alive. This letter, although clearly misplaced, must be roughly contemporary with two other letters, G88 and G118 and possibly postdates the closely contemporary G94, G96 and G98.[63] But G116 also has a brother and G110, immediately preceding the first mention of illness, contrasts Theophylact's catarrh and fear of the Vardar with his brother's health and eagerness to travel. If this was Demetrios, there was a certain irony in Theophylact's characterisation of the Vardar as a river of Hades. In view of earlier letter-bearing expeditions in winter Demetrios might figure as a casualty of Byzantine letter-exchange. Gautier thought otherwise,[64] and postulated a 'robust brother' for G110, offering in justification G70 'my brothers your pupils.' In G42 and G46 he thought he detected a possible candidate, ὁ καλός Ἰωάννης. While it is very unclear when Theophylact uses ἀδελφός to indicate a blood relationship (except at G122 where he clearly distinguishes) he uses ὁ καλός Ἰωάννης also to and of John Opheomachos.[65] Given that the manuscript order cannot stand in its entirety, it seems more economical to assume one brother, Demetrios, a last letter-bearing journey at

---

Anopalaiokastro legomeno idrumenes, ed. L. Petit, 'Le monastère de Notre-Dame de Pitié en Macédoine,' *IRAIK* 6 (1908), 1-153 at 30.

[62] G120, to John Pantechnes, 555.30: παρὰ τοῦ δούλου καὶ ἀποστάτου; 555.34-5: τῇ σαύρᾳ γοῦν ταύτῃ θαλφθείσῃ ταῖς τῶν εὐεργεσιῶν τοῦ βασιλέως ἄκτισι. Uspenskii and Jireček thought it was a popular uprising and Vasilevskii argued that it was Bohemond; Mitropolit Simeon, *Pismata na Teofilakt Ochridski archiepiskop Bulgarski* (Bulgarskata Akademija na Naukitie, 15, Sofia, 1931), 165-166.

[63] Here the problem is the dating of Constantine Doukas's tour of duty at Boleron-Strymon-Thessalonike. He was there in 1118, Lavra, no. 64.61-62, ed. P. Lemerle, A. Guillou and N. Svoronos (Archives de l'Athos, 5, Paris, 1970), 332. See D. Polemis, *The Doukai, A Contribution to Byzantine Prosopography* (University of London Historical Studies, 22, London, 1968) no. 30, p. 76.

[64] Gautier, *Théophylacte,* I, 15-16.

[65] G71 addresses Opheomachos Ὦ καλὲ Ἰωάννη and G69 starts, II, 377.2: τί τοῦτο; Καὶ ὁ καλὸς Ἰωάννης. On the problem of ἀδελφός see below 4.1, 173-175; G122, II, 561.2 uses συνεπίσκοπε to distinguish between Theophylact's natural brother, ἀδελφός, and his suffragan, normally also ἀδελφός but here συνεπίσκοπος.

the beginning of the imperial visits to Thessalonike, so perhaps 1105-06; illness and death in 1106-07 followed by Theophylact's collapse, his postponed visit to Constantinople, his seasickness and recovery and return to Ochrid in 1108. No proposed solution is ultimately convincing.

Apart from these events and episodes, the letters fall into various sequences. We can sometimes see the development of a relationship over a long period,[66] sometimes the tour of duty of an official or even Theophylact's dealings with the holders of one particular local government post over the whole span of the archiepiscopate.[67] We can follow Michael Pantechnes from his status as Theophylact's pupil through his appointment as doctor to the imperial court, his proximity to Theophylact during the Bohemond war, to the death of his father, perhaps one of the latest events of the correspondence.[68] We can see Gregory Kamateros from an early stage still *logariastes tou genikou*, to his position as *hypogrammateuon* to Alexios, and his proximity to Prespa perhaps as a function of this post. When Theophylact wrote G127 to him he had just been promoted to the post of *protasekretes* and the rank of *nobellissimos*, and had been on campaign with the emperor for some time. We do not see his operation as tax collector for the provinces or his marriage and elevation to logothete of the sekreta and *sebastos*.[69]

Officials came and went in Theophylact's universe, though we shall see that he took good care to nurture his relationship with them. We can see the arrival of Nicholas Anemas, we have a letter to him after he had been in Bulgaria some time and another to him after he had left. We hear of the appointment of Gregory Pakourianos (possibly to the theme of Ochrid), with a letter to him while in Bulgaria, another possibly after his departure and in G79 he is referred to as having left. The appointment of Constantine Doukas to the rule of the Vardar is heralded in two letters which probably place it in the 1100s; we have also Theophylact's adventus letter and a letter written during his tenure. Letters are preserved to all the *doukes* of Dyrrachion before Alexios Komnenos (first attested in 1107): to John Doukas and John Komnenos as we have seen and then to John Bryennios after 1097.[70]

We can follow the course of some cases with which Theophylact was concerned—the case of the *aule* at Mogila in G26 and G17, the case of the

---

[66]   See the case studies in 4.3 below, 204-214.

[67]   See my 'Patronage in Action; the Problems of an Eleventh-century Bishop,' *Church and People in Byzantium*, ed. R. Morris (Birmingham, 1990), 125-147.

[68]   On Michael Pantechnes see below, 182 and 'The Network'.

[69]   On Gregory Kamateros see below, 182-183 and 'The Network'.

[70]   On Nicholas Anemas see below, 183; Gregory Pakourianos, 186; Constantine Doukas, 187. On the *doukes* of Dyrrachion see my 'Patronage.'

priests of Pologos in G12 and G19—and we can observe his modus operandi in the cases of the Kittaba monastery, the *protostrator* and the canons and the church land at Diabolis. I deal with all these below.[71] But one case, that of the village of Ekklesiai and Theophylact's difficulties with fisc and *paroikoi*, stretches through the correspondence and is extraordinarily difficult to reconstruct. With the synod of Prespa and the death of Demetrios it was one of the loose ends that Failler considered Gautier had not tied up before he died.[72] Harvey has recently given an excellent reason why it may never be possible to arrive at a final solution.[73] But it may at least be demonstrated that Theophylact's difficulties at Ekklesiai were not restricted, if indeed certainly connected, to the undoubted crisis which broke between 1097 and 1105. A difficulty which all admit in dealing with the issue is that Theophylact does not always bother to identify the village he is speaking about, and that we cannot always be sure whether he is writing about 'churches' or the place Ekklesiai. But it seems that the village's name is used in G31, G90 and G111.[74] There are references to a Vardar village in G88 and G118.[75] From G111 and G112 (taken with G113, ἡ δὲ ἐνταῦθα ἐπιμονή) it appears that Theophylact spent a considerable amount of time there, particularly during the period of the second Norman war, and Demetrios may have died there.[76] But in G31, which we have seen may date to 1093 or 1094, Theophylact is already talking of his difficulties at Ekklesiai as the tenth wave of his troubles, and his current difficulties, an unwelcome *anametresis*, as succeeding a crisis caused by a eunuch. A follow-up letter, G38, indicates the difficulties of persuading Gregory to act against imperial interests. G90, a letter sent to the *chartophylax* in the depths of winter, expresses Theophylact's fear that he may have to abandon Ekklesiai.[77] This letter (in view of the climate of calumny)[78] may[79] be

---

[71] 4.3, 205-211 and fig. 6.

[72] *Théophylacte*, II, 5.

[73] A. Harvey, 'The Land and Taxation in the Reign of Alexios I Komnenos: the Evidence of Theophylakt of Ochrid,' *REB* 51 (1993), 139-154 on the problems which faced all landowners in the reign of Alexios.

[74] G31, to Gregory Kamateros, II, 233.15-16; G90, to the *chartophylax,* II, 469.10; G111, to Nicholas Kallikles, II, 535.5 and 535.15.

[75] G88, to John *grammatikos* of Palaiologos, II, 461.11; G118, to Constantine Doukas, II, 549.13.

[76] G113, to bishop of Kitros, II, 539.3; G111, to Nicholas Kallikles, II, 535.15-20; G112 to Nicholas Kallikles, II, 537.3.

[77] G31, to Gregory Kamateros, II, 233.11-17; G38, to Gregory Kamateros, 259.21-26; G90, to the *chartophylax*, II, 469.9-11.

[78] Letters G60 (Bishop of Triaditsa), G61, G85, G87, G96, G100 seem particularly afflicted with the problems of calumny, but see above, 17-18.

[79] This is what I argued in 'Patronage' but 1) as the reading in G85 is uncertain, 2) since

related to G85 strengthened by G89, which deal with the confiscation of a village, and to G96 and G98, the most explicit of all his letters on his troubles with the fisc.[80] In another complex of letters Theophylact asks the assistance of George Palaiologos, the *protostrator* Michael and Constantine Doukas to persuade the praktor Iasites not to order an *anagraphe*; in G126 he thanks Palaiologos for his success.[81] In G111 during the illness of Demetrios he tells Nicholas Kallikles of his troubles at Ekklesiai and sends some villagers to seek his assistance; G112 thanks Nicholas for his assistance. We may be sure that the three occasions on which Theophylact appears to use the name expressly denote different stages of his difficulties over the village. But certain dating of this tangled case will almost certainly elude us.

Other ways of looking at the ordering and articulation of the correspondence have been tried by various scholars. Some (fortunately not the same scholars who regard Theophylact as a hypochondriac) have looked to his illnesses for assistance.[82] Is the sciatica of G103 the same as the pain in his side of G48? Is the illness from which he rises for the synod in G108 the same as that which keeps him in bed in G106? Was he visited (G107) by the ex-*basilissa* (Pentegostis to Ekklesiai, let us say) before 1094 or in Constantinople around 1095 or in 1108, or by the *augousta* on campaign near Thessalonike in

---

Harvey is certain that G85, G89, G96 and G98 belong to the same affair, and 3) since G96 and G98 can also be read as being focused on Ochrid, some caution is advisable. I am grateful for advice from Michael Angold and Alan Harvey on this point. Angold, *Church and Society*, 161, unfortunately does not offer an alternative reconstruction, but refers in each case to a single letter, to G111 as (clearly) referring to the Ekklesiai case and to G85 (possibly) to another village near Ochrid.

[80]   G85, to Adrian the Grand Domestic, II.445-451, but at 451.31 note τὸ ἐν Ἀχρίδι τῆς ἐκκλησίας χωρίον; G89, to Adrian, 465-467; G96, to Nikephoros Bryennios, II, 483-493 at 493.140; G98, to Adrian, 499-505 at 503.71.

[81]   G88, to John, *grammatikos* of Palaiologos, and to be shown also to George Palaiologos, II, 461.11-14; the letter to the *protostrator* Michael has not survived. G88, 461.20. G118, to Constantine Doukas, II, 549.13-19. G126, II, 569 may be thanks for services requested in G88, 463.28-29.

[82]   On Theophylact's illnesses see Gautier, II, 542, n. 2 and below, 102-103. On hypochondria in Byzantine literature see H. Hunger, 'Allzumenschliches aus dem Privatleben eines Byzantiners: Tagebuchnotizien des Hypochonders Johannes Chortasmenos,' *Polychronion. Festschrift F. Dölger* (Heidelberg, 1966), 251. He compares him to Aelios Aristides and to Theodore Prodromos who wrote a poem on his illness, ed. C. Gallavotti, 'Novi Laurentiani codicis analecta,' *SBN* 4 (1935), 220-222; for hypochondria in writers of the Second Sophistic see G.W. Bowersock, *Greek Sophists in the Roman Empire* (Oxford, 1969), 71-75 citing the correspondence of Fronto and Marcus Aurelius as a departure in ancient letter-writing. By the time of Theophylact, as we see below, 3.2.ii, 104, what may appear to be hypochondria is expected subject-matter for epistolography.

September 1105 - January 1106 or November 1107 - spring 1108? Does the malaria-like illness of G120 precede or follow the collapse of G121? There may be 'grave dangers in psychoanalysing the dead',[83] but diagnosing their illnesses is not exactly safe either.

We have some view of the movements of Theophylact around his archdiocese, or perhaps within a very restricted part of it. He visits Pelagonia in 1092 or 1093, Diabolis before 1097, Prespa for the *panegyris* of 15 May 1103 (and for one or more synod as well) and promises a visit to the metropolitan of Naupaktos when he is in Kanina. He plans to visit Gregory Kamateros who is with the emperor on campaign and talks of what may be two other visits to army camps in the early years of his episcopate. Between 1096 and 1105 he flees from the fisc to Pelagonia, and during the second Norman war he is to be found on his estate at Ekklesiai. G4 and G120 suggest two visits to Constantinople, one combining a visit to Nicomedia (?1095), the other in 1108.[84]

We see above all the rhythm of the year and realise the seasonality of letter-exchange as much as of military activity. 'That we send our brother to you in winter is a measure of the great urgency of our need.' 'Seeing him at such a time undertaking such a long voyage you will assume the greatness of the pressure which has made him set out from here.'[85] Lent is a great time for letter-exchange and for gifts of fish.[86] Spring and summer see visits to army camps, *panegyreis* and synods but also busy letter-activity.[87] Spring comes after the winter of calumny; 'my soul has come through the winter torrents.'[88]

About Theophylact's letter-collection it may first of all be said that it is a collection, not a correspondence. We have indications of a few letters received by Theophylact and of his reactions to them, and of some gifts he received.[89] We can also see the political effect of some of his letters. But whoever collected

---

[83] R.H. Bainton, 'Interpretations of the Reformation,' *AmHR*, 66 (1960), 81.

[84] See above, 2.5, 55, n. 234 and Table X.

[85] G90, to the *chartophylax*, II, 469.2-3; G93, to Nicholas Kallikles, II, 477.8. The exception marks the rule here.

[86] E.g. G13, II, 171.17 notes the season: ἐπεὶ δὲ νηστείας καιρὸς καὶ ἰχθυοφαγίας. G10, G11, G12, G13, G15 were also written before Easter.

[87] G110, G111, G112, G113, G118 belong to spring. Army camps: G77, to the bishop of Kerkyra, II, 411.68-82; G30, to the *chartophylax* Nikephoros, II, 229.4; poems 11 and 12, I, 367. *Panegyris*: G78, to Gregory Taronites, II, 415.17-18. For the synod, see above, 89-91. For zephyrs and the *kausteros* (unidentified enemy), G76, to Mermentoulos, II, 403.22. On seasonality, M. Bartusis, 'The Rhythm of the Chancery: Seasonality in the Issuance of Byzantine Imperial Documents,' *BMGS* 13 (1989), 1-21: March to June is the busiest time.

[88] G61, to ?John Komnenos, II, 351.22; G63, to ?the bishop of Pelagonia, II, 359.34, quoting from Ps.123:4-5.

[89] See Tables VII and IX below.

them was concerned with his words, not, as we shall be later, with the interactions of his network. We probably should think also of a core of the letters relating to the archiepiscopate c.1088-1108, 133 in all. Three of these letters belong to his very early days in Ochrid; the Bohemond war and the death of John Pantechnes mark the end of this sequence. They may be very broadly in chronological order but a considerable number of letters can be shown to be out of order, and there seem to be bands of disturbance around the overlap of the constituent parts (B and A) of the collection and at the very end. In addition G133 should be inserted towards the end of the sequence, somewhere before the death of Demetrios. G134, to Demetrios on the liturgy, belongs to a rather different genre, of canonical response, but it certainly should be dated to the period of the core of the collection. Gautier's first three letters, rather longer than most of the letters from Bulgaria, find their place in the 1080s and should be preceded by the consolatio on the death of Michael Psellos. G135, the fragment to Tibanios the Armenian, occurring in cod. Reginae Suecorum 57 and identified there as from a letter, most probably dates to later in the archiepiscopate.

Above all we may be clear that Theophylact may have been an antiquarian and a hagiographer but he was not a diarist or an annalist. He saw time as a succession of πονηραὶ ἡμέραι, of waves of misfortune, of a sea of troubles, ἔξωθεν μάχαι, ἔσωθεν φόβοι,[90] concerns and worries which could always be lightened for him by human interaction and the concerns of the mind.

3.2 Preoccupations and concerns of the letters

In contradistinction to the grand affairs of state and major events of Theophylact's life anxiously sought but rarely found above, this section deals with the typical content of the letters, the topical, the timeless and the everyday.

i. *Logoi and technai*
It is a commonplace of descriptions of the Byzantine letter that it moves in a timeless, looking-glass land with a classical landscape.[91] Theophylact's

---

[90] For πονηραὶ ἡμέραι, Ps.93(94).13, see G35, G54, G56, G65. For ἔξωθεν μάχαι, 2Cor.7:5, see G57, II, 323.3; G75, II, 399.8-9.

[91] See my 'The Classical Tradition in the Byzantine Letter,' *Byzantium and the Classical Tradition*, ed. M. Mullett and R. Scott (Birmingham, 1981), 75-93, and the classic statement

landscape is not however conventional or idyllic, and can be somewhat more threatening, as we shall see,[92] but his commitment to the timeless episteme of *logoi*[93] is tempered only by the pressures of the everyday. Gout can hamper Theodore Smyrnaios's speech; it is the harpies, the tax-officials, who have snatched away Theophylact's books.[94] He frequently recalls his previous career as rhetor, and constantly draws on the old relationships of teacher and pupil.[95] He appears to have discussed books with his friend Nicholas bishop of Kerkyra; 1125-26 may have seen them reading Symeon the New Theologian. His answer to the faintheartedness of Anemas is to cheer him by sending a Chrysostom; when ill himself and worried about his brother he asks Nicholas Kallikles to lend him a small medical library; a Galen and a set of commentaries on Hippocrates, a treatise on the doctrines of Hippocrates and Plato.[96]

He presents himself as Plato, not just as Plato to Pakourianos's Dionysios, but also as Plato to Theophylact Romaios's Aristotle; Romaios has let this characterisation down by being too Pythagorean and failing to write; Theophrastos and the Demetrios of the *Peri Hermeneias,* he argues, are true pupils of Aristotle. A philosopher for Theophylact keeps his head in the air and his feet on the ground, a wise precaution, perhaps, after the Italos trial. Platonic vocabulary is not as frequent as one might expect from someone in close contact with Psellos; but it is philosophy, believes Theophylact, which distinguishes humans from animals.[97]

---

of this stereotype, H. Hunger, 'On the Imitation (MIMHCIC) of Antiquity in Byzantine Literature,' *DOP* 23-24 (1969-70), 28-29.

[92] See above, 2.5, 54-57 for the landscape; for how he peopled it, below, 3.2.iv, 124-125.

[93] This word in Theophylact's letters conveys our concepts both of learning and literature, G6, I, 149.36; G42, II, 273.29; G76, II, 403.11, 16.

[94] G28, to Theodore Smyrnaios, II, 223.2-3; G29, to Mermentoulos, II, 225.11-12.

[95] Previous career: G71, to Opheomachos, II, 383.10-12; G8, to John Doukas, II, 153.5-6; G9, to the Caesar Melissenos, II, 157.12-13; G81, to Gregory Taronites, II, 427.5-6. Drawing on old teaching relationships: see G84, to Niketas the nephew of Leo of Chalcedon; 441.2-9; G104, to John Attaleiates, *protonotarios* of the *doux* of Attaleia, II, 519.2-11.

[96] For Symeon the New Theologian see the pair of poems in Paris. suppl. gr. 103, fol. 16, ed. Gautier, I, 352-5; for Anemas and Chrysostom (Dio or John?), G34, II, 243.21; for the medical books, G112, to Nicholas Kallikles, II, 537.6-16, and for the return, poem 3, I, 350-351. On Dio in Theophylact's other work see K. Praechter, 'Antike Quellen des Theophylaktos von Bulgarien,' *BZ* 1 (1892), 399-414.

[97] For Plato and Dionysios, G55, to Pakourianos, II, 317-319.2-20; for Plato and Aristotle/Pythagoras, G42, II, 271; for the uses of philosophy, G46, to Theophylact Rhomaios, II, 289.16-17 (but quoting the *Iliad*). There is certainly no sense of any political unwisdom in discussing philosophy at this time.

In G127 he explores other arts in a parodic tour de force to Gregory Kamateros, or rather the arts as practised by one Theodore Chryselios, the renaissance man of late eleventh-century Macedonia. He is a local official who combines the art of war with that of geometry, arts separated, Theophylact points out, since Archytas; governing the Vardar has taught him arithmetic, which he practised half the night; measuring land has taught him how to make mistakes in geometry. Theophylact envisages him turning to harmonics, the sister of arithmetic, to play a formidable brass instrument. Then to astrology, not just because it is akin to geometry but also because of its affinity (in respect of spheres) to polo. And so to chariot-driving on the plains of Thessaly, and the only art of present use to Theophylact, choral singing. In G66 the offer of an accomplished singer, Gregory the *psaltes*, has to be declined since to accept him would be in breach of the canons. But Theophylact's view of the importance of music—and of candlelight—in a church is clear from G22 and G53.[98]

But his own *techne* was writing, and we shall see him at work. One aspect of his literary art bears also on his reading: the works Theophylact quotes from. The Psalms are clearly most favoured with 234 quotations, closely followed by Isaiah (37), Matthew (40), the *Iliad* (41) Luke (35), 1 Corinthians (24), 2 Corinthians (22), *Odyssey* (21), Proverbs (15), Jeremiah (14), Euripides (12). He cites six plays of Euripides, four of Aristophanes and three of Sophocles. There are only three references to Plato and two to Aristotle but five to Empedocles. Herodotos and Lucian join Hesiod and Pindar, Oppian and Lykophron. He repeats a few favourite quotations, but casts his net fairly wide. But this is not the full range of his own reading, even as we know it in the collection from references in passing. It is arguable that Theophylact uses quotation and imitation from a deliberately restricted range of texts, the school syllabus, for a social purpose, to attach himself more closely to the common past of his correspondents.[99]

---

[98] G127, to Gregory Kamateros, II, 573.42-579.113; G66, to the *chartophylax*, II, 365-367; G22, the deserted *katholikon*, to John Komnenos, II, 203.9-21; G53 to bishop Gregory Kamateros on the effects of an absentee bishop, II, 307.16; G15 to Diabologyres on how to provide for converted heretical congregations, II, 179-181.

[99] On quotations in Byzantine letters see A.R. Littlewood, 'A Statistical Survey of the Incidence of Repeated Quotations in Selected Byzantine Letter-writers,' *Gonimos, Neoplatonic and Byzantine Studies presented to L.G. Westerink at 75* (Buffalo, NY, 1988), 137-154. The application of Littlewood's techniques to Theophylact supports his overall conclusions and suggests that Theophylact's quotation practice is not out of line with the twenty-three collections he examined. Littlewood's top ten authors were also Theophylact's with the substitution for Empedocles for Plutarch. His reluctance to repeat quotations is, at 91.8%, slightly above average.

Certainly a range of literacy practices, even within Bulgaria, is taken for granted in the correspondence. Theophylact refers back to previous letters;[100] we can add at least sixteen and probably twenty-one letters mentioned in it to the collection as we have it.[101] He talks of writing iambics as a revenge against an enemy who had inspired only laments previously; he offers to copy out and bring or send the *akolouthia* for converted Armenians;[102] fifteen letters mention documents of one kind or another.[103] We can begin to imagine the archiepiscopal cadaster, but he is by no means the only person brandishing documents; G60 shows a Bulgar monk who has obtained βασιλικὰ ἔγγραφα to support him against his bishop.[104]

On two occasions in the letters Theophylact advises correspondents on reading, in one case what to read and in another how to read. G29 is addressed not to an old pupil, but to a friend, a powerful lawyer in Constantinople, Nicholas Mermentoulos. The Academy should lead to the Stoa; the *Iliad* to tragedy and comedy. He is to read pastoral but to take care with its erotic content. Then the Pentateuch and the prophets, next the New Testament. And then he is to frequent the Gregories and the Basils and their blessed circle. Lastly he is to pray that Theophylact should not through his responsibilities in Ochrid forget what Greek sounds like.[105]

How one should read is also of concern to Theophylact. G36, to his friend the bishop of Pelagonia, is a call to read the bible, to allow the Lord to accompany his friend on the road of life, talking to him through the prophets, the apostles, the evangelists and ancient history (ἐν ἱστορίαις ἀρχαίαις). He anticipates a complaint from the friend, that Scripture is obscure; not, says Theophylact, if you receive it well. Christ's disciples were taught by puzzling

---

[100] G7 refers to G5 but probably not to G6; G60 refers to G58; G89 refers to G85; G127 may refer to G115 or G116, but see Table II; G87 refers to letters written to the bishops of Pelagonia, Strumitsa and Malesova. For a full list see Table III.

[101] See below, Table II.

[102] For the iambic revenge, G76, to Mermentoulos, II, 405.24; cf. the invective of poem 8, to a hardened evil-doer, I, 358-361; poem 9, to someone who criticised other ordained persons, I, 360-365; poem 13 to a licentious eunuch, I, 366-369. For the *akolouthia*, G15, to Diabologyres, II, 181.28.

[103] Documents are mentioned as follows: G9 *prostagma*, G12 *pittakion* and *sigillion*; G17 *sigillion*; G18, *pittakion, chrysoboullon*; G19, *pittakion, chrysoboullon*; G22, imperial *sigillion*; G26, *praktikon* and *prostaxis*; G38, *praxis* and *hypomnesis*; G49, *pittakion*; G60, *basilika engrapha; semeioma;* G66, *engraphon*; G79, *prostagma*; G85, *chrysoboullion, semeioma, engraphon*; G96, *prostaxis*; G98, *prostaxis*. See Table VI for documents requested.

[104] G60, to the bishop of Triaditsa, II, 345.37.

[105] G29, to Mermentoulos, II, 225.13-33. Gautier in *Théophylacte*, I, 27 listed Mermentoulos with other pupils of Theophylact, but there is no evidence to support the proposal.

parables; only the crowds of people who failed to make an effort and to ask for explanation were left in the dark. Only open your eyes, says Theophylact, and you will see the light. And that light is a light for one's own times, as he makes clear in G56. Theophylact is no intentionalist.[106]

Books then, and learning, and the art of speech, are all important to Theophylact; they may bring one to the truth; they may also console one in the *ponerai hemerai* and draw one closer, on Jacob's ladder or by the golden chain to the community of the wise and the good and to their creator.

ii. *Sickness and medicine*

If timelessness is the keynote of Theophylact's thinking about books, the preponderance of materia medica in Theophylact's letters[107] looks very topical in a text of the end of the eleventh century.[108] What has not yet been defined is the precise relation between the epistolarity of references to sickness and the fashionable interest in medicine.

At first sight however, Theophylact's explicit use of sickness and medicine in his discourse appears out of keeping with the restrained elegance of the letter form:

> You ask how things are with me; not altogether well, and that is an understatement. Fever smoulders within me and already I am in advanced ill-health. Dry and spittle-less coughs trouble me. I have a long-standing pain in my side.[109]

> Many things impel me to come to the tents, which you, the new Israel, have pitched as you wander in our desert. But two streams prevent me coming. The first is common and epidemic and stuffs up my head, producing catarrhs and coughs and makes me (not without reason) afraid of chest complaints. For what would not happen to me if I exposed myself to the elements when I am in such a state while lurking in my hole? The second stream is that of

---

[106] G36, to the bishop of Pelagonia, II, 249-251; cf. G56, to the bishop of Semnea, 321.8-12.

[107] This was noticed from the early years of the twentieth century, see J. Kohler, *Der medizinische Inhalt der Briefe des Theophylaktos von Bulgarien* (Diss., Leipzig, 1918). See also now A. Leroy-Molinghen, 'Médecins, malades et remèdes dans les lettres de Théophylacte de Bulgarie,' *Byz* 55 (1985), 483-492.

[108] A.P. Kazhdan, 'The Image of the Medical Doctor in Byzantine Literature of the Tenth to the Twelfth Centuries,' *DOP* 38 (1984), 44-51; A. Kazhdan and A. Epstein, *Change in Byzantine Culture in the Eleventh and Twelfth Centuries* (The Transformation of the Classical Heritage, 7, Berkeley and Los Angeles, 1985), 155-156.

[109] G48, to Michael Pantechnes, II, 295.2-5.

the neighbouring river, which the ancient Greek language called Axios but the new barbaric language calls Vardar.[110]

As for me, most brilliant master, when I boarded the boat (it was the day when I was expecting the periodic return of my illness) there happened to me something unexpected: nausea and then a flow of saliva and vomiting resulted in the outflow of undigested and separating material and at the end, some quantity of bile. After a short interval of time, the same thing happened again, except with more bile, which on ejection tasted more bitter. I was waiting for the symptom of quartan fever to manifest itself as usual, but without doubt that had been vomited at the same time as the liquid and the bile, and I was convinced that my fear had been vain. The day of the periodic return of the illness came round and I, who am very cowardly, was in despair, but God was the same and did not change. The evil disappeared and no-one knows where it has hidden. And here I am safe and sound at Thessalonike, I who was seriously ill, delivered from all ills. As the proverb says: bile has its uses.[111]

Other letters refer to illness in passing; his correspondents were kept au fait with his condition. As he said to Mermentoulos, 'you know our weaknesses.'[112] It is all too easy to portray Theophylact as a hypochondriac.[113] But parallels may be found for his descriptions of illness. The first passage could be compared with Gregory of Nazianzos, ep. 80, where he begins: 'you ask what my situation is like; it is extremely miserable.' He goes on to list his troubles, not all physical, but in exactly the same tone as Theophylact's gloomy recitation.[114] For the long-winded listing of complaints, one may compare St Basil:

In the first place I have been detained by certain worldly business; then I have been wasted by constant and violent attacks of fever so that there does seem to be something thinner than I was: a thinner version of myself. And besides all this, bouts of quartan ague have gone on for more than twenty turns. now I do seem to be free from fever, but I am in such a feeble state that I am no stronger than a cobweb.[115]

---

[110] G110, to Niketas, the doctor of the emperor, II, 531.4-7.

[111] G120, to the *magistros* kyr John Pantechnes, II, 14-28.

[112] G76, to Mermentoulos, II, 403.21.

[113] See above, 3.1, 96, n.82.

[114] Gregory of Nazianzos, ep. 80, ed. P. Gallay, *Saint Grégoire de Nazianze, Lettres* (Paris, 1967), I, 103.

[115] Basil, ep. 193, ed. R.J. Deferrari, *Saint Basil, the Letters* (London and Cambridge, Mass., 1930), III, 84.

For the gruesome concentration on purely medical aspects of suffering, George Tornikes's discussion of the last illness of Theodotos II in 1154 might be compared with Theophylact's seasickness:

> In fact the right hand of the dead patriarch had gone black during his illness, whether by accident caused by the fact that blood fled from the extremities first, or else, as I think, because of constriction by a string.[116]

Sickness, like separation and (as we shall see) friendship, appears to be built into the Byzantine letter. Complaint is one of the commoner ways for disease to be introduced. Complaints at the beginning of letters, complaints in passing, complaints at the end of letters: Theodore of Nicaea ends with a description of the calming effect of a friend's letter 'on me, who cannot bear the harshness of the stifling heat and the mosquitoes and am wasting away with stomach pains and lack of sleep.'[117]

Replies to letters like this also exist. They normally exhort the writer to have patience and rely on God. Symeon Magistros trusts that relief provided by divine providence will ensure that the pain arising from his correspondent's illness will not increase. When the writer has heard of the correspondent's illness from someone else, his reply is not always so restrained. Nikephoros Ouranos says, 'I was prostrated with shivering as a report announcing your illness completely maimed my soul and my tongue.' The polite enquiry is also common. Gregory of Nazianzos begins a letter to Philagrios: 'How are you getting on with your health? You give me no means of knowing. As for your spirit, I shall not ask for news, for I know it is in excellent state.' 'Get well' wishes are not uncommon, occasionally with unusual twists. 'Get better,' writes Alexander of Nicaea to Gregory of Ankyra, 'for if you do not I shall die.'[118]

Sickness often acts as an excuse for lazy letter-writers or visitors: Basil says, 'Why do you not visit me, dear friend, that we may discuss such matters in each other's company? For by reason of my infirmities, I am like a plant held always to the same place.' The effects of illness on literary output is

---

[116] George Tornikes, ep. 7, ed. J. Darrouzès, *Georges et Démétrios Tornikès, Lettres et discours* (Paris, 1970), 209. On the identification of the patriarch see R. Browning, 'An Unidentified Funeral Oration on Anna Comnena,' *PCPS* n.s. 8 (1962), 2-3; Darrouzès, 204, n.1; 208, n.7.

[117] Theodore of Nicaea, ep. 37, ed. J. Darrouzès, *Épistoliers byzantins du Xe siècle* (AOC, 6, Paris, 1960), 303.

[118] Symeon Magistros, ep. 37, ed. Darrouzès, *Épistoliers byzantins*, 125; Nikephoros Ouranos, ep. 36, ed. Darrouzès, ibid., 236; Gregory of Nazianzos, ep. 92, ed. Gallay, II, 112; Alexander of Nicaea, ep. 8, ed. Darrouzès, ibid., 82-83.

noticed: Hierotheos complains that 'bodily sickness enfeebles the spirit; an inflammation stops the tongue.'[119] Sickness can cause pleas for help, for prayers or for doctors.

Diagnosis is rare in letters, but to set beside Theophylact's letter to the bishop of Kitros about Demetrios there is Hierotheos's letter to the *grammatikos* John.

> You cause yourself the fire which burns and the fever which reduces you to nothing. You are a victim of gormandising and voracity, of guzzling meat, fish, vegetables, cheese, milk and fruits—all against the advice of doctors and of your holy wife. Pull yourself together.[120]

Finally, there are many passages which link the theme of sickness with the other great themes of Byzantine letters, friendship and separation. Symeon Magistros considered that sickness and separation were trials wished by providence. They were seen as related problems by Gregory of Nazianzos and Hierotheos. Friendship is proved by the ability to empathise with one's friends' illnesses, thus Gregory to Eudokios: 'Sickness is cured by friendship. What better remedy than a friend's conversation?'[121]

So at the time when Theophylact wrote, there was a long-standing association of sickness with letters. A statement of one's physical condition was expected by the recipient of the letter. Michael Psellos wrote, 'How are you? Are you well in body and soul? I do not ask about your virtues, for I can see them perfectly clearly, but about your happiness or depression. I hope body and soul are well.' Julian replied to such a request, 'In all respects my bodily health is fairly good, and indeed my state of mind is no less satisfactory. I fancy there can be no better prelude than this to a letter from one friend to another.' The reason for this expectation should be sought in the idea of the letter as an icon of the soul, and the reality of letters as a means of creating and maintaining personal relations. It was important for correspondents to give and exchange all information possible to build up this spiritual portrait of the other. And it need not be so surprising that the physical condition was to be drawn as well as the spiritual state; after all, in

---

[119] Basil, ep. 9, ed. Deferrari, I, 98; Hierotheos, ep. 71, see Darrouzès, 'Un recueil épistolaire du XIIe siècle: Académie Roumaine cod. gr. 508,' *REB* 30 (1972), 215; ep. 82, see Darrouzès, 216; Theodore of Nicaea, ep. 19, ed. Darrouzès, *Épistoliers byzantins*, 287.

[120] G113, to the bishop of Kitros, II, 539.9-16, cf. Hierotheos, ep. 48, see Darrouzès, 212.

[121] Symeon Magistros, ep. 36, ed. Darrouzès, 124; Gregory of Nazianzos, ep. 64, ed. Gallay, I, 83; Hierotheos, ep. 66, see Darrouzès, 214; Gregory, ep. 216, ed. Gallay, II, 106 and ep. 87, ed. Gallay, 108.

descriptions of saints, physical health was a vital ingredient in establishing an icon type.[122]

The association of letter and sickness is seen at another level; disease permeates the language of the Byzantine letter. The evils of Theophylact's archdiocese are a *nosos* and anything which helps him is a *pharmakon* or *therapeia*. The sinning hieromonk of G11 is a plague and a pest which must be driven out. The bishop of Triaditsa is like a sick man who is reproved by his doctor for drinking wine with a fever and then refuses to drink water. Healing words, ἰατρός, ἐκθεραπεύω, ἰῶμαι, φάρμακον, are applied to God, the emperor, the archbishop, and his friends.[123] The sustained nature of the imagery is striking, but it is not new. Particularly in early Christian writing, medical images were common. Anthony was a physician to all Egypt, Christus medicus is a commonplace of patristic literature. Bishops heal maladies of the church.[124]

For Theophylact the best healer was a friend who wrote a letter. To deprive him of letters was to deprive a sick man of medicine. 'It was very pleasant to receive your letter...In my present depression you poured me a medicine, banishing care.' Letters are 'the medicine that releases from toil', the medicine which brings oblivion. John Peribleptenos is told to write more frequently and cool Theophylact's overheated body and to offer means of medicine and general help to the afflicted. The theorists had said it before, 'to

---

[122] Michael Psellos, ep. 45, ed. E. Kurtz and F. Drexl, *Scripta minora*, II (Milan, 1941), 76; Julian, ep. 72, ed. W.C. Wright, *The Works of the Emperor Julian*, III (London, 1923), 234. See Doula Mouriki's investigation of an icon-type in 'The Portraits of Theodore Stoudites in Byzantine Art,' *JÖB* 20 (1971), 249-280.

[123] The pest: G11, II, 165.36: ὡς λοιμὸς καὶ νόσημα ἐπιδήμιον. The bishop of Triaditsa: G60, II, 347.76-78; another type of bad patient is recalled in G86, II, 461.5-7, suggesting a consciousness of preventative medicine; the evils of the diocese as a νόσημα, G97, to John Peribleptenos, II, 495.23-26; cf. *Al.*, I.x.1, L, I, 36.21-37.5 (Roussel, Basilakios, Robert Guiscard as mortal plagues in the body politic); Theophylact feels the pains of his archdiocese as the head feels pain in the limbs, G45, to the patriarch, II, 285.69. Help as θεραπεία, ἰατρεία: Melissenos in G13, II, 171.9 is the λυσίπονον φάρμακον; John Komnenos in G12, II, 167.18 can provide the μάλαγμα for the πληγή; the emperor is a better doctor than the archbishop, G58, to the bishop of Triaditsa, II, 327.14-18; God is the only λύτης καὶ ἰατρός of all ills, G57, to the bishop of Vidin, II, 325.35.

[124] E.g. Basil, ep. 82, ed. Deferrari, II, 9, cf. Michael Psellos, ep. 96, ed. Kurtz-Drexl, 194; R. Arbesmann, 'The Concept of Christus Medicus in St Augustine,' *Traditio* 10, 1-28; H.J. Frings, *Medizin und Artzt bei den griechischen Kirchenvätern bis Chrysostomos* (Bonn, 1959); R. Murray, *Symbols of Church and Kingdom* (Cambridge, 1975), 199-203.

heal desire with letters', and the idea was picked up by Gregory of Nazianzos, Procopius of Gaza and Theodore of Kyzikos.[125]

So in both subject-matter and imagery Theophylact is following long-established literary convention although in his vivid powers of description and in his inspired conviction of the relevance of medicine to his own situation he passes beyond it. But Theophylact's interest in medicine went deeper than this: he had medical friends and he read medical books.

So far we have seen medicine used indiscriminately to his correspondents. But among these were three doctors, and it is usually clear when he is writing to one of them. To Nicholas Kallikles he writes:

> But you unsparingly pour into the chalices the drastic antidotes for the diseases which attack me, the god-given medicine and your panacea; also that important drug made from the bodies of vipers. I expect this pouring out to happen in Thessalonike and in Ekklesiai a draining. In both places there is weakness and paralysis. So will it be in vain that I call upon my Asklepios in this very great trouble?

To Michael Pantechnes:

> From somewhere else another arrow pierces my heart, and nowhere is there a Paieon, nowhere a second Machaion or Podaleiros to pull out the arrow, suck the blood and offer sweet ointments.[126]

Theophylact delights to flatter his correspondents by using allusions suitable to their craft. Both these doctors are well known figures of Alexios's reign, thanks to their attendance at the death-bed of the emperor.[127] Niketas the imperial doctor to whom Theophylact addressed G110 is known from no

---

[125] G33, to Mermentoulos, II, 241.8-9; G75, to the bishop of Kerkyra, II, 399.5-6; G13, to Caesar Melissenos, II, 171.9-10; G97, to John Peribleptenos, II, 497.30-31. For a model, 61γ, Libanios, *Epistolimaioi charakteres*, ed. V. Weichert, *Demetrii et Libanii qui feruntur typoi epistolikoi et epistolimaioi charakteres* (Leipzig, 1910), 38: τοῖς γοῦν γράμμασι θεραπεύειν τὸν πόθον επειγόμεθα. See for example Gregory of Nazianzos, ep. 70, ed. Gallay, I, 90; Procopius of Gaza, ep. 31, ed. R. Hercher, *Epistolographi graeci* (Paris, 1873), 543; Theodore of Kyzikos, ep. 55, ed. S. Lampros, *NE* 20 (1924), 151.

[126] G111, to Nicholas Kallikles, II, 535.2-8; G48, to Michael Pantechnes, II, 295.11-14.

[127] *Al.*, XV.xi.2, L, III, 230.24 for Nicholas; XV.xi.3, L, III, 231.2-4 for both. Nicholas is mentioned in Theodore Prodromos's *Iatros e demios?* and in Ptochoprodromos, II, 415, ed. L. Hesseling and H. Pernot, *Poèmes prodromiques en grec vulgaire* (Amsterdam, 1910); ed. H. Eideneier (Neograeca medii aevii, 5, Cologne, 1991), 171. Kazhdan, 'Doctor,' 44 on Pantechnes; P. Gautier, *Michel Italikos, lettres et discours* (AOC, 14, Paris, 1972), 46-49 on Michael Pantechnes, 50-52 on Lizix.

other source, but I see no reason to deny his existence.[128] In addition, letter G97 to John Peribleptenos, who is also otherwise unknown, has an extended medical image found elsewhere only in the letters to doctors:

> You know that now more than ever we need conversation, no less than someone who is ill needs an Asklepios or a Paieon. Don't talk to me of the remedies which I have, or say that because I have these boxes about me I can without difficulty combat the illness, whether with a mixture, an ointment or a plaster. No, for we see that even the doctors of the body are powerless against their own illnesses...[129]

He may have been, like Theophylact, an interested non-practitioner. Theophylact's involvement may be seen from his request to Nicholas Kallikles for the loan of some medical textbooks, where he claims a theoretical interest only, and from his letter to the bishop of Kitros about the illness of his brother, where he describes his condition and discusses his treatment. He may have been no more knowledgeable than this. But his close acquaintance with doctors and general concern with medicine are of particular significance at the time he was writing.[130]

In the twelfth century medicine appeared to be at the centre of intellectual life. Most letter-writers were in touch with doctors, and it is very clear that like Theophylact, but unlike Anselm and Peter the Venerable,[131] they were not consulting doctors by letter, they were writing to doctors as to other correspondents. Indeed Michael Italikos held the prestigious position of *didaskalos ton iatron* before becoming archbishop of Philippopolis, and many of the twelfth-century letter-writers had medical correspondents.[132] Darrouzès

---

[128] As Gautier does, *Théophylacte*, II, 70. Caution surely suggests there may have been more imperial doctors than are known to us.

[129] G97, to John Peribleptenos, II, 495.21-29. But note also 495.19: οἱ τοῖς Λατίνων λόγοις ἐνσεμνυνόμενοι, which may mean he was a monk with a legal training; Gautier agrees he may belong to the monastery of the Peribleptos, see R. Janin, 'Le monastère de la Théotocos Péribleptos à Constantinople,' *AcadRoumBullSectHist* 26 (1945), 192-201; *La géographie ecclésiastique de l'empire byzantin*, I, *Le siège de Constantinople et patriarchat occuménique*; II, *Les églises et les monastères*, 2nd edn (Paris, 1969), 227-231.

[130] G112, to Nicholas Kallikles, G, II, 537.5-8; G113, to the bishop of Kitros, II, 539.9-16.

[131] E.g. Peter the Venerable, epp. 158 a, b, ed. G. Constable, *The Letters of Peter the Venerable* (Cambridge, Mass., 1967), I, 379-383; Anselm, epp. 36, 44, ed. F.S. Schmitt, *Anselmi opera omnia*, III (Edinburgh, 1946), 143-144, 156-157.

[132] See Gautier, *Michel Italikos*; Michael Choniates wrote to two doctors, Tzetzes to two, and to two members of the Pantokrator staff; Michael Italikos to a doctor called Leipsiotes and to the *aktouarios*; he and Theodore Prodromos, who wrote poems about

suggested that the interest of George Tornikes in medicine might be attributed to his family relationship with Theophylact,[133] but this explanation is not necessary. The prestige of doctors and of medicine had risen at the end of the eleventh century; intellectuals had taken the discipline to their hearts, and charitable foundations included hospitals.[134] Doctors rose to the rank of *proedros*.[135] Kazhdan has sensibly connected this with the decline of the traditional holy man,[136] but this is only part of the story. Suspicion of medicine remained, but doctors were very visible, not least in satire, an indicator of the fashionable status of the subject. Satire does not however

---

doctors, both wrote to Lizix, who is a candidate for identification with the third doctor, Michael the eunuch, at the deathbed of Alexios.

[133] Darrouzès, *Tornikai*, 26.

[134] On hospital-building, T.S. Miller, *The Birth of the Hospital in the Byzantine Empire* (Baltimore, 1985); 'The Byzantine Hospital,' *DOP* 38 (1984), 53-63; see A. Philipsborn, 'Der Fortschritt in der Entwicklung des byzantinischen Krankenhauswesens,' *BZ* 54 (1961), 338-365; for *xenones* in the Mangana quarter see John Skylitzes, *Synopsis Historion*, ed. J. Thurn, *Synopsis historiarum, editio princeps* (CFHB, 5, Berlin and New York, 1973), 477; for the hospital church of St George, Janin, *Églises et monastères*, 78; for Pantokrator, *Typikon tes basilikes mones tou Pantokratoros*, 904-1389, ed. Gautier, 'Le typikon du Christ Sauveur Pantokrator,' *REB* 32 (1974), 83-111; P. Codellas, 'The Pantocrator: Imperial Medical Center of the XIIth Century in Constantinople,' *Bulletin of the History of Medicine* 12 (1942), 392-410; *Typikon emou tou sebastokratoros Isaakiou kai uiou basileos kyrou Alexiou tou Komnenou epi to kainisthenti par hemon neosystato monasterio kata ten pentekaidekaten indiktiona tou hexakistichiliostou exakostiostou exekostou etous, en o kai kathidrutai to tes kosmosoteiras mou kai theometoros kai en pollois euergetidos dia mouseiou eikonisma*, ch. 70, ed. L. Petit, 'Typikon du monastère de la Kosmosoteira près du Aenos (1152),' *IRAIK* 13 (1908) 17-77 at 53.26-56.8. For other social services see e.g. *To typikon to ekethen para tou megalou domestikou tes duseos kyrou Gregoriou tou Pakourianou pros ten par'autou ktistheisan monen tes hyperagias Theotokou tes Petritziotisses*, ch. 28: old people's homes, 29: hospices, lines 1510-1589, ed. P. Gautier, 'Le typikon du sébaste Grégoire Pakourianos,' *REB* 42 (1984), 5-145 at 110-115; for the *Orphanotropheion, Al.*, XV.vii.4, L, III, 215; Zonaras, 24, ed. Büttner-Wobst, III, 744-745.

[135] On the title of *proedros* see R. Guilland, *Recherches sur les institutions byzantines*, 2 vols (Berlin and Amsterdam, 1967), I, 34, 38, 200, 303, 307, 346; Oikonomides, *Listes de préséance*, 299.

[136] Kazhdan, 'Doctor,' but see P.R.L. Brown, 'The Rise and Function of the Holy Man in Late Antiquity,' *JRS* 61 (1971), 98: 'in his relation to contemporary medical science, the holy man appears far more often than one might at first sight suppose in a merely supporting role.' See P. Hordern, 'Saints and Doctors in the Early Byzantine Empire: the Case of Theodore of Sykeon,' *The Church and Healing*, ed. W.J. Shields (Studies in Church History, 19, Oxford, 1982), 1-13; S. Ashbrook Harvey, 'Physicians and Ascetics in John of Ephesus: an Expedient Alliance,' *DOP* 38 (1984), 87-93.

necessarily mean disapproval[137] and Theophylact shows a positive attitude when he notes that

> For those who are sick in body it is the woman's part to beat the breast, strike oneself and tear the face, but it is the doctor's part to calm everything and to think out a solution for the sick man.

This is a long way from the hysterical cries of the patients of St Artemios; 'Where now are the braggarts, Hippokrates and Galen and the tens of thousands who call themselves physicians?'[138]

Yet a fashionable interest seems to have preceded institutional grounding. Anna Komnene shows a considerable informed interest in medicine but when she lists her educational accomplishments in her preface medicine is not among them. Nor is it listed by Psellos in his account of his studies in the *Chronographia*, although his account of the last illness of Isaac Komnenos claims otherwise:

> After greeting me he remarked with a cheerful look, 'You come at an opportune moment' and promptly gave me his hand to feel his pulse, for he knew that beside my other activities I had also practised medicine. I recognised the illness from which he was suffering, but made no immediate comment.[139]

Proximos, aktouarios and *didaskalos ton iatron*, the main teaching posts in medicine, appear to be early twelfth-century creations.[140] But the interest in

---

[137] If parody may indicate some involvement with the values of the genre, H. Dubrow, *Genre* (The Critical Idiom, 42, London and New York, 1982), 24, the same may be said for satire and society. For twelfth-century satire see *Timarion*, ed. R. Romano, *Timarione, Testo critico, introduzione, traduzione, commentario e lessico* (ByzetNeohellNap, 2, Naples, 1974), 72 and Theodore Prodromos, e.g. *Iatros e demios?* ed. G. Podestà, 'Satire lucianesche di Teodoro Prodromo,' *Aevum* 21 (1947), 12-21. Barry Baldwin, *Timarion, translated with Introduction and Commentary* (BTT, Detroit, 1984) seeks (unnecessarily?) for a doctor author, adding Michael Italikos to the previous candidates Nicholas Kallikles and Theodore Prodromos. Theophylact, G78, II, 417.28 has Roman doctors cutting and burning as an image for the fisc, but so does Basil, ep. 299, ed. Deferrari, IV, 216; Kekaumenos, 125, ed. B. Wassilewsky and V. Jernstedt, *Cecaumeni strategicon et incerti scriptoris de officiis regiis libellus* (St Petersburg, 1896), 53 is characteristically uncharacteristic.

[138] G53, to Gregory Kamateros, II, 309.44-48; cf. *Miracula Artemii*, no. 24, ed. A. Papadopoulos-Kerameus, *Varia graeca sacra* (St Petersburg, 1909), 34.

[139] *Al.*, preface, L, I, 3; Michael Psellos, *Chronographia*, VI.36, ed. E. Renault, *Michel Psellos, Chronographie*, II (Paris, 1928), 129.

[140] V. Grumel, 'La profession médicale à l'époque des Comnènes,' *REB* 7 (1949), 42-46; Michael Pantechnes held the post of *proximos* and in G99 and in G129 is described as τῷ ἰατρῷ τοῦ βασιλέως; he is *aktouarios* by the time of Michael Italikos's monody, op. 9, ed.

medicine which is patent by then was already visible in the mid-eleventh century. Psellos wrote six medical works; others by Damnastes, Stephen Magnetes and Symeon Seth indicate a considerable flurry of activity.[141] Theophylact is simply reflecting this interest and expressing it in a literary form which was inherently open to medical imagery and content. Theophylact's letters are the point at which we can see medical imagery, accounts of diseases, doctor-litterati, respect for healing and an academic curiosity about the body all together for the first time. But despite—even because of—the new explicitness all this is still recognisable as quintessentially epistolary.

iii. *Friendship*

While the letter is in Darrouzès's words 'essentially φιλικός',[142] friendship has been seen as an especial concern of the eleventh and twelfth centuries both in the medieval west and in Byzantium.[143] Indeed it is possible to use Anselm as a foil for Theophylact's friendship discourse, examining the relative importance in the letters of Theophylact of his friends, of the abstract idea of friendship and of friendship expressed in the letter.

These concepts may not have appeared distinct to Theophylact. Letters created and maintained friendships; friendships filled letters, often to the exclusion of everything else. Friends might be known only by letter, as idealised embodiments of a literary theory. Demetrios in the *Peri Hermeneias* expressed it like this: 'A letter is designed to be the heart's good wishes in brief.' So from very early in the history of Greek letter-writing the letter and friendship were inextricably entangled; that amicitia or philia belonged in the

---

Gautier, 111-115; Nicholas Kallikles was *archiatros* and *didaskalos*, ed. Sternbach, 325, 392; Michael Italikos was *didaskalos ton iatron* before the death of Eirene Doukaina, 1133 or 1138.

[141] See O. Temkin, 'Byzantine Medicine: Tradition and Empiricism,' *DOP* 16 (1962), 95-115.

[142] Darrouzès, *Épistoliers byzantins*, 48.

[143] F. Tinnefeld, 'Freundschaft in den Briefen des Michael Psellos, Theorie und Wirklichkeit,' *JÖB* 22 (1973), 151-168 and its discussion by A.P. Kazhdan, 'Predvaritel'nye zamechaniia o mirovozzrenii vizantiiskogo mistika x-xi vv. Simeona,' *BS* 28 (1967), 19-20 (and in all his recent books) and my 'Byzantium, a Friendly Society?' *P&P* 118 (1988), 3-24, in which I stress the social importance of friendship in eleventh- and twelfth-century Byzantium. For the west, B.P. McGuire, *Friendship and Community: the Monastic Experience 350-1250* (CS, 95, Kalamazoo, 1988), ch. 6, 'The Age of Friendship,' 231-295 gives a welcome sense of development and a clear view of the difference between ascetic and worldly milieux; J. McEvoy, 'Notes on the Prologue to Saint Aelred of Rievaulx's *De spirituali amicitia*, with a translation,' *Traditio* 37 (1981), 396-411 does more than he claims.

letter was as much a commonplace for patristic writers as for modern scholars.[144]

The ancient theory of friendship, too, as expressed in Plato, Aristotle and Cicero, was well digested by the writers of the fourth and fifth centuries and integrated with the newer theory of the letter. Both Greek and Latin writers show this fusion together with Christian ideals of sancta societas, of friendship in Christ, and a general spiritualisation of ideals of friendship under considerable neoplatonic influence.[145]

Within this received common ground there was considerable opportunity for individuality. Some authors are clearly more interested in friends than in friendship. Paulinus of Nola makes his various correspondents very real to the reader; he had after all reshaped his entire circle of friends after conversion.[146] But to see the three strands already combined we must go to the Cappadocians. This is Basil:

> Ever great and many are the gifts of our master, and neither can their greatness be measured nor their multitude enumerated. And one of the greatest is even this present one—that he has granted us, who are very widely separated by an interval of space to be united to one another through communication by letter. And a double means of acquaintance has been granted us; one by meeting and the other by intercourse by letter. Since, then, we have become acquainted with you through what you have said...not by having your bodily characteristics imprinted upon our memory, but by coming to know the beauty of the inner man through the variety of his discourse...For by this we shall be able to be near each other in spirit even if in our earthly habitation we are most widely parted.[147]

---

[144] Demetrios, *Peri Hermeneias*, 231, ed. W. Rhys Roberts, *Demetrius on Style* (Cambridge, 1902), 176.

[145] On ancient theories of friendship see L. Dugas, *L'amitié antique d'après les moeurs populaires et les théories des philosophes* (Paris, 1904); J.-C. Fraisse, *Philia. La notion d'amitié dans la philosophie antique* (Paris, 1974); K. Treu, 'Freundschaft,' *Reallexikon für Antike und Christentum* 8 (1972), 418-434. See G. Karlsson, *Idéologie et cérémonial dans l'épistolographie byzantine* (Uppsala, 1962), ch. 3B, 'Spiritualisation de la thème d'amitié,' 58-60. C. White, *Christian Friendship in the Fourth Century* (Cambridge, 1992) shows how some fourth-century writers continued the classical approach while others, notably the Cappadocians, reinterpreted classical theory in a new synthesis with Christian thought.

[146] On Paulinus's friendships see P. Fabre, *S. Paulin de Nole et l'amitié chrétienne* (Paris, 1949).

[147] Basil, ep. 197, ed. Deferrari, III, 90. K. Treu, 'Philia und Agape: zur Terminologie der Freundschaft bei Basilius und Gregorius Nazianzenus,' *StudClass* 3 (1961), 421-427. On varieties of Cappadocian friendship in action (and opposition) see R. van Dam, 'Emperors, Bishops and Friends in Late Antique Cappadocia,' *JThS* 37 (1986), 53-76.

Friendship is almost better served by letters than by personal contact. In a letter to Peter of Alexandria he writes:

> Eyes are promoters of bodily friendship, and the intimacy engendered through long association strengthens such friendship. But true love is formed by the gift of the spirit, which brings together objects separated by a wide space and causes loved ones to know each other, not through the features of the body, but through the pecularities of the soul. This indeed the favour of the Lord has wrought in our case also, making it possible for us to see you with the eyes of the soul, to embrace you with the true love and to grow one with you, as it were, and to enter into a single union with you through communion according to faith.[148]

Again the idea of distance, but also that of the union of souls surfaces here. Sidonius Apollinaris expressed this quite simply in a letter to Acquilinus, 'simus animae duae, animus unus'. This idea is taken up and played with many times in the Greek middle ages: it is used by Theodore of Stoudios and Michael Psellos, its implications are seen by Anselm and parodied by Michael Italikos. But it is to be found earlier, in the myth told by Aristophanes in Plato's *Symposium*.[149]

Most patristic ideas, and the many other commonplaces of letter-friendship—the winged visit, 'another self', the union of souls—continued to attract Byzantine letter-writers. The sense of continuity may even have been conscious. In Theodore of Stoudios, Ignatios of Nicaea and the tenth-century letter-writers the topoi reappear. Writers looked for new ways of expressing the old ideals. 'Loving friends are like plants,' suggested Symeon Magistros, 'and qualities of the spirit are like leaves of the tree.' 'Friendship without letters,' thought Leo of Synada, 'is a lamp without oil.'[150]

In the west this was not true in the same way, despite the circle of Alcuin and Charlemagne. Gerbert's letters contained some lyrical passages of praise for friends and friendship, but his greater gift was for invective. Friendship was to return fully in the twelfth-century renaissance when the reading of Cicero was revived. Letters, sermons, prayers attest this revival.

---

[148] Basil, ep. 133, ed. Deferrari, II, 302.

[149] Sidonius, ep. V.9, ed. W.B. Anderson, *Sidonius, Poems and Letters* (London and Cambridge, Mass., 1965), II, 202; Theodore of Stoudios, in a *kontakion* to Basil, ed. J.B. Pitra, *Analecta sacra*, I (Paris, 1876), 346; Michael Psellos, ep. 45, ed. Kurtz-Drexl, 75.14; Michael Italikos, ep. 1, ed. Gautier, 59; Anselm, ep. 3, ed. Schmitt, *AOO*, III, 103; Plato, *Symposion*, 189-191.

[150] Theodore of Stoudios, ep. 504 (II.148), ed. G. Fatouros, *Theodori Studitae epistolae* (CFHB, 31, Berlin and New York, 1992), II, 745-746; Symeon Magistros, ep. 35, ed. Darrouzès, 123; Leo of Synada, ep. 34, ed. Darrouzès, *Épistoliers byzantins*, 192.

Systematic treatises codify these discoveries: Ailred of Rievaulx revised his *De spirituali amicitia* between 1164 and 1167, and Peter of Blois wrote his *De christiana amicitia* in the 1190s. An earlier stage of the revival, when the reading of Cassian was more influential, is represented by Theophylact's contemporary Anselm.[151]

Anselm and Theophylact have often been compared,[152] but 'even so there was a formidable gulf between an essentially Greek prelate, such as Theophylact, and Anselm'.[153] How deep was this gulf on friendship?

Anselm is for our purposes an excellent foil for Theophylact. His career is roughly analogous, for he was appointed to Canterbury four years after Theophylact arrived in Ochrid, and died about the time of Theophylact's last surviving letters. The comparison with Anselm is also helpful because of what Southern has called his 'gift for friendship';[154] it was a concept he understood supremely well and took great trouble to express. And in that he drew on the *Collationes* of Cassian he had behind him the consensus of the eastern Mediterranean in the fourth century. What he lacks is the rhythm of centuries-long reworking of ceremonial themes.

---

[151] On Alcuin, see A. Fiske, 'Alcuin and Mystical Friendship,' *Studi medievali*, 3 ser., 2 (1961), 551-575; for Gerbert see H. Platt Lattin, *The Letters of Gerbert with his Papal Privileges* (New York, 1961), 147; 159; 166. On the revival of friendship in the medieval west see C. Morris, *The Discovery of the Individual 1050-1200* (London, 1972). J. Leclercq, *Monks and Love in Twelfth-Century France: Psychohistorical Essays* (Oxford, 1979) is particularly interesting on the erotic vocabulary of Bernard of Clairvaux. For Cassian see Collatio XVI, *De amicitia*, ed. M. Petschenig, *Johannis Cassiani conlationes XXIIII* (CSEL, 13, Vienna, 1886), 437-462; Aelred, *Amicitia* and *Speculum caritatis*, ed. A. Hoste and C.H. Talbot, *Aelred opera omnia*, I, *Opera ascetica* (CCCM, 1, Turnhout, 1971), tr. M. Laker (CF, 5, Kalamazoo, 1974). F.M. Powicke, *The Life of Ailred of Rievaulx by Walter Daniel* (London, 1950); Peter of Blois, *De amicitia christiana* and *De charitate dei et proximi*, PL, 207, 807-958. See R.W. Southern, 'Peter of Blois: a twelfth-century humanist,' *Medieval Humanism and Other Studies* (Oxford, 1970), 105-132.

[152] For the classic comparison of Theophylact's liberal stance on theological differences between east and west to Anselm at the Council of Bari in 1098 see S. Runciman, *The Eastern Schism. A Study of the Papacy and the Eastern Churches during the Eleventh and Twelfth Centuries* (Oxford, 1955), 72-77.

[153] A.A.M. Bryer, 'Cultural Relations between East and West in the Twelfth Century,' *Relations between East and West in the Middle Ages*, ed. D. Baker (Edinburgh, 1973), 78-79. He goes on, 'in everything save a determination to maintain a sympathetic and open mind on the superficial differences between the two churches', reinforcing Runciman's point.

[154] On Anselm's career see R.W. Southern, *St Anselm and his Biographer. A Study of Monastic Life and Thought, 1059-1130* (Cambridge, 1963), and now *Anselm, a Portrait in a Landscape* (Cambridge, 1990). On his thought see G.R. Evans, *Anselm* (London, 1989). On friendship see Southern, *Humanism*, 13; *Portrait*, 138-165.

There are certain difficulties in working with Anselm's letters.[155] For one thing there are two distinct collections put together for different reasons. The first, ordered by Anselm himself, is predominantly a dossier of his friendships, centring on his life at Bec; the second collection is a much less ordered agglomeration of political documents relating to his rule at Canterbury. Although in date and in the administrative background the second collection would seem the fairer parallel with Theophylact, I have chosen to study rather the earlier collection, which deals extensively with friendship, rather than the later one which hardly mentions it. This is perhaps the most striking difference between the writers; when administrative worries arise, Anselm appears to shelve his friendships, but Theophylact cultivates them all the more assiduously and derives great comfort from them. But there is at least a reasonable correspondence in number: 139 in Anselm's first collection to 135 in Theophylact's. If we bear these difficulties in mind it should be possible to proceed to compare the two writers' views of friends, friendship and the role of the letter within friendship.[156]

I discuss below, in chapter 4, the difficulties of detecting a friend in Theophylact's correspondence. For western letters these problems were foreseen by Morey and Brooke in 1965: 'The result is that it is extremely difficult for us to discriminate between the language of acquaintance and the language of intimacy. A kindly, diplomatic and charitable man like Peter the Venerable seems to be on terms of close friendship with everyone in Christendom.'[157] The discussion which follows depends in some measure on the results of my efforts. But for Anselm the position is a little easier than for Peter the Venerable or Theophylact.

Anselm's friends are relatively easy to determine. For one thing his friendships 'were famous in their own day'[158] and they are recorded by Eadmer his biographer. For example, when he consulted Lanfranc on the wisdom of entering the religious life, Eadmer makes a point of telling us that he consulted Lanfranc as a friend.

> He had many other friends, but his devotion to Lanfranc was so great that if as they were going through a forest on the way to Rouen Lanfranc had said

---

[155] See Southern, *Portrait*, Appendix, 458-481.

[156] On the manuscript tradition of Anselm's letters see A. Wilmart, 'La tradition des lettres de S. Anselme. Lettres inédites et de ses correspondants,' *RevBen* 43 (1931), 38-54; F.S. Schmitt, 'Zur Entstehungsgeschichte der handschriftlichen Sammlungen der Briefe des hl. Anselm von Canterbury,' *RevBen* 48 (1936), 300-317; Southern, *Biographer*, ch. I.4, 'The Letters of Friendship;' *Portrait*, Appendix.

[157] A.C. Morey and C.N.L. Brooke, *Gilbert Foliot and his Letters* (Cambridge, 1965), 13.

[158] Southern, *Humanism*, 13.

to him, 'Stay in this wood and see you never come out as long as you live',
Anselm would have obeyed the command.

Eadmer describes the impact of the death of Osbern on Anselm, points out
the role of friends in the various stages of the editing of Anselm's works and
the delight everyone took in his conversation: 'A charming sweetness
proceeded from his conversation, which drew all men to him in friendship
and affection.'[159]

Besides, the first collection is so ordered that the recipients are easy to
identify, and that order is Anselm's own. They are all monks, from his early
days at Bec; he does not seem to have achieved that intimacy again after his
appointment to Canterbury. Lanfranc remained an important friend to whom
he wrote seventeen letters with great affection and gift-giving.[160] Gondulf
entered Bec on the same day as Anselm, and theirs was a very special bond
although Gondulf was ten years older. Twelve letters to Gondulf survive,
spanning the time he was at Canterbury with Lanfranc and after his election
to the see of Rochester; he was still there when Anselm was appointed to
Canterbury, and he was instrumental as a go-between with the King during
Anselm's exile. During this later period the letters are more business-like;
students of the collection do not believe that the relationship actually deteriorated.[161] The Gondulf correspondence is interesting because one can see some
development and also how very painful a friendship with Anselm might be;
for their ideas on the letters as vehicles of friendship differed, and Gondulf's
letters must have been long pleas for more letters. This had little success, for
Anselm simply reiterated his theories of friendship. So Gondulf took to
enlisting the support of their friends, which got back to Anselm but had no
effect. He tried another tack and sent him presents instead, presents which he
had to acknowledge. This was apparently no more successful, and yet this was
the man whom Anselm described as 'altera anima mea'. He was cruel
apparently not because he thought too little of friendship, merely reiterating
its formulas without meaning them, but because he thought too much and believed friends were one soul: what then was the point of writing?[162]

---

[159]   Eadmer, *De vita et conversatione Anselmi Cantuarensis archepiscopi*, ed. R.W.
Southern, *The Life of St Anselm, Archbishop of Canterbury by Eadmer, edited with
introduction, Notes and translations (from the Latin)* (Oxford, 1962), 10-11, 19, 28-31.

[160]   I.e. epp. 1, 14, 23, 25, 27, 31, 32, 39, 49, 57, 66, 75, 89, 90, 103, 124, 137.

[161]   I.e. epp. 4, 7, 16, 28, 34, 41, 51, 59, 68, 78, 91, 141. See A. Fiske, 'St Anselm and
Friendship,' *Studia Monastica* 3 (1961), 259-290 at 261-2 on the change of emphasis from
affectus to *effectus*.

[162]   Anselm, ep. 16, ed. Schmitt, III, 121.

Other friends who emerge from the letters of Anselm are Maurice, a devoted pupil (who fell ill, causing him much distress, and then recovered and became the superior of a new college of Bec at Confluentium), and Henry, who went with Lanfranc to Canterbury and eventually became prior there.[163] A counterpart to Gondulf is the friend Gilbert Crispin. Anselm has preserved only four letters to him, yet at his parting he really seems to have felt anguish:

> The gifts of your sweet nature, most sweet friend, are very sweet to me, but cannot in any way console my heart which is desolate for you from the desire for your love. For surely if you sent every kind of aromatic scent, every metal that gleams, every kind of precious stone, every variety of weave, my torn soul would reject them, indeed it would not be able to find consolation for its mangling unless it could receive that other part of itself.[164]

Yet it is important to note that Anselm could be effusive also to those he had never met; it is very dangerous to try to establish friendship from the content of his letters alone. Though many of his letters are simple thanks for gifts or letters of advice or exhortations to join the monastic life they are couched in effusive terms. Here is a letter to two young relatives he had not yet met:

> My eyes eagerly long to see your faces, most beloved; my arms stretch out to your embraces; my lips long for your kisses; whatever remains of my life desires your company, so that my soul's joy may be full in time to come.[165]

Theophylact's friends form a sizeable sector of the network of his collection,[166] drawn from Constantinople and Bulgaria, his contemporaries and the young, whom he greatly enjoyed and deliberately cultivated, scholars and doctors and lawyers and soldiers and churchmen. Some he knew from his time in Constantinople,[167] some he knew also through their family;[168] others he appears to know through the everyday concerns of Bulgaria.[169] When a Constantinople friend appeared near Ochrid[170] it was the signal for rejoicing, and hope that practical difficulties could be smoothed over. With bishops like

---

[163] The letters to Maurice: epp. 42, 43, 47, 60, 64, 69, 74, 79, 97. To Henry: epp. 5, 24, 33, 40, 50, 53, 67, 73, 93, 110, 121, 140.

[164] Anselm, ep. 84, ed. Schmitt, III, 208-9. The other letters to Gilbert Crispin are ep. 106, III, 239; ep. 130, III, 272-273; ep. 142, III, 288-289.

[165] Anselm, ep. 120, ed. Schmitt, II, 258; cf. Southern, *Biographer*, 72-73; Morris, *Individual*, 96.

[166] See below, 200 and fig. 7.1.

[167] E.g. his colleagues Theodore Smyrnaios and Niketas *ho tou Serron* and ex-pupils.

[168] E.g. Michael Pantechnes.

[169] E.g. Gregory Kamateros.

[170] E.g. Nicholas Anemas, John Opheomachos.

Nicholas of Kerkyra, Chrysoberges of Naupaktos, Theodoulos of Thessalonike and the bishop of Semnea he shared worries and case-histories, wrapped up in elegant riddles so as not to bore his friend.[171] To the bishop of Kitros also he confided the story of the illness and death of his brother, the closest relationship of the correspondence.[172] His nearest friend appears to have been the bishop of Pelagonia with whom on occasion he stayed.[173] Many of his friends were powerful and famous;[174] others are quite unknown.[175] To some of these he addressed his most characteristic letters of friendship.

His letters to friends are of different kinds: long tours de force, like G127 to Gregory Kamateros, scrappy little notes built on a single conceit, like some to Michael Pantechnes,[176] more crafted short letters, like those to Nicholas Kallikles.[177] The letters to his doctor friends build on medical vocabulary as well as on parables and psalms.[178] But to friends like Mermentoulos the Grand *droungarios* of the Watch, to John Peribleptenos, perhaps a monk at the Peribleptos, John the philosopher, John the *maistor*, as well as to Opheomachos and Anemas, who like Gregory Kamateros appear in Bulgaria, he offers a particular kind of brilliant, sparkling communication.

They may be letters of praise, comparing the speech of the other to Hymettos honey,[179] or letters of advice on reading,[180] or complaints of rusticity.[181] Monsters and sickness are usually absent here, for most of these friends provide a distraction rather than a solution for his cares of the archdiocese. What they can do for him is to keep writing, to pour into his chalice the honey of Hymettos or the vine of experience which can keep alive the web of learned relationships[182] which acted for Theophylact like a safety-net. They are literary, short and full of charm and wit and wordplay and

---

[171] G77 to the bishop of Kerkyra has the image of each bishop in turn pouring out before the other his cup (of troubles).

[172] G121, II, 559.

[173] G21 warns him of impending reshuffles; G36 discusses reading and the scriptures; G64 gives him an introduction to the patriarch; G63 may console him on the death of a protector.

[174] For example Gregory Kamateros, Michael Pantechnes.

[175] For example Machetares, Theophylact Romaios, John Opheomachos, Nicholas Anemas, John Peribleptenos.

[176] For example G130, II, 585.

[177] G94, built on the story of Alkmaion; G111, built on Nicholas pouring out his remedies; G112 built on the book-exchange.

[178] See above, 107-108.

[179] G25, to Mermentoulos, II, 213.13-17.

[180] G29, to Mermentoulos, 225.13-227.32.

[181] See below, 5.3 and 5.6, 256, 271-276.

[182] E.g. G77, II, 407.20-21.

shared quotations, here classical rather than biblical. When they write to him they are praised, when they fail to write their neglect is noted.[183] Very rarely do these letters ever touch on sordid reality; they celebrate friendship, learning and letters.

Yet examining their vocabulary in comparison with Anselm's shows the reticence of the Byzantine letter. Only the two *threnoi* on Demetrios point up the affect, παμπόθητε, of G133;[184] few even of the last type of friendship letter approach it. Michael Pantechnes is φίλτατε; Opheomachos and Anemas are θαυμάσιε and ποθεινότατε;[185] but it is Machetares to whom Theophylact expresses his most developed theory of friendship and the letter.[186] In contrast, another letter which begins promisingly, 'you always kindle my desire' goes on to depict the other's climb to goodness on the ladder of Jacob. It is possible that this letter is to the Tarchaneiotes who consulted Theophylact on spiritual matters and who received two letters of parainesis, neat homilies by letter.[187]

What did Anselm and Theophylact think about friendship? For Anselm this is the core of the matter; for him a friend was more an idea than a person.[188] The importance of friendship can be seen in the fact that he put the letters of friendship into a collection while the letters of his later political life were left to be collected by another. Its importance can be seen by the number of synonyms he uses for the emotion—affectus, caritas, amicitia, dilectio—and in the prayer he wrote for his friends.[189] Friendship to Anselm was a duty imposed by God, but it was different from the social duty observed by Sidonius; it was a simple duty to love and to bring the beloved through love to God. Love is a virtue, and Anselm is very concerned about true love, but he does not admit the hierarchy of love such as was expressed in Cassian.[190] His love was inexpressible, but he found ways in which to express it: it burns, it is sweet, it gives joy and makes the lover drunk.

---

[183] E.g. G54, to the patriarch, II, 313.7-16; G44, to Machetares, II, 277.14-18.

[184] G133, to Demetrios, II, 591.2.

[185] See below, 4.2, 182-183, and 'The Network'.

[186] G44, to Machetares, II, 277-279.

[187] G16 and G20.

[188] Southern, *Biographer*, 76.

[189] Anselm, or. 18, ed. Schmitt, III, 71-2; B. Ward, *Prayers and Meditations of St Anselm* (Harmondsworth, 1973), 212-215. See also her *Anselm of Canterbury: a Monastic Scholar* (Fairacres Publications, 62, Oxford, 1973). I am very grateful to Sister Benedicta for guidance and discussion of this section, long ago now.

[190] Cassian, *Collatio* XVI.xiv, ed. Petschenig, 418-419.

Although true love, once kindled, burns for ever without the help of fanning, yet it is enjoyed by friends in no small measure through either the frequent sharing of company in person, or, when friends are parted, by constant reminders through a third person.

For what is sweeter, what more pleasant, what is a greater consolation for love than love?

Whenever you are pleased that something is pleasing to me, then that itself pleases me, the more so in that it was pleasing to begin with. You say that you are happy because I (to say nothing of other matters) have taken delight in our beloved young man, your nephew. And so I am happy with your happiness, and the joy which I had in that young man, though it is always strong, is renewed as it grows.

And thus let the familiar habit of virtue and the long-accustomed love affect your mind like intoxication, so that not only may everything you do be touched by the love inside you, but also that your mind may be amazed that anyone should be actually incapable of feeling the same drunkenness in himself.[191]

Anselm's love involves desire: 'And so it is that because I am not able to have you with me, while I desire you and you me, I love you more not less.' And it is totally sure of itself:

Although a space of time or place separates us, by divine will, no cause has, or shall have, the power to diminish my love for you, which divine grace protects. And since it is certain that to your heart a similar feeling towards me is clinging, there is no doubt in me that you wish always to know all about me as I do all about you.[192]

Like Aristotle he saw the beloved as another self, ἄλλος ἐγώ, and finds the power of love great enough to overcome the temporal difficulties of absence, which caused, because of the union of souls, a scissura animae, and of social inequality, which occurred when a friend was elevated to a bishopric; however, 'pristina familiaritas et familiaris amicitia ad aequalitatem me sublevat.'[193] For Anselm friendship was the closest one could get in the present life to heaven.

Theophylact too understood the value of friendship, though he rarely expressed his view without reference to the concrete circumstances of friends

---

[191] Anselm, epp. 50, 115, 32, 7, ed. Schmitt, III, 163, III, 250, III, 140, III, 109.
[192] Anselm, epp. 69, 54, ed. Schmitt, III, 189, 168.
[193] Anselm, ep. 91, ed. Schmitt, III, 218.

or their letters. (He uses φιλία far less frequently than φίλοι.)[194] He wrote poems for his friends, but not about friendship. And his friendship was of a more instrumental variety than Anselm's. He quotes Empedocles to Theodore Smyrnaios as part of a conceit on the headless monsters of Ochrid; in another letter he invokes friendship in order to persuade an official to do what he wishes; he talks of a crime against friendship and accuses Mermentoulos of thinking too little of it.[195]

In G41 to Anemas there is a long consideration of the relationship of separation and friendship. This passage is unique as an expression of Theophylact's view of friendship:

> Truly, a true friend is depressed when deprived of his beloved. But when he has been a neighbour of the desired one and he was expecting to embrace him soon, then his heart is torn. However, since the mind both sees and hears, as the Pythagorean Epicharmos says, and if you can see me in this way, O dearest of men and so the most desired, do not blame too much the distance and the separation from the one you love. Be satisfied with the greater, even if you are deprived of what is the lesser. For it is better to see us with the mind, which bodily seeing lacks.[196]

Finally, what did Anselm and Theophylact think about friendship and the letter? Here their roles are reversed. It is Theophylact whose ideas are more thoroughly worked out while Anselm seems indifferent or even hostile to the role of the letter in friendship. It is difficult to tell what value Anselm placed on his own letters. Queen Matilda wrote that they had the gravity of Fronto, the copiousness of Cicero, the acuteness of Quintilian, the teaching of Paul, the diligence of Jerome, the elaboration of Gregory and the perspicacity of Augustine. She does not consider their qualities as carriers of friendship.[197] Eadmer also overlooks this quality in his discussion of Anselm's letters.

> Meanwhile he also wrote many letters, in some of which he sought to obtain for his correspondent those things which their varying business required, and in others he sent reasoned replies to people seeking his advice about their affairs. As for those which he was obliged to write for other reasons, we pass over them in silence.[198]

---

[194] Seven times as against twenty-two.

[195] For Empedocles see G6, II, 147.8-12; for the law of love and the official John Serblias, G49, II, 297.5-7. For the crime against φιλία see G42 to Romaios Theophylaktos, II, 271.27-29; G47, II.293. On instrumental friendship see my 'Friendly Society?' and below, 4.2, 189.

[196] G41, to Anemas, II, 269.2-9.

[197] Anselm, ep. 384, ed. Schmitt, V, 327; Southern, *Biographer*, 192.

[198] *VAnselmi*, xx, ed. Southern, 32.

Not a word here about friendship. Nor is there much more in Anselm himself. He talks of letters flying to his correspondent, a concept fairly common in Byzantium, and on which Theophylact elaborates.[199] But in general, and for Anselm surprisingly, the letter was irrelevant. If the souls of the writer and the beloved were one, what did they have to say to one another? Why should he describe his love when a true image of it lived in the heart of the beloved in the form of the beloved's love for him?[200] If hearts are truer media of expression than words, why write about love instead of feeling it?[201] If the lovers are one soul, all that belongs to one belongs to the other, so how can one give the other a gift?[202] This is an old problem which was solved in antiquity, but still crops up as a pleasantry in the letter-exchange of Theodore Prodromos and Michael Italikos—but it was no more than a joke to them whereas to Anselm (and to his correspondent) it was serious.[203]

But for Theophylact, a discussion of friendship necessarily entailed a discussion of letters of friendship. His idea of the sublimity of human friendship in relation to God is not so very far away from Anselm's except in that it presupposes letters of love as the ladder which leads the friends to God. Unlike Anselm, he uses the images of moisture rather than of fire; for Theophylact friendship soothes, drops dew on the distressed friend. For Theophylact how could this be done without letters?[204]

In G16 he says that the greetings of friends are like wings to the runner; we have seen him echo Gregory of Nazianzos's view of the letter as feast. Another correspondent is compared to the phoenix because he suddenly makes a reappearance by letter just when Theophylact had lost hope of their friendship. He describes the effect of the letters on him of 'the sweetest of men'. He talks of the 'the honey of your goodness, of which, ever since I tasted it, the sweet flavour has remained'. Theophylact, confessing himself madly in love, explains that since he has no means of sprinkling his longing with dew, he will play subtle tricks to gain this by letter. Elsewhere the letter

---

[199] Anselm, ep. 16, ed. Schmitt, III, 121. Theophylact, G64, II, 361.8-10.

[200] Anselm, ep. 41, ed. Schmitt, III, 152.

[201] Anselm, ep. 59, ed. Schmitt, III, 174. Anna Komnene could actually have told him the answer, for she notes that Aristotle says that lack of communication dissolves many friendships, *Nic.Eth.*, 8.6, see *Al.*, XIII.iv.1, L, III, 100.17-18: σπάνις γὰρ προσηγορίας κατὰ τὸν Σταγειρίτην πολλὰς φιλίας διέλυσε.

[202] Anselm, ep. 34, ed. Schmitt, III, 141-142.

[203] See R. Browning, 'Unpublished Correspondence between Michael Italicus, Archbishop of Philippopolis, and Theodore Prodromus,' *BB* 1 (1962), 288.

[204] For imagery of water, dew, cooling and refreshment see particularly G22, G73, G75, G91, G92, G106, G109, G131.

is more than second best; it is a gift from God to friends, and letters of love return the love of the friends to the source of all love.[205]

These then are the views of Theophylact and Anselm on friendship, friends and the letter. There are surface similarities between their views; the relationship of human and divine love seems very similar, as does the insistence on pothos and the persistent consciousness of friendship in separation. Even details can tie up; compare Theophylact writing to Michael Pantechnes on his appointment as imperial doctor and Anselm to Gondulf when elevated to the see of Rochester.[206] But their views are in fact very different. Anselm's approach is much more idealistic than Theophylact's; he values the idea of friendship rather than the individuals who enact it or the means by which they do so. Theophylact's is an essentially practical approach; he values the means rather than the ideal, the network rather than the individual. His love is built on need, mutually understood if not shared, while Anselm's is a love without need, more perfect but less satisfying. For Anselm a supreme aim in life was *verus amor* : for Theophylact what mattered most was an ἀληθινὸς φίλος.

iv. *Everyday problems*

If Theophylact's thoughts on reading show timeless concerns and if medicine and friendship in his letters reveal eleventh-century preoccupations, the everyday also had an important place in his letters. They serve both business and pleasure; they divert, but each one makes a unique contribution to the world outside letters. They were 'real letters'.[207] Some commentators have shrunk from this view; Darrouzès described Byzantine letters as being 'un genre littéraire noble, qui s'évade loin des realités de la vie quotidienne'.[208] But

---

[205] G16, II, 185.29; G25, II, 213.2; G76, II, 405.5-8; G86, II, 453.2; G10, II, 161.2-6; G44, II, 277-279.

[206] G102, to his pupil Michael Pantechnes the doctor, II, 515.2-5: 'I do not know whether to rejoice with you or sympathise with you on entering the imperial court. For the opinion of many argues the former, but the facts of the matter the second.' Cf. Anselm, ep. 78, ed. Schmitt, III, 200: 'on the one hand I rejoice with your paternity as with one with whose past life the grace of God has shown itself to be pleased in that it seems proper to count you among the princes of the church. On the other hand, I am forced to commiserate with your fraternity as one who, by being raised to greater heights, has been weighed down with a greater burden.'

[207] For discussions of whether Roman letters were 'real' or not, see A.N. Sherwin-White, *The Letters of Pliny: a Historical and Social Commentary* (Oxford, 1966), 11-18; D.A. Russell, 'Letters to Lucilius,' *Seneca*, ed. C.D.N. Costa (Birmingham, 1974), 77-79; M. Griffin, *Seneca. A Philosopher in Politics* (Oxford, 1976), 414-419; M.J. McGann, *Studies in Horace's First Book of Epistles* (Coll.Lat., 100, Brussels, 1969), 89-100.

[208] Darrouzès, *Épistoliers byzantins*, 48.

St Basil in a letter to Amphilochios had suggested something quite different: 'There is nothing to prevent my letters being, as it were, a daily record of my life, recounting to your charity the happenings of each day. For me it brings relief to communicate our affairs to you, and you, I know, are anxious about nothing so much as our affairs.'[209]

Theophylact saw his problems as monsters:

> For I had not quite escaped from the lion when a bear came upon me, and as
> I rush away and just rest my hands on the wall of the house, a deadly snake
> puts its head out of its hole, which makes my distress all the more acute.[210]

Nor did they go away. He remembers the hydra of Lerna[211] which grew as fast as Herakles could cut off its limbs. (Herakles though had only twelve labours to perform.) Some of the monsters may be identified: Briareus normally represents the praktors with their hundred heads (Theophylact's addition) and hundred arms.[212] Others like Typhon, Euroklydon, Polyphemos the Cyclops[213] may be particular individuals. And there is a general sense in which Bulgaria is presented as a waste land populated by monsters: Kedar, a desert with scorpions, the land of the Laestrygonians.[214] Theophylact is Daniel in the lions' den, Samson being blinded, a lion set upon by dogs.[215] Often he refers generally to the difficulties he met every day as an archbishop. In the correspondence they appear as vague and nightmarish, except when specific action is requested. But rarely is there a policy statement, rarely a recapitulation of difficulties. And Vailhé's penetrating comment on the double difficulty faced by Byzantine archbishops of Ochrid, how to promote Greek over Bulgarian while defending Ochrid against the patriarchate,[216] seems some

---

[209] Basil, to Amphilochios, ep. 231, ed. Deferrari, III, 358.

[210] G75, to the bishop of Kerkyra, II, 401.27-30.

[211] G85, to Adrian the Grand Domestic, II, 401.27-30.

[212] G55, to Pakourianos, II, 347.21; G61, ?to John Komnenos, II, 351.12-13.

[213] For Typhon see G96, to Bryennios, gambros of the emperor, II, 483.23 (bracketed with Briareus); for Euroklydon, G31, to Kamateros, II, 233.2; Scylla and Charybdis in the same letter, 233.18 are a troublesome eunuch; for Polyphemos the Cyclops, G127, to Gregory Kamateros, II, 573.25, where he teases his correspondent, urging him to guess who the Cyclops is. In G76 there is ὁ δεινὸς καυστηρός (=Sirius).

[214] For Kedar see G90, to the *chartophylax*, II, 469.7; G79, to the Grand Domestic, II, 423.69; poem 1, to Bryennios, I, 26; a desert with scorpions, G37, to Symeon the abbot of Anaplous, II, 253.5-7; the land of the Laestrygonians, G69, to Opheomachos, II, 377.2.

[215] Daniel in the lions' den, G61, ?to John Komnenos, II, 351.5-6; Samson: G89, to Adrian the emperor's brother, II, 465.21; the lion: in the same letter, II, 465.18.

[216] S. Vailhé, 'Achrida,' *DHGE*, I (Paris, 1912), 325.

distance from the perspective of the correspondence: Theophylact is not treading a tightrope; he is in the arena pursued by monsters.

This section seeks to depict the problems, not explain them, or (as I do later in the chapter) analyse how Theophylact sought to solve them. But to gain a balanced view of the collection it is important to know how many letters deal with problems and in what ways. Xanalatos wrote a seminal study of taxes and tax-officials in Theophylact's letters, but he based it on only thirty-four letters.[217] Was this the tip of the iceberg?

Only forty of Theophylact's letters appear to be entirely problem-free, and of these half are letters in which a recital of his problems would be intrusive; formal 'adventus' letters, recommendatory and consolatory letters,[218] two letters of pure *parainesis*, the letter on the liturgy, letters of praise, thanks and congratulations, and letters sent with gifts. Of the letters which deal with problems, only three might automatically be expected to deal with his problems (the arrival-in-see letters), and thirteen could be regarded as dealing with other people's problems. A rough count suggests that about eighty touch on his problems and fifty-five do not. This of course includes a vast range from mention in passing through heavily veiled allusion, lengthy complaint and specific request to the itemised precision of G96 and G98. (No critic of the vacuity of Byzantine letters could fail to be impressed by those.) Few give any overview, and there is of course absolutely no reason to believe they are complete.

G45, to the patriarch, is more comprehensive than most: Theophylact thanks him for understanding

> the thorns and thistles of archbishops today; their pricks have reduced us to misery, because they elevate the daring of sinners who kill the widow and the orphan and assassinate everyone, the poor and the stranger, without there being anyone to rescue and save them. Everything is pillaged and carried off, without anyone to redeem or restore it. Deceivers rule over us; our praktors glean the last grains cut by the sickle. All those in power are younger in age and in wisdom. They are also innovating in injustice,

---

[217]   D.A. Xanalatos, *Beiträge zur Wirtschafts- und Sozialgeschichte Makedoniens im Mittelalter, hauptsächlich auf Grund der Briefe des Erzbischofs Theophylaktos von Achrida* (Munich, 1937), which systematises Theophylact's tax-problems and sets them in a wide social and economic context. The letters cited by him are G9, G10, G12, G17, G18, G22, G24, G26, G30, G32, G37, G45, G48, G52, G53, G55, G56, G57, G59, G66, G67, G68, G71, G75, G79, G82, G85, G88, G96, G98, G111, G114, G120, G129, among which he makes heaviest use of G22, G26, G45, G96, G111.

[218]   On these see below, 3.3, 135-148.

thinking up new forms of greed and renewing their vicious spirit in their guts.[219]

G48, to Michael Pantechnes, begins with Theophylact's physical condition and goes on

> But the height of my ills is my worries, unspeakable and inconsolable, about the state of the people and of the church. It is not only the cares about here. While I am at Ochrid, I am shot with arrows from Glavenitsa and Vidin and Sthlanitsa, and you too must put up with the discomfort of these barbarian names, you who are feasting on Hellenism...[220].

Some are revealed only by contrast. G57, to the bishop of Vidin, is intended to cheer him up by explaining how Theophylact can cap every one of his worries:

> Are your praktors cruel? They are not more sharp than ours around here who take one in every five children into slavery, exactly as they do with cattle, taking a fifth or a tenth. Are Cumans attacking you from outside? What are they compared with residents of Ochrid who regard going up [to Constantinople] as a weapon of honour and a crown, destroy and ravage everything without there being anyone to rescue or save? Are your citizens revolting? Do you have wicked townspeople? They are children compared with our Bulgar citizens, or rather, so as not to undervalue the evil which savages us [at Ochrid], what are they compared with our savage Mokrenoi? I have compared all this with what it is like at Ochrid, which you know from living a long time in this vale of tears, so that you may see, by synekdoche, the part for the whole.[221]

So far we have heard about invasion, officialdom and rebellion, ἔξωθεν μάχαι, ἔσωθεν φόβοι. But the recital of placenames points also to the clergy and the church in general. Individual letters bear out worries on all these issues. Invasion is almost the least of Theophylact's worries, though he records the passing of the First Crusade and the second Norman war, and the Byzantine army could cause its own problems. In G13 he welcomes Melissenos on a recruiting tour of Macedonia, but has to ask John Komnenos in G24 to have Ochrid left alone. G111 probably points to the requisition of his house in Thessalonike for the army which stayed there on and off from 1105 to 1108. G32 blames *katepano* and *kastroktistes* for many of his woes. He

---

[219] G45, to the patriarch, II, 281.16-25.
[220] G48, to Michael Pantechnes, II, 295.5-11.
[221] G57, to the bishop of Vidin, II, 323.21-325.35.

visits army camps more than once and reports his dislike of the journey and his feeling of being unwelcome.[222]

On the doubtful loyalty of the citizens of Ochrid we hear almost nothing else, except that Bulgarians are often ready to ally with the lowest representatives of the official class against him. The immoral hieromonk of G11 got mixed up with the praktor Iasites's entourage, as did the paroikos Lazaros in G96 and G98. He points out that representatives of the fisc have sought out members of the faithful disciplined by Theophylact for heresy or immorality and made common cause with them; officials stir up a dissident bishop.[223]

This is one of very few references to heresy in the collection. Others are Theophylact's enthusiastic congratulation of a suffragan bishop Diabologyres who has converted an Armenian community (G15) and the whole sequence of letters to the bishop of Triaditsa who had done likewise and was insisting on parading them in front of the emperor in Constantinople (G58, G59, G60, G87). The fragment of a letter (or speech) to the Armenian Tibanios or Tigranes more probably refers to a general doctrinal issue than to Theophylact's own domestic problems.[224] In any case there is absolutely nothing in the collection to support Chalandon's claim that 'toute la correspondance de Théophylacte est pleine d'allusions aux Bogomiles'.[225]

---

[222] On the First Crusade, G52, to the bishop of Kitros, II, 303.4, 16. On the second Norman war, G120, to John Pantechnes, II, 555.29-36, assuming Bohemond is the δοῦλος καὶ ἀποστάτης of 30-31. G13, to the caesar Melissenos, II, 171-172; G24, to John Komnenos, II, 209.22-211.25 on τῇ τῶν πεζῶν ἐκβολῇ. G111, to Nicholas Kallikles, II, 535.11-13. G32, to Anemas, II, 237.18-19 on *kastroktistes* and *katepanos*. On journeys to army camps G77, to the bishop of Kerkyra, II, 411.68-74 (in prospect); G30, to Nikephoros the *chartophylax*, II, 229.2-4 (in retrospect); poems 11 and 12, I, 366-367. See below, Table X.

[223] G11, to John Komnenos, II, 163.8-164.28 on the hieromonk and Iasites; G96, to Nikephoros Bryennios, II, 485.48-487.52 but surely not 'sans doute Iasites' as Gautier has it (486, n.14); G98, to Adrian Komnenos, II, 501.55-503.61.

[224] For the aptly named achievements of Diabologyres (which is a proper name, or could be the bishop of Diabolis) G15, II, 179-181; for the conversions of the bishop of Triaditsa, G59, II, 339.31-48. G135, to Tibanios the Armenian, II, 595-597, should be read with other speeches for the disputations at Philippopolis. See below, 239-243.

[225] Chalandon, *Les Comnène*, I, 319, n.4. Nor is there much to support the characterisation in D. Obolensky, *The Bogomils: a Study in Balkan Neomanichaeism* (Cambridge, 1948, repr. London, 1972) of Macedonia as the cradle of Byzantine Bogomilism. Though the *Life* of Hilarion of Moglena shows a mixed population including Bogomils in one area of the archdiocese in the mid-twelfth century, E.Kałužniacki, *Werke des Patriarchen von Bulgarien Euthymios (1375-93)* (Vienna, 1901), 27-58, there is no earlier evidence. And if its roots were so deep in the mountain villages of Macedonia it is hardly

Other problems with the church are endemic. The problems of his suffragan bishops are painted clearly in long parainetic letters to them as well as letters attempting to solve their problems. Both manpower and morale seem to have been perceived as problematic. A letter to the bishop Gregory Kamateros is apparently a reply to one reporting that his church had been burnt down. G122 reveals that the bishop of Debra was absent from his see. The bishop of Glavenitsa was so demoralised by G40 that Theophylact sends him on a rest cure to Niketas Polites. G22 is an eloquent description of what happens to a church without a bishop; the church at Diabolis,[226] one of Boris's ἑπτὰ καθολικά, is without chant or candlelight, like the vineyard of David open to all comers; its *paroikoi* have fled and set themselves up in the forest; no priest or deacon is left in this most splendid of the churches of Bulgaria. Theophylact sees manpower as vitally important and G18 to the *doux* of Skopje reveals his appointments policy. Only Vidin at that time was without a bishop and for that see it was vital to have someone with experience in both spiritual and material affairs.[227]

Problems could also be caused by bishops.[228] The bishop of Triaditsa's harsh treatment of one Bulgar monk, and possibly of another from the monastery of St John there, drew the censure of the whole synod of bishops. He was also responsible for a dispute with the bishop of Lipenion which could not be solved without his appearance at the synod.[229] Other monastic problems arise only in connection with outside bodies. In G12 and G19 Theophylact takes up the case of the priests of Pologos with the *doux* of Dyrrachion;[230] G30 is a reply to a question raised by the *chartophylax* about a community to which he refers by the name Ἁγιοσερρῆται. It is extremely unclear to what he is referring, whether a monastery in Serres (out of Theophylact's jurisdiction) or a monastery of St Sergios in Constantinople. It seems to have been a problem of mutiny within the community allied to an

---

likely that Bogomilism should have flourished so easily in towns and the capital; see D. Gress-Wright, 'Bogomilism in Constantinople,' *Byz* 47 (1977), 163-185.

[226] Art historians and more recently Angold, *Church and Society*, 170, have assumed that this church is Hagios Achilleios on Mikre Prespa, which we know Theophylact visited, see above, 89-90, below, 237-239, but the letter first thanks the *doux* for services rendered in Prespa and Diabolis and then goes on to ask for further help in Diabolis.

[227] G53, to Kyr Gregory Kamateros, but clearly addressed to a metropolitan II, 307-311; G122, to the bishop, 561.12-15; G40, to Niketas Polites, II, 267.1-8; G22, to John Komnenos, II, 303.9-204.24; G18, to the *doux* of Skopje, II, 191-192.

[228] G75, to Nicholas of Kerkyra, II, 401.36-37.

[229] G58, to the bishop, II, 327.2-19; on Lipenion, 333.99-103 and from the synod, G59, II, 341.74-79; on the monk, of the *kastron* of St John, G59, II, 341.79-88.

[230] G12, II, 167.6-7; G19, II, 195, both to John Komnenos.

appointments problem; Theophylact is prepared to settle for the lesser of two evils and to go up to Constantinople if necessary. We hear no more.[231] Theophylact is scrupulously correct on the question of monastic stability, sacrificing in G66 the opportunity of acquiring a *psaltes* because he had a letter only from his abbot (rather than from the powerful *charistikarios* of the monastery as well) allowing him to move. Theophylact consults the *chartophylax*, but again we hear no more.[232] A final case is of a monastery founded against Theophylact's wishes and supported as stauropegic by patriarchal authority. Here, as only otherwise in G18, where a local official is seeking to meddle in church appointments, we see Vailhé's Theophylact, fighting off the ambitions of the patriarchate, or Kazhdan's Theophylact, 'above all concerned for the rights and privileges of the archdiocese of Ochrid'.[233] There is no sign of the old eleventh-century disputes with neighbouring metropolitans; the collection shows good relations with Naupaktos and Thessalonike, and the patriarchate is normally supportive.[234]

So were the various local officials (as opposed to the fisc); Theophylact was very concerned that they should be so. Sometimes it is difficult to tell whether a *doux* or a tax-official is referred to—like Romanos Straboromanos in G17 for example or the grasping Makrembolites in G23. But we can see his relations with three *doukes* of Dyrrachion, a *doux* of Skopje, a *doux* of Veroia, an *archon* of Prespa, a 'ruler' of the Vardar and three officials appointed to

---

[231] G30, to Nikephoros the *chartophylax*, II, 229.19-231.26. Gautier emends, unconvincingly, the Ἁγιοσερρῆται of the three manuscripts to Ἁγιοσεργῖται, on the analogy of Ἁγιοσαββῖται, and assumes on the basis of ἀναβῆναι, 231.25, that the monks are in Constantinople. On both these cases in context see now Morris, *Monks and Laymen*, 151.

[232] G66, to Nikephoros the *chartophylax*, II, 365-367. Angold, *Church and Society*, 169 suggests that Theophylact had been the subject of a complaint by the patriarch; there is no direct evidence of this, and the structuring of the letter might even suggest that—far from Theophylact protesting too much—Gregory was a gift from the *chartophylax* which Theophylact is reluctantly declining. Caution is advisable here.

[233] For the Kittaba case, G82, to Michael *ho tou Chalkedonos*, II, 435.16-31, see below, 205 and fig. 6. For the issue of the bishopric of Vidin, G18 to Taronitopoulos, *doux* of Skopje, II, 191-193. See S. Vailhé, 'Achrida,' *DHGE*, I (Paris, 1912), 325; A. Kazhdan (with G. Constable), *People and Power in Byzantium: an Introduction to Modern Byzantine Studies* (Washington, DC, 1982), 28.

[234] The letter G35, to Chrysoberges metropolitan of Naupaktos, shows Theophylact preparing to come and see him at Kanina, II, 245.20-24; the letter G72, to Theodoulos metropolitan of Thessalonike, is full of fellow-feeling and fellow-suffering; G54, to Nicholas III Grammatikos, is grateful for the letter and presents.

unknown posts very near Theophylact.[235] Elsewhere I have dealt with Theophylact's method for dealing with local officials,[236] but it is clear that they are always regarded as potential allies, not as the creators of Theophylact's problems. In G79 we have a portrait of Theophylact's ideal official (Gregory Pakourianos, idealised for Gregory's relative and Theophylact's patron Adrian the Grand Domestic), which may perhaps alert us to the dangers of the position for Theophylact: he is a lily and a rose and his sweet smell rises from the poor to God. Now that he has left, who will conserve landowners' property? Who will lead to comfort those who have fallen on hard times? Who will allow orphans to testify that by being deprived of relatives they received the support of such a powerful man? Who will deliver *prostagmata* to put a limit to widowhood? Who will have eyes which will weep for the victims of injustice? Who will defend the poor against the depredations of the rich and what advocate will the rich find against the criminal and defamatory poor? What servant will the cohort of servants of God find? Who will now be deprived of necessities so that the Bulgars cannot complain?[237]

In fact Theophylact depicts officials as presenting a cushion between himself and the fisc. The real villain of the collection is the *demosion*. Individuals make an appearance from time to time: the eunuch of G31; Blachernites of G129 who was good at losing *paroikoi*; Senachereim and his emulator; Michael Antiochos—against whom Theophylact invoked the support of a holy man, Neilos, to prevent him from being sent anywhere near Ochrid. Iasites appears twice at markedly different dates but operating the same methods.[238] But the whole point of describing the fisc as the Hydra, or Briareus, is that individuals do not matter; there is always another head or limb to appear when one is cut off.

---

[235] John Doukas, John Komnenos and John Bryennios of Dyrrachion, Constantine Komnenos, *doux* of Veroia (? = the διενεργῶν in Veroia of G49); Makrembolites, archon of Prespa (only very possibly the Makrembolites of G23 or the Eumathios of G21), Constantine Doukas, ruler of the Vardar; the three officials in unknown posts are Nicholas Anemas, John Opheomachos and Gregory Pakourianos. Gregory Taronites is mentioned as concerned with Vodena, G49, II, 297.10-11.

[236] In 'Patronage.'

[237] G79, to Adrian the Grand Domestic, II, 419.18-59.

[238] Senachereim the Assyrian appears in G77, to the bishop of Kerkya, II, 407.22 and his emulator at 23-29. On the identification see Gautier, *Théophylacte*, II, 89-90. Even if he is the Theodore Senachereim of Xenophontos in 1083, the ὁ Ἀσσύριος points to a mocking use of II Kings 18:13. For Michael Antiochos, see poem 10, I, 365. A Michael Antiochos was implicated in the Anemas conspiracy. For Iasites see G11, to John Komnenos, II, 163.26 in spring 1092 and G88, to John Grammatikos of Palaiologos, II, 461.13-14, possibly ten years later, during the worst of the trouble over the Vardar village.

G79 describes the effects of the *demosion*: insolence and greed have infected the praktors, who destroy rather than collect. They regard divine and imperial law as cobwebs; they triumph over a fly but are torn by a wasp. The property of Christian people is ruined and devastated without anyone to save it—until of course Gregory came along. Officers of the fisc are responsible for many of his ills; they force him to flee to Pelagonia, they prevent him from reading, his sins heap up disasters and come home to roost in the form of a tax-collector. They are of course executioners not extortioners, δήμιοι not δημόσιοι. The letters are a litany of taxes, the *kanonikon*, the *zeugologion*, the *dekatosis*, *kastroktisia*, fishing-tax, mill-tax, general *epeiriai*.[239]

Several cases may be followed through in the correspondence, but there is one key document. In G96, Theophylact accuses the *demosion* directly. He makes nineteen different charges, all relating to recent events and against the background of a history of threats to a village of the church of Ochrid. He complains about the behaviour of a Bulgar peasant called Lazaros: his revolt against the church, his association with heretics and the immoral, his recruitment by the fisc, his accusation that Theophylact had caused a fire and other calumnies. (G98 has him accepting hospitality and clothing from the praktors.) Theophylact makes specific charges against the fisc of overriding exemptions: they have ignored the free *zeugarion* of the *klerikoi*; they have ignored the *exkousseia* from *dekatosis*; *klerikoi* have been made to pay double mill-tax and more than laymen on *strougai*; marsh is assessed as if it were good land; his *exkousseia* on the first five animals has been ignored; his *paroikoi* have been threatened; a survey has been bungled. Harvey has recently analysed this letter in terms of the general fiscal difficulties of the empire on the eve of the fiscal reforms of Alexios I. Theophylact's picture of fiscal depredation is set in a comprehensible economic context; Theophylact's problems here are those of any large landowner at the time.[240]

Some problems were very personal. His various illnesses and failures of morale,[241] the five letters on the illness and death of his brother dominate the

---

[239] Fleeing to Pelagonia: G94, II, 479.4-8; the hands of the praktors prevent him working: G29, to Mermentoulos, II, 225.11; sins and their penance: G106 (to a high ecclesiastic of smart family) I, 523.10-11. For the pun, G94, II, 479.8. For the taxes see Xanalatos, *Beiträge* and Harvey, 'The Land,' 143-149.

[240] G96, to Nikephoros Bryennios, II, 483-493. Harvey, 'The Land.'

[241] Some can be distinguished, the sore hip in G108 at Ochrid, the chest complaint, perhaps at Ekklesiai in 1106 in G110; the collapse after Demetrios's death, the malaria of G120 in 1108. In G48 he self-diagnoses a fever, a dry cough and a pain in his side. See above, 3.2.ii, 102-111, for explanations of his explicit expression.

correspondence.[242] But equally personal and threatening are problems of communication. Travel is a terrible burden to Theophylact; the Vardar an apparently impenetrable barrier.[243] The journey to the military camp is toilsome and many-dayed. But worse is the failure of communication. G18 shows what happens when a document fails to arrive. The spectre of calumny may be seen throughout. It is a constant fear and on occasion a concrete problem, as when the bishop of Triaditsa or Lazaros and his gang spread specific rumours.[244] In general the fisc and the people of Ochrid believed that

> my mountains flow with milk, that I am stuffed with I know not how many talents for my supplies, that I am immensely rich and live like a satrap, that in comparison to the riches of the archbishop those of the Persian would seem shabby, that the palaces at Susa and Ecbatana are mere huts compared with my airy, high-rise residence, where in summer I cool the furnace of my fleshiness

and that 'the archbishop of all Bulgaria ladles out with a corn ladle the gold of everyday.'[245] This he accepted with wry recognition. But the campaign of Lazaros and the *demosion*, some time between 1097 and 1103, was so efficient that he began to fear that people were starting to believe the rumours. Then he begins to quote Psalm 37.12: 'my friends and my near ones are drawn up against me.' He begins to fear that people have stopped writing to him. The campaign is now a threat to more than his estates; his very means of operation, by letters, is in peril.[246]

For the most part however Theophylact's Bulgaria is infested by the monsters of his worries and problems, his 'cares unspeakable and incorrigible about the state of the laity and the church'.[247] Theophylact's monsters can usually be traced to their lairs in classical mythology, though the Bible is the source of serpents and scorpions and the lions of Daniel who knew no fast.[248] The monsters may confuse the issues for modern scholars; for Theophylact they put a decent cloak on sordid problems while depicting a nightmarish set

---

[242] G133, II, 591; G111, II, 535.23-5; G113, II, 539.2-16; G121, II, 559; G122, II, 561. See above, 91-94, below, 244-246.

[243] G77, II, 413.85-86 expresses Theophylact's views on travelling. See C. Galatariotou, 'Travel and Perception in Byzantium,' *DOP* 47 (1993), 221-241.

[244] G18, G60, G61, G85, G87, G96, G97, G99, G100 are the letters most troubled with calumny.

[245] G96, II, 487.63-69; G129, to Michael Pantechnes, II, 583.7-9. For the truth of the rumours see above, 2.5, 62, n. 264; 67.

[246] G97, to John Peribleptenos, II, 495.7-10; G93, to Nicholas Kallikles, II, 477.2.

[247] G48, II, 295.5-6.

[248] G37, II, 253.6-7, Deut. 8:15, Daniel 14:38.

of worries; in the next chapter I consider how Theophylact dealt with them. But the monsters were a suitably epistolary way of describing his problems, and the next section will look further at the rhetoric of the letters.

3.3 The rhetoric of the collection

By rhetoric I mean various things. In general I take rhetoric to mean the art of persuasive communication, but I also take it to mean, in Byzantium, the verbal (and significantly oral) part of ceremonial, the maintenance of due proportion and order.[249] This brings it much closer to etiquette, to a comforting and recognisable practice that makes sure that the right thing is said on the right occasion, rather than the agonistic tour de force often imagined with Plato in mind, and caricatured, by those who disapprove, as 'empty rhetoric'.[250] Byzantine rhetoric is anything but empty in that it meets an everyday need which is answered in later societies by the etiquette book, the toastmaster's guide or the handbooks still published today for the deportment of weddings. The difference in Byzantine society was that the results were regarded as worthy of literary evaluation and of performance by persons of high social status. But I use 'rhetoric' in a both narrower and wider sense here to signify the reasons why Theophylact's preoccupations were packaged as they were. From this I exclude some very worthy aims. I am not embarking upon a truly rhetorical analysis of the letters, a task which is certainly a desideratum. I also leave aside an analysis by level of style, and by prose-rhythm.[251] I am as ever primarily concerned with the collection *as letters* and what in rhetoric is relevant to its epistolarity. What I offer is thoughts on

---

[249] Despite paying lip-service to the importance of imperial ceremony in Byzantium, scholars came late to analysing even imperial ceremony rigorously; see now M. McCormick, 'Analysing imperial ceremonies,' *JÖB* 35 (1985), 1-20 and *Imperial Victory. Triumphal Rulership in Late Antiquity, Byzantium and the Early Medieval West* (P&PP, Cambridge, 1986); S. MacCormack, *Art and Ceremony in Late Antiquity* (The Transformation of the Classical Heritage, 1, Berkeley, 1981); Averil Cameron, 'The Construction of Court Ritual: the Byzantine Book of Ceremonies,' in *Rituals of Royalty. Power and Ceremonial in Traditional Societies*, ed. S. Price and D. Cannadine (Cambridge, 1987), 106-136.

[250] For the best attack as well as the best defence, see B. Vickers, *In Defence of Rhetoric* (Oxford, 1988); see also *Rhetoric Revalued. Papers from the International Society for the History of Rhetoric* (Binghampton, NY, 1982).

[251] Such as for example the work of Anastasi and Maisano for rhetoric, Hunger and Ševčenko for level of style and Hörandner and Katičić for prose-rhythm: on Theophylact see the pioneering study of R. Katičić, 'Die akzentuierte Prosarhythmus bei Theophyakt von Achrida,'*Živa Antika*, 7 (1957), 66-84.

the principles of *dispositio* in the letters. It should now be apparent that I do not regard rhetoric as a one-way communication system: letters are an interactive form and Theophylact regarded an active reader as a good one. Rhetoric does not necessarily entail authorial intention.[252]

Theophylact was also very modest about his own rhetorical achievement.

> I am not a God. Why count me among the immortals? Certainly, Zeus the God of friendship teaches you to lie, even though you maintain truth in the judgements of Themis, of which you are the first. But it is enough for me to be ranked as we were before, at dekadarch or if you prefer triakontarch; as for the glory of chiliarch or strategos, I know this rank only to say yes, sir. So do not attribute to me the judgement of a Longinos, and be prepared also not to appear to others to judge contrary to the canons of Longinos.[253]

How much did the 'canons' of Longinos, or any other theorist, matter? In the late eleventh century in the west letter-writers were equipped with a new aid, the *ars dictaminis*. Before any other prose or verse genre, letters received exhaustive treatment in prescriptive works largely emanating from Bologna in the early twelfth century. But they go back to pioneering works by the monk Alberic which have a clear link to the traditional rhetoric of the schools. In view of the close links between Byzantium and Monte Cassino in the eleventh century, it is a prima facie possibility that Alberic was inspired to include letter-writing in his textbooks by his familiarity with the practice and theory of Byzantine letter-writing.[254] But to our knowledge, the Byzantines never possessed anything as formalised and helpful as the *artes*. Byzantine letter-writers were assisted above all by *mimesis* of accepted models of letter-writing

---

[252] G56, to the bishop of Semnea, II, 321.8-14. Alistair Fowler on the other hand, in 'Apology for Rhetoric,' *Rhetorica* 8 (1990), 103-118 sees the advantages of rhetoric for intentionalism.

[253] G29, to Mermentoulos, II, 225.2-8.

[254] Alberic of Monte Cassino, *Breviarium de dictamine*, partly ed. L. Rockinger, *Briefsteller und Formelbücher des elften bis vierzehnten Jahrhunderts* (Quellen und Erörterungen zur bayerischen und deutschen Geschichte, 9, Munich, 1863), II, 29-46; *Dictaminum radii*, ed. D.M. Inguanez and H.M. Willard (Miscellanea Casinense, 14, Monte Cassino, 1938); H. Hagendahl, 'Le manuel de rhétorique d'Albericus Casinensis,' *Class et Med* 17 (1956), 63-70; C.H. Haskins, 'The early artes dictandi in Italy,' *Studies in Medieval Culture* (Oxford, 1929), 170-192'; J.J. Murphy, *Rhetoric in the Middle Ages: A History of Rhetorical Theory from St Augustine to the Renaissance* (Berkeley, Los Angeles and London, 1974), 203-212. The connection between Byzantium and Monte Cassino has been much exaggerated, see G. Loud, 'Montecassino and Byzantium in the Tenth and Eleventh Centuries,' *The Theotokos Evergetis and Eleventh-century Monasticism*, ed. M. Mullett and A. Kirby (BBTT, 6.1, Belfast, 1994), 30-55.

practice,[255] but also by various types of theoretical work,[256] none of which much resembles the western *ars dictaminis*. I shall here set Theophylact's practice against two kinds of rhetorical theory.

i. *The Typoi epistolimaioi*

The first of these is the *Typoi*, of which two have survived. Their dates within late antiquity are uncertain, and their authorship even more so, but there seems little reason to doubt that they were available in some form to Byzantines composing letters.[257] The *Typoi* tell little that could not be learned elsewhere, but they do offer, like *progymnasmata*, sample efforts, fair copies, and they also list what are effectively genres, which could be deduced from practice. Some of these genres are peculiarly epistolary,[258] some simply relate to the same genre as it might be discussed in a handbook like Menander[259] or put into practice in a speech or a poem. They provide for vital social occasions, but since times had moved on, the *Typoi* no longer provided for all eleventh-century eventualities. And so some of the genres found in Theophylact's collection are instantly recognisable from the *Typoi* and possibly from Menander as well, but others make sense only in a Byzantine context. That Theophylact was genre-conscious and made use of some of the possibilities which come with genre we have seen already.[260] I here simply point to examples in Theophylact's collection of genres of both kinds, those drawn from the *Typoi* and those answering to later needs. For the first kind I take the *systatike*, the recommendatory letter, and the *paramythetike* or consolatory letter (together with other death genres); for the latter the 'arrival letter', otherwise known as the 'first letter-on-arrival-in-see', and the 'adventus letter' to an incoming governor. In one case, the consolatio, I look at the context of epistolary death-writing.

Theophylact wrote three clearly systatic letters; six others may also be considered. Some letters which recommend someone may not have been

---

[255] There are few echoes of earlier letter-writers in Theophylact: a letter of the emperor Julian; a letter of Synesios.

[256] Theophylact mentions the *Peri Hermeneias* as well as Longinos and we may be fairly sure that something like Menander Rhetor was available to him. He taught rhetoric and was clearly aware of the basic text-books of the Second Sophistic, see epp. 1 and 2.

[257] Weichert, *Demetrii et Libanii* dates 'Demetrios' to some time between the first century BC and the middle of the first century AD, and 'Proklos/Libanios' to the late fourth century AD. Eleven manuscripts attribute the work to Libanios, six to Proklos.

[258] E.g. *systatike, eucharistike, erotike, philike*.

[259] E.g. *paramythetike, symbouleutike, eutike, presbeutike*.

[260] See above, 2.1, 21 and my 'The Madness of Genre,' *Homo Byzantinus. Papers in Honor of Alexander Kazhdan*, ed. A. Cutler and S. Franklin, *DOP* 46 (1992), 240-243.

carried by him (G104, G32), others recommend someone already known to the recipient (G28, G93), and yet other letters (G112) were carried by the bearer which are not specifically systatic. I dealt above with the difficulties of detecting the bearer. But G40, G114 and G27 are clearly written to introduce and recommend the bearer to someone, while G112, G28 and G64 demand some discussion.

G27, to Gregory Kamateros, is a letter of introduction on behalf of the grandson of Michael Psellos. Theophylact uses a challenging opening, based on a reference to *Il.* 22.389: 'Even if in Hades the dead are forgotten, I at least will show the recognition I owe to a friend in terms of those he has left behind.' Theophylact then identifies the dead friend as Michael Psellos and elaborates on his eloquence and his *beneficia*. 'I know I benefited greatly from the muse of that man.' He passes directly to the bearer, his relationship and his current predicament (never spelled out but evoked with pathos): 'Don't think I am writing simply to ease my conscience, but believe it is from the depths of my heart.' He then recalls his relationship to Psellos and envisages him returning to haunt the ingrate Theophylact. 'Yes, by the charms of that man I shall suffer, afflicted by justice, God and the tongue of Psellos.' His conclusion is the request: bluntly he asks Gregory to release Theophylact from torment by giving Psellos's grandson a job. Theophylact points out Gregory's prominent position and how easy it would be for him to oblige. And he ends abruptly with his customary prayer.[261]

G112 and G114 are not unlike this letter, except that they are not primarily systatic. G112 thanks Nicholas Kallikles for his efforts on behalf of Theophylact over the Ekklesiai affair, and then asks another favour, the loan of some medical books. A last note tells Nicholas that the bearer is to be recommended to his friendship by the excellent Smyrnaios.[262] G114 is a brief note to Michael Pantechnes with his customary (to this correspondent) flippancy. 'You cause me a lot of trouble. Some people thinking that the excellent and honest man that you are is totally devoted to me never cease to bang at the door of my tranquillity to get me up to write them an introduction. And as I am normally lazy and convinced that your influence is nothing like as great as they imagine, I hesitate to give in, but when they use violence I yield and promise to write for them to your magnificence.' The bearer turns out to be a relative of the wisest and cleverest Smyrnaios. 'If you are able to render him some service,' says Theophylact, 'glory to him who has given you the ability to render service. If not, glory to him anyway. No harm to you anyway, for your power is as nothing to your will.' What we see here

---

[261] G27, to Gregory Kamateros, II, 219-221.

[262] G112, to Nicholas Kallikles, II.537.17-18: τῇ ἀγάπῃ σου συσταθήσεται.

is subversion of the *systatike* indeed, in which Theophylact runs down the power of the addressee rather than emphasising it, and blames the importunacy rather than praises the virtues of the bearer.[263]

The tone of G40 is very different. Here Theophylact asks a favour for one of his suffragan bishops (of Glavenitsa) from a friend (Niketas Polites) who is also a metropolitan. In the first sentence he begins with the formula of friendship, οἴκωθεν οἴκαδε (which is an instant signal of a *systatike*), names the bearer of the letter, uses the form of address to a bishop not of his own archdiocese, and admits it was his idea to send the bishop-bearer. He means business. He then sets out the general problem of the bishop's depression, explaining that he did his best to lift it himself and should not be blamed for neglect. He then mentions a specific problem which Niketas can help with, and asks him to give the bishop a pleasant stay, shielding him from people he does not wish to see. He ends with an assurance that today (the day of delivery in epistolary time) Niketas is doing Theophylact a favour, but tomorrow he will be doing good to a good man. And in his closing prayer, the first and great archbishop Christ presides over this act of collegial support.[264]

G64 looks as though it could have been planned as a duplicate, but turned out differently. It is a letter to the patriarch on behalf of the bishop of Pelagonia. The first sentence emphasises the relationship between Theophylact and the patriarch and the balance of *officia* and *beneficia* between them. Then the bishop of Pelagonia makes an appearance because of his wish to meet the patriarch and gain from him 'refreshment'. But instead of explaining the bishop's need, Theophylact emphasises the good fortune of the bishop in seeing the patriarch at close quarters and asks for the patriarch's prayers for himself.[265]

Systatic letters are unusual among Byzantine letters in that they require the intrusion of a third person into essentially monoaxial discourse.[266] The five elements of a formal *systatike* are 1) the writer, 2) the receiver, 3) the relationship between them, 4) the bearer, his virtues, connections, needs and 5) the specific request made on his behalf from the writer to the receiver. Theophylact's letters show that rhetoric is no straitjacket for the practising epistolographer even when the type is well known from the time of Cicero.[267] The weight given to each of the elements varies in each case.

---

[263] G114, to Michael Pantechnes, II, 541.

[264] G40, to Niketas Polites, II, 267.

[265] G64, to Nicholas the patriarch, II, 361.

[266] For exceptions among Theophylact's letters see above 2.1, 18-19.

[267] Cicero, *Ad familiares*, 13 is composed entirely of seventy-nine letters of recommendation, see L. Wilkinson, *CHCL*, 247-249. On classical recommendatory letters

The letter to Gregory Kamateros on behalf of Psellos's grandson concentrates almost entirely on the fourth and fifth elements of the *systatike*. The normal balance of reinforcing the primary relationship is overridden and the effect of the plight of the young man and the strength of Theophylact's recollections of the grandfather are all the greater. Theophylact also fails to underline the possibilities of the parallelism between the Theophylact-Gregory and Psellos-Theophylact relationships. It is not that he is too proud to point out something so obvious; he does so in G28, when asking Theodore Smyrnaios to look after Demetrios. Gregory's attachment is taken for granted; it is enough for Theophylact to play up the nature of his own distress so that Gregory will help him and so the young man.

In G114, the letter to Pantechnes on behalf of the relative of Theodore Smyrnaios, elements 1) 2) and 3) dominate, 4) is just about identified and 5) is left obscure. (G112, also carried by him, to Nicholas Kallikles, simply identifies the fourth element). Here a close relationship with Michael Pantechnes has a quite different effect. There they are so sure of the relationship that even the bearer suffers in the general undermining of normal ceremonial. It is hardly likely that Theophylact is describing accurately the request for an introduction, but it is clear that he is not asking for anything specific from Michael. In G40, to Niketas Polites for the bishop of Glavenitsa, 1) and 2) are drawn by the lines of ceremonial and the assumption that the other will have the same principles of concern for a bishop as Theophylact. But the emphasis is upon 4) and 5). G64, to the patriarch for the bishop of Pelagonia, lays the emphasis on 1), 2) and 3), but 4) and 5) are also present. To explain the differences would need a full analysis of the relationships of all these correspondents as well as an understanding of the urgency of the particular request. What is clear is that the provisions for a *systatike* make a very wide range of variations possible and Theophylact is equal to the opportunity.

Another type of letter which should be examined in detail is the *paramythetike*, the consolatio. In the collection G132 consoles a brother of Psellos for the death of Psellos, G73 consoles a patron for the loss of his brother-in-law; G37 is a celebration rather than a consolation to a spiritual father for the death of his own spiritual father and G39 consoles a friend for

---

see C.W. Keyes, 'The Greek Letter of Introduction,' *AmJPhil* 56 (1935), 28-44; C.-H. Kim, *Form and Structure of the Familiar Greek Letter of Recommendation* (Society of Biblical Literature Dissertation Series, 4, Ann Arbor, 1985); H. Cotton, 'Greek and Latin Epistolary Formulae: Some Light on Cicero's Letter-Writing,' *AmJPhil* 105 (1984), 409-425; and, more generally on the relationship between Greek theory and Latin practice, K. Thraede, *Grundzüge griechisch-römischer Brieftopik* (Zetemata, 48, Munich, 1970).

the loss of his father.[268] The genre should be seen in the context of rhetorical provision for death in Byzantium and for the capacity of the letter for dealing with death. Death was well regulated in Byzantine society,[269] and many though not all of the classical death-genres were still available to the eleventh-century writer.[270] It is often difficult to pin down the social setting of any one genre;[271] descriptions of funerals are as rare as descriptions of the moment of death.[272] Alexiou suggests that the ritual lament retained its significance throughout the period, and it is clear that its rhetorical (and male) counterpart, the *epitaphios logos*,[273] did so too. Other death-writings may have found their audience among literary salons or perhaps on commemorative occasions in private houses.[274]

---

[268]   G132, to a brother of Psellos, II, 589; G37, to Symeon the *hegoumenos* of the monastery of Anaplous, II, 253-257; G73, to Nikephoros Melissenos on the death of the *sebastokrator* Isaac, II, 389-393; G39, to Michael Pantechnes, II, 263-265. Other candidates are G63, where Theophylact assures the bishop of Pelagonia that another good official will come along and G133, described as a *paramythetike* in one manuscript.

[269]   J. Kyriakis, 'Byzantine Burial Customs: Care of the Deceased from Death to the Prothesis,' *GOThR* 19 (1974), 58; M. Alexiou, *The Ritual Lament in Greek Tradition* (Cambridge, 1974); for modern parallels see L.M. Danforth, *The Death Rituals of Rural Greece* (Princeton, 1982).

[270]   The *epikedeion* was a casualty; for various stages of its earlier popularity see F. Cairns, *Generic Composition in Greek and Roman Poetry* (Edinburgh, 1972), 90-99; Alexiou, *Ritual Lament*, 84, 107-108; already in the tenth century it was treated as a verse genre synonymous with the *epitaphion* or *epithanation*, *Souda*, ed. A. Adler (Leipzig, 1931), 360.

[271] For exceptions among Theophylact's letters see above 2.2, 27-28. On circumstances for *epitaphioi logoi*, e.g. the orations pronounced on Nicholas Hagiotheodorites by Euthymios Malakes in Constantinople when the death was first announced, and by Eustathios in Thessalonike when the cortege bringing him back to the capital had stopped along the Via Egnatia, see A. Papadopoulos-Kerameus, *Noctes Petropolitanae* (St Petersburg, 1913), 154-162; J. Darrouzès, 'Notes sur Euthyme Tornikès, Euthyme Malakès et Georges Tornikès,' *REB* 23 (1965), 158.

[272]   For such descriptions see Gregory of Oxeia, ep. 2, ed. P. Gautier, 'Les lettres de Grégoire, higoumène d'Oxia,' *REB* 31 (1973), 213; Euthymios Tornikes's description of the last moments of the logothete is described by Darrouzès, 'Les discours d'Euthyme Tornikès (1200-1205),' *REB* 26 (1968), 94 as 'une pièce unique pour plusieurs siècles'. The death of saints is regularly and schematically described at this date.

[273]   On *epitaphios logos* see Menander Rhetor, II.XI, ed. D.A. Russell and N.G. Wilson, *Menander Rhetor* (Oxford, 1981), 171-179.

[274]   Cf. the second of two speeches of Gregory Antiochos on the death of his father in Esc. Y Π 0, 2v-6v; 7-14r, described by Darrouzès, 'Les discours d'Euthyme Tornikès (1200-1205),' *REB* 26 (1968), 63. It is admittedly hard to imagine the performance of some enkomia, see P. Gautier, 'Éloge funèbre de Nicolas de la Belle Source par Michel Psellos, moine à l'Olympe,' *Byzantina* 6 (1974), 19.

Function as well as occasion played a part; the Byzantines knew well which genres were intended to praise, which to mourn and which to console.[275]

Of the genres which praised, the *epitaphios logos* had great popularity, more perhaps even than the *basilikos logos*, certainly more than the inaugural lecture.[276] Some works are called *epitaphios* which were not pronounced at the funeral, like Gregory Antiochos's speech one hundred and twenty days after the death of Manuel; often however these have the general title of *enkomion*. The other prose genre was the monody,[277] which belonged to the class of genres which mourned; it was remarkably popular,[278] perhaps because it was less formal than the epitaphios, gave full scope for personal response[279] and allowed a much freer choice in the combination of the various elements of the scheme, *threnos* and *enkomion*, past, present and future.[280] As in the letter, brilliance in the monody involved conciseness.[281] The verse genres also flourished; even if no popular lament has survived, writers like John Mauropous and Nicholas Kallikles specialised in the epitaph (which may well

---

[275] Contra A. Vogt and I. Hausherr, 'Oraison funèbre de Basil I par son fils Léon VI le Sage,' *OCP* 26 (1932), 24-25: 'les distinctions anciennes avec leurs termes propres sont tombées: toute oraison funebre est un épitaphe.' Titles of genres are certainly used in a sense inconsistent with classical usage, but many of these changes had occurred by the time of Late Antiquity or the Second Sophistic, cf. Menander, *Peri epideiktikon*, ed. Russell and Wilson, 171, and writers could depart from the received form for literary effect, e.g. Euthymios Tornikes's funeral oration on Demetrios, ed. Darrouzès, *REB* 26 (1968), 106. Michael Italikos differentiates *enkomion* from monody, see Gautier, *Michel Italikos*, 111; Eustathios discusses the properties of the *epitaphios logos*, E. Miller, *Catalogue des manuscrits grecs de la bibliothèque de l'Escurial* (Paris, 1848), 201-202.

[276] For a preliminary listing of twelfth-century examples see my *Theophylact*, fig. II, 832-836.

[277] See Menander, II.XVI, *Peri Monodias*, ed. Russell and Wilson, 200-206; A. Garzya, 'Monodie inédite de Nicéphore Basilakes,' *BS* 30 (1969), 201-202; J. Soffel, *Die Regeln Menanders für die Leichenrede in ihrer Tradition dargestellt, herausgegeben, übersetzt und kommentiert* (Beiträge zur klassischen Philologie, 57, Meisenheim am Glan, 1974); D. Hadjis, 'Was bedeutet Monodie in der byzantinischen Literatur?' *Byzantinische Beiträge*, ed. J. Irmscher (Berlin, 1964), 177-185.

[278] There are four examples by Michael Italikos alone, nos. 3, 7, 9, 11, ed. Gautier, 81-88, 102-104, 110-115, 129-134.

[279] Though famous scholars must have competed for the opportunity to pronounce the official funeral oration on distinguished persons and particularly the imperial family, it was also common practice for the role to be filled by close relatives and pupils of the deceased, see *Theophylact*, fig. II. This issue needs further consideration.

[280] Menander, II.XVI, ed. Russell and Wilson, 205.

[281] Menander, ibid., 207: 'mourners do not tolerate long delays or lengthy speeches at times of misfortune and unhappiness' (tr. Russell and Wilson).

have been inscribed)[282] and Theophylact's are by no means the only *threnoi* of his time.[283] The consolatio combined the functions of lament and epitaphios while adding the personal element of condolence. It must praise the dead man's achievements and express the loss felt by friends and family before allaying the grief of the bereaved by pointing to the blessed state of the deceased and exhorting the bereaved to rejoice.[284]

So much for the type; what about the form? Letters have the advantage over speeches and poems in dealing with death in that they are habitually concerned with human emotion. They have several disadvantages. Firstly the restraint which we have seen was expected of the Byzantine letter. Unrestrained grief, just like unrestrained gossip, would appear out of place. Secondly the strong sense of genre excludes the tragic.[285] Thirdly, letters are habitually concerned with a single relationship, that of writer and recipient. But like the *systatike*, the *paramythetike* was structurally designed to incorporate a third person. And it appeared naturally epistolary; for many medieval letter-writers the letter was itself a consolation.[286] But though *consolationes* account for perhaps half of Byzantine letters dealing with death, other treatments of death are to be found.

Death can be represented as a nuisance, as in Basil's letter after the death of one of his servants, or as a pretended excuse for not writing. Or it can be used in a jocular announcement: 'Know then that my soul only just missed taking up residence in Hades,' or a writer may with great formality express the simple message, 'I was surprised to have a letter from you; I thought you were dead.' There are letters thanking the correspondent for a consolatio, like Michael Italikos's letter to his brother after the death of Constantine Hagiotheodorites, which points out the great drawback of the the consolatio,

---

[282] See W.A. Buckler, 'Deux inscriptions de Constantinople,' *Byz* 3 (1926), 305-309; S. Petrides, 'Épitaphe de Théodore Kamateros,' *BZ* 19 (1910), 8-10.

[283] On the *threnos*, see Alexiou, *Ritual Lament*, though she is weakest on rhetoric and omits most of the Komnenian material. Though in Greek tradition the threnos belongs to the women's side of mourning, eleventh- and twelfth-century examples are by men, see *Theophylact*, fig. II. It is interesting to note in view of Theophylact's poems 14 and 15 that several (e.g. by Isidore Meles, Christopher of Mytilene) are by brothers.

[284] Menander, II.IX, *Peri paramythetikou*, ed. Russell and Wilson, 161-165; J. Bauer, *Die Trostreden des Gregorius von Nyssa in ihren Verhältnissen zur antiken Rhetorik* (Marburg, 1892); there is no general study of the Byzantine *consolatio* to compare with C. Favez, *La consolation latine chrétienne* (Paris, 1937).

[285] Niketas Magistros, ep. 12, ed. L.G. Westerink, *Lettres d'un exilé* (Paris, 1973), 85, answers criticism of (another's) overplaying grief in a letter.

[286] E.g. Basil, ep. 220, ed. Deferrari, III, 274-276.

that it cannot erase the memory of the beloved. Letters can give practical advice to the bereaved or apply the imagery of death to the writer himself.[287]

The converse of the consolatio, the announcement of death, is a common genre in the letter, like Theophylact's G121 and 122. Occasionally we see the two frames of a consolatio, such as Niketas Magistros's announcement of the death of what he calls a second father and then the reply to the correspondent who had in a consolation praised the first letter's eloquence. It is the second letter which describes how he received the news of the death and the effect this had on him, how emotion touched his spirit so that he could think of nothing else and how it would remain with him for the rest of his life.[288]

But the quintessentially epistolary funerary genre is the consolatio. This is not to say that there are no consolatory speeches or poems, but they are not common. Nor is the consolatio always entirely free-standing; there is a consolatory element included in the *epitaphios logos*.[289] But the epistolary consolatio should not be seen as simply a truncated form of the *paramythetikos logos*, or even of the *epitaphios*. There is an element of *enkomion* in the *paramythetikoi*; both are concerned with the men's part rather than the women's, but their function is different.[290] There are however differences between *paramythetikos logos* and consolatory letter; one is the intimacy of a single recipient, another is the immediacy of a letter which presents itself as written as soon as the news is heard rather than composed at leisure to be delivered on a future occasion; the emotional time is very different.

This intimacy and immediacy is often well exploited by Byzantine epistolographers, at their best expressing in terms of the relationships of the correspondents their respective relationships with the dead.[291] Alexiou's statement of the functions of the traditional lament can also be applied to the consolatio: 'Objectively it is designed to honour and appease the dead, while

---

[287] Basil, ep. 3, ed. Deferrari, I, 26-28; Michael Italikos, op. 27, ed. Gautier, 182; John, monk of Mt Latros, ep. 5, ed. Darrouzès, *Épistoliers byzantins*, 214; Niketas Magistros, ep. 19, ed. Westerink, 99; Michael Italikos, ep. 4, ed. Gautier, 89-91; Niketas Magistros, ep. 22, ed. Westerink, 109; Nicholas Mystikos, ep. 104, ed. R.J.H. Jenkins and L.G. Westerink, *Nicholas I Patriarch of Constantinople, Letters* (DOT, 2, CFHB, 6, Washington, DC, 1973), 384.

[288] Niketas Magistros, epp. 1, 3, ed. Westerink, 54-55, 58-60.

[289] For consolation in *epitaphios logos* see Menander, *Peri epideiktikon*, XI, ed. Russell and Wilson, 176-178.

[290] See E.R. Curtius, *European Literature and the Latin Middle Ages*, tr. W.R. Trask (London, 1952), 80; A.R. Littlewood, 'Byzantine Letter-writing in the Tenth Century,' *ANRW*, III (Berlin, still forthcoming) makes the point well.

[291] Gregory of Nazianzos, ep. 76, ed. Gallay, I, 94.

subjectively it gives expression to a wider range of conflicting emotions',[292] of which sympathy is only one.

Given this spectrum of opportunity, where do Theophylact's *consolationes* fit? Again their range is great. At one end is G37, hardly a *consolatio* at all. It is addressed to the *hegoumenos* of Anaplous and is carried by one of the monks of the monastery. Theophylact retails his reaction to the news for which he had been burning, and his entourage's reaction to his reaction to the news of the death of the ex-abbot of the monastery. Theophylact launches immediately into his previous worries about the abbot's wish to become an *enkleistos*, apostrophising the devil and his temptations. But the old man is now beyond the devil's temptations and has found his way to heaven, from which the devil once fell. All is well. Theophylact then recounts again his reaction, of pleasure and happiness, of fraternal joy. A *consolatio* is quite out of place in this story of a monastic happy ending, and Theophylact turns to bemoaning his own troubles and embraces the monks, his brothers.[293]

In contrast, G132 is a short, but formally correct *consolatio* to the brother of Psellos. He begins with an assurance that he understands the other's emotional state. He explains his own distress, as befitting friendship, and suggests that he is doubly afflicted, by his own distress and by his inability to console his friend in person. That is why he consoles him by letter with the thought that his brother is not dead but has migrated to God, and that he has been delivered from a life full of care and illnesses and has attained the Lord, who is full of grace. He ends almost curtly: 'You are not the only one to know his life; we all know who he was.' This letter begins properly with mourning, the brother's and Theophylact's, and adroitly shifts the emphasis into an exhortation to the brother to accept the death in the proper spirit. It might perhaps have been inappropriate to mourn the great Psellos in a more obviously eloquent—or personal—manner.[294]

Considerations of propriety also prevail in G73, to Nikephoros Melissenos on the death of the *sebastokrator*, at the other end of Theophylact's range. It is long (556 words), elaborate and obscure, full of the ceremonial demanded on the death of an imperial personage. It opens with a neat reversal of function: 'Holy lord, your letters always drop the dew of consolation upon us' and the death is introduced as part of information Theophylact had received about his correspondent's state of health and spirit. Immediately he brings in the consolation of God's calm and hopes that the caesar will find it

---

[292] Alexiou, *Ritual Lament*, 55.
[293] G37, to the *hegoumenos* of Anaplous, II, 253-257.
[294] G132, to the brother of Psellos on his death, II, 589.

equally comforting. He then with ultimate tact raises the question of the caesar's own preparation for death, which he mourns in advance and brings the subject back to the relations of Theophylact and the caesar. It is a letter from client to patron, making the proper moves at the proper time. He ends with a gift of fish and hopes for the bodily and spiritual refreshment of his patron. Imperial imagery, ceremonial balancing and archiepiscopal *parainesis* produce another variation on the theme.[295]

A last consolatio, to Michael Pantechnes after the death of his father, also sticks closely to the rules. Of these letters it is the closest to the classic tripartite division of mourning, consolation and exhortation. It begins on a high note of mourning and the first paragraph after a double anaphora (οἴχεται, οἴχεται; ποῦ, ποῦ, ποῦ, ποῦ) sums up ἀλλὰ βαβαί, οἷον πέπονθα, how I suffered. His is the duty to mourn the great John, now brilliant in glory, in the presence of Jesus. His second paragraph centres on Michael's reaction. The star has deserted the earth but has become a sun with God. And imperceptibly Theophylact moves into *parainesis*. 'To think of his qualities, consider also that heaven is worthy of them. Why weep for someone returning to his own...?' and by the end of the paragraph Michael is urged to rejoice. It is selfish to prefer our pleasure in living with John when he is better off in heaven. The final paragraph is more personal, alluding to the close relationship between Theophylact and Michael. Michael is to remind us of the deceased, his gentleness to subordinates, his pleasantness, his circumspection and wisdom, his piety and fear of God. Michael will show that his branches from John's root carry all the fruits and show the joys of God and man. This is a much more personal though correct consolatio.[296]

These genres of recommendation and consolation can easily be put in a long pattern of epistolary exemplars. My two other genres cannot, at least not in quite the same way. While the 'arrival-in-see letter' can easily be paralleled from other writers of the eleventh and twelfth centuries[297] and is a kind of *epibaterion*,[298] a speech on arrival, it has particular poignance for the circumstances of the period. And while the 'adventus letter' to an incoming governor is a kind of *prosphonetikon*, a speech of address, or a special kind of

---

[295] G73, to the caesar, II, 389-393.

[296] G39, to Michael Pantechnes, II, 263-265.

[297] E.g. George Tornikes, ep. 21, to the metropolitan of Athens, ed. Darrouzès, 152-157.

[298] On the *epibaterion* (second variety, on arrival at a city other than the arriver's *patris*) see Menander, III, ed. Russell and Wilson, 94-115; it is inverted since the hallmark of the genre is joy.

epibaterion,[299] it takes on its own colour from the particular needs of late eleventh- and twelfth-century official and patronage relations.

Three of Theophylact's letters appear to have been written very soon after his arrival at Ochrid. G5, to Adrian the Grand Domestic, opens with a series of addresses and oppositions designed to establish the relationship between himself and Adrian.[300] He then turns to his own position. Evils have piled up on one another like Ossa on Pelion or the Giants' battlements at Chalane. He solicits the other's ear for an account of his condition. The listener is to contrast what is said with what is not said—which may be more eloquent. The whole of the second paragraph is built on the myth of Herakles as the slave of Omphale. Theophylact develops the story using Plutarch to describe the nature of the servitude, buttling, under the instruction of a eunuch who pulls his hair because he doesn't like hair. Herakles grinds corn with women who sing raucously like donkeys ignorant of rhythm. So suffered, says Theophylact, the son of Zeus, until the time came for him to be delivered. Theophylact then draws the moral of his narrative. Herakles was favoured in comparison with Theophylact. His captress was a beautiful queen; Theophylact is the captive of barbarian slaves, dirty, smelling of sheepskin and as poor in resources as they are rich in evil. The point of the letter is reached: he asks Adrian to deliver him from this slavery lest he die of shame before his time. The real shame, he remarks dryly, is with those who tolerate it.

G6, probably to Theodore Smyrnaios, is in similar vein. He begins with a quotation from Euripides, 'this man is no longer himself'. 'I hadn't yet reached Ochrid when already, unhappy lover, I longed for the city which holds you.' He launches into another tour de force, this time a landscape of Hades, with poisonous breaths and Empedoclean monsters with neckless heads. He draws the parallel quickly: 'For what Achridiot is not a neck without a head, not knowing how to honour God or man? It is in the middle of monsters like this that I am condemned to live...' His ambitions are dashed; his honoured position as eagle on the sceptre of Zeus is cast down so that he walks on foot and lives in the mud with frogs. And they, not usually offered Zeus's bird to play with, jump on his back, muddy and stinking, and cry discordantly like beasts of the marsh, imagining they sing a song of victory, but beak and claws are still to be drawn. The eagle looks to the sun, but its rays are unclear; his correspondent is in full view and illumines also the little eaglets around him. Is it in vain, asks Theophylact, that the eagle wishes to

---

[299] On the *prosphonetikon*, Menander, X, ed. Russell and Wilson, 164-171; on the *epibaterion*, III (third variety, address to a governor), ed. Russell and Wilson, 95-103. On *adventus*, see MacCormack, *Art and Ceremony*, 17-89.

[300] G5, to Adrian the Grand Domestic, II, 143.2-3.

live among the blessed? If so may Theodore be condemned to inhabit this lake of evils and the frogs it spawns! A quick reference to gout establishes the interactive note, and a final long prayer wishes the other relief from pain and Theophylact deliverance from his ills.[301]

G7, to the *didaskalos* of the Great Church, Niketas *ho tou Serron*, is much shorter and apologises for not drawing up before his eyes the vast stage of his tragedies. He refers him instead to two other letters to other people; he solicits the prayers of the *didaskalos tou evangeliou* which he is sure will be heard, to improve his position.[302]

These letters have much in common. They depict life in the provinces to a metropolitan audience; all present a picture of bleak exile and deprivation, and above all a sense of humiliation and ill-fittedness. Herakles is too clumsy to pour wine; the eagle is ill adapted for life on the marsh. They are liminal letters from a *maistor ton rhetoron* suddenly become a bishop. He looks back to his colleagues and a major patron, and maintains his relationship with them through elaborate and elegant description of his woes, suiting the more complicated Empedoclean myth to the teacher surrounded by pupils (his eaglets), the simpler myth of Herakles to the soldier. Nothing can be learned from them about actual conditions in Ochrid or Theophylact's actual reactions to what he found; his reactions were determined before he reached Ochrid, and the need to establish his credentials as unchanged is clear. It would have been impossible for him to arrive in Ochrid and paint a picture of the idyllic Macedonian highlands and his splendid cathedral; essential rather to mark his new position vis à vis his old.

The last genre (the adventus letter) was of less emotional and more political importance. Four 'first letters to incoming governors' are preserved in the collection, and they bear a common pattern. The officials are John Komnenos and John Bryennios of Dyrrachion, Constantine Doukas of 'the Vardar' and Gregory Pakourianos, Theophylact's favourite official, to whose Dionysios he plays Plato.[303]

---

[301]   G6, II, 147-149. The identification by A. Leroy-Molinghen, 'Le destinataire de la lettre Finetti I de Théophylacte de Bulgarie,' *Byz* 36 (1966), 431-437, of the recipient as Theodore Smyrnaios is surely correct. Gautier's convenient attribution of what would otherwise be a lost letter to the *epi ton deeseon* mentioned in G7, II, 151.8-9 makes nothing of the teaching role apparent in the letter, but Gautier suggests that (like Eustathios of Thessalonike) he may have combined the jobs of *epi ton deeseon* and *hypatos ton philosophon*. G6 and G28 are surely to the same recipient, ἀνθρώπων...χαριέστατε, who like the Theodore Smyrnaios of the *Timarion* suffered from gout.

[302]   G7, II, 151. There is surely some element of parody here.

[303]   John Komnenos, G10, II, 161; John Bryennios, G86, II, 453-455; Constantine Doukas, G118, II, 549; Gregory Pakourianos, G68, II, 373-375.

In these letters Theophylact bemoans the fact that he cannot render *proskynesis* in person to the official, but proceeds to do so by letter.[304] He has first to counter the accusation of excess *parresia*, in deigning to address someone he had never met.[305] He wishes him good fortune in his new tasks,[306] alludes to the wretched state of the church in Bulgaria and ways in which he can help;[307] the bearer will describe this fully;[308] the official is god-like,[309] youthful and vigorous[310] (or of mature years),[311] like his father[312] (or a welcome new broom)[313] and Theophylact prays to God to give him every assistance in his task.[314]

Two rather different examples are also preserved, to Nicholas Anemas and to John Opheomachos. It is quite possible that Theophylact knew these officials before they arrived in Bulgaria; the letter to Bryennios also suggests prior acquaintance. G32, to Anemas, begins with a quotation from the *Orestes* of Euripides and proceeds via Aristophanes to explain it. Nicholas is his φιλτάτη μοι κεφαλή and Theophylact is excited and jubilant at his arrival. He then breaks into the psalms and Isaiah to hymn it. Anemas is to be the man who chases away evil. In the past, says Theophylact, this has been caused, now by the *kastroktistes*, now by the *katepano*. But now all will be different and *logos* will reign. A final note asks his help for Constantine Choirosphaktes, whom (a joke?) he characterises as ἀφελέστερος καὶ μαλακώτερος, weak and feeble.[315]

G69, to John Opheomachos, is yet another variant, a parainetic version. 'What is this?' he says, 'Even the good John has been sent to battle with Laestrygonians and Cyclopes.' Theophylact warns him to emulate Odysseus in cleverness in dealing with evil, and wishes him the *moly*, which Odysseus needed to remain himself, to help him. If John plays his cards right he will be able to return in a cloud of success safe and sound to his near and dear. Theophylact predicts Olympic victories which he will celebrate like

---

[304] G118, to Constantine Doukas, II, 549.6-7.
[305] E.g. G68, to Gregory Pakourianos, II, 373.3-4.
[306] E.g. G10, to the son of the *sebastokrator*, II, 161.6-7.
[307] E.g. G10, II, 161.16-17.
[308] E.g. G86, to Bryennios, II, 453.23-24.
[309] E.g. G10, II, 161.13-14.
[310] E.g. G68, to Gregory Pakourianos, II, 373.13-15.
[311] E.g. G86, to Bryennios, II, 453.2 (subtly).
[312] E.g. G10, to the son of the *sebastokrator*, II, 161.11-12; G118, to Constantine Doukas, II, 549.19-21.
[313] E.g. G68, to Gregory Pakourianos, II, 373.15.
[314] E.g. G68, II, 375.37-38.
[315] G32, to Nicholas Anemas, II, 237-239.

Simonides or Bacchylides or Pindar.[316] Another tour de force, built on a single quotation[317] rather than the ebullient mixing of G32, but in a similar tone. In both cases he is speaking to a younger acquaintance or friend who is coming for a tour of duty in Bulgaria, rejoicing at his arrival and wishing him well for his stay. They have a shared culture, his friends can read his riddles. He assumes their support, querying only their ability to win the palms.

ii. *Characteristics of the letter*

So in Theophylact's letters distinct genres (or types) may be distinguished, which create a loose framework for letters which fall into that genre. We have seen how Theophylact varies the range and tone of the same type and on occasion how new types have been created for new circumstances.[318] Rhetoric is clearly here an aid to composition. But the theoretical literature of rhetoric did not restrict itself to lists of types, and we have seen that systematic instructions on letter-writing were not available to him. Treatment of the letter comes more in passing references, at the most an excursus like that of 'Demetrios' in the *Peri Hermeneias*. Byzantine letters, and Theophylact's with them, conform to Demetrios's requirements. There are epistolary subjects as well as styles (logic and science are excluded); a letter is not just one side of a conversation, but more elaborate; it is a brief token of friendship and the icon of the soul. It demands a combination of two styles: the charming and the plain.[319]

But there is another view of the Byzantine letter and how it should be written. Gregory of Nazianzos, a model of epistolary style for many Byzantines,[320] described the essential characteristics of a good letter as

---

[316] G69, to John Opheomachos, II, 377.

[317] Homer, *Od.* 10.305, but the whole letter is Odyssean.

[318] A full comparative analysis of the letters of Psellos and John Mauropous is needed before suggesting with any confidence that Theophylact is initiating a genre. See however my 'Originality in the Byzantine Letter: the Case of Exile,' *Originality and Innovation in Byzantine Literature, Art and Music*, ed. A.R. Littlewood (Oxford, 1995), 39-58 and 5.3, 256-260, below.

[319] Demetrios, *Peri Hermeneias*, 223-234, ed. R. Roberts, *Demetrius on Style* (Cambridge, 1902), 173-177.

[320] Photios, ep. 207 (233), ed. B. Laourdas and L.G. Westerink, *Photii epistolae et Amphilochia*, II (Leipzig, 1984), 107; for John Mauropous, see A. Karpozilos, *The Letters of Joannes Mauropous, Metropolitan of Euchaita* (CFHB, 34, Thessalonike, 1990), 33-34; Joseph Rhakendytes, *Rhetorike Synopsis*, ed. C. Walz, *Rhetores graeci*, III (Stuttgart and Tübingen, 1834), 559; see Theophylact, G60, to the bishop of Triaditsa, II, 345.44-46; G29, to Mermentoulos, II, 227.29-30.

συντομία, σαφήνεια and χάρις:[321] brevity, clarity and grace. I shall look at each of these in turn in the letters of Theophylact.

Syntomia

Theophylact cannot have been unaware of the theoretical idea of the *metron* of a letter. The author of the *Peri Hermeneias* declared that 'a letter is the heart's good wishes in brief'[322] and notes that expanded letters cease to be letters and become treatises. Elsewhere the idea of clarity and brevity is compared to the process of aiming a bow.[323] This idea is often to the fore of letter-writers' minds.[324] But brevity is not always thought to be a good thing in practice. Gregory of Nazianzos in letter 73 apologises, and sometimes we may gain an impression that the *metron* is being invoked as an excuse for not writing at length, for fear that the recipient should feel he is not getting good value from his correspondent.[325] Gregory in his letter to Nikoboulos, despite his general recommendation of brevity, suggests that a writer would adapt his length to his subject.[326]

Of Theophylact's letters only thirteen[327] are longer than 750 words and most are around 300. He is aware of considerations of length, apologising[328] for inadequate coverage, blaming his health for a brief letter[329] or the sudden appearance of a letter-bearer.[330] The *metron* is evoked in G82, where he is clearly regretful that he was not able to complain at greater length.[331] Exceptions should perhaps be examined. The long letters fall into different categories. Some are business letters which spell out explicitly the business on hand, emphasising over and over again salient points (like the letters to the bishop of Triaditsa[332] and to the bishop Gregory Kamateros[333]), or massing

---

[321] Gregory of Nazianzos, ep. 51, to Nikoboulos, ed. Gallay, I, 66.

[322] Demetrios, *Peri Hermeneias*, 228, ed. Roberts, 174.

[323] 'Proklos', *Epistolomaioi charakteres*, ed. Hercher, *Epistolographi Graeci*, 7.

[324] E.g. Gregory of Nazianzos, ep. 50, ed. Gallay, I, 64; Nicholas Mystikos, ep. 4, ed. Jenkins and Westerink, 24-26.

[325] E.g. Gregory of Nazianzos, ep. 73, ed. Gallay, I, 92; ep. 54, ed. Gallay, 70; Basil, ep. 12, ed. Deferrari, I, 104; ep. 19, ed. Deferrari, 122.

[326] Gregory of Nazianzos, ep. 51, ed. Gallay, I, 66.

[327] G4, G45, G53, G58, G59, G60, G77, G79, G81, G85, G96, G98, G127. There is a noticeable gap between the longest of the 'short' letters (550 words), G73, to the caesar and the shortest of the 'long' letters, G4, to the ex-*basilissa* (770 words).

[328] G7, to the *didaskalos* of the Great Church, II, 151.2-6.

[329] G124, to the *chartophylax* Nikephoros, II, 565.2-3.

[330] G117, II, 547.2-3.

[331] G82, to Michael *ho tou Chalkedonos*, II, 435.25.

[332] G58, 59, 60; II, 327-349.

[333] G53, II, 307-311.

relevant detail to convince the recipient of the urgency and severity of the complaint (like the letters of the Lazaros crisis[334]); it may be that Theophylact had long resigned himself to the need for detail to his major patrons.[335] Some are long because the recipient had asked for explanation or expansion,[336] others simply apparently because Theophylact lost the power to control his material.[337] A final group is of letters which are carefully crafted and of great literary pretension where length is demanded by the form. G4 to the ex-*basilissa* Maria is a tour de force of travel, G81 to Gregory Taronites an extended *enkomion*, G127 to Gregory Kamateros a sparkling satiric conceit based (also exceptionally) on a third person, Theodore Chryselios.[338] Length then was sometimes politically necessary, sometimes a fault of composition and sometimes a luxury to be indulged in for special correspondents on special occasions.

Especial brevity is also worth examining. Health accounts for several of the very short letters (around 100 words or less). G103 to the Bulgarians he taught, G107 to the *despoina*, G124 to the ex-*chartophylax* Nikephoros.[339] Letters of considerable emotional content may be very brief.[340] G125 plays on a proverb: the point of the letter is to urge someone to do what he was doing already, so ceases to let him get on with it; G119 is a simple gift tag.[341] The remaining brief letters are addressed (or could be assigned to) Michael Pantechnes, with whom Theophylact appears to have had a particularly easy relationship marked by friendly sarcasm. G114 is the subverted *systatike*; G115 is a simple rule for gauging Theophylact's situation; G116 a simple line to accompany an unknown bearer; G129 is an invitation to come and stay; G130 provocatively claims its writer is glad not to have letters from Michael; G131

---

[334] G96 and 98, II, 483-493, 499-505.

[335] G79 and G85, II, 414-423, 445-451; both to Adrian the Grand Domestic.

[336] G85 is a reply to such a request; the previous letter was a προφητικόν γράμμα. G127 is a reply to a letter in which he was asked who the Kyklops was; G77 seems to be a clearer version of G75.

[337] G45, II, 281-287.

[338] G4, to Maria the ex-*basilissa*, II, 137-141; G81, to Gregory Taronites, II, 427-433; G127, to Gregory Kamateros, II, 571-579.

[339] G103, to the Bulgars he taught, II, 577.4-5; G107, to the *despoina* who visited him when he was ill, II, 525.1; G124, to the ex-*chartophylax* Nikephoros, II, 565.

[340] G133, to his brother Demetros when sick, II, 591; G132, the consolatio to the brother of Psellos, II, 509; G122, to the bishop of Debra after the death of Demetrios, II, 561.

[341] G125, II, 567, based on *Par.Gr.*, I, 191; G119 to Constantine Doukas, II, 551, a gift of fish, possibly for a feast of the Virgin.

complains of the quality or quantity of letters coming from him.[342] With his closest associates Theophylact would offer both extremes of length; his *metron*, used for ordered conventional communication with less intimate correspondents, measured 300 or 400 words a time.

Sapheneia

Clarity was Gregory of Nazianzos's next criterion for a good letter.[343] It is questionable whether Theophylact would have agreed with him. Jenkins in his famous criticism of Byzantine letters suggested an alternative aesthetic: 'to us a letter is a message accompanied by an expression of personal regard; a Byzantine letter is an impersonal rhetorical flourish which either contains no message at all, or if it does, the message is couched in so obscure and allusive a fashion as to be nearly unintelligible.'[344]

This shows considerable misunderstanding of Byantine epistolarity. Theophylact always has a message to convey, even if that message is simply the desire for communication. Pray for me, write me a letter, talk to the *protostrator*, arrange a *prostaxis* for me, don't believe the bad things they are saying about me; the message of every letter stands out clearly, normally towards the end of the letter before the final prayer. Nor was his rhetoric impersonal; we have seen it finely attuned to the recipient. But obscurity there certainly is in Theophylact's as in many Byzantine letters.

Theophylact has a way of describing this obscurity. Though in a letter to Nicholas Kallikles he writes: 'Let no one say I rant vainly on, weaving riddles,'[345] this is precisely what Theophylact does in his letters, and γρίφους πλέκειν, riddle-weaving, is part of his stock-in-trade. To Niketas the Didaskalos he says,

> and if I speak in obscure words and in riddles I shall perhaps not be accused of acting improperly when I speak like this to one so experienced and practised in these matters.[346]

And again to Opheomachos,

---

[342]   G114, II, 541, see above, 136-137. G115, II, 543.4-6, assigned by Gautier to Kamateros; G116, also assigned by Gautier to Kamateros, II, 545.2-3; G129, II, 583; G130, II, 585; G131, II, 587.

[343]   Gregory of Nazianzos, ep. 51, to Nikoboulos, ed. Gallay, I, 67.

[344]   R. Jenkins, 'The Hellenistic Origins of Byzantine Literature,' *DOP* 17 (1963), 45.

[345]   G111, to Nicholas Kallikles, II, 535.8-10.

[346]   G91, to the teacher of the Great Church (probably to Niketas *ho tou Serron*, but there is a problem with the form of address), II, 471.7-9.

Surely I didn't retail puzzles to you, and riddles and surely you do not need
the solution, or have I led you into the labyrinth and do you need Ariadne's
thread to reach the way up and the exit?[347]

He is clearly ambivalent about his use of obscurity, but he is not alone in
using it. His riddles, woven with allusions, half-mentioned facts and disguised
personalities are personal but not unparalleled.[348] The image of weaving is not
inapposite; any Byzantine, especially middle Byzantine, letter is a careful tissue
of meanings and allusions, quotations, proverbs, mythological characters and
biblical parables.

What does Theophylact mean on the five occasions on which he speaks
of weaving riddles? All five letters are concerned with Theophylact's
sufferings (although this is not particularly remarkable in the correspondence).
All express his feelings in an allusive and tantalising way: 'My experience with
you, O good John, is like the hares' experience of the frogs in the fable.' Or,
'You do to us what the Myceneans did to Orestes.'[349]

Certainly, as he tells us in G54, he hesitates to enlighten the
surrounding of dark speech.[350] In two cases his sufferings seem to be caused by
the correspondent, in three to be alleviated by him. All hit on a strong image
and sustain it through a long, intricate passage, varying between sixty and 200
words. In G109 the troubles burn like a furnace or a bonfire and the
correspondent by not writing pours on them not water but the naphtha from
Babylon. But Theophylact has a way for the correspondent to release all the

---

[347] G71, to Opheomachos, II, 383.19-21. Cf. G109, to the *epi ton deeseon*, II, 529.14.
And for the labyrinth motif, see Gregory of Nazianzos, ep. 16, ed. P. Gallay, I, 23.

[348] γρῖφος and αἴνιγμα were of course technical terms in classical and Byzantine
rhetoric, and were often mentioned in discussions of allegory and emphasis. See Quintilian,
Institutio oratoria, 8.6.52, ed. M. Winterbottom (Oxford, 1970), II, 473: sed allegoria quae
est obscurior 'aenigma' dicitur. The two terms were originally thought of as largely
distinct, for example Pollux, *Onomastikon*, 6.109, ed. E. Bethe, *Lexicographi graeci*, IX.ii
(Leipzig, 1931), 31: αἴνιγμα καὶ γρῖφος; τὸ μὲν παιδίαν εἶχεν, ὁ δὲ γρῖφος καὶ σπουδήν,
but Theophylact does not seem to distinguish. See G. Kustas, *Studies in Byzantine Rhetoric*
(Analekta Vlatadon, 13, Thessalonike, 1973), 193, n.7; W. Schulz, RE, sv Rätsel.

[349] G71, to Opheomachos, II, 383.2-3; G109, to the *epi ton deeseon*, II, 529.2-3. Both are
challenging openings. What did the hares do to the frogs? In Aesop fable 191 they learned
that the frogs' cowardice was worse than their own. What did the Mycenaeans do to
Orestes? ostracise him? The explanation follows: μισου'μεθ' οὕτως ὥστε μὴ προσεννέπειν,
Eurip, *Or.*, 428 cf. the beginning of G93 to Nicholas Kallikles, again with the quotation, II,
477.2.

[350] G54, to the patriarch, II, 313.21-22: Ὀκνῶ γὰρ αὐτὸς διαφωτίσαι τὴν τοῦ
σκοτεινοῦ λόγου περιβολήν.

force of the Nile onto the leaping flames.[351] In G91 the image is also of burning
and his correspondent is pictured holding a pitcher of cooling water.[352] In G54
the letter is a guiding hand leading Theophylact back from the hurricane and
the abyss and drawing him out of the mud of pollution.[353] In G111 the
correspondent is called Asklepios, pouring out all the most effective kinds of
medicines for Theophylact's current problems.[354]

The basic image is much elaborated and subordinate images make the
texture even more dense; the hero of Salamis (Themistocles? or Ajax?) is
introduced in G71, Cleopas in G54 and in G91 there is an echo of the Good
Samaritan.[355] The long flow of elaborate complaint is broken up by questions
and exhortations. After the opening fable G71 is built on a series of questions:
Why are you transfixed by fear? You know how our life was: uninvolved and
simple and reeking of books and ancient civilisation? But you, why did you
turn your back like the bad man in the story? Why did you show cowardice at
the rattle of the chariots? The horses have no charioteer, no passenger, no
warrior. They pull their chariots noisily, unbridled and disordered. Check
their impetus, resist them and they will immediately abandon their course, or
leap on their backs and your horsemanship will save you...[356] The
thoroughness of the conceit here might lead us to believe that Opheomachos
had actually deserted in battle, were it not for the warning that Theophylact
has woven *griphous kai ainigmata* to cover a message like 'Your behaviour
towards Bulgaria is like that of a soldier who deserts in battle.'

All these techniques are apparent in other letters as well. The mournful
tone of G54 is echoed in G37 and G51;[357] the fable reference in G71 can be
paralleled by that in G108;[358] the parable in G91 by the parable of the sower in
G112 and of the talents in G20.[359] Though medical imagery and monster
imagery are more common,[360] as we have seen, there are other cases of martial

---

[351] G109, to the *epi ton deeseon*, II, 529.6-10 and 12-14. (He has simply to release
Theophylact's *gambros ep' adelphidi* from military service.)

[352] G91, to the *didaskalos* of the Great Church, II, 471.2-5.

[353] G54, to the patriarch, II, 313.7-9, using Ps.54:9; Ps.70:20.

[354] G111, to Nicholas Kallikles, II, 535.2-4, for the δραστικὰς ἀντιδότους, the panacea,
the viper serum; he is revealed as Asklepios in 7-8.

[355] G71, II, 383.6; G54, II, 313.15-16; G91, II, 471.4.

[356] G71, II.383.7-14. Three *Iliad* quotations are worked into the tissue, but the
paragraph ends triumphantly with Habbakuk 3:8.

[357] G37 is gloomy but vigorous; G51 gloomy but short.

[358] G108, II, 527.10-12: the cantors are really grasshoppers or cicadas who feed on song
alone.

[359] G112, to Nicholas Kallikles, II, 537.4 and 12-14; his reading will fall on productive
soil, Luke 8.8; G20, to Tarchaneiotes, II, 197.3-15, more explicitly and didactically.

[360] See above, 3.2 ii, 106-107, for the medical imagery; 3.2 iv, 124-125 for the monsters.

imagery[361] and the introduction of otherwise irrelevant classical figures.[362] The mixing of quotations from Homer and the prophets[363] is also characteristic of Theophylact's style.

So what marks these letters off from others that Theophylact should particularly draw attention to his enigmatic style? Surely only that Theophylact here both combines fanciful and ambitious imagery and also wants to be sure that action will be taken. To friends who can do nothing to alleviate his misfortunes Theophylact may write long and veiled complaints about evil ones, enemies and the *ponerai hemerai*,[364] but in these 'enigmatic' letters the complaints must be understood and acted upon. G91 says, 'Help me, I know you won't let me down.' G109 says, 'You have been making life harder for us. If you were to let Tornikios off military service it would help. You don't need an Oedipus to solve this one.' G111 says, 'Help me, for you are particularly suited to do so—and this is what happened.' G71 says, 'You've let us down rather badly in Bulgaria by not being firmer. Take a leaf out of my book. You don't need Ariadne's thread—you know the situation.' G85 talks about clouds of calumny then admits to covering the sun with the clouds of *asapheia,* but he wants Adrian to ignore the accusations against him and to prevent the village being taken away from him. G79 says, 'I'm already dead and only you can resuscitate me. Shall I pull back the veil of *asapheia* and show you the sense of these words? I have lost a good governor; I need your consolation.' By contrast G54 thanks the patriarch for his help, but refuses to cast light on the enveloping darkness of his speech; he does not need to, since he has no specific request; this is a letter reinforcing their relationship, thanking the patriarch for his gifts and asking for continued support.

So the same techniques appear elsewhere in the collection, whether or not they are identified by Theophylact as riddle-weaving. Is Theophylact alone in cultivating this style? A suggestive parallel is with the fourteenth-century *pletenie sloves* (braiding of words) of Epiphanios the Wise,[365] and Jakobson tried to relate this use of 'long rhetorical passages, strings of epithets,

---

[361] G29, to Mermentoulos, approximates teaching posts to ranks in the army, II, 225.2-6; G99, to Pantechnes, has him fighting on Theophylact's side, II, 507.5.

[362] Herod Antipas in 574, II, 395.10; Anarcharsis and Solon in G79, II, 419.12-13; Erostratos (the arsonist of the temple of Artemis at Ephesos) at G98, II, 501.34.

[363] E.g. G77, particularly the middle section, II, 409; G32 plants a quotation from Euripides and another from Aristophanes at the beginning, then offers a paragraph of cento, largely from the psalms.

[364] E.g. G75, to the bishop of Kerkyra, G45, to the patriarch, II, 407-413, 281-287.

[365] F. Kitch, *The Literary Style of Epifanij Premudrij. Pletinije Sloves* (Slavistische Beiträge, 96, 1976), R.R. Milner-Gulland, 'Russia's Last Renaissance,' *Literature of Western Man*, III, ed. D. Daiches (London, 1974), 448.

conglomerations of synonyms and subtle variations on one theme' to 'synchronic international correspondences and the trend of the time which required speaking in riddles'.[366] But the breadth of the literatures he drew on and their many disparities[367] do not offer very helpful explanations for Theophylact's riddles. More domestic connections can also be drawn. Riddle collections were popular in the eleventh and twelfth centuries, and the technique of schedography can also be viewed in this light.[368] But even earlier Byzantine letter-writers were increasingly unwilling to name names or describe actual events.[369]

Consider the way in which Niketas Magistros for the sake of decency and politeness wraps up his refusal of a pension from John the *patrikios* and *mystikos*:

> They say that the Spartan legislator, to whom the god divulged the oracle at Delphoi—I think his name was Lykourgos, if that interests you—among other laws enacted this one; that the city should be deprived of gold. And Solon of Athens proclaimed Tellos the Athenian, Biton and Kleobis to be more fortunate than Croesus and by so doing mocked gold and riches. As for the men who went with Agamemnon, it was with other commodities,
> > some with bronze, some with shining iron,
> > some with slaves, some with cattle
> that they obtained their wine. And I, a Spartan on my father's side, an Athenian on my mother's, own only iron, not gold, carry on my business with iron only, and deal with those who love me with the means at my disposal. [370]

He does eventually reach the point. Michael Italikos, although his letters have normally more obvious point than Theophylact's, has the same penchant for sustaining an image through a letter. The idea of a literary banquet in letter 18, the rhetorical questions and classical allusions in letter 20 and the elaborate beginning to letter 23 all recall Theophylact.[371] But a closer parallel might be a letter like that of Theodore of Nicaea to the *chartophylax*, where he pleads with him to prevent people spying on him under the pretence of help or

---

[366] R. Jakobson, 'The Puzzles of the Igor Tale,' *Speculum* 27 (1952), 43-66.

[367] E.g. Geoffroi de Vinsauf's *ornatus difficilis*; Snorri Sturlusun's *kennings*.

[368] A. Garzya, 'Literarische und rhetorische Polemiken der Komnenenzeit,' *BS* 34 (1973), 1-14; for a riddle-collection see M. Treu, *Eustathii Macrembolitae quae feruntur aenigmata* (CXXIIX Programm Königl. Friedrichs-Gymnasiums zu Breslau, 1893), 1-47.

[369] This is not the 'deconcretisation' described by Karlsson, which is a stringing together of (in particular) friendship topoi while any real message is missing; what we are dealing with is the expression of a message in disguise.

[370] Niketas Magistros, ep. 2, ed. Westerink, 57.

[371] Michael Italikos, epp. 18, 23, 20, ed. Gautier, 156, 174, 164.

George Tornikes' vagueness about his situation in letter 12 or his exhortations to John Pantechnes in letter 26 to 'avoid the darkness'.[372]

But it may be a mistake to look only in letters for parallels, or indeed surprising to find them in letters at all. What Theophylact is talking about is surely only the old literary device of *asapheia*,[373] analysed successfully in the eleventh- and twelfth-century *basilikos logos*.[374] Kustas has well shown the theoretical history of obscurity from Aristotle through Longinos, Seguerianos and the *Peri Hermenias* and through Theon and Hermogenes to John of Sardis, the anonymous scholia *Eis Peri Ideon*. He argues that 'obscurity becomes established as a definite literary standard in the tenth and eleventh centuries by men such as Geometres and Sikeliotes.'[375]

Kustas overstates his case, 'that one of the key principles of Byzantine rhetorical theory is that obscurity is a virtue of style' or 'one of the main features and presuppositions of Byzantine literature' or a 'touchstone of rhetoric'.[376] Most references to *asapheia* are in passages which tell the student how to avoid it; there is no Byzantine equivalent to the lost work of Galen, *On clarity and unclarity*, mentioned in his *Peri ton idion biblion*[377] and commentators and theorists from Hermogenes to Plethon[378] allow only a limited role to obscurity. As Sikeliotes cautiously put it: 'not every form of obscurity is blame-worthy.'[379] But it may be said that there is some evidence for an increased interest in *asapheia* in the tenth and eleventh centuries and an awareness of its literary possibilities.

But wherever *asapheia* might be tolerated, the letter was expected to show *sapheneia*. Commentators who explain Aristotle's deliberate use of

---

[372] Theodore of Nicaea, ep. 39, ed. Darrouzès, *Epistoliers byzantins*, 305; George Tornikes, epp. 12, 26, ed. Darrouzès, 134, 170.

[373] On ancient *asapheia* see M. Fuhrmann, 'Obscuritas. Das Problem der Dunkelheit in der rhetorischen und literatur-aesthetischen Theorie der Antiken,' *Immanente Aesthetik. Kolloquium Köln 1964. II, Poetik und Hermeneutik* (Munich, 1966), 47-72. For the association of γρῖφος with *asapheia* see J. Sikeliotes, *Eis tas ideas tou Hermogenous*, 6.199.29-31, ed. C. Walz, *Rhetores graeci*, VI (Stuttgart and Tübingen, 1834), 199.

[374] J. Lefort, 'Rhétorique et symbolique: l'obscurité dans le discours à l'empereur au XIe-XIIe siècles,' communication to the *XV IntCong* (Athens, 1976). I am grateful to the author for a copy of this paper.

[375] Kustas, *Byzantine Rhetoric*, 63-100 at 95.

[376] Ibid., 12, 93.

[377] Ed. J. Marquardt, *Galeni scripta minora*, II (Leipzig, 1891), 124.16.

[378] Plethon, *Syntome peri tinon meron tes rhetorikes*, ed. C. Walz, *Rhetores graeci*, VI, 587.4-9. The specific cases Plethon excludes from the rule are 'figured topics and imitative forms of composition written by authors deliberately obscure and verbose'.

[379] John Sikeliotes, *Exegesis eis tas ideas tou Hermogenous*, ed. C. Walz, *Rhetores graeci*, VI, 203.5.

obscurity in the *Categories* point out that where clarity is especially called for, as in letters, he more than provides 'that combination of clarity and grace which the epistolary style requires'.[380]

Yet among the *typoi epistolikoi* are the allegorical, the *allegorikos*, to be used 'when we wish only the person to whom we are writing to understand and by writing one thing mean another', and the riddling, the *ainigmatike* 'when one thing is said and another meant'.[381] The same writer points up a problem in the theorists: the conflict between decoration and clarity, in Gregory of Nazianzos's terms, *sapheneia* and *charis*. Proklos says that one must decorate with clarity, brevity and *archaismos lexeon*. 'In some cases the charms of history will fill the letter, the memory of myths and ancient writers and proverbs and the teachings of philosophers are used.'[382] There is similar ambiguity in Gregory; on clarity he says 'It is equally disagreeable to think out a riddle and to have to interpret a letter,' but on grace he says letters should not be left ἀκόσμητα καὶ ἀκόρητα, unadorned and untrimmed,

> with for instance a style destitute of maxims and proverbs and pithy sayings, or even jokes and riddles, by which language is sweetened. Yet we must not seem to abuse these things by an excessive employment of them.[383]

In general Theophylact follows closely Gregory's advice and practice; 'these forms of speech are to be used in the same moderation as purple in woven garments' but the practice of his day was different from Gregory's, and complaints of obscurity are common. Symeon Magistros complains to a certain metropolitan that he cannot understand his letter; if the latter wishes to be obscure, he says his desire has been fulfilled, but if he wished to be understood he must cultivate clarity. In another letter he pointedly praises another friend for his clarity. Theodore, metropolitan of Nicaea, complains to Zacharias, the *kouboukleisios* of the *oikonomos* that he has received a letter he cannot understand, in fact Pythagorean riddles.[384]

Clarity was especially sought when language was likely to be a problem anyway: Arethas's 'letter to the emir at Damascus' was for a long time not attributed to him because of the relative simplicity of the language, but a

---

[380] Simplicius, *Eis tas kategorias tou Aristotelous*, ed. C. Kalbfleisch (CAG, 8, Berlin, 1908), 7.50-54. Cf. Demetrios, *Peri Hermeneias*, 223, ed. Roberts, 172.

[381] Demetrios, *Typoi epistolikoi*, 15, ed. Weichert, 8; Proklos/Libanios, *Peri epistolimaiou charakteros*, ed. Weichert, 32.

[382] Ibid., 21.

[383] Gregory of Nazianzos, ep. 51, ed. Gallay, 67.

[384] Symeon Magistros, epp. 94, 23, ed. Darrouzès, 154, 114; Theodore metropolitan of Nicaea, ep. 7, ibid., 277.

marginal annotation explains the oddity thus: 'It is simply phrased for the understanding of the Arabs.' It should be noted, however, that diplomatic letters do not usually show this tendency; the need for a grand style normally carries with it obscurity as well as length.[385]

Both Arethas and Psellos had to meet the charge of obscurity. Arethas's ep. 17 is in reply to a friend who sent back one of his works because he could not understand it, and Psellos's ep. 174, justifies the use of obscurity in philosophy. Both defend their position by pointing to earlier authors and by claiming to follow the rhetorical rules of Hermogenes. All Psellos's examples are philosophers, but Arethas cites Thucydides, (surprisingly) Herodotos—and Gregory of Nazianzos. We should not conclude that either was justifying obscurity in principle (indeed Psellos elsewhere praises clarity), simply their own writing.[386]

And so when Theophylact was writing, letters were still supposed to be clear, but both in theory and in practice *asapheia* was not always condemned as a vice. For the techniques of *asapheia* were also those of *charis*; this is a structural tension in the *dispositio* of a Byzantine letter. If to Gregory *charis* lay in decoration with maxims and proverbs and pithy sayings, with jokes and riddles, where is the dividing line to be drawn? For Theophylact surely where charis produces incomprehensibility. The pursuit of *asapheia* may well have been pragmatic, for its political advantages were enormous.[387] But it had its limitations. Dark words are fine if he wants to evoke sympathy in his reader and protect himself from calumny, but his correspondent must have at least

---

[385] Arethas, ep. 26, ed. L.G. Westerink, *Arethae scripta minora*, I (Leipzig, 1968), 233-245; P. Karlin-Hayter, 'Arethas' letter to the emir of Damascus,' *Byz* 19 (1959), 282-291. On grandeur see Demetrios, *Peri Hermeneias*, 234, ed. tr. Roberts, 177: 'such letters must be composed in a slightly heightened tone.' On diplomatic letters see my 'The Language of Diplomacy,' *Byzantine Diplomacy. Papers from the Twenty-fourth Spring Symposium of Byzantine Studies, Cambridge, March 1990*, ed. J. Shepard and S. Franklin (SPBS, 1, Aldershot, 1992), 203-216.

[386] Arethas, ep. 17, ed. Westerink, I, 186-191; Michael Psellos, ep. 174, ed. K.N. Sathas, *Mesaionike bibliotheke*, V (Paris, 1876), 441-3. On Psellos's literary criticism see A.R. Dyck, *Michael Psellos: the Essays on Euripides and George of Pisidia and on Heliodorus and Achilles Tatius* (ByzVind, 16, Vienna, 1986). The most frequent example of *asapheia* quoted in the middle ages is Thucydides' summers and winters chronology; in the eleventh century Doxapatres, *Homilia eis Aphthonion*, ed. C. Walz, *Rhetores graeci*, II (Leipzig, 1854), 219-227 there is a strong sense of *asapheia* as a narrative vice: the writer must not mention too many things at once, nor confuse his chronology or use long digressions or be garrulous, use abstruse allegory or technical vocabulary.

[387] See for example, Julian, ep. 6, quoted above, 2.1, 17 and the political uses of letters under Alexios, see my 'Diplomacy', 205-210.

Ariadne's clue. So that his message could get through, *syntomia* had to be sacrificed on occasion and so did *charis*; he simply could not afford *asapheia*.

Charis

Is it possible to reconstruct what Theophylact would have understood by *charis*? Or the principles of *dispositio* in a Theophylact letter?

We can find in Theophylact's letters all the techniques of decoration that the theorists list: maxims and proverbs, pithy sayings, history, myths and philosophy as well as jokes and riddles.[388] But we may suspect that surface decoration was normally subordinated to structural considerations. In a letter to his pupils justifying his decision not to introduce Hermogenes, *Peri Ideon* into his teaching he claimed that he hoped to restore rhetoric to its original state. Simplicity, nobility and appropriateness are for him cardinal virtues—which he strongly objects to being categorised as rusticity—and opposes any style which praises mere 'prettiness or charm or a dropsical glittering of words'.[389] Instead Theophylact's letters tend to have an organic unity. This may be a set of interlocking quotations from the psalms or the prophets or on a parable. But it is interwoven with quotations and imagery into a complex whole, which may be an extended conceit to be taken literally at the reader's peril.

G112, to Nicholas Kallikles, opens with an apology and asks for books but is built on the parable of the sower. The sustained conceits of the 'arrival letter' invoked Isaiah as well as Plutarch, tragedy and the *Iliad* as well as philosophy. To Anemas he combines quotations from the Old Testament with Echo and Tantalos. G108 to Makrembolites knits together the miracle of the lame man, wordplay on the name of the *archon* and the fabulous grasshoppers who fed on song alone. In G94 he depicts himself as Alkmaion, chased from country to country but by the end of the letter still manages to evoke his correspondent as Paieon, doctor of the gods.

In general he suits his imagery to the recipient:[390] to his academic friends he talks of tragedies;[391] with successful warriors military imagery;[392] a letter to a doctor is an opportunity for a virtuoso performance with all the jargon he can

---

[388] For maxims see e.g. G38; for proverbs see e.g. G125; for pithy sayings (or challenging openings) e.g. G130; for history e.g. G55; for myths e.g. G5; for philosophy e.g. G42; for riddles see above, 151-155; for a joke, e.g. G32; to these may be added fables, e.g. G71 and parables, e.g. G20.

[389] G2, to his pupils, I, 147.23-149.15.

[390] For example the nocturnal play in G76 on Mermentoulos's office of Grand *droungarios* of the Watch, II, 403.6-8.

[391] G95, to Theodore of Smyrna, G7, to Niketas *ho tou Serron*, II, 481.2-3, 151.4.

[392] G65, to Gregory Taronites, G69, to Opheomachos, II, 363.18-22, 377.

remember from Galen and the most bizarre diseases he could ever have suffered.[393] He peoples his letter with sympathetic personalities from the bible or mythology, the suffering like Orestes, Job, Jonah, Samson, Daniel, and the good like the Muses, Solomon and Nestor. His persecutors are found names of their own, Briareus, Charybdis or Argos, or are lost in a series of *deinotatoi* and *panponeroi* who stalk through the correspondence and the *ponerai hemerai.*[394]

He uses his quotations in different ways; Hunger generalises on the use of quotation in letters: 'quoting abundantly, sometimes using a mass of quotations, which one might call a kind of mannerism...in some cases the mixture of pagan and christian quotation was a pattern that was popular with many writers and can be traced back even to Clement of Alexandria.'[395] But Theophylact does not always mix his biblical and his classical quotations, and he does not mass the classical ones together. Classical quotations often appear in a prominent place, at the beginning or end, or expressing the main message of the piece and always to some literary effect.[396] Quotations are omitted entirely from business letters, like those to provincial officials, and from letters of high emotional content.[397] In general, classical allusions are used to lighten the emotional spectrum, to cheer, amuse and dazzle, whereas a cento of biblical quotations creates an atmosphere of deep gloom.[398] Quotations depend also on the recipient; classical quotations are for the inner circle of his correspondence, the truly intellectual companions who were his pupils, his friends and his teaching colleagues; a biblical atmosphere is suited to his suffragans and for other pastoral letters.[399] Quotations are a highly precious device to be disposed with discrimination, single jewels in rich settings rather than clusters. And they are vital to the structure of the letter, which shows similar variety.

Some letters are structurally straightforward with an introduction, an elaboration and a request before the final prayer; others wander gloomily in

---

[393] See above, 3.2.ii, 107-108.

[394] See above, 3.2.iv, 124-125.

[395] Hunger, 'Mimesis,' 30.

[396] At the beginning: G6, II, 147.2; G27, II, 219.2; at the end, G47, II.293.15. G31 sends the message with the double quotation from Homer, *Il.*, 24, 528-530 and Hesiod, *Works*, 179.

[397] G23, to John Komnenos, II, 207; G123, to Constantine Komnenos, II, 563.

[398] E.g. the balance in G127, to Gregory Kamateros, is on the classical side with four classical references to three biblical ones including the Song of Songs, while G77, to the bishop of Kerkyra, has eighteen biblical references to four Homeric.

[399] Cf. G76, to Mermentoulos, (Herodotos, *Odyssey*, Aristophanes, *Iliad*, Oppian) with G87, to the bishop of Triaditsa, (Psalms, Gospels, Epistles).

pages of depression before coming to the point; others show a polemic energy, like the letter to the bishop of Vidin, where Theophylact matches him, problem for problem.[400] All have a purpose, whether it is a specific request, or the maintenance of communication, and the purpose will affect the form of the letter.

So letters were recognised by Theophylact and his correspondents as conforming to a type, whether ancient or more recent, and were (with certain exceptions) expected to be brief, clear and decorated. But it is at least arguable that sometimes neither the demands of politics nor of literature shaped his letters. G93, to Smyrnaios, says

> If you want to hear tragedies, o consul of Christian philosophers and of philosophical Christians, ask for letters from our friendship, for they will contain nothing but lamentations and weeping, since our situation is the subject. But if you have had enough of tragedy and you have a lot around you, you won't need any more coming from Bulgaria. Don't ask for letters laying open our affairs, for even if we wanted to, we could not write about anything else. For the tale of our misfortunes falls automatically upon the pen; to write is to write of misfortunes. May you be above such suffering, so that the oppressors of virtue do not succeed in everything, and may the Lord deliver us from this weakness, not because of our justice, but because of his own goodness.[401]

There are limits in Theophylact's discourse to a sense of genre, to brevity, clarity and grace.

---

[400] Straightforward four-point structure: G11, G12, G34. Missing elements: G5 lacks the prayer, to reinforce the request, 'Get me out!' added: the fragrant paragraph in G4. Gloomy meanderings: see the wave-pattern of G31, to Gregory Kamateros, II, 233-235. G57, to the bishop of Vidin, 323-325; for the matching problems, 323.21-325.32.

[401] G95, to Theodore Smyrnaios, II, 481.

Theophylact's synod-church: Hagios Achilleios, Prespa

CHAPTER FOUR

COLLECTION AND NETWORK (II)

And so for Theophylact the text could be affected by the world. We have seen how he promoted active reader-response;[1] his view of letters is also profoundly referential and instrumental. 'Blessed be God who among other examples of His outpouring goodness has given us letters by which friends greet their friends and slaves may address their masters from afar.'[2] There is a world outside the text and the text is instrumental in articulating it. In this chapter I want to look at the collection as evidence for network, 'the social relations in which every individual is embedded'.[3]

4.1 Detecting Theophylact's network

Theophylact's collection offers us a rare opportunity in Byzantium to look at a single personal network, and, in a very few cases, to observe that network in use. There are advantages in applying some techniques of anthropological network analysis,[4] but there are also problems.[5] But a methodology which looks towards interaction, and therefore communication, would seem to be well adapted to a letter-collection, promising us in the determination of

---

[1] G56, to the bishop of Semnea, II, 326.9-14.

[2] G10, to John Komnenos, II, 161.2-4.

[3] J. Boissevain, *Friends of Friends. Networks, Manipulators and Coalitions* (Oxford, 1974), 24.

[4] See J. Boissevain and J. Mitchell, *Network Analysis: Studies in Human Interaction* (The Hague and Paris, 1973); J.C. Mitchell, *Social Networks in Urban Situations* (Manchester, 1969); S. Leinhardt, *Social Networks: a Developing Paradigm* (New York, 1977) for the golden age of networks in anthropology, which is rather underplayed in J. Scott, *Social Network Analysis. A Handbook* (London 1991), ch. 2, 'The Development of SNA,' esp. diagram 7.

[5] See R. Cormack, 'Additional Notes and Comments,' *The Byzantine Eye: Studies in Art and Patronage* (Variorum, CS, 296, London, 1989), 16 on the unhelpfulness of an understanding of Cicero's letter-collection for explaining the Roman Revolution. We may well be left in the same position at the end of the present exercise, but it is probably unfair to expect transactional evidence to answer structural questions and the understanding gained from the exercise is of a rather different kind.

personal relations sophistication beyond the scope of role-based structural-functionalist analysis.[6]

Network analysis proceeds from the social relations of a given individual. Those that are known personally form the first order zone; those known to them are the second order zone and so on. These links are potential communication channels which may or may not be used to carry transactions, which are defined as 'an interaction between two actors that is governed by the principle that the value gained from the interaction must be equal to or greater than the cost'.[7] The transaction may be reciprocal, and the pattern of transactions may be viewed as a relation of exchange: relations between individuals may be symmetrical or asymmetrical according to the pattern of exchange.

Students of networks then proceed to an analysis of the nature of these relationships, which may be seen as role relations,[8] the norms and expectations that apply to the occupant of a particular position; it is assumed however that each person will fill many roles; neighbour, husband, employee, football club member. The assumption is that relations which are multiplex, where individuals meet in overlapping role relations, offer greater accessibility and thus responsiveness to pressure than does a single-stranded relation.[9] Transactional content in given relationships may be spelt out. For example: cash + affection + miscellaneous gifts + sex = husband/wife; conversation + joking behaviour + job assistance + personal service + cash assistance = work associates; greetings + civilities + conversation + visits = instrumental friends in rural society. The next step is to consider directional flow,[10] frequency and duration of interaction,[11] the symmetry or asymmetry of the relationship.[12]

---

[6] This was the original justification of the network approach, see Boissevain, 1-23; J. Clyde Mitchell, 'The Concept and Use of Social Networks,' *Social Networks in Urban Situations. Analyses of Personal Relationships in Central Africa* (Manchester, 1969), 1-50 at 8, a response to questions of its time, which struck a chord also with social historians: see R.M. Smith, 'Kin and Neighbours in a Thirteenth-century Suffolk Community,' *Journal of Family History*, 4 (1979), 219-256 at 220 on the work of John Bossy. The classic structural-functionalist essay in Byzantine Studies is P.R.L. Brown, 'The Rise and Function of the Holy Man in Late Antiquity,' *JRS* 61 (1971), 80-101. For studies of Theophylact's role, see e.g. D. Xanalatos, 'Theophylaktos ho Boulgaros kai he drasis autou en Achridi,' *Theologia* 16 (1938), 228-241.

[7] Boissevain, *Friends*, 25.

[8] M. Banton, *Roles. An introduction to the study of social relations* (London, 1965).

[9] Boissevain, *Friends*, 32.

[10] Ibid., 33-34.

[11] Ibid., 34-35.

[12] This concept of symmetry owes more to anthropological and historical studies of patronage, see E. R. Wolf, 'Kinship, Friendship and Patron-client Relations in Complex

It is then possible to turn to the whole network and its structural criteria: size (including potential links), density (the degree to which the members of a person's network are in touch with each other independently of her,[13] degree of connection (the average number of relations each person has with others in the same network)[14] and centrality, an indicator of the subject's ability to manipulate the maximum number of people and pieces of information.[15] Clusters can be analysed: a cluster is a compartment of a network which has a relatively low ratio of external relations as compared to internal relations—a clique or closed circle. When the structure is analysed, an individual's use of the network can be determined; dynamically the network can be tested in a given situation.

Less objective criteria are taken into consideration in the depiction of zones of intimacy, which range from a personal cell through intimate zones to an effective zone of pragmatic exchanges, a nominal zone of mere acquaintances and an extended zone moving into the second order. This pattern, which changes with every transaction, may be tested against the objective criteria in transactional exchanges to arrive at a more nuanced picture of the individual's network.[16]

There is no great difficulty in translating these terms of analysis into the conventions of the Byzantine letter. We may see Theophylact's first order zone as anyone directly addressed or mentioned in such a way as to make it clear they were acquainted either face-to-face or through writing, his second order zone as anyone in contact with his correspondents or known acquaintances. Role relations and transactional content can also be translated easily: in the eleventh and twelfth centuries in Byzantium, ritual kinship, teaching relationships, patronage involving money may similarly be differentiated by the transactional content of riddles, gifts of fish, visits and so on. For football team read deme; for club read confraternity. The next steps of directional flow, frequency and duration, symmetry are all potentially detectable in Byzantium, depending on the kind of evidence involved, and it should not be impossible to look at density, degree of connection and centrality. The final stage, that of the use of a network, I have already attempted.[17]

Societies,' *The Social Anthropology of Complex Societies,* ed. M. Banton (ASA Monographs, 4, London, 1966), 1-22 at 16ff.

[13] Boissevain, *Friends,* 37.
[14] Ibid., 40.
[15] Ibid., 41.
[16] Ibid., 45-48 and diagram 2.10.
[17] 'Patronage'.

But however sympathetic we may be to the application of this approach, there are obvious difficulties in applying it fully to Byzantine letter-collections. Historians have, after a pioneering start by Smith and others, been slow to take advantage of network analysis, and in particular of its more developed manifestations.[18] Clearly completeness is a problem: our records, however impressive compared with other periods of Byantine literary history, cannot measure up to field notebooks.[19] The main problem is of omission or even survival; there is no reason to believe that all social relations of any Byzantine writer are recorded in his writings. Proximity might exclude everyday relations, unless Byzantines corresponded as frequently as eighteenth-century Londoners.[20] Convention would exclude the domestic, the banal, the less than socially acceptable;[21] chance would account for a great deal else. A crude indication of what may be lost is to compare Boissevain's subject Pietru Cardona with Theophylact: a first order zone of 1,750 persons as against 127.[22] Our knowledge of the dynamics of a network may suffer accordingly in the restricted availability of case studies which may be detected in a collection. Another problem is that it is tempting to take a collection as synchronic, like the anthropologist's notebook, but a synchronic network cannot demonstrate a changing pattern of transactions; this erodes many of the claims made for the technique. A quick look at Theophylact's second order zone shows up the problems clearly; of his correspondents only

---

[18] The approach as I present it here represents a fairly early stage in SNA, before what Scott, *Social Network Analysis*, 33ff. calls the 'Harvard breakthrough' in harnessing graph theory, algebraic and computational techniques to quantify networks. See D. Postles, 'Reviewing Social Networks: using UCINET,' *History and Computing* 6 (1994), 1-11 on historians and advanced techniques. His differentiation between early SNA and current practice, of the star-system of every individual as against a complete sociogram of all relations in a society, suggests contrarily why the early stage is more appropriate to a study based on a single letter-collection.

[19] See though Scott, *Social Network Analysis*, 3 and fig. 1.1 on suitability of types of data for types of analysis; in this historical texts outclass ethnographic research in suitability. See also A.D.J. MacFarlane, 'History, Anthropology and the Study of Communities,' *Social History* 5 (1977), 631-652 on the superiority of historical data and the contribution historians can make to refining social scientists' techniques.

[20] Did Theophylact correspond with anyone in Ochrid? Contrast Richard Steele, 7 May 1787: 'Dear Prue, I am just drinking a Pint of Wine and will come home forthwith. I am with Mr Elliot settling things. Yrs ever ever, Richd Steele' in the *Faber Book of Letters*, ed. F. Pryor (London, 1990), xi.

[21] See above, and further discussion in chapters 2.1, and 3.2, on subjects excluded from letters, to take only one example.

[22] Boissevain, *Friends*, 97-146. But see the analysis in Smith, 'Kin and Neighbours,' of 13,592 interactions in the village of Redgrave between 1259 and 1293.

Nicholas Kallikles in his occasional poetry has anything like a network to offer; only Michael Psellos, probably dead ten years before Theophylact's collection really gets under way, has a comparable letter-collection.[23] (The twelfth century promises much more.)[24] A final difficulty in using a letter-collection in this way is that it is not a network of *potential* communication channels; rather of *actual* ones. We simply cannot see non-serviced relations.[25]

Further problems arise when we look at the nature and quality of relationships. Here, with no interviews, we are in difficulties. If in ignorance, the anthropologist can ask her subject. For her, intimacy is always determined that way.[26] We must proceed quite differently and the detection of relationship in Byantine literary texts presents a series of quite complex difficulties. We may be sure that we are better off using a letter-collection than any other type of source; a history may allow 'social localisation',[27] but the interactive nature of the letter, its concentration on emotion and affect, the existence of named correspondents is far more suited to network analysis. Letters can be used for all the basic questions: who knew whom, and the nature, quality and use of the relationship. They can also be used to determine intimacy. But letters have their own problems. For example they concentrate on the relationship between writer and recipient, leaving us thoroughly ignorant about the social relations of writers who have not left a letter-collection. We should also beware the illusory charge of intimacy the genre carries with it: 'a kindly, diplomatic and charitable man like Peter the Venerable seems to be on terms of close friendship with everyone in Christendom.'[28]

It should here be noted that the difficulties do not arise from any inappropriate graft of the methods of social anthropology onto Byzantium.

---

[23] Nicholas Kallikles, ed. R. Romano, *Nicola Callicle, Carmi, Testo critico, introduzione e traduzione, commentario e lessico* (ByzetNeohellNap, 8, 1980); most poems date from the late years of Alexios or the reign of John. For Psellos, the letters, ed. Sathas and Kurtz-Drexl, should have been joined by Gautier's edition of the 47 unpublished letters discovered since, see J. Darrouzès, 'L'activité scientifique de Paul Gautier,' *REB* 42 (1984), 368, and it is to be hoped that the task will be completed and the dating issue clarified. Even if Psellos were alive in the 1090s, see above, 48, n. 196, it does not appear that the letter-collection reflects it.

[24] See my *Theophylact*, fig. II, 813-847.

[25] Much of the anthropological discussion focuses on this distinction.

[26] Boissevain, *Friends*, 117.

[27] See the technique developed by Alexander Kazhdan to devastating effect in 'The Social Views of Michael Attaleiates,' *Studies on Byzantine Literature of the Eleventh and Twelfth Centuries* (Cambridge, 1984), 23-86.

[28] A. Morey and C.N.L. Brooke, *Gilbert Foliot and his Letters* (Cambridge, 1965), 13 and see above, 3.2, 115.

The problems are there anyway.[29] Stiernon's researches into the kin structure of the twelfth-century Komnenoi[30] show that for example the word γαμβρός must be translated with great care. Even outside kin there are other known difficulties: Kazhdan's work on the relationship of Theodore Prodromos and Niketas Eugenianos reveals the necessity to examine rigorously the evidence for relationship.[31] So far unexamined in Byzantium is the tension between *eros* and *agape* which concerns some students of the twelfth-century West: 'modern readers of the letters of Anselm of Canterbury and the poems of Jaufre Rudel have sometimes concluded that the monk was in love with his friend and the poet not in love with his lady.'[32] The expression of the erotic in Byzantium is another story,[33] but intimacy is very much part of our problem.

We should not however acknowledge defeat: Byzantine letters actually carry certain advantages over other forms of evidence. Not only do they foreground personal relations, but they regulate them with a ceremonial which can be extremely revealing. This ceremonial is what Zilliacus called the 'Anredeformen und Höflichkeitstiteln,'[34] the delicate balance of superlative adjective and abstract noun which can help us to pinpoint social status and occupation and, in relation to the writer, role, relationship and intimacy. Zilliacus studied these forms because he saw in them one of the strongest signs of 'Byzantinism', of artificiality of social relations stretching from the Achaemenid court to officials in nineteenth-century Germany. Societies change however and personal relations change. In Byzantium *taxis* and ceremony were of extreme importance and we may therefore expect the way someone is addressed to reflect a contemporary reality rather than an

---

[29] See the brilliant chapter, 'What's in a Name? The Vocabulary of Love and Marriage,' in J. Boswell, *The Marriage of Likeness. Same-Sex Unions in Pre-Modern Europe* (London, 1995), 3-27.

[30] In the classic series of articles, 'Notes de prosopographie et de titulature byzantines, 1-5,' in *REB* 19 (1961), 273-283; 21(1963), 178-198; 22 (1964), 184-198; 23 (1965), 222-243; 24 (1966), 89-96.

[31] A. Kazhdan, 'Bemerkungen zu Niketas Eugenianos,' *JÖB* 16 (1967), 101-117.

[32] C. Morris, *The Discovery of the Individual 1050-1200* (London, 1972).

[33] Note how the latest works on western medieval friendship are all concerned to distance themselves from J. Boswell, *Christianity, Social Tolerance and Homosexuality* (Chicago and London, 1980). The XXI Spring Symposium of Byzantine Studies on 'Desire and Denial' (Brighton, 1997) addressed the issue.

[34] H. Zilliacus, *Untersuchungen zu den abstrakten Anredeformen im Griechischen* (Helsingfors, 1953); see also L. Dineen, *Titles of Address in Christian Greek Epistolography to 527AD* (Catholic University of America Patriarchal Studies, 18, Washington, DC, 1929); P. Koch, *Die byzantinischen Beamtentitel von 400 bis 700* (Diss., Jena, 1903). I am greatly indebted in this chapter to Marie Taylor Davis for bibliographical help and for stimulating discussion over many years.

unchanging archaism. I would not claim that the forms adopted by one necessarily work for all epistolographers; there appears to be considerable idiosyncrasy of usage from writer to writer. And some types of relationship show up more clearly than others. The technique cannot be used in isolation; often it can be reinforced by the addition of generic analysis.[35] But inasmuch as Theophylact in 111 of the 135 letters uses these forms, it is worth attempting to interpret them.

His use of them is rich; he uses perhaps one-fifth of those collected by Zilliacus from the whole of patristic and papyrus literature. In letters to high court dignitaries or clerics protocol played a large part. In addressing the caesar and the brothers of the emperor imperial vocabulary was in order, together with the imperial virtues of *chrestotes*, *megaleiotes* and *philanthropia*;[36] members of the class of *sebastoi* are often greeted as *pansebaste*;[37] *megalepiphanestate* seems to have been reserved for members of the court down to *kouropalates*, that is a wider group.[38] A slightly lower social group,

---

[35] See my 'Madness of Genre,' on the relationship of Theophylact and Gregory Taronites.

[36] G73, to the caesar, addresses him as *despota mou hagie* and refers to his *basileia*, *chrestotes* and Theophylact's *chthamalotes*; G9, to the caesar, emphasises his *basileia* and *megaleiotes*, and addresses him as before and as *basileu philodorate kai chrestotate*; G13 addresses him as *despota mou hagie* and *despotes*, marking out his *basileia* as against Theophylact's *tapeinotes*. G79, to Adrian the Grand Domestic, calls him *pansebaste megiste mou antileptor*; G85, to Adrian, calls him *kyrie mou*, *kyrie* and refers to *megaleiotes*, *agathotes*, *philanthropia*. G89 makes him *hagie mou authenta* and *megaleiotes*; G5 calls him *hagie mou authenta* and contrasts his *hupsos* with Theophylact's *tapeinotes*. G96, to the *panhypersebastos* Bryennios, refers to his *basileia*.

[37] On the dignity of *sebastos* and in general on the Komnenian system of precedence see N. Oikonomides, 'L'évolution de l'organisation administrative de l'empire byzantin au XIe siècle,' *TM* 6 (1976), 126-127 and the series by Stiernon, 'Notes de prosopographie,' where note the use of the prefix *pan* to create a form of address; Theophylact nowhere reaches the exuberance of Gregory of Oxeia's *panhyperprotosebastohypertate despota* for a *sebastohypertatos*, ep. 5, ed. Gautier, 'Grégoire, higoumène,' 222. Theophylact uses *pansebaste* for the following correspondents: John Doukas, G8: *pansebaste mou antileptor*; Constantine Doukas, G118 and G119: *pansebaste mou authenta kai megiste antileptor;* John Komnenos, G10: *pansebaste mou antileptor*; G11: *pansebaste mou authenta kai antileptor*; G12: *pansebaste mou authentes* (and *antileptor*); G24: *pansebaste emon antileptor* (though in G22 and G23 he is addressed as *pammegiste)*; G61: *pansebaste mou antileptor*; Adrian Komnenos, G79: *pansebaste mou megiste antileptor*; George Palaiologos, G126: *pansebaste mou authente*; the sebastos Pakourianos; G55: *pansebaste mou en kurio huie*; G80: *pansebaste mou huie*; G68: *pansebaste*. Another favoured abstract is *agathotes*.

[38] See P. Gautier, *Nicéphore Bryennios, histoire; introduction, texte, traduction et notes* (CFHB, 9, Brussels, 1975), 316, n.2. Theophylact addresses as *megalepiphanestatos* the following correspondents: Bryennios, G86; the *doux* of Dyrrachion Bryennios, G105: *megalepiphanestate mou authenta*; Gregory Taronites, G81: *megalepiphanestate moi en Kyrio*

perhaps of the official class, would seem to be addressed as *hyperlampre* or *lamprotate*.[39] But it should be emphasised that with Theophylact this protocol is not adhered to in a rigid way: it is not possible to infer the precise rank of a correspondent from his form of address though with a writer like Theophylact it may sometimes be possible to identify correspondents from their form of address.[40] Protocol also played its part with letters to clerics; subordinates were addressed as equals, equals as superiors and superiors with *douleia*. The commonest form to suffragans is *timiotate adelphe*,[41] although *hierotate* is used almost interchangeably with *timiotate*, and to colleagues *timiotate despota*.[42] The *chartophylax* is *pater hemetere*,[43] the patriarch *despota mou hagie*.[44]

Since the seventh-century texts studied by Zilliacus certain changes have occurred. *Makarios* no longer refers only to the dead and may apply to laymen; *hosiotatos*, which in the seventh century was an episcopal title, is Theophylact's regular adjective for Symeon the *hegoumenos*; the simple monk is *eulabestatos*. *Eugeneia* no longer maintains its female connotations[45] and imperial rhetoric, now entering a newly formal period, has had its effect also: *basileia* and some compounds of *megas* are reserved for emperor, caesar and

---

huie kai authenta; Tarchaneiotes, G16: *megalepiphanestate hemon authentes; makariotate kai megalepiphanestate moi authenta*; probably G43: *megalepiphanestate moi authenta*.

[39] These include Gregory Kamateros, G27: *lamprotate*; G31: *panhyperlampre moi en Kurioi huie kai authenta*; Mermentoulos, G29 and G76: *panhyperlampre*; John Attaleiates, G104, *lamprotate moi en Kyrio huie*; Michael Pantechnes, G114, G128: *hyperlampre en kurioi huie*; Rhomaios, G46: *lamprotate moi en kurioi huie*.

[40] It should be noted that Theophylact himself believed it was possible to deduce rank from titles, see his hypothesis to Luke, PG 123, 685: 'He writes to Theophilos, a senator and perhaps an *archon*. For *kratistos* is used of archontes and governors (ἡγεμόνων) as indeed Paul says to the governor Festus, *kratiste* Festus.'

[41] Bishop of Vidin, G57: *adelphe timiotate*; Triaditsa, G58: *timiotate adelphe*; G87: *timiotate adelphe*; Pelagonia, G21: *timiotate adelphe*; G53, to the bishop Gregory Kamateros: *adelphe timiotate*. Cf. G52, to the bishop of Kitros: *adelphe hierotate*; G58, to the bishop of Triaditsa: *hierotate adelphe*.

[42] Bishop of Kitros, G52: *timiotes;* G121: *timiotate adelphe kai despota*; also to the *chartophylax* Nikephoros, G30: *timiotate despota*; G51: *timiotate despota kai pater emetere*; Niketas *ho tou Serron*, G70: *ten sen timioteta*; the *didaskalos* of G91: *timiotate moi en kurioi huie*; favoured virtues for fellow archbishops and metropolitans are *timiotes, hagiosyne, hagiotes*.

[43] G51; addresses range from *timiotate despota*, G30, through *hagie despota kai pater*, G66, G83, G90, to the effusive *panagie despota*, G124, to the ex-*chartophylax*. Virtues emphasised are *chrestotes, hagiotes, hagiosune, timiotes*.

[44] The range here is from *hagie despota* through *hagie pater kai despota* and *panagie despota* to *panagiotate despota*: G64, G45, G54.

[45] E.g. G37, G49, G52, G68, of Gregory Pakourianos, and G38, of Gregory Kamateros.

the ex-*basilissa*. *Kyr* and *kyrios* are little used and most officers and nobles may be addressed as *authentes*.[46]

Theophylact's use of the forms must be seen against a background of expected protocol. Clearly with some forms he had little choice; the form of address came with the job.[47] But this was not always so; in most cases considerable freedom was possible in the balancing of the three elements which made up the form of address, namely the adjective which usually denotes status, the noun (*authentes, adelphos, despotes, huios, pater, antileptor*), which indicated the relative position of writer and recipient, and the optional virtues which usually attached to the noun. Further, the writer was free to use the opposite of these virtues or abstracts (*tapeinotes, chthamalotes*) to describe himself. The frequency of use and the position of the terms could each subtly alter the tone of the letter.

Theophylact often disposes with forms altogether,[48] and it is interesting that it is in what appear to be the purest friendship letters, both long and short: intimacy then would seem to be revealed not by the prolific use of vocatives but the reverse, except for a *potheinotate, philtate* or *thaumasie*.[49] Forms are also omitted where the letter focuses on a third person,[50] although not in recommendatory letters where relationships (writer to sender, writer to bearer, bearer to mutual friend) are of the essence. Theophylact often substitutes an unusual word not in the repertoire[51] or creates a whole phrase for one of his correspondents.[52] He may play on the protocol, creating a neat form of address out of a title[53] or ironically emphasising a virtue missing in his

---

[46] *Basileia*: e.g. Nikephoros Bryennios, G96; Maria, G4; Melissenos, G13. *Megiste*: Adrian the Grand Domestic, G89. *Kyrios*: Adrian, G85. The persons designated as *authentes* are Gregory Taronites, G81; Nikephoros Bryennios, G96; Constantine Doukas, G118; George Palaiologos, G126; Adrian the Grand Domestic, G5; John Komnenos, G11; Gregory Kamateros, G31.

[47] Like *panagie despota* for the patriarch or *pansebaste* for a *sebastos*.

[48] E.g. G125, II, 567; G127, II, 571-579.

[49] E.g. G34, to Anemas, II, 243.2: *andron emoi potheinotate*; G99, to Michael Pantechnes, II, 507.3: *moi philtate*; G71, to Opheomachos, II, 383.7: *o thaumasie*.

[50] E.g. G127, 132.

[51] E.g. *hierotate moi kephale* (the adjective is formal, the noun personal) to the bishop of Semnea, G74. Cf. G56, to the bishop, when the formal address, *timiotate adelphe*, is preceded by Προσαγορεύω σε τὴν φίλην ἐμοὶ κεφαλήν.

[52] E.g. *tou theou anthrope*, Theophylact's regular form for the metropolitan of Kerkyra, G75, G77, as well as the more formal *timiotate despota*.

[53] E.g. *Ho ton en philosophois christianon, he ton en christianois philosophon hypate* to the *hypatos ton philosophon* Theodore Smyrnaios; he does (unlike e.g. Mouzalon) avoid the temptation to pun, e.g. *semnotes* to the bishop of Semnea.

correspondent,[54] or avoiding an obvious term when ambiguity would have been painful.[55] But his main aim seems to have been to personalise the protocol: a formula once arrived at for a correspondent tends to have become permanent, specific to that correspondent. A kind of intimacy is created out of formality. It is helpful to focus on forms of address as well as the subject matter and tone of letters in order to determine gradations of intimacy as well as types of relationship in Theophylact's network.

So in examining Theophylact's network the stages are clear. 1) Prosopography, much of which has been established by the patient work of Gautier and others.[56] I record only where I differ from earlier scholars. But prosopography is not enough. 2) Detection of relationship, whether patron, friend, colleague, pupil, and any indication of the development of that relationship, multiplexity and directional flow (frequency seems fraught with difficulty) over time. 3) Justification of intimacy zoning. 4) Theophylact's use of that relationship. I employ Boissevain's categories where they are helpful; frequently the evidence does not allow this. In the next section I present the network with some tentative conclusions and in the last section of this chapter I discuss its use by Theophylact. I now turn to some outstanding problems of analysis in Theophylact's collection.

i. *Kin and non-kin*

Kinship became politically important at the end of the eleventh century[57] and we should not be surprised to see a stress on kinship in the correspondence,

---

[54] E.g. the use of *praotes* to the bishop of Triaditsa (under attack for his harshness) in G59.

[55] In G122, to the bishop of Debra, he uses *synepiskope* where *adelphe* would be more normal; the occasion is the death of his own brother Demetrios.

[56] For families, e.g. D. Polemis, *The Doukai, A Contribution to Byzantine Prosopography* (University of London Historical Studies, 22, London, 1968); K. Barzos, *He Genealogia ton Komnenon*, 2 vols (Byzantina keimena kai meletai, 20, Thessalonike, 1984); W. Seibt, *Die Skleroi: eine prospographisch-sigillographische Studie* (ByzVind, 9, Vienna, 1976), J.-F. Vannier, *Familles byzantines, Les Argyroi, X-XII siècles* (ByzSorb, 1, Paris, 1975), Darrouzès, *Tornikai*; for offices, R. Guilland, *Recherches sur les institutions byzantines*, 2 vols (Berlin and Amsterdam, 1967); J. Darrouzès, *Recherches sur les ὀφφίκια de l'église byzantine* (Paris, 1970); for a text, B. Skoulatos, *Les personnages byzantins de l'Alexiade. Analyse prosopographique et synthèse* (Louvain, 1980). All these will be incorporated and checked from the primary sources in the *Prosopography of the Byzantine Empire*, III. For a vital methodological observation see P. Karlin-Hayter, '99. Jean Doukas,' *Byz* 42 (1972), 259-265.

[57] See A. Kazhdan, 'Small Social Groupings (Microstructures) in Byzantine Society,' *JÖB* 32/2 (1982), 3-11, for a challenging argument which overprivileges the nuclear family.

nor to see non-kin relationships described in kinship terms.[58] Twenty-two times Theophylact addresses his correspondent as ἀδελφέ,[59] nine times as πάτερ[60] and eighteen times as 'son', whether formally as υἱέ or more intimately τέκνον μου or combinations with παί.[61] Theophylact's own family, the Hephaistoi, appear seldom.[62] He sometimes defines third persons in kinship terms which can cause problems of identification. (Is the son of τοῦ πανσεβάστου αὐθέντου ἡμῶν of G88 the same as the πανσέβαστον υἱὸν τοῦ χρηστοῦ πρωτοστράτορος of G127?[63] Can the πανευγενέστατός σου γαμβρός of G79 really be the recipient's nephew-in-law? Can Theophylact's γαμβρός ἐπ' ἀδελφιδῇ in G109 be identified with George Tornikes's maternal uncle?[64] I have assumed so.) And Theophylact sometimes addresses a correspondent—sometimes, but not always, in the early stages of a correspondence—in terms of a more illustrious relative.[65]

A particular problem in Theophylact's collection is in the use of the word ἀδελφός. It is used regularly of his suffragan bishops[66] and also for his own brother Demetrios whose illness and death provide one of the few events

---

[58] E. Gellner, 'Patrons and Clients,' *Patrons and Clients in Mediterranean Society,* ed. E. Gellner and J. Waterbury (London, 1977), 1: 'patronage often utilises the vocabulary of kin.'

[59] In G15, G21, G36, G40, G52, G53 (three times), G56, G57, G58, G59, G60, G63, G72, G82, G87, G88, G106, G113, G121, G133; in G64 and G77 bishops are referred to in the third person.

[60] In G3, G37, G51, G64, G66, G75, G77, G83, G90. In G45 and G52 he refers to the patriarch and abbot Symeon as *pater;* in G84 to himself.

[61] *huie*: G31, G46, G55, G80, G81, G91, G92, G104, G108, G115, G116, G128, G131; *teknon mou*: G102, and *tekna*: G1; *pai*: G39, G84, and *paides*: G2.

[62] G17, II, 189.35-36; G8, II, 155.30-33; G109, II, 529.11-13.

[63] Gautier makes a good case on the basis of a parallel in Anna Komnene, *Alexiad,* III.i.1, ed. B. Leib, *Anne Comnène, Alexiade. Règne de l'empereur Alexis I Comnène (1081-1118),* 3 vols (Collection byzantine, Paris, 1937-1945), I, 103.2: τὸν ἐπ' ἀνεψιᾷ γαμβρὸν αὐτῶν Μιχαήλ, though this does spell it out. G79 fits very well into the story of Gregory Pakourianos in Bulgaria as presented by G68 *(adventus)*, G55 *(agroikia)*, G67 (telling Kamateros of his arrival); G80 (a tiff dissolved), G79 (after his departure).

[64] See J. Darrouzès, *Georges et Dèmètrios Tornikès, Lettres et discours* (Le monde byzantin, Paris, 1970), 25-26.

[65] E.g. Taronitopoulos in G18, Mermentopoulos in G47, John Komnenos the son of the *sebastokrator* in G10, G11, G19, G26 and G123 to Constantine Komnenos. Adrian is always called the brother of the emperor and Bryennios referred to as the *gambros*—but this is how power lay under the Komnenoi: not so much a put-down, more evidence of *parresia.*

[66] E.g. the bishop of Pelagonia in G21 and G36, G63, Vidin in G57, Triaditsa in G58, G59, G60, G87. See R. Maisano, 'Sull' uso del termine ἀδελφός nel *Prato* di Giovanni Mosco,' *Koinonia* 6 (1982), 147-154.

of the collection.[67] In the vocative it is always a bishop; the lack of forms of address in the letter to Demetrios conforms to the impression of intimacy we gain from the relationship; even the formal opening of the defence of eunuchs uses the dative, and the lemma of the reply on the liturgy helpfully adds ἑαυτοῦ.[68] The problem arises in the third person. G122 distinguishes carefully between the suffragan addressee, τιμιώτατε συνεπίσκοπε and his χρηστότατος ἀδελφός, i.e. his brother Demetrios.[69] Other examples are less clear. Is the συνάδελφος of G61 the same as the ἀδελφός who bears G7, G90, G91, G93, G94, G110, G116? I suspect not.[70] Other people's brothers are more easily distinguished by a possessive: Chrysoberges' brother Nicholas in G35, Adrian's brother Alexios in G85, G89, G98, Theodore Smyrnaios's brother Paul in G28, Psellos's brother Michael in G132.[71] In G37 τὸν ἀδελφὸν is a monk of Anaplous, in G77 τῷ ἀδελφῷ is probably the bishop of Triaditsa.[72] Plural brothers seem less likely to be kin: in G37 they are the monks of Anaplous, in G87 the bishops of the archdiocese;[73] ἀδελφότης in G37 refers to the monastic brotherhood and in G58 and G87 the college of bishops.[74] Only in G70 to Niketas *ho tou Serron* is there a doubt about οἱ δὲ ἐμοὶ μὲν ἀδελφοί, σοὶ δὲ μαθηταί who balance so clearly the form in G37, τοὺς σοὺς υἱούς, ἐμοὺς δὲ ἀδελφούς.[75] And the lack of a possessive in G110 leaves that also ambiguous.[76] Every case must be decided on its merits; I suggest above[77] that this difficulty does not justify inventing a robust brother John for

---

[67] Demetrios is sick in G111, G113 and G133 and dead in G121, G122 and poems 14 and 15, I, 369-377. See above, 3.1, 91-94 on the dating and below, 5.2, 244-247 for analysis.

[68] *In Defence of Eunuchs*, no.7, Gautier, *Théophylacte*, I, 291.1: Λόγος ἀδελφῷ μὲν εὐνούχῳ χαρίζεται...; G134 πρὸς τὸν ἑαυτοῦ ἀδελφὸν Δημήτριον, II, 593.1.

[69] G122, II, 561.2-3: Ὁ μὲν χρηστοτατός μοι ἀδελφός, τιμιώτατε συνεπίσκοπε, ὑπὸ Κυρίου προσληφθείς...

[70] It will need a careful search of uses in other eleventh- and twelfth-century letters in my network study of Byzantine literary society 1050-1250 before we can confirm the suspicion that συνάδελφός is more likely to mean colleague than friend.

[71] G35, to Chrysoberges metropolitan of Naupaktos, II, 245.23: περὶ τοῦ ἀδελφοῦ σου, κυροῦ Νικολάου; G28, to Smyrnaios, II, 223.20: τῷ σῷ Παύλῳ; G132: Πρὸς ἀδελφὸν τοῦ Ψελλοῦ θανόντος, II, 589.10: ὁ σὸς ἀδελφός. The address: τῷ μεγάλῳ δομεστίκῳ κῦρ Ἀδριανῷ τῷ ἀδελφῷ τοῦ βασιλέως is unambiguous.

[72] G37, to the *hegoumenos* of Anaplous, Symeon, II, 253.10; G77, to the bishop of Kerkyra, II, 411.63-64.

[73] G37, II, 257.54; Ἀσπάζομαι πάντας τοὺς σοὺς υἱούς, ἐμοὺς δε ἀδελφούς; G87, II, 459.37: παρὰ πλειόνων ἀδελφῶν ὁ δεσμός.

[74] G37, II, 253.20; G58, II, 333.102; G87, II, 457.5.

[75] G70, II, 381, 26; G37, II, 257.54, both valedictory greetings.

[76] G110, II, 531.19: στέλλω τὸν ἀδελφὸν, ᾧ...but taken with G90, G91, G93, all of which have the possessive, it is most likely to be an actual brother.

[77] 93-94.

Theophylact. A rather different problem arises out of Theophylact's use of υἱός: who were Theophylact's sons?

ii. Sons and lovers

Theophylact addresses eight of his correspondents as λαμπρότατε, ὑπερλάμπρε, μεγαλεπιφανέστατε, πανσέβαστε or τιμιώτατέ μοι ἐν Κυρίῳ υἱέ. These are John Attaleiates, Michael Pantechnes, Gregory Kamateros, Theophylact Romaios, Gregory Taronites, Makrembolites *archon* of Prespa, Gregory Pakourianos and the *didaskalos* of the Great Church of G91.[78] He also addresses Niketas *ho tou Chalkedonos* as παῖ ἱερώτατε and calls Michael Pantechnes on occasion τέκνον μου and ὦ καλὲ παῖ.[79] Nearly all may be seen to have some kind of filial or semi-dependent relationship with Theophylact; he is concerned about their progress, rejoices in their successes and fears for their morals. What exactly was the relationship? An obvious suggestion is that they were ex-pupils and it is apparently on this basis that Gautier lists Theophylact's alumni.[80] But Kazhdan has taught us to be cautious on this issue, and we should examine the evidence. External evidence may sometimes help; Gregory Kamateros is identified as a pupil on those grounds.[81] Michael Pantechnes is admitted by the lemma of G102 as is Nicholas, deacon and *kanstresios* of Hagia Sophia, and future bishop of Malesova, the addressee of Theophylact's *logos* against the Latins.[82] Others are specifically (and rather crudely) identified as ex-pupils: Niketas *ho tou Chalkedonos* and John Attaleiates.[83] The parallelism of G28 establishes the kin relationship of Paul Smyrnaios and Demetrios Hephaistos, and also the teaching relationship of

---

[78] John Attaleiates, *lamprotate/chrestotate* in G104; Michael Pantechnes, *hyperlampre* G115, 116, 128, 131; Gregory Kamateros, *panhyperlampre* in G31, Theophylact Romaios, *lamprotate* in G46; Gregory Taronites, *megalepiphanestate* in G81 and G92; Makrembolites, *epiphanestate* in G107; Pakourianos is *pansebaste* in G55, G68 and G80; the *didaskalos* is *timiotate* in G91.

[79] Niketas G84, II, 441.2; Michael in G102, II, 515.2; G39, II, 265.35.

[80] Gautier, *Théophylacte*, I, 27-28. But he includes also Niketas bishop of Malesova, Nicholas Mermentoulos, Paul Smyrnaios, Nicholas Anemas, John Opheomachos, Niketas o tou Chalkedonos.

[81] George Tornikes, ep. 10, ed. Darrouzès, 129.

[82] G102, II, 515.1: τῷ μαθητῇ αὐτοῦ, τῷ Παντέχνῃ, κυρῷ Μιχαήλ, τῷ ἰατρῷ, I, 247, title: Προσλαλιά τινι τῶν αὐτοῦ ὁμιλητῶν περὶ ὧν ἐγκαλοῦνται Λατίνοι.

[83] Theophylact calls in the debt (τὸ χρέος, τὸ ὀφειλόμενον) of teaching: G84, to Niketas, II, 441.5-9 and 443.26-28; G104, to John, II, 519.3-8.

each with the other's brother.[84] In every other case we should be hesitant. Even Constantine the young co-emperor is a dubious case.[85]

Other possibilities are that it is a relationship of ritual kinship[86] or spiritual kinship[87] or patronage.[88] In view of Theophylact's orders we should discard the first. The last looks attractive. We know that Theophylact privileged his relationships with the young,[89] and what is more likely than that these represent 'young friends' recruited by the old teaching relationship or like Pakourianos and Makrembolites by proximity in Bulgaria? Yet we should be wary of assuming that it is a relationship of protector to protégé: a generic analysis of the letters to Gregory Taronites presents Theophylact far more in the role of client than patron.[90] A last possibility is spiritual kinship, at that time of great social importance. The emperor Alexios on his mother's orders took holy men on campaign with him; sewing circles in the capital brought monks and rich women together.[91] Letters exist from Michael Psellos as spiritual father and spiritual son; the former is the only one in the collection to address its addressee as 'son.'[92] But Theophylact was not a monk (and his attitude to monks was cause for mirth in his household),[93] and the only two letters of clear parainetic force which are not to suffragan bishops, to Tarchaneiotes, do not use this form.[94] It may well be that he would not use the form anyway because of the advanced age and social splendour of Tarchaneiotes; it remains true that the letters to Tarchaneiotes certainly do

---

[84] G28, II, 223.19-22: Ὁποῖον ἂν ἐβούλου με εἶναι τῷ σῷ Παύλῳ ὑπ' ἐμοὶ τελουμένῳ σοφίας τι μυστήριον, τοιοῦτος γενοῦ τῷ ἐμῷ Δημητρίῳ τὰ φιλοσοφίας ὑπὸ σοὶ ὀργιάζοντι.

[85] All the evidence is internal.

[86] On ritual kinship in Byzantium see R. Macrides, 'The Byzantine Godfather,' *BMGS* 12 (1987), 139-162; see also her 'Kinship by Arrangement. The Case of Adoption,' *DOP* 44 (1990), 109-118.

[87] See R. Morris, 'The Political Saint of the Eleventh Century,' *The Byzantine Saint*, ed. S. Hackel (Studies Supplementary to Sobornost, 5, Birmingham, 1981), 43-50; J. Turner, *St Symeon the New Theologian and Spiritual Fatherhood* (Leiden, 1990); F. Hausherr, *Direction spirituelle en orient autrefois* (OCA, 14/4, Rome, 1955).

[88] See M.E. Mullett, 'Patronage in Action: the Problems of an Eleventh-century Bishop,' *Byzantine Church and People*, ed. R. Morris (Birmingham, 1990), 125-147 and 'Byzantium, a Friendly Society?' *P&P* 118 (1988), 3 -24,

[89] G35, to Chrysoberges, metropolitan of Naupaktos, II, 245.9-12.

[90] M.E. Mullett, 'The Madness of Genre,' *Homo Byzantinus. Papers in Honor of Alexander Kazhdan*, ed. A. Cutler and S. Franklin, *DOP* 46 (1992), 243.

[91] See Morris, 'Political Saint,' esp. 48-49.

[92] Michael Psellos, ep. 27, to Olympites the monk, ed. Sathas, 262; ep. 189, υἱῷ πνευματικῷ, ed. Kurtz-Drexl, 209-212.

[93] G37, to Symeon, *hegoumenos* of Anaplous.

[94] G16 and G20.

not help to identify Theophylact's 'sons' as spiritual sons. Again each case must be taken on its merits.

iii. *Patrons, clients and friends*
We have seen that Theophylact in theory distinguished clearly between these relationships;[95] in practice it is no easier to draw hard and fast lines in Byzantium than in many other societies.[96] He only once describes himself in what may be client status, to caesar Melissenos, but the description of Demetrios as σύνδουλος in G4 must be read in relation to Maria, the addressee: Demetrios, like Theophylact, is her slave.[97]

The concern of Theophylact for symmetry and reciprocity may be seen from G28,[98] and I have made this the basis of my distinctions between the relationships. In practice Theophylact seems to have several patrons at a time, and he is careful to oil the wheels of the relationship; he also has a wide circle of friends, some of whom are seen in the correspondence as only instrumental,[99] others as only emotional,[100] some as both.[101] Probably all his friendships were expected to work. A (cynical but operable) rule of thumb is to take it that the praise of friendship may well denote instrumentality. It is sometimes equally difficult in the shifting expectations of the role of the local official to distinguish between official and patron; I have attempted to do so elsewhere,[102] but it is a question which needs constant alertness.

My criteria for intimacy need a little discussion. First, affect, rare though it is in the collection, and misleading as it may be.[103] On the basis of the rest of the Demetrios dossier I have taken the letter to Demetrios as being likely to

---

[95] G10, II, 161.2-4. We have also seen above, 119-121, that he had a clear idea what a friend was.

[96] See my 'Friendly Society?'; for other societies see S.N. Eisenstadt and L. Roniger, *Patrons, Clients and Friends: Interpersonal Relations and the Structure of Trust in Society* (Cambridge, 1984).

[97] G13, II, 171.15-16: τοῖς ὑπ' αὐτοῦ ἐλεουμένοις; G4, II, 141.54: εἰς τὸν σύνδουλον καὶ ἀδελφόν μου Δημήτριον.

[98] G28, II, 223.15-23.

[99] E.g. John Serblias, G49.

[100] E.g. Romaios Theophylaktos, G42, G46.

[101] On the difference see R. Reina, 'Patterns of Friendship in a Guatemalan Community,' *American Anthropologist* 61 (1969), 44-50; Y.A. Cohen, 'Patterns of Friendship,' *Social Structure and Personality: a Case Book* (New York, 1961), 351; but R. Paine, 'In Search of Friendship,' *Man* n.s. 4 (1969), 505: 'is not all friendship ultimately instrumental?'

[102] 'Patronage,' 135-137.

[103] On affect J. Pitt-Rivers, *People of the Sierra* (London, 1954), 140; Wolf, 'Kinship, Friendship and Patron-Client Relations,' 13.

convey Theophylact's warmest expression of a close relationship,[104] and have looked for similarities elsewhere. The brevity, the lack of formal address forms, the presence of *anthropon* or *andron* or *potheinotate* or *philtate* may be indicators here,[105] while the bald statement that ἀεί μοι τὸν πόθον ἀνάπτεις may cut less ice.[106] Second, circumstantial indications: the people Theophylact stayed with or invited to stay with him; the people to whom he confided the story of the illness and death of his brother or lent his books I have assumed are among his intimates.[107] Third, shared interests, in medicine or books or shared troubles like those of the episcopate, or shared intimates, especially where these relations are multiplex I suggest indicate intimacy.[108] And finally I have taken the stylistic brilliance and lighthearted wordplay of some of the letters[109] to suggest that these relationships were valued by Theophylact because they distracted him from the *ponerai hemerai*.

4.2 Theophylact's first order zone

This section first presents (in words and diagrams) and then analyses Theophylact's network. Fig. 1 represents Theophylact's first order zone as it is known from his letter-collection. Rather than list members of the network alphabetically (many are known from incomplete names)[110] or by Gautier's numbers (his list is incomplete and often fuses several individuals under a single head),[111] or by *taxis* (even with Stiernon and the synodal attendance lists

---

[104] G133, II, 591.

[105] *Anthropon*: Theodore Smyrna in G6 and G28; *andron*: Mermentoulos in G33 and Anemas in G34 and G41. Michael Pantechnes is *philtate* in G99; the bishop of Semnea is *phile emoi kephale* in G56; Opheomachos is *thaumasie* in G71.

[106] As in G43, II, 275.2 which speaks more of patronage than friendship.

[107] He invites Michael Pantechnes to stay, visits the bishop of Pelagonia, talks of the impending visit of the *sebastos* (John Doukas!). He tells the bishop of Kitros and the bishop of Debra about the death of his brother. He lends a Chrysostom to Anemas, borrows a Galen at least from Nicholas Kallikles and may have shared reading with Nicholas of Kerkyra.

[108] For example the metropolitan of Naupaktos, Nicholas Kallikles, Niketas *ho tou Serron*.

[109] For example G25, to Mermentoulos, G32, to Anemas, G46, to Romaios Theophylactos, G71, to Opheomachos, G108, to Makrembolites, G123, to Constantine Komnenos, G127, to Gregory Kamateros.

[110] I.e. Christian name or surname only, or a nickname, e.g. Diabologyres.

[111] I, 37-38. For example no.24, 'Michel et Nikétas, diacres;' no.21, 'Pantechnès, Michel et Jean.' I offer 57 correspondents to Gautier's 46.

quite a task in itself),[112] I have represented it at a fairly late stage in the process of analysis I describe above.[113] That is, I have already decided on issues of prosopography (though I record dissident views), and on the nature of the relationship with Theophylact, whether uniplex or multiplex.[114] I have recorded the uses of that relationship, to form the basis of my discussion of Theophylact's uses of network below in 4.3. I have also decided on questions of intimacy, and both diagram and discussion show the network arranged according to intimacy zones.[115] At the centre is Theophylact, around him a *personal cell*, and, moving outwards, an *intimate zone* and an *effective zone*. All these contain persons addressed in the correspondence. Beyond the effective zone is a *nominal zone* containing persons simply mentioned in the collection. On the outside is the *extended zone*, at which point the second and third order zones begin. These are not shown in fig. 1, but fig. 2 shows these ramifications spreading outwards from Theophylact's personal cell.[116] Each of these diagrams represents a series of decisions taken on the basis of the criteria discussed in 4.1 above and allows us to characterise members of Theophylact's network and their relationship with him. It is then possible to analyse Theophylact' network. Fig. 3 taken with fig. 1 enables a comparison of the evidence of the collection with that of Theophylact's other works; it also compares the latter with the first order zone of Nicholas Kallikles from the evidence of his occasional poems. Fig. 4 accompanies the section which attempts to characterise the network in terms of its sociological makeup. Figs. 5-7, which shows Theophylact's use of network, accompany section 4.1 below. Bibliography and detailed breakdown of the detection of relationships in all these figures are to be found below, 'The Network,' 347-381.

So returning to fig. 1, I shall describe the network in each of the intimacy zonings in turn, beginning at the centre with Theophylact's personal cell and moving outwards.

i. *Personal cell*
An anthropologist's definition of a personal cell is that it is 'usually composed of Ego's closest relatives and possibly, a few of his [or her] most intimate

---

[112] For synodal lists see now conveniently (but for secular persons only) P. Magdalino, *The Empire of Manuel I Komnenos, 1143-1180* (Cambridge, 1994), 182-185 and appendix 2, 501-509; L. Stiernon, 'Notes de prosopographie.'

[113] The Prosopography of the Byzantine Empire is presently evolving means of demonstrating criteria for these decisions in a relational database.

[114] Cf. diagram 2.2 in Boissevain, *Friends*, 29.

[115] Cf. the diagram 2.10 in ibid., 47.

[116] This builds on the diagram 2.1 in Boissevain, *Friends*, 26.

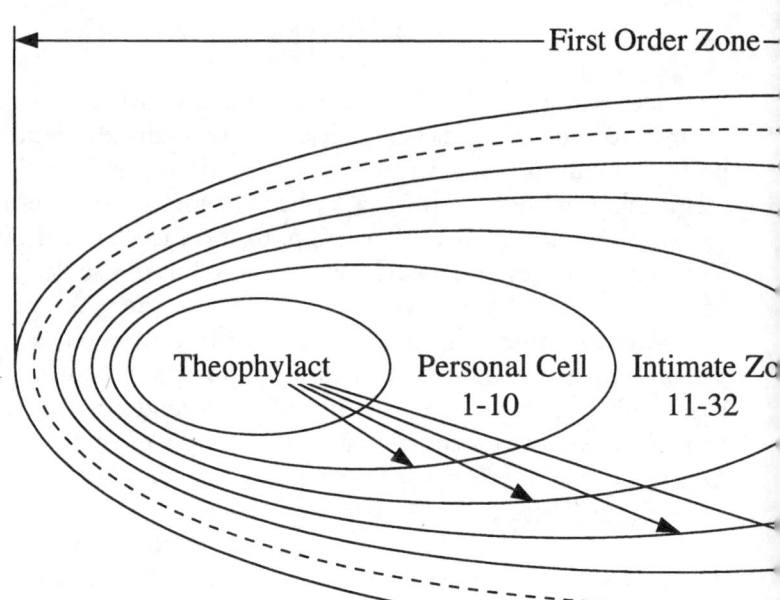

First Order Zone—

Theophylact

Personal Cell
1-10

Intimate Zo
11-32

FIRST ORDER ZONE
Personal cell
(1) Demetrios Hephaistos
(2) Nicholas Anemas
(3) Nicholas Kallikles
(4) Gregory Kamateros
(5) Nicholas Mermentoulos
(6) John Opheomachos
(7) Michael Pantechnes
(8) Nicholas bp of Kerkyra
(9) bp of Kitros
(10) bp of Pelagonia
Intimate zone
(11) Nikephoros Bryennios
(12) Constantine Komnenos
(13) Machetares
(14) Makrembolites
(15) Gregory Pakourianos
(16) John Pantechnes
(17) John Peribleptenos
(18) Niketas Polites, bp
(19) Theophylact Romaios
(20) Theodore Smyrnaios
(21) Tarchaneiotes
(22) Niketas *ho tou Serron*
(23) Nikephoros *chartophylax*
(24) Niketas *chartophylax*
(25) Peter, *chartophylax*
(26) Chrysoberges, bp of
    Naupaktos
(27) Theodoulos, bp of
    Thessalonike

(28) bp of Semnea
(29) Symeon, abt, Anaplous
(30) John the maistor
(31) John the philosopher
(32) Niketas, imperial doctor
Effective zone
(33) John Attaleiates
(34) John Bryennios
(35) Diabologyres, bp
(36) Constantine Doukas
(37) Eirene Doukaina
(38) John Doukas
(39) Michael Doukas,
    protostrator
(40) Gregory Kamateros, bp
(41) Adrian Komnenos
(42) John Komnenos
(43) patriarch Nicholas
(44) Nikephoros Melissenos
(45) George Palaiologos
(46) Psellos, brother
(47) John Serblias
(48) Gregory Taronites
(49) John Taronites,
(50) Maria, *basilissa*
(51) Maria of Bulgaria,
    protovestiaria
(52) Michael *ho tou Chalkedonos*
(53) Niketas *ho tou Chalkedonos*
(54) John, *grammatikos* of
    Palaiologos
(55) Tibanios, Armenian

(56) Grand *oikonomos*
(57) *epi ton deeseon*
(58) bp of Debra
(59) bp of Triaditsa
(60) bp of Vidin
(61) Recipient of G106
(62) (Undisciplined) pupils
(63) Bulgar pupils
(64) Rodomir Aaron
(65) Constantine Doukas
(66) Nicholas, *kanstresios*
(67) The monk Neilos
(68) A libidinous eunuch
(69) A grieving person
(70) A 'wicked slave'
(71) Condemner
Nominal zone
(72) Symeon Blachernites
(73) Theodore Chryselios
(74) Nicholas Chrysoberges
(75) Constantine Choirosphaktes
(76) Iasites, praktor
(77) Alexios I Komnenos
(78) Isaac Komnenos, *sebastokrator*
(79) Demetrios Kritopoulos
(80) N. Kritopoulos
(81) Michael Beses Lampenos
(82) N. Makrembolites
(83) N. Medenos
(84) Michael Psellos
(85) Psellos, grandson
(86) Senachereim

Figure 1: Theophylact's first order zone

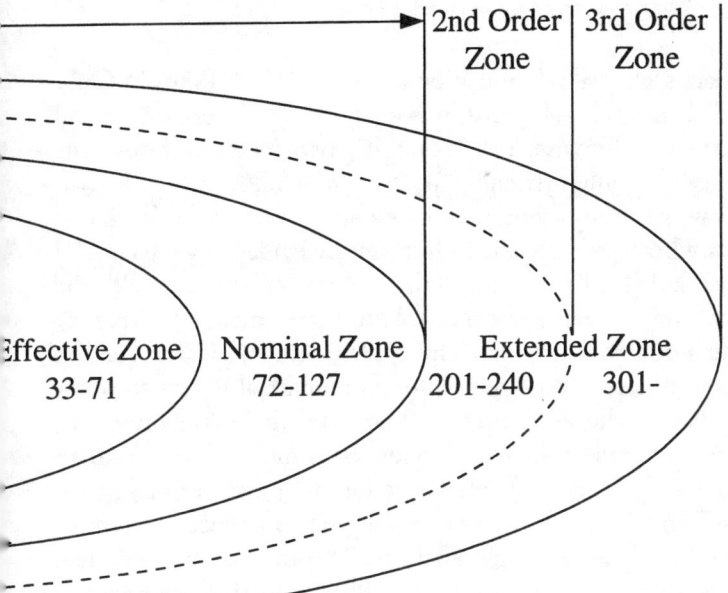

2nd Order Zone | 3rd Order Zone

Effective Zone 33-71 | Nominal Zone 72-127 | Extended Zone 201-240 / 301-

(87) The 2nd Senachereim
(88) Paul Smyrnaios
(89) N. Smyrnaios
(90) Romanos Straboromanos
(91) Tornikios
(92) Michael *ho tou Polyeuktou*
(93) Nicholas *ho tou Boutou*
(94) Eumathios, *megalepiphanestatos*
(95) Gregory *psaltes*
(96) John, *ho kalos*
(98) Theodosios
(97) Lazaros
(99) bp of Side
(100) bp of Glavenitsa
(101) bp of Lipenion
(102) bp of Malesova
(103) bp of Strumitsa
(104) monk of Anaplous
(105) member of Theo-
phylact's household
(106) *ho paron anthropos*
(107) immoral hieromonk
(108) Bulgar *geron*
(109) 2nd Bulgar *geron*
(110) eunuch praktor
(111) Ex-abt, Anaplous
(112) Two bearers
(113) Relatives in Euripos
(114) Priests of Pologos
(115) *Hagioserretai*
(116) Villagers of Ekklesiai
(117) Pupils of Niketas (22)

(118) Monks of Anaplous
(119) All the bps of Ochrid
(120) Michael Antiochos
(121) Anna Dalassene
(122) John II Komnenos
(123) Symeon, abt of
eunuchs on Athos
(124) bp of Edessa
(125) bp of Petra
(126) bp of Pydna (=Kitros)
(127) bp of Thessalonike
Extended zone:
SECOND ORDER ZONE
(201) Nicholas Adrianoupolites
(202) Leo Anemas
(203) Michael Anemas
(204) N. Anemas
(205) N. Anemas
(206) Anna Arbantenissa
(207) John Arbantenos
(208) Nikephoros Diogenes
(209) N. Dokeiane
(210) Anna Doukaina
(211) Anna Doukaina
(212) Eirene Doukaina
(213) Alexios Doukas
(214) N. Doukas, son of
protostrator
(215) Michael Italikos
(216) Michael Doukas
Kamateros
(217) Anna Komnene

(218) Eirene Piroska
Komnene
(219) Eudokia Komnene
(220) Maria Komnene
(221) Theodora Komnene
(222) Isaac Komnenos
(223) Michael (??Lizix)
(224) Andronikos Doukas
Palaiologos
(225) Theodore Prodromos
(226) Nicholas Skleros
(227) John Skylitzes-
Thrakesios
(228) John Zonaras
(229) Roger, *sebastos*
(230) Stephen-Symeon the
Sanctified
(231) Ex-bp, archimandrite
of the Mangana
(232) Cyril Phileotes
(233) Niketas Stethatos
(234) Manuel Straboromanos
(235) George Tornikes
(236) Euthymios Zigabenos
(237) Eustratios of Nicaea
(238) Leo of Chalcedon
(239) Hosios Meletios
(240) Gregory, abt of Oxeia
Extended zone:
THIRD ORDER ZONE
(301) Symeon the New
Theologian

Figure 1: Theophylact's first order zone

friends'.[117] Theophylact's closest relationships are of different kinds.[118] Only one relative is included, and this relationship is qualitatively different from all others in the collection. Otherwise, two ex-pupils, two fellow-bishops, one nearby suffragan, two young friends posted to Bulgaria, and two Constantinopolitans with common interests make up his personal cell, that is those correspondents who appear closest to him on the evidence we have. All but Demetrios are addressed in more than one letter; not all the correspondents to whom he addressed most letters are included: Gregory Kamateros (5-7 letters) and Michael Pantechnes (9-10 letters) clearly qualify, but John Komnenos (7-8 letters) does not. Though individual letters to other correspondents may betray the same traits as letters to obvious members of the personal cell, there is usually insufficient evidence of multiplexity or affect for these correspondents to qualify: I include letters to John Peribleptenos, John the philosopher and John the *maistor* among Theophylact's letters of friendship,[119] but they are eclipsed in closeness to Theophylact by episcopal correspondents whose closeness is of a different kind, and this difference is reflected in the letters.

I describe elsewhere[120] the nature of Theophylact's relationship with his brother as presented in the correspondence and his poems, and it must serve as a measure of warmth in his other relations. We meet DEMETRIOS (HEPHAISTOS) (1)[121] as the trusted letter-bearer, the member of the *kyklos* to whom and from whom greetings are borne, as dangerously ill and then, movingly, as dead. We see his connections—as dear to the emperor, fellow-client of Maria and student in Constantinople. Only one letter catches the tone of their relationship, but it is consistent with the third-person references to the most important person in Theophylact's life and network.

MICHAEL PANTECHNES (7) is the correspondent to whom most letters have been preserved. Here we see in the letters an ex-pupil for whom Theophylact maintains continuing concern at various crises of his life, the death of his father, his appointment to court. Brief, witty letters informed by their teaching relationship run throughout, supported by visits, poems and their shared interest in medicine. GREGORY KAMATEROS (4) is the other ex-pupil we can see in the collection, again at various stages of his career.

---

[117] Boissevain, *Friends*, 47.

[118] For detailed documentation of each correspondent see below, 'The Network,' 347-381.

[119] See above, 3.2, 118.

[120] See above, 91-94; below, 244-246.

[121] Nowhere is Demetrios called by both names. Numbers in brackets refer to 'The Network', below, 347-381.

Theophylact congratulates him on promotion, thanks him for helpful interventions in Bulgaria and asks him to engineer others. The relationship appears more instrumental than with Michael Pantechnes, but letter G127 is unparalleled in the collection,[122] and they were clearly on visiting terms. There is no sense in the letters of the ambition and social-climbing at which Niketas Choniates hints—unless the satire of G127 could be turned also against its recipient.

NICHOLAS ANEMAS (2) and JOHN OPHEOMACHOS (6) are young friends (the first is called φίλος ἀληθινός) who appear as officials in Bulgaria. The letters show considerable affection (*philtate, potheinotate, thaumasie*) for friends who are not here described as 'sons'. In each case we see their arrival and a point during their tour of duty; with Anemas we also see his departure with the *propemptikon* of G41. All letters to them are short, teasing, brilliant with word-play and quotation.

Though the world of Constantinople is very much in Theophylact's mind as he measures himself against its achievements and expectations, only two other correspondents of that world seem to reach his innermost circle. One is NICHOLAS MERMENTOULOS (5), *Grand droungarios of the Watch*, who received five letters from Theophylact, including requests which reveal how much he valued his letters. The tone is light in all of them and the content is friendship and learning; the lack of ceremonial forms of address is made up for by extravagant forms playing on the superlatives attached to court titles like *hyperlampros* and *hyperteros*. Theophylact appears to have used his friendship for consolation rather than anything more practical. The other is NICHOLAS KALLIKLES (3), to whom four letters are preserved, all from a late stage in the collection. Nicholas is known from his own poems as well as his career as a doctor, though little of his personality emerges, a difficulty which has made it difficult to attribute to him the *Timarion*. From the collection he appears as a friend with common interests and sense of humour, a crucial role at court and a willingness to lend Theophylact his books.

Very different are the letters to Theophylact's three closest episcopal correspondents. NICHOLAS, *metropolitan of* KERKYRA (8) appears as an episcopal counterpart with whom Theophylact can be frank (though far from transparent) about his worries. The two long letters G75 and G77 pour out their troubles antiphonally with much riddling and centos of the psalms. It is without surprise that we learn that Nicholas attempted to resign his episcopate, possibly at the synod of 1094 and of the specific troubles he lists in his poem of resignation; in this we have a clearer, though still obscure, view of

---

[122] See above, 150.

his cup of bitterness hinted at by Theophylact in the two letters. I have suggested that the coincidence of poems on Symeon the New Theologian by them both, dated to 1125/26, may indicate a continuing connection between them of book-exchange. N.N., *bishop of* KITROS (9) is shown in his four letters to be another fellow-sufferer, though as a suffragan of Thessalonike unequal in *taxis* to Theophylact. They exchange gifts with some ceremony, and the news of the crossing of the First Crusade, but the bishop's claim to be in Theophylact's personal cell lies in his choosing him to receive the news of the death of Demetrios. N.N., *bishop of* PELAGONIA (10) receives affectionate communications about everyday matters; they are on visiting terms and Theophylact looks after his interests by advice, speedy warnings and metropolitan introductions as appropriate.

ii. *Intimate zone*

In anthropological practice this zone is defined as 'very close friends and relations with whom Ego maintains active, intimate relations' and 'both friends and relatives with whom he maintains more passive relations but who nonetheless are emotionally important to him'.[123] I have not distinguished within this zone but have included any correspondent for whom there is evidence of affect.[124] Twenty-one qualify: ex-colleagues, ecclesiastical superiors, fellow-bishops and officials. It is worth noting though that thirteen of these are known from one letter only; more letters might change their intimacy rating considerably; it is sometimes even on this evidence difficult to exclude them from the personal cell.

Into this zone come the two members of the imperial family for whom Theophylact shows more than expected emotion. Although Maria the ex-*basilissa* draws from him his most courtly expressions and clearly acted as patroness over some time, and though Adrian the Grand Domestic (41) takes her place as chief patron in the latter part of the collection, NIKEPHOROS BRYENNIOS (11), *panhypersebastos* then *caesar*, appears more multiplex, son of another correspondent of Theophylact, patron when times were hard, and recipient of a poem such as Theophylact sent to his friends. This is one case where the evidence for intimacy is provided not by a letter but by another work of Theophylact. CONSTANTINE KOMNENOS (12) is known as *Grand droungarios of the Watch* (and/or *Grand Droungarios*) largely from synods and seals; Theophylact's G123 is a puzzling letter (narrative, using direct speech, short, without forms of address) which indicates something other than an

---

[123] Boissevain, *Friends*, 47.

[124] For affect see Wolf, 'Kinship, Friendship and Patron-Client Relations,' 13; Pitt-Rivers, *The People of the Sierra*, 139-140.

impersonal official relationship, such as he had with Constantine's elder brother John. A charming compliment to a friendly governor, it also suggests a warmer relationship.

In this zone also appear Theophylact's academic friends in Constantinople, whom he was so eager to contact on his arrival in Bulgaria. THEODORE SMYRNAIOS (20) the *hypatos ton philosophon* appears with the gout also attested in *Timarion* as teacher of Demetrios and brother of Theophylact's pupil Paul. Theophylact is very conscious of reciprocity in this relationship, and the word-play does not reveal close attachment. There is though some duration, from appointment to at least the calumny crisis, and Theophylact takes the opportunity to complain of his troubles, in a suitably veiled way. The relationship with NIKETAS *ho tou Serron* (22), *didaskalos of the Great Church*, another ex-colleague and *oikoumenikos didaskalos,* is revealed over a similar period, Demetrios again appearing as a participant in the relationship. Difficulties over attribution of letters mean this relationship is hard to tease out.

Ecclesiastical colleagues are also found in this zone: relations with the three *chartophylakes*, NIKEPHOROS (23), NIKETAS (24) and PETER (25) are affectionate but business-like, benevolence and concern characterising all; Demetrios was sent to Peter. Four other episcopal correspondents appear in this zone with five letters between them. N.N. *bishop of* SEMNEA (28) received two, fairly obscure letters praying for assistance to subvert the fisc; shared problems appear to be the basis of the relationship. Theophylact seems on slightly closer terms with N. CHRYSOBERGES, *metropolitan of* NAUPAKTOS (26) whom he planned to visit and whose brother, Nicholas, he knew, and with THEODOULOS N., *metropolitan of* THESSALONIKE (27), whose shared woes were geographically close. Slightly older correspondents appear to be JOHN PANTECHNES, *magistros* (16), whose death is announced in G39; G120 to him is addressed as to an elevated friend, with much literary artistry; and N. TARCHANEIOTES (21), who appears to be an older, grander figure who has sought his spiritual advice. It is to him though that Theophylact makes what might otherwise be thought an unambiguous statement of affection: 'you always kindle my desire.' I suggest this should be read in a spiritual sense, of desire for God, and that care be taken elsewhere with affirmations of this kind. SYMEON, *hegoumenos of* ANAPLOUS (29), is greeted in an affectionate tone, with shared friends, and news, gossip and prayers form the transactional content; he is clearly a friend rather than a spiritual father. NIKETAS, *the imperial doctor* (32) is another correspondent without forms of address, which often suggests special intimacy; he and Theophylact were clearly on visiting terms and Demetrios was a shared concern.

But the largest group in this zone is of intellectual friends in the capital who might, with more letters, qualify for Theophylact's personal cell. JOHN PERIBLEPTENOS (17) may be the καλος Ἰωάννης of G42 and G46, certainly G101 addresses him as such; informality and elaborate medical vocabulary suggest shared interests. JOHN *the philosopher* (31) and JOHN *the maistor* (30) are greeted without forms of address, but there is very little to go on. THEOPHYLACT ROMAIOS (19) is a 'son', and the content of the letters is light with classical allusions and jokes as well as advice. Other 'sons', this time in Bulgaria are N. MAKREMBOLITES (14), to whom Theophylact addresses a brilliant tour de force about organising a synod, and GREGORY PAKOURIANOS (15), Theophylact's favourite local governor, whom he addresses with respectful forms and some affection: to Theophylact he and Gregory are Plato and Dionysios.

iii. *Effective zone*
This is defined by Boissevain thus: 'then there is a circle of persons who are important to him in a more pragmatic sense for economic and political purposes and the logistics of everyday life. A number of the people in this zone are there because of their own networks. As these contain strategic persons who may be useful to Ego, he keeps his relations with them warm so he can gain access to the friends of his friends.'[125] Theophylact's effective zone of twenty-eight persons includes superiors and inferiors in an official sense, his current pupils, local functionaries, an opponent in debate, patrons and instrumental friends.

Strictly speaking, the patriarch NICHOLAS KYRDINIATES, *patriarch* NICHOLAS III GRAMMATIKOS (43) was not Theophylact's superior since he held an autocephalous see, but the letters to him, and to N.N. *the Grand oikonomos* (56) are encrusted with the politeness owed to a superior. The letter to the Grand *oikonomos* dates from Theophylact's teaching days in Constantinople; the three letters to Nicholas are taken up with complaints, gifts, prayers, but do not face the issues of disagreement between Ochrid and the patriarchate. The asymmetry is very clear. Theophylact's suffragan *bishops of* DEBRA (58), VIDIN (60), TRIADITSA (59) and perhaps DIABOLIS (35) are in this zone, together with a GREGORY KAMATEROS, *bishop of* N. (40), recipient of G53, otherwise unknown. I discuss below, 4.4, the letters relating to certain cases; these letters have in common their sympathy and concern, but also a sense that this is all part of the job. *The recipient of G106* (61) who appears to be a high ecclesiastic

---

[125] Boissevain, *Friends*, 47.

from a smart family is addressed with apparent affection, but the letter appears to be merely establishing contact.

Current pupils are addressed: a group from Theophylact's teaching days, *(undisciplined) pupils* (62) in G1 and G2 and his *Bulgar pupils* (63) in G103. The first two are long, speeches rather than letters, justifying his philosophy of teaching and addressing them as *O syneton moi akroaterion*; the last is a short letter which involves reproach as well as an apology for illness.

Four local functionaries may be found in this zone, all *doukes* of Dyrrachion or the Vardar.[126] JOHN BRYENNIOS, *doux of Dyrrachion* (34), despite Theophylact's more friendly relations with his son the caesar, is treated with formality: the transactional content is praise and fish, since we possess an adventus letter and another accompanying a gift of fish. CONSTANTINE DOUKAS, *ruler of the Vardar* (36) is the official we hear of in passing more than meet in addressed letters; we again have an adventus letter and a letter accompanying a gift. Theophylact's expectations outweigh any particular individuality of correspondent or relationship. JOHN DOUKAS, *doux of Dyrrachion*, then *megas doux* (38) is the classic official recycled as patron. There is a hint of hero-worship about the relationship, not surprising perhaps where the architect of the Komnenian reconquest was concerned. JOHN KOMNENOS, *doux of Dyrrachion* (42) on the other hand is the other pole of a purely official and difficult relationship which curiously shows no sign of the crisis which must have occurred when Theophylact denounced him to the emperor.[127] The tone adopted by Theophylact is cool, respectful and businesslike throughout.

The opponent is TIBANIOS *the Armenian* (55), who is simply a theological opponent, addressed with no forms; it is unclear whether the letter is a letter, or delivered as a speech or simply written to contribute to a debate. Other opponents are largely relegated to the nominal zone; it seems that letters, with some exceptions like those to the bishop of Triaditsa (59), were not the place where Theophylact chose to confront his opponents. Another exception is JOHN TARONITES, *doux of Skopje* (49), whom Theophylact showers with polite forms of address while making it quite clear that he is

---

[126] I discuss in more detail Theophylact's handling of them in 'Patronage.'

[127] *Al.*, VIII.vii.3, L, II, 147-151. But see K. Roth, *Studie zu den Briefen des Theophylaktos Bulgarus* (Ludwigshafen am Rhein, 1900) and Angold, *Church and Society*, 161. Some of this can easily be disposed of, for example the statement that Theophylact was forced to go to Constantinople to explain himself, the blunt accusation of G24 which is more a statement of fact and plea for help, the 'food-for-thought' prayer to the Virgin which is rather more subtle, as a variation on Theophylact's normal ending. What is agreed is that relations with this *doux* were not easy.

angry with him for trying to influence the appointment of a bishop. Other letters let us know that both the patriarch and MICHAEL DOUKAS, *protostrator* (39) have in different ways violated the rights of Ochrid. Michael reappears as a patron, asked to put in a good word with his son, recently appointed to the rule of the Vardar.

Seven other patrons make an appearance in this zone. They are identified as such by an adulatory tone, the piling on of forms of address, specific requests for favours and a clearly asymmetrical relationship. Some are longer-lived than others. We see MARIA *of Alania, basilissa* (50) in one letter only, but it is a highly crafted letter to make clear the relationship between them, which is one of personal patronage.[128] What we do not see is how her gentle slide from power compelled Theophylact to seek other patrons, the most powerful of whom in the 1090s was ADRIAN KOMNENOS, *Grand Domestic* (41). The relationship can be followed in five letters, from Theophylact's arrival to the Lazaros crisis, but the relationship is extremely formal—and productive—throughout. GEORGE PALAIOLOGOS (45) enters fairly late in the collection, but is seen as heroically successful: he is likened to Herakles. Visitors to Bulgaria could be brought into play; NIKEPHOROS MELISSENOS (44) between an adventus letter and a consolatio on the death of the *sebastokrator* is both thanked for a favour and asked for another; the *despoina* who visited him in his illness, EIRENE DOUKAINA, *despoina* (37) is thanked, but we see her no more. Another imperial lady, MARIA *of Bulgaria, protovestiaria* (51), is asked to control her son Michael; there is no evidence of any other connection. These are both tantalising references, but we must simply accept that we are unlikely to learn any more.[129] With GREGORY TARONITES (48) we have a much better view of a patron who began as a 'son'. In four letters we see him from before his Pontic campaigns to after his release from imprisonment; the treatment in the collection adds to, and corrects, the account in the *Alexiad*. The relationship is clearly asymmetrical, multiplex and not excluding the possibility of intimacy, though the letters preserved are panegyric in tone.[130]

It is this tone and the asymmetry which make it easy to distinguish patrons from instrumental friends. Five such may be found in this zone. JOHN SERBLIAS (47) is treated with business-like efficiency, so that one might believe

---

[128] See my 'The "Disgrace" of the Ex-Basilissa Maria,' *BS* 45 (1984), 202-211.

[129] I have with some hesitation excluded from the network as not herself entering the world of the letters yet another imperial lady, Maria, elder sister of Alexios I Komnenos. In G18, II, 191, Theophylact exhorts her son John Taronites 'on the prayers of your holy mother' to investigate the missing *pittakion*.

[130] See my 'Madness of Genre,' 233-243.

he is being dealt with as an official, were it not for the request; he is addressed with equality as *O kale* and *O makarie* and there is no evidence of affect. N.N., *the epi ton deeseon* (**57**) again seems not to be consulted in an official capacity, though there is again no evidence of affect. In two other cases Theophylact calls in the debt of teaching: NIKETAS *ho tou Chalkedonos* (**53**) is asked to act in the case of the *protostrator's* canon-breaking, and JOHN ATTALEIATES, *protonotarios of the doux of Attaleia* (**33**) is asked to go to the help of the metropolitan of Side; in both Theophylact's call on old affection (they are 'sons' as well as pupils) is rather calculating. He also trades on the relation between Niketas and MICHAEL *ho tou Chalkedonos* (**52**) to get the latter to stop the patriarch's meddling, though he uses a form which suggests that he is presenting his relation as slightly asymmetrical in order to win the other's favour. In contrast his relation with JOHN, *grammatikos of Palaiologos* (**54**) is built on respect, and his appeal—'become Herakles, killer of brigands!'—open-ended, while the use of *adelphe kai despota* suggests a respectful equality. In all these cases symmetry marks them out from patrons, while the absence of evidence of affect differentiates them from 'emotional' friends.

iv. *Nominal zone*
This is what anthropologists call 'persons Ego knows but who mean little to him pragmatically and emotionally. He is acquainted with them but that is about all.'[131] I include in this group persons mentioned by Theophylact in the letters, but who are not directly addressed by him in the collection. Some may have been emotionally as important to him as many in zones i-iii, but we cannot see this. Nor can we analyse as carefully the nature of the relationship or the level of intimacy. We are forced back on taking Theophylact's word for it, where indeed we have it: we have seen that the Byzantine letter did not encourage the naming of third persons.

This zone includes 36 individuals and several groups. These groups include *two bearers* (**112**), *Theophylact's relatives in Euripos* (**113**), *the priests of Pologos* (**114**), *the monks of Anaplous* (**118**) and *the Hagioserretai* (**115**), *the villagers of Ekklesiai* (**116**), *the pupils of* NIKETAS *ho tou Serron* (**117**), *all the bishops of Ochrid* (**119**). The individuals range from ALEXIOS I KOMNENOS, *emperor* (**77**) and his brother ISAAC KOMNENOS, *sebastokrator* (**78**) to the vivid vignettes of low-life characters like LAZAROS the revolting *paroikos* (**97**), N. IASITES, *the praktor* (**76**), and N.N., *immoral hieromonk* (**107**). Some are very well known and otherwise well-connected like MICHAEL PSELLOS, *hypatos ton philosophon* (**84**) or CONSTANTINE CHOIROSPHAKTES (**75**) or ROMANOS

---

[131] Boissevain, *Friends*, 47-48.

STRABOROMANOS (90); others like DEMETRIOS (79) and N. KRITOPOULOS (80), MICHAEL BESES LAMPENOS (81), MICHAEL *ho tou Polyeuktou* (92), NICHOLAS *ho tou Boutou* (93), and THEODORE CHRYSELIOS (73), were clearly vital figures in the local politics of the day but have left no other mark. We meet various unsavoury taxmen—SYMEON BLACHERNITES (72), N. SENACHEREIM (86), MAKREMBOLITES (82) and EUMATHIOS, *megalepiphanestatos* (94)—as well as *psaltes* GREGORY (95), whom Theophylact is reluctant to return, and the Bulgar *geron* (108) whom Theophylact defended. Various relatives appear, of Theophylact and his friends (74, 85, 88, 89, 91) and various more or less anonymous bearers (89, 98, 104, 105, 106), together with five more bishops, three, of LIPENION (101) STRUMITSA (103) and MALESOVA (102), mentioned in passing, but two others, of SIDE (99) and of GLAVENITSA (100), described as being in need of care and attention. Given the rarity of third persons in Byzantine letters each one must have had good reason to appear in the collection. These shadowy figures bring up the rear in Theophylact's first order zone, but there is a little further to go.

v. *Extended zone: second and third order zones*

Here we come to the limits of the analysis we have set ourselves. This in Boissevain's terms is 'the ragged edge of his primary zone, the collection of people whose faces he recognises, or those who remember they have met him though he no longer remembers them. These persons, and those beyond his first order zone, form the extended zone of his network.'[132]

There are obvious difficulties in trying to move beyond the first order zone in a letter-collection, but the attempt can teach us a great deal. In the network table I have recorded under 'connections' only blood relations of persons in Theophylact's first order zone and connections clearly documented in the sources, including predecessors and successors in post. This of course presents limitations. It is in fact reasonable to assume that all suffragans of the archdiocese of Ochrid knew one another, that all imperial doctors, or Constantinopolitan teachers or members of a family knew one another. Beyond that we may be in an area of unrecorded density.

There is also a difficulty, acknowledged by network theorists,[133] of physically depicting all the relationships into the second and third order zones, even those chosen by the rigorous if absurd criteria suggested above. But it is important to attempt at least a pilot sketch, for it is only by going beyond the

---

[132] Boissevain, *Friends*, 48.

[133] M. Noble, 'Social Networks in Family Analysis: its use as a conceptual framework,' J. Boissevain and J. Clyde Mitchell, *Network Analysis. Studies in Human Interaction* (The Hague and Paris, 1973), 3-13 at 11.

first order zone that we can attempt to assess the density of Theophylact's network and his centrality. In fig. 2 and its accompanying key I take Theophylact's personal cell and follow through the known relationships of the individuals within it. Of the ten relationships five offer us no further connections, but the other five produce an interesting picture. For four of these, Nicholas Kallikles, Gregory Kamateros, Michael Pantechnes and the bishop of Kitros, there is independent evidence, and the diagram follows it through. DEMETRIOS (HEPHAISTOS) (1) produces, from the collection and other works of Theophylact, nine connections. NICHOLAS ANEMAS (2) produces none, except possibly the conspiratorial brothers Michael, Leo and two others. NICHOLAS KALLIKLES (3) has a network most comparable (in the collection) to Theophylact's own and it is fully illustrated below in fig. 3.2; only four of his twenty-one connections are already in Theophylact's network, an interestingly low density, perhaps explained by the fact that his poems date mostly from the reign of John II Komnenos. The connections largely represent the patrons for his occasional verse, members of the Komnenos family and other aristocratic families. Gregory Kamateros (4) from varied evidence, documentary and narrative, offers six more, of whom three are already in Theophylact's network; the others are the rebel NIKEPHOROS DIOGENES (208) and the poet THEODORE PRODROMOS (225). Of NICHOLAS MERMENTOULOS (5) nothing is known except his career; it is likely that he knew the other holders of his post in the late eleventh century: JOHN THRAKESIOS SKYLITZES (227), NICHOLAS SKLEROS (226) and JOHN ZONARAS (228). With JOHN OPHEOMACHOS (6) we draw a complete blank. With MICHAEL PANTECHNES (7) we are again assisted by varied evidence and can produce six connections, three of whom are already in Theophylact's network: Nicholas Kallikles, John Pantechnes (16) his father and Niketas the imperial doctor (32). We meet now MICHAEL ITALIKOS (215), MICHAEL ?LIZIX (223) and at last ANNA KOMNENE (217). NICHOLAS, *metropolitan of* KERKYRA (8) though we have several of his own works, offers us no individuals in his resignation poem[134] though Nicholas Adrianoupolites (201) tells us that the whole synod heard and took courage from Nicholas's poem.[135] *The bishop of* KITROS (9) connects Theophylact again to Eirene Doukaina (37), but also to N., *ex-bishop and archimandrite of St George in the Mangana* (231).

While a high proportion (21/45) of these contacts keep us within Theophylact's first order zone, simply increasing its density, some take us beyond, even if we record only the most obvious connections. In this zone

---

[134] *Paraitesis*, 105, ed. Lampros, 34.
[135] Ed. Lampros, 'Ho Markianos Kodix 524,' *NE* 8 (1911), 7. The lines also appear in his publication of Nicholas's poem, numbered as 306-310, ed. Lampros, 41.

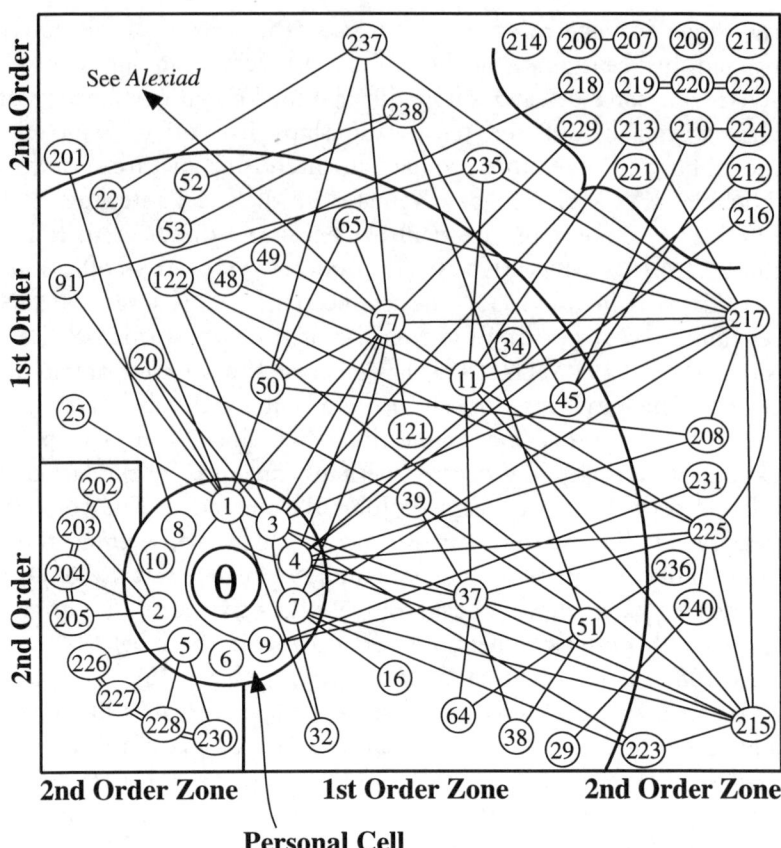

2nd Order Zone   **1st Order Zone**   **2nd Order Zone**

Personal Cell

(1) DEMETRIOS HEPHAISTOS: evidence of Theophylact only
      Nicholas KALLIKLES (3), G93, Gautier, II, 477.
      Gregory KAMATEROS (4), G127, Gautier, II, 571.
      Theodore SMYRNAIOS (20), G28, Gautier, II, 223.
      Niketas *ho tou Serron* (22), G7, Gautier, II, 151.
      Peter, *chartophylax* (25), G90, Gautier, II, 469.
      Niketas, imperial doctor (32), G110, Gautier, II, 531-533.
      Maria, basilissa (50), G4, II, 141.
      Alexios I KOMNENOS (77), poem 14.85, Gautier, I, 375.
      N. TORNIKIOS (91),G109, to the *epi ton deeseon*, Gautier, II, 529.

(2) NICHOLAS ANEMAS: not known, unless the brothers of *Al.*,XII.5-6, L, III, 67-75:
      Leo ANEMAS(202)
      Michael ANEMAS (203)
      N ANEMAS (204)
      N ANEMAS (205)

Figure 2: Ramifications of Theophylact's personal cell

(3) NICHOLAS KALLIKLES: evidence of his poems; not of *Timarion*:
      Gregory KAMATEROS (4), poem 18, ed. Romano, 92-93.
      Eirene DOUKAINA (37) (Polemis 26), poem 6, ed. Romano, 8.
      George PALAIOLOGOS (45), poem 9.6-7, ed. Romano, 84.
      Alexios I KOMNENOS (77) (Barzos 15), poems 24, 25, ed. Romano, 101-104.
      John II KOMNENOS (122) (Barzos 34), poems 2, 31, ed. Romano, 78-80; 112-116.
      Eirene DOUKAINA (212)(Polemis 32), poem 21.7-8, ed. Romano, 96.
      Alexios DOUKAS (213) (? = Barzos 65, but Barzos: = 67), poem 36, ed. Romano, 121.
      N. DOUKAS, son of the *protostrator* (? = 36)(Polemis 30), poem 30, ed. Romano, 111-112
      Anna ARBANTENISSA (206), poem 26, ed. Romano, 104-105
      John ARBANTENOS (207), poem 1, ed. Romano, 77-78.
      N. DOKEIANE (209), poem 22, ed. Romano, 97-100.
      Anna DOUKAINA (210) (Polemis 27), poem 9.4-5, ed. Romano, 83.
      Anna DOUKAINA (211) Polemis 127), poem 23, ed. Romano, 100-101.
      Michael Doukas KAMATEROS (216), poem 21, ed. Romano, 26-27.
      Eirene Piroska KOMNENE (218), poem 28, ed. Romano, 106.
      Eudokia KOMNENE (219) (Barzos 37), poems 16, 17, ed. Romano, 91-92.
      Maria KOMNENE (220)(Barzos 33), poem 27, ed. Romano, 105.
      Isaac KOMNENOS (222) (Barzos 36), poem 8, ed. Romano, 82-83.
      Andronikos Doukas PALAIOLOGOS (224), poems 9, 10, 11, 12, 13, ed. Romano, 83-88.
      ROGER, *sebastos* (229), poem 19, ed. Romano, 93-95.
      Theodore SMYRNAIOS (20), poem 30, ed. Romano, 111-112.

(4) GREGORY KAMATEROS: varied evidence.
      Nicholas KALLIKLES (3), Kallikles, poem 18.
      Eirene DOUKAINA (37), Niketas Choniates, *Chronike Diegesis*, ed. van Dieten, 9.
      Alexios I KOMNENOS (77), Al.,IX.viii.1; G127, ed. Gautier, II, 579.
      Nikephoros DIOGENES (208), *Al.*, IX.viii.1, L, II, 178.
      Michael ITALIKOS (215), Michael Italikos, 12, ed. Gautier, 135-138.
      Theodore PRODROMOS (225), monody, ed. Majuri, 'Anecdota Prodromea', 528-536.

(5) NICHOLAS MERMENTOULOS: nothing known except career, Guilland, *Institutions*, 563-587
      John THRAKESIOS-SKYLITZES (227)
      Nicholas SKLEROS (226)
      John ZONARAS. (228)
      STEPHEN-Symeon the Sanctified (230)

(6) JOHN OPHEOMACHOS: nothing known.

(7) MICHAEL PANTECHNES: varied evidence.
      Nicholas KALLIKLES (3) (at the deathbed of Alexios, *Al.*, XV.xi.
      John PANTECHNES (16), G39, ed. Gautier, II, 263-265.
      Niketas the imperial doctor (32), Al., XV.xi.
      Michael ITALIKOS (215), Michael Italikos, 9, ed. Gautier, 110-115.
      Anna KOMNENE (217), Al, XV.xi.
      Michael ?Lizix (223), Al XV.xi; ? = Michael Italikos, 25, ed. Gautier, 178.

(8) NICHOLAS of KERKYRA: own works
      Nicholas ADRIANOUPOLITES (201)

(9) N.N. bishop of KITROS: another letter
      Eirene DOUKAINA (37)
      ex-bishop and archimandrite of St George in the Mangana (231)

(10) N.N. bishop of PELAGONIA: nothing known.

Figure 2: Ramifications of Theophylact's personal cell

should also be placed connections of Theophylact's second order zone who are also connected to members of his first order zone beyond the personal cell. Here we meet other writers of the period: *St* CYRIL PHILEOTES (232) whose network overlaps considerably with Theophylact's; NIKETAS STETHATOS (233), whose circle is quite different apart from the *chartophylax* NIKETAS (?=24); GEORGE TORNIKES (235), who is of a distinctly different generation and has connections with the Komnenoi and Kamateroi of that generation; and EUTHYMIOS ZIGABENOS (236), with court and monastic connections. *Hosios* MELETIOS (239) offers a circle of aristocratic visitors (as well as more humble monks) which overlaps with Cyril's circle as well as with Theophylact's. GREGORY, *hegoumenos of Oxeia* (240) connects—possibly—to Theophylact's *hegoumenos* SYMEON (29), again to THEODORE PRODROMOS (225), to another Anemas and another *porphyrogennete* THEODORA KOMNENE (221), as well as court figures of the mid-twelfth century.

And it is then possible to arrive at a third order zone for Theophylact arising only out of his personal cell. Here problems of chronology are particularly acute: NIKETAS STETHATOS (233) would produce SYMEON THE NEW THEOLOGIAN (301), by whom Theophylact was impressed, but who died (1022) a century before Theophylact read (1125/26) his hymns! It is also noticeable that very few candidates for the third order zone, unless in this way chronologically outside Theophylact's span, do not also find themselves either in Theophylact's first or second order zones. Theophylact was well connected, either through his friends or through his friends-of-friends. This can be demonstrated by a simple comparison (fig. 3), but it may be that a letter-collection confers an unfair advantage on its author.

So it remains to probe how far this impression of well-connectedness is an illusion arising from the kind of evidence we possess for Theophylact. So far we have looked only at his letter-collection. If we look at the great mass of his remaining oeuvre, his first order zone increases by at most eleven persons, probably ten, not all of whom can be identified. We may divide these persons into those who are addressed (who constitute part of Theophylact's effective zone), and those who are mentioned (who join those mentioned in the letters in Theophylact's nominal zone).

In the effective zone we meet RODOMIR AARON (64) with his own imperial connections to Eirene Doukaina (37) and Maria of Bulgaria (51), the monk NEILOS (67) who cannot certainly be identified with Neilos of Calabria, and the young co-emperor CONSTANTINE DOUKAS (65) as well as *a libidinous eunuch* (68), *a grieving person* (69), *a 'wicked slave'* (70) and *someone who condemned consecrated persons* (71). In the nominal zone we find MICHAEL ANTIOCHOS, *the Grand Hetairiarch* (120), *the co-emperor* JOHN II KOMNENOS

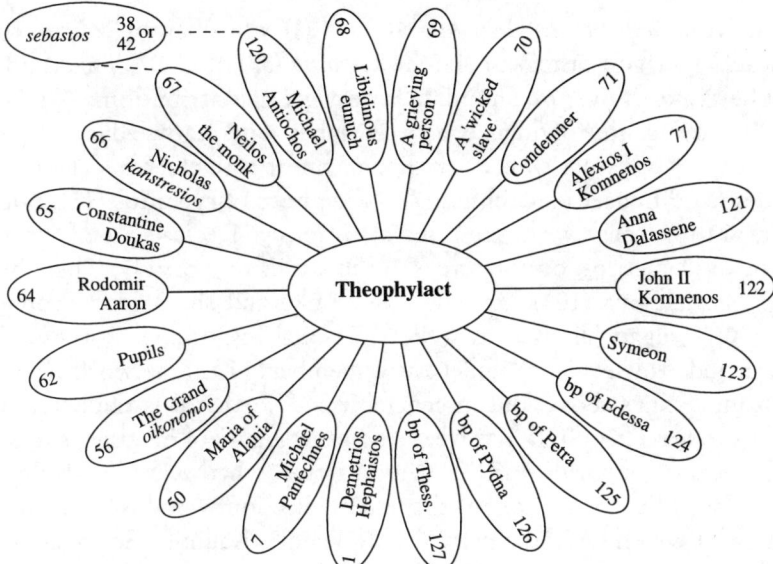

Figure 3.1 Theophylact's network as known from texts other than the collection
See below, *The Network*, 375-376

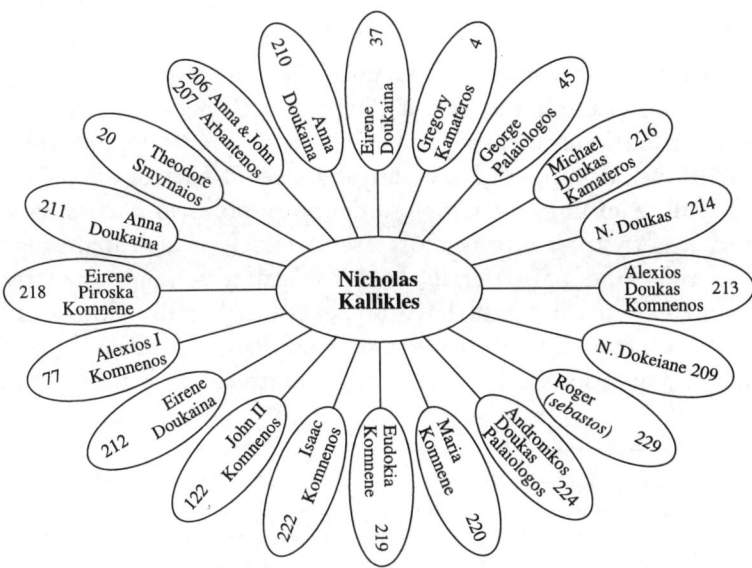

Figure 3.2 Nicholas Kallikles's network as known from his occasional poems
See above, Fig 2 and below, *The Network*, 378-379

Figure 3: Theophylact and Nicholas Kallikles

(122) and the *despoina* ANNA DALASSENE (121) who may of course, though practicalities suggest otherwise, be the *despoina* (37) of G107. This is not, in a first order zone of over one hundred, a very great contribution.

But using this evidence also enriches our knowledge of persons already in Theophylact's network. Poems on or to Demetrios (1), Nicholas Kallikles (3), Michael Pantechnes (7), Nikephoros Bryennios (11), Nicholas of Kerkyra (8)[136] help with questions of intimacy. Dedications of works, on eunuchs to Demetrios, on the errors of the Latins to (possibly) Theophylact's bishop of Malesova (101), on Mark and Luke and the Minor Prophets to Maria (50),[137] suggest literary as well as personal inspiration. For simplicity's sake I include this evidence under these members of the network in the first order zone listings above. But in general it is clear that it is the letters which enable us to see Theophylact as we see no other figure of his time, surrounded by his personal world. Fig. 3 demonstrates what we would know of Theophylact's first order zone if the letter-collection were lost, and compares it with what we know of the network of Nicholas Kallikles. So we are now in a position to draw some tentative conclusions about the structure of Theophylact's network. I save questions of its use for the next section, and for figs. 5-7.

vi. *Analysis and conclusions*

Some conclusions will have to wait until more network studies have been carried out: for example the size of Theophylact's network is very difficult to assess without comparative studies. Political questions, like the balance of Doukai and Komnenoi, have already been touched on: it is always difficult in Byzantium to attempt to delineate political parties, and this is not what a network study is most useful for. It is also inappropriate to apply to this kind of material the statistical techniques used by social anthropologists: density will have to be assessed impressionistically, and degree of connection is probably also unavailable in Theophylact's case. But on some questions it is worthwhile counting, particularly in order to

---

[136] Poems 14 and 15, ?3, 2, 1, 4, I, 369-377; 351; 349-351; 347-349; 353-355.

[137] *In Defence of Eunuchs*: see the beginning of both the iambic and the prose *protheoria*, II, 289.1-2: Ἀδελφός ἐστιν αἴτιός μοι τοῦ λόγου,/ εὐνοῦχος ὤν, ἄγαλμα κοσμίου βίου; II, 291.1-2: Λόγος ἀδελφῷ μὲν εὐνούχῳ χαρίζεται, πικραινομένῳ πρὸς τὰ κατ' εὐνούχων ἁπλῶς λογόμενα, II, 289-291. *On the Errors of the Latins*, Προσλαλιά τινι τῶν αὐτοῦ ὁμιλητῶν, II, 247. On Mark and Luke: Vind. gr. 219 (=theol. gr. 90, the presentation copy to Maria) de Rubeis, *De Theophylacti gestis et scriptis*, PG 123, 35: Τῆς βασιλίσσης ἐννόημα Μαρίας,/ ψυχῆς ἀληθῶς ἔργον εὐγενεστάτης,/ ὁ δὲ τρυγήσας τοὺς μελλιρρύτους λόγους/ Θεοφύλακτος ποιμενάρχης Βουλγαρίας.

recognise the various sectors of the network. And it should be possible to pick up evidence of clusters if that evidence exists. Other simple questions asked by anthropologists of their networks may certainly be directed to Theophylact.

Age and gender for example. His network is almost entirely male: four imperial women are the exceptions. Several eunuchs are included, Demetrios (1), Gregory, the eunuch praktor (110), the libidinous eunuch (68) and possibly the metropolitan of Thessalonike (127?=27).[138] In this he is probably not exceptional; few women epistolographers are known,[139] and Theophylact lived at the end of the period of eunuchs' influence[140] as is demonstrated by the treatise for Demetrios. Yet it is a period notably rich in women patrons, to one of whom he dedicated two works. More interesting is the age balance of the collection: although Theophylact says he prefers to confide in the young and in his own generation,[141] only twenty-seven are clearly younger than him; sixteen are clearly older, and the rest are treated as of roughly equivalent age. Also characteristic of a Byzantine letter-network as distinct from a twentieth-century one recorded by an anthropologist, is the

---

[138] It is assumed rather than proven that Demetrios is the eunuch brother, on the grounds of the iambic prologue. I, 289, cf. poems 14-15, I, 369-377. He must have one other sibling, see Darrouzès, *Tornikai*, 25. For Gregory see G66, II, 367.39-40; in G31 we meet a eunuch he nicknamed Scylla and Charybdis, II, 233.17-18. In G96, II, 491.107 we meet a tiny community of eunuch-monks. In poem 13, I, 367-369 he pillories a eunuch for his debauchery. In the dialogue *In Defence of Eunuchs* contemporary bishops who are eunuchs are mentioned: the bishops of Petra, Edessa-Moglena, and of Pydna-Kitros and Thessalonike, who may be Theophylact's correspondents.

[139] For women epistolographers see A.C. Hero, *A Woman's Quest for Spiritual Guidance; the Correspondence of Princess Irene Eulogia Choumnaina Palaiologina* (Brookline, 1986). For Eirene-Eulogia Choumnaina Palaiologina see V. Laurent, 'Une princesse byzantine au cloître,' *EO* 29 (1930), 29-62; 'La direction spirituelle à Byzance,' *REB* 14 (1956), 48-87; A.C. Hero, 'Irene-Eulogia Choumnaina Palaiologina, Abbess of the Convent of Philanthropos Soter in Constantinople,' *ByzForsch* 9 (1985), 119-147. For Eugenia-Eulogia, see V. Laurent, 'La direction spirituelle des grandes dames à Byzance,' *REB* 8 (1950), 64-84; Alice-Mary Talbot has collected a total of 195 letters from the ninth to fifteenth centuries addressed to women; she regards this as an early stage in the task however; I am grateful to her for sharing her work with me.

[140] Kazhdan and Epstein, *Change*, 70, see eunuchs as one of the casualties of the family government of Alexios I, remarking, 67, that 'for whatever reason eunuchs were important both in myth and reality in the tenth and eleventh centuries.' In Theophylact's G5 to Adrian the Grand Domestic, his Herakles myth draws colour and veracity from the chief eunuch at the court of the Lydian queen Omphale.

[141] G35, to Chrysoberges metropolitan of Naupaktos, II, 245.9-12.

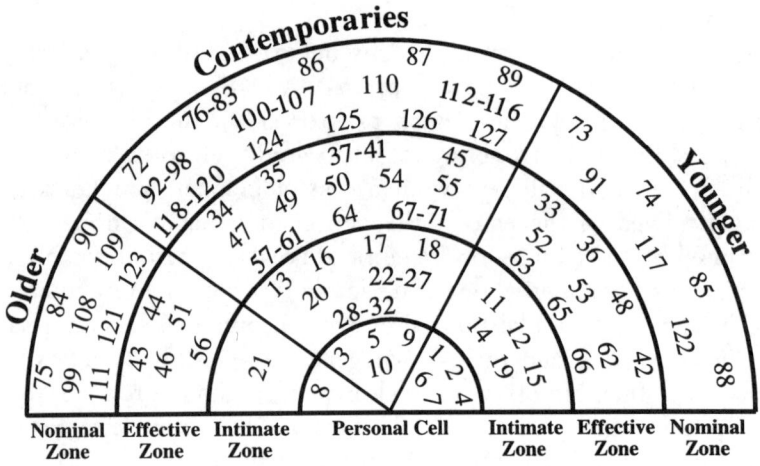

4.1: Age

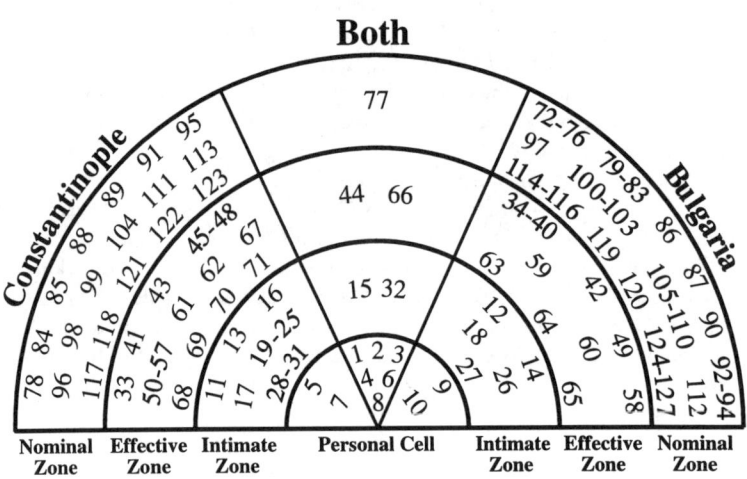

4.2: Residence
Figure 4: Analysis by age, gender, residence and taxis

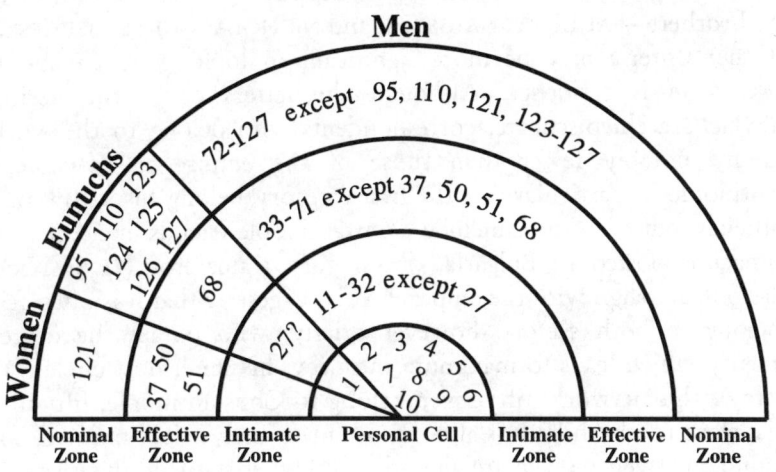

4.3: Gender

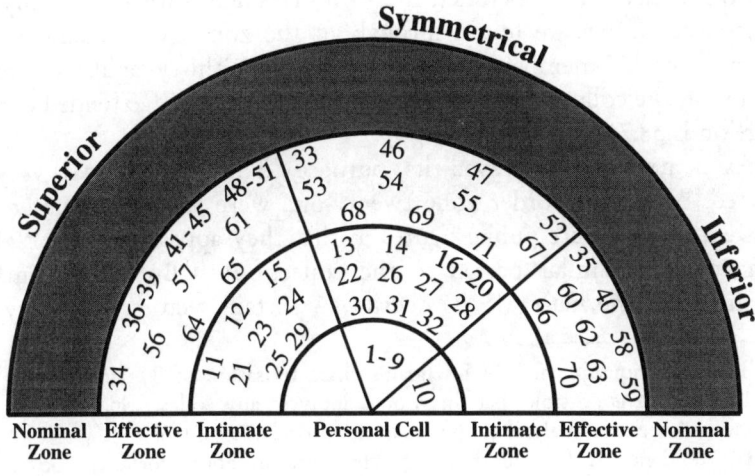

4.4: Taxis

Figure 4: Analysis by age, gender, residence and taxis

clear preponderance of friends over family:[142] only Demetrios (1), TORNIKIOS (91) and the relatives in Euboia (113) appear in the collection. Demetrios however is a significant exception, and Theophylact is also aware of other people's brothers—PAUL SMYRNAIOS (88) and NICHOLAS CHRYSOBERGES (74).

Other criteria may be more significant in looking at Theophylact's network. One is residence. Although the letters cover the period of Theophylact's archiepiscopate, correspondents who belong to the world of Ochrid are notably fewer than those of the empire as a whole, and Constantinople in particular. To the first category belong his suffragans and local officials, but even these include Constantinople friends like Anemas and Opheomachos posted to Bulgaria, or Gregory Kamateros (4) or Nicholas Kallikles on campaign with the emperor. It is suggestive that it is often friends who belong in both sectors, however briefly, who obtain the degree of multiplexity which leads to maximum intimacy, his innermost circle. Of the members of this network, fifty-seven belong to Constantinople, fifty-nine to Bulgaria, eleven to both.[143] It is also important to analyse its symmetry: of his correspondents twenty-seven are viewed as of higher status in the relationship from the point of view of *taxis*; ten of lower. Thirty-four appear to have been of equal status, or to have crossed the *taxis* boundaries, and many in the outer zones cannot be tied down. Profession seems immaterial: thirty-five are churchmen—only seven monastic—and academics account for only one in twenty of the network. Doctors (three or four), soldiers (three certainly), desk administrators (four) are found throughout the zones. One characteristic is striking: of the 127 members of the first order zone thirty-eight are seen to be put to use in the collection; if we exclude the nominal and extended zones the proportion is 38:71.

As a network it served its purpose. Theophylact was very well connected: of his first order zone twenty-one were related to the emperor. And twenty-seven were public figures in that they appear in Anna's *Alexiad* (which covers a similar period to the collection).[144] But this points to a disadvantage of the network: its density.[145] Certain sectors were very dense

---

[142] This is curious in view of Kazhdan's characterisation of Byzantium as a family-oriented society. It is possible that this would apply to any ecclesiastic, east or west. An answer awaits a separate analysis of laymen in the period as a control.

[143] The tendency is for correspondents involved in both worlds to be closest to Theophylact, those of Constantinople next and those of Bulgaria in the outer zones.

[144] I.e. one-eighth of the actors in the *Alexiad* are part of his network; a quarter of his network is mentioned in the *Alexiad*.

[145] By density, network theorists mean 'the extent to which links which could possibly exist among persons do in fact exist', or alternatively, perhaps more helpfully, 'the degree to which the members of a person's network are in touch, independently of him'.

indeed. Of Theophylact's first order zone, fifteen attended the synod of Blachernai; among his effective zone are the five first names on that attendance list. In no sense could he be regarded as central, and so his role as a broker was minimal.[146] His only centrality is where the worlds of Ochrid and Constantinople overlap, and where he saw his role as interceding on behalf of his flock with the great and the good.

4.3 The uses of network

Theophylact uses the image of a net, but he sees himself as caught in it rather than saved by it: it is applied to his problems rather than their solution.[147] But a substantial proportion[148] of the letters in the collection ask for a concrete and tangible action, not for prayers or a letter of friendship, and they ask it of someone not directly responsible to Theophylact. A job for a friend,[149] a document in a case,[150] a respite from recruitment,[151] help for a friendly official,[152] release from military service,[153] support for his villagers,[154] a helpful appointment[155]—all could be arranged through his network. In this section the cases we have seen so far in this chapter in 3.1 as chronological puzzles and in 3.2 as monsters reappear *in motion*.

Perhaps more to the point, relationships we have observed and distinguished above are put to use. Theophylact was a great seizer of opportunities: John Doukas went from Bulgaria to Attica as part of his reconquest expedition, and Theophylact saw an opportunity (in fact two) to ask him to look after his relatives in Euboia.[156] An ex-pupil in a post in Attaleia gave him the chance to alert someone to the needs of the bishop of

---

Boissevain, *Friends*, 37; K.E. Campbell, 'Networks Past: a 1939 Bloomington Neighbourhood,' *Social Forces* 69 (1990), 139-155 at 142.

[146] See Boissevain, *Friends*, ch. 6, 'Social Manipulators: Brokers as Entrepreneurs,' 147-169; A.C. Mayer, 'The Significance of Quasi Groups in the Study of Complex Societies,' *The Social Anthropology of Complex Societies*, ed. M. Banton (ASA Monographs, 4, London, 1966), 97-122.

[147] G75, to the metropolitan of Kerkyra, II, 401.37.

[148] 48 of the 135 letters.

[149] G27, to Gregory Kamateros, II, 221.25-29.

[150] G49, to John Serblias, II, 297.11.

[151] G24, to John Komnenos, II, 209.10-16.

[152] G21, to the bishop of Pelagonia, II, 199.6-8.

[153] G109, to the *epi ton deeseon*, II, 529.11-13.

[154] G111, to Nicholas Kallikles, II, 535.18-20.

[155] G8, to John Doukas, II, 155.30-33; G17, II, 189.36-37.

[156] G8, II, 155.30-33; G17, II, 189.36-37, both to John Doukas.

Figure 5: Theophylact's network in action: requests
other than for letters and prayers

Letter	Recipient	Relation	Request	For	Response?
G8	John Doukas	patron	help	relatives in Euripos	?
G9	caesar Melissenos	patron	kanonika of other villages	Theophylact	?
G11	John Komnenos	official	get rid of hieromonk and stop him talking to Iasites	Theophylact	?
G12	John Komnenos	official	exemption from services	priests of Pologos	pittakion granted
G17	John Doukas	official	sigillion giving Mogila village	Theophylact	?
G19	John Komnenos	official	follow-up on Pologos: have JK's pittakion implemented	priests of Pologos	?
G21	bishop of Pelagonia	suffragan	look after...	Demetrios Kritopoulos	?
G22	John Komnenos	official	sigillion to ensure the position of the	paroikoi of Diabolis	?
G23	John Komnenos	official	support lawsuit against Nicholas ho tou Boutou	Michael Beses Lampenos	?
G24	John Komnenos	official	stop the depopulation of Ochrid by recruitment	Ochrid	?
G26	John Doukas	official	asks for assurance of aule and intercession with emperor	Theophylact	?
G27	Gregory Kamateros	'son'	give a job to...	Psellos's grandson	?
G28	Smyrnaios	brother's teacher	look after...	Demetrios	?
G31	Gregory Kamateros	'son'	have anametresis of Ekklesiai overturned	Theophylact	GK baulks
G32	Nicholas Anemas	official	look after...	Constantine Choirosphaktes	?
G35	metropolitan of Naupaktos	colleague	be nice to...	brother Nicholas	?
G36	bishop of Pelagonia	suffragan	read the scriptures		?
G40	Niketas Polites	friend	sort out Koprinista and look after	the bishop of Glavenitsa	?
G49	John Serblias	friend	give Gregory Taronites decree about Vodena; ask for pittakion	?Theophylact	?
G55	Gregory Pakourianos	official	help with tax	Theophylact	GP does
G58	bishop of Triaditsa	suffragan	come to synod and help geron	archdiocese	Bishop refuses
G59	bishop of Triaditsa	suffragan	come to synod	archdiocese	Bishop refuses
G61	?John Komnenos	?official	do not listen to calumny	Theophylact	?
G64	patriarch	senior	look after...	the bishop of Pelagonia	?
G66	chartophylax	senior	rule on psaltes Gregory	Theophylact	?

G67	Gregory Kamateros	'son'	brief Gregory Pakourianos	Theophylact	?
G71	John Opheomachos	friend/ official	not to abandon the struggle in Bulgaria	Theophylact	?
G72	Theodoulos, metropolitan of Thessalonike	colleague	mutual support and help in combating Amalek	Theophylact and general good	?
G79	Adrian the Grand Domestic	patron	help after the departure of Gregory Pakourianos	Theophylact	?
G82	Michael *bo tou Chalkedonos*	acquaintance	speak to the *chartophylax* about the patriarch's meddling at Kittaba	Theophylact	?
G84	Niketas *bo tou Chalkedonos*	ex-pupil	involve mother of *protostrator* in case; carry letters to both	Theophylact	?
G85	Adrian the Grand Domestic	patron	counter calumny and stop *anagrapheus* taking village	Theophylact	AK does?
G88	John, *grammatikos* of Palaiologos	friend	show letter to George Palaiologos	Theophylact	?
G89	Adrian the Grand Domestic	patron	intercede with emperor to stop *anagraphe*	Theophylact	?
G90	*chartophylax*	senior	counteract rumours	Theophylact	?
G91	*didaskalos* of the Great Church	ex-colleague	prayers and efforts (refuting calumny?)	Theophylact	?
G93	Nicholas Kallikles	friend	look after...	Demetrios	?
G94	Nicholas Kallikles	friend	help! (in Lazaros crisis)	Theophylact	?
G96	Nikephoros Bryennios	patron	*prostaxis* for village	Theophylact	?
G98	Adrian the Grand Domestic	patron	intercede with emperor	Theophylact	?
G99	Michael Pantechnes	friend, 'son'	refute calumny with emperor	Theophylact	?
G100	John the philosopher	friend	refute calumny	Theophylact	?
G104	John Ataleiates	'son', ex-pupil	look after...	Theophylact	?
G108	Makrembolites	'son'	see to victualling of synod	metropolitan of Side synod	?
G109	*epi ton deeseon*	friend	let Tornikios off military service	Tornikios brother	?
G110	Niketas imperial doctor	friend	look after ...	Theophylact	?
G111	Nicholas Kallikles	friend	help (by approaching emperor) with house at Thessalonike and village of Ekklesiai	Theophylact	received and helped villagers returned with poem?
G112	Nicholas Kallikles	friend	send medical books	Theophylact and Demetrios	?
G114	Michael Pantechnes	'son', ex-pupil	help...	N. Smyrnaios	?
G118	Constantine Doukas	official	look after villagers of Ekklesiai	Theophylact	?
G122	bishop of Debra	suffragan	get back to post	diocese	?
G125	?	?	come to help of	Theophylact	?
G129	Michael Pantechnes	'son', ex-pupil	visit!	Theophylact	?

Side.[157] But it would be a mistake to imagine that Theophylact was simply opportunistic; he worked hard at his friendships and all his relationships. Had his relations with John Doukas while *doux* of Dyrrachion not been so good he could not have tried to recycle him as patron in Euboia.

Theophylact can frequently be observed servicing a relationship. His practice with officials is perhaps easiest to see, since he often wrote a welcoming adventus letter.[158] Other letters (which doubtless Jenkins and Schubart would write off as vacuous) keep the wheels oiled with gifts for officials, promises of visits for officials and suffragans, jokes and riddles and brilliant word-play with his intimates. Even when he had no requests of his own he kept his lines open, and we see him sometimes undertaking negotiations[159] on behalf of other people. He takes the part of Michael Beses Lampenos in a lawsuit with *ho tou Boutou*, telling one *doux* what his predecessor had ruled.[160] He makes the point that the Pologos case, which he takes up with John Komnenos, is not directly his affair.[161] And he pleads eloquently with John Komnenos to prevent the depopulation of Ochrid through the recruiting drive during the Dalmatian wars.[162] He does not appear to be acting as broker (nor does he need one); he is exercising his network and building up other people's obligations to him.[163]

But a more cogent reason for constant use of his network was simply as an information system. It was important for him to learn of impending reshuffles so that action might be taken: he learns of a complicated changeover of officials in Macedonia and immediately informs the bishop of Pelagonia—who needs to know, but who can also help in looking after Demetrios Kritopoulos (who has many enemies) during his inspection of the outgoing *strategos*'s handling of things.[164] He knows of the appointment of Constantine Doukas to the 'rule of the Vardar' in time to set up a complicated structure of reactions to the news.[165] He learns of the possible advent of Michael Antiochos in time to ask the monk Neilos to prevent the appointment.[166]

Some of his transactions were very simple. Melissenos's help with the *kanonika* appears to have been straightforward, since Theophylact pushes his

---

[157] G104, II, 519.6-8.

[158] See above, 3.3, 146-148.

[159] G26, to John Komnenos, 215.2: μεσιτεύειν is the word he uses.

[160] G23, to John Komnenos, II, 207.

[161] G12, II, 167-169; G19, II, 195, both to John Komnenos.

[162] G24, II, 209-211.

[163] Cf. the Maltese dictum quoted in Boissevain, *Friends*, 164: 'do much for people, but ask for little in return.'

[164] G21, to the bishop of Pelagonia, II, 199.

[165] See below, 210-211.

[166] Poem 10, I, 365.

luck and asks for more.[167] Requests to friends to look after particular officials or bishops must have suggested themselves as the need arose. Many transactions were possible without involving Constantinople at all. In the Mogila case, for example, he took the problem to the outgoing *doux* of Dyrrachion, John Doukas, currently in Euboia engaged on the reconquest, telling him that a property, an *archaia aule* given to the archbishopric by chrysobull, had been confiscated by Romanos Straboromanos. (An earlier stage of the case may also be referred to in G26 where a village with an *aule* and an *hospition* is appropriated by the state because it was not recorded in the *praktikon* as belonging to the church.)[168] He built wherever possible on success. When John Komnenos had been instrumental in 'refreshing' Diabolis and Prespa he brought the sad case of the abandoned cathedral before the other's attention:[169] an official's task was never done.

But sometimes he needed to work through Constantinople. The Kittaba case shows him making something of a fuss, not directly with the patriarch but with someone who would feel strongly about the misappropriation of church property: Michael, the nephew of Leo of Chalcedon. If Michael was in the patriarchal civil service he might have been in a position to cancel the stauropegic status of the monastery at Kittaba without involving the patriarch, or threatening Theophylact's blossoming relationship, based on complaints and prayers and gifts.[170] The Vodena case shows him activating an instrumental friendship with John Serblias (or at least he claims a friendship) while putting the other in the wrong for not having written, rather as he does with the *epi ton deeseon* before dropping upon him the request to release Tornikios from military service. John Serblias was to act as go-between with Gregory Taronites, passing on to him the news about Vodena and requesting from him a *pittakion* to guide the *doux* of Veroia. Why this case could not be

---

[167] G9, II, 157.

[168] G17, to John Doukas, assuming that John Komnenos had not yet been appointed, II, 187.24-29. G26 is surely wrongly addressed and is also to John Doukas, II, 215-217, while in post, so before G17. Gautier believes the village of G26 is Ekklesiai, which Harvey refutes. It may be wisest to bear in mind that G17 and G26 may refer to separate villages, but for illustration I reconstruct in fig. 6 below the less cautious scenario.

[169] G22, II, 203.3: καὶ Πρέσπαν ἅμα καὶ Διάβολιν ἀναψύξας; 9-42 is the new proposal.

[170] G82, to Michael *ho tou Chalkedonos*, II, 435.16-437.54. For Theophylact's relations with the patriarch see G45, 54, 64.

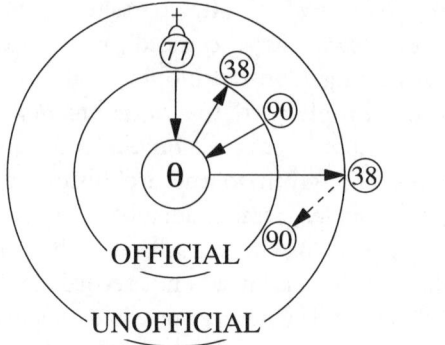

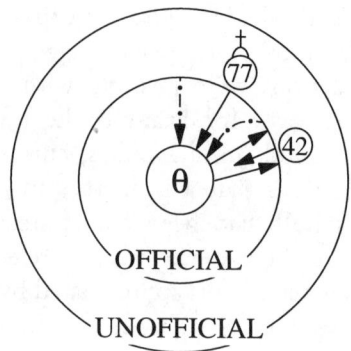

6.1 The Mogila case

1. Village long owned by the church with an *hospition* and *aule;* chrysobull for the *aule*
2. confiscated by emperor
3. Theophylact does not argue about village, but
4. G26 to John Doukas queries *prostaxis* about *hospition* and *aule*
5. Romanos Straboromanos occupies the property
6. after John Doukas leaves writes G17 to ask him to use his influence with Romanos Strabo--romanos and to get a *sigillion* for the *aule*.

6.2 The Pologos case

1. Problem: *exkousseia* for all taxes except *zeugologion* for priests of Pologos has been ignored
2. Alexios I Komnenos provides a chrysobull
3. ignored by John Komnenos
4. G12 asks John Komnenos for a *pittakion*
5. provided by John Komnenos but not implemented
6. G19 asks John Komnenos to enforce it

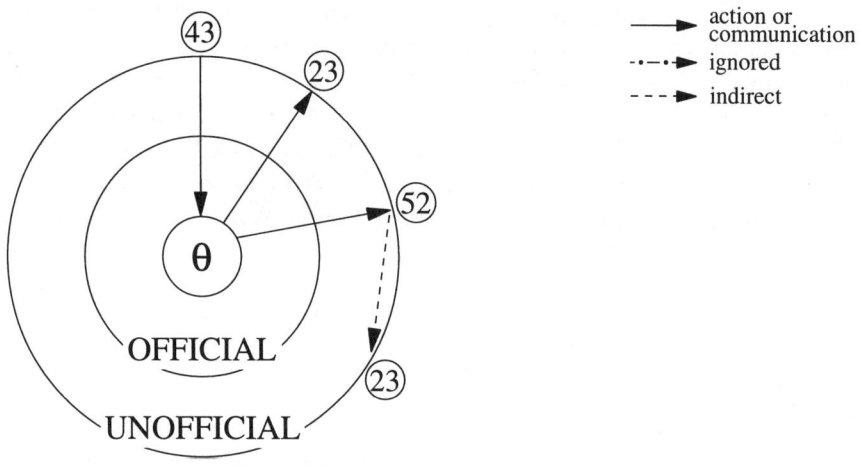

6.3 The Kittaba case

1. The patriarch has founded a stauropegic monastery without reference to Theophylact
2. Theophylact protests in Lost 9 to the *chartophylax* and asks in G82 Michael *ho tou Chalkedonos* to speak to the *chartophylax* about it

Figure 6: Theophylact's network in action: cases

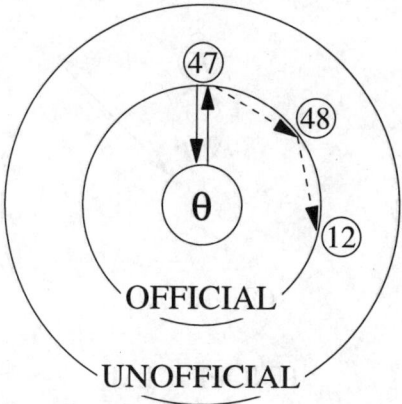

6.4 The Vodena case

1. John Serblias has destroyed a document
2. Theophylact asks him in G49 to give Gregory Taronites the decree about Vodena
and to ask Gregory to give a *pittakion* to the governor of Veroia telling him what to do

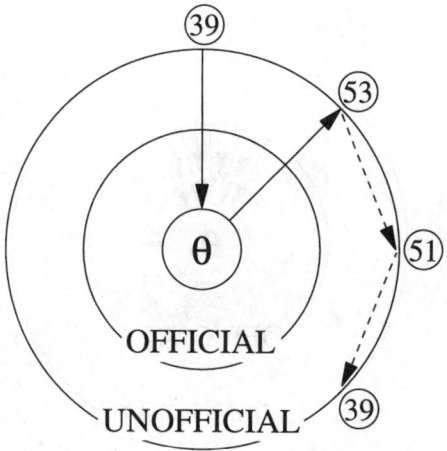

6.5 The case of the *protostrator* and the canons

1. The protostrator Michael Doukas has offended against the canons
2. G84 to Niketas *ho tou Chalkedonos* asks him to give two letters to Maria of Bulgaria, *protovestiaria*
Lost 16 to Maria asks her to give Lost 15 to her son and persuade him to mend his ways
Lost 15 to Michael asks him to desist
3. In Lost 17 the *protostrator* is approached as a patron; the dating òf this case is probably 1094, but
the date of G84 is unknown. Maria the *protovestiaria* died before the Kecharitomene *typikon*.

6.1-5 The cases of Mogila, Pologos, Kittaba, Vodena, the *protostrator*

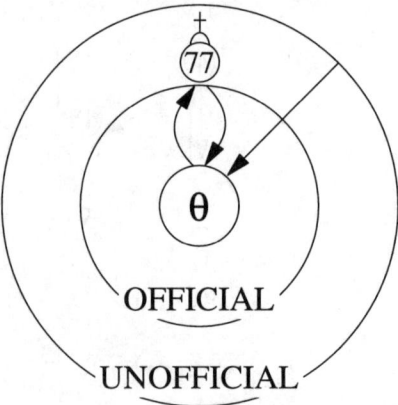

6.6 The case of τὸ ἐν ᾿Αχρίδι τῆς ἐκκλησίας χωρίον

6.6.1 1. exchange of the village for some pasturage: *entallages engrapha*; *chrysoboullos logos*
2. recent calumny

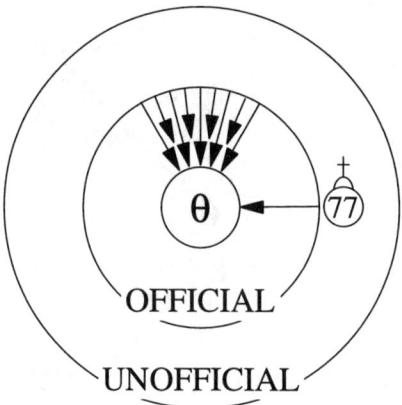

6.6.2 when the Kerkopes were harassing Herakles: *basilikon semeioma*

Figure 6: Theophylact's network in action: cases

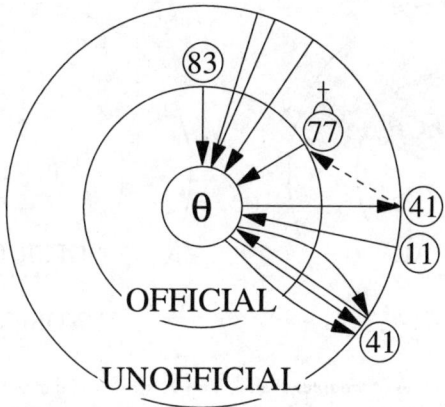

6.6.3. 1.*Anagrapheus* (? =Medenos G98) has just (G85) gone and ruled that the village is to be confiscated
Theophylact is the plaything of 2 Bulgars/calumny/ emperor undoes at night the good he does by day
2. Adrian Komnenos to keep emperor straight: Bryennios (G96, 491.121) acquired a *prostaxis*
Lost 10 to Adrian Komnenos: prophetic
3. G85 to Adrian Komnenos: asks to deal with emperor
4. G89 to Adrian Komnenos: asks to talk to emperor

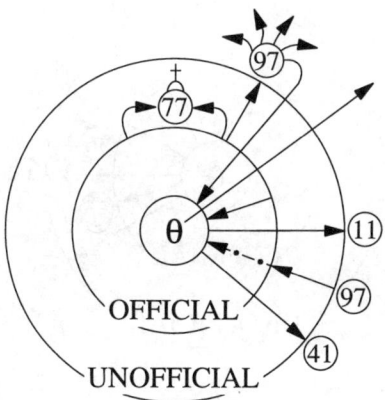

6.6.4.1 Typhon and Briareus directly intervene with the emperor: recruit Lazaros who travels round & recruits enemies of Theophylact, accuses Theophylact of fire in Ochrid
2. Theophylact had fled to Pelagonia (G94, G96)
3. accuses Theophylact of wealth, pile on extra taxes; refuse *paroikoi* given to the church, threatens to keep on the extra taxes despite the *prostaxis* so that he will yield the village and it will become Lazaros's
4. G96 to Nikephoros Bryennios: Theophylact demands a *prostaxis*
Lazaros deserts the village and to Constantinople to get *prostaxis* overturned; chrysobull ignored
5. G98 to Adrian Komnenos

6.6 The case of the village of the church in Ochrid

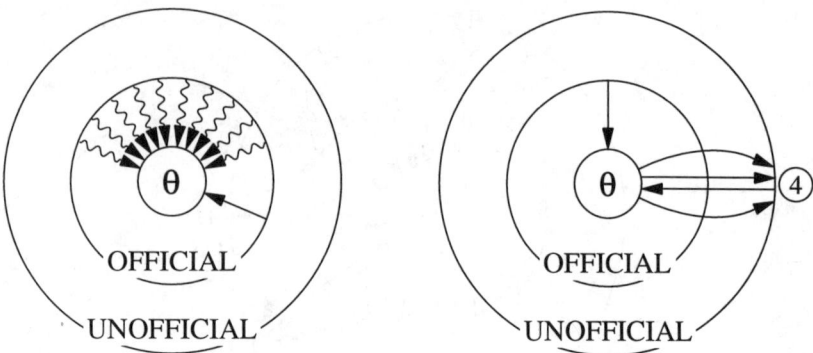

6.7.1 First phase: the waves of troubles: before 1094-95 synod and during the campaigns of 1093-95 after tenth wave of troubles: the eunuch (Scylla & Charybdis),

6.7.2 Second phase: Theophylact puts his foot wrong
1. Euroklydes: a problematic *anametresis*
2. Theophylact will reproach Gregory Kamateros in person after the synod (G31)
3. Demands *praxis* to be registered (G38)
4. Gregory Kamateros reacts unfavourably
5. G38 to Gregory Kamateros: why accuse us of obstructing referral to emperor of the village issue?

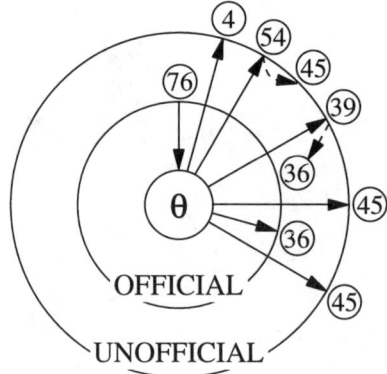

6.7.3 Third phase: Vardar village
1. Iasites has taken nearly all the goods of the village
2. G127 to Gregory Kamateros: has heard that Constantine Doukas has been appointed to the Vardar
G88 to John *grammatikos* of Palaiologos (remind George Palaiologos to do what I asked)
Lost 15 to *protostrator* Michael Doukas: brief your son not to send *anagrapheus* to village
Lost 18 to George Palaiologos: deal with praktor
3. G118 to Constantine Doukas: now you are here, remember us and our village
4. G126 to George Palaiologos: you have helped by intervening with the praktor

Figure 6: Theophylact's network in action: cases

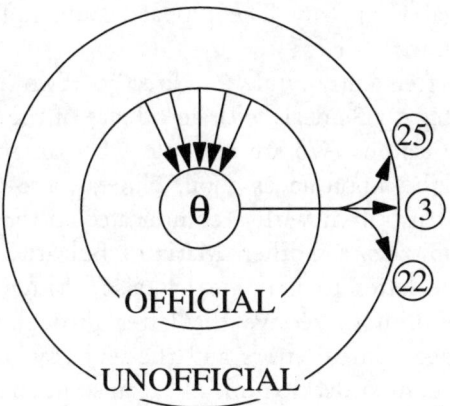

6.7.4 Fourth phase: the winter crisis
1. Tempted to abandon Ekklesiai (the troubles are so bad)
2. Sends Demetrios to Constantinople in the middle of winter with G90, G91, G93 to do his best

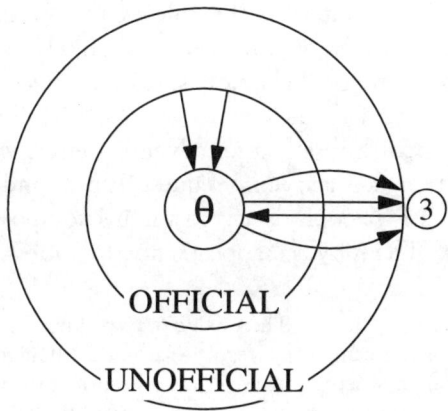

6.7.5 Fifth phase: Second Norman war (1105-07: emperor based in Thessalonike)
1. Ekklesiai taxed until empty while house in Thessalonike has been used for billets
2. G110 Nicholas Kallikles arrives with the army to Thessalonike; Demetrios goes to greet him
3. G111 to Nicholas Kallikles: stop this emptying in Ekklesiai (and billeting in Thessalonike): look after my villagers when they come to you; Demetrios ill
4. G112 to Nicholas Kallikles: yesterday I asked your help for them: request did not fall on stony ground; medical books

6.7 The case of Ekklesiai

sorted out in Bulgaria, or why Theophylact could not approach Gregory direct is not at all clear.[171]

Theophylact frequently works indirectly. Two letters in particular show tortuous strategy. G84 deals with an offence of the *protostrator* Michael Doukas against the canons. We are not told what offence or how it affects Theophylact. He lights upon an ex-pupil, Niketas, also a nephew of Leo of Chalcedon, and entrusts him with a complicated mission. Theophylact has written to the *protostrator*'s mother, Maria of Bulgaria, and he asks his ex-pupil to deliver the letter to her. He has also written to the *protostrator* himself and wishes him to receive the letter through his mother, which Niketas is to arrange. Three letters and the embassy of the young deacon Niketas are planned in order to unleash against Michael the full force of mother-power so formidable at the time.[172]

G88 relates to the Ekklesiai saga[173] and shows a crucial moment in that case. He writes to the secretary of George Palaiologos (unfortunately we cannot understand the nature of that relationship) filling him in on the latest depredations of Iasites the tax-man and asking John, much as he did with Niketas in the *protostrator* case, to pass on a letter to Michael Doukas, because his son has just been appointed to the rule of the Vardar and will be in a position to prevent an *anagraphe*. It also seems likely that (as with G84) a letter came also to George Palaiologos, asking his help (at all events Theophylact writes him a thank-you letter in G126). Finally, Theophylact addresses the young man himself in an adventus letter, which, unusually for Theophylact, actually makes a specific request. It is an indication that perhaps by this stage of the case Theophylact is losing his composure. But also at this moment in the case Theophylact appears not to mobilise one of his usual

---

[171]   G49, to John Serblias, II, 297. There is no way of knowing whether this is at the beginning or the end of the career of Gregory Taronites (though John Serblias's career would suit the later date), or whether the governor of Veroia is the Constantine Komnenos of G127. Cf. the letter to the *epi ton deeseon*, G109, II, 529. John Serblias was a Constantinopolitan civil servant (who witnessed documents in 1099 and 1109). No connection with Bulgaria is known, so it seems he is being appealed to in Constantinople from Bulgaria.

[172]   G84, II, 441-3. On mother-power, see my 'Maria' and 'Alexios I Komnenos and Imperial Revival,' *New Constantines, The Rhythm of Imperial Renewal in Byzantium, 4th-11th Centuries,* ed. P. Magdalino (SPBS, 2, Aldershot, 1994), 259-267 and see also in that volume, L. Brubaker, 'To Legitimize an Emperor: Constantine and Visual Authority in the Eighth and Ninth Centuries,' 139-158. See also Barbara Hill, *Patriarchy and Power in the Byzantine Empire from Maria of Alania to Maria of Antioch, 1080-1180* (PhD Diss., Belfast, 1994).

[173]   I am assuming that Ekklesiai = the Vardar village on grounds of geography. On this troublesome case see above, 95-96 for dating and 131-133 for the issues.

weapons: Gregory Kamateros, whom he informs about the appointment of Constantine but of whom he makes no request.[174] This might perhaps have something to do with the history of the case.[175]

However the tangled narrative is reconstructed,[176] it is clear that the problem develops through various phases. A very late stage is represented by G111 and the embassy of villagers from Ekklesiai which resulted in some solution before G112;[177] a much earlier stage is recalled in G31, when Theophylact describes his troubles in Ekklesiai as like wave after wave of difficulty. A previous wave was caused by the eunuch, but now with the *anametresis* a much worse wave is upon him. He appears to be asking Gregory to set it aside, a request which appears to have been too much even for Gregory's benevolence. Certainly G38 shows Theophylact very much on the defensive after an accusation from Gregory that he was being asked to do something illegal. This difficulty may well explain why in G88 Theophylact mobilised four other relationships in his network in preference to Gregory.[178]

The Ekklesiai case involved at one time or another six of Theophylact's most effective major patrons and friends. These he used sparingly after local resources had been exhausted, and normally only one at a time, even if the approach to the one patron was somewhat complicated. It is interesting to observe who are the three people who receive 'arrival-in-see' letters: two colleagues who must be persuaded he can still write—and his major patron Adrian Komnenos who must by the beginning of Theophylact's archbishopric have overtaken the ex-*basilissa* Maria in influence and access. It was he, together with the caesar Melissenos, who was seen by the *sebastokrator* Isaac to be attacking his son John, *doux* of Dyrrachion, in the Komnenian

---

[174] G127, which is long and fanciful, exceptional both to Gregory and the collection, II, 571.16-17, in which relations with Gregory seem excellent.

[175] G88, to John *grammatikos* of Palaiologos (who Gautier suggests is a hieromonk), II, 461.11-18. The letter to Michael Doukas has not survived, nor has that to George Palaiologos. For the thank-you letter see G126 to Palaiologos, II, 569. The adventus letter to Constantine Doukas, G118, II, 549.

[176] See above, fig 6, 210-211, and for previous attempts of mine, 'Patronage,' 125-126; *Theophylact*, 547. I more and more see the need for caution in assuming that letters belong to the same case. It may very well be that G85 and G89 refer to a village other than Ekklesiai (perhaps in Ochrid); Alan Harvey is clear that this is connected to the Lazaros crisis of G96 and G98. In fig. 6 I try to show clearly Theophylact's actions in each stage of this and of the Ekklesiai/Vardar village affair.

[177] G111, to Nicholas Kallikles, II, 535.15-22; G112, II, 537.2: χθές, using the parable of the sower.

[178] G31, to Gregory Kamateros, II, 233.17-20; G38, to Gregory, II, 259.21-34.

family row—and so to be defending Theophylact.[179] He was also invaluable in the Lazaros crisis over the village of the church in Ochrid. Theophylact's friendship with the Bryennios family also stood him in good stead when John came to Bulgaria and Nikephoros married Anna; only G96 shows Nikephoros Bryennios as patron, acting in tandem with Adrian. It is the only example in the collection of one patron duplicating another's efforts. This may be an indicator of the level of Theophylact's distress at this point; another is the length and comparative clarity of G96 and G98. The end of the collection sees Theophylact better supplied with patrons than at the beginning.[180]

But using major patrons was only one way of operating the network, and good relations with officials should make it a rare one. Friends could be used all the time for passing on information, and for occasional services when necessary. Gregory Kamateros's appointment as *hypogrammateuon* in 1094[181] was extremely useful to Theophylact, since he was now so close to the emperor. This must partly explain why the relationship with Gregory appears so different from the one with Michael Pantechnes, who is rarely called upon to render a specific service, though he too joins the ranks of courtiers. Only in G127 do we see the friendship between Theophylact and Gregory extend beyond instrumentality; only in G99 is Michael given a task. Another friendship which exploited closeness to the emperor is that with Nicholas Kallikles: G111 asks for two favours at once, though other letters simply ask for books or for assistance for his brother. But any relationship could be brought into play, and Theophylact appears to be ruthless in calling in debts, as in the two letters to John Attaleiates and to Niketas *ho tou Chalkedonos*, where he reminds them of their debt to him as their teacher. The occasion when all friendships were needed was the calumny crisis when Lazaros (building on the efforts of the bishop of Triaditsa, Iasites and the 'two

---

[179] G5, 6, 7, to Adrian the Grand Domestic, Theodore Smyrnaios and Niketas *ho tou Serron*, plus another letter to the *epi ton deeseon*. It is not known who this is, but Constantine Choirosphaktes and John Taronites are possible candidates. On genre see above, 145-146. For Adrian's role in the Komnenian family row see Anna, *Al.*, VIII.viii.3, L, II, 150.23-25. Anna shows no surprise that Melissenos was also present.

[180] John Bryennios was appointed some time after 1096, the last reference to John Komnenos in Dyrrachion, receiving Hugh de Vermandois, and before 1107 when Alexios Komnenos is attested there. The marriage of Anna and Nikephoros occurred some time after the last reference to Constantine Doukas in summer 1094 and before the first reference to Nikephoros, *gambros* of the emperor in 1097. G96 to Nikephoros is noticeably longer than to G98 to Adrian, who perhaps needed less explicit instruction. By the end of the collection Maria's political influence was over and Melissenos and Adrian and John Pantechnes were dead; all Theophylact's young friends had been recruited as well as George Palaiologos, Nikephoros Bryennios and, on a good day, the *protostrator* Michael.

[181] *Al.*, IX.viii.1, L, I, 23-35.

Bulgarians') had circulated so many rumours about Theophylact that he feared they were being believed and that people were possibly dropping him. His whole network was under threat and he reacted accordingly. While Nikephoros and Adrian were concentrating on the practical issues, Michael Pantechnes is recruited to make sure the emperor has the story straight, and John the philosopher is thanked and urged to do more to counteract rumours; earlier the *chartophylax* had been asked to make sure that whoever was stirring the pot should see that it was to no avail. So in crisis all kinds of relationships could be mobilised.[182]

This only emphasised the importance of servicing all relationships. I have analysed[183] how this is done with local governors, a kind of ten point plan: 1) try and influence his appointment (G127); 2) warn suffragans of his advent (G21); 3) write him an obsequious letter on arrival (G10); 4) keep him happy by gifts of fish, letters, visits, etc. (see Table IX); 5) try to get him to protect the interests of the church (G22); but 6) simultaneously use the patronage network (G13); 7) if he fails to come up to scratch, delate on him to the emperor (*Al.*,VIII.vii); 8) write to him on his replacement telling him what a marvellous governor he has been (G41); 9) try to influence the choice of his successor (poem 10); 10) try to use him after he has been appointed elsewhere (G17). The importance of good governors was clear; Theophylact thanked Gregory Kamateros for Pakourianos's appointment and praised him also to Adrian the Grand Domestic; he clearly had high hopes of Constantine Doukas turning out the same way. It was of course not always possible to keep relations sweet; the failure of communication and the attempt to usurp the archbishop's prerogative result in an outspoken letter (G18) studded with ultra-polite forms of address. Theophylact refuses to deal with a criticism of Gregory Kamateros in writing, and will have it out with him after the synod. Even the paragon Pakourianos has apologised by the time of G80;

---

[182]   G93 asks Nicholas to help his brother, G94 asks in a general way for help in Theophylact's tax troubles; G112 asks for books. For the calumny crisis, see G85, G87 (bishop of Triaditsa); G88 (Iasites); G93; G96 (Lazaros) and G98(Lazaros); G98 (two Bulgars). It can also be picked up in quotation from Ps.37.12 and in a more anxious approach to *siope*. For Michael Pantechnes see G99, II, 507, for John the philosopher, G100, II, 509; for the *chartophylax* (Peter), II, 469.16.

[183]   'Patronage,' 141.

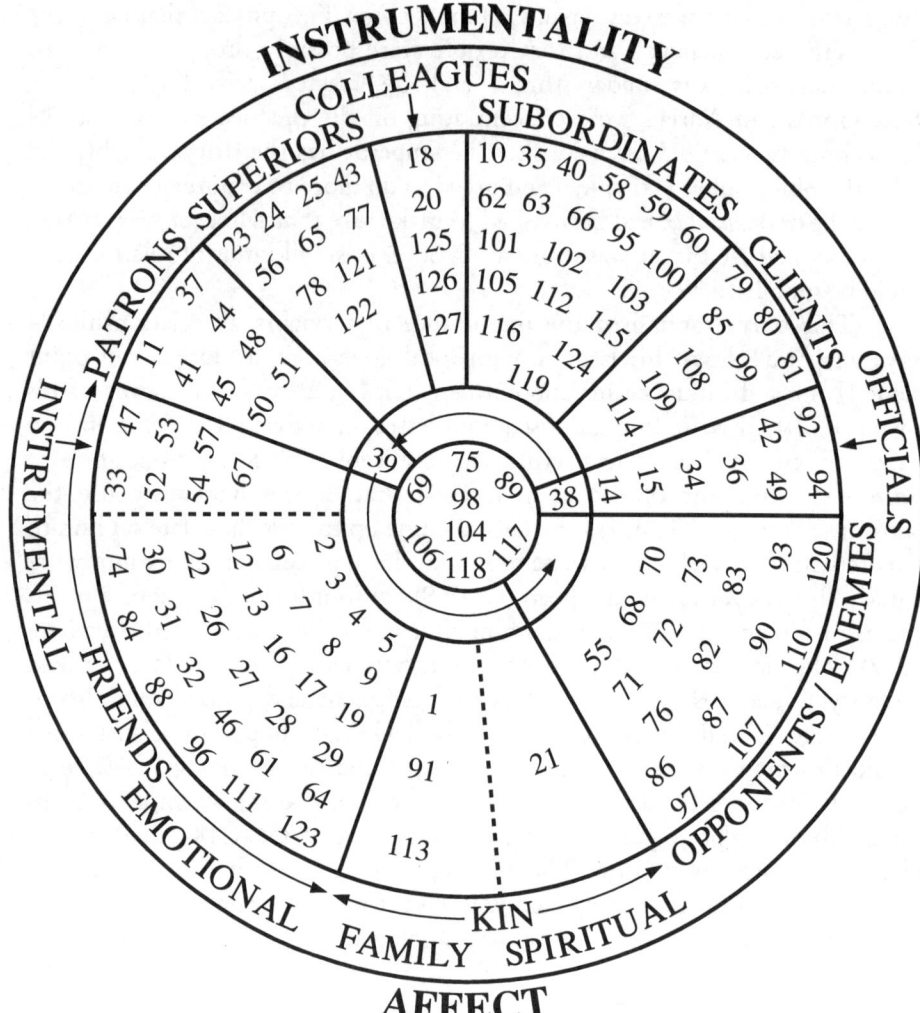

Figure 7.1: Theophylact's network in action: instrumental
and non-instrumental

Figure 7: Theophylact's network in action: instrumental and non-instrumental

	Addressee	Role/relation	Use	Case	Evidence	Affect?	Used?
1	Demetrios	brother/friend	letter-bearer; with tax-problems		Poems 14 and 15;	Yes	Yes
2	Nicholas Anemas	official/friend	not seen		G32, G34, G41	Yes	Not seen
3	Nicholas Kallikles	friend	to look after Demetrios		G93	Yes	Yes
4	Gregory Kamateros	'son', friend	to arrange a job; to override a tax-assessment; to find a job for a client; to brief a new official		G27, G31, G38, G67	Yes	Yes
5	Nicholas Mermentoulos	friend	to console		G33	Yes	Yes (emotional)
6	John Opheomachos	official/friend	not seen		G69, G71	Yes	Not seen
7	Michael Pantechnes	'son', pupil, friend	to speak well of Theophylact to the emperor	Lazaros affair / calumny crisis	G99	Yes	Yes (emotional)
8	Nicholas of Kerkyra	colleague, friend	share problems	Triaditsa affair	G75, G77	Yes	Yes (emotional)
9	N.N., bishop of Kitros	colleague, friend	to confide in	death of Demetrios	G121	Yes	Yes (emotional)
10	N.N., bishop of Pelagonia	suffragan, friend	not seen		G21, G36,?G63	Yes	Not seen
11	Nikephoros Bryennios	patron, friend	to counteract the alliance of Iasites and Lazaros	Lazaros affair	G96, poem 1	Yes	Yes
12	Constantine Komnenos	official, ?friend	not seen		G123	Yes	Not seen
13	N. Machetares	friend	not seen		G44	Yes	Not seen
14	N. Makrembolites	'son', official	official	synod of Prespa	G108	Yes	Yes (official)
15	Gregory Pakourianos	'son', official	general assistance, protection from fisc		G55, G79	Yes	Yes (official)
16	John Pantechnes	elevated friend	not seen		G120	Yes	Not seen
17	John Peribleptenos	friend	to counteract calumny	Lazaros crisis	G97	Yes	Yes (emotional)
18	Niketas Polites	friend	to look after the bishop of Glavenitsa and solve Koprinistra problem		G40	Yes	Yes
19	Theophylact Romaios	'son'	not seen		G42, G46	Yes	Not seen
20	Theodore Smyrnaios	ex-colleague	to look after Demetrios		G6, G28, G95	Some	Yes (emotional)
21	N. Tarchaneiotes	older recipient of spiritual advice	not seen, but monetary?		G16, G20	No	Not seen
22	Niketas *ho tou Serron*	ex-colleague	general assistance in crisis	calumny crisis	G91 (if to him)	Not much	Yes (emotional)

23	Nikephoros *chartophylax*	official	not seen		G51, G66	Some	Not seen
24	Niketas *chartophylax*	acquaintance	not seen		G83	Not seen	Not seen
25	Peter *chartophylax*	friend, contact	to look after Demetrios	winter crisis	G90	Some	Yes (emotional)
26	N. Chrysoberges	colleague, friend	not seen		G35	Some	Not seen
27	Theodoulos N	colleague, friend	to share problems		G72	Some	Not seen
28	N.N. bishop of Semnea	colleague, friend	not seen		G56, G74	Some	Yes (emotional)
29	Symeon, *begoumenos*	friend	?		G37	Yes	Not seen
30	John the *maistor*	?	?		G62	?	?
31	John the philosopher	friend	to combat calumny	calumny crisis	G100	Yes	Yes (emotional)
32	Niketas, imperial doctor	friend	to look after Demetrios		G110	Yes	Yes (emotional)
33	John Attaleiates	'son', ex-pupil	to help bishop of Side		G104	Not seen	Yes
34	John Bryennios	official	general assistance		G86, G105	Not seen	Yes
35	N. Diabologyres	suffragan	not beyond duty		G15	Not seen	Not seen
36	Constantine Doukas	official	help with Vardar village	Ekklesiai case	G118, G119	Not seen	Yes
37	Eirene Doukaina	patroness	not seen		G107	Not seen	Not seen
38	John Doukas	official, patron	to help with hospition and aule; help Θ's relations	Mogila case	G26, G17, G8	Hero-worship	Yes
39	Michael Doukas	patron; opponent	to soften up son; to stop violating the canons	Vardar village Canons case	G88, G84	Not seen	Yes
40	Gregory Kamateros	suffragan	not beyond duty		G53	Not seen	Not seen
41	Adrian Komnenos	patron	to stop an *anagraphe*; to intercede with the emperor	Village in Ochrid, Lazaros	G85, G89, G98	Not seen	Yes
42	John Komnenos	official	to deal with immoral hieromonk; to help bishop of Devol, to uphold *exkousseia* of priests of Pologos; stop recruitment in Ochrid area; settle a lawsuit; general help with fisc	Pologos case	G10, G11, G12, G19, G22, G23, G24, ?G61	Not much	Yes
43	Patriarch Nicholas III	senior churchman	moral support; look after the bishop of Pelagonia		G54, G64	Inappropriate	Yes (emotional)
44	Nikephoros Melissenos	patron	obtain *kanonika* of villages		G9	Inappropriate	Yes
45	George Palaiologos	patron	help in avoiding *anagraphe*; intervention with praktor	Vardar village	G88, G126	Inappropriate	Yes
46	N. Psellos	friend	not seen		G132	Not seen	Not seen

47	John Serblias	friend	to get a *pittakion* from Gregory Taronites for the official at Vodena	Vodena case	G49	Not much		Yes
48	Gregory Taronites	'son', patron	give *pittakion* as above	Vodena case	G49	Possibly	Yes
49	John Taronites	official	not seen		G18	Not seen	Yes
50	Maria of Alania	patroness	not seen (in past?)		G4	Yes	Not seen
51	Maria of Bulgaria	acquaintance	to stop her son from breaking canons	Canons case	G84	Not seen	Yes
52	Michael *bo tou Chalkedonos*	acquaintance	to stop patriarch from meddling	Kittaba case	G82	Not seen	Yes
53	Niketas *bo tou Chalkedonos*	ex-pupil, 'son'	deliver Θ's letters to (51) and (39)	Canons case	G82	Some	Yes
54	John, *grammatikos* of Palaiologos	not clear	give letter to (45) and consult Θ's interests	Vardar village	G88	Some	Yes
55	Tibanios the Armenian	opponent	not seen		G55	Inappropriate	Inappropriate
56	N.N. Grand *oikonomos*	superior	to get Θ a pay-rise		G3	Not seen	Yes
57	N.N. the *epi ton deeseon*	friend	to free Tornikios from military service		G109	Not seen	Yes
58	N.N. bishop of Debra	suffragan	simply to do duty		G58	Not seen	Not seen
59	N.N. bishop of Triaditsa	suffragan	not seen	Triaditsa case	G58,G59, G60, G87	Not seen	Not seen
60	N.N. bishop of Vidin	suffragan	not seen		G57	Not seen	Not seen
61	Recipient of G106	?friend	not seen		G106	Some	Yes
62	(undisciplined) pupils	pupils	not seen		G1 and G2	Not seen	Not seen
63	Bulgar pupils	pupils	not seen		G103	Not seen	Not seen
64	Rodomir Aaron	host	not seen		poems11 and 12	Not seen	Not seen
65	Constantine Doukas	addressee	inappropriate		PB	Inappropriate	Inappropriate
66	Theodore,deacon and *kanstresios*	addressee, 'son'	inappropriate		Errors of Latins	Inappropriate	Inappropriate
67	monk Neilos	contact	to persuade the *sebastos* to keep Gregory Antiochos away		poem 10	Not seen	Yes
68	libidinous eunuch	enemy	not seen		poem 13	Not seen	Not seen
69	grieving person	no evidence	not seen		poem 6 and 7	Not seen	Not seen
70	'*poneiros doulos*'	enemy	not seen		poem 8	Not seen	Not seen
71	condemner of holy persons	enemy	not seen		poem 9	Not seen	Not seen

Theophylact could be formidable on occasion, and he asked a great deal of his friends and protectors.[184]

But he did not expect them to last for ever. G63 is a fascinating letter to a suffragan and would make sense in terms of the understanding he displayed in G21 if it were destined for the bishop of Pelagonia. It is about the death of a protector and praises his efforts in trying to ensure a peaceful life for Theophylact. But he makes the point that it is God who protects, through the intermediary of the deceased. Was Israel left leaderless after Moses? Did not Elisha succeed Elijah? He expects that things will go even better in future to remind both writer and recipient that it is not through human strategy and effort but through the goodness and the powerful word of God that they are directed. The poor suffragan's *mikropsychia* and lowness of morale are castigated, but Theophylact admits he has had a little time to recover from the blow, and recommends trust in the Lord, wishing his bishop the consolation of the Spirit. It is in parts very close to a consolatio, and could almost be the reply to a consolatio, were it not for the sense that the suffragan is distressed at the loss of a patron for the archdiocese. We have no idea who this protector might be.[185]

We have seen Theophylact's network in action. It was always necessary as an information-gathering operation, and various parts of it were mobilised as appropriate. He worked where possible through official channels, calling on his major patrons in more difficult cases, working obliquely so as to protect other sectors of the network. As well as patrons instrumental friends seem to have been used, and old debts called in on occasion. When the whole network was threatened, Theophylact called on otherwise entirely 'emotional' friends to counteract the rumours. And we should not forget the less obvious uses of network: the majority of the letters which make no specific request and the sizeable minority of the letters which do not mention problems. These letters serviced relationships which might be manipulated later, but they also maintained Theophylact's morale, cheered his spirit, amused and delighted him, in writing as well as in receiving.[186]

---

[184] 'Patronage,' 141. See G67 (the good governor has arrived) and G79 (the good governor has gone) for Gregory Pakourianos: G127 and G88 show us Theophylact's aspirations at the moment of appointment. G18, to John Taronites, II, 191.2-193.42, G31, to Gregory Kamateros, II, 235.32. G80 begins καὶ Κύριος παρεβίβασε τὸ ἁμάρτημά σου (Kings 12:13), II, 425.2-9: he notes that among Pakourianos's virtues is that he is no Pharisee.

[185] G63, II, 357-359.

[186] See my 'Classical Tradition,' 92-93 and M. Solarino, 'Un intellettuale in provincia: Teofilatto di Achrida,' *Syndesmos: Studi in onore di Rosario Anastasi* (Catania, 1991), 63-82 at 82.

It is important not to reduce Theophylact's network to the question of patronage. The concept of symmetry applied to the collection shows that the picture is more complex. On the other hand the systemic importance of patronage in Byzantine society remains to be determined,[187] but Theophylact's network provides some pointers. There was, as far as we can see, no problem for example for Theophylact in running multiple patrons, and reciprocity in his collection need certainly never be immediate.[188] Anthropologists and sociologists have discussed at some length the societies in which patronage flourishes.[189] Byzantium might not at first sight look a very promising prospect with its reliance both on kinship and on bureaucracy. I have argued that the conditions of the eleventh and twelfth centuries, a period of rapid social change followed by a more rigid kin-based order, encouraged the manipulation of friendship ties, and, by implication, of patronage.[190] But when I came first to analyse Theophylact's use of patronage I was puzzled to discover him, for all his dexterity—and we have seen him only once make a false move—more often in the role of client than of patron.[191] Alan Harvey has provided a convincing explanation of this difficulty: he sets Theophylact's collection in the context of Alexios's financial difficulties and the fiscal confusion on the eve of Alexios's tax reforms of 1106-09. 'That a landowner as well connected as Theophylact had so much difficulty with tax-officials was indicative of the general effectiveness of imperial fiscal policy, which enabled Alexios to secure his rule and withstand the external threats to the empire.'[192] Every victory of Theophylact in the area of taxation at least was at the expense of imperial policy; their interests were diametrically opposed. This understood, the apparent powerlessness of Theophylact appears more comprehensible, and his achievement as a manipulator even more

---

[187]   T. Johnson and C. Dandeker, 'Patronage: Relation and System,' *Patronage in Ancient Society*, ed. A. Wallace-Hadrill (London, 1989), 219-241.

[188]   Both appear problematic in *Patronage in Ancient Society*, in the paper by R. Saller, 'Patrons and Friendship in Early Imperial Rome: Drawing the Distinction,' 49-62, and in reaction to reviews of R. Saller, *Personal Patronage in the Early Empire* (Cambridge, 1982).

[189]   E. Gellner, 'Patrons and Clients,' *Patrons and Clients*, ed. E. Gellner and J. Waterbury (London, 1977), 1-6, see my 'Patronage'; S.N. Eisenberger and L. Roniger, *Patrons, Clients and Friends. Interpersonal Relations and the Structure of Trust in Society* (Themes in the Social Sciences, Cambridge, 1984). For the Byzantine state see J.F. Haldon, 'The Army and the Economy: the Allocation and Redistribution of Surplus Wealth in the Byzantine State,' *MedHistRev* 7.2 (1992), 133-153.

[190]   'Friendly Society,' 18-20.

[191]   'Patronage,' 133-143.

[192]   Harvey, 'The Land,' *REB* 51 (1993), 139-154 at 154.

impressive.[193] But power in patronage lies with the client as well as the patron: patrons need to build up a following in competition with other patrons.[194] But Theophylact was physically distant from the centre of power, the emperor, and to succeed he needed to keep his lines of communication clear. We are brought back again to the supreme importance of epistolary communication in maintaining patronage, or any social relation, over the geographical span of the empire.

We have now looked at Theophylact's letter-collection as literary artefact, as the embodiment of eleventh- and twelfth-century concerns, as an example of an old and valued genre, and as the traces of a system of human relationships. It is time to move again beyond the collection.

---

[573] *Pace* Angold, *Church and Society*, 164, I have never 'doubted the effectiveness of Theophylact's defence of his church's interests.' We have in this chapter seen his remarkable skills in action. As I argue in 'Patronage,' he appears in the collection more in the role of client than of patron and very seldom, for reasons I explain above, 200-201, in the role of broker.

[194] J. Boissevain, 'Patronage in Sicily,' *Man* 1 (1966), 8-33, described by A. Weingrod, 'Patronage and Power,' *Patrons and Clients*, 47 as 'a kind of clients' view of the world'; cf. D. Braund, 'Function and Dysfunction; Personal Patronage in Roman Imperialism,' *Patronage in Ancient Society*, 148, on competition for clients.

CHAPTER FIVE

AUTHOR AND MAN

5.1 Theophylact as *auctor*

So far we have considered Theophylact's letter-collection as a text, as a series of 135 letters which preserve only part of a social and literary whole. This is my emphasis throughout this book, but in using the modifier 'Theophylact's' I open the question not only of text and reader, but also of author. This may seem ill-advised. It was in 1968 that Barthes proclaimed 'the death of the author' in an attempt to subvert some of the most cherished presuppositions of his day: he saw culture as 'tyrannically centred on the author, his person, his tastes, his passions'. To begin with, his objections seem New Critical in a desire to liberate the artefact from the artist's personality, but it soon becomes clear that he regards New Critics as having consolidated the place of the Author and looks forward to a time when the author will be cleared away and the reader seen as the one place where a multiplicity of meanings is fused: 'the birth of the reader must be at the cost of the death of the author.'[1]

It is clear that this desire to focus on the reader is fully in keeping with the preferences of late twentieth-century scholarship: in this I collude. But the author has proved harder to bury than to kill. Foucault finds that to talk about a work precludes an author, but the author is not totally eliminated. A milieu may privilege a genre so that its producers may be accounted authors or it may not; his example is of a private letter: 'it may have a signatory but does not have an author'. He is forced to fall back on the idea of 'author function' in order to achieve a desired sophistication of analysis of the use of the first person, the epistolary (usually present) tense and so on in a given text, rather as Wayne Booth needs his Implied Author. It is only in an imaginary society of his own that he is able to pose questions about discourse which take no account of authenticity and authority.[2]

---

[1] R. Barthes, 'The Death of the Author,' *Image-Music-Text*, ed. tr. S. Heath (London, 1984), 142-148.

[2] M. Foucault, 'What is an Author?' tr. J.V. Harari, *Textual Strategies: Perspectives in Post-structural Criticism* (Cornell, 1979), 141-160, repr. P. Rabinow, *The Foucault Reader* (Harmondsworth, 1984), 101-120; cf. C. Wayne Booth, *The Rhetoric of Fiction*, 2nd ed. (Chicago, 1983), 264-266. For the centrality of the reader see the excellent S. Suleiman and I.

Alexander Nehamas neatly detaches the necessity for a concept of the author from any sense of authorial authority; to Barthes's idea of an author visiting his text like a guest may be added Nehemas's sense of a reader recreating the author in an intelligent consideration of what that reader as literary historian may or may not expect to recreate of the original circumstances of the text. 'Texts belong to the past; their understanding belongs to the future.'[3] It is unlikely that the Yale critics, in their most European mood, would accept this division between text and *hors-texte*. Yet even they cannot dispense entirely with the concept of author, nor with the idea of literature.[4] It would seem to be premature,[5] in concentrating on our text, to ignore the authorial sense of that 'Theophylact' we have mentioned so often.

The 'historical horizon of its origination'[6] comes closer to the birth than the death of the author. Literary theorists are prone to look at the romantic period or the nineteenth century as the heyday of the concept of the author; sometimes they allow themselves to flirt with the Renaissance.[7] Recent work however on the western medieval commentary tradition allows the

---

Crosman, *The Reader in the Text. Essays on Audience and Interpretation* (Princeton, 1980); H.R. Jauss, *Towards an Aesthetic of Reception*, tr. T. Bahti (Brighton, 1982); W. Iser, *The Implied Reader: Patterns of Communication in Prose Fiction from Bunyan to Beckett* (Baltimore, 1974); U. Eco, *The Role of the Reader. Explorations in the Semiotics of Texts* (London, 1981).

[3] A. Nehamas, 'The Postulated Author: Critical Monism as a Regulative Ideal,' *Critical Inquiry* 8 (1981), 133-149 at 149. Cf. at 144: 'to interpret a text is to place it in a context.'

[4] G. Hartman's *Criticism in the Wilderness* (New Haven and London, 1980) is subtitled *The Study of Literature Today*; he plays down the author but creates instead, chapter by chapter, a canon of critics. Derrida in *Signéponge/Signsponge* (New York, 1984), 11, assiduously though he sponges, concedes that 'ma chose aujourd'hui' is Francis Ponge. And, while only tenuously a Yale critic, H. Bloom, *The Anxiety of Influence. A Theory of Poetry* (London and Oxford, 1973) depends on the relationship of two kinds of author, the ephebe and the precursor.

[5] See the brilliant S. Burke, *The Death and Return of the Author. Criticism and Subjectivity in Barthes, Foucault and Derrida* (Edinburgh, 1994).

[6] Jauss, 'Literary History as a Challenge to Literary History,' repr. *Towards an Aesthetic of Reception*, 18; T. Bennett, 'Texts in History,' *Poststructuralism and the Question of History*, ed. D. Attridge, G. Bennington and R. Young (Cambridge, 1989), 63-81 at 76-77 defends Lukács against the charge of a simplistic view of origination.

[7] For the Renaissance, G. Hartman, 'Literary Criticism and its Discontents,' *Critical Inquiry* 2 (1976), 204-205; for romanticism and the nineteenth century see T. Eagleton, *Literary Theory. An Introduction* (Minneapolis, 1983), 74, 184; H.R. Jauss, 'The Alterity and Modernity of Medieval Literature,' *NLH* 1 (1979), 385-390. See M. Nesbitt, 'What was an Author?' *Everyday Life*, ed. A. Kaplan and K. Ross (YFS, 73, Yale, 1987), 229-257, for the contribution of the French copyright law of 1793.

medieval view of the *auctor* to emerge—an ancient *auctor*, and one with authority. To be worth reading, a book had to be by an *auctor*. Levels of authorship can be distinguished: the scribe, the compiler, the commentator, the *auctor*. Stages of development may be discerned (the addition of secular authorities to biblical or patristic ones; the conviction that the thought of an author is best understood in the context of his work as a whole; the treatment of authors as familiars in the early Renaissance) and then the application of all these attitudes to living authors detected.[8]

Was there anything parallel to the *auctor* in Byzantium? Neither συγγραφεύς nor ῥήτωρ has the same resonance, but the lack of a word does not mean that the concept did not exist. Certainly the importance of tradition and of Holy Writ in Orthodoxy might suggest so, as in the use of actual volumes in iconoclastic debates to authenticate quotations.[9] And if there is a point at which the author might be born, it would surely be in the eleventh century (rather than Minnis's thirteenth) when, as we saw above in chapter 2.6, we can begin to see an 'author in the text'.[10] But other characterisations of the role of writers in eleventh- and twelfth-century Byzantium would appear to deny this possibility: if twelfth-century writers are regarded as artisans and if the patron is accorded the palm of creativity and intention, there would be very little scope for an author.[11] Is this view then to prevail? Or is there a limited sense in which there was a sense of authorship in Byzantium?

---

[8]   A. Minnis, 'Discussions of "authorial role" and "literary form" in late medieval scriptural exegesis,' *Beiträge zur Geschichte der deutschen Sprache und Literatur* 99 (1977), 37-65; A.J. Minnis, *Medieval Theory of Authorship. Scholastic Literary Attitudes in the Later Middle Ages*, 2nd edn (London, 1988).

[9]   There is as yet no general study of the Bible in Byzantium. For the brandishing of codices at the time of iconoclasm (the council of 787), see C. Mango, 'Books in the Byzantine Empire AD 750-850,' *Byzantine Books and Bookmen* (Washington, DC, 1975), 29-45 at 30-31.

[10]   See R. Scott, 'The Classical Tradition in Byzantine Historiography,' *Byzantium and the Classical Tradition*, ed. M. Mullett and R. Scott (Birmingham, 1981), 61-74; A. Kazhdan with G. Constable, *People and Power in Byzantium. An Introduction to Modern Byzantine Studies* (Washington, DC, 1982), 100-101; R. Beaton, '"De vulgari eloquentia" in Twelfth-century Byzantium,' *Byzantium and the West, c.850-c.1200*, ed. J.D. Howard-Johnston (Amsterdam, 1988), 261-268; J. Ljubarskij, 'Writers' Intrusion in Early Byzantine Literature,' *XVIII IntCong, Major Papers* (Moscow, 1991), 433-456; see also a forthcoming study in *DOP* by Michael Angold on the autobiographical impulse from the eleventh to the thirteenth centuries culminating in the autobiographical accounts of Blemmydes and Michael VIII.

[11]   P. Magdalino, 'Byzantine Snobbery,' *The Byzantine Aristocracy, IX-XIII Centuries*, ed. M.J. Angold (BARIntSer, 221, Oxford, 1984), 67-68. The role of the patron has been much exaggerated in recent years, so that Catia Galatariotou for example can regard Neophytos of Paphos as author of the paintings of the cave. See the important corrective of R.

Writers are acclaimed on occasion: the priest Michael's claim to know all of Theodore Prodromos's oeuvre by heart is an interesting example.[12] Certainly we should not imagine any sense (as in the west) that only an ancient author could be an *auctor*: Byzantines saw no division between the Roman empire and their own[13] and their most favoured literary models came from various periods of classical antiquity and the Byzantine middle ages. Frequent colophons and epigrams show this interaction between litterati of the present and authors of the past and the ubiquitous use of τοῦ αὐτοῦ shows a concern in principle for authorship, even if the result can often be otherwise. The Byzantines were not snobbish either about genres; there seems to be no hierarchy which would exclude a certain kind of writer from the status of author. In particular epistolographers take their place with writers of other rhetoric and we are not in the position—like students of French early modern letters[14]—of having to justify the literary credentials of the letter. Nor indeed have Byzantinists relegated the letters of Byzantine writers to second-class status, belonging in a 'life and letters' biography,[15] though this is less a theoretical decision than an oddly happy result of the general neglect of the literary study of Byzantine literature: the study of the author in Byzantium is at a very early stage.

There is interesting work to be done on the place of anonymity in Byzantine literature, and the invention of historical contexts, as for example with pseudo-Dionysios the Areopagite. But it is too early to be sure whether there is a real change in the status of the author between the *gerontika* of John Moschos in the seventh century and Paul Evergetinos in the eleventh: John presents all his sources as oral testimony and foregrounds the frame story of his travels with Sophronios; Paul lists his source texts in a careful and

---

Cormack, 'Patronage and New Programs of Byzantine Iconography,' *XVII IntCong* (New Rochelle, NY, 1986), 609-638, repr. *The Byzantine Eye. Studies in Art and Patronage*, X (London, 1989).

[12] Michael Italikos, ep. 1, to Theodore Prodromos, ed. P. Gautier, *Michel Italikos, Lettres et Discours* (AOC, 14, Paris, 1972), 64.

[13] For Byzantine views of the past, see *Reading the Past in Late Antiquity*, ed. G. Clarke, B. Croke and R. Mortley (Canberra, 1990), 205-223; *The Perception of the Past in Twelfth-century Europe*, ed. P. Magdalino (London and Rio Grande, 1992); R. Macrides, 'Perception of the Past in the Twelfth-century Canonists,' *To Byzantio kata ton 12° aiona: kanoniko dikaio, kratos kai koinonia*, ed. N. Oikonomides (Hetaireia Byzantinon kai Metabyzantinon Meleton, 3, Athens, 1991), 589-599.

[14] J.G. Altman, 'The Letter Book as a Literary Institution 1539-1789: toward a Cultural History of Published Correspondences in France,' *Men/Women of Letters*, ed. C.A. Porter (YFS, 71, Yale, 1986), 17-62.

[15] Cf. the attitude of V. Kaufman, *Post Scripts. The Writer's Workshop* (Harvard, 1994), 1: 'there is nothing more tedious in a writer's work than his correspondence.'

scrupulous order and it is a task for modern scholarship to detect what parts of the work (or of his parallel collection of catecheses) are his own. The popularity of florilegia in the middle Byzantine period needs to be examined for what it can tell us about the author: does it indicate respect or cavalier treatment to excerpt, rearrange, preserve, 'mis'represent?

Equally we can learn a great deal from author-portraits in Byzantine art, though we cannot yet see a clear pattern of development here either. The Byzantines inherited from Roman art various ways of picturing the author at various stages of the process of creation, which perhaps reflect different views of the role and status of the writer: the evangelist-model is a craftsmanlike, work-in-progress view, which assimilates the author to the labour of the scribe, while representations of the author offering his work to the patron (or dedicatee, or recipient) raise the issues of the primacy of patronage.[16] Only the frontal view of the enthroned author celebrates achievement and recognition of authority. These seem very different iconographies, and might suggest radically opposed roles for the author—yet the historian Constantine Manasses was represented both as enthroned *auctor* and as *technites* delivering the artefact to his patroness—and as writer-on-the-hoof, scribbling in the presence of recipient and Creator. To find a twelfth-century historian as evangelist-scribe we need only turn to Niketas Choniates.[17] In the late period there seems to be a trend towards showing authors as men, rather than makers—or perhaps in terms of their most prestigious roles: Manuel II as emperor, Pachymeres as deacon of the Great Church, Kantakouzenos as emperor and monk.[18] But hymnographers are in the fourteenth century shown in pendentives on the old evangelist-model; by now theologians have joined the historians and liturgists, and the prototype epistolographer was represented from the twelfth century at least.[19]

In the middle Byzantine period there is a sense that authors had to make room for patrons, literally in some cases, like the marginalising of David,[20] or

---

[16] J. Spatharakis, *The Portrait in Byzantine Illuminated Manuscripts* (Leiden, 1976), esp. 248-250.

[17] Vind. phil. gr. 49, fol. 10r, Vind. hist. gr. 91, fol. 1r; Vat. slav. 2, fol. 1v; Vind. hist. gr. 53, fol. 1v; see Spatharakis, figs 100-102; 98.

[18] E.g. ms Ivoires 100, fol. 2r; Monac. gr. 442, fol. 6v; Paris. gr. 1242, fol. 123v; see Spatharakis, figs 93, 106, 87.

[19] For hymnographers see the parekklesion at Chora, for Manuel II as theologian Paris. suppl. gr. 309, fol. VI; for historians see above, n.15, for St Basil as liturgist Hagia Sophia, Ochrid; St Paul sends and receives letters at Monreale.

[20] In the frontispiece of Harvard College Library, cod. gr. 3, fol. 8v, the psalmist David watches from the other side of a column the *deesis* group and kneeling *ktetor* under the canopy, see Spatharakis, fig. 15.

the heavy court presence in the eleventh century where scribe and emperor, emperor and empress, emperor and bureaucrats, author and emperor were all needed to preface a single manuscript.[21] But there is sometimes instead of authority, a sense of interaction between the author and his readership in a synchronity redolent of the underworld of the *Timarion*. Hippocrates the author enthroned on one page faces Apokaukos the owner, plushily seated on the facing page, at least his equal.[22] An abbot's investiture is celebrated by each evangelist in turn, culminating in the gift of the staff by St. John.[23] Complicated literary relationships can be represented: in a manuscript of the homilies of John Chrysostom on Matthew the two authors (John and Matthew) face, and (we are told in an inscription) intercede for, the imperial owners of the volume.[24] The source-authors of a work offer their texts in scrolls to the patron who commissioned it (leaving out the compiler) who then offers the resulting codex to Christ.[25] Complications of text and patronage are also represented: to the Theotokos as patroness of a monastery the two founders offer first the church and then the *typikon*, revised by the second founder.[26] We need to look further in each period at the complicated relations of patron, author, scribe and illustrator and the varied roles of author as technician, entertainer and inspired *vates* in the years around 1100. Alexios may have had his Muses (whatever this tells us), but Ptochoprodromos would soon complain of the meagre returns on literary craft.

Some authors staked their claim to a literary identity by collecting their own works.[27] Whether or not Theophylact was among these, he was acclaimed as a writer in a poem which puts him in the company of Psellos, George of Pisidia, Christopher of Mitylene, and someone called Leo, all now dead:

---

[21] Coislin 79, fol. 1r, 1v, 2r, 2v; see Spatharakis, figs 69-72.

[22] Paris gr. 2144, fols 10v-11r; see Spatharakis, fig. 96.

[23] Paris. gr. 74, fols 61v, 101v, 213r; see Spatharakis, figs 29, 33, 36. Luke is missing but can be reconstructed from other manuscripts.

[24] Sinai. gr. 364, fols 2v-3r; see Spatharakis, fig. 66.

[25] Vat. gr. 666, fols 1v, 2r and 2v; see Spatharakis, figs 78-80. Is it modesty or a proud appeal to the authority of the saintly contributors that we should read in this omission?

[26] Lincoln. gr. 35, fols 10v and 11r; see Spatharakis, figs 152-153.

[27] See N. Basilakes, *Prologos*, ed. E. Miller, *Annuaire de l'Institut* 7 (1873), 135-137; see A. Garzya, 'Il prologo di Niceforo Basilace,' *Boll. del comm. per la preparazione dell' Edizione nazionale dei classici greci e latini* n.s. 19 (Rome, 1971), 55-71; 'Intorno al Prologo di Niceforo Basilace,' *JÖB* 18 (1969), 57-71; Michael Choniates, *Protheoria*, ed. S. Lampros, *Michael Akominatou tou Choniatou ta sozomena* (Athens, 1879), I, 3-5. See R. Browning, 'The Patriarchal School at Constantinople,' *Byz* 32 (1962), 178-179 on a collected edition of George Tornikes taken over wholesale into a thirteenth/fourteenth-century miscellany and on twelfth-century material in these collections in general.

You, *hypertimos* Psellos, the Pisidian, and Christopher,
Leo and Theophylact, the bishop of Bulgaria.[28]

The gathered worthies though are cited simply to throw the achievement
of another writer into higher relief; the poem goes on

You underwent a dreadful and a terrifying penalty,
You moved to below earth before you'd any knowledge of
These verses, which were sent me by the composer of the poetry.

The lines may not match up to Minnis's commentaries as evidence, but they
do show Theophylact in respected company. There is also no doubt that his
books were read: Michael Choniates himself copied the commentary on the
epistles of St Paul, and was very concerned to get it back after the loss of his
library. Demetrios Chomatianos quoted his predecessor's work *On the Errors
of the Latins* and supported its stance. By the fourteenth century we know
Theophylact's letters were in demand, as part of an ascetic and theological
assortment, and in company with Michael Choniates, Gregory of Nazianzos's
letters and Theophylact's own early works.[29]

It is not clear however that it was always Theophylact's literary
qualities which were in demand. His curious *Nachleben* has often been
noted. A demonisation was under way early, and it has been revived in
recent years:[30] the Dominican author of *Contra errores Graecorum* alleges
Theophylact was sent by Photios to the Bulgarians, where he doctored
Chrysostom, cutting out anything that was favourable to the Latins and to

---

[28] Cod. Vind. theol. gr. 242; ed. K. Krumbacher, *Geschichte der byzantinischen Literatur*
(Munich, 1847), 441: the lines are lines 81-82 of a poem, 68, ascribed to Michael Psellos, ed.
L.G. Westerink, *Michaelis Pselli poemata* (Leipzig, 1992), 454: Σὺ δ'αὖ ὑπέρτιμε Ψελλέ,
Πίσιδη, Χριστοφόρε/Λέων καὶ Θεοφύλακτε, προέδρε Βουλγαρίας.

[29] On Michael Choniates' eagerness to lay his hands on Theophylact's commentaries on
the *Epistles* see epp. 106, 146, ed. Lampros, II, 241-2, 295-6. Theophylact's commentaries on
the *Gospels* were already in the monastery of Michael Attaleiates by 1100 at the latest,
Diataxis, ed. P. Gautier, 'La diataxis de Michel Attaliate,' *REB* 39 (1981), 1-143 at 123. On
this gift of the monk Michael to the monastery see P. Lemerle, *Cinq études*, 97-98. For
Demetrios Chomatianos see M. Angold, *Church and Society in Byzantium under the
Comneni, 1081-1261* (Cambridge, 1995), 532. On the manuscript tradition see E.
Marsenger, *Der Mattäuskommentar des Theophylaktos von Achrida* (Schweidnitz, 1924),
Beck, *Kirche und theologische Literatur*, 649-651. For the fourteenth-century readership of
Theophylact see above, 81-82.

[30] See below, chapter 4.5, 262-271 and my 'Byzantium and the Slavs; the views of
Theophylact of Ochrid,' *Studies in Memory of I. Dujcev*, II, ed. A. Djourova (Sofia,
forthcoming) for misconceptions of Theophylact's role. They are mostly attributable to
Zlatarsky, *Istoriia na Bulgarskata durzhava.*

papal claims.[31] But in late and post-medieval Bulgar legend he was elevated
to the patriarchate of Trnovo and a posthumous and apparently spurious
canonisation[32] and in the stormy controversies of Reformation Europe he was
treated as a kind of honorary church father, revered by two such different
figures as Erasmus and archbishop Laud. Erasmus was originally under the
misapprehension that Theophylact was indeed an early Father, but his
honorary status appears widespread in the Reformation. Augustine Lindsell's
edition of Theophylact's commentaries on the *Epistles* was the first book to be
printed (in 1636) by archbishop Laud's Greek press in London, the second
being his correspondent Niketas *ho tou Serron*'s biblical catena. *Habent sua fata
libelli*: so, it would seem, do their authors.[33]

5.2 The letters in the oeuvre

Foucault in his search for someone to blame for the privileged position of the
author settled on St Jerome. His four-fold criteria for determining
inauthenticity (inferiority, inconsistency of argument, a different style, tell-
tale anachronisms) Foucault saw as compelling a standard level of quality, a
field of conceptual coherence, stylistic uniformity and a view of the author as
a historical figure.[34] Put this way round (and I leave aside the question of

---

[31] PG 140, 487-574, at 520. My thanks here to Michael Angold.

[32] I. Snegarov, 'Les sources sur la vie et l'activité de Clément d'Ochrida,' *BB* 1 (1963),
111-114. Note though that N. Velimirović, *The Prologue from Ochrid, Lives of the Saints and
Homilies for Every Day in the Year* (Birmingham, 1985), I, 395 has a mention for
Theophylact of Ochrid on 31 December. Vol IV, which should contain that day, has not
yet appeared.

[33] For Erasmus see M.A. Screech, *Ecstasy and the Praise of Folly* (London, 1980), 150ff.,
but his honorary status appears widespread in the Reformation, see S.L. Greenslade, *The
English Reformers and the Fathers of the Church* (Inaugural Lecture, University of Oxford,
1960), 5. On Laud see H. Trevor-Roper, *Archbishop Laud, 1573-1640* (London, 1940), 275.
On reasons for the interest in the contemporary Orthodox among English reformers see
G.J. Cuming, 'Eastern Liturgies and Anglican Divines, 1510-1662,' *Studies in Church
History* 13 (1976), 231-238; H.R. Trevor-Roper, 'The Church of England and the Greek
Church at the Time of Charles I,' *Studies in Church History* 15 (1978), 213-240.

[34] Foucault, 'What is an author?' 110-111, quoting Jerome, *De viris illustribus*, PL 23,
637-766 in which he discerns various criteria: ch. 1, 638: style; ch. 4, 646: *vetustate jam et
usu*; ch. 5, 647: style again, but allowing for sensitivity to the recipient (Paul writes as a
Hebrew to the Hebrews); ch. 7, 651: authorial ignorance; ch. 25, 678: difference *elegantia et
phrasi*; ch. 41, 691: a biographical argument in letters; ch. 56, 703: difference of style,
though he accepts, ch. 117, 747, that the same author could write both for and against a
proposition.

whether this was fair to Jerome) implicit assumptions about what an author is may be revealed. If an author need not have not all these things, then there is hope for Theodore Prodromos and Procopius yet.[35] How about Theophylact? Is there a single voice bombinating in his oeuvre?

It is a very large oeuvre, four volumes of Migne's Patrology, and comprises a wide range of writing: exegesis, polemic, hagiography, homiletic, epideictic rhetoric, and poems. To do justice to it would require a series of studies and a series of scholars expert in each part of it. For present purposes I can only sample and take cases where there appears to be a fruitful intertextuality between letters and another part of the oeuvre. Nor should we lay too much weight on Foucault's categories. I have already forsworn evaluation in this book, and we shall look at the author as historical figure in the second half of this chapter. Here we look only for a single voice. Minor matters of inconsistency may be noted but over such a large mass of material and from the 1070s to the 1120s details may well be different. When Theophylact is confused over where the Nikopolis is where St Paul stayed,[36] or when he appears to be inconsistent over the virtues and vices of eunuchs,[37] any number of explanations may be forthcoming. And to find stylistic or substantive inconsistency we do not need to leave the collection: there are significant differences for example between the letters from Bulgaria and the early letters.[38] But we have also seen that the commentaries can inform us about letters and the letters inform us about reading scripture. Theophylact may have made generic distinctions but one work could inform another.

It remains unclear whether the various Theophylacts of modern scholarship can be reconciled. He has been seen[39] as a witness of the First

---

[35] For spirited defences of the right of an author to have more than one voice see Averil Cameron, *Procopius and the Sixth Century* (London, 1985) and R. Beaton, 'The Rhetoric of Poverty: the Lives and Opinions of Theodore Prodromos,' *BMGS* 11 (1987), 1-28.

[36] G35, to Chrysoberges metropolitan of Naupaktos, II, 245.25-247.26; *Comm. in Titum*, PG 125, 169B, where he locates Nikopolis in Thrace.

[37] Compare poem 13.3-5, I, 369: Ἐγὼ δ' ἐν εὐνούχοις σε θήσομαι τέρας/ὡς πρὸς καθαρότητα παρεφθαρμένον with G66, to the *chartophylax*, II, 367.39-40: τοῦ τοιούτου...καί, ὃ σπάνιον εὐνούχοις, χρηστοήθους καὶ ἁπλουστάτου.

[38] G1, G2, G3 are each longer than all but the longest of the Bulgarian letters and are very highly decorated throughout; the first two are studded with mixed quotations throughout, the third, to the Grand *oikonomos*, keeps to the Bible. For quotation practice in the Bulgarian letters see above, 3.2, 100 and 3.3, 159-161.

[39] F. Chalandon, *Les Comnène*, I, *Essai sur le règne d'Alexis I Comnène* (Paris, 1900), 160; B. Leib, *Rome, Kiev et Byzance à la fin du XIe siècle* (Paris, 1924), 42; S. Runciman, *A History of the Crusades* (Cambridge, 1951), I, 170.

Crusade, a curiously Anselm-like liberal in the controversies with Rome,[40] a valuable source for the use of the classics,[41] for the history of Bulgaria[42] or provincial economic history[43] or heresy[44] or Byzantine feudalism,[45] as a representative prelate[46] and as an original writer.[47] But to reconcile these views may be too ambitious for the present. Let us look instead at a series of oppositions and listen for that single voice.

i. *The letters and panegyric*

Two speeches survive from Theophylact's career as rhetor in Constantinople, the speech to Constantine Doukas frequently known as the *Paideia Basilike (PB)* and the speech to Alexios Komnenos *(AK)*.[48] The first dates from between the accession of Alexios and the birth of John; the second has been convincingly dated to 6 January 1088 by Gautier. It is not possible to arrive at a firm date for the *PB*; the reference to an annual tax suggests a regular occasion, but the absence of reference to Alexios suggests that it was delivered in Maria's court at the Mangana rather than in the presence of the emperor. Although the two speeches appear very different in tone and structure, so much so that not until Gautier was the *PB* identified as a *basilikos logos*, there are distinctive similarities. Both are *double* panegyrics, in that the emperor's mother is praised in each case; the play on *mantis* in *AK* and *didaskalos* in the

---

[40]   S. Runciman, *The Eastern Schism* (Oxford, 1955), 72-77; A.A.M. Bryer, 'Cultural Relations between East and West in the Twelfth Century,' *Relations between East and West in the Middle Ages*, ed. D. Baker (Edinburgh, 1973), 78-79; J. Draeseke, 'Theophylaktos' Schrift gegen die Lateiner,' *BZ* 10 (1901), 512-523.

[41]   K. Praechter, 'Antike Quellen des Theophylaktos von Bulgarien,' *BZ* 10 (1901), 512-523.

[42]   V.G. Vasilevskii, 'Vizantiia i Pechenegi,' *Trudy*, I (St Petersburg, 1908), 1-175 esp. Appendix III, 'Feofilakt Bolgarski e ego sochineniia,' 134-149; Zlatarsky, *Istoriia na Bulgarskata durzhava*, II, 252-366.

[43]   D. Xanalatos, *Beiträge zur Wirtschafts- und Sozialgeschichte Makedoniens auf Grund der Briefe Theophylakts von Achrida* (Diss., Munich, 1937)

[44]   D. Obolensky, *The Bogomils. A Study in Balkan Neomanichaeism* (Cambridge, 1948), 171-172; D. Panov, 'Bogomil'skoe dvizhenie v Makedonii na osnovanii pisem Feofilakta Okhridskogo,' *XIV IntCong* (Bucharest, 1976), III, 721-727.

[45]   B.A. Nikolaev, *Feodalni otnosheniia v pokorenata ot Bizantiia Bulgarskia otrazeni v pismata na Teofilakt Okhridski archiepiskop Bulgarski* (Sofia, 1971); I.A. Božilov, 'Pismata na Teofilakt Ochridski kato istoricheski izvor,' *Isvestiya na Durzhavnite Archivi*, 14 (1967), 60-100.

[46]   R. Janin, *DTC* 15 (1946), 538.

[47]   Janin, ibid.

[48]   Gautier, *Théophylacte*, I, 179-211, 215-243.

PB, the evocation of the *choros* or *kyklos* in each and the conclusion with references to the art and practice of rhetoric are further parallels.[49]

In both, Theophylact appears to be speaking as *maistor ton rhetoron*. Gautier's view that Theophylact did not hold the office appears to conflict with one lemma, two letters and the twelfth-century list of the archbishops of Bulgaria.[50] It is not unreasonable to see the conclusion of the 1088 speech with its Hadrianic comparison as a direct reference to Alexios's creation of the post of *maistor* and the reinstitution of the Epiphany speech. The way in which Theophylact 'hands over' to his pupils seems characteristic of the behaviour of twelfth-century *maistores*. It is just possible that he was *maistor* for the 1088 speech but not for the *PB* and that the *maistor*[51] on that occasion handed over to Theophylact, as Constantine's teacher, to praise the young co-emperor.[52] But it is more likely that an alternative court demanded an alternative rhetor.

The *PB* is different largely because it is addressed to a child-emperor and contains suitably (but also very fashionable) parainetic material. Advice on forms of government and the importance of friendship could be regarded as having topical as well as timeless importance. The imperial virtue emphasised, because within the child's capacity, is *philanthropia*; this finds a place also in *AK*, but *phronesis* and *sophrosyne* and especially *andreia* are celebrated there, with an emphasis on foreign policy. Although Theophylact says he will leave out material already celebrated by rhetors, and *patris*, *genos*, *genesis* and *paideia* are abandoned for fuller emphasis on virtues and *synkrisis*, it is a straightforwardly Menandrian composition.[53]

---

[49] On the double nature of the speeches see my 'The "disgrace" of the ex-basilissa Maria,' *BS* 45 (1984), 202-212 at 208; but note R. Anastasi, 'Sul logo basilikos di Teofilatto per Alessio Comneno,' *Orpheus* 3 (1982), 358-362 on the two emperors and my discussion in 'The Imperial Vocabulary of Alexios Komnenos,' *Alexios I Komnenos*, I, *Papers*, ed. M.E. Mullett and D.C. Smythe (BBTT, 4.1, Belfast, 1996), 359-397 at 384-387.

[50] See the lemma of *VClem*, PG 126, 1194: καὶ μαίστορος τῶν ῥητόρων χρηματίσαντος ἐν Κωνσταντινούπολει. For the bishop list, which simply calls him ῥήτωρ, see Gelzer, *Patriarchat von Achrida*, 6-7; G9, to the caesar Melissenos, II, 157.12-13: τὸν ἦν ὅτε δριμὺν ῥήτορα sets his previous position in the imperial context of the caesar whom he addresses as βασιλεῦ; G8, to John Doukas, similarly recalls former glories, more specifically in describing himself as κορυφαῖος γενόμενος of the ῥητόρων χορός. On the origins of, and recruitment for, the post see R. Macrides, 'Nomos and Kanon on Paper and in Court,' *Church and People in Byzantium*, ed. R. Morris (Birmingham, 1990), 61-85 at 70, n.46.

[51] Possibly the John of the Italos trial of 1082, see J. Gouillard, 'Le procès officiel de Jean l'Italien,' *TM* 9 (1985), 61-85 at 70, n.46.

[52] P. Magdalino, *The Empire of Manuel I Komnenos* (Cambridge, 1993), 416.

[53] On *parainesis*, see above, 2.6, 76 and my 'Imperial Vocabulary,' 379-384; the imperial virtues are used by Kazhdan to suggest that ideological changes emphasised the military,

If we now turn to the collection we should search less for references to Alexios,[54] though they exist—and are understandably less panegyric than in the speech—than for epistolary panegyric. Three of the letters are panegyric in tone and topoi. None comes so embarrassingly (or dangerously) close to a *basilikos logos* as to be misunderstood, but all bear some resemblance to the genre.

G8, to John Doukas,[55] is a victory letter after his successful expedition of reconquest against Tzachas, emir of Smyrna. Theophylact begins with a direct reminiscence of his former position, after calling for the *schole* to compose and deliver his speech. 'Who will reunite for me a *choros* of rhetors of which I am *koryphaios*? I will give them the note, to carry out in public the dance of words.' But his vocabulary, while totally victorious, is now more suited to his position; it is a tissue of quotations from the psalms. After a request on behalf of his relatives in Euboia, Theophylact wishes John more glory and for his enemies to bite the dust. G17[56] is written in spring and refers to the perennially imperial image of the sun. John has left Bulgaria, but his rays still shine upon it (and on Euboia); the imperial virtue here celebrated is *philanthropia*.

G81 comes in a sequence of letters from Theophylact to Gregory Taronites which appear to have been carried by a servant of Gregory's. G65 is a brief exhortation to a 'son' to make good, excelling in both war and peace, pacifying the nations and emulating Prometheus; *parainesis* and panegyric are mixed here as in the *PB*. G78 is written at an early stage of the Pontic expedition, in May 1103, and wishes Taronites victory; and G92 is a *prosphonetikon* on Gregory's return to Constantinople.[57] G81 is a long

---

'Certain Traits of Imperial Propaganda in the Byzantine Empire from the Eighth to the Fifteenth Centuries,' *Prédication et propagande au Moyen Age, Islam, Byzance, Occident* (Paris, 1983), 13-28, but a more subtle emphasis within conventional *parainesis* and panegyric is surely involved; on *patris* and *genos* in this period see P. Magdalino, 'Honour among Rhomaioi: the framework of social values in the world of Digenes Akrites and Kekaumenos,' *BMGS* 13 (1989), 183-218. No other Epiphany speech to Alexios has survived and only one other *basilikos logos* by Manuel Straboromanos, ed. P. Gautier, 'Le dossier d'un haut fonctionnaire d'Alexis Ier Comnène, Manuel Straboromanos,' *REB* 23 (1965), 168-204 at 181. On the misnamed Fürstenspiegel see W. Blum, *Byzantinische Fürstenspiegel: Agapetos, Theophylakt von Ochrid, Thomas Magister* (Bibliothek der griechischen Literatur, 14, Stuttgart, 1981), esp. 81-98; G. Prinzing, 'Beobachtungen zu den "Integrierten" Fürstenspiegeln der Byzantiner,' *JÖB* 38 (1988), 1-38 and my 'Imperial Vocabulary.'

[54] G127, to Gregory Kamateros, II, 579.118-126 (positive); G102, to Michael Pantechnes, II, 515.9-10 (negative).

[55] II, 153-155.

[56] II, 187-189.

[57] G81, II, 427-439; G65, II, 363-5; G78, II, 415-417; G92, II, 473-475.

celebration of the achievements of Gregory; with one victory he has subdued two peoples, the Turk and the Frank. As in *AK* he continues this ethnocentric celebration, emphasising the rhetorical nature of his letter while saying that what he is offering is not the eloquent flattery of a rhetor. He notes the length of the letter, but deplores the fact that no letter could be long enough to do justice to Gregory's virtues. There is reference also to a θέατρον τοῦ λόγου, suggesting a Constantinopolitan focus[58] for the Pontic achievements praised in Bulgaria.

These letters, seen in the light of imperial panegyric, establish an asymmetrical relationship, probably of patronage, between Theophylact and the *laudandi*; they also allow us to observe Theophylact recalling a former role and including a genre within the form of the letter. I show elsewhere[59] how this inclusion allows us to decide on conflicting evidence in the sources.

ii. *The letters and the Lives*

Of all Theophylact's works the two hagiographical works are the least securely attributed, but it is a safe assumption that if they are Theophylact's, they belong to the period of the episcopate. The long *Life* of St Clement (*VClem*) is transmitted in nine manuscripts, separately from his other works; the *Martyrion* of the Fifteen Martyrs of Tiberioupolis (*XV*) is preserved in a single manuscript.[60] Although Milev had established Theophylact's authorship of the *VClem* in the 1950s, Gautier's (still unpublished) doctoral thesis of 1968 argued that although verbal parallels between the texts establish a single authorship, and although the *VClem* must be dated to the late eleventh and early twelfth centuries on the basis of references to the Pecheneg invasions at the end, the positive attitude to Bulgaria could not be a product of Theophylact's pen. Recently Obolensky has reviewed the evidence and made an overwhelming case for Theophylact's authorship of both texts, based on the manuscript tradition, verbal parallels with other works of Theophylact

---

[58]   See my 'Aristocracy and Patronage in the Literary Circles of Komnenian Constantinople,' *The Byzantine Aristocracy, IX-XIII Centuries*, ed. M. Angold (BARIntSer, 221, Oxford, 1984), 173-201 for *theatra*.

[59]   'The Madness of Genre,' 233-243. On the context of Alexian panegyric see my 'Imperial Vocabulary', 359-397, esp. 363-379. On inclusion, see Cairns, *Generic Composition*, ch. 7, 158-176; A. Fowler, *Kinds of Literature. An Introduction to the Theory of Genres and Modes* (Oxford, 1982), 179-181.

[60]   For the *Long Life* see PG 126, 1194-1240, N.L. Tunickij, *Monumenta ad SS Cyrilli et Methodii successorum vitas resque gestas pertinentia* (London, 1972), 66-140 and A. Milev, *Grutskite zhitiia na Kliment Okhridski* (Sofia, 1966), 76-146. For the XV Martyrs see *Historia martyrii XV martyrum*, PG 126, 152-221. On the manuscript tradition see A.I. Milev, *Zhitie na Kliment Okhridski* (Sofia, 1955).

and internal chronological evidence.[61] Interestingly, among his parallels are references by the author to the barbarism of the Bulgars, which are very familiar to a reader of the collection.

The *Lives* place local Bulgarian history in a wider Byzantine context: the *XV* opens with a long historical section on Constantine and Constantius before the emperor Julian is introduced, in a section reminiscent of that on Justianian in the treatise on eunuchs. The *VClem* starts with Cyril and Methodios, more notably Byzantine than Clement.[62] But full justice is done to local cults: the story of the translation of the XV appears to be based on an eyewitness account, and St Germanos is introduced so as to include all the local good; one of the XV, interestingly as we shall see, was present at the Council of Nicaea. Bulgar rulers, Boris in particular but also Symeon, are given full credit as good rulers. In general both *Lives* are long and do not conform closely to hagiographic conventions and standard episodes; their concern is with local cults and their place in history.[63]

Various letters in the collection have a bearing on local history. The most obvious is G22, in which Theophylact thanks John Komnenos for 'refreshing' Prespa and Diabolis, and then asks for further help for the *episkope* of Diabolis, which is in great trouble: the church has no chanting or candles burning, the bishop and all the clergy have left and the *paroikoi* have fled to the woods and all this 'in the most splendid of the Bulgarian churches'. Theophylact went himself to see and wept at the sight. The solution is simple: a *sigillion* to protect the episcopate from the tax-men. Then everyone will come out of their hiding places, the church will flourish again, lamps will be lit and psalms will be sung. Theophylact reiterates: the danger is great, the solution is simple. And there is good reason for John to oblige: it was one of the most blessed of churches, which the most Christian Boris, basileus of the

---

[61] M. Jugie, 'L'auteur de la vie de Clement d'Achrida,' *EO* 23 (1924), 5-8; P. Gautier, *Deux oeuvres hagiographiques du pseudo-Théophylacte* (Thèse de doctorat du 3e cycle, Université de Paris, Faculté de lettres et sciences humaines, Sorbonne, 1968); D. Obolensky, 'Theophylaktos of Ohrid and the authorship of the Vita Clementis,' *Byzantium. A Tribute to Andreas N. Stratos* (Athens, 1986), I, 601-618. See I.G. Iliev, 'The Manuscript Tradition and the Authorship of the Long Life of St Clement of Ohrid,' *BS* 53 (1982), 68-73 and N. Dragova, 'Theophylact of Ochrida's Old Bulgarian Sources on Cyril and Methodius,' *Études balkaniques* n.s. 28 (1992), 107-110 both of whom support Theophylact's authorship.

[62] In the *VClem* Clement makes his entrance at the end of ch. 2 with the other disciples, PG 126, 1196, Milev, 80 and again in ch. 9, 1218, Milev, 82 and ch. 12, 1216, Milev, 84, but only in ch. 15 (of 29), 1220, Milev, 88 does he take centre stage in his own saint's life; only at ch. 12 (of 55), 108, in the *XV*, does the narrative reach Macedonia.

[63] For the translation of the XV, PG 126, 204-210. See Obolensky, *Portraits*, 74-75; for St Germanos, *XV*, PG 126, 201; for the Virgin, *VClem*, PG 126, 1229, ed. Milev, 132.

Bulgars, built as one of his seven *katholika*. He built it; may John restore it.[64] Art historians have tried to make sense of this letter but it defeats analysis in terms of artistic patronage, unless Theophylact is taking advantage of a known interest of John's in architecture or in patronage to gain economic advantage for the bishopric. It does however connect with two passages in the *VClem*: XVII,[65] in which he tells how Boris assigned three grand houses to Clement in Diabolis; in XXIII, the *VClem* describes the building of seven *katholika* like a seven-branched candlestick and three churches in Ochrid. The *katholika* are not named.[66]

Another case of the use of local history in the letters is more complex. It involves the synod of Prespa, which we have already examined.[67] We have seen Theophylact's interest in Boris, the first Christian tsar of Bulgaria, but he was also prepared to praise Symeon.[68] We now see him building on a local tradition strongly associated with a more recent enemy of Byzantium, tsar Samuel. The home of the synod is known: from the combination of G78 and G108, it must be the basilica of St Achilleios on the island of the same name in Mikre Prespa, the smallest of the group of three major lakes of the Macedonian highlands. It is the largest middle Byzantine basilica in present-day Greece, and it has several remarkable features, including a tomb in the *diakonikon* and four tombs in the south aisle. There are three layers of wall painting in the church including two inscriptions round the conch of the apse, substantial remains of painting in the *diakonikon* and isolated figures in the north arcade. In the lowest register of the large apse are inscribed eighteen arches and in each one is painted the name of a see of the archdiocese of Ochrid, a monumental bishop-list.[69]

---

[64] G22, II, 203-205.

[65] *VClem*, XVII, 54, PG, 126, 1224, ed. Milev, 124; XXIII, 67, 1229, ed. Milev, 132-134.

[66] PG 126, 1224 and 1229. The identification of these *katholika* is thorny. It seems agreed that one church in Ochrid is a *katholikon* as it is mentioned as such in the *VClem*, probably Diabolis (G22) and possibly Bregalnitsa, *XV*, 201, though other sources attribute its building to Tsar Michael. A.P. Vlasto, *The Entry of the Slavs into Christendom. An Introduction to the Mediaeval History of the Slavs* (Cambridge, 1970), 166, lists them as Prespa, Ochrid, Mesembria, a church at Vodoča near Strumitsa and the church at Cherven, but he does not give his arguments. See Milev, *Grutskite Zhitiia*, n.155; A. Cankova-Petkova, 'Contributions au sujet de la conversion des Bulgares au christianisme,' *BB* 4 (1973), 31-32.

[67] See above, 89-91.

[68] *VClem*, XIX, 60, PG 126, 1225, ed. Milev, 128.

[69] G78, II, 415.17: ἀπιόντι γὰρ πρὸς τὸν μέγαν Ἀχίλλειον; G108, II, 527.7: κατὰ τὴν Πρέσπαν. See above, 89-91, for discussion. On the church see P. Miliukov, 'Khristianskiia drevnosti zapadnogo Makedonii,' *IRAIK* 4 (1899), 21-149; I. Ivanov, 'Tsar Samuilovata stolitsa vu Prespa, istoriko-arkheologicheski belezhki,' *Izvestiya Bulgarsko Arkheol.*

Although the church was excavated in the 1960s[70] dating evidence was not conclusive, but the evidence of the bishop-list (and of dendrochronology?) is consistent with its construction by tsar Samuel.[71] Skylitzes tells us that 'Samuel translated the relics of St Achilleios, bishop of Larissa, and laid them in Prespa, for his royal seat was there.' The interpolations of Michael of Diabolis add that Achilleios attended the Council of Nicaea in the time of Constantine with Reginos of Skopelos and Diodoros of Trikke, and that Samuel built a large and beautiful house in his name. Certainly there was a church there dedicated to Achilleios in 1073, when Skylitzes Continuatus tells us that it was plundered by Alamanoi and Varangians, probably ill-controlled mercenaries of Saronites's army.[72]

Why did Samuel build the church on Prespa, and why did Theophylact over a hundred years later hold a local synod not in the archiepiscopal see but in Samuel's basilica, presumably restored after the 1073 destruction? The answer lies in the life of Achilleios. Both questions may be answered by the single piece of information that Michael of Diabolis chose to record about him: not that he was *poliouchos* of Larissa, but that he attended the council of

---

Druzhestvo 1 (1910), 55-80; G. Soteriou, 'Ho byzantinos naos tou agiou Achilleiou tes Prespas kai ai Boulgarikai peri tes idruseos tou apopseis,' *Praktika Akademias Athenon* 20 (1945), 8-14; K. Pelekanides, *Byzantina kai Metabyzantina Mnemeia tes Prespas*, 64-78; D. Stričević, 'La rénovation du type basilical dans l'architecture ecclésiastique des pays centrales des Balkans aux IXe-Xe siècles,' *XII IntCong*, I (Belgrade, 1963), 195-201; A. Grabar, 'Deux témoignages archéologiques sur l'autocephalicité d'une église: Prespa et Ochrid,' *ZRVI*, 8 = *Mélanges Ostrogorsky*, 2 (1964), 163-168; J. Ferluga, 'La date de la construction de l'église de S. Achillée de Prespa,' *Zbornik za Likovne Umetnosti*, 2 (1966), 3-8.

[70] See the full three-volume report of N. Moutsopoulos, *He basilike tou hagiou Achilleiou sten Prespan. Symbole ste melete ton Byzantinon mnemeion tes perioches* (Aristoteleio Panepistemio Thessalonike: Kentro Byzantinon Ereunon, Thessalonike, 1989).

[71] See my 'The monumental bishop-list at Prespa,' *A Mosaic of Byzantine and Cypriot Studies for A.H.S. Megaw*, ed. J. Herrin, M.E. Mullett and C. Otten-Froux, forthcoming, and the recent work of P. Kuniholm, who is waiting for further material before he can complete his sequence and date construction beams from the tree-ring data.

[72] Skylitzes, *Synopsis Historion*, ed. Thurn, 330. On the interpolations see B. Prokić, *Die Zusätze in der Handschrift des Johannes Skylitzes, codex Vindobonensis hist. graec. LXXIV. Ein Beitrag zur Geschichte des sogennanten westbulgarischen Reiches* (Munich, 1906) and J. Ferluga, 'John Skylitzes and Michael of Devol,' *ZRVI* 10 (1967), 163-170. Skylitzes Continuatus, ed. E. Tsolakes, *He synecheia tes Chronographias tou Joannou Skylitzes* (Thessalonike, 1968), 166. For the date: it seems reasonable to follow Tsolakes with his new dating for the Serbian rising to 26-31 August 1073, which follows from his emendation τρίτοι for πρῶτοι, 162.18, although he does not answer all the arguments of B. Radočić, 'Peri tes exegeseos tou Konstantinou Bodin,' *XII IntCong* (Belgrade, 1964), II, 185-187.

Nicaea. The special features of the church, the *diakonikon* tomb and the bishop-list in the apse, are mirrored in the features Michael of Diabolis chose to elaborate: St Achilleios in Prespa is a synod church purpose-built for a synod-saint, to provide ultra-Byzantine ecclesiastical respectability for his patriarchate, in a place with special significance for him.[73]

And when Theophylact chose to hold his synod there, he must also have been aware of the strong associations with Samuel: he may be buried there, and Attaleiates' account of his death certainly places it in the reeds of Prespa. Despite these factors, or perhaps because of them, Theophylact supported the cult (he attended the *panegyris* in 1103), arranged for the 'refreshment' of Prespa and honoured the original function of the church of St Achilleios with its built-in synod features.[74]

iii. *The letters and polemic*

Only one full-scale piece of religious polemic by Theophylact has survived,[75] and the generic term 'polemic' describes it badly. It is the *proslalia* to his ex-pupil Nicholas on the accusations against the Latins. Gautier, its most recent editor, is not sure whether it belongs to the debates over union of 1088-89 or to the visit of Peter Grossolano to Constantinople in 1112.[76] In it, although he lists various grievances against the church of Rome (the Saturday fast, the azymes, the calculation of Lent, clerical celibacy and lack of regulation of lay marriage, tonsure, gold rings and silk vestments, proskynesis, monastic meat-eating, he makes a point of differing from the current view that these are

---

[73] For the diakonikon tomb and the bishop list see Moutsopoulos, *He Basilike*, I, 158-192; on Samuel and his pretensions to patriarchate and empire see A. Leroy-Molinghen, 'Les cométopoules et l'état de Samuel,' *Byz* 39 (1969), 479; *Iliada godini od vostanieto na Komitopulite i sozdava njet na Samuilavata Dr ava*, ed. M. Apostolski, S. Antoljak and B. Panov (Skopje, 1971); A. Nikoloff, *Samuel's Bulgaria* (Cleveland, 1969); S. Runciman, *A History of the First Bulgarian Empire* (London, 1930), esp. 230-232.

[74] For the death of Samuel see Attaleiates, *Historia*, ed. I. Bekker, *Michael Attaliota* (CSHB, Bonn, 1853), 230. For tomb G see Moutsopoulos's excavation reports, 'Le tombeau du tsar Samuil dans la basilique de saint Achille à Prespa,' *Etudes balkaniques* 1 (1984), 114-126 and H. Andonovski, 'La tombe de Samuel, est-elle trouvée?' *Iliada Godini*, 191-202.

[75] *On the Errors of the Latins*, ed. Gautier, I, 247-285.

[76] Gautier, I, 105-114. On the attempts at union of 1089 with the visit of the abbot of Grottaferrata and cardinal deacon Roger see W. Holtzmann, 'Die Unionsverhandlungen zwischen Kaiser Alexios I. und Papst Urban II. im Jahre 1089,' *BZ* 28 (1928), 62-63. On the visit of Peter Grossolano in 1112, see J. Darrouzès, 'Les conférences de 1112,' *REB* 23 (1965), 51-59; V. Grumel, 'Autour du voyage de Pierre Grossolanus, archevêque de Milan à Constantinople en 1112,' *EO* 32 (1933), 22-33.

serious differences justifying a division between the churches. To him only the
question of the procession of the Holy Spirit is important, and he deals with it
in detail. The purpose of the piece is not to engage in debate with a Latin, but
to tell his pupil, a patriarchal civil servant, what to think and how to proceed.
His chosen image (very reminiscent of the letters) is of a doctor, caring not for
specific organs but for the body as a whole. In its courageous abandonment of
much of the literature of polemic and its tolerant, diplomatic and pragmatic
position it has much in common with the treatise on eunuchs, where
Theophylact insists on interpreting the spirit rather than the letter of the
law.[77]

We have seen that there is little in the correspondence which deals with
doctrine: the letter to the bishop of Pelagonia on scripture, the two pastoral
letters to Tarchaneiotes and not much else. Of the heresy problem, which we
might have expected to loom large in Theophylact's consciousness, we have
evidence only of his efforts with Armenians. The letters to the bishop of
Triaditsa tell us only of his success; the letter to Diabologyres shows an
everyday concern: what to do with a converted community. It is concerned,
correct and pragmatic. The bishop is not to close churches, but to rededicate
the sanctuary and make signs of the cross with holy oil, and allow the
congregations back. He is prepared to reordain Armenian priests who have
become orthodox and to allow them to use their liturgy if it does not differ
from that of Chrysostom; their psalms must also be checked. Again we see the
sympathetic, pragmatic approach, changing only what absolutely needs to be
changed. Theophylact was a stickler for the canons, and took a poor view of
vows abandoned, but he was always prepared to show *oikonomia* where it
would help.[78]

---

[77] For Saturday fast, *On the Errors of the Latins*, I, 269-270; for the azymes, I, 261-264;
the calculation of Lent, I, 249.10; for clerical celibacy, 249.10-12; beardless priests, 249.12-
13; rings and vestments, 249.14-125; monks eat meat, 249.15 and throw proskynesis to the
floor, 249.16. Most of these merit very few words. For the substantive issue see 251-260;
271-285 is concerned with healing the breach. For the medical image, II, 273.25-34; cf. G53,
II, 309.44-50. For oikonomia see *In Defence of Eunuchs*, I, 395.17-23; *On the Errors of the
Latins*, I, 279-285.

[78] G15, II, 179-181; G96 tells us that Theophylact had been active in condemning
people for heresy, II, 485.38. On the canons see below, 263. For the letter to the bishop of
Pelagonia, see G36, II, 249-251; the pastoral letters to Tarchaneiotes G16 and G20, II, 183-
185, 197. On heresy in the archdiocese see Obolensky, *Bogomils*, 111-229; D. Angelov,
'Aperçu sur la nature de l'histoire des Bogomiles en Bulgarie,' *Hérésies et sociétés dans
l'Europe préindustrielle, 11e-18e siècles*, ed. J. Le Goff (Paris and The Hague, 1968), 75-81,
and above, chapter 2.5, 59, n. 251 and 3.2 iv, 127, n.225. It is very hard to know whether
the hereticorum castrum of *Gesta Francorum*, I, ed. R. Hill (London, 1962), 8 and Peter

G135 is rather different. It is a fragment, and the lemma of the single manuscript declares it to be from a letter addressed to the Armenian Tibanios. It is possible that the addressee is in fact Tigranes, who is named by Anna as one of the Armenians whose contacts with Neilos the Calabrian so disturbed Alexios, and who reappears at the time of the disputations at Philippopolis (though Anna notes that the Armenians were condemned along with Neilos) in 1114. On that occasion Eustratios of Nicaea delivered a speech against Tigranes, and Alexios addressed one to 'an Armenian'. But a local addressee for G135 should not be ruled out.[79]

Two questions need to be asked: whether it is in fact a letter, and when it should be dated. Both may be considered by comparing it with other works against Armenians of the period. The literature on that other question of union is hardly less than on the Latins; there were probably more Armenians in Constantinople than there were Latins; Dagron has suggested that debate with Armenians set the pace for debate with Latins.[80] To the eleventh-century invectives by Euthymios, monk of the Peribleptos, and Isaac the convert, and the section in Euthymios Zigabenos, *Panoplia Dogmatike*, should be added polemic by Andronikos Kamateros, Michael *ho tou Anchialou* and ep. 45 of Michael Italikos. Still unpublished are five treatises of Niketas Stethatos in Mosq. 4443.[81]

It is difficult to be very certain of where Theophylact's work in its truncated form fits. It begins 'It is a great folly to think that after union (the

---

Tudebod, PL 155, 767 was Bogomil, Armenian—or Orthodox! (see my *Theophylact*, 354, n. 45). For Theophylact on the canons and vows see below, chapter 4.4, 263.

[79] G135, II, 595-7; Anna Komnene, *Al.*, XIV.viii.1-ix.5, L, III, 177-185; Eustratios of Nicaea, *Elenchos kai anatrope*, ed. A. Demetrakopoulos, *Ekklesiastike Bibliotheke*(Leipzig, 1866), I, 160-198; Alexios I Komnenos, *Ekdotheis par autou pros Armenious doxazontas kakos mian physin epi Christou*, ed. A. Papadopoulos-Kerameus, *Analekta Ierosolymitikes Stachylogias*, I (St Petersburg, 1891), 116-120; for translation with text and commentary see *Alexios I Komnenos*, II.

[80] P. Charanis, *The Armenians in the Byzantine Empire* (Lisbon, 1963); R. Janin, 'L'église arménienne,' *EO* 17 (1916), 5-32; S. Vailhé, 'Formation de l'église arménienne,' *EO* 16 (1913), 109-126, 113-211; G. Dagron, 'Minorités ethniques et religieuses dans l'orient byzantin à la fin et au XIe siècle: l'immigration syrienne,' *TM* 6 (1965), 214, n.184.

[81] Euthymios, monk of the Peribleptos (Invective I), *Logos steliteutikos kata Armenion*, PG 132, 1155-1218; 'Isaac' (Invective II), *Kai hoti posai haireseis eisi ton auton skoteinon peri to phos Armenion*, PG 132, 1217-1237, see V. Grumel, 'Les invectives contres les Arméniens du Catholic Isaac,' *REB* 14 (1956), 174-194; Euthymios Zigabenos, *Panoplia dogmatike*, PG 130, 19-25; cf. *Al.*, XV.ix.1, L, III, 223; Michael *ho tou Anchialou*, *Antigramma pros touton ton Katholikon*, PG 133, 224-232; Michael Italikos, ep. 45, ed. Gautier, 285-301; for five treatises by Niketas Stethatos in Mosq. 4443 (Vladimir 232), see Dagron, 'Minorités ethniques,' 214, 185.

divine and human natures of Christ) are one.' It deals at some length with the different possible types of union of natures and wills, using the analogies of iron in the fire and of the pouring together of two liquids. He takes trouble to show the points of agreement between the two churches. As theology it cannot have added much to the clarity or profundity of thought on the question but as polemic it has a directness which may well have been effective. Like Theophylact's *proslalia* on the Latins, and unlike Euthymios Zigabenos, it concentrates on the central issue rather than on peripherals like non-celebration of the Annunciation, azymes and the mixing of wine, the sacrifice of animals, the celebration of Christmas, the addition to the Trisagion, having this in common with Eustratios of Nicaea's speech, which was delivered after Alexios's. Of all eleventh- and twelfth-century polemic, G135 is closest to Alexios's *logos* against a single Armenian. The central issue, the image of iron in the fire, (developed further by Alexios), the form and style are very close. They share an emphatic repetition: Theophylact frames his letter, 'I say; you say... I agree, but...,' so Alexios perpetually addresses his opponent often using this as a link device between one section and the next. 'In vain, Armenian...,' 'I ask, Armenian...,' 'So what, Armenian?' Eustratios's speech, which is entirely credible as a follow-up to Alexios's, is less direct and more of a treatise. It seems most likely that all three were written for the same occasion, whether the trial of Neilos or the disputation at Philippopolis. (Eustratios is known to have taken part in both.)[82]

It is not impossible that G135 is actually a fragment of a speech. Certainly its style is quite different from the rest of Theophylact's collection, and illustrates very clearly the point of the remark in the *Peri Hermeneias* that although letters should be plain they should not simply be one half of a dialogue. The short sentences, the piled up questions which 'Demetrios' cites are precisely what distinguishes the style of G135 from that of other letters.[83] Its subject matter is not non-epistolary, as may be seen from Michael Italikos's

---

[82]　Anna's account of the trial of Neilos, *Al.*, X.i.1-6, L, II, 186-189 focuses rather surprisingly on his undesirable contacts with Armenians. She adds that the Armenians were tried in the public synod with Neilos, but she does not mention their fate. No attendance list or acts are preserved, simply Neilos's retraction, on which see Gouillard, 'Le synodikon de l'Orthodoxie, édition et commentaire,' *TM* 2 (1967), 202-206, text at 299-303, and a mention in the 1117 speech of Niketas *ho tou Serron*. The dating of the trial is very uncertain, after Italos's trial and before that of Blachernites. On Neilos see J. Hussey, *Church and Learning in the Byzantine Empire, 867-1185* (Oxford, 1937), 95-96. On Eustratios of Nicaea see Niketas of Heraclea, *Logos apologetikos kai elenchitikos*, ed. J. Darrouzès, *Documents inédits*, 304ˑ.

[83]　*Peri Hermeneias*, 223-4, 226, ed. R. Roberts, *Demetrius on Style* (Cambridge, 1902), 173-177.

letter to the *sakellarios*,[84] and it might perhaps be viewed as a postal contribution to a debate, which may have set the agenda and prompted Alexios's use of the iron image. Alternatively it may have tactfully alluded to it in retrospect. It is certainly not incompatible with G15 on the conversion of the Armenians or with the *proslalia*.

iv. *The letters and the poems*

Of all Theophylact's works it is the poems[85] which dovetail best with the letters. We have seen one reason for this, that poems were sometimes sent with letters as gifts, or to multiply further the multi-media experience. Poems sometimes dedicate other works, like the poem to his brother which introduces the treatise on eunuchs,[86] or the four lines which precede the commentary on St Mark and St Luke in what may be a presentation copy to Maria.[87] Some poems were sent with—or instead of—letters, like poem 1, to Bryennios, who had asked for a letter.[88] Poem 2 is very close to the message of G129,[89] poem 3 suggests that G112 had its effect,[90] poem 4 (taken with a similar one by Nicholas of Kerkyra also dated to 1125/26) suggests that it travelled with a letter and a copy of the hymns of Symeon the New Theologian.[91] Poems 10 and 11-12 expand Theophylact's network to include a monk Neilos to whom he appeals to have Michael Antiochos kept away from the Ochrid region, and Rodomir Aaron, who entertained Theophylact in his tent on one of his visits to a military camp.[92] Poems 8, to a hardened villain, 9, to someone who had condemned consecrated persons, 13, to a licentious eunuch, extend as invectives our knowledge of Theophylact's range, but we know from G76 that he took refuge in writing iambics against someone who had caused him

---

[84] Michael Italikos, ep. 45, ed. Gautier, 295-301.

[85] Ed. Gautier, *Théophylacte*, I, 347-377.

[86] Ibid., I, 289-291.

[87] Vind. theol. gr. 90, see H. Hunger, *Katalog der griechischen Handschriften der österreichischen Nationalbibliothek*, 3/1 (Vienna, 1976), 105-166; ed. de Rubeis, PG 123, 35.

[88] Poem 1, I, 347-349. It is nice to note that occasionally the boot could be on the other foot.

[89] Poem 2, I, 349-351, cf. G129, to Michael Panteches, II, 583.

[90] Poem 3, I, 351, cf. G112, to Nicholas Kallikles, II, 537.5-8.

[91] See J. Koder and J. Paramelle, *Syméon le Nouveau Théologien, Hymnes* (Paris, 1969), I, 65-67. For Theophylact's letters to Nicholas see G75 and G77.

[92] Poems 10, 11, 12, I, 365-367. See I. Djurić, 'Teofilakt Okhridski pod shatorom Arona,' *ZRVI* 27/28 (1989), 69-91.

to think in elegiacs.[93] Poems 6 and 7 console and brace, showing Theophylact's
characteristic pragmatism and sympathy.[94]

But without poems 14 and 15 we should be in a very much worse
position to understand the central event of the collection, the death of
Theophylact's brother Demetrios. We have seen that three letters, including
the 'new' letter 133, deal with the illness and two with the death, and that the
most likely date for them all is 1107. G133 appears to come first in the
sequence, although it is not preserved with the rest of the collection, but as
part of the 'C' group of manuscripts. Theophylact tells his brother that he has
only just heard that he is ill, and describes the effect upon him of the news: his
heart is bruised, grief causes his thoughts to sink, a cloud of depression settles
on his spirit. 'How am I not to groan, how not to be pained and distressed,
when I learn what serious evils have touched you, you the light of my eyes,
the consolation of my spirit?' God and the Theotokos are invoked to bring
him back to health, and Theophylact urges him to write and tell him of his
recovery.[95] By G111 that recovery appears less likely, and a bulletin on his
brother's illness forms the conclusion of the letter to Nicholas Kallikles. G113
is an account of the illness to the bishop of Kitros, explaining the symptoms,
Theophylact's hopes and fears, the treatment he prescribes and his feeling of
responsibility. G121 to the bishop of Kitros is written after the death,
apologising for not writing and depicting the death as the last straw: 'as if all
the other burdens were not enough to lower my spirits, the death of my
brother has been added, a brother on whom my breath depended, who was
everything to me, who would have thrown himself on fire and sword, as they
say, so that I could be kept free from worry and distress. And now I am
deprived of him how I am unable to express my needs from elsewhere...' He
asks for the other's prayers and warns that he is descending on the same
journey as his brother.[96] G122 is a shorter letter, possibly written at a later
stage. He begins with the announcement of the death, and his own
abandonment in the village of grief, the tents of obscurity, the valley of tears,
exposed to all the winds of evil. He describes how he lamented for his brother

---

[93] Poems 8, 9, 13, I, 359-365, 367-369; cf. G76, II, 405.23-25 for iambic revenge.

[94] Poems 6 and 7, I, 355-359, cf. the letters of consolation, see above, chapter 3.3, 143-
144 and the letters to ailing suffragans, G57, II, 323-4; G40, II, 267.2.

[95] See above, 91-93 on the ordering and 84, n. 27-28 on the date. In the only manuscript
we have, see A.M. Bandini, *Catalogus codicum manuscriptorum bibliothecae Mediceanae
Laurentianae,* repr. Leipzig, 1961, II, 41-42, it is found with two *consolationes,* to Michael
Pantechnes and to the brother of Psellos; its lemma shows that the compiler of the
manuscript regarded it as a *paramythetike.* For the text, G133, II, 591.

[96] G111, to Nicholas Kallikles, II, 535; G113, to the bishop of Kitros, II, 539; G121, to
the bishop of Kitros again, II, 559; G122, to the bishop of Debra, II, 561.

as much as nature and the old Adam demanded, but then turned his eyes to the Word, knowing that he would not be left without assistance. The bishop's prayers—and his return to his flock—are requested. The letters have taken us from first knowledge to recovery from mourning, and they give us a sense of the intimacy of the relationship, Theophylact's dependence on his brother and his feelings of loss. The narrative is jerky like all letter-narrative, and emotion is expressed in a controlled manner comprehensible to the correspondents. It does not range backwards and forwards over time, nor does it assess more than in passing the brother's personality, attributes or achievements.

The poems, 14 in anacreontics and 15 in iambics, which name the brother as Demetrios, appear to belong to the period described in G122 of Theophylact, ἀποκλαυσάμενοι...τὸν ἀδελφόν. They are long, eloquent and express painful loss.

> I long for an ocean of tears
> To mourn my brother,
> Who shone before me in the road,
> Fated to darkness.
> I stumble along the dark way
> Because of his death who has suffered extinction.
> My heart in every fibre
> Is gripped by Niobe's grief.
> If God were to shape me into stone
> I would again bewail my suffering.
> Time is no healer;
> Suffering lasts and stays fresh.

Each stanza ends with an appeal to the forces of nature to add their strength to Theophylact's grief. 'Stop your course, ye streams of water and all you rivers, flowing torrents of tears.' We see more of the illness, confirmed as consumption, complicated by fever; Demetrios's youth is emphasised; his network is depicted in terms of those who will mourn for him: he was dear to the emperor, who loves only the good, and appreciated by the senate and the emperor's entourage. Nor is he forgotten by the family: 'you hear the moans and lamentations which rise from Euripos on your behalf.' He ends: 'Who will put an end to the floods of my tears?'[97] Poem 15 is

---

[97] Poem 14, I, 369-375; the refrain 13-14, I, 371 is followed by an appeal to an oak-forest, to poverty, to the sun, to all good hearts and to the unfortunate generation and the family. For the emperor, 85, I, 375, the senate, 91 and Euripos, 98.

shorter, thirty-two lines, and elaborates on Demetrios's role as described in G121.

> Who will contain the violent attacks of the praktors?
> Who will close the frog-mouths of the *sekretika*?
> Who will be the friend of wise judges?
> Who will be respected by senators for the worth of his character?
> To whom shall I reveal the pain of my suffering
> Now that I no longer have a doctor for my torment?

Demetrios gave him advice, administered his affairs and was to him an effective right arm, the support for his feet, mind, hearing, breath and heart. Again Theophylact mentions Demetrios's youth, contrasting him as an elderly child with himself a childish old man. 'O living death, do not abandon me totally, me the living, dead by being deprived of you.'[98] Only the poems concentrate on Theophylact's feelings for his brother; in the collection he steps in and out on the margins of Theophylact's life, visiting friends,[99] studying with Theodore,[100] carrying letters,[101] enquiring about liturgical embraces[102] or complaining of eunuchs' bad press.[103] But the collection at least allows us to witness more than a single emotional moment, and occasionally to see Demetrios in relation to others of Theophylact's correspondents. Letters tell us different things, because they are letters, but the emotional truth of letters and poems appears the same.

And so in all these cases we hear a single voice, and it is the voice which sounds in the letter-collection. Our study thus far bears some resemblance to Theophylact's favourite figure, *synekdoche*.[104] If the voices had been different, it would have been appropriate to return to generic considerations; as it is, we have yet to look at Theophylact's as against other people's letters. 'An author,' say Kazhdan and Franklin, '—even a Byzantine author—deserves to be regarded as an entity, not to be torn to pieces in the interests of proving the eternal stability of genres.'[105] I take issue with this statement elsewhere;[106] here I

---

[98] Poem 15, I, 377.

[99] G123, to Constantine Komnenos, II, 563.2-9.

[100] G28, to Theodore Smyrnaios, II, 223.19-23. G7, to Niketas *ho tou Serron*, II, 151.9.

[101] ?G4, G5, G6, G7, G61, G90, G91, G93, G110, G116, G123, G127. For evidence see Table VIII below.

[102] G134, I, 335-343.

[103] Verse *protheoria*, I, 290.3-4, prose *protheoria*, I, 291.2-3.

[104] G57, II, 325.34.

[105] A. Kazhdan and S. Franklin, *Studies on Byzantine Literature of the Eleventh and Twelfth Centuries* (Cambridge, 1987), viii.

[106] 'Madness of Genre.'

would simply remark that while a text is to be tested against both genre and oeuvre it also deserves to be read for itself.

5.3 Other people's letters

Kazhdan's objection to generic analysis appears to be based on an opposition to an 'eternal stability' of genres, in which no-one any longer believes. In fact theorists who are prepared to work with genre are more interested than most in the question of change.[107] Kazhdan's own book on change in Byzantine culture, it was well observed,[108] defined neither change nor culture. Yet change is an issue of overwhelming and controversial importance in the study of Byzantine society where an underlying assumption for generations has been of an unchanging edifice; and indeed evidence may easily be found to indicate that the Byzantines themselves did not welcome or value innovation.[109] For genre theorists every new text changes a genre.[110] Critics would say that in a literature where tradition and convention are privileged as much as in Byzantium opportunity for change is slight. Individuality, perhaps, a personal response, a special *variatio* of traditional features, creative imitation, but not innovation. Yet empirically observed, both Byzantine literature and art did change, and they are frequently viewed in a complex relationship with contemporary society.[111] What has not been investigated is the processes of change, or the ways in which change was assimilated to an ideology of non-

---

[107] See for example Fowler, *Kinds*, 37. For the formalists, genre was important in the dynamics and shifts of one genre to another, see J. Tynjanov, 'On Literary Evolution,' *Readings in Russian Poetics,* ed. L. Metejka and K. Panaska (Cambridge, Mass., 1971), 66-78. For reception theorists like Jauss it is genre which allows him to propose 'Literary History as a Challenge to Literary Theory,' *NLH* 2 (1970), 7-38.

[108] R. Cormack, '"New Art History" vs "Old Art History": writing Art History,' *BMGS* 10 (1986), 230.

[109] But see *Originality and Innovation in Byzantine Literature, Art and Music,* ed. A.R. Littlewood (Oxford, 1995); Kazhdan's opening essay, 1-14, this time focuses on the 'change factor' in Byzantium.

[110] Fowler, *Kinds*, 23.

[111] See for art the series of articles by A. Epstein (=Wharton) on political art: 'The Political Content of the Bema Frescoes of St Sophia in Ohrid,' *JÖB* 29 (1980), 315-329; 'The Middle Byzantine Churches of Kastoria in Greek Macedonia, their Dates and Implications,' *ArtBull* 62 (1980), 191-207; 'Frescoes of the Mauriotissa Monastery near Kastoria: Evidence of Millenarianism and Anti-semitism in the wake of the First Crusade,' *Gesta* 21 (1982), 21-29. For literature see Hunger's interpretation of the twelfth-century romances in *Antiker und byzantinischer Roman* (Heidelberg, 1981); *Der byzantinische Katz-Mäuse Krieg* (Graz, 1968), 55-65.

change.[112] A diachronic approach is needed. If it is important to set Theophylact's letter-collection against other parts of his oeuvre, from the point of view of the cultural history of Byzantium, it must also be viewed as one letter-collection among others.[113]

We have already seen Theophylact conforming to the expectations of the receivers of letters, reflecting the new status of medicine and its practitioners and revealing the (recently increased) social importance of friendship.[114] I here take the example of the consciousness of exile in Byzantine letter-writers in an attempt to place Theophylact's collection.

A consciousness of separation is, we have seen, part of the epistolarity of the Byzantine letter and Theophylact is no exception. But Theophylact is also conscious of exile, of local as well as personal deprivation. 'No sooner do I find myself in Ochrid, than I long for the city which holds you.'[115] This places it in a long tradition of writing in Greek about exile. From Homer to the most modern of popular songs Greeks have written and sung about leaving home, 'home thoughts from abroad', the condition of exile, death in exile and homecomings.[116] Xeniteia is the extended theme of the whole of the Odyssey and essential to the plot of the ancient Greek novel; Archilochos, Alcaeus and even Sappho perhaps had all known exile; it is a necessary concept for the understanding of the Phoenissai, the Medea, the Philoktetes.

---

[112] For kainos-neos see the debate over the nomenclature of Symeon the (New) Theologian, and most recently in E.M. Collins, Prayer and Mystical Theology in Eleventh-century Byzantium (PhD Diss., Belfast, 1991); for imperial ideology see P. Magdalino, 'Observations on the Nea Ekklesia of Basil I,' JÖB 37 (1987), 51-64. For approaches to the processes of change in literature which might be applied with profit to Byzantium see Poststructuralism and the Question of History, ed. D. Attridge, G. Bennington and R. Young (Cambridge, 1989), 7ff.; J. Frow, Marxism and Literary History (Oxford, 1986); for reception theory and change see R. Beaton in The Medieval Greek Romance, 5, 10-11, and for genre theory R. Cohen, 'Innovation and Variation: Literary Change and Georgic Poetry,' Literature and History (Los Angeles, 1974).

[113] Detailed comparisons of Theophylact's collection with those of his closest contemporaries, John Mauropous, Michael Psellos and Michael Italikos, must await another study; here I take a thematic approach for the sake of a longer perspective.

[114] Above, 3.2, 102-111 and 111-123.

[115] G6, to Theodore Smyrnaios, II, 147.2-3.

[116] I am not concerned here to prove continuity: I simply point to the wealth of inspiration for any kind of exile-writing in Greek by Byzantines. My examples are necessarily highly selective, as are those of G.T. Zoras, H xeniteia en te hellenike poiesei (Athens, 1953), which is sadly lacking in Byzantine examples. On the travel genres of antiquity see Cairns, Generic Composition, 38-49, 52-56. For pointers to aspects of Greek experience of exile, equally selective, see M. Mentzou, Der Bedeutungswandel des Wortes Xenos (Diss., Hamburg, 1963); R.F. Spencer, Emigration and Anthropology (Washington, DC, 1970); G. Herman, Ritualised Friendship and the Greek City (Cambridge, 1987).

Philosophers debated the proper attitude to exile: Plutarch regarded exile as an adversity to the extent that it is felt to be so; his friend is exhorted to see the whole world as his *patris*.[117] Similar ideas found currency in Christianity: the idea that the whole of life is an exile from heaven is common to Empedocles and to Christian thinking.[118] One sense of *xeniteia* in the early Christian centuries was of a kind of martyrdom, in which the ascetic ideal of anachoresis was carried to its logical conclusion. One of John Moschos's monks, abba Olympios, had as his three principles of living to avoid heretics, to keep hold of tongue and stomach, and to say always that he was an exile.[119]

A crucial position is occupied by John Chrysostom. He adopts views from the philosophical tradition: exile is like a stone which feels heavier to some than to others; the whole *oikoumene* is one's native land; no-one can take away virtue or wisdom.[120] But his own history of exile, and his letters from exile, set a pattern for the Byzantine centuries. After his confrontation with Arcadius and Eudoxia and his removal from the patriarchate in 403 he was taken by ship to the mouth of the Black Sea and from there to Praentum near Nicomedia. He was recalled but again exiled in 404 and taken overland to Koukousos, a journey of ten weeks' duration and was then kept in a fortified post in primitive conditions. The winters of 404-5 and 405-6 he survived with great difficulty, in constant danger of attack from marauding Isaurians and equally constant fear of being moved. In 407, his fear was realised and he had reached Comana in Pontos before he died. He left behind a corpus of consolations to his followers on his absence, and despite all his stoicism, vivid accounts of the real horrors of exile.[121] His status as exile-martyr in a virtuous

---

[117] Plutarch, *Peri phyges*, ed. P.H. de Lacy and B. Einarson, *Plutarch's Moralia* (London and Cambridge, Mass., 1959), VII, 518-571.

[118] Empedocles, *Katharmoi*, fr. 115, ed. H. Diel and W. Kranz, *Die Fragmente der Vorsokratiker* (Berlin, 1956), I, 358; R. Markus, *Christianity in the Roman World* (London, 1974), 30-31.

[119] John Moschos, *Pratum Spirituale*, ch. 12, PG 87.3, 2861: ξένος εἰμι. H. von Campenhausen, *Die asketische Heimatlosigkeit im altkirchlichen und frühmittelalterlichen Mönchtum* (Tübingen, 1930). Peregrinatio was practised most spectacularly in Georgia, finally reaching Iviron, and in Ireland at Skellig Mhicil.

[120] John Chrysostom, *Pros ten makarian Olympiada kai pros pantas tous pistous*, ed. A.M. Malingrey (SC, 103, Paris, 1964); ep. 9 to Olympias, ed. A. M. Malingrey, *Lettres à Olympias* (SC, 13, Paris, 1947), 150.

[121] See the letters to Olympias, epp. 1, 2, from Nicaea, 3, 4, from beyond Caesarea, 5, 6, arriving at Koukousos, ed. Malingrey, 95, 96, 97, 98, 100, 102. Palladios, *Dialogus de vita S. Joannis Chrysostomi*, 38, ed. P.R. Coleman-Norton (Cambridge, 1928), 68; on his posthumous glory F. Halkin, *Douze récits byzantins sur S. Jean Chrysostome* (SubsHag, 60, Brussels, 1977). He died before reaching Pitsounda, which ironically attained spurious

cause is emulated by a series of political churchmen in later centuries, some of whom make conscious use of the model in their letters: Theodore of Stoudios, Joseph the Hymnographer, the patriarch Ignatios, Photios, Nicholas Mystikos all qualify; Symeon the New Theologian at Paloukiton is the last in a long line, suffering *exoria* 'as did our fathers of old'.[122]

But exile was not only a status for ecclesiastical politicians to aim at; it was a legal penalty used throughout the middle Byzantine period.[123] Letters from 'legal' exiles abound in Byzantine letter-collections. Let us take four examples from the tenth century: Leo Choirosphaktes, Niketas Magistros, Alexander of Nicaea and Theodore of Kyzikos. Leo Choirosphaktes was a casualty of the time of the tetragamy crisis, although the reasons for his exile are not at all clear. Some have suggested that he was suspected of an intrigue with Andronikos Doukas during an embassy to Baghdad, while his editor, George Kolias, argued that he was accused of atheism.[124] While his detractors certainly charged him with being a Hellene, it seems unlikely that this would be enough to ruin what had been a long and distinguished diplomatic career. He wrote eight letters from his imprisonment at Petra, some abject supplications, others appeals for help from his friends. He was acutely aware of the physical conditions of his imprisonment:

> Hear, o emperor, hear, and hear favourably my prayer. Save me, save me, appearing *ex machina* like a delivering saviour. Yea, save me, for good deeds

---

posthumous glory on the strength of his exile; see A.A.M. Bryer, 'Cities of Heraclius,' *BMGS* 4 (1978), 28.

[122] On Theodore see P. Alexander, 'Religious Persecution and Resistance in the Byzantine Empire of the Eighth and Ninth Centuries: Methods and Justifications,' *Speculum* 52 (1977), 238-264; on Joseph the Hymnographer see Niketas David, *Eis ton bion tou en hagiois patros hemon Ioseph tou hymnographou*, PG 105, 940-976; for the patriarchs Ignatios and Photios, F. Dvornik, *The Photian Schism* (Cambridge, 1948), 161-171; Nicholas Mystikos, ep. 32, ed. Jenkins and Westerink, 224; *Vita Euthymii*, 19, ed. tr. P. Karlin-Hayter, *Vita Euthymii patriarchae CP, Text, Translation, Introduction and Commentary* (Bibliothèque de Byzantion, 3, Brussels, 1970), 120-121; Niketas Stethatos, *Bios kai politeia tou en hagiois patros hemon Symeon tou neou theologou, presbyterou, hegoumenou mones tou hagiou Mamantos tes Xenokerkiou*, 11-12, ed. I. Hausherr, *Un grand mystique byzantin: vie de Syméon le nouveau théologien* (OC, 12, Rome, 1928), 131-156; for the quotation, *VSymeon*, 12.105, ed. Hausherr, 147.

[123] The legal and political history of Byzantine exile has yet to be written. See E. Evert-Kappesowa, 'L'archipel de Marmara comme lieu d'exile,' *ByzForsch*, 5 (1977), 23-24. For a list of eleventh-century exiles see my *Theophylact*, 600-601.

[124] See G. Kolias, *Léon Choirosphaktès, magistre, proconsul et patrice, biographie-correspondance. Texte et Traduction* (Texte und Forschungen zur byzantinisch-neugriechischen Philologie, 31, Athens, 1939), 15-20, 53-60; P. Karlin-Hayter, 'Arethas, Choirosphaktes and the Saracen Vizir,' *Byz* 35 (1965), 455-468.

are not unrewarded by God. Have you no pity for my abundant tears
flowing so frequently? Does not my unkempt hair move you to sympathy?
Nor the fact that I have lice in greater abundance than Kallisthenes? Nor that
I am more squalid than Zenon? Nor that through lack of exercise I have
dropsy as bad as Philoktetes? Nor that I have lost my salary for so many
years?[125]

Various letters to the emperor trace his various moods: a brief incredulous
note on his arrival,[126] a desperate outpouring on the evils of his surroundings;[127]
a learned and polished plea for the ending of his exile;[128] a counterpart using
strings of quotations from the psalms instead of citations of famous classical
exiles,[129] and a dignified reminder to the emperor of his service to the state on
his embassies to the Bulgars and the Arabs.[130] Leo's letters are to be dated to
about 910; by June 913 he was back in Constantinople, writing court poetry
for the new emperor Constantine Porphyrogennetos[131] and running the risk of
further punishment.

Niketas Magistros is a different case.[132] He fell out of favour sometime in
927-28, was deported and tonsured, and settled on his own property on the
south-east shore of Hellespont. This area he calls Hermotos, and there he
stayed for eighteen years, during which he wrote the thirty-one surviving
letters. He ignored his tonsure and decided to live as a gentleman farmer and
retired statesman. He designed the pattern of his life with dignity; he had the
means to build a chapel, buy books and import horses from Greece. But he
feels the lack of metropolitan society.

These fields, these trees do not wish to teach me to write letters, nor have
the Muses taken me up like the shepherd of Askra to teach me their song,
nor has the Pythian taught me (unlike Ismenias) to play the flute. Those who
in the city, both men and books, taught me to speak and write have sent me
here as you see, deprived of everything in these thickets and these hills.[133]

---

[125] Leo Choirosphaktes, ep. 21, ed. Kolias, 107.

[126] Ep. 20, ed. Kolias, 97-98.

[127] Ep. 21, ed. Kolias, 99-107 at 101.

[128] Ep. 21 at 107.

[129] Ep. 22, ed. Kolias, 109.

[130] Ep. 23, ed. Kolias, 112-114. For the embassies see respectively epp. 1-14, ed Kolias,
77-91 and epp. 25-9, ed. Kolias, 91-94.

[131] See Kolias, 17, 54, 60.

[132] On Niketas and his letters see L.G. Westerink, *Nicétas Magistros, Lettres d'un exilé
(928-946)* (Le monde byzantin, Paris, 1973).

[133] Ep. 3, ed. Westerink, 59.

Herakles! What evils, what misfortunes I have suffered! How many are the ills which the Divinity has poured upon me! He has dimmed my two givers of light, has sliced off the two nostrils by which I breathed the air and smelt the breath of life. He has taken away my children, sent me away from those close to me and kept me far from my friends. He has, despite my inexperience, forced me to cultivate a little parcel of hilly land, to observe the circular course of the stars and the fruitfulness of climate and soil—things I never learned before.[134]

Here we have the impression that he is facing his exile constructively; certainly there are no self-pitying recitals of the hardships he has to endure or the inclemency of the climate. He wrote also a letter of praise of his Hermotos and took offence when John the *patrikios* praised instead Bithynian Olympos. Hermotos, insisted Niketas, was a paradise and his greatest consolation. Nor is there the perpetual harping on the glories of Constantinople one might expect; rather he praises his *patris*, Larissa in Thessaly.[135]

In two letters he tries to make peace with the authorities in Constantinople, both respectful, restrained models of diplomacy.[136] At one time he thinks a return is possible, but like Odysseus he is blown back to exile. He takes it in remarkably good part, finding comfort in his estates, his reading and his friends.[137] He fears his literary skill is fading and catches up on his reading of Demosthenes. He wrote to Alexander of Nicaea and Theodore of Kyzikos while they were still in power; each was himself subsequently to suffer the pain of exile. To Alexander he quotes Nicander, 'a long distance separates us', and exchanges books with him; to Theodore he mentions the building of his church, for which the other had sent him some candles.[138] His great consolation was letters; while upbraiding a correspondent for *agraphia* he compares his exile to the length of the Trojan war.[139]

With Alexander of Nicaea we are back in the world of politics and stinking prisons. He was metropolitan of Nicaea until 944 when he was exiled, again for no clear reason.[140] The seventeen letters he wrote on his exile are full of complaint, self-pity and perpetual intrigues to secure the vote of this or that bishop for his return. He describes the way he was arrested, his journey by boat to the monastery of Satyros and his eventual imprisonment

---

[134] Ep. 19, ed. Westerink, 99.

[135] Ep. 20, ed. Westerink, 101; ep. 23, ed. Westerink, 113.

[136] Ep. 7, ed. Westerink, 69-71; ep. 15, ed. Westerink, 92.

[137] Ep. 17, ed. Westerink, 95.

[138] Ep. 9, ed. Westerink, 79; ep. 8, ed. Westerink, 71-3.

[139] Ep. 10, ed. Westerink, 79. He was in fact in exile for eighteen years.

[140] On Alexander of Nicaea see P. Maas, 'Alexandros von Nikaia,' *BNJ* 3 (1922), 333-336; Darrouzès, *Épistoliers byzantins* (AOC, 6, Paris, 1960), 27-32.

in a cave in the monastery of Monobata.[141] 'It is impossible to recount all my ills', he writes to the metropolitan of Philippi, but mentions the hostility of the bishops, the harshness of his servitude and describes his prison as a stinking tomb. In addition he had a terrible disease and also gout.[142] Elsewhere there is a different mood: he confesses to Eusebios that he has hopes of returning to see his house again, and tells Eustathios of Side that the fidelity of his friends comforts him. But then politics gain the upper hand once more, and he is writing to George of Hierapolis telling how well he had followed the commandments of God and suggesting that he persist in trying to obtain Alexander's release.[143]

Few letters are preserved from the exile period of Theodore of Kyzikos compared with his happy correspondence with Constantine Porphyrogennetos. It may well have been that after the death of this ruler he was without the support of a protector and he was at the mercy of the patriarch Polyeuktos. It certainly seems that shortly after 959 he was exiled to Nicaea, where he wrote twelve letters.[144] In letter 19 he blames the patriarch for his fall; in letter 21 he is already in exile and speaks of consolations: his urgent need is not to escape from exile, but to save his soul through this trial. In the next letter he explains the condition of his detention at Nicaea in a little house. He asks friends to use their influence with the emperor but in general writes with patience and resignation. He has still time for friends in his trouble, and pretends that separation from a particular monk is his only adversity. In general the tone of these exile letters has more of an eye to the next world than to this.[145]

Resignation, constructive retreat, indignant complaint and perpetual intrigue all have their place as reactions to exile in these tenth-century letters. But little is said of what is lost in all this, even in Niketas Magistros; physical conditions and questions of guilt and innocence obsess writers more than deprivation of office or of Constantinople. If we seek expressions of regret and loss, we must look to other than political exiles, for example to Philetos Synadenos, judge at Tarsos, or Nikephoros Ouranos, governor of Antioch.

---

[141] Ep. 1, ed. Darrouzès, 68-71.

[142] Ep. 6, ed. Darrouzès, 80-81.

[143] Epp. 12, 14, 17, ed. Darrouzès, 88, 91, 95-96.

[144] On Theodore of Kyzikos and his part in tenth-century politics see Darrouzès, *Épistoliers byzantins*, 55-61. For his letters see S. Lampros, 'Epistolai ek tou Biennaiou Kodikos Phil. gr. 342,' *NE* 19 (1925), 269-290; 20 (1926), 31-46, 139-157; Darrouzès, *Épistoliers byzantins*, 317-341.

[145] Ep. 21, ed. Darrouzès, 334-336; ep. 22, ed. Darrouzès, 355; ep. 27, ed. Darrouzès, 338.

I would not have chosen life with Calypso rather than the smoke of
Constantinople. I am absolutely possessed by the thought of the many
sources of pleasure which are there on all sides: the size and beauty of its
churches, the length of its colonnades and the extent of its walks, its houses
and all the other things which enrich our image of Constantinople;
gatherings of friends and conversations, and indeed the greatest of all, my
gold-pourer and my mouth, that is to say *your* mouth and its flowers and
characterisations, the flow of graces and the waters of teaching.[146]

Here we seem closer to Theophylact's sense of loss and exile. But for a
comparable group of letters dealing with exile we must look ahead to the
twelfth century, when exile appears to be in fashion. The poetry of John
Mauropous,[147] Nicholas of Kerkyra,[148] Nicholas Mouzalon,[149] Theodore
Prodromos,[150] Constantine Manasses[151] and Michael Choniates,[152] the speeches
of Manuel Straboromanos[153], histories written by[154] and about exiles[155] and the
letters of a high proportion of the epistolographers of the period[156] are concerned with exile. Exile, more than friendship, sickness, riddles or death is the

---

[146] For the letters of Philetos Synadenos, see Darrouzès, *Épistoliers byzantins*, 48-49, 249-
259, see particularly epp. 11 and 12 on Tarsos and Antioch; Nikephoros Ouranos, see
Darrouzès, 44-57. Nikephoros Ouranos, ep. 47, ed. Darrouzès, 246, tr. Littlewood. Note
the play on Homer, *Od.*, I.57.

[147] Poems 47 and 48, ed. P. de Lagarde and J. Bollig, 'Johannis Euchaitorum
metropolitae que in codice Vaticano Graeco 676 supersunt,' *Abhandlungen der historisch-
philologischen Classe der königlichen Gesellschaft der Wissenschaften zu Göttingen* 28 (1882),
24-27.

[148] Ed. S. Lampros, *Kerkyraika anekdota* (Athens, 1882); see Gautier, 'Le synode,'265-269.

[149] Ed. S.I. Doanidou, 'He paraitesis Nikolaou tou Mouzalonos apo tes archiepiskopes
Kyprou. Anekdoton apologetikon poiema,' *Hellenika* 7 (1934), 109-150; P. Maas and F.
Dölger, 'Zu den Abdankungsgedicht des Nikolaos Muzalon,' *BZ* 35 (1935), 2-14; J.
Darrouzès, 'L'éloge de Nicolas III par Nicolas Mouzalon,' *REB* 46 (1988), 5-53.

[150] Poems 40 and 79, ed. W. Hörandner, *Theodoros Prodromos. Historische Gedichte*
(WByzSt, 11, Vienna, 1974), 391-393, for the return of an exile, the *sebastokrator* Isaac; for
the dialogue, *Apo apodemias te philia*, PG 133, 1321-1332.

[151] Constantine Manasses, *Hodoiporikon*, ed. K. Horna, 'Das Hodoiporikon des
Konstantinos Manasses,' *BZ* 13 (1904), 313-355.

[152] Ed. S. P. Lampros, *Michael Akominatou ta sozomena* (Athens, 1871-80), II, 375-398.

[153] For Manuel Straboromanos, see P. Gautier, 'Le dossier de Manuel Straboromanos,'
REB 23 (1965), 168-204.

[154] Anna wrote from the seclusion of Kecharitomene, Zonaras from Hagia Glykeria,
Glykas possibly in prison, Manasses possibly from an exile-see, Kinnamos (like Psellos)
while out of favour, Choniates after the fall of the City.

[155] See for example, *Al.*, IX.x.2, L, II, 185 on how to spend a good exile and catch up on
your reading even when blinded.

[156] See my 'Originality in the Byzantine Letter: the Case of Exile,' *Originality and
Innovation*, 39-58.

most characteristic theme of Komnenian literature.[157] And with the innate epistolary leaning towards separation, letters express it best.

This has been noticed before, but oversimplified: exile authors have been uniformly classified as 'ageing professors whose entire lives had been spent in the study and teaching of rhetoric, philosophy and theology.'[158] In fact exile writers of the period fall into several categories: politico-legal exiles,[159] monastic exiles,[160] non-episcopal official exiles,[161] episcopal official exiles[162] and refugee bishops.[163] With the fall of Constantinople to the Latins in 1204 an additional factor is introduced, for all writers are now exiles.[164] What is

---

[157] See my 'The Classical Tradition in the Byzantine Letter,' *Byzantium and the Classical Tradition*, ed. M. Mullett and R. Scott (Birmingham, 1981), 75-93 at 91.

[158] R. Browning, 'Unpublished Correspondence between Michael Italicus Archbishop of Philippolis and Theodore Prodromus,' *BB* 1 (1962), 27, and see the remarks of W. Hörandner, 'La poésie profane au XIe siècle et la connaissance des auteurs anciens,' *TM* 6 (1976), 253, n.53. It is to be hoped that further research into episcopal careers in the eleventh and twelfth centuries will throw light on this question: at present it appears that bishops could be appointed from about the age of 35 onwards, even then hardly old age.

[159] E.g. Nikephoros Basilakes, see A. Garzya, *Storia e interpretazione dei testi bizantini* (London, 1974), esp. VIII, IX, XII, XX (vii).

[160] E.g. Hierotheos monachos, see J. Darrouzès, 'Un recueil épistolaire du XIIe siècle: Acad. roum. cod. gr. 508,' *REB* 30 (1972), 199-229.

[161] An example is Gregory Antiochos, on an official mission to Bulgaria in 1173, see J. Darrouzès, 'Notice sur Grégoire Antiochos,' *REB* 20 (1962), 61-92 and 'Deux lettres de Grégoire Antiochos, écrites de Bulgarie vers 1173,' *BS* 13 (1962), 276-284; A. Kazhdan, 'Grigorii Antioch, zhizn' i tvorchestvo odnogo chinovnika,' *VV* 26 (1965), 77-92, 'Gregory Antiochos: writer and bureaucrat,' *Studies On*, 196-223.

[162] Theophylact is an excellent example.

[163] On these, which include John the Oxite, Niketas metropolitan of Ankyra, Basil metropolitan of Reggio, see S. Vryonis, *The Decline of Hellenism in Asia Minor and the Process of Islamization from the Eleventh through the Fifteenth Century* (Berkeley, Los Angeles and London, 1971), 194-210; V. Tiftixoglou, 'Gruppenbildungen innerhalb des konstantinopolitanischen Klerus während der Komnenenzeit,' *BZ* 62 (1969), 25-72; J. Darrouzès, *Documents inédits d'ecclésiologie byzantine* (AOC, 6, Paris, 1960), 3-53, 66-74; R. Morris, *The Byzantine Church and the Land in the Tenth and Eleventh Centuries* (unpublished DPhil thesis, Oxford, 1978), 3-40.

[164] Most notably Michael Choniates but also Basil Pediadites, John Apokaukos, George Bardanes, Euthymios Tornikes; see I.C. Thallon, *A Medieval Humanist: Michael Akominatos* (repr. New York, 1973); for Basil Pediadites see *Kerkyraika Anekdota*, 48-49; for Apokaukos, see M. Wellnhofer, *Johannes Apokaukos Metropolit von Naupaktos in Aetolien c. 1155-1233* (Freising, 1913); on George Bardanes, E. Kurtz, 'Georgios Bardanes Metropolit von Kerkyra,' *BZ* 15 (1906), 603-613; M. Roncaglia, *Georges Bardanès, métropolite de Corfou et Barthélemy de l'ordre franciscain* (Studi e Testi Francescani, 4, Rome, 1953); for Euthymios Tornikes see Darrouzès, *Tornikai*, 7; 'Notes sur Euthyme Tornikès, Euthyme Malakès et Georges Tornikès,' *REB* 23 (1965), 149-155.

remarkable amid this variety of experience is the homogeneity of this exile discourse.

Unlike the political exiles of the tenth century there is far less emphasis on physical discomfort although such matters are often mentioned in passing. *Penia* is a constant complaint; so is the climate and its implications for health. The state of the church and populace is a matter for concern, and the physical condition of the metropolitan church serves as metaphor for much else. But in general what comes over is a sense of contrast and of loss—books, the sight of Hagia Sophia, the face of the correspondent. Past glories are regretted and the provinces contrasted to their detriment with the bright lights of Constantinople. The writers dwell on their success or failure in bearing exile, which they all see, whatever their status, as ἐξωρισμός, ἀειφυγία, ὑπερορία. *Odyssey* imagery is rife; monsters prowl. For those happily in Constantinople there are proper responses to the exiled: their letters prove that Philippopolis or Athens or wherever their correspondent may be is the home of Muses and Graces. But the most characteristic expression of exile is the complaint of *barbarismos* and *agroikia* which is found in all the twelfth-century writers: time taken up with administrative worries and distance from Constantinople turn these writers into barbarians.[165] All this is instantly recognisable from Theophylact.

It is important to define the limits of this phenomenon. We should not expect to find exile-writing everywhere either in twelfth-century writing generally or even in the letters of the period. The sentiments are often confined to a few letters, often written at the beginning of a posting, or after some time when the effects of *barbarismos* might have been expected to be felt. Not every epistolographer in the twelfth century wrote exile letters: Nicholas Kataskepenos and Michael Glykas belonged to a different, monastic, circle; Theodore Prodromos and John Tzetzes were too metropolitan to do more than reply to exile letters.[166] A writer like Neophytos of Cyprus, although very conscious of the evils of exile, was hardly affected at all: he was outside the charmed circle.[167]

---

[165] On all this see my 'Originality,' 39-58 at 44-45.

[166] Other 'outsiders' include Gregory of Oxeia, Theoreianos, Michael *ho tou Anchialou*, Theodore Balsamon, Demetrios Tornikes and the *hegoumenos* of St George Mangana.

[167] Neophytos on exile: ὁ ξένος πάντα θλίβεται, ὁ ξένος πάντα κλαίει,/Ὁ ξένος πάντοτε θρηνεῖ, παραμυθίαν οὐχ ἔχων. See I.P. Tsiknopoulos, 'He poietike paragoge tou enkleistou agiou Neophytou,' *Kypriakai Spoudai* 16 (1952), 47-49 and C. Galatariotou, *The Making of a Saint. The Life, Times and Sanctification of Neophytos the Recluse* (Cambridge, 1991). One of the very few failings of this splendid book is not to consider how little representative Neophytos was of, and how little in touch with, metropolitan culture; it fails to do justice to Neophytos's eccentricity.

It would also be untrue to suggest that this kind of exile-writing was a totally new phenomenon. We saw in Niketas Magistros and Philetos Synadenos pointers to the developed discourse of the twelfth century. Nicholas Mystikos in the early tenth century was aware of the horrors of episcopal service abroad: 'I myself reflect...on the desolate nature of the place and the ways of the men with whom you live and the strangeness of their manners.'[168] But it is in Michael Psellos's replies to officials serving in local government in Greece that we come closest to this imagery.[169] And with John Mauropous's unhappy stay at Euchaita, this line of discontented officials which runs from Philetos Synadenos to Psellos's correspondents finds its first episcopal sufferer. John writes vividly about his surroundings:

> There is a great emptiness in the land, without dwellings, charm, trees, foliage, wood or shade, all full of wildness and neglect, lacking much in report or fame.[170]

But there is no mention in the letters from Euchaita of the topoi which are to become so familiar later: *exorismos, aeiphygia, amousia* and *barbarismos*. To place a terminus ad quem is not easy either. The events of 1204 clearly have no great impact on the use of exile imagery, nor does the increasing growth of feelings of loyalty to the *patris* rather than the metropolis find literary shape. Early thirteenth-century writers in Nicaea have other concerns; with Akropolites and Blemmydes, even Niketas Choniates, we are in another world. But George Bardanes, taught by Michael Choniates in Athens, faithfully mirrors the writing of his teacher.[171] So our exile discourse appears limited to the period between the 1090s and the 1230s.

Can it be explained within the traditions of *xeniteia* in Greek literature and of separation in the letter? I suspect not without reference to wider social

---

[168] Nicholas Mystikos, ep. 79, ed. tr. R.J.H. Jenkins and L.G. Westerink, *Nicholas I Patriarch of Constantinople, Letters* (DOT, 2, CFHB, 6, Washington, DC, 1973), 334.

[169] E.g. Michael Psellos, ep. 80, to the *kourator* of Cyprus, ed. E. Kurtz and F. Drexl, *Scripta minora*, II, 100-101.

[170] John Mauropous, ep. 64, ed. tr. A. Karpozilos, *The Letters of John Mauropous, Metropolitan of Euchaita* (CFHB, 34, Thessalonike, 1990), 173; in contrast to the sermons he pronounced at Euchaita, ep. 184, ed. Lagarde, 160-165. The generic difference is essential here; see A. Kazhdan, 'Some Problems in the Biography of Mauropous,' *JÖB* 43 (1993), 87-111 and at 105.

[171] This clearly depends on the preservation of letters of the right kind and the right date. With John Mesarites, John Kamateros and Michael Autoreianos only dogmatic and administrative letters have survived; the letters of Nikephoros Chrysoberges and Manuel Karantenos have not yet been edited; for Constantine Stilbes, see J. Diethart, *Der Rhetor und Didaskalos C. Stilbes* (Diss., Vienna, 1971).

developments. One is the magnetism of Constantinople during the eleventh century.[172] Another is the influx into the city of exiles from Anatolia in the 1070s and 1080s. They are for the most part anonymous; even bishops are hard to document, and they must have been only a small proportion of the Christian population of Anatolia.[173] But Beaton has plausibly suggested that it is in resettled Anatolian communities in Constantinople that another kind of exile literature should be sought: the nostalgic recreation of border society in the heart of Constantinople in the Grottaferrata Digenes, and the 'traumatisme de Manzikiert' of the Hades scene of *Timarion*.[174]

Indirect evidence for the impact of uprooted metropolitan bishops certainly exists. The rowdiness of the synod of 1084 with its open split between archontes and metropolitans and the very curious role of the refugee patriarch Nicholas seem attributable to a strong metropolitan presence in the City, and especially in synod;[175] the loud and courageous opposition to Alexios by Leo of Chalcedon, John the Oxite and Niketas of Ankyra[176] may be more easily understood in the context both of the *scholazontes* themselves with time on their hands in Constantinople and of loyal and vocal support in the synod. The attempts to disperse the clergy to their sees wherever possible as in the posting of John the Oxite, the imperial legislation of 1094[177] and specifically

---

[172] For the magnetism of the capital see above, chapter 2.4, 44-45. I am grateful in what follows to Rosemary Morris for many discussions along these lines, and for so much more.

[173] See above, chapter 2.4, 47, n.186. For the most serious study, Vryonis, *Decline*, 143-287; M.F. Hendy, *Studies in the Byzantine Monetary Economy, c.300-1450* (Cambridge, 1985), 100-133. We know very few by name. Niketas of Ankyra might have been their spokesman were he not an individualist, Nicholas Grammatikos was a refugee though not a metropolitan and John the Oxite did not take up his see until 1091. We know nothing of reactions within the group. There seems no justification for Darrouzès's comment, 'sans être de ses intimes', *Documents inédits*, 41.

[174] R. Beaton, 'Cappadocians at Court: Digenes and Timarion,' *Alexios I Komnenos*, I, 329-338.

[175] V. Grumel, *Regestes*, no.938, III, 40-41; Niketas of Ankyra, *On Ordinations*, ed. Darrouzès, *Documents inédits*, 177-207; Tiftixoglu, 'Gruppenbildungen,' 44-46; R. Morris, *The Church and the Land*, 39.

[176] On the Leo case see above, 72, n. 305. For John the Oxite see the three studies of Gautier, 'Jean V l'Oxite,' *REB* 22 (1964), 128; 'Diatribes de Jean l'Oxite,' *REB* 28 (1970), 5-17; 'Réquisitaire du patriarche Jean d'Antioche contre le charisticariat,' *REB* 33 (1975), 77-132. On Niketas of Ankyra see Darrouzès, *Documents inédits*, 37-53. Each case must be viewed on its merits.

[177] Alexios's two acts may appear contradictory but are the two sides of the coin of imperial policy. The *prostagma*, Dölger, *Regesten*, no.278, ed. P. Zepos, *Jus Graecoromanum* (Athens, 1931), I, 35-61 was designed to end the undesirable and destructive lingering of Balkan bishops in the capital. The *prostaxis*, Dölger, *Regesten*, no.1172, ed. Zepos, I, 325-326, was designed to provide financial support for the refugees with no visible means of

the edict on the reform of the clergy in 1107[178] would seem to be an imperial response to the problem. It is even possible to view the admonition which provoked Niketas of Ankyra's *On Synods*[179] as an attempt of the same kind, and to see in the stirring up of heresy trials in the 1090s and the 1110s together with the reform of the *nomokanon* attempts by Alexios to distract the refugees from their obsession with 'elections and ordinations'. All this evidence suggests that there was a large, vocal and politically threatening metropolitan presence in Constantinople. The *synodos endemousa* was an established and functioning institution; this was a time when, as Darrouzès points out,[180] crucial constitutional questions of church authority were in flux: above all, it was a time when the ambitious cleric would want to be in Constantinople. Theodore Balsamon cynically remarked that if episcopal dignity were to be detached from its exercise in a see, there would be far more bishops out of their dioceses than in them.[181] To be 'exiled' from Constantinople at this date meant not only exile from the heart of the empire, from the *theatra* and literary society, but also from major participation in major changes in the government of the church. There were good reasons for a sense of loss on leaving the City, for consciousness of exile and for its literary representation.

For someone like Theophylact a see was indeed *aeiphygia*, a life sentence. Although practice had loosened up considerably from the early days of the church, particularly with the current need for *metathesis* and *epidosis*, and although the reign of Alexios saw a rash of resignations, debate was still alive in the twelfth century on both the right of resignation and the propriety of translation.[182] By the early thirteenth century the position was rather differ-

---

support and in so doing preserved intact the episcopal corps for mobilisation in the course of the reconquest, see Vryonis, *Decline*, 207; Tiftixoglu, 'Gruppenbildungen,' 49. The fact that no synods appear to have been called between 1095 and 1107 (John the Oxite complained, see his ep. 2, ed. Gautier, 144) may suggest another imperial ploy.

[178] Dölger, *Regesten*, no. 1236, ed. Gautier, 'L'édit d'Alexis I sur la réforme du clergé,' *REB* 31 (1973), 165-201; Darrouzès, *Offikia*, 72-75. See Morris, *The Church and the Land*, 40, on the edict as part of Alexios's reconquest policy.

[179] The admonition seems to date to before July-August 1084, see Darrouzès, *Documents inédits*, 45.

[180] Darrouzès, *Documents inédits*, 6. On the *synodos endemousa*, see above, 90-91 and n. 53.

[181] Balsamon, 16 Constantinople, PG 137, 1072-1073.

[182] On the processes of *metathesis* (translation) and *epidosis* (the temporary combination of two poor bishoprics to provide sufficient support for one poor bishop) see Vryonis, *Decline*, 207-8 and Darrouzès, *Documents inédits*, 46. On resignations apart from the three preserved documents see the discussion of the 1151 Mouzalon issue in Darrouzès, *Documents inédits*, 69-71. Note that Niketas of Ankyra was quoted in the Mouzalon case as

-ent. The loss of Constantinople together with the consolidation of local
loyalties like the Helladic connection[183] and the tendency towards a hereditary
episcopate through the medium of the *ho tou* network meant that although
letter-writers might still write in terms of barbarism and exile, the sharp sense
of deprivation and of a general consciousness of exile was missing. The pull of
Constantinople, the nostalgia for Anatolia, the heavy tactics of refugee
metropolitans combined to create the conditions for a literary fashion.
Theophylact the Author could be held responsible for transforming these
conditions into discourse.

*   *   *

But what of Theophylact the Man? Cardinal Newman was sure that not only
author but also man was illuminated by a letter-collection. 'It has ever been a
hobby of mine (unless it be a truism, not a hobby) that a man's life lies in his
letters.' Letter theorists agreed with him: was not the letter an icon of the
soul?[184] Yet, whether portrait or life,[185] there is much doubt as to whether the
biography of medieval subjects is possible.[186] What we can say from
Theophylact's collection is that he leaves open to us a multitude of ways of
viewing him.

We have seen him in the collection as Nestor, the aged counsellor,[187] as
Plato,[188] as 'among the clients' of Melissenos,[189] as Daniel in the lion's den,[190] as

---

well as the case of Hilarion of Mesembria, who resigned in the wrong way. See K.M.
Rhalles, *Peri paraiteseos episkopon kata to dikaion tes orthodoxias anatolikes ekklesias* (Athens,
1911).

[183] For the Helladic connection which bound together the influential group of twelfth-
century clerics which comprised the Tornikai, Euthymios Malakes, Michael Choniates and
John Apokaukos see J. Darrouzès, 'Notes sur Euthyme Tornikès, Euthyme Malakès et
Georges Tornikès,' *REB* 23 (1965), 148-167, esp. 162.

[184] A.R. Littlewood, 'The Ikon of the Soul: the Byzantine Letter,' *Visible Language* 10
(1976), 197-226.

[185] Obolensky, *Portraits* and R.W. Southern, *Saint Anselm: a Portrait in a Landscape*
(Cambridge, 1990) do not problematise the difference.

[186] The doubt surfaced after Peter Brown's brilliant biography of Augustine, as scholars
measured what they knew of their subject against that work. Note also Christopher
Brooke's dictum, 'It is rarely possible to know a man solely from his letters.'

[187] G99, to Michael Pantechnes, II, 587.23-24.

[188] G55, to Pakourianos, is built on the story of Plato's stay with Dionysios of Syracuse,
II, 317.9-20.

[189] G13, to caesar Melissenos, II, 171.16.

[190] G61, to John Komnenos, II, 35.5-7.

Samson,[191] as a noble lion assaulted by dogs,[192] as a soldier fighting Amalek,[193] as a useless dolphin who once was a useful ox,[194] as the leader of the dance of rhetors[195] and as the bishop who intercedes constantly for his people.[196] These last two roles are suggested in a more comprehensive description of himself to the ex-*basilissa* Maria. 'And that is why I descend among the Bulgarians, I who am a true Constantinopolitan, and strangely enough a Bulgarian, exuding like them the smell of sheepskin...'[197] Bulgarian and Constantinopolitan: we are reminded of Dennis's stricture about Byzantine letters: 'they live in one world and speak in another'.[198] It is not that Theophylact can inform us about the relationship of capital to province which many have thought so important and defined so crudely;[199] rather that the dichotomy can inform us about Theophylact. He lived in both worlds and wrote about both of them.

5.4 Theophylact the Constantinopolitan

Theophylact liked to remind himself (G8, G9, G81) of his former position as rhetor, and he kept in touch with former colleagues, still teaching in Constantinople, Niketas *ho tou Serron* and Theodore Smyrnaios.[200] He also kept in touch with some pupils, sharing with them a delight in λόγοι or taking advantage of their strategic position.[201] He maintained an interest in medicine and exchanged books with friends; we have one book, a Gospels with the commentary of pseudo-Peter of Laodicea, which contains work in

---

[191] G89, to Adrian, II, 465.20-24.
[192] G89, to Adrian, II, 465.18.
[193] G72, to Theodoulos, metropolitan of Thessalonike, II, 387.6-10.
[194] G134, to Demetrios, I, 335.1-3, 343.11-13.
[195] G8, to John Doukas, II, 153.5-6.
[196] G26, to the son of the *sebastokrator*, II, 215.2.
[197] G4, to Maria, II, 141.58-62.
[198] G. Dennis, *The Letters of Manuel II Palaeologus, Text, Translation and Notes* (DOT, 4, CFHB, 8, Washington, DC, 1977), xviii.
[199] E.g. I. Ševčenko, 'Constantinople Viewed from the Eastern Provinces in the Middle Byzantine Period,' *Eucharisterion: Essays Presented to Omeljan Pritsak on his Sixtieth Birthday by his Colleagues and Students,* ed. I. Ševčenko and F.E. Sysyn = *Harvard Ukrainian Studies* 3-4 (1979-80), 712-747; A. Epstein, 'Art and Hegemony in Byzantium, 9th to 12th Century,' *XXVI International Congress of the History of Art* (Washington, DC, 1986), abstracts, 9.
[200] G6, II, 147-149; G7, II, 151; G28, II, 223; G95, II, 481.
[201] See above, 99, 212.

his own hand.[202] He responded to calls to participate in the polemic of the day.[203] He maintained his links with friends and patrons in Constantinople and dedicated some of his commentaries to an old patroness, whose influence was now eclipsed.[204] Much of his time in Bulgaria may have been taken up with the composition of his commentaries, but he was above all conscious[205] of the difference between his old life, simple and business-free, redolent of books and ancient civilisation, and the new, more active, life.

That activity involved him in administration and in pulling strings, to maintain the integrity of his archdiocese and his considerable estates. In both roles he acted as a Constantinopolitan; there is no reason to believe that he would have acted any differently had he been a bishop in Pamphylia or held estates in Cyprus, though some of the problems he faced would have been different. We have been able to analyse in detail those epistolary transactions which are preserved of his efforts to mitigate imperial policy on the *exkousseiai* of the archdiocese. His letters also allow us an assessment of his conduct as archbishop.

He was by any account a prelate who looked after his flock.[206] For one thing he was present in Bulgaria, by no means easily to be assumed,[207] and we have evidence for at most two visits to the capital during his episcopate.[208] He was not, for example, at the synod of Blachernai at the end of 1094.[209] And he took his position seriously. He made visits,[210] though perhaps not to the outlying parts of the diocese, and held at least one, perhaps more, provincial

---

[202] On book exchange see above, 99. For the Theophylact autograph, and its colophon, Coislin 21, fol. 20, see R. Devréesse, *Bibliothèque nationale: catalogue des manuscrits grecques*, II, *Le fonds Coislin* (Paris, 1945), 17-18.

[203] *On the Errors of the Latins*, I, 247-285, possibly G135, II, 595-597.

[204] Gautier, I, 66-67 says it is impossible to decide whether the commentaries in question date from before or after the 1094 conspiracy. On the slow slide from power see my 'Maria'.

[205] G71, to Opheomachos, II, 383.9-12.

[206] For bishops who did not measure up see Mouzalon, *Paraitesis*, 306-377, ed. Doanidou, 120-122; Galatariotou, *Making of a Saint*, 193.

[207] For a welcome corrective to the widespread impression of episcopal absenteeism see Hendy, *Studies in the Byzantine Monetary Economy*, 76-77.

[208] G4, to Maria, II, 137-141 at 137.3-4; G120, to John Pantechnes II, 553-557. He has arrived at Thessalonike, 555.1, and, 557.46-7, sets out for Ochrid. Presumably he started in the City. G120 is dated to 1108 (the δοῦλος καὶ ἀποστάτης of 555.30-31). G4 cannot be dated closely (c. 1095) but it is unlikely to be as late as 1108. Theophylact is leaving Constantinople after a vain attempt to visit Maria on the Princes' Islands.

[209] Gautier, 'Le synode.'

[210] See above, 55, 97, Table X, for Theophylact's visits and, 89-91, for the synod.

synods. His emphasis on canonical propriety is noticeable,[211] as is his firm line on immorality. (He was aware that this did not endear him to some of his flock.)[212] He took a personal interest in the conversion of Armenians and showed concern for proper liturgical provision.[213] He urged the reading of the scriptures.[214]

But it is in his dealings with his suffragans that we see him at his best. In G18 we are fortunate to have a policy statement on appointments. 'Bishops,' he writes, 'have been appointed by me either for their work in this church and their discretion and dignity' like the bishops of Morava and Prisdiana, or they are chosen from those who 'in Constantinople have been brilliant in thought and teaching' like the bishops of Kastoria and Belgrade (and later perhaps the bishop of Malesova), or they are chosen from 'those who were conspicuous in the monastic life', like the bishop of Triaditsa.[215] This shows an intelligent policy of enriching the archdiocese with different abilities while allowing local talent to be rewarded. He was no fool either; his appreciation of the special skills needed for Vidin are borne out by the problems of the holder of that see revealed in G57.[216] We should not be surprised that Theophylact chose bishops himself: by the eleventh century the appointment was normally in the hands of the metropolitan (or here the archbishop);[217] Bulgaria could never have known the early stage of acclamation.[218]

---

[211] G66, to the *chartophylax*, II, 365-6, is scrupulous about taking on a cantor with inadequate documentation, 365.21 referring specifically to the canons; G84, to Niketas *ho tou Chalkedonos*, deals with a violation of the canons by the son of the *protostrator*, II, 441.13. In G108, to Makrembolites, it is the voice of the canons which raises him from his sickbed, II, 527.3. The canons are almost certainly 5 Nicaea, modifed by 37 In Trullo; see Balsamon, PG 137, 640 on 8 In Trullo.

[212] G11, to John Komnenos, II, 8-12, deals with the immoral hieromonk who has thrown off his habit, lives with a woman and glories in his lust. G96, II, 488.38-39, tells how Lazaros sought out anyone who had been disciplined for polygamy or illegitimate marriage and 'since he found many of these' Lazaros proceeded to put them to use.

[213] G15, to Diabologyres, II, 179.11-14. Psalmody has to be inspected as well as the liturgy.

[214] G36, to the bishop of Pelagonia, II, 249-251.

[215] G18, II, 191.20-31.

[216] G18 on requirements for Vidin, II, 193.34-35; G57, II, 323-325 on the problems of one incumbent.

[217] Except in the case of disputed elections which even by the time of Euthymios of Sardis were referred to the synod of Constantinople. See Darrouzès, *Documents inédits*, 109-114 for Euthymios's treatise.

[218] See P. L'Huillier, 'Quelques remarques à propos des élections épiscopales dans l'Orient byzantine,' *REB* 25 (1967), 101-105 on the development from acclamation to the archbishop's choice of one of three candidates put up by the suffragans and then to Balsamon's expectation of Constantinople elections.

He was very conscious of the importance of the right incumbent, but also of avoiding an interregnum. G22 is an eloquent statement of what happens when a bishop is forced out of his see.

> What is this danger? There is no chant and no lights because it is without a bishop. In fact, placed on the main road, like David's vineyard, which flourished, but was pillaged by all who passed, it has no bishop in residence because its bishop cannot bear to offer his back to the whips and his cheeks to the blows, and naturally once the bishop has fled on account of these terrible insolent persons, no one else stays near the church, for the rest of the body follows the head...[219]

Even the temporary problems of a see deprived of its bishop are noted in G59 and G60. And G15 suggests that Theophylact would expect to be with a suffragan at a crucial moment like the conversion of an Armenian community.[220]

The morale of his suffragans was clearly also much on his mind. He praises where praise is due. He takes care to keep the bishop of Pelagonia informed, visits him and advises him on reading.[221] When the bishop of Debra has had to leave his see, possibly because of Bohemond's invasion, he confides to him his own despair and loneliness on the death of his brother, before urging him to return to his flock as soon as possible.[222] When the bishop of Vidin writes with a miserable account of his problems—praktors, Cuman incursions, insurrectionary citizens—Theophylact sends a bracing letter matching problem for problem, playing the trump card of the other's familiarity with Ochrid.[223] G53 is a long, patient discussion of the problems of a suffragan whom the lemma calls Gregory Kamateros. The bishop's church appears to have been damaged, and the bishop has punished his flock by abandoning them. Theophylact begins with a tissue of quotations from the prophets, then urges Gregory to pull himself together and show his intelligence and magnanimity to the full. He then launches into the parallel of the temple at Jerusalem, its destruction and rebuilding in even greater glory. He ends sympathetically. It is an understanding letter, interceding between bishop and flock, calling for a cool head and a warm heart.[224] In another letter, G40, we see his kindness to another suffragan, the bishop of Glavenitsa. He there

---

[219] G22, to the son of the *sebastokrator*, II, 203.9-21.

[220] G59, to the bishop of Triaditsa, II, 341.70-74, emphasised the implications of the other's obstinacy; G15, to Diabologyres, II, 179.15ff.

[221] G21, II, 199-201, briefs his suffragan; G36, II, 249-251, advises on reading the scriptures. Theophylact is in Pelagonia in G17, to John ?Doukas, II, 187.19; G94, to Nicholas Kallikles, II, 479.6; G96, II, 487.55.

[222] G122, II, 561.

[223] G57, II, 323-325, see above, 126.

[224] G53, to Gregory Kamateros, a bishop, II, 307-311.

writes to another bishop, Niketas Polites, commending the other, and explaining that the problem is of morale. The bishop of Glavenitsa was a fainthearted man, and took on the burden of episcopacy unwillingly, and withdrew from the hopeless weight of business as fast as others try to snatch it from him. Theophylact has persuaded him to undertake the journey; he asks Niketas to look after him and to protect him from unwelcome meetings. Niketas is to play Herakles and kill some monster in Koprinista.[225] The bishop of Pelagonia also receives his recommendatory letter to the patriarch in Constantinople when he needs time away, and he is possibly the recipient of a letter, G63, of consolation to a suffragan on the burning of a church.[226] Theophylact is in all these cases the considerate, patient, thoughtful, inspiring archbishop.

Only with the bishop of Triaditsa do we see relations with a suffragan deteriorate. There is some indication that relations had not always been bad: the impression that Nicholas of Kerkyra knew and was fond of the bishop,[227] the recognition of his age and monastic holiness,[228] which connect with the bishop mentioned in the policy statement of G18. There is also a sense of regret that things have gone so far, and a suggestion that Theophylact is covering himself, first in G58 with the collegial views of those around him, and then in G59 with those of the synod, lest his own views and sentence be thought harsh.[229] (That the other does regard him as harsh and vengeful we learn from G87.) What all thought regrettable was the bishop's harshness to the monk. The entourage in G58 poses the hypothetical question: what would he have done if you had given him someone to punish? He would have used the highest sanctions at his disposal, they sadly agree. Theophylact had other grievances. Certainly there was the fact that his earlier ruling had been ignored and the monk forced to go outside the archdiocese for assistance; perhaps the fact that the bishop, unlike Diabologyres, has not involved Theophylact in the success with the Armenians and his breach of the canons in failing to come to the synod. None of this was nearly as damaging as his rumour-mongering, which hit Theophylact on a very sensitive spot. Here, uniquely (though we learn that he did so elsewhere), he confronts an opponent with his

---

[225] G40, to Niketas Polites, II, 267.2-6.

[226] G64, to the patriarch, II, 361.4-5; G63, II, 357-359.

[227] G77, to the bishop of Kerkyra, II, 411.56-57: the word φιλάδελφος is used. See above, 84, n.29 and 88, n.45; the identification remains uncertain.

[228] G60, to the bishop of Triaditsa, II, 349.95-6: ἀρχιερεῖ μοναχῷ καὶ ἤδη γέροντι; cf. G18, II, 193.24-5: ἐν μοναστηρίῳ τῷ μοναδικῷ βίῳ ἐμπρέψαντες.

[229] G58, to the bishop of Triaditsa, II, 327-335, emphasises the moment of the arrival of the *geron*, while *archontes* of church and state were going into church, 327.2-3; 329.26 recalls these and puts words into their mouths, 28-31. G59 is addressed τῷ αὐτῷ ἀπὸ τῆς συνόδου.

crime. 'For who does not know how your *timiotes*, during your stay in Constantinople, spread myriad calumnies against me, so that there can be no-one, great or humble, who has not been deafened by the lies you have spread?' The letter however is in response to a submission from the bishop, and replies in generous mood, taking account of the other's infirmity and finally closing the dispute.[229] Theophylact was fortunate that this case ended as it did, not because he handled the difference with less than tact, concern for all parties and a due sense of canonical propriety, but because the other was apparently so hostile and difficult. We are fortunate (compared with students of, for example, the collection of Michael Choniates), to see this dispute in some detail, and Theophylact comes out of it well.[230]

So Theophylact the Constantinopolitan, with the consolation and support of his network and his books, maintains the values of the City in extremely difficult circumstances, supporting his subordinates where necessary, confronting and exhorting them where circumstances demanded. He has no time for shirking, or for abandoning vows, or for transgressing canons, or for unnecessary harshness but he understands human frailty and can deal with it. He is also prepared to act as protector and go-between for his people in general. This leads us into a discussion of Theophylact the Bulgarian.

5.5 Theophylact the Bulgarian

Until very recently this section-heading would have appeared a contradiction in terms; it is still controversial. Theophylact was long thought of as the prime representative of Byzantine imperialism during the period of Byzantine rule in Bulgaria, with a mission to destroy local Slavonic culture, or alternatively as a metropolitan emigré, exiled from the life of the court by an ill-advised allegiance and venting his spite against his flock in xenophobic outbursts. Writings of dubious authorship were ascribed to Demetrios

---

[229] G87, to the bishop of Triaditsa, II, 457.13-17.

[230] But see M.D. Spadaro, 'Archontes a confronto nella periferia dell'impero sotto la basileia di Alessio I Comneno,' *Syndesmos. Studi in onore Rosario Anastasi* (Catania, 1991), 83-114 for a less flattering assessment; I can find no support in the collection for her suggestion that it shows an inexperienced Theophylact early in his career.

Chomatenos rather than to him when they showed any knowledge of Slavonic or sympathy towards the Bulgars.[231]

Recently this harsh interpretation of Theophylact's role has been considerably modified through the patient researches of scholars largely from the Balkans. The work of Snegarov and Xanalatos[232] has been well continued by Božilov, Iliev, Maslev and Nikolaev in Bulgaria and by Panov in Yugo-slavia.[233] This shift of emphasis is well documented in the change of attitude in various works by Obolensky: in 1948 he stated that 'the gulf which separated the higher clergy from the people and the mutual hatred between Bulgarians and Greeks can be well judged from the expressions of contemptuous disgust with which the Greek archbishop Theophylact of Euboea...refers to his Bulg-arian flock.' But by 1971 Obolensky remarks, 'This fact alone should be sufficient to put us on our guard against the popular picture of Theophylact as a fanatical enemy of Slavonic culture.'[234] In my doctoral thesis of 1981, in Obolensky's *Six Byzantine Portraits*, in his article on the *Vita Clementis* and in mine on Theophylact's views of the Slavs[235] a sympathetic view of Theophylact's role and stance are taken.

---

[231] Most influential was Zlatarsky, *Istoriia na Bulgarskata durzhava*, but see the extensive bibliography cited by D.A. Xanalatos, 'Theophylaktos ho Boulgarias kai he drasis autou en Achridi,' *Theologia* 16 (1938), 235-236. For a decision on authorship made on these grounds see Vlasto, *The Entry of the Slavs into Christendom*, 165.

[232] The view of Theophylact as enlightened pro-Bulgar is to be found in I. Snegarov, *Istoriia na Okhridskata arkhiepiskopiia* (Sofia, 1924), I, 222-224; D. Xanalatos, *Beiträge*; R. Katičić, 'Biographika peri Theophylaktou archiepiskopou Achridos,' *EEBS* 30 (1960-61), 364-385.

[233] Further nuancing of the picture has resulted from the great volume of work produced in the last twenty years by these scholars, for example the monographs by N.A. Nikolaev, *Feodalni otnosheniia v pokorenata ot Bizantiia Bulgariia otrazeni v pismata na Teofilakt Okhridski archepiskop Bulgarski* (Sofia, 1951) and B. Panov, *Teofilakt Ohridski kako izvor za srednovekovnata istorija na Makedonskijot narod* (Skopje, 1971). See on the question of role the sensible approach of E.S. Papayanni, 'Hoi Boulgaroi stis epistoles tou Theophylaktou Achridas,' *I. Panhellenio Istoriko Synedrio. Praktika* (Thessalonike, 1989), 63-72.

[234] D. Obolensky, *The Bogomils*, 169; *The Byzantine Commonwealth. Eastern Europe, 500-1453* (London, 1971), 285.

[235] Mullett, *Theophylact*, esp. 312-488; Obolensky, *Portraits*, 34-82; Obolensky, 'Theophylaktos of Ohrid and the authorship of the Vita Clementis;' M.E. Mullett, 'Byzantium and the Slavs; the views of Theophylact of Ochrid,' *Studies in Memory of I. Dujčev*, II, ed. A. Djourova (Sofia, forthcoming). This paper was written for the Washington Congress in 1986.

Yet in several recent general works, all from the West, the old view has been forcibly put. In 1964 Ševčenko contrasted the apostles to the Slavs, Cyril and Methodios with Theophylact: 'Since they were typical, if highly refined, products of Byzantine culture, they redeem it of some of its responsibility for the mixture of arrogance and pusillanimity with which it imbued a Theophylactus of Ochrida—relegated here to a footnote, where he belongs.' (The footnote continues in this vein, ending with perhaps the worst insult he could think of: 'he behaved as English officials, jogging along in some far-off colony of the empire, might have behaved half a century ago.'[236]) More recently in an article on the paintings of Theophylact's cathedral, the church of the Holy Wisdom at Ochrid, Ann Wharton Epstein, leaning heavily on the works of Zlatarsky, interpreted the artistic programme of his predecessor Leo in terms of Theophylact's writings and his assumed role in Bulgaria. 'Just as Basil crushed the Bulgarian army, so the Byzantine bishops castrated Bulgarian literary culture. No doubt they were chosen for the position because of their cultural background; they were there to impose Greek on the people.'[237] In 1983 John Fine attributed to Theophylact an intensification of the Byzantine policy of hellenisation. 'Theophylact closed Slavic schools, introduced Greek language services in many places and encouraged the translation from Slavonic into Greek of many local texts...there also seems to have been a systematic destruction of Slavic manuscripts.'[238] (Some of these charges need immediate response: there is no evidence that Theophylact opened or closed any school; the only evidence on Greek language services is the *akolouthia* for the converted Armenians; the only evidence for the destruction of manuscripts is one of silence: it is claimed by the Yugoslav scholar Mošin that no Slavic manuscript from before 1180 has survived within Bulgaria, but this assertion is not accepted by all scholars and directly contradicts the views of Dostál.)[239] The evidence for this picture of 'arrogance and pusillanimity' is invariably that of the letters, those 'outspoken epistles' which give 'scandalous sidelights on the relations between Byzantine clerics

---

[236] I. Ševčenko, 'Three Paradoxes of the Cyrillo-Methodian Mission,' *Slavic Review* 23 (1964), 226-236 at 229, n.32.

[237] A.W. Epstein, 'The Political Content of the Paintings of Agia Sophia at Ohrid,' *JÖB* 29 (1986), 315-329 at 323.

[238] J. Fine, *The Early Medieval Balkans: a Critical Survey from the Sixth to the Late Twelfth Century* (Ann Arbor, 1983), 220.

[239] A. Dostál, 'Les relations entre Byzance et les Slaves (en particulier les Bulgares) aux XIe et XIIe siècles du point de vue culturel,' *XIII IntCong* (Oxford, 1966), 173-174; V. Mošin, 'O periodizatsii russko-iuzhnoslavianskikh literaturnykh sviazei X-XV vv.,' *Trudy otdela drevnerusskoi literatury* 19 (1963), 54-69.

and their Bulgarian and Macedonian flock.'[240] It has even been suggested that not only were relations between Theophylact and his flock bad, but that the Bulgarians had driven him to drink.[241]

So it is to the collection that we must turn to assess these views. Another view, that Theophylact 'was above all concerned with the privileges and possessions of his church',[242] is difficult to assess from the collection. Possessions, certainly, for we have seen Theophylact, no catspaw of imperial government, in constant struggle with the fisc. And we have seen also his straight-backed reaction to patriarchal interference in a monastery, and to an official's attempt to nominate a bishop.[243] The Theophylact who self-mockingly uses his title, *ho archiepisokopos tes pases Boulgarias*, in a trifle to a friend,[244] but who scrupulously observed canonical and liturgical obligations, may well have been so motivated. We cannot know.

The collection and its expectations however may illuminate the 'often quoted passages of the letters'[245] which created the demonisation of Theophylact. The same quotations, from very few of the letters, appear in book after book. In G6 he refers to his life as Zeus's eagle among the frogs of the lake of Ochrid,[246] in G44 to those Greekless villages where there is no-one to teach him anything good,[247] in G50 he is listened to 'as is a lyre by asses'[248] and in G103 rails at Bulgarians, whether taught by him or chastised by him.[249] In G110 and G82 he apologises for the use of foreign, i.e. Slav, names.[250] Generally disenchanted descriptions of the province may be found in G24 and G90 and to a lesser extent in G25, G29 and G30.[251] In G4 and G5 he ventures

---

[240] Ševčenko, 'Three Paradoxes,' 231.

[241] D.M. Lang, *The Bulgarians* (Ancient Peoples and Places, 84, London, 1976), 72.

[242] Kazhdan with Constable, *People and Power in Byzantium*, 28.

[243] G82, to Michael *ho tou Chalkedonos*, II, 435-437; G18, to Taronites, *doux* of Skopje, II, 191-193.

[244] G129, to Michael Pantechnes, II, 583.7.

[245] Ševčenko, 'Three Paradoxes,' 231.

[246] G6, to Theodore of Smyrna, II, 147.12-14.

[247] G44, to Machetares, II, 277.12: Ἐν...οὕτω βαρβάροις χωρίοις.

[248] G50, to Pantechnes, II, 299.3, quoting the proverb, *Par.Gr.*, I, 291.

[248] G103, τοῖς παιδευθεῖσιν ὑπ' αὐτοῦ Βουλγάροις, II, 517.8-10.

[250] G110, to the doctor of the emperor kyr Niketas, II, 531.8-9; G82, to Michael *ho tou Chalkedonos*, II, 435.16.

[251] G24, to John Komnenos, II, 209.7-13; 211.26-27; G25, to Mermentoulos, II, 213.6-8; G90, to the *chartophylax*, II, 469.5-9; G29, to Mermentoulos, II, 225.10-12; G30, to the *chartophylax* Nikephoros, II, 229.10-15.

to remark that the Bulgars smell of sheep-or goatskin.[252] In G57 he makes a specific charge against the inhabitants of Ochrid,[253] in G89 he puts all his troubles down to the efforts of two Bulgars,[254] in G96 he describes the Bulgarian nature as the nurse of all evil,[255] and in G101 uses the image of the Gadarene swine to suggest that the devil had lodged firmly in Bulgarian bodies.[256] Some references disappear once Theophylact's practice of extended metaphor is recognised: the *paian* of G6 is part of the image of the eagle among the frogs, just as is the *panegyris* of the grasshoppers in G108.[257]

The other references must be seen in the context of the collection, in respect of the timing of their use and in respect of the correspondent. In G57 Theophylact matches the complaint of his suffragan about the Cumans with a slight on the loyalty of the people of Ochrid. The precise background of this complaint is obscure, but it has (plausibly) been associated with the passage in Anna where she describes the episode in 1082 when Bohemond was summoned to Ochrid by the citizens, but was prevented from capturing the city by Ariebes the military governor. Although this took place before Theophylact's time in Bulgaria it is unlikely that the disposition or the loyalty of the citizens would have changed so quickly. The question of inhabitants of Ochrid 'returning from the City' must be seen in the context of Theophylact's troubles over calumny. In this case Theophylact's charge may have been justified.[258]

The most damning passage cited by those who condemn Theophylact's xenophobia is the claim in G96 that the Bulgarian nature is the nursery of all evil. Here Theophylact is not making an indiscriminate taunt, but complaining about a specific peasant, Lazaros, who is guilty of a list of offences against him, including that of having accused him to the emperor of criminal arson. He may be one of the Bulgars of G89; the identity of the other is much debated. We have seen throughout that the Lazaros crisis affected

---

[252] G4, to Maria, II, 141.58-62 presents himself as emitting an authentically Bulgarian smell; G5, to the Grand Domestic, II, 145.35-38.

[253] G57, to the bishop of Vidin, II, 325.25-35. There is an element here of exaggeration of his own troubles in order to impress the bishop and make him realise he is not alone.

[254] G89, to Adrian the Grand Domestic, II, 465.12-13 (but then he was in Bulgaria).

[255] G96, to Nikephoros Bryennios, II, 485.34-35.

[256] G101, to John Peribleptenos, II, 513.10-12.

[257] G6, to Theodore Smyrnaios, is the frog-song, II, 147.18-19; G108 to Makrembolites, II, 527.10-12.

[258] *Al.*, V.v.1, L, II, 22.12-16.

Theophylact's writing. Emotional stress can surely be pleaded for him here; G101 may belong to the same crisis.[259]

G6 is explained by its place in the correspondence, as an 'arrival letter' from the ex-*maistor ton rhetoron* to the *hypatos ton philosophon*. Other letters also make sense in terms of their recipients: his pupil Michael Pantechnes, his friend the lawyer Mermentoulos, the imperial doctor Niketas, his old patroness the ex-*basilissa*.[260] They expect a disparaging view of his surroundings, the more grotesque the better. The specific charges of G57 are provoked only by his suffragan's difficulties, those of G96, 89, 101 by his own despair. The vocabulary of sheepskin and asses however is much more directed to its receivers and designed to amuse.

It could be argued that what matters is not particular references but the overall tone, condescending, critical and patrician. This is a matter of reading; it is not my reading. The 'sympathetic' view of Theophylact's episcopate also depends on a reading of the collection, as well as on other works in which we have heard the same voice. We have seen him combating heresy not as an extirpator of Bogomil Bulgarian culture but in the tradition of St Clement, moving slowly among isolated settlements with *akolouthiai* and holy oil. We have seen him defend not only the rights of Ochrid against the central government but those of a Bulgar monk against an over-harsh diocesan bishop. We have seen him prepared to appoint Bulgars, or at least locals, to sees. He saw himself in danger of being accused not of harshness towards his flock but of weakness towards them; he defends himself energetically:

> For anyone who would criticise an archbishop for making representations in support of his burdened people sets his net absolutely beyond the limits of sense and reason.[261]

It is also possible to go further and argue that far from trying to eradicate Bulgarian national culture Theophylact was himself converted to it. It is by

---

[259] G96, II, 485.34-35; on the identity of the Bulgars of G89: Maslev, *Studia*, 80-1; Gautier, II, 44. Simeon, *Pismata*, 145-146 thought they were *praktores*; Zlatarsky, *Istoriia*, II, 348-349, thought they were bishops. G101, II, 513.3-6: again there is much speculation on the enemy possessed by a demon, Simeon, *Pismata*, xxiii; Snegarov, *Archiepiskopiia*, 220; Maslev, *Studia*, 424.

[260] Recipients: Pantechnes of G56, Mermentoulos of G25, G29; Niketas of G110; Maria of G4.

[261] G24, to John Komnenos, II, 209.4-6.

no means proven that he did not learn at least a little Slavonic.[262] Though he affects to despise the Bulgar forms of placenames, such as Vardar for Axios, he actually uses them and records them, though pretending to punish an over-privileged correspondent who was always 'feasting on Hellenism': he produces them with a flourish, as a mark of learning.[263] Certainly he seems to have acquired for himself the services of a competent translator.[264] The eleventh and twelfth centuries in Ochrid were a time of flourishing local antiquarianism: if Theophylact was trying to extirpate local culture, he was extraordinarily unsuccessful. According to Dostál if not Mošin, the Ochrid scriptorium flourished: such works as the Gospel of Dobromir and the Boiana Gospel may date from this time.[265] It may have been Theophylact's policy of appointment which brought to the episcopal throne of Diabolis bishop Michael, who, presumably able to write without fear of attack from the fisc, in the year 1118 copied out the history of Skylitzes adding to it vital information about Bulgarian history in the reign of Samuel and afterwards. Such information as the rise of the Komitopouloi, the date of Samuel's death, and the names of churches are known only from this source.[266] It is also interesting in that it contains a mention of the archdiocese of Ochrid being a continuation of Justinian's autocephalous see of Prima Justiniana. Before Prinzing, this equation, as so often, was attributed to Demetrios Chomatenos and not to Theophylact. The equation of the two sees might have resulted from the need of the clergy of Ochrid to prevent the loss of any more bishoprics to the encroaching metropolitans of Thessalonike, Naupaktos and Dyrrachion, although the collection shows only good relations with neighbours.[267] But a bishop-list of the twelfth century (Gelzer taxis 'C') shows

---

[262]   A. Leroy-Molinghen, 'Trois mots slaves dans les lettres de Théophylacte de Bulgarie,' *AIPHOS* 6 (1938), 111-117. Bilingualism in the letters is fairly superficial and can be paralleled in other writers, e.g. Anna Komnene.

[263]   G48, to Michael Pantechnes, II, 295.10-11.

[264]   On the question of the use of Slavonic originals for the *VClem* see S. Maslev, 'Zur Quellenfrage der Vita Clementis,' *BZ* 70 (1977), 310-315; Obolensky suggests, *Portraits*, 79, on the basis of a φέρονται in *VClem*, 22-66, that Theophylact may not have seen manuscripts of Clement's hymns himself 'perhaps because he was unable to read Old Church Slavonic'; this does not convince.

[265] A. Dostál, 'Les relations,' 173-174.

[266] Prokić, *Die Zusätze*; J. Ferluga, 'John Skylitzes and Michael of Devol,' *ZRVI* 10 (1967), 163-170.

[267] Skylitzes Interpolatus, ed. Thurn, 365, interpolation in mss U and E: ὁ δὲ βασιλεὺς ἐκύρωσε καὶ αὖθις τὴν ἐπισκοπὴν (ἀρχιεπισκοπὴν E) Βουλγαρίας αὐτοκέφαλον, καθὰ καὶ πα^λ (πάλιν E) ἐπὶ τοῦ γέροντος Ρωμανοῦ, πληροφορηθεὶς ἀπὸ τῶν διατάξεων Ἰουστινιανοῦ τοῦ βασιλέως αὐτὴν εἶναι τὴν πρώτην Ἰουστινιανήν, ἣν ἐκεῖνος πατρίδα

Theophylact's favourite trick of listing alternative Greek and Slavonic placenames: we may here see traces of Theophylact's research work in his archdiocese.[268]

We have already noted Theophylact's interest in early Bulgarian history, and his support of local cults, the Virgin, the XV Martyrs, St Achilleios.[269] Doubt may still persist about the *Lives* attributed to him, but when a late-eleventh- to twelfth-century building phase turned up at the church of the Fifteen Martyrs at Strumitsa, its excavators had no difficulty in connecting it with the antiquarian interests of Theophylact of Ochrid.[270] Theophylact's encouragement of the cult of Achilleios at Prespa we have seen as remarkable in its time; whether it was Bulgarian tradition or antiquarian revival to have held a synod at all in a place so imbued with the aura of Samuel it was hardly the act of a Byzantine archbishop concerned above all to castrate Bulgarian culture. I suggest that in choosing to hold a synod at all, and in holding it in a traditional location with strong memories of Samuel, Theophylact showed a sensitivity to Bulgarian practice credible in the antiquarian of Strumitsa and Prima Justiniana, the defender of local rights and people, the hagiographer who based his *Life* on Slavonic originals and the bishop who saw himself as the successor of Clement. Byzantines, or at least one Byzantine, however patrician in outlook, however imbued with Constantinopolitan culture and however concerned by virtue of his office to uphold Byzantine rule in Bulgaria, could still be genuinely attracted to the Slavs and their history.

Magdalino has rightly raised the issue of motivation. 'If he cultivated the Cyrillo-Methodian heritage, this was for the same reason that metropolitans of Athens indulged in classical nostalgia—because it once

---

ἑαυτοῦ φησιν (ἔφησεν E) ἔχουσαν τηνικαῦτα ἐπίσκοπον Καστελλίωνα; G. Prinzing, 'Zur Entstehung und Rezeption der Ohrider Justiniana-Prima-theorie im 12. Jahrhundert,' *BB* 5 (1978), 269-287. On the encroaching metropolitans see above, chapter 2.5, 65-66.

[268] H. Gelzer, 'Ungedruckte und wenig bekannte Bistümerverzeichnisse der orientalischen Kirche,' *BZ* 1 (1892), 257; A. Diller, 'Byzantine Lists of Old and New Geographical Names,' *BZ* 63 (1970), 27-42, notes the Bulgar predilection for alternative names, some the Bulgarian equivalent, others doublets of places geographically apart.

[269] For the Virgin, see e.g. *Logos eis ten heorten tes hyperagias despoinas hemon Theotokou*, PG 126, 129-144; G13, II, 171.17-20; V. Zlatarsky, 'Namiestnitsi-upraviteli na Bulgariia prez tsaruvaneto na Aleksiia Komnin,' *BS* 4 (1932), 139-145 at 145. For the XV Martyrs and St Achilleios see above, 5.2, 235-239.

[270] D. Koco and P. Miljković-Pepek, 'Rezultatite od arheoloskite iskopuvanja vo 1973 g.vo crkvata "Sv. 15 Tiveriopolski mačenici"—Strumitsa,' *Arheološki Muzej na Makedonija*, 7.9 (Skopje, 1978), 93-97 at 96 and 97.

belonged to the distinguished tradition of his see and to capitalise on it was part of his pastoral duty.'[271] This seems to me not at all inconsistent with the view of Theophylact presented in the collection. But the difference between Athens and Bulgaria was one of language as well as time. Theophylact like Michael Choniates[272] bemoans past glories, and the loss of the golden age and the coming the *ponerai hemerai*. But because of the accident of his posting, to be a good antiquarian Byzantine constrained him to be a good antiquarian Bulgarian. 'I, quite simply a Constantinopolitan, and, strange to say, a Bulgarian.'[273]

5.6 Theophylact the exile

And so Theophylact lived, now dashing off a letter to protect his archdiocese, now picking up his Galen or consoling a friend in Constantinople. But G4 offers another self-image of Theophylact: ἀείφυγος,[274] the eternal exile. And this image offers a way of viewing the entire collection. It explains why Bulgaria is so little described, why the Vardar appears as a barrier between Theophylact and his correspondent, why barbarism is an issue. Bulgaria in the letters is Kedar of the Bible,[275] a desert inhabited by scorpions,[276] or a dismal swamp,[277] these desolate places,[278] where Laestrygonians and Cyclopes lurk[279] and the harpies snatch away books.[280]

'Αποδημῶν is a favourite word of his, βαρβαρισμός is another.[281] In a letter to the caesar Melissenos he refers to his surroundings as the τῇ βαρβάρῳ

---

[271] P. Magdalino, review of Obolensky, *Portraits*, in *History* 74 (1989), 500-501.

[272] Michael Choniates, *Epi te archetypo anistoresei auton, toutesti tes poleos ton Athenon*, ed. S. Lampros, *Michael Akominatou tou Choniatou ta sozomena*, II, 397-398. See also S.G. Mercati, 'Intorno all' elegia di Michele Acominato sulla decadenza della città di Atene,' *Eis Mnemen S. Lamprou* (Athens, 1935), 423-427, tr. P. Magdalino, *Perception of the Past*, x; on twelfth-century views of history see R. Macrides and P. Magdalino, 'The Fourth Kingdom and the Rhetoric of Hellenism,' ibid., 117-156; R. Macrides, 'Perception of the Past,' 589-599.

[273] G4, to Maria, II, 141.58-60.

[274] G4, II, 141.63.

[275] G79, II, 423, quoting from Ps.119 (120).5; G90, II, 469.7. Cf. poem 1.26-27, I, 349: 'Αλλ' ἔσχον αὐτὸν ἡ Κηδάρ ἡ Βουλγάρων,/ἀπορριφέντα τῆς Θεοῦ συνουσίας.

[276] G37, II, 253.6-7.

[277] G6, II, 147.13-18.

[278] G30, to the *chartophylax* Nikephoros, II, 229.11-12.

[279] G69, to Opheomachos, II, 377.2-3.

[280] G29, to Mermentoulos, II, 225.10-12.

[281] G34, to Anemas, II, 243.5.

καὶ καθ' ἡμᾶς οἰκουμένη.[282] A whole world of barbarism is envisaged to balance the world of hellenism he knew well. Nothing good is to be learned in these barbarian regions, a desert, inaccessible and waterless, needing the nectar of his correspondent's letter.[283] He begs Michael *ho tou Chalkedonos* not to laugh at the barbarian name Kittaba, but thrusts Glavenitsa, Vidin, Sthlanitsa, under the nose of Michael Pantechnes.[284] He both suffers this *amousia*, this *agroikia* and has absorbed them. Mermentoulos's function is to lead him to Kalliope; enslaved as he is by the *amousia* of ἐνταῦθα, he needs to be reminded and brought back to τὰ οἰκεῖα. Why has Mermentoulos not written? Could it be the *agroikia* that Theophylact has contracted among the barbarians?[285] Barbarism is inside him; far from extirpating anyone else's culture he needs to hold on to his own. He compares himself to the exiled Orestes; the children of Israel are never far, and the driving out of the Bulgar *geron* strikes a personal chord.[286]

G34 shows him examining the phenomenon for the benefit of a young friend recently posted to Bulgaria. 'You tell me my own dream,' he begins, 'in saying that you have become a barbarian in the middle of Bulgarians.' Anemas has either simply complained of *amousia* or has quoted from Euripides, *Orestes* 485, one of Theophylact's most frequently quoted plays, and a quotation previously used by Apollonios of Gaza, Philetos Synadenos and John Geometres.[287] In Theophylact's reply, a proverb, the *Peri Hermeneias*'s preferred decoration for letters, and one used before him by Julian in a letter,[288] precedes the citing of that quotation: epistolary credentials are established. But Anemas is not to be allowed the monopoly of this comfortably classicising feeling: the cup of *agroikia* precedes the Solomonic cup of wisdom, complete with reference from *Proverbs*. He establishes his affection for Anemas, quoting from the *Song of Songs,* then calls him to order.

---

[282] G13, to the caesar Melissenos, II, 171.2.

[283] G44, to Machetares, II, 277.12-15.

[284] G82, II, 435.16; G48, II, 295.8.

[285] G25, II, 213.6-8.

[286] Orestes, G109, to the *epi ton deeseon*, II, 529.2; for the children of Israel in the desert G37, II, 253.5-6; for the *geron*, G59, II, 341.79-86. For *agroikia* within see G29, to Mermentoulos, II, 225.8-10.

[287] G34, to Anemas, II, 243.2-3. Eur. *Or.*, 485. See Apollonios of Tyana, ep. 34, Philetos Synadenos, ep. 74, ed. Darrouzès, *Epistoliers byzantins*, 254. Cf. also Libanios, ep. 499, ed. R. Foerster, *Libanii opera* (Leipzig, 1921), X, 475.

[288] *Par.Gr.*, II, 565: τὸ ἐμὸν ὄναρ μοι λέγεις; cf. Julian, ep. 45, ed. W.C. Wright, *The Works of the Emperor Julian* (London and Cambridge, Mass., 1969), III, 141.

'We who have been for a long time in Bulgaria[289] have *agroikia* sharing our way of life and our hearth. But you, feigning ignorance before those who know, be not downcast, for it is only yesterday that books left your hands and the voices of the wise were sounding in your ears.' Having established seniority, he relents and sends the Chrysostom. It is neatly done, and only Michael Choniates's more literal use of the *Orestes* passage[290] will later improve on it.

Yet this feeling of becoming, strange to say, a Bulgarian, is not to reject it. Theophylact did his duty, in a determined and spirited way. He had no intention of being recalled. To Gregory Pakourianos, the good young governor, he recalls:

> I used to bemoan my fate, most honoured son in the Lord, and call it malignant and unhappy since it brought me to this extremity, where live envy and rancour and crowds of other faults, where the voice of reason is hated more than perfume by dungbeetles. But now I am led to give thanks to my fate for settling me among these barbarians and enriching me by giving me you as a listener.[291]

G71 to Opheomachos is built on the fable of the frogs and the hares, after Theophylact has discovered someone less able than himself to cope with Bulgaria. He reminds him of the radical contrast between Theophylact's life as a rhetor and his new role. Opheomachos is to overcome his feebleness; after all Theophylact has not turned and fled. Ἀλλ' ἔτλην καὶ ἔμεινα. 'But I suffered and I stayed.'[292]

*　　*　　*

The following epigram is preserved in two manuscripts of Theophylact's Gospel commentaries. It records the truth of his own word for

---

[289] II, 243.17: Ἡμῖν μὲν οὖν ὡς χρονίοις οὖσιν ἐν τῇ Βουλγάρων... cf. again Eur.*Or.*, 485.

[290] Michael Choniates, ep. 28, ed. Lampros, II, 44: βεβαρβάρωμαι χρόνιος ὢν Ἀθήναις...For other twelfth-century uses see my 'Originality,' n.66.

[291] G55, to Pakourianos, II, 317.2-7.

[292] G71, to Opheomachos, II, 383.12; a cumulatively heroic effect, recalling Odysseus and Diomedes holding firm when the Greeks wanted to flee in battle, Achilles addressing the Achaeans after the death of Patroclus, and Odysseus's refusal to succumb to despair after the winds of Aeolus carried him away from Ithake, quoting from Homer, *Il.*, 11.317; 19.308, *Od.*, 10.53.

himself, ἀείφυγος, and the end of his exile in Bulgaria:

> A comprehensible commentary on the Gospel according to John
> Is the work of Bulgaria's bishop, for whom Euboia was home.
> Words were his life, his portion the work of God
> His resting-place a sepulchre in Bulgaria's sod.[293]

> Εὔληπτον ἐξήγημα τοῦ Βουλγαρίας
> εὐαγγελίων τῶν κατὰ Ἰωάννην,
> ᾧ πατρὶς ἦν Εὔβοια καὶ βίος λόγοι,
> θεῖος δὲ κλῆρος καὶ τάφος Βουλγαρία

---

[293] Cod. Laur. gr. 6-26, fol. 243; Paris. suppl. gr. 219, fol. 294, Gautier, I, 12.

Theophylact's patronage? Hagios Achilleios at Prespa: the second
layer of wall-painting

CHAPTER SIX

CONTEXT AND TEXT

The preceding chapter shows that exile is a vital consideration in our examination of Theophylact as author (in that his vocabulary of exile radically changes the genre) and Theophylact as man (in that this is how he portrayed himself). We have also seen in 5.5 that topoi of exile should not be taken naively without consideration of when, where and to whom they are used.

> Quod quicumque leget (si quis leget) aestimet ante
> compositum quo sit tempore quoque loco.
> Aequus erit scriptis, quorum cognoverit esse
> exilium tempus barbariamque locum.[1]

Ovid's words might speak also for Theophylact. But they also recall us to current Ovidian scholarship.[2]

In that classicists were considerably, though rather late, influenced by New Criticism and have hence been extremely sensitive to questions of persona (although perhaps not in a very even manner)[3] it is unlikely that Ovid would, at least recently, have been pilloried as attempting to eradicate the indigenous culture of Tomi. In fact classicists have even more recently come to terms with the possibility that Ovid never even went to Tomi, that not only does he offer an exile-persona but also that his is a fictional setting.[4] Byzantinists have been very slow to adopt the notion of persona: even begging-poetry, which in western medieval poetry has for some time been read in this manner, was read as hard fact for patronage studies. The

---

[1] Ovid, *Tristia*, III.14.27-30.

[2] I am indebted to Elizabeth Fisher for this thought; she replied to an earlier version of chapter 5.5 above with the dictum: 'they would never do this to Ovid.'

[3] See W.S. Anderson, 'Roman Satire and Literary Criticism,' *Bucknell Review* 12 (1964), 106-113 = *Essays in Roman Satire* (Princeton, 1982), 3-10; M.J. McGann, *Studies in Horace's First Book of Epistles* (CollLat, 100, Brussels, 1969), 96 and n.1; N. Rudd, 'Theory: Sincerity and Mask,' *Lines of Enquiry* (Cambridge, 1976), 145-181. Against the use of persona: R.O.A.M. Lyne, *The Latin Love Poets. From Catullus to Horace* (Oxford, 1980), viii.

[4] The outlines of a debate on this subject can be traced in *Liverpool Classical Monthly* 10 (1985), 19-22 (A.D. Fitton-Brown), 48 (A.W.J. Holleman); 12 (1987), 23 (H. Hoffmann).

Prodromic question cried out for an interpretation along these lines; only recently has it been offered.[5]

But the question of fiction is even more germane to our problem. Recent studies, as we have seen, have pointed to a revival of fiction at the end of the eleventh century with the domestication of Arabian tales, the after-dinner stories of Kekaumenos, the Anatolian epic.[6] Theophylact himself experiments with a fictional setting,[7] itself a revival of tradition.[8] The treatise on eunuchs for his brother presents the defence as a conversation overheard in Thessalonike at a time when the emperor was also there. One summarised neatly all the conventional criticisms of eunuchs, before the other, a eunuch himself, 'smiled discreetly, for he was the most charming and the best educated of men, a living refutation of the criticisms' and launched into a reply. At the end, the pair get up and embrace one another, the eunuch takes in his arms the child, his nephew, who was listening to them avidly, and they separate. This, says Theophylact, is the ἀγώγιμον[9] which with difficulty he has brought his brother from Thessalonike, for he is not Simonides or Hippias, even if his memory remains at its peak even in his old age.[10]

[5.] F. Cairns, 'The Archpoet's Confession,' *MLJ* 15 (1980), 87-103; 'The Archpoet's Jonah Confession: Poem II,' *MLJ* 18 (1983), 168-193; R. Beaton, '"De vulgari eloquentia" in Twelfth-century Byzantium,' *Byzantium and the West c.850-c.1200*, ed. J.D. Howard-Johnston (Amsterdam, 1988), 261-268; R. Beaton, 'Ptochoprodromika 3: he ethopoiia tou ataktou monachou,' *Ste Mneme Stamate Karatza* (EEPS, Thessalonike, 1990), 101-107; M. Alexiou, 'The Poverty of Écriture and the Craft of Writing: towards a Reappraisal of the Prodromic Poems,' *BMGS* 10 (1986-87), 1-40.

[6] See above, 2.6, 76-77. See now for a new approach to fictionality R. Ronen, *Possible Worlds in Literary Theory* (Literature, Culture, Theory, 7, Cambridge, 1994).

[7] But see M.D. Spadaro, 'Un inedito di Teofilatto di Achrida ed un horismos di Alessio Comneno; problemi di chronologia,' *Quaderni del Siculorum Gymnasium, 8, Studi di filologia bizantina*, 2 (Catania, 1980), 159-181, who argues that the setting must be true because there would be no point in it otherwise.

[8] On the revival of the dialogue form in middle Byzantine satire see C. Robinson, *Lucian and his Influence in Europe* (London, 1979), 66-81; on the revival of satire see the broad brush of Barry Baldwin, 'A Talent to Abuse: Some Aspects of Byzantine Satire,' *ByzForsch* 8 (1982), 19-28; on Prodromos R. Beaton, 'Hoi satires tou Theodorou Prodromou ki hoi aparches tes neoellenikes grammateias,' *Ariadne* 5 (1989), 207-214; there is a narrow line between the revived satire e.g. Prodromos, *Apodemia te philia*, PG 133, 1321-1332 and *dramatia* e.g. Michael Haploucheir, *Dramation*, ed. M. Treu, *Städtisches evangelisches Gymnasium zu Wadenburg i. Schl.* 4 (1874), 1-6. The question of parody needs reassessment.

[9] Gautier translates 'marchandise' from ἀγώγιον, (wagon) load, but it may in this context mean 'love-potion', LSJ, sv ἀγώγιμος, III: ἀγώγιμον, τό.

[10] *In Defence of Eunuchs*, I, 291-292; 331.

This raises the question of the status of Theophylact's letters. Are they reliable, factual letters?[11] Or might they too be tainted with this fashionable fiction? What about G133, to Demetrios? Why are Ovid's letters treated with more circumspection? Is it that others of his works are recognised as fictional? Or is that they clearly belong to the category of poetic discourse? The use of verse is a distancing feature, but in Byzantium, and especially at this date, there was considerable confusion about the relative status of prose and verse,[12] and the elaborate prose style of the letter had its own distancing effect.

Is it possible to determine the factual reliability of Theophylact's letter-collection? I suspect it is not. In historiography and in hagiography time-honoured techniques have been evolved to sift wheat from chaff, fact from fiction. Epistolography is different. No source-criticism can pare down to the trustworthiness of Theophylact; no Bollandist could establish or demolish his canonicity. Yet 'the reader is always obliged to seek to measure the sincerity of a letter.'[13] For it is in the nature of epistolography to present not only a mirror, but also a mask. 'Demetrios' (and Cardinal Newman) believed that letters were the icon of the soul; Dr Johnson did not.

> It has been so long said as to be commonly believed, that the true characters of men may be found in their letters, and that he who writes to his friend lays his heart open before him. Such were the friendships of the *Golden Age*, and are now the friendships only of children. Very few can boast of hearts which they dare lay open to themselves, and of which, by whatever accident exposed, they do not shun distinct and continued view; and certainly what we hide from ourselves we do not shew to our friends. There is, indeed, no transaction which offers stronger temptations to fallacy and sophistication than epistolary intercourse.[14]

---

[11] On definitions of 'real letters' in the ancient world see above, 3.2, 123, n.207.

[12] The distinction between prose and verse, never great in Byzantium, where prose forms could take on the characteristics of poetry, became with the even more highly polished rhetorical products of the eleventh century even less clear, culminating with the development of the *politikos stichos* as a middle way, an *ametros metros*: it was used from the middle of the eleventh century as a teaching medium, is found in monasteries and court circles and was invaluable: it was clear, easy to memorise—and it built bridges out of the mandarin class to a wider world. See M.J. Jeffreys, 'The Nature and Origins of the Political Verse,' *DOP* 28 (174), 143-145.

[13] C.A. Porter, foreword to *Men/Women of Letters* (YFS, 71, Yale, 1986), 1-16 at 4.

[14] Ep. 559, ed. R.W. Chapman, *The Letters of Samuel Johnson* (Oxford, 1952), II, 228; see J. Diester, 'Samuel Johnson on Letters,' *Rhetorica* 6.2 (1988), 145-166. On the related issue of sincerity see Nicholas Spice reviewing Maynard Solomon on Mozart, *London Review of Books*, 14 December 1995, 6: 'Hildesheimer's case rests on an interpretation of the letters. Like an old hand biting a coin to find out if it is genuine, he tests them for sincerity but

But fallacy and sophistication do not of themselves require fictionality. Let us compare with Theophylact's a straightforwardly fictional (and modern) presentation of what could in fact represent Theophylact's own fate: Cavafy's Βυζαντινὸς "Αρχων, ἐξόριστος στιχουργῶν.[15]

Byzantine *archon*, in exile, writing verses

The light-weight may call me light-weight.
In serious matters I was always
Most punctilious. And I will insist
that no-one knows better than I
the Fathers and the Scriptures and the Canons of the Councils.
In every quandary of his, Botaneiates
in every problem with the church
took my advice, mine first.
But exiled here (let that expert in evil
Eirene Doukaina watch out) and dreadfully bored,
it is not at all strange that I should amuse myself making
hexastichs and octostichs—
that I should amuse myself with myths of
Hermes and Apollo and Dionysos
or heroes of Thessaly and the Peloponnese.
And that I should compose the most correct of iambics
which—you'll allow me to say this—the litterati
of Constantinople do not know how to compose.
More than likely, this correctness is the reason for their blame.

The speaker could be Theophylact, in that it is an *archon* who was in Constantinople in the 1070s, exiled through the agency of Alexios's *augousta*, bemoaning his fate and consoling himself with literature; the signals of 'Scriptures', 'Doukaina', 'litterati' (λόγιοι) are particularly Theophylactine. A closer look erodes this impression: the speaker writes verses like Niketas Magistros rather than exile letters like Theophylact and his twelfth-century successors; Eirene Doukaina would not have had the power so early in

---

fails to ask himself whether sincerity is an appropriate construct to apply to eighteenth-century letter-witing, or indeed to letter-writing in any age.'

[15] Ed. G.P. Savvides, *K.P. Kabaphe, Poiemata, II (1919-1933)* (Athens, 1963), 21. For other readings of this poem see P.A. Agapitos, 'Byzantium in the Poetry of Palamas and Cavafy,' *Kampos* 2 (1994), 1-20 at 15-16 and S. Ekdawi, 'Cavafy's Byzantium,' *BMGS* 20 (1996), 17-34 at 33, which offers additional autobiographical significance. I am grateful to Sarah Ekdawi for helpful correction and stimulating discussion, to Peter Mackridge for learned advice and to Georgia and Alexandros Alexakis for lending me their text for a Washington summer.

Alexios's reign if Zonaras is to be believed.[16] Nor does Cavafy claim historical authenticity, in contrast to his two other Alexian poems: 'Anna Komnene' self-consciously begins Στὸν πρόλογο τῆς 'Αλεξιάδος; 'Anna Dalassene' begins Εἰς τὸ χρυσόβουλλον ποὺ ἔβγαλ' ὁ 'Αλέξιος Κομνηνός.[17] But as in those poems Cavafy offers an *ethopoiia* revealing, unknown to the speaker, a personality which is vain, pedantic, querulous and quarrelsome, just as the hypocrisy of the mother-and-son team and the devoted daughter and wife are revealed in the Anna poems with deft economy. As in those poems historical points[18] are made: the regency could not have worked; Anna was personally ambitious; exile was a political tool in the eleventh century. But its fictionality is clear: the speaker cannot after all be identified; the knowing presence of the poet looks on ironically.

Theophylact's letter-collection covers some of the same ground. Both offer autobiographical statements with varying degrees of self-revelation, realism, artificiality and self-awareness. Theophylact's collection presents a more attractive subject (but then it would, wouldn't it?), who is less bitter and lonely and more skilfully manipulative, in poetic prose, with more sense of place. It is though a portrait of more than one man, of a whole network of contemporaries strung around the empire; it is more diffuse, and the elements in common with Cavafy's portrait are scattered through the minutiae of provincial life; its addressees are inscribed and ever-present, whereas Cavafy's *archon*'s invocation of the addressee in line 17 takes the reader by surprise. It is a portrait over time in contrast to Cavafy's snapshot. It is a portrait which the reader colludes in making, in drawing the connections; if there is a collector other than Theophylact (s)he is self-effacing to the opposite extreme of Cavafy. These differences are overwhelmingly those required by epistolarity; the similarities are those of autobiography.

If letters require fallacy and sophistication, autobiography, according to George Moore, offers an opportunity for self-creation.[19] 'Autobiography is not

---

[16] See among others the papers by M.J. Angold, B. Hill and M.E. Mullett, *Alexios I Komnenos*, I, *Papers of the Second Belfast Byzantine International Symposium*, ed. M.E. Mullett and D.C. Smythe (BBTT, 4.1, Belfast, 1996), esp. 403-404.

[17] Ed. Savvides, 20, 56.

[18] See R. Beaton, 'The History Man,' *C.P. Cavafy*, ed. M. Alexiou=*Journal of the Hellenic Diaspora* 10 (1983), 23-44, on how the ποιητὴς ἱστορικός 'subverted history from within' and D. Haas, 'Cavafy's Reading Notes on Gibbon's Decline and Fall,' *Folia Neohellenica* 4 (1982), 25-96 at 81-85 for Cavafy's knowledge of the Komnenian period.

[19] E. Grubgeld, *George Moore and the Autogenous Self. The Autobiography and Fiction* (Syracuse, NY, 1994), 185; quoting, 182, George Moore on autobiography and letters, 'Egotism is the god that inspires the letter-writer and good letters are all about the letter-writer.'

a genre or a mode but a figure of reading or of understanding that occurs, to some degree, in all texts',[20] and it is its fictive potential which has attracted most interest in recent scholarship.[21] This was a potential open to Theophylact, as the autobiographical mode made its appearance in *typika*, *prooimia*, histories,[22] and free-standing occasional poems in the early twelfth century before developing to its most elaborate form in the thirteenth-century writings of Neophytos the recluse, Nikephoros Blemmydes and Michael VIII.[23]

We have seen the metaphors of self Theophylact employs, and his skilful handling of the central problem of autobiography: how to handle the identity of author, subject and narrator.[24] We need not be constrained by rigid definitions of autobiography, for example that narrative is intrinsic to autobiography[25] or that autobiography 'as a genre involves the recapturing of a self lost in time past and renewable only through memory',[26] though it may be true that 'the issues of time and memory have occupied the great autobiographers'.[27] There is certainly in Theophylact no 'obsessive preoccupation with the chronological aspect of time',[28] but we can all think of autobiographers of whom this is also true. Pike's remark, that autobiography

---

[20] P. de Man, 'Autobiography as De-facement,' *MLN* 94 (1979), 919-930 at 921.

[21] E.g. B. Pike, 'Time in Autobiography,' *Comparative Literature* 28 (1978), 326-342 at 337: 'not all fiction is autobiographical but...all autobiography is fiction.' See also P.J. Eakin, *Fictions in Autobiography: Studies in the Art of Self-invention* (Princeton, 1985); M. Sprinker, 'Fictions of the Self; the End of Autobiography,' *Autobiography. Essays Theoretical and Critical*, ed. J. Olney (Princeton, 1980), 321-342.

[22] See R. Morris, *Monks and Laymen in Byzantium, 843-1118* (Cambridge, 1975), 122-123, for the element of self-justification in the *prooimia* of monastic *typika*. Authorial intrusion in historiography is well handled by R.J. Macrides in 'The Historian in the History,' *In Honour of Robert Browning*, ed. C. Constantinides and E. Jeffreys (Venice, 1996), 205-224.

[23] See Michael Angold's forthcoming study on autobiography in *DOP*, and for an example of religious autobiography, J. McGuckin, 'The Notion of the Luminous Vision in Eleventh-century Byzantium: Interpreting the Biblical and Theological Paradigms of St Symeon the New Theologian,' *Work and Worship at the Theotokos Evergetis, c. 1050-1200*, ed. M. Mullett and A. Kirby (BBTT, 6.2, Belfast, 1997), forthcoming.

[24] E.W. Bruss, 'Eye for I: Making and Unmaking Autobiography in Film,' *Autobiography*, ed. Olney, 296-320, explores this problem to explain why there is no real cinematic equivalent for autobiography.

[25] See Grubgeld, *George Moore*, 187.

[26] S. Burke, 'Writing the Self,' *Authorship from Plato to the Postmodern: a Reader* (Edinburgh, 1995), 304.

[27] Burke, 'Writing the Self,' 304.

[28] Pike, 'Time,' 327.

does not necessarily consist of remembered empirical experience,[29] both allows us to consider the collection as autobiography and examine its creative (or fictive) function. It contrasts two phases of the writer's life, portrays significant figures in it, allows us to see his family through his relations with a patron, his teacher through his relations with a client. There is, if not an obsession with chronology, a sense of development from the newly arrived bishop, desperate to locate himself in the agenda of the *theatra* of Constantinople and suffering every shift of public opinion in the City, through the mature figure who reproaches young friends for their desertion and excessive complaints and comes to appreciate his antiquarian surroundings, to the decisive prelate who speeds to be back with his flock at a time of political difficulty. What we do not have is a chronological account from birth, education, vocation—but this is something we find at the time only in hagiography.[30] We can only expect his autobiography to be that of his own day, and, with the exception of hagiography, when the telling of the story of a man's life is vital to provide a model for those who come after,[31] that story from the cradle is less important than portraits at the crucial and relevant stages. Memoirs, typika and testaments are the striking homes of autobiography in this period: Kekaumenos tells stories to prepare the young for similar trials; Eustathios Boilas tells us how he made his pile as well as how he wishes to distribute it; monastic heroes tell us how they have governed their houses as well as how they wish them to be governed in future. It is only later that Neophytos will write what appears to be *his own saint's life*. What we can most hope for at the end of the eleventh century is writers peering round a curtain from the wings of a performance of another actor's story: Psellos in Isaac Komnenos's tent, Anna looking down from a balcony on palace events. Against this context Theophylact's collection appears a welcome concentration on the capturing of a self for the appreciation of the reader.

---

[29] Ibid.

[30] The Menandrian structure which determined encomia, funeral orations, *prosphonetika* and other rhetorical genres shared—and had influenced—the topics of *patris, genos, genesis* and *paideia*, but the mode there is of celebration, whereas in hagiography it is traditionally narration.

[31] It can be argued that hagiography had at this stage become less a simple narrative, more a sophisticated art form; the *Life of Cyril Phileotes* is generically double: a saint's life is carefully welded to an ascetic compilation with several included genres; the *Lives* of Meletios must be read in competition with each other, with the context of the philosophical debates of the capital and with the spicing of parody. On Meletios see the forthcoming volume of Pamela Armstrong.

From this generalisation should be excepted two texts which have hitherto been neglected as proto-autobiographies, but which both turn on an autobiographical event, not irrelevant to Theophylact's life: the resignation from an episcopal see. They are the iambic poems on *paraitesis* of Nicholas, metropolitan of Kerkyra and of Nicholas Mouzalon, autocephalous archbishop of Cyprus.

Nicholas of Kerkyra's 305 verses, preserved in three manuscripts and edited by Moustoxidi and Lampros in the nineteenth century,[32] were delivered at a synod which is believed to be the synod of Blachernai of 1094, at which he was certainly present;[33] five additional lines record their effect on the synod—and the devil.[34] Poems on the Holy Cross and John Chrysostom are preserved, as is a 43-line prologue, addressed to the emperor, on the *200 Kephalaia* of Maximos Confessor.[35] Nothing is otherwise known of him except that he was the recipient of G75 and G77 and like Theophylact wrote a poem on the hymns of Symeon the New Theologian.[36] His verses are gloomy, dark and vague; reminiscent of the language of Theophylact's most monstrous[37] letters: the *ponerai hemerai*, the cannibal Laestrygonians are here too;[38] he inhabits Theophylact's dream.

In contrast Mouzalon's 1,057 verses[39] appear structured and lively, a more active attempt to defend himself against any charge of dereliction of duty, by the account of his first reactions to Cyprus, by a dialogue with a friend, by five cases experienced on the island, by extended farewells to the island, his colleagues and his flock. He names names (almost) and describes

---

[32] S.P. Lampros, *Kerkyraika anekdota ek cheirographon Hagiou Orous, Kantabrigias, Monachou kai Kerkyras, nun to proton demosieuomena* (Athens, 1882), 30-41; A. Moustoxidi, *Illustrazioni corciresi* (Milan, 1814), II, appendix V, xx-xxx. I am grateful here to Anthony Hirst.

[33] P. Gautier, 'Le synode de Blachernes (fin 1094). Étude prosopographique,' *REB* 29 (1971), 213-284 at 219.

[34] Gautier, *Théophylacte*, II, 88, notes that Marc. gr. 524, fol. 1v, ed. S. Lampros, 'Ho Markianos Kodix 524,' *NE* 8 (1911), 7, attributes these lines to Nicholas Adrianoupolites.

[35] Lampros, *Kerkyraika anekdota*, 27-28; Moustoxidi, *Illustrazioni corciresi*, II, xxx.

[36] Ed. Gautier, I, 352-355; J. Koder, 'Die Hymnen Symeons, des neuen Theologen. Untersuchungen zur Textgeschichte und zur Edition des Niketas Stethatos,' *JÖB* 15 (1966), 153-199 at 189; cf. J. Koder, *Syméon le nouveau théologien, Hymnes*, I (SC, 156, Paris, 1969), 64-67.

[37] See above, 124-125.

[38] Lines 69, 271, ed. Lampros, 32, 40.

[39] Ed. S.I. Doanidou, 'He paraitesis Nikolaou tou Mouzalonos apo tes archiepiskopes Kyprou. Anekdoton apologetikon poiema,' *Hellenika* 7 (1934), 109-150; see also P. Maas and F. Dölger, 'Zu dem Abdankungsgedicht des Nikolaos Muzalon,' *BZ* 35 (1935), 1-14.

atrocities. It is in the presence of the emperor[40] a powerful denunciation of the civil power in the island and the effects of the *demosion* as well as a self-portrait of a man who cared too much about his flock to remain powerless to assist them. It is a narrative of a tour of duty and credible in terms of autobiography, although like Nicholas of Kerkyra's poem, it seldom uses the first person. Mouzalon appears to have retired to the Kosmidion before his call to the patriarchate in Constantinople in 1147.[41]

These two works, one by a friend, the other by a contemporary in the closest job to his own (the only other autocephalous archbishopric), offer a useful foil to the autobiographical nature of Theophylact's collection. Nicholas's shorter poem develops several of the themes of despair also to be found in the collection without adding any sense of perspective; Mouzalon's longer, more narrative work is written at a single moment of emotional time in contrast to the more varied and developing reactions of Theophylact. Porter's observation that letters are written forwards whereas autobiography is written backwards[42] may be superficially true, but the narrative effect can sometimes be different; the very diffuseness of a letter-collection and its sense of growth over time can enhance and enrich the autobiographical effect. Mechanistic attempts to give autobiographical status only to the editor of a collection[43] seem equally ill-founded; though we cannot know whether heavy editing took place on Theophylact's collection it was certainly less than in many other letter-collections, and it is the sense of transitory and irrelevant detail in Theophylact's collection which gives credence to a deeper consistency of background which carries through from letter to letter and creates a quite distinctive imaginative world of its own; Smith's dictum that

---

[40] Lines 205-206 (Ἀλέξιος τὸ θαῦμα τῶν βασιλέων), ed. Doanidou, 117, suggest it; cf. the ἀλέξημα of Nicholas of Kerkyra, line 42, ed. Lampros, 31. See my 'The Imperial Vocabulary of Alexios I Komnenos,' *Alexios I Komnenos*, 372. But for a seductive alternative view see P. Karlin-Hayter, 'The Tax-collectors' Violence Drove the Archbishop into the Cloister?' *Stephanos. Studia byzantina ac slavica Vladimiro Vavřínek ad annum sexagesimum quintum dedicata*= *BS* 56 (1995), 171-182; on 179 she puts the case for the Alexian dating before proposing a date in the 1140s; she does not however take other autobiographical resignation texts into consideration.

[41] *De translationibus*, 57, ed. J. Darrouzès, 'Le traité des transferts. Édition critique et commentaire,' *REB* 42 (1984), 183; J. Darrouzès, 'L'éloge de Nicolas III par Nicolas Mouzalon,' *REB* 16 (1988), 5-53.

[42] Porter, *Men/Women*, 3.

[43] E. Showalter, Jr, 'Authorial Self-consciousness in the Familiar Letter: the Case of Madame de Graffigny,' *Men/Women*, 113-130 at 126-127.

letters reflect a context while poems create a context[44] is certainly not borne out by these examples. But while the collection has a strong autobiographical impact, this in no way implies a lack of epistolarity: the constant sense of the presence of the addressee, the sense of reciprocity and balance ensure that the person of Theophylact at the centre does not dominate the whole.

If in a letter-collection 'coherence replaces correspondence as the primary standard of judgment' and 'the letters of a master escape from their origins as reservoirs of fact' we may be clear we are in the world of letters rather than of autobiography. There can be no doubt that Theophylact created a consistent, vital and self-supporting world for his readers, for generations of receivers, indeed alternative worlds. These are the exotic world of Bulgaria and the familiar and enclosing classical companionship of Byzantium. Other scholars, with an understandable local concern, have exploited the letter-collection to illuminate the first, the world of Bulgaria. I believe though that the collection tells us far more about Constantinople than about Bulgaria, and that like other Byzantine letter-collections it tells us above all about individuals, their relationships and their ideas, in this case about the personal relations and the preoccupations of the Byzantine elite in the generation after Manzikiert. The plot of Theophylact's letter-collection is that of the interrelations of those worlds in the mind and the actions of its central figure Theophylact.

*   *   *

In a recurring dream, I advance through long rooms lined with gilt looking-glasses, passing waiters carrying great silver trays of canapés to find Theophylact standing quietly at the end of the very last room. We talk, with great understanding of one another, about issues of his day and mine, while I rediscover his characteristic humanity and generosity and charm. Finally as I move to say goodbye, he says, gently, with a little smile, 'You do know, don't you, that it wasn't like that at all?'

In this study we have explored all the implications of this dream: the limitations of surviving evidence, the difficulties and opportunities for the historian in dealing with privileged text as well as the role of the author in drawing upon fictionality, autobiography and the persona in the construction of history as fiction. We have also seen enough to understand that my dream is essentially irrelevant to the central exercise of this book: the consideration of 'the

---

[44] B. Herrnstein Smith, *On the Margins of Discourse* (Chicago and London, 1978), 33, well refuted by B. Redford, *The Converse of the Pen. Acts of Intimacy in the Eighteenth-century Familiar Letter* (Chicago and London, 1986), 9.

continual mutual interaction' of the 'actual world' and the 'represented world' which according to Bakhtin leads to 'the renewing of the work through the creative perception of listeners and readers'. In that sense there is nothing beyond the text, though we have mobilised overlapping contexts of milieu, genre, oeuvre, some more obviously intertextual, some apparently[45] extra-textual, in order to identify individuality and posit the relationship of the collection to other realities. We have identified also certain techniques and innovations, the 'how?' as well as the 'what?' of letter-writing in the belief that there may be wider implications for other privileged discourse in Byzantium: letters—'la lettre, l'épître, qui n'est pas un genre mais tous les genres, la littérature même'—are for Derrida a *synekdoche*.[46] We do not yet know what constituted privileged text, belles lettres, literature in Byzantium:[47] for Theophylact it was λόγοι; by this he means learning and literature, both their production and their reception, whether visually or orally.There is a problem here which needs a wider answer and further work. The study of what Byzantines have to say about earlier writers, the teasing out of rhetorical commentary, the pointing up of contrasts in art and literature, the examination of parody, dream, fiction, the balancing of levels of language and style, all may help to decide—and then to move on to the even trickier issue of evaluation. The question 'what is literature?' is of perennial interest to theorists; it should be to Byzantinists—and to historians in general.[48]

In the past, historians have gutted letter-collections for facts. They have also expressed frustration at the paucity of facts for them to gut. This kind of historian will find my reading of a single letter-collection disappointing, for it does not aim at traditional positivist goals like new prosopographical identifications or the discovery of new manuscript readings. Many of these tasks still remain to be done, and I have identified some: the codicology of the

---

[45] Like C.J. Wickham, *Gossip and Resistance among the Medieval Peasantry* (Inaugural Lecture, Birmingham, 1995), though not as elegantly, I have tried and failed to get round Derrida's strictures on the *hors-texte*, and like Wickham I believe that the significance lies in the trying.

[46] J. Derrida, *La carte postale: de Socrate à Freud et au-delà* (Paris, 1980), 'Envois,' 88.

[47] R. Browning, 'Tradition and Originality in Literary Criticism and Scholarship,' *Originality in Byzantine Literature, Art and Music,* ed. A.R. Littlewood (Oxford, 1995), 17-28 does not take the opportunity; T. Conley, *Cambridge History of Literary Criticism,* II, ed. A. Minnis (Cambridge, forthcoming) surveys the obvious ground; M. Angold, 'Were Byzantine Monastic Typika Literature?' *The Making of Byzantine History,* eds R. Beaton and C. Rouché (KCL, 1, London, 1993), 46-70, addresses many useful questions of eleventh- and twelfth-century monasticism, and highlights the interesting issue of the autobiographical preface, but does not explore or answer his own question.

[48] For a pointer see 'An Interview with Pierre Macherey,' *Red Letters* 5 (1977), 3: 'In particular historical periods literature exists in different forms. What needs to be studied is the difference between these forms. Literature with a capital 'L' does not exist.'

collection, the rhetorical analysis of the letters, the intertextuality of Theo-phylact with—in particular—Psellos. And inasmuch as this reading is cautious about referentiality in general, and suspicious in particular of the non-fictional status of this work, it might be thought by other kinds of historian also to subvert its own pretensions as a work of cultural history. Yet conversely it may also prove frustrating for a certain kind of literary scholar: it insists on a historicist setting of the collection in Komnenian contexts rather than on demonstrating its worth as a masterpiece of world literature, and so beginning to make the case for the rehabilitation of Byzantine literature as a whole. Even for other kinds of literary scholar it may seem over-concerned with the social editing of discourse, with its greater stress on genre, on network-analysis, on communication, than on the indeterminacy of post-modernism. And within the limited scope of the study of Byzantine literature it neglects currently fashionable approaches and avoids a thoroughgoing pursuit of a single method: its eclecticism neither interrogates Theophylact with Kazhdanian ruthlessness nor ushers the archbishop to the psychiatrist's couch. I would argue of course that this eclectic mix of historicist criticism and post-empiricist history is essential for my reading of this important text.

What this book does do is examine a major letter-collection in a systematic way, giving careful consideration to its whole as well as its parts. It situates the collection in the interactions of an individual's network as well as the preoccupations of a powerful elite with a strong sense of group identity. It touches on issues of performance and processes of communication and above all the contribution of epistolarity to the nature of the text: its reciprocity, its com-pression, its role as a public vehicle for private emotion, its play on the realities of presence and absence. The text is not seen as innocent: its political impact as well as its literary sophistication are delineated in the epistolary world it portrays, a mirror for the Byzantine world of the turn of the eleventh and twelfth centuries. And it is seen as a polished, playful, sophisticated achievement of a remarkable literary society. I hope my book will inspire others to do as much for other texts, and indeed for this one, for despite my unwillingness to evaluate,[49] it must be clear that I believe there is still a great deal to say about Theophylact's letter-collection. Mine is simply one reading of one text, and of the epistolarity of that text. But what we may be sure of[50] is that the author of that text will not speak for himself.

---

[49]   It would of course for example have been possible to apply Redford's evaluative criteria of autonomy, fertility and versatility; it seems more important to me to engage with Altman's more functional criteria of mediation, confidentiality, reading, closure, patterning and temporal polyvalence as they are found in the collection.

[50]   *Pace* A. Failler, 'Introduction' to *Théophylacte*, II, 5.

THE COLLECTION

Explanation of headings

Number in Gautier's edition, addressee as in mss
Correspondent: as in chapter 3.5 above and 'The Network' below, 347-382; bracketed numbers in bold are the numbers in Theophylact's network

Date: as proposed in this study, see above, chapter 3.1 **Editions:** first Gautier then earlier editions; for a full concordance see
Place: as proposed in this study; of dispatch and Table I
destination unless both parties are in CP or Bulgaria

Incipit: first few words of the letter **Desinit:** last few words of the letter
Message: the reason for sending the letter as expressed **Genre:** a preliminary suggestion of
in it and any other observations, see
above, chapter 3.3

Subject matter: for historical events, cases, crises mentioned, see chapter 3.2 above
Structure: see chapter 3.3. above, xxx-xxx

Tone: an impressionistic characterisation of the letter **Bearer:** where mentioned
as a whole in the letter; see also Table VIII.
Length: in words **Sent with:** other letters or works,
gifts; see Table IX

Bibliography: major secondary works which discuss or use this letter
Discussed above: pages above where this letter is discussed, **any in detail**

? = unknown; ?Alexios = possibly Alexios; Θ = Theophylact; O = Ochrid;
CP = Constantinople

G1, to his pupils who have been undisciplined

Correspondent: (undisciplined) pupils (**62**); see also G2

Date: c.1080   **Editions:** Gautier, I, 131-142

Place: within Constantinople

Incipit: ποῦ ποτέ εἰσιν οἱ τὸ αὐστηρὸν ἡμῖν   **Desinit:** καὶ πρεσβευταὶ πιστευόμεθα

     Genre: really a letter? Gautier, I, 130, n.1

Message: self-defence   **Subject matter:** pupils' complaints

Structure: 1) where are my detractors? let them hear Θ; 2) disorder causes disaster in nature; 3) in society; 4) in Greek antiquity; 5) defence of disciplinary practice; 6) relations with students; 7) advice; 8) ends with prayer to the God of order.

Tone: vigorous   **Bearer:** ?

Length: 1619   **Sent with:** ?

Bibliography: Gautier, I, 47; Gautier, 'L'épiscopat,' 165-166.

Discussed above: 43, 49, 173, 231.

G2

Correspondent: pupils (**62**); possibly those of G1

Date: c. 1080   **Editions:** Gautier, I, 131-142

Place: within Constantinople

Incipit: ἔδει μέν με λέγειν   **Desinit:** ἐκκλησίας ἀπελαυνόμενος

Message: justification of syllabus and teaching   **Genre:** really a letter?

Subject matter: old and new rhetoric

Structure: 1) this subject will produce bitter words, for situations determine the language used; 2) Θ's mission is to restore rhetoric to its pristine nobility; 3) many students have benefited from Θ's gifts; others have been prevented by long-established vice from so doing and they corrupt their contemporaries; 4) differences with students and his patience; 5) a minority of students wanted to read Hermogenes; Θ refused and is pilloried, but does not care; 6) violent disaccord among students; confrontation between master and pupil in class; 7) Θ will fight on, confident in the future and looking after his own affairs; 7) urges pupils to do likewise; they will be grateful for his teaching; down with rebels!

Tone: determined   **Bearer:** ?

Length: 2307   **Sent with:** ?

Bibliography: Gautier, I, 47; Gautier, 'L'épiscopat,' 165-166; Chrestides, 'Echidnai,' 119.

Discussed above: 49, 159, 173, 231.

G3, to the grand *oikonomos*, brother of the patriarch

Correspondent: N.N., grand *oikonomos* (**56**)

Date: c. 1080   **Editions:** Gautier, I, 131-142

Place: within Constantinople

Incipit: μικρόν μοι πρὸς σέ   **Desinit:** πρὸς τελείωσιν ἄγοντας

Message: request for a pay-rise   **Genre:** really a letter?

Subject matter: recipient

Structure: 1) this *logos* is a small present; 2) thanks for noticing Q's grievance: he is underpaid; 3) praise of the patriarch and the *oikonomos*, compared respectively to Moses and Aaron; the *oikonomos* must put to flight the calumniators who block his brother's goodness; 5) this *epainos* was written in a short time snatched from teaching; Θ will write a better one when his pay-rise comes through.

Tone: respectful   **Bearer:** ?
Length: 941   **Sent with:** ?
Bibliography: Gautier, I, 47; Gautier, 'L'épiscopat,' 161.
Discussed above: 173, 231.

G4, to the *despoina kyra* Maria
Correspondent: MARIA of Alania, *basilissa* (50)
Date: ?summer 1095 (Alexios in Nicomedia)   **Editions:** Gautier, II, 131-142;
Place: from ?Ochrid to the Princes' Islands   Lami 1, 501-6
Incipit: δέσποινά μου ἀγία, πολλοῖς μέν   **Desinit:** καὶ δεκτὸν θυμίαμα
Message: apology for failing to say farewell to her **Genre:** apologetic *hodoiporikon* (delayed
while he was in Constantinople   *syntaktikon*
Subject matter: Theophylact's journey
Structure: (free of all but biblical allusion): 1) unhappy stay of Θ in CP; greater unhappiness now
that he has failed to say farewell to her; 2) detailed description of his journey, alleging interference
by the *doux* of Dyrrachium; 3) Θ deserved to fail in his aim, since the desire of the wicked shall
perish, Ps.111(112).10; 4) asks M to show him her continued favour, and to help his brother
Demetrios by keeping the promise she had previously given; 5) his exile in Bulgaria; 6) references
to incense suggesting a gift.
Tone: ceremonial, inventive, using powers to the full **Bearer:** ?
Length: 744   **Sent with:** incense (or scented wood)
Bibliography: Roth, *Studie*, passim; *Acta Albaniae*, no.72, p. 23; Chalandon, *Les Comnène*, I, 6;
Leroy-Molinghen, 'Prolégomènes,' 254; Simeon, *Pismata*, xiv-xv, xxv, xxx, xxxiii, 180-187; Maslev,
Studia, 74-75; 131-133; Ducellier, *Façade*, 97; Mullett, 'Maria,' 202, 206-207, 210; Papayanni,
'Boulgaroi,' 64-65; Polemes, 'Paratereseis,' 376-377; Angold, *Church and Society*, 164.
Discussed above: 16, 34, 36, 69, 84, 87, 97, 149-150, 161, 171, 177, 246, 261, 266, 270, 271-274.

G5, to the Grand Domestic
Correspondent: ADRIAN KOMNENOS, the Grand Domestic (41); see also G79, G85, G89, G98
Date: c. 1088-89   **Editions:** Gautier, II, 143-145; Lami
Place: from Ochrid to ?Constantinople   2a, 505-510
Incipit: ἀγιέ μου αὐθέντα   **Desinit:** ἀνασχομένοις τυχὸν δυσκλεές
Message: request to AK to release him from his   **Genre:** first letter on arrival in see =
servitude in Bulgaria; complaint   inverted *epibaterion*
Subject matter: *barbarismos*
Structure: built on the myth of Herakles and Omphale: 1) fragmentary greeting linked with myth
of Pelion and Ossa; 2) Θ asks AK to listen; 3) relates the myth (Hera, Hebe, Aphrodite and Zeus
make appearances) with squalid details of Herakles's slavery; 5) Θ is also a slave; he asks AK to free
him otherwise he will die before his time; the ending is abrupt, possibly incomplete.
Tone: desperate; finely crafted   **Bearer:** ?
Length: 213   **Sent with G6, G7 and Lost 1**
Bibliography: Simeon, *Pismata*, 187-192; Leroy-Molinghen, 'Destinataire,' 432; Gautier,
'L'épiscopat,' 161; Katičić, 'Korespondencija,' 183; Maslev, *Studia*, 17, 133; Papayanni, 'Boulgaroi,'
64-65; Solarino, 'Un intellettuale,' 72; Mullett, 'Slavs.'
Discussed above: 84, 88, 101, **145**, 159, 161, 169, 171, 214, 243, 270.

G6

Correspondent: THEODORE SMYRNAIOS (20); see also G28, G95

Date: c. 1088-1089

Place: from Ochrid to CP

Incipit: ὅδ' ἀνὴρ οὐκέτ' αὐτός· ἐκνεύει πάλιν

Message: maintenance of communication

Editions: Gautier, II, 147-149; Lami 2b, 507-510; Finetti 1, 307-310

Desinit: τὸ κόνδυ τῆς πτώσεως

Genre: first letter on arrival

Subject matter: nostalgia for CP; description of his situation

Structure: 1) begins with Eur., *Ph.*, 920; describes the inhabitants of Ochrid in terms of Empedocles's monsters; 2) compares his own situation to that of the eagle of Zeus, brought low; 3) contrasts his situation with that of Theodore in the full light of imperial favour, using Hom., *Od.* 6, 44-45; 5) prays for deliverance or consolation for himself; and deliverance or relief for Theodore from 'the cruel beast' (his gout). Allusive and learned framework of quotation.

Tone: vigorous and querulous

Length: 414

Bearer: ?

Sent with: G5, G7, Lost 1

Bibliography: Leroy-Molinghen, 'Destinataire,' 431-437; Chalandon, *Les Comnène*, I, 7; Obolensky, *Bogomils*, 170, n.1; Darrouzès, *Tornikai*, 227; Obolensky, *Byzantine Commonwealth*, 224; Gautier, 'L'épiscopat,' 161-165; Simeon, *Pismata*, xxii-xxiii, 1-2; Nikolaev, *Feodalni*, 53; Panov, *Teofilakt*, 302, 320; Maslev, *Studia*, 16-17, 88-92; Obolensky, 'Byzantine Impact,' 156; Papayanni, 'Boulgaroi,' 64-65; Mullett, 'Slavs.'

Discussed above: 13, 21, 55, 84, 88, 99, 101, **145-146**, 160, 178, 214, 246, 248, 261, 269-270; 274-276.

G7, to the *didaskalos* of the Great Church, kyr Niketas *ho tou Serron*

Correspondent: NIKETAS *ho tou Serron*, *didaskalos* of the Great Church (22); see also G70, G91

Date: c. 1088-1089

Place: from Ochrid to ?CP

Incipit: ἐβουλόμην μὲν καὶ πρὸς τὴν σὴν ἱερότητα

Message: to tell Niketas briefly about his troubles

Editions: Gautier, II, 151; Lami 3, 509-510

Desinit: σου ῥημάτων ἀκούσεται.

Genre: first letter on arrival

Subject matter: the letters also carried by the bearer

Structure: 1) Θ's frustrated desire to tell all; 2) N must learn from the letter to the Grand Domestic (G5); 3) if this is clear enough, Θ asks him to tell others about his sufferings; 4) if he needs more detail, the bearer will show him a letter to the *epi ton deeseon* (Lost 1); 5) asks that N tries to change his situation by prayer; 6) God will listen.

Tone: neutral

Length: 123

Bearer: ὁ σὸς μαθητὴς καὶ ἀδελφὸς ἐμός

Sent with: G5 and G6

Bibliography: Simeon, *Pismata*, 192-193; Gautier, 'Le synode,' 247; Katičić, 'Biographika,' 367; Maslev, *Studia*, 35-36; 133.

Discussed above: 16-17, 35, 84, 88, 101, **146**, 149, 214, 244.

G8, to the *sebastos* John, brother of the wife of the emperor

Correspondent: JOHN DOUKAS, *doux* of Dyrrachion, then *megas doux* (38); see also G17, ?G26

Date: ?summer 1091 or 1092 (Gautier: end 1092 beg. 1093)

Place: from Bulgaria to Hellas

Incipit: τίς ἄν μοι σχολήν

Editions: Gautier, II, 153-155; Finetti 5, 309-312; Lami 4, 511-4

Desinit: καὶ οἱ ἐχθροί σου χοῦν λείξουσι.

Message: to ask help for his relatives in Euripos (**113**)

Subject matter: praise of the recipient

Genre: panegyric

Structure: 1) opens with rhetorical conceit; 2) long tissue of quotations from Psalms, Isaiah, Luke and ICor., describing the benefits brought by JD to Bulgaria; 3) points out that he has praised God's gifts to JD in God's own words; 4) asks him to continue his benefits, specifically by helping Θ's relatives; 5) ends with prayer for JD's further glory.

Tone: adulatory   **Bearer:** ?
Length: 329   **Sent with:**?
Bibliography: Gautier, 'Diatribes,' 15; 'L'épiscopat,' 163-164; 'Défection,' 215-227; Roth, *Studie,* 14-15; Polemis, *Doukai,* 69, n.15; Katičić, 'Biographika,' 365, 372; Simeon, *Pismata,* viii, xii, 2-3, 193-195; Zlatarsky, 'Stellvertretende Verwalter,' 129; Panov, *Teofilakt,* 15, 234-235; Maslev, *Studia,* 19-23; Solarino, 'Un intellettuale,' 72.
Discussed above: 41, 86, 99, 169, 173, 201, **234,** 261.

G9, to the caesar
Correspondent: NIKEPHOROS MELISSENOS (44) (Maslev: Alexios I.) See also G13, G73
Date: before 1104 (Maslev: before 1005)   **Editions:** Gautier, II, 157-159; Lami 5,
Place: from Ochrid to ?   511-514
Incipit: δέσποτά μου ἅγιε   **Desinit:** ἀπειροπλάσιον τοῖς
φιλοτιμήμασι
Message: to thank the caesar for his efforts on Θ's   **Genre:** *parakletike*
behalf; to get the *kanonikon* of villages.   **Subject matter:** the *prostagma* on the
    kanonikon. Not the *prostaxis* of G96, G98.
Structure: 1) begins with address; 2) Θ has often praised NM for all his good works, in a balance of *beneficia,* but now the lightness of his words is outweighed by the greatness of the other's works; 3) the *prostagma* has been added on, like Pelion on Ossa; 4) NM's deeds vanquish even τὸν ἦν ὅτε δριμὺν ῥήτορα; 5) the ruler is an *eikon*; God the archetype; 6) Θ claims to hear a sweet voice speaking; 7) imagined conversation of NM and Θ, in which Θ is given the *kanonikon* of more villages; 7) God will lavishly reward NM.
Tone: enthusiastic   **Bearer:** ?
Length: 304   **Sent with:** ?
Bibliography: Simeon, *Pismata,* 195-197; Maslev, 'Melissenos,' 179-186; Papachryssanthou, 'Date,' 250-255; Guilland, *Recherches,* II, 25-43; Xanalatos, *Beiträge,* 31, 39; Litavrin, *Bolg. i Viz.,* 361; Panov, *Teofilakt,* 106; Maslev, *Studia,* 45-49, 133; Mullett, 'Patronage,' 135.
Discussed above: 99, 101, 125, 169, 205, 261.

G10, to the son of the *sebastokrator*
Correspondent: JOHN KOMNENOS, *doux* of Dyrrachion (42) also G11, G12, G19, G22, G23, G24, ?G61
Date: spring 1092   **Editions:** Gautier, II, 161; Lami 6, 513-
Place: from Ochrid to Dyrrachion?   514
Incipit: εὐλογητὸς ὁ θεός   **Desinit:** ὕψει σου ἀντιλαμβανόμενον
Message: to greet the new governor   **Genre:** adventus letter
Subject matter: formal
Structure: 1) praised be God for letters; 2) wishes JK good health; 3) he must help the poor and imitate God; 4) may God watch over him as he protects Θ's lowliness.
Tone: correct   **Bearer:** ?
Length: 185   **Sent with:** ?

Bibliography: Simeon, *Pismata*, 197; Roth, *Studie*, 12; Gautier, 'Diatribes,' 11-12; Xanalatos, *Beiträge*, 58; Panov, *Teofilakt*, 218; Maslev, *Studia*, 49-59, 133-134, 159, 184, 306, 527; Mullett, 'Patronage,' 136.
Discussed above: 27, 29, 38, 86, 97, 125, 146-147, 162, 169, 173, 177, 215.

G11, to the *sebastos kyr* John, the son of the *sebastokrator*

Correspondent: JOHN KOMNENOS (42), *doux* of Dyrrachion; see also G10, G12, G19, G22, G23, G24, ?G61

Date: ?spring (τῶν κυριακῶν τῆς ἀπόκρεω) ?1092   Editions: Gautier, II, 163-
Place: from Ochrid to Dyrrachion?   165; Lami 7, 513-516
Incipit: ἐπειδὴ Θεὸς τοῖς πτωχοῖς   Desinit: ἀνώτερον καὶ κακώσεως
Message: asks JK to take action   Genre: *parakletike*
Subject matter: a renegade hieromonk
Structure: 1) protect the poor; 2) behaviour of the hieromonk: sexual immorality; behaviour of the hieromonk: worse, he is involved with Iasites's (76) men; 3) Θ's attempt to deal with him has failed; now he asks JK to drive the demon out; JK must have pity on the poor and on the hieromonk's soul; he must be driven from these parts (if Θ catches him he'll expire in a tower as a public menace); 4) may God protect JK.

Tone: not over-hopeful   Bearer: ?
Length: 367   Sent with: ?

Bibliography: Gautier, 'Le synode,' 251; Roth, *Studie*, 11-12; Obolensky, *Bogomils*, 200, n.5; Simeon, *Pismata*, xxix, 197-199; Litavrin, *Bolg. i Viz.*, 318; 325; Maslev, *Studia*, 49-59; 134-135.
Discussed above: 19, 97, 106, 127, 130, 161, 169, 173, 263.

G12, to the same

Correspondent: JOHN KOMNENOS, *doux* of Dyrrachion (42); see also G10, G11, G19, G22, G23, G24, ?G61

Date: ?1090s; before G19   Editions: Gautier, II, 167-169; Lami 7,
Place: from Ochrid to Dyrrachion   515-518
Incipit: τῶν θείων ἀνδρῶν   Desinit: ἰχθύας ταρίχους ἑκατόν
Message: asks JK to issue a *pittakion*   Genre: *presbeutike*
Subject matter: Pologos case
Structure: 1) the gifts of divine men are not subject to second thoughts; 2) Θ puts the case for the monks of Pologos (113); why has JK subverted a *sigillion* of Alexios? 3) asks for a *pittakion*; JK must ensure that Θ's priests are not used by the so-called mediators for private services; 4) may God protect JK; gift of 100 (perfect number) sacred fish.

Tone: business-like, tough   Bearer: ?
Length: 319   Sent with: 100 salt fish

Bibliography: Simeon, *Pismata*, 200-204; Leroy-Molinghen, 'Prolégomènes,' 255-260; Dölger, *Regesten*, 1286; Roth, *Studie*, 12-13; Leroy-Molinghen, 'Trois mots slaves,' 116-117; Nikolaev, *Feodalni*, 45; Xanalatos, *Beiträge*, 41; Panov, *Teofilakt*, 84, 137, 189, 204; Maslev, *Studia*, 49-59; 135; 184; Papayanni, *Ta oikonomika*, 265, 268; 'Phorologikes plerophories,' 396-402; Mullett, 'Patronage,' 125-127; Harvey, 'The Land,' 150; Morris, *Monks and Laymen*, 261; Angold, *Church and Society*, 164.
Discussed above: 28, 86, 95, 97, 101, 106, 125, 128-129, 161, 169, 204.

G13, to the caesar Melissenos

Correspondent: NIKEPHOROS MELISSENOS (44) (*pace* Maslev, arguing that *basileia* would not be used of a caesar, but Gautier refutes). See also G9, G73

Date: before Lent 1091, recruiting before Pecheneg defeat of 29 April

Editions: Gautier, II, 171-173; Lami 9, 517-520

Place: from Ochrid to a nearby Vlach region

Incipit: δέσποτά μου ἅγιε

Desinit: ὡς δοῦλος ἀνάξιος

Message: greets NM and sends him fish

Genre: adventus letter

Subject matter: troubles, very vague

Structure: 1) NM is θέος ἐλευθέριος in Θ's βαρβαρῷ οἰκουμένῃ; a medicine, a tower of strength; 2) Θ hopes this letter will dissipate all his troubles; invites NM to take on his problems; 3) since it is Lent, the Theotokos sends the other 200 salted fish; the number is explained.

Tone: close to obsequious

Bearer: ?

Length: 217

Sent with: 200 salted fish

Bibliography: Simeon, *Pismata*, 204-205; Gautier, 'L'épiscopat,' 162; Maslev, 'Melissenos,' 179-186; Uspenskij, *Obrazobanie*, 25-26; Maslev, *Studie*, 45-46; 135-136; Mullett, 'Patronage,' 135, 'Slavs.'
Discussed above: 33, 86, 97, 106-107, 127, 169, 171, 177, 215, 260, 275.

G14, to the bishop of Kitros

Correspondent: N.N., bishop of KITROS (9); see also G52, G113, G121

Date: ?

Editions: Gautier, II, 175-177; Meurs 14, 381-382

Place: ?

Incipit: ὄντως τῷ πνευματικῷ

Desinit: ὑπὲρ ἡμῶν ἐξαιτούμενος.

Message: thanks the bishop for a gift

Genre: *eucharistike*

Subject matter: gift of rosewater and four fragrant sticks

Structure: 1) spiritual and worldly; 2) aspects of the bishop's gifts; symbolic interpretation; 3) may Θ, aided by the bishop's prayers, practise the teachings conveyed by the gifts; 4) ends with wish that bishop may not cease to pray for this.

Tone: friendly

Bearer: ?

Length: 305

Sent with: ?

Bibliography: Simeon, *Pismata*, 61-62; Maslev, *Studia*, 76-77.
Discussed above: 34, 81.

G15, to Diabologyres

Correspondent: N. DIABOLOGYRES, bishop of N (35)

Date: Easter, early 1090s (1090 if *sebastos* = John Doukas)

Editions: Gautier, II, 179-181; Lami 10, 519-520

Place: from ?Ochrid ?Ekklesiai to ?Diabolis

Incipit: εὖγε ὅτι προσθήκη

Desinit: ἀπὸ παντὸς ἐχθροῦ.

Genre: *syncharitike*

Message: request to make arrangements for liturgy

Subject matter: heresy

Structure: 1) Θ congratulates the bishop on Armenian conversions; 2) arrangements for dealing with converts: akolouthia, oil and priests; 3) Θ realises that his presence is sought but the *sebastos* (John Doukas? Komnenos?) is coming, perhaps to stay with him; so asks to be kept informed; 4) thanks the bishop for the gift of a horse; 5) asks if the bishop possesses the necessary akolouthia; if not Θ will have it copied; 6) the bishop must not cease attending to psalmody and the beauty of the church; 7) may God protect him from every enemy.

Tone: cheerful

Bearer: ?

Length: 316   **Sent with:** ?
Bibliography: Simeon, *Pismata*, 205-207; Gautier, 'L'épiscopat,' 164, n.33; Panov, *Teofilakt*, 312-313; Maslev, *Studia*, 136; Mullett, 'Patronage,' 130; Angold, *Church and Society*,170.
Discussed above: 97, 127, 173, 240, 263-264.

G16, to Tarchaneiotes

Correspondent: N. TARCHANEIOTES (21); see also G20, G43

Date: ?	**Editions:** Gautier, II, 183-185; Lami 11,
Place: ?	520-522
Incipit: ὄντως εἰκὼν ὁ λόγος	**Desinit:** μέγας ἀπόστολος ἐνετείλατο
Message: thanks for T's letters and advice on	**Genre:** *parainetike*
his attitude to wealth	**Subject matter:** heavenly and earthly riches

Structure: studded with quotations from Ps., NT, Eccle.; 1) Θ thanks T for his generous letter; 2) Θ queries his own credentials as adviser to T; 3) good and bad riches, cf. Job; 4) value of friends' words; 5) may God give aid to T.

Tone: encouraging	**Bearer:** ?
Length: 253	**Sent with:**?

Bibliography: Simeon, *Pismata*, 207-208; Gautier, 'Le synode,' 255.
Discussed above: 119, 123, 170, 176, 240.

G17, to the brother of the wife of the emperor, kyr John

Correspondent: JOHN DOUKAS, *Doux* of Dyrrachion, then *Megas Doux* (38) See also G8, ?G26

Date: spring 1092	**Editions:** Gautier, II, 187-189; Lami 12,
Place: from Pelagonia to somewhere further south	521-524
Incipit: Νῦν ἔγνωμεν οἷον	**Desinit:** σου χειρὶ ἀντιλαμβανόμενον
Message: to ask him to restrain Romanos	**Genre:** *parakletike*
Straboromanos (90)	**Subject matter:** Mogila case

Structure: 1) JD is the sun at which Θ closed his eyes; 2) he misses those virtues on account of which JD as sent by God (on account of Θ's sins he has departed); 3) he will govern Bulgaria again; 4) even though he is further south now, his rays still reach as far as Pelagonia where Θ is; 4) specific help requested against Straboromanos and a *sigillion* for the *aule* in Mogila; 5) like a true Doukas let him cleave to that goodness and generosity, from which Θ and his family would wish to benefit.

Tone: ceremonial but businesslike	**Bearer:** ?
Length: 364	**Sent with:** ?

Bibliography: Simeon, *Pismata*, 208-209; Gautier, 'L'épiscopat,' 172; 'Défection,' 215; Litavrin, 'Tmutorakan,' 228; Roth, *Studie*, 15; Zlatarsky, 'Stellvertretende Verwalter,' 144; Xanalatos, *Beiträge*, 58; Litavrin, *Bolg. i Viz.*, 83; Panov, *Teofilakt*, 81, 100, 146, 189; Maslev, *Studia*, 19-23; 137; Mullett, 'Patronage,' 125-127; Angold, *Church and Society*, 161.
Discussed above: 66, 84, 86, 94 125, 129, 173, 201-204, 205, 215, 2314, 264.

G18, to Taronitopoulos, the *doux* of Skopje

Correspondent: JOHN TARONITES, *doux* of Skopje (49)

Date: before 1094 (Diogenes crash)	**Editions:** Gautier, II, 191-193; Lami 13a,
Place: from ?Ochrid to ?Skopje	523-526
Incipit: Εἰ μὲν παραφρονήσαντα	**Desinit:** ὡς Ἡσαΐας εἶπεν, ἀθόλωτον

Message: answers the query of JT about an episcopal   **Genre:** *apologetike* + *aparnetike*
election
Subject matter: a lost letter; policy of appointing bishops; an election to Vidin
Structure: 1) begins provocatively by raising the possibility of Θ's madness; he would have had to
be mad not to reply to a letter of JT; 2) defends himself against the charge that he received the
missing *pittakia*, demanding that the bearers reveal to whom they gave the letter; swears by the
prayers of JT's holy mother that he did not receive it; 3) Θ's policy in appointing bishops;
acceptability of JT's choice: only Vidin is now vacant, but Θ cannot find a candidate wise in both
spiritual and worldly matters; 4) answers the criticisms that he had failed to write to the *proximos*
and failed to send his cleric; 5) who is doing the stirring? May God both chastise and heal him and
preserve JT as a river of peace.
Tone: emphatic   **Bearer:** ?
Length: 319   **Sent with:** ?
Bibliography: Simeon, *Pismata*, 209-212; Gautier, 'Le synode,' 236-237; Adontz, 'Taronites,' 583;
Leroy-Molinghen, 'Deux Jean Taronites,' 152; Dölger, *Regesten*, 1286; *Acta Albaniae*, 74; Leroy-
Molinghen, 'Prolégomènes,' 254; Litavrin, *Bolg. i Viz.*, 289, 338; Katičić, 'Biographika,' 375;
Banescu, *Les duchés*, 150, 160; Zlatarsky, 'Stellvertretende Verwalter,' 154; Katičić,
'Korespondencija,' 185; Panov, *Teofilakt*, 95, 171; Maslev, *Studia*, 59-63, 139, 239, 240; Obolensky,
Portraits, 78; Mullett, 'Patronage,' 131, 140; Angold, *Church and Society*, 166.
Discussed above: 36, 89, 101, 125, 128-129, 132, 173, 220, **263**, 265, 269.

G19

Correspondent: JOHN KOMNENOS, *doux* of Dyrrachion (**42**), identified by Leroy-Molinghen;
see also G10, G11, G12, G22, G23, G24, ?G61
Date: after G12; 1092-1097 or later   **Editions:** Gautier, II, 195; Lami 13b,
Place: from Ochrid to ?Dyrrachion   523-526
Incipit: missing (*pace* Gautier); first words are   **Desinit:** πρὸς αὐτὸν εἰρηνεύοντα
οἱ δ' ἐν τῷ Πολόγῳ
Message: to have JK's *pittakion* put into force   **Genre:** *presbeutike*
Subject matter: Pologos case
Structure: 1) Situation of the priests of Pologos (**113**) is no better than before; 2) Θ has already
made his position clear; 3) those who prevent JK acting are the enemies of goodness; 4) distinction
between clergy and common people must be observed; 5) may God guard JK in peace.
Tone: determined   **Bearer:** ?
Length: 118   **Sent with:** ?
Bibliography: Leroy-Molinghen, 'Prolégomènes,' 260; Maslev, *Studia*, 49-59; Papayanni, *Ta
oikonomika*, 267; ' Phorologikes plerophories,' 402; Harvey, 'The Land,' 150.
Discussed above: 101, 128-129, 173, 204.

G20, to Tarchaneiotes

Correspondent: N. TARCHANEIOTES (**21**); see also G16, ?G43
Date: ?   **Editions:** Gautier, II, 197; Lami 14, 525-
Place: ?   526
Incipit: καὶ τίς ἡμῶν   **Desinit:** τοῦ πνεύματός σου
Message: pastoral   **Genre:** *parainetike*
Structure: 1) happiness of Θ in serving a great man like T; 2) parable of the talents; the gift of
reason is like a coin with the imperial image; 3) Θ deposits his little coin with T for him to

multiply (the little coin is Ps 36:1: 'do not envy evildoers'); in this way he will have life; 4) ends with prayer.

Tone: imaginative, obscure **Bearer:** ?
Length: 250 **Sent with:** ?
Bibliography: Simeon, *Pismata*, 212-213.
Discussed above: 119, 153, 159, 176, 240.

G21, to the bishop of Pelagonia
Correspondent: N.N., bishop of PELAGONIA (10); see also G36, ?G63
Date: ? **Editions:** Gautier, II, 199-201; Lami 15,
Place: from Ochrid to ?Pelagonia 527-528
Incipit: ἐπυθόμην, τιμιώτατε ἀδελφέ **Desinit:** ἁγίου ἐπισκοπῇ ἐπισκέψαιτο
Message: to prepare the bishop and ask him to help **Genre:** briefing
the theme officials
Subject matter: changeover of *strategos* and *anagrapheus* in theme of Ochrid? Pelagonia?
Structure: (very straightforward quotations from OT and NT) 1) Θ has heard that there has been a shake-up in local government; 2) asks the bishop to give guidance to the Kritopouloi, especially Demetrios Kritopoulos (79); 3) the bishop's interests coincide with those of a new official; 4) may God give understanding and his blessing to the bishop.
Tone: matter-of-fact **Bearer:** ?
Length: 210 **Sent with:** ?
Bibliography: Simeon, *Pismata*, 213-214; Litavrin, *Bolg. i Viz.*, 300-301; Katičić, 'Korespondencija,' 187; Panov, *Teofilakt*, 85, 101; Maslev, *Studia*, 83, 141; Angold, *Church and Society*, 166.
Discussed above: 118, 130, 170, 173, 204, 199, 202, 215-220, 264.

G22, to the son of the *sebastokrator*
Correspondent: JOHN KOMNENOS (42), *doux* of Dyrrachion; see also G10, G11, G12, G19, G23, G24, ?G61
Date: 1090s **Editions:** Gautier, II, 203-205; Lami 16,
Place: from?Ochrid to Dyrrachion 533-536
Incipit: Παμμέγιστέ μου αὐθέντα **Desinit:** σὲ ποιῶν ἀκριβέστατον
Message: request for a *sigillion* **Genre:** *parakletike*
Subject matter: the abandonment and restoration of an ancient bishopric and church at Diabolis
Structure: 1) Θ thanks JK for his efforts in refreshing Prespa and Diabolis; 2) suggests he turn his hand to the church/bishopric at Diabolis, compared to the vine of Ps.79.9-19; 4) details observed by Θ on his inspection: no bishop, priest, deacon, music or light, no inhabitants; 5) request for *sigillion*; 6) the *doux* should be like Boris; 7) may God grant JK to be energetic and like his father.
Tone: lyrical description **Bearer:** ?
Length: 383 **Sent with:** ?
Bibliography: Simeon, *Pismata*, xxv, 214-216; Litavrin, *Bolg. i Viz.*, 80, 329; Pelekanides, *Prespa*, 69; Xanalatos, *Beiträge*, 37; 48; 75; Obolensky, *Bogomils*, 197; Roth, *Studie*, 11; Dölger, *Regesten* 1286; Katičić, 'Korespondencija,' 183; Nikolaev, *Feodalni*, 107; Panov, *Teofilakt*, 183; Maslev, *Studia*, 49-59; 141; Papayanni, *Ta oikonomika*, 265; 'Phorologikes plerophories,' 403; 405; 'Boulgaroi,' 64-65; Angold, *Church and Society*, 170; Mullett, 'Bishop-List.'
Discussed above: 55, 100, 101, 122, 125, 128, 169, 205, 215, **236-237**, 264.

G23, to the same

Correspondent: JOHN KOMNENOS, *doux* of Dyrrachion (42); see also G10, G11, G12, G19, G22, G24, ?G61

Date: soon after 1092
Place: from Ochrid to Dyrrachion
Editions: Gautier, II, 207; Lami 17, 531-532

Incipit: Δυσαπάλλακτον χρῆμα φιλόδικος ἄνθρωπος **Desinit:** ἐργαζόμενον θέλημα
Message: denunciation of Nicholas *ho tou Boutou* (93) **Genre:** *presbeutike*
Subject matter: lawsuit decided under John Doukas but revived by Nicholas
Structure: 1) begins bluntly; 2) explains the problem, 3) let Nicholas learn not to challenge good judgements; oral and documentary evidence will reveal the truth; let Nicholas be punished; 4) JK protects us; God protects and will always protect him.
Tone: business-like **Bearer:** ?
Length: 194 **Sent with:** ?
Bibliography: Simeon, *Pismata*, 216-217; Banescu, *Les duchés,* 156; Zlatarsky, 'Stellvertretende Verwalter,' 142; Maslev, *Studia*, 49-59, 151, 510.
Discussed above: 86, 129, 160, 169, 204.

G24, to the same

Correspondent: JOHN KOMNENOS, *doux* of Dyrrachion (42); see also G10, G11, G12, G19, G22, G23, ?G61

Date: 1093-94
Place: from ?Ochrid to Dyrrachion
Editions: Gautier, II, 209-211; Lami 18, 531-534

Incipit: ἴσως μὲν ὀχληρός **Desinit:** καὶ τὰ ἀνθρώπινα
Message: plea to the *doux* not to exploit Ochrid **Genre:** *presbeutike*
Subject matter: *ekbole ton pezon* at time of invasion of Serbs and Dalmatians
Structure: 1) beginning fragmentary? 2) Θ announces his embassy; 3) theme of O is so small it will disappear if made to carry such a burden; two other ambassadors; 4) sums up: O is the size of Mykonos not Pelagonia; 5) may the Theotokos look after JK.
Tone: eloquent **Bearer:** ?the two fellow-ambassadors?
Length: 276 **Sent with:** ?
Bibliography: Simeon, *Pismata*, 217; Xanalatos, *Beiträge*, 61; Ahrweiler, *Administration*, 88; Nikolaev, *Feodalni*, 109; Litavrin, *Bolg. i Viz.*, 320, 335; Panov, *Teofilakt*, 77; Maslev, *Studia*, 49-54, 142; Obolensky, *Portraits*, 58; Papayanni, 'Phorologikes plerophories,' 401; Angold, *Church and Society*, 164; Mullett, 'Slavs.'
Discussed above: 62, 67, 86, 125, 127, 169, 187, 201, 204, 269-271.

G25, to Mermentopoulos

Correspondent: NICHOLAS MERMENTOULOS (5); see also G29, G33, G47, G76
Date: ?
Place: ?
Editions: Gautier, II, 213; Lami 19, 533-534

Incipit: ἑορτή μοι τὰ πρὸς σὲ γράμματα **Desinit:** τῷ ἀγαθῷ ὁδηγῶν
Message: communication **Genre:** request for letters
Subject matter: letter-exchange
Structure: 1) it is a feast to send letters to NM and a greater one to hear from him; 2) let NM's letters guide Θ to Kalliope's hearth and rescue him from the tyranny of *amousia*; 3) NM has charmed Θ with his words in the past; may Θ be similarly charmed while they are apart; 4) let NM bestow honey from Hymettos on Θ who will thank him; 4) may the Lord protect him.

Subject matter: letter-exchange
Tone: brilliant   **Bearer:** ?
Length: 184   **Sent with:** ?
Bibliography: Simeon, *Pismata*, 218; Nikolaev, *Feodalni*, 55, 142; Panov, *Teofilakt*, 533; Solarino, 'Un intellettuale,' 72.
Discussed above: 28, 34, 118, 123, 178, 269-271, 275.

G26, to the *sebastos*, the son of the *sebastokrator*

Correspondent: Gautier suggests JOHN DOUKAS, *doux* of Dyrrachion, then *Megas Doux* (**38**)
See also G8, G17.
Date: ?1089-1092?   **Editions:** Gautier, II, 215-217; Lami 20,
Place: from ?Ochrid to ?Dyrrachion   533-536
Incipit: ἐγὼ δὲ καί   **Desinit:** ὡς οἶδας, ἡμέτερον
Message: request for clarification and mediation with **Genre:** *parakletike*
the emperor over church property   **Subject matter:** ?Mogila case?
Structure: 1) Θ had been asked to intercede on behalf of others with the emperor, but is himself in difficulties; 2) a village long owned by the church has been confiscated by the emperor; 3) he does not argue about the village, but does not accept that the emperor issued a *prostaxis* which dealt with the *hospition* or the *aule*; 4) has sent off bearer; let the *prostaxis* be read out; 5) since the land does not appear to belong to the church *zeugologion* will be paid; a reference to mote, beam, gnat and camel (Matt. 7.3; 23.24); challenges the other to carry out the order about the *aule;* 6) may the Theotokos (proprietress of the land and the *aule*) guard JD.
Tone: business-like   **Bearer:** ὁ παρὼν ἄνθρωπος
Length: 284   **Sent with:** ?
Bibliography: Simeon, *Pismata*, 218-219; Nikolaev, *Feodalni*, 72; Xanalatos, *Beiträge*, 30, 58; Litavrin, *Bolg. i Viz.*, 84, 147; Panov, *Teofilakt*, 82, 109; Maslev, *Studia*, 49-59; Papayanni, 'Phorologikes plerophories,' 405; Mullett, 'Patronage,' 129; Solarino, 'Un intellettuale,' 78; Harvey, 'The Land,' 151; Angold, *Church and Society,* 164.
Discussed above: 86, 101, 125, 169, 173, 199, 204, 261.

G27, to Kamateropoulos

Correspondent: GREGORY KAMATEROS (**4**); see also G31, G38, G67, G127, ?G115, ?G116
Date: after the death of Psellos (?1078 ?1097)   **Editions:** Gautier, II, 219-221; Meurs
Place: ?   15, 385-386
Incipit: εἰ καὶ θανόντων   **Desinit:** κακίας τε καὶ κακώσεως
Message: request to GK to give the bearer a job   **Genre:** *systatike*
Subject matter: death of Psellos (**84**)
Structure: 1) Θ quotes Hom., *Il.*, 22.389; 2) Θ owes a great deal to Psellos; 3) recommends the unhappy bearer who is Psellos's grandson; 4) Θ could not fail to help; 5) asks GK's help; 6) may God protect him.
Tone: reminiscent   **Bearer:** Psellos's grandson
Length: 287   **Sent with:** ?
Bibliography: Gautier, 'Monodie inédite,' 159-164; Katičić, 'Biographika,' 365; Simeon, *Pismata*, x, 62-63; Panov, *Teofilakt*, 14-17; Cheynet, *Pouvoir et contestations*, 256; Solarino, 'Un intellectuale,' 64
Discussed above: 49, 81, 84, **136**, 201.

G28, to Smyrnaios

Correspondent: THEODORE SMYRNAIOS (20), see Leroy-Molinghen. See also G6, G95
Date: before 1094-5 (then protoproedros)   **Editions:** Gautier, II, 223; Meurs 16,
Place: ?   385-388; Lami 21, 535-536
Incipit: μὴ καὶ τὴν γλῶτταν   **Desinit:** ἀνθρώπων ἐμοὶ χαριέστατε
Message: enquiry about the other's *agraphia*;   **Genre:** *philike*
expression of anxiety about his brother
Subject matter: Theodore's education of Demetrios; friendship
Structure: 1) pleasantry about TS's gout and complaint about τῶν νῦν καιρῶν; 2) Θ is delighted
with TS's teaching of Demetrios and hopes he will have favoured treatment; 3) he would like TS to
treat Demetrios as he himself treated Paul, TS's brother; 4) ends with cheerful good wish and
address.
Tone: friendly   **Bearer:** ?
Length: 208   **Sent with:** ?
Bibliography: Simeon, *Pismata*, 220-221; Gautier, 'L'épiscopat,' 165; Leroy-Molinghen,
'Destinataire,' 435; Katičić, 'Biographika,' 371.
Discussed above: 81, 99, 136, 174, 176, 177, 246, 261.

G29, to Mermentoulos

Correspondent: NICHOLAS MERMENTOULOS (5); see also G25, G33, G47,G76
Date: after mid-1092 (career)   **Editions:** Gautier, II, 225-227; Meurs18,
Place: from Bulgaria   389-392
Incipit: οὐ τίς τοι θεός εἰμι   **Desinit:** ἐργοῖς ἐμοὶ πανυπέρλαμπρε
Message: literary communication and guidance   **Genre:** *pros philon aspastike*; plays with
                                                       epic, tragedy, pastoral
Subject matter: literature; *praktores*
Structure: 1) begins with quotation from *Od.*; disputes NM's high assessment of his literary skills;
2) the *praktores* are harpies who have snatched up his books; 3) let NM give himself to reading
philosophy, the *Iliad*, tragedy and comedy, without negecting pastoral (even if his Muses
disapprove of its eroticism); 4) but he must also feed on the bible and Fathers; 5) let him join in
praying that he does not forget Greek; 6) may he hear and see NM again; 7) ends with form of
address.
Tone: light, complex, brilliant   **Bearer:** ?
Length: 365   **Sent with:** ?
Bibliography: Simeon, *Pismata*, 66-68; Litavrin, *Bolg. i Viz.*, 241; Polemes, 'Paratereseis,' 377;
Solarino, 'Un intellettuale,' 72.
Discussed above: 81, 101, 118, 131, **134**, 170, 269-271, 274.

G30, to the *chartophylax kyr* Nikephoros

Correspondent: NIKEPHOROS *chartophylax* (23); see also G51, G66, G74, G124, ??G83
Date: before 1094 (ex-*chartophylax*); Maslev: 1107-08 **Editions:** Gautier, II, 229-231; Lami 22,
Place: from Ochrid to ?CP   535-538
Incipit: ἐκ τῆς ἐπιπόνου   **Desinit:** τὴν ἡμετέραν ἀσθενείαν
Message: there is no obvious *hegoumenos* at the **Genre:** briefing
monastery; Θ has everything in hand   **Subject matter:** the *hagioserretai* (114)

Structure: 1) Θ has just returned from a long journey to an army camp; 2) he has received a letter from N; 3) complains about Bulgaria; 4) does not know how to deal with the question of the *hagioserretai;* let N fight the good fight.

Tone: intimate   **Bearer:** ?
Length: 260   **Sent with:** ?
Bibliography: Simeon, *Pismata*, 221-222; Gautier, 'Le synode,' 281; Maslev, 'Melissenos,' 182, n.21; Gautier, 'Chartophylax,' 163; Maslev, *Studia*, 75-76, 143; Morris, *Monks and Laymen*, 151.
Discussed above: 27, 84, 97, 125, **129**, 170, 269, 274.

G31, to Kamateros

Correspondent: GREGORY KAMATEROS (4); see also G27, G38, G67, G127, ?G115, ?G116
Date: ?1093-95? (campaigns; Gautier: spring)   **Editions:** Gautier, II, 233-235; Lami 23,
Place: from Ochrid to ?in Bulgaria?   537-540
Incipit: οὐ παύσεταί ποτε   **Desinit:** κακίας ἀνώτερον καὶ κακώσεως
Message: request for help with his fiscal problem **Genre:** *parakletike*
Subject matter: Ekklesiai case
Structure: 1) Θ, under pressure from a 'murderer' has come through fire and water; Homer and Hesiod have words relevant to his situation; 2) image of a stormy voyage through the sea of taxation threatened by a eunuch (Scylla or Charybdis) and a hurricane (Acts 27.14); God has given him GK to save his ship; 3) Distress when he learned of the tax-assessment of the village; 4) Θ cannot come to see GK until after the synod at Hagios Achilleios is over; 5) may God who has given GK the power to help Θ increase it and guard him.

Tone: worried   **Bearer:** ?
Length: 420   **Sent with:** ?
Bibliography: Simeon, *Pismata*, 222-223; Pelekanides, *Prespa*, 65; Litavrin, *Bolg. i Viz.*, 82, 88-89; Maslev, *Studia*, 65-68, 143-145; Mullett, 'Patronage,' 125-127; Angold, *Church and Society,* 161, 168; Mullett, 'Bishop-List.'
Discussed above: 18, 56, 66, 89-91, 95-96, 124, 130, 160-161, 170, 171, 173, 175, 197, 213, 220.

G32 to Anemas

Correspondent: NICHOLAS ANEMAS (2); see also G34, G41
Date: ?   **Editions:** Gautier, II, 237-239; Meurs 19,
Place: ? within Bulgaria   391-392, Lami 24, 539-542;
Incipit: φίλον λόγου θέλγητρον   **Desinit:** ἀνώτερον καὶ κακώσεως
Message: welcome to NA and request for help for **Genre:** adventus with included *systatike*
Constantine Choirosphaktes (**75**)
Subject matter: arrival of new governor (acquaintance of Θ)
Structure: 1) begins with adapted quotation of Eur. *Or.*, 211-212; adds Ar. *Pl.*, 288 and then a tissue of psalms and Isaiah to indicate triumph and joy at NA's arrival; Θ's enemies are put to flight; 2) three of these are picked out; Θ will proclaim NA's success; 3) please help poor simple Constantine Choirosphaktes (**75**) (joke?); 4) ends with usual prayer.

Tone: jubilant   **Bearer:** just possibly CC
Length: 267 in longer version   **Sent with:** ?
Bibliography: Simeon, *Pismata*, 68-70, 223-224; Xanalatos, *Beiträge*, 70; Gautier, 'Le synode,' Maslev, *Studia*, 36-37, 109-110; Mullett, 'Classical Tradition,' 92-93; Papayanni,'Phorologikes plerophories,' 397.
Discussed above: 18, 34, 36, 81, 125, 127, 136, **147-148**, 154, 159, 178.

G33, to Mermentoulos

Correspondent: NICHOLAS MERMENTOULOS (5); see also G25, G29, G47, G76
Date: ?
Place: ?
Incipit: εἰ μὲν ἔγνως
Message: request for letters
Subject matter: communication

Editions: Gautier, II, 241; Lami 25, 541-542
Desinit: ἔχω τοῦ ᾄσματος
Genre: *antalepistalike*

Structure: 1) Θ praises NM's letters; 2) whether Θ is happy or unfortunate, NM should write; 3) since NM is so busy let him just strike up the music and Θ will perfom the whole song.
Tone: fanciful
Length: 149
Bibliography: Simeon, *Pismata*, 225.
Discussed above: 29, 30, 106-107, 178.

Bearer: ?
Sent with: ?

G34, to Anemas

Correspondent: NICHOLAS ANEMAS (2); see also G32, G41
Date: late in collection: τοσούτων ἐτῶν; after G32 and before G41
Place: within Bulgaria
Incipit: τὸ ἐμὸν ὄναρ μοι λέγεις
Message: encouragement; exchange of books
Subject matter: barbarism; learning

Editions: Gautier, II, 243; Meurs 21, 395-396; Lami 26, 41-544
Desinit: μετὰ τῆς πράξεως
Genre: *paratharryntike*

Structure: 1) begins with *Par.gr.*, II, 565 (also used by Julian, ep. 45); 2) the cups of rusticity and wisdom; Solomon and the Song of Songs; wisdom hides herself from Θ, who is an unhappy lover and in danger of becoming a *mythos*, Echo's lover or Tantalos; contrast between Θ who has been in Bulgaria a long time and NA, who still has the voices of the wise in his ears; 3) sends him a copy of Chrysostom; 4) may Christ, the source of wisdom, give NA understanding and strengthen him on the road.
Tone: friendly, sparkling
Length: 227

Bearer: ?
Sent with: a work of Chrysostom

Bibliography: Katičić, 'Biographika,' 366; Simeon, *Pismata*, xxiii, 63-64, 71-73; Maslev, *Studia*, 36-37; Mullett, 'Classical Tradition,' 92-93; Papayanni, 'Boulgaroi,' 64-65; Mullett, 'Patronage,' 129; Solarino,'Un intellettuale,' 72-3; Mullett, 'Slavs.'
Discussed above: 81, 161, 171, 178, 274, **275-276**.

G35, to Chrysoberges, metropolitan of Naupaktos

Correspondent: N. CHRYSOBERGES, metropolitan of NAUPAKTOS (26)
Date: ?
Place: from ?Ochrid to Naupaktos
Incipit: διήλθομεν διὰ πυρός (also G31)
Message: share troubles; Θ's advice to him on relations with C's brother Nicholas (74)
Subject matter: episcopal troubles and family relations

Editions: Gautier, II, 245-247; Lami 27, 543-546
Desinit: τοῦ ἐξαιρεῖσθαί σε
Genre: *schetliastike+parainetike*

Structure: 1) Θ has come through fire and water with C's help; 2) he asks C to rejoice with him and to pray that God's goodness may remain with them; 3) when Θ is in Kanina he will visit C; 4) Θ had wanted to advise him to be kind to his brother, but was embarrassed; he is confident that C will act with fraternal concern; 5) asks for C's prayers; 6) may the Lord be with him.

Tone: neutral
Length: 332
Bibliography: *Acta Albaniae*, 71; Simeon, *Pismata*, 226-227; Maslev, *Studia*, 18, 145; Mullett, 'Classical Tradition,' 92-93; Obolensky, *Portraits*, 79; Angold, *Church and Society*, 168.
Discussed above: 55, 98, 129, 174, 176, 197, 231.

Bearer: ?
Sent with: ?

G36, to the bishop of Pelagonia

Correspondent: N.N., bishop of PELAGONIA (10); see also G21, ?G63
Date: ?
Place: from ?Ochrid to ?Pelagonia
Incipit: ὁ τοῦ Θεοῦ
Message: pastoral
Subject matter: reading

Editions: Gautier, II, 249-251; Lami 28, 545-546
Desinit: κακίας σκότους ἀνώτερον
Genre: *parainetike*

Structure: 1) the miracle of letters; 2) begs the bishop to attend to the work in hand, the zealous preaching of the Divine Word; 3) replies to the complaint that the message of the Scriptures is obscure; 4) the disciples asked questions and received illumination; it is necessary now to open one's eyes in active reading and receive illumination even if partial; 5) the bishop must not disdain the lamp of divine law, and must keep himself above the darkness of evil.

Tone: hortatory
Length: 451
Bibliography: Simeon, *Pismata*, 227-228; Obolensky, *Portraits*, 79.
Discussed above: 29, 39, 101-102, 118, 173, 240, 263.

Bearer: ?
Sent with: ?

G37, to the *hegoumenos* of the monastery of Anaplous, *kyr* Symeon

Correspondent: SYMEON, *hegoumenos* (29)
Date: ?after synod of Blachernai
Place: Ochrid to ?Kyr Philotheos
Incipit: καὶ πῶς ἂν τὸν παρόντα
Message: communication

Editions: Gautier, II, 253-257; Lami 29, 547-550
Desinit: ἁγίων ἐν φωτί
Genre: mixed

Subject matter: the ex-*hegoumenos*, the ὁσιώτατος καὶ τρισμάκαρ πατήρ
Structure: 1) how could Θ have overlooked the present bearer? he was delighted to see him and to hear the news, especially about the ex-*hegoumenos*; 2) had been worried when the ex-*hegoumenos* became a recluse and feared for the monastery, but rejoiced to hear of his death—a reaction which provoked the ribaldry of Θ's circle; 3) tells in general but graphic terms of his troubles; 4) needs the community's prayers; 5) sends greetings to the monks; 6) may Symeon present his monks to the Father.

Tone: affectionate

Length: 341
Bibliography: Simeon, *Pismata*, 228-231; Nikolaev, *Feodalni*, 54; Xanalatos, *Beiträge*, 55, 59; Maslev, *Studia*, 44, 145-147; Mullett, 'Classical Tradition,' 92-93; Obolensky, *Portraits*, 78; Mullett, 'Patronage,' 129; Solarino,'Un intellettuale,' 73; 78.
Discussed above: 35, 38-39, 83, 124-125, 132, 139, **143**, 170, 173, 174, 176, 274.

Bearer: monk of Anaplous; also carried G52?

Sent with: ?

G38, to kyr Gregory Kamateros

Correspondent: GREGORY KAMATEROS (4); see also G27, G31, G67, G127, ?G115, ?G116

Date: ?after G31 ?1093-5
Place: ?within Bulgaria?
Incipit: εἶδον ἐγὼ πατέρας Αἰθίοπας
Message: apology and reproach
Subject matter: ?Ekklesiai affair

Editions: Gautier, II, 259-261; Lami 30, 549-552
Desinit: καταφυγὴ καὶ κραταίωμα
Genre: *apologetike*

Structure: 1) Fond Ethiopian fathers and judges who are excessively attached to ther own verdicts offer an analogy to GK; 2) he must be brave in the face of Θ's enemies; 3) Θ did not try to prevent GK referring the question of the *chorion* to the emperor—unless his demand to have the *praxis* registered had this effect; 4) after that Θ hugged the *hypomnesis* to himself with delight; whoever GK believes to be responsible for his present embarrassments, he must gird himself against Θ's enemies; 6) it would have been better if GK had written earlier what he has now written to Θ; 7) ends with prayer.

Tone: querulous
Length: 341

Bearer: ?
Sent with: ?

Bibliography: Simeon, *Pismata*, 232-233; Maslev, *Studia*, 65-68; Harvey, 'The Land,' 149.
Discussed above: 95-96, 101, 169, 213.

G39, to kyr Michael Pantechnes

Correspondent: MICHAEL PANTECHNES (7); see also G48, G50, ?G94, G99, G102, G128, G129, G130, G131, ??G115, ??G116

Date: after G120 if that is to John: 1108+
Place: from ?Ochrid to ?CP
Incipit: οἴμοι ὅτι ἀπόλωλεν
Message: consolation for Michael
Subject matter: the death of his father John

Editions: Gautier, II, 263-265; Lami 31, 551-554
Desinit: τῆς ἐκεῖθεν πιότητος
Genre: *paramythetike*

Structure: 1) begins with exclamation of grief; 2) the virtues of the dead man; 3) too much weeping is bad; MP should rejoice that his father has reached heaven; 4) MP should make recompense, by bearing fruit, to God the gift of his father John.

Tone: respectfully ceremonial
Length: 495

Bearer: ?
Sent with: ?

Bibliography: Gautier, *Michel Italikos*, 47; Katičić, 'Biographika,' 385; Simeon, *Pismata*, xxxiii, 233-234; Polemes, 'Paratereseis,' 377, 379.
Discussed above: 138-139, **144**, 175, 185.

G40, to kyr Niketas Polites

Correspondent: NIKETAS POLITES, bishop of N (18)

Date: ?
Place: Ochrid to unknown see
Incipit: οἴκοθεν οἴκαδε, παρ' ἡμῶν
Message: plea to NP to look after the bishop
Subject matter: troubles of the bishop of Glavenitsa (100)

Editions: Gautier, II, 267; Lami 32, 553-556
Desinit: ἀνώτερον καὶ κακώσεως
Genre: *systatike*

Structure: 1) echoes Pind. *Od*.6.99 (cf. Libanios, ep. 149); low morale of the bishop; 2) Θ has held out hope of help from NP; let there be no disappointment; 3) urges NP to a labour of Hercules in cleaning up Koprinista for 'our brother'; 4) NP will remember this as a good deed to a good man; 5) ends with the usual prayer.

Tone: neutral   Bearer: bishop of Glavenitsa
Length: 195   Sent with: ?
Bibliography: *Acta Albaniae*, 70; Simeon, *Pismata*, 234-236; Maslev, *Studia*, 148.
Discussed above: 128, 137, 173, 265.

G41, to Anemas
Correspondent: NICHOLAS ANEMAS (2); see also G32, G34
Date: after G32 and G34   Editions: Gautier, II, 269; Lami 33,
Place: within Bulgaria   55-556
Incipit: ἀληθῶς μὲν ἀνιᾶται   Desinit: ἀνώτερος καὶ κακώσεως
Message: farewell   Genre: *propemptikon*
Subject matter: friendship; the departure of NA
Structure: 1) a friend parted from his beloved is upset, but his heart is torn when he thinks he was
on the point of embracing him; 2) quotes Epicharmos on seeing and hearing with the mind; this is
better and NA should embrace it; 3) God does not always bring about what is expected; his will
prevails, quoting Isa.14:27; 5) wishes him well on return to γλυκείᾳ πατρίδι καὶ τοῖς φιλτάτοις;
6) ends with usual prayer.
Tone: very affectionate   Bearer: ?
Length: 147   Sent with: ?
Bibliography: Simeon, *Pismata*, 236; Maslev, *Studia*, 34-37, 150.
Discussed above: 121, 183, 215.

G42, to Theophylaktos Romaios
Correspondent: THEOPHYLACT ROMAIOS (19); see also G46
Date: ? = G46, ??G69, G71   Editions: Gautier, II, 271-273; Lami 34,
Place: ?Ochrid to CP   555-558
Incipit: Αὐτὸς δὲ οὐχ ἅπαξ   Desinit: ἀνώτερον καὶ κακώσεως
Message: complaints of silence   Genre: *philike*
Subject matter: philosophy and rhetoric; letter-writing
Structure: 1) Not a word from TR; silence is all right if he is a Pythagorean, but not if he studies
the Peripatetics; 2) he seems to be treating Θ, his old teacher, as Aristotle did Plato; 3) TR's possible
excuses for not writing: business, and indirect communication through the letters of John (*maistor*
(30)? *philosopher* (31)? Opheomachos (6)?); 4) Θ will not accuse TR of the crime against *philia* and
logoi if he keeps writing to John, for Θ's people will benefit; 5) may God, the father of wisdom,
keep TR (usual prayer).
Tone: light, didactic   Bearer: ?
Length; 346   Sent with: ?
Bibliography: Simeon, *Pismata*, 236-238; Maslev, *Studia*, 39-40.
Discussed above: 28, 93, 99, 159, 177.

G43, to the same (but see below)
Correspondent: too grand for Theophylact Romaios (19). Tarchaneiotes(21)?
Date: ?   Editions: Gautier, II, 275; Lami 35, 557-
Place: ?   558
Incipit: ἀεί μοι τὸν πόθον ἀνάπτεις   Desinit: ἀνώτερος καὶ κακώσεως
Message: communication; thanks for beneficia?   Genre: *parainetike*

Subject matter: spiritual progress
Structure: 1) Θ tells the other that he always kindles his desire because he is always surpassing himself in   goodness; 2) the ladder of Jacob: the present a step to the future; 3) urges the other to greater spiritual heights; 4) God will not overlook his goodness; 5) usual prayer.

Tone: encouraging; grateful   **Bearer:** ?
Length: 133   **Sent with:** ?
Bibliography: Simeon, *Pismata*, 238; Maslev, *Studia*, 39-40.
Discussed above: 29, 170, 178

G44, to Machetares
Correspondent: N. MACHETARES (13)

Date: early   **Editions:** Gautier, II, 277-279; Finetti 3,
Place: from Bulgaria   311-314
Incipit: εἰ ὁ Θεὸς ἀγάπη ἐστίν   **Desinit:** ἀνώτερον καὶ κακώσεως
Message: consolidate friendship, but...   **Genre:** (negative) reply to request
Subject matter: friendship, *barbarismos*
Structure: 1) love letters, the ladder of Jacob and the golden chain of Homer; letters lead friends to God; 2) problems of *barbarismos*; 3) tells M, the Platonist, to avoid *ta theia* and scrutinising the human soul and asks him to be a friend within these limits; 4) usual prayer
Tone: eloquent   **Bearer:** ?
Length: 300   **Sent with:** ?
Bibliography: Simeon, *Pismata*, xxiii, 3-4; Snegarov, *Archiepiskopiia*, 202; Maslev, *Studia*, 17, 92; Polemes, 'Paratereseis,' 377; Solarino, 'Un intellettuale,' 73; Mullett, 'Slavs.'
Discussed above: 29-30, 119, 123, 269-271.

G45, to the patriarch
Correspondent: NICHOLAS KYRDINIATES, patriarch NICHOLAS III GRAMMATIKOS (43); see also G54, G64

Date: ? (Gautier :1097-1105, = G96 = G98)   **Editions:** Gautier, II, 281-287; Finetti 4,
Place: ?Ochrid to ?CP   313-317
Incipit: πῶς ἐτόλμησας, φαίη ἄν τις   **Desinit:** πρεσβείαις, πανάγιε δέσποτα
Message: request for prayers in trouble with *demosion*   **Genre:** *parakletike*
Subject matter: ceremony and *parresia*; Θ 's problems
Structure: 1) prepares the ground by asking himself how he dare address one so great: he can because the patriarch is father as well as lord and understands the problems of being an archbishop; 2) detailed account of his difficulties; 3) specific complaints against praktors, cf. task-masters of Pharaoh; 4) Job and Jeremiah set the tone for general self-pity and insistence on helplessness; 5) asks for the patriarch's prayers; 6) apologises for the length of the letter; 7) may the Lord give relief in response to the patriarch's prayers for all; final vocative.
Tone: self-pitying and eloquent   **Bearer:** ?
Length: 980   **Sent with:** ?
Bibliography: Xanalatos, *Beiträge*, 53, 61; Simeon, *Pismata*, xxviii-xxix, 4-7; Nikolaev, *Feodalni*, 85; Litavrin, *Bolg. i Viz.*, 331; Panov, *Teofilakt*, 78, 99, 111; Maslev, *Studia*, 25-26; 92-94; Papayanni, 'Phorologikes plerophories,' 397, 405; Polemes, 'Paratereseis,' 377-378; Solarino,'Un intellettuale,' 78.
Discussed above: 17, 106, 125-126, 149-150, 154, 170.

G46, to Romaios

Correspondent: THEOPHYLACT ROMAIOS (19); see also G42

Date: ?

Place: probably from Bulgaria to CP

Incipit: ἐκκεκώφηκέ μοι τὰ ὦτα

Message: communication

Subject matter: friendship, philosophy

Editions: Gautier, II, 289-291; Finetti 5, 317-320

Desinit: ἀνώτερον καὶ κακώσεως

Genre: *pros philon aspastike*

Structure: 1) John has deafened Θ with praise of TR; 2) mesh of quotations from Hesiod, Pindar, Plato, Homer: good influence of philosophy on TR; 3) he must be the right kind of philosopher; 4) may the Logos of God enlighten him and (usual prayer).

Tone: light, brilliant, complex

Length: 264

Bearer: ?

Sent with: ?

Bibliography: Simeon, *Pismata*, 7-8; Maslev, *Studia,* 39-40; 94; Mullett, 'Classical Tradition,' 92-93; 'Patronage,' 129.

Discussed above: 93, 99, 173, 178, 186.

G47, to Mermentopoulos

Correspondent: NICHOLAS MERMENTOULOS (5); see also G25, G29, G33, G76

Date: ? (Gautier: 1093-94; Maslev: 1090-92)

Place: probably from Bulgaria to CP

Incipit: περὶ ἐμοῦ δ' οὐδεὶς λόγος

Message: request for a letter

Subject matter: *sige*

Editions: Gautier, II, 293; Finetti 6, 319-320

Desinit: σῴζειν τὸν Νέστορα

Genre: request for letter

Structure: 1) quotes Arist., *Frogs*, 87: not a word about me! this applies to NM who has left Θ dry and withered; 2) why? mistrust of Θ's rusticity? 3) legal conceit; 5) quotes Hom., *Il.,* 8.104, with a significant change.

Tone: light, brilliant

Length: 147

Bearer: ?

Sent with:?

Bibliography: Simeon, *Pismata*, 8; Maslev, *Studia*, 18; Mullett, 'Patronage,' 129; 'Slavs.'

Discussed above: 160, 173.

G48, to kyr Michael Pantechnes

Correspondent: MICHAEL PANTECHNES (7); see also G39, G50, ?G94, G99, G102, G128, G129, G130, G131, ??G115, ??G116

Date:?

Place: from Ochrid

Incipit: ἐρωτᾷς πῶς ἔχει τὰ ἡμέτερα

Message: reply to query about his health; grumbles

Editions: Gautier, II, 295; Finetti 7, 321-322

Desinit: πᾶσιν ἱλαρωτέροις ἀνάπαυσιν

Genre: *schetliake*

Subject matter: Θ's ill-health; problems in three corners of archdiocese

Structure: 1) question and answer; 2) enlarges on physical misfortunes; 3) troubles of people and church in Glavenitsa, Vidin and Sthlanitsa; 4) none of the physicians of myth is to hand; 5) hopes MP is in easier circumstances; 6) may God give relief to Θ and happy rest to MP.

Tone: vehemently complaining, but still wordplay

Length: 198

Bearer: ?

Sent with: ?

Bibliography: Simeon, *Pismata*, xxx, 9; *Acta Albaniae*, 69; Xanalatos, *Beiträge*, 60; Maslev, *Studia*, 28-32, 94; Obolensky, *Portraits*, 54; Papayanni, 'Phorologikes plerophories,' 401; 'Boulgaroi,' 64-65; Angold, *Church and Society*, 168; Mullett, 'Slavs.'
Discussed above: 96-97, 102, 107, 126, 132, 272.

G49, to kyr John Serblias

Correspondent: JOHN SERBLIAS (47)

Date: ? late (not Adontz: 1091-92; Gautier: 1093-94)　Editions: Gautier, II, 297; Finetti 8, 321-322

Place: from ?Bulgaria to ?CP

Incipit: Σὺ δέ, ὁ καλός　Desinit: τὰ καλὰ ἀμελείας

Message: attempt to persuade JS to show the letter to　Genre: *parakletike*
Gregory Taronites (48) and get a *pittakion* from him　Subject matter: the election to Vodena

Structure: 1) the actions of JS are calculated to confirm Θ's strictures; 2) he must not honour friendship like this, but must desire for his friend what he desires for himself; 3) he must not destroy the *dikaiomata* he is given; 4) he should give Gregory Taronites the decree about Vodena and ask for a *pittakion* telling the governor of Veroia what to do; 5) if the decree has been issued he must still do this, if not, he must be sure he is in no danger from failing through excessive speed (sarcasm, presumably); 6) may JS be guarded by the Lord from the traps of the devil and from carelessness with regard to the good.

Tone: caustic; businesslike　Bearer: ?

Length: 174　Sent with: ?

Bibliography: Simeon, *Pismata*, 9; Adontz, 'Observations,' 407-413; Laurent, 'Bulles métriques," *Hellenika* 7 (1934), 291; Gautier, 'Le synode,' 236; Adontz, 'L'archevêque,' 584; Leroy-Molinghen, 'Deux Jean Taronites,' 152; Maslev, *Studia*, 27-28; Mullett, 'Madness of Genre,' 240-243.
Discussed above: 28, 101, 130, 170, 177, 205, 212.

G50, to Pantechnes

Correspondent: MICHAEL PANTECHNES (7); see also G39, G48, ?G94, G99, G102, G128, G129, G130, G131, ??G115, ??G116

Date: ? (Gautier: 1093/4; Maslev: 1100)　Editions: Gautier, II, 299; Finetti 9, 323-324

Place: from Ochrid to ?CP

Incipit: ἀλλ' οἴ γε 'Αχριδιῶται μέλος ἐμόν　Desinit: ἑκάτερος ἐναποσταλάξαντες

Message: communication　Genre: *pros filon aspastike*

Subject matter: Θ and the people of Ochrid

Structure: 1) the insensitivity and ignorance of the people of Ochrid; Θ's loquacity and madness; 2) advice and good wishes for MP; 4) those whom MP greeted warmly reciprocate.

Tone: intimate　Bearer: ?

Length: 73　Sent with:?

Bibliography: Simeon, *Pismata*, 10; Maslev, *Studia*, 28-32, 94-95; Solarino, 'Un intellettuale,' 73; Mullett, 'Slavs.'
Discussed above: 269-271.

G51, to the *chartophylax kyr* Nikephoros

Correspondent: NIKEPHOROS *chartophylax* (23); see also G30, G66, G124, ??G83

Date: 1089-95; before synod of Blachernai　Editions: Gautier, II, 301; Finetti 10, 323-324

Place: ?

Incipit: Εἰ καὶ ὁ ἐχθρός   **Desinit:** τῶν πονηρῶν πράξεων
Message: asks him to continue to pray for and advise Θ**Genre:** *parakletike*
Subject matter: an unknown crisis
Structure: simple: 1) the devil is loose in God's holy place (Ps.73.3), but the Lord is with Θ, thanks to N's words and prayers; 2) he must not cease to ensure God's continuing protection by means of these.
Tone: mysterious   **Bearer:** ?
Length: 109   **Sent with:** ?
Bibliography: Simeon, *Pismata*, 10; Xanalatos, *Beiträge*, 61; *Maslev*, Studia, 75-76; Gautier, 'Chartophylax,' 159-195; Mullett, 'Classical Tradition,' 92-93; 'Patronage,' 129
Discussed above: 83, 170.

G52, to the bishop of Kitros

Correspondent: N.N., bishop of KITROS (9); see also G14, G113, G121
Date: 1097   **Editions:** Gautier, II, 303-305; Finetti 11
Place: Ochrid to Kitros   323-326
Incipit: πολὺν ἐσιγήσαμεν χρόνον ἀλλήλοις   **Desinit:** ἀνώτερον καὶ κακώσεως
Message: to make contact   **Genre:** *pros philon aspastike*
Subject matter: First Crusade; difficulty of communications
Structure: 1) neither has written to the other recently; 2) Θ offers his first excuse: the passage of the Franks; 3) second excuse: not finding a suitable letter-bearer; 4) but now he has become accustomed to the Frankish outrage and as well a monk of abbot Symeon has turned up; 5) asks after the bishop's health; 6) Pauline echoes (and one quotation); 6) faith in the bishop's prayers; 7) usual prayer.
Tone: expansive self-pity; little decoration   **Bearer:** monk of Anaplous
Length: 371   **Sent with:** ?G37
Bibliography: Simeon, *Pismata*, 10-11; Chalandon, *Les Comnène*, I, 160; Runciman, 'Journey,' 208; Mercati, 'Gli aneddoti,' 136; Nesbitt, 'Rate,' 167-181; Uspenskij, *Obrazobanie*, 11; Leib, *Rome, Kiev et Byzance*, 238; Xanalatos, *Beiträge*, 78; Panov, *Teofilakt*, 321, 340; Maslev, *Studia*, 76-77, 95-96.
Discussed above: 28, 35, 83, 84, 85, 125, 127, 170, 173.

G53, to *kyr* Gregory Kamateros

Correspondent: GREGORY KAMATEROS, bishop of N (40), to a suffragan bishop, noted by Vasilievskij; Gautier suggests GK, bishop of Sthlanitsa. Diabolis, after G22, is also possible.
Date: ?   **Editions:** Gautier, II, 307-311; Finetti 12,
Place: ?Ochrid to suffragan see   325-330
Incipit: καιρός μοι τὸ προφητικόν   **Desinit:** δυναμούμενος χάριτι
Message: cheer up   **Genre:** *paramythetike*; τὸ προφητικόν
Subject matter: destruction of a church
Structure: 1) 'it is time to speak prophetically': emotional tissue of quotations from psalms and prophets on the destruction of a church and God's anger at Θ; 2) GK must show fortitude and magnanimity; 3) story of the burning and rebuilding of the temple at Jerusalem; 4) assurance that new temple would surpass the old; GK should take encouragement from that; 5) may GK benefit from this being fortified by the Paraclete against grief.
Tone: hortatory   **Bearer:** ?
Length: 914   **Sent with:** ?

Bibliography: Simeon, *Pismata*, 11-14; Maslev, 'Melissenos,' 182; V. Vasilievskii, review of Uspenskii, *Obrazovanie* in *Zhurnal ministerstva narodnogo prosvescenija* 204 (1879), 329.
Discussed above: 21, 100, 110, 125, 128, 149, 170, 173, **264.**

G54, to the patriarch

Correspondent: NICHOLAS KYRDINIATES, patriarch NICHOLAS III GRAMMATIKOS(43); see also G45, G64

Date: ? (Gautier: 1097-1105)	**Editions:** Gautier, II, 313-315; Finetti ,
Place: ?Ochrid to CP	13, 329-324
Incipit: καὶ τίς ἡμῶν	**Desinit:** ἡμῖν τῆς συγχωρήσεως
Message: thanks for the patriarch's letter and gift	**Genre:** *eucharistike*

Subject matter: gift received
Structure: two-fold, divided by ὀκνῶ γὰρ αὐτὸς διαφωτίσαι τὴν τοῦ σκοτεινοῦ λόγου περιβολήν: 1) describes the effect on Θ of the patriarch's letter with general biblical imagery; 2) finds allegorical and moral significance in the 24 sticks of incense (not 12 pairs of hiking boots) and 4 pieces of ?cinnamon sent to him; if he has failed to understand let the patriarch give him illumination.

Tone: grateful	**Bearer:** ?
Length: 422	**Sent with:** ?

Bibliography: Simeon, *Pismata*, 14-15; Maslev, *Studia*, 25-26, 96.
Discussed above: 28, 34, 39, 98, 119, 129, 152-154, 170.

G55 to Pakourianos

Correspondent: GREGORY PAKOURIANOS (15), son-in-law of Nikephoros Komnenos. See also G68, G80, ??G43

Date: ? late in the collection	**Editions:** Gautier, II, 317-319; Finetti
Place: within Bulgaria	14, 333-336.
Incipit: πάλαι τὴν ἐμαυτοῦ θρηνῶν τύχην	**Desinit:** ἀνώτερον καὶ κακύνσεως
Message: attempt to persuade GP to temper the effects of the fisc	**Genre:** *parakletike* (much sweetening)

Subject matter: exile, tax-problems and the alleviating influence of P
Structure: built round the story of Plato's journey to Sicily; 1) Θ used to lament his exile; 2) but now GP is there; 3) Θ is more fortunate than Plato for he will now live without fear of the *demosion* (Briareus); 4) GP should transcend the claims of justice; 5) request is moderate in order to teach GP to be moderate in his comments; 6) may God strengthen GP in wisdom and (usual prayer).

Tone: intimate, hopeful, fanciful	**Bearer:** ?
Length: 492	**Sent with:** ?

Bibliography: Katičić, 'Pros Pakourianous,' 386-397; Xanalatos, *Beiträge*, 55, 61; Simeon, *Pismata*, xxiii, xxiv, 15-17; Tivčev and Cankova-Petkova, 'Relations féodales,' 109; Panov, *Teofilakt*, 84; Maslev, *Studia*, 23-34 96-98; Mullett, 'Classical Tradition,' 92-93; Polemes, 'Paratereseis,' 378; Solarino,'Un intellettuale,' 73; Mullett, 'Slavs.'
Discussed above: 18, 21, 99, 124, 125, 159, 168, 173, 260, **276.**

G56, to the bishop of Semn(e)a

Correspondent: N.N. metropolitan of SEMNEA (28); Gautier suggests this is an otherwise unknown suffragan see called after the river Semnica. See also G74.

Date: ?
Place: ?from Ochrid to Semnea in Asia Minor:
Incipit: Προσαγορεύω σε τὴν φίλην ἐμοὶ κεφαλήν
Message: to ask the bishop to pray for him
Genre: *pros philon aspastike*

Editions: Gautier, II, 321; Finetti 15, 35-36
Desinit: αὐτοῦ τὴν ἄνεσιν
Subject matter: troubles

Structure: 1) greets the bishop and asks for his prayers; 2) each has his own woes and some that are common to all; Satan has taken hold of the praktors; 3) it is not for nothing that they carry a sword (cf. Rom.13.4.); 4) Θ asks for prayers that their sword may be blunted or rather completely broken.

Tone: resigned
Length: 170

Bearer: ?
Sent with: ?

Bibliography: Simeon, *Pismata*, 17; Xanalatos, *Beiträge*, 69; Maslev, *Studia*, 78-79; 98; Mullett, 'Patronage,' 125-127, 136; 'Semnea,' 247-250.

Discussed above: 39, 98, 102, 125, 134, 162, 171, 173, 178.

G57, to the bishop of Vidin

Correspondent: N.N., bishop of VIDIN (60)
Date: 1095 or other time of Cuman trouble
Place: Ochrid to Vidin
Incipit: Λυπηρὰ μὲν τὰ κατὰ σέ
Message: reply to the bishop's complaints
Subject matter: praktors, Cumans, unruly citizens

Editions: Gautier, II, 323-325; Finetti 16, 335-336
Desinit: ἐπικαμπτόμενον εὑρήσομεν
Genre: *paratharruntike*

Structure: (hangs on the question: τίς γάρ, εἴπέ μοι, τὴν ἐκ τῶν πονηρῶν τούτων ἡμερῶν ἄνεσιν ἔχει, and on the exhortation, μὴ οὖν, ὡς σὺ μόνος δεινὰ πάσχων, μικροψυχότερον διάκεισο) 1) expresses his distress at the problems the bishop has to face; 2) poses his question; 3) encouraging platitudes; 4) exhortation; 5) parallels between his own problems and the bishop's; 6) prayers and supplications will bring God's favour.

Tone: impatient, hortatory
Length: 371

Bearer: ?
Sent with: ?

Bibliography: Simeon, *Pismata*, xxiii, xxv, xxviii, 18-19; Nikolaev, *Feodalik*, 55; Xanalatos, *Beiträge*, 54, 79; Litavrin, *Bolg. i Viz.*, 320; Panov, *Teofilakt*, 78, 123, 181; Maslev, *Studia*, 77-78; 98-99; Mullett, 'Classical Tradition,' 92-93; Cheynet, *Pouvoir et contestations*, 389; Angold, *Church and Society,* 161; Mullett, 'Slavs.'

Discussed above: 17, 57, 87, 98, 106, 125, **126**, 161, 170, 173, 244, 264, 270-271.

G58, to the bishop of Triaditsa

Correspondent: N.N., bishop of TRIADITSA (59); see also G59, G60, G87
Date: ? before 1094-95 (if G75, G77 refer to him)
Place: ?Prespa to Triaditsa
Incipit: ἐνέτυχε μὲν ἡμῖν ὁ παρὼν γέρων
Message: attempt to persuade him to reconsider the case of the *geron* (108) and come to the synod
Subject matter: the synod

Editions; Gautier, II, 327-335; Finetti 17, 337-344
Desinit: τοῦ πνεύματός σου
Genre: *oneidistike*

Structure: 1) sets the scene at the synod as the *geron* presents himself; 2) his case; 3) synod's view of the bishop; 4) tells bishop what he must do and requires his attendance at synod; 4) threat of excommunication; 5) may the God of peace be with his spirit.

Tone: concerned, measured   **Bearer:** ὁ παρὼν γέρων
Length: 1035   **Sent with:** ?

Bibliography: Zlatarsky, *Istoriia*, II, 337-346; Simeon, *Pismata*, xxvi, 19-22; Panov, *Teofilakt*, 322; Maslev, *Studia*, 72, 100; Polemes, 'Paratereseis,' 378; Obolensky, *Portraits*, 51; Spadaro, 'Archontes,' 84ff, 92; 94-96; Angold, *Church and Society*, 168; Mullett, 'Bishop-List.'

Discussed above: 35, 84, 85, **89-90**, 91, 101, 106, 128, 149, 170, 173, 174, **265-266**.

G59, to the same, who is refusing to attend, from the synod

Correspondent: N.N., bishop of TRIADITSA (59); see also G58, 60, 87

Date: after G58   **Editions:** Gautier, II, 337-341; Finetti
Place: ?from Prespa to Triaditsa   18, 343-350
Incipit: ἀνεγνώσθη, τιμιώτατε ἀδελφέ   **Desinit:** ἐπιδεικνυμένην τοῦ Πνεύματος
Message: to persuade him to the synod   **Genre:** *kategorike*

Subject matter: the conversion of Armenians; dispute with bishop of Lipenion; the *geron* (107)

Structure: 1) the bishop's letter has been read out to all the synod, and all congratulate him on the conversion of Armenians; 2) all grieve that he refuses to come; 3) his reasons seem inconsistent and insufficient; 4) his presence is necessary; he is threatened with suspension; 5) the *geron* is still suffering ; the wrong must be righted; 6) let this be brought about by the bishop under the protection of the Lord.

Tone: stern   **Bearer:** ?
Length: 882   **Sent with** G60

Bibliography: Dölger, *Regesten*, 1290; Zlatarsky, *Istoriia*, II, 337-346; Simeon, *Pismata*, xxvi, 22-25; Snegarov, *Archiepiskopiia*, 236; Maslev, *Studia*, 72; Polemes, 'Paratereseis,' 378-379; Obolensky, *Portraits*, 51; Spadaro, 'Archontes,' 84ff, 93, 96-97; Angold, *Church and Society*, 168; Mullett, 'Bishop-List.'

Discussed above: 39, 84, 85, 89-90, 125, 127, 128, 149, 172, 173, 264, **265-266**.

G60, to the same from the archbishop

Correspondent: N.N., bishop of TRIADITSA (59); see also G58, G59, G87

Date: after G58   **Editions:** Gautier, II, 343-349, Finetti
Place: Prespa to Triaditsa   19, 349-354
Incipit: ὅσα μὲν ἐπὶ τῇ τοῦ σοῦ γράμματος **Desinit:** ἤδη γέροντι πρέπουσαν
Message: to explain condemnation   **Genre:** *kategorike*

Subject matter: the bishop's letter; the monk

Structure: (loose, as in all the letters of this crisis): 1) The bishop has been sent a letter giving the synod's reply to his letter conveying his refusal to come; the present, private, letter answers the bishop's very clever defence offered in reply to Θ's letter about the *geron* and the ban on liturgical celebration; 2) accuses him either of not reading his letter or of failing to understand its meaning; defends its tone; denies condemning the bishop in his absence; 3) criticises the bishop's handling of the monk; 4) vigorous attack on the excuse at the end of the bishop's letter that he could not come to the synod because Θ was so angry with him; 5) may the Lord change the bishop's savagery to gentleness.

Tone: reproachful   **Bearer:** ?
Length: 954   **Sent with:** G59

Bibliography: Dölger, *Regesten* 1290; Zlatarsky, *Istoriia*, II, 337-346; Simeon, *Pismata*, 25-28; Panov, *Teofilakt*, 340, 366;   Maslev, *Studia*, 872, 102; Obolensky, *Portraits*, 51; Spadaro, 'Archontes,' 93, 97-101; Angold, *Church and Society*, 167; Angold, *Church and Society*, 168; Mullett, 'Bishop-List.'
Discussed above: 43, 84, 85, **89-90**, 95, 101, 106, 127, 132, 149, 173, **265-266.**

G61, Letters of the blessed archbishop of Bulgaria kyr Theophylact

Correspondent: Gautier suggests JOHN KOMNENOS, *doux* of Dyrrachion (**42**), see also G10, G11, G12, G19, G22, G23, G24

Date: spring
Place: within Bulgaria
Incipit: ἐγὼ δὲ καὶ χάριν
Message: to answer accusations against him
Subject matter: the fisc

Editions: Gautier, II, 351-353; Meurs1, 357-360
Desinit: ἀνώτερον καὶ κακώσεως
Genre: *apologetike*

Structure: 1) Θ's detractor is to be thanked because Θ has received a letter from the *sebastos*; and has been given permission to reply; 2) he is accused of obstructing the fisc, which attacks the innocent and the guilty; 3) all this belongs to last winter and its floods of calumny; 4) Θ will not be drowned but purified; 5) his brother will tell the other how powerless he is here; 6) the *sebastos* must not listen to calumny; 7) usual prayer.

Tone: flattering, confident
Length: 368
Bearer: a bishop (ὁ συνάδελφός μου)
Sent with: ?

Bibliography: Simeon, *Pismata*, 31-36; Maslev, *Studia*, 102-104; Mullett, 'Classical Tradition,' 92-93; 'Patronage,' 129.
Discussed above: 17, 18, 35, 97, 132, 169, 246, 260.

G62, to the maistor kyr John

Correspondent: JOHN the maistor (**30**)
Date: ?
Place: ?
Incipit: οὔτ' ἐμοὶ σχολὴ μακρά
Message: ?
Subject matter?
Structure: ?
Tone: ?
Length: 19
Bibliography: none
Discussed above:

Editions
Gautier, II, 355; Meurs 2a, 359
Desinit: missing: ends λυπεῖν τὸ πρᾶγμα
Genre: ?

Bearer:?
Sent with:?

G63

Correspondent: certainly a bishop, perhaps Pelagonia (**10**). See also G21, G36
Date: ?
Place: within Bulgaria
Incipit: missing; begins with ὡς ἐξὸν γίνεσθαι
Message: consolation
Subject matter: the death of a protector

Editions: Gautier, II, 357-359; Meursius 2b, 360-362
Desinit: καὶ ὁμοδυνάμου Πνεύματος
Genre: *paramythetike*

Structure: 1) no point in pursuing the impossible; 2) enjoy the peace brought by 'that man's' death; 3) such an attitude is self-regarding, but it would be a mistake to be too attached to him and not to look to God, our protector; he was his intermediary, and will be replaced; 4) things will go better than in the past; 4) these thoughts will help to avoid feebleness of spirit; the rock of Christ is a sure refuge; flood image; 5) may God console the bishop.

Tone: encouraging   **Bearer:** ?
Length: 373   **Sent with:** ?
Bibliography: Simeon, *Pismata*, 36-38.
Discussed above: 97, 118, 173, **220**, 265.

G64, to the patriarch kyr Nicholas

Correspondent: NICHOLAS KYRDINIATES, patriarch NICHOLAS III GRAMMATIKOS (43); see also G45, G54

Date: before 1111   **Editions:** Gautier, II, 361; Meursius 3,
Place: Ochrid to CP   361-364
Incipit: οὐ μᾶλλον δίδωμι   **Desinit:** ἅγιε πάτερ καὶ δέσποτα
Message: recommendation of bishop of Pelagonia (10)   **Genre:** *systatike*
Subject matter: delights of knowing the patriarch

Structure: (simple with only one ICor. 13.12 quotation): 1) in writing this letter Θ does himself a favour no less than he confers one; 2) the bishop of Pelagonia (10) has asked him to write this introduction and is grateful for it, not realising how pleased Θ is to write to N; 3) how fortunate the bishop is to see the patriarch face to face; Θ is content to see his great qualities in the mirror of letters; 4) asks the patriarch to pray for him; ends with address, cf. G45.

Tone: correct   **Bearer:** bishop of Pelagonia (10)
Length: 246   **Sent with:** ?
Bibliography: Simeon, *Pismata*, xxi, 38-39; Maslev, *Studia*, 25-26; Mullett, 'Patronage,' 139; Polemes, 'Paratereseis,' 379.
Discussed above: 28, 118, 122, **136-138**, 169, 171, 265.

G65, to the nephew of Taronites, *kyr* Gregory

Correspondent: GREGORY TARONITES (48); See also G78, G81, G92

Date: ?before summer 1094 (Diogenes crash)   **Editions:** Gautier, II, 363; Meursius 4,
Place: ?   363-366
Incipit: ἐσιώπησα, μὴ καὶ ἀεὶ σιωπήσομαι   **Desinit:** ἀνώτερος καὶ κακώσεως
Message: maintenance of relationship   **Genre:** panegyric
Subject matter: GT's military career

Structure: 1) opens with Isa.42.14; 2) Θ has been silent because of the *ponerai hemerai*; 3) now he breaks silence since he feels somewhat better and has the opportunity of a bearer; 4) enquiry about GT's well-being is followed by praise of his personal qualities and his civil and military achievements; 5) Θ asks how he is getting on, listing various soldierly activities and hopes GT will surpass Θ's hopes; 6) a letter would be most acceptable; 7) ends with usual prayer.

Tone: enthusiastic, fond   **Bearer:** τοιοῦτος διάκονος
Length: 252   **Sent with:** ?
Bibliography: Simeon, *Pismata*, 39-40; Adontz, 'L'archevêque,' 583; Leroy-Molinghen, 'Grégoire Taronite,' 589-92; Gautier, 'Le synode,' 269, 162; Xanalatos, *Beiträge*, 34; Maslev, *Studia*, 75-76, 104-105; Mullett, 'Classical Tradition,' 92-93; 'Madness of Genre,' 240-243.
Discussed above: 83, 98, 159, **234**.

G66, to the *chartophylax* kyr Nikephoros

Correspondent: NIKEPHOROS *chartophylax* (23); see also G30, G51, G124, ??G83
Date: 1089-95; before synod of Blachernai   **Editions:** Gautier, II, 365-367; Meursius 5
Place: ?Ochrid to ?CP   365-368
Incipit: Οὐχ οὕτως ἀφιλόκαλος   **Desinit:** ταῖς σαῖς ἁγίαις εὐχαῖς
Message: to justify declining the offer of a *psaltes*   **Genre:** *apologetike*
Subject matter: The proposed stay of Gregory the *psaltes* (95) at Ochrid
Structure: 1) Θ has been impressed by Gregory; 2) worries about his canonical position; 3) tells N the procedure he has followed, insisting on Gregory gaining release from both his abbot and his *charistikarios*; asks N if permission of abbot alone would suffice; 4) he will refer the bothersome problem to God, 5) may he be preserved through N's prayers from the scandals of this world.
Tone: straightforward   **Bearer:** ?
Length: 415   **Sent with:** ?
Bibliography: Simeon, *Pismata*, 40-43; Gautier, 'Le synode;' 269; 'Chartophylax Nicéphore,' 162; Xanalatos, *Beiträge*, 34; Panov, *Teofilakt*, 94; Maslev, *Studia*, 75-76, 104-105; Mullett, 'Patronage,' 140; Angold, *Church and Society,* 169.
Discussed above: 83, 100, 101, 125, **129**, 170, 173, 197, 263.

G67, to *kyr* Gregory Kamateros

Correspondent: GREGORY KAMATEROS (4); see also G27, G31, G38, G127, ?G115, ?G116
Date: ??late in the collection? (cf. Phoenix & Nestor)   **Editions:** Gautier, II, 369-371; Meurs
Place: from Ochrid to ?   6, 367-370
Incipit: βαβαί, φαίης ἄν   **Desinit:** πρὸς ὄρνιθα θεῖον
Message: thanks for appointing a good person to   **Genre:** *eucharistike + parakletike*
Ochrid; also request for him to brief Pakourianos
Subject matter: appointment of Gregory Pakourianos
Structure: 1) letters to GK from Θ are rare; 2) when you are busy it is as hard to receive letters as to write them; 3) gratitude for sending a good *archon* to Ochrid; 4) GK must brief him; 5) GK should advise him to show more respect for Θ; in that way GK, the divine bird of Zeus, will be unaffected by cawing detractors (Pi., *Ol.,* 2.158-159).
Tone: persuasive; pleasant   **Bearer:** ?
Length: 384   **Sent with:** ?
Bibliography: Simeon, *Pismata*, 44-46; Zlatarsky, 'Stellvertretende Verwalter,' 147; Xanalatos, *Beiträge*, 69; Maslev, *Studia*, 65-68; 105-106; Mullett, 'Classical Tradition,' 92-93; 'Patronage,' 132; Polemes, 'Paratereseis,' 379; Angold, *Church and Society,* 163.
Discussed above: 125, 173, 220.

G68, to Gregory Pakourianos, the gambros of the grand *droungarios*

Correspondent: GREGORY PAKOURIANOS (15); see also G55, G80
Date: ?   **Editions:** Gautier, II, 373-375; Meurs
Place: within Bulgaria   7, 369-372
Incipit: ἀρά σοι θρασύς   **Desinit:** ἀνώτερον καὶ κακώσεως
Message: to welcome GP   **Genre:** 'adventus'
Subject matter: Pakourianos's arrival
Structure: 1) is Θ audacious in advising GP whom he has never met, or is he naive in sharing his wealth wth those he does not know?; 2) young and powerful, GP must be on his guard; his

goodness unites him with God; 3) he should be like God to those in need of kindness, especially to clergy; 4) if he disregards the law of the present day he will avoid envy, not criticism; 5) ends with usual prayer.

Tone: ceremonial, kindly; parainetic   Bearer: ?

Length: 345   Sent with: ?

Bibliography: Simeon, *Pismata*, xxix, 46-50; Tivčev and Cankova-Petkova, 'Relations féodales,' 109; Panov, *Teofilakt*, 128, 156; Maslev, *Studia*, 32-34, 106-107; Polemes, 'Paratereseis,' 379.

Discussed above: 125, **146-148**, 170, 173, 175.

G69, to Opheomachos

Correspondent: JOHN OPHEOMACHOS (6); see also G71

Date: ?before G71,?G46, G42   Editions: Gautier, II, 377; Meurs 8, 371-374

Place: Ochrid?

Incipit: Τί τοῦτο; καί   Desinit: σεμνοτέρῳ λεγομένους ὀκρίβαντι

Genre: adventus   Message: to encourage JO in his task

Structure: (richly-textured): 1) the good John has been sent to combat Laestrygonians and Cyclopes; 2) if he emulates Odysseus and uses his intelligence, he will return safely; 3) Θ waits to sing chants of victory for his Olympian victor, comparable with those of Bacchylides, Simonides and Pindar, though treating of a more glorious subject.

Tone: light, learned, affectionate   Bearer: ?

Length: 126   Sent with: ?

Bibliography: Simeon, *Pismata*, 51-53; Maslev, *Studia*, 38-39, 107; Mullett, 'Classical Tradition,' 92-93.

Discussed above: **147-148**, 159, 274.

G70, to the *didaskalos kyr* Niketas *ho tou Serron*

Correspondent *didaskalos tou euangeliou*: NIKETAS *ho tou Serron, didaskalos* of the Great Church; (22), see also G7, G91

Date: 1090-94/5   Editions: Gautier, II, 379-381; Meurs 9,
                                                                              373-374
Place: ?

Incipit: Καὶ ὁ τοῦ εὐαγγελίου ἐξηγητής   Desinit: περισπώντων πειρασμῶν
ἐκβασιν

Message: accusation of economy with the truth   Genre: (playful) *kategorike*

Subject matter: unknown episode

Structure: 1) challenging beginning: the interpreter of evangelical truth has been caught out lying—or is it an *oikonomia* which uses praise to underline Θ's childishness?; 2) accepts latter view; 3) if something more profound has led N to praise Θ he must give an explanation; 4) N's action is at odds with today's mores when a good man is one not completely possessed by evil; 5) respectful greetings from him and Θ's 'brothers' N's pupils (116); 6) requests prayers that Θ will emerge from his difficulties.

Tone: teasing   Bearer: ?

Length: 270   Sent with: ?

Bibliography: Simeon, *Pismata*, 54; Katičić, 'Biographika,' 367; Panov, *Teofilakt*, 292; Maslev, *Studia*, 35-36; 107-108.

Discussed above: 83, 93, 170, 174.

G71, to Opheomachos

Correspondent: JOHN OPHEOMACHOS (6); see also G69
Date: ?late in archiepiscopate; after G69, ?G46, G42   **Editions:** Gautier, II, 383-385;
Place: within Bulgaria   Meurs 10, 373-374.
Incipit: ἐγὼ δε τοῦτ' ἐκεῖνο πρὸς σέ   **Desinit:** κακύνσεως καὶ κακώσεως
Message: plea not to abandon the struggle in Bulgaria   **Genre:** paratharryntike
Subject matter: riddles
Structure: 1) Θ's attitude to JO is like that of the hares to the frogs in the fable: having discovered that JO makes Θ's cowardice seem small he strides heroically towards him; 2) Θ's new active life is very different from his old scholarly one but he has persisted; JO has shown himself afraid of the rattle of war-chariots; 3) Θ has been speaking in riddles about Bulgarian affairs not real war; he will come out on top with God as his ally; 4) may JO in this way please God, give joy to Θ and (usual prayer).
Tone: light, intimate, gently reproachful   **Bearer:** ?
Length: 321   **Sent with:** ?
Bibliography: Simeon, *Pismata*, 54-56; Xanalatos, *Beiträge*, 61; Maslev, *Studia*, 38-39, 108; Mullett, 'Patronage,' 129; Solarino,'Un intellettuale,' 74.
Discussed above: 81, 99, 125, **152-154**, 159, 178, 262, 276.

G72, to the metropolitan of Thessalonike kyr Theodoulos

Correspondent: THEODOULOS N., metropolitan of THESSALONIKE (27)
Date: ?   **Editions:** Gautier, II, 387; Meurs 11,
Place: ?from Ochrid ?toThessalonike   375-378
Incipit: τοῦτο μόνον ἔχοντες   **Desinit:** ἀποίσῃ τὸ ὄφελος
Message: mutual support   **Genre:** parakletike
Subject matter: Amalek: the devil (Gautier; others have believed him to be Bohemond)
Structure: 1) our only consolation in these *ponerai hemerai* is communication and reciprocal prayer; 2) T must help by combating Amalek; 3) appeal for help against him; 4) this also to T's advantage.
Tone: collegial   **Bearer:** ?
Length: 134   **Sent with:** ?
Bibliography: Simeon, *Pismata*, 56-57; Katičić, 'Biographika,' 368; Panov, *Teofilakt*, 323; Maslev, *Studia*, 40-44, 70-72; Angold, *Church and Society*, 169.
Discussed above: 81, 129, 262.

G73, to the caesar

Correspondent: NIKEPHOROS MELISSENOS (44)(but see Maslev); see also G9, G13
Date: 1102-04   **Editions:** Gautier, II, 389-393; Meurs12,
Place: ?Ochrid to ?CP   377-380
Incipit: δέσποτά μου ἅγιε, ἀεί μοι   **Desinit:** τὰ καθ' ἡμᾶς φυσικά
Message: maintenance   **Genre:** paramythetike
Subject matter: the death of the *sebastokrator* (78)
Structure: 1) NM's letters always comfort Θ; 2) Θ has heard that NM has been unwell and is suffering because of the death of the *sebastokrator*; 3) he has the intelligence to use this grief to lead him to better things; 4) NM knows how unstable all things are; 5) Θ's grief has been assuaged by NM's response to the death; 6) may the gift of fish from the Theotokos give him appetite and strength; symbolism of their number.

Tone: formal consolation   **Bearer:** ?
Length: 556   **Sent with** 500 fish, some baked into
                                                rolls, others smoked
Bibliography: on the date, Papachryssanthou, 'Date;' Guilland, *Recherches*, II, 30-31; Chalandon, *Les Comnène*, I, 273; Simeon, *Pismata*, 57-59; Maslev, 'Melissenos,' 186; Gautier, 'L'obituaire,' 249; Gautier, 'Le synode,' 225; Panov, *Teofilakt*, 109, 157; Maslev, *Studia*, 45-49; Polemes, 'Paratereseis,' 380.
Discussed above: 25, 29, 84, 122, 139, **143-144**; 169.

G74 to the bishop of Semnea

Correspondent: N.N. metropolitan of SEMNEA (28); see also G56
Date: ?   **Editions:** Gautier, II, 395-397; Meurs 13,
Place: ?   381-382
Incipit: Καί κεν τὸ βουλοίμην   **Desinit:** τὸν λίθον μετακινήσαιμεν
Message: to tell the bishop of his troubles **Genre:** *pros philon aspastike*
Subject matter: evildoers
Structure: 1) it would be good if those who harm Θ were reformed by the deaths of other evildoers; 2) but they become hardened like Pharaoh of old, or wounded wild animals, or 3) as in the story of Herod son of Antipater, when all the notables of the council of the Jews were killed at the time of his death; 4) because they are wounded, today's beastly Herodians wish to bring others down with them; 5) evil is ingrained in them, but we must pray for their improvement; 6) urges the bishop to pray for them and to exhort others to do likewise.
Tone: sad and wise   **Bearer:** ?
Length: 296   **Sent with:** ?
Bibliography: Simeon, *Pismata*, 59-61; Katičić, 'Korespondenicija,' 186; Maslev, *Studia*, 78-79; Mullett, 'Semnea.'
Discussed above: 81, 171.

G75, to the metropolitan of Kerkyra

Correspondent: NICHOLAS, metropolitan of KERKYRA (8); see also G77
Date: before synod of 1094-95   **Editions:** Gautier, II, 398-401; Meurs
Place: Ochrid to Kerkyra   17, 387-390
Incipit: Πῶς ἂν εἴποις   **Desinit:** πανίερε καὶ ἅγιε δέσποτα
Message: shares his problems with fellow-sufferer **Genre:** *schetliastike*
Subject matter: heavily veiled (as the bishop, G77, pointed out); enemies
Structure: 1) thanks N for his comforting letter; his enemies have grown powerful while his friends and those near him stand aloof; 2) let N use his knowledge and wisdom on behalf of Θ; 3) expatiates on evils; there are monsters on all sides; 4) he must observe discretion (fellow clergy and bishops have spread the net of oppression); 5) let N pray that Θ escape his false brethren and for them to escape the devil; 6) ends with prayer (God's grace be with N's spirit) and the address.
Tone: intimate, obscure, comfortable   **Bearer:** ?
Length: 435   **Sent with:** ?
Bibliography: Lampros, *Kerkyraika anekdota*, 30-41; Moustoxidi, *Illustrazioni corciresi*, xx-xxx; Simeon, *Pismata*, 64-66; Nikolaev, *Feodalni*, 105; Xanalatos, *Beiträge*, 55; Panov, *Teofilakt*, 83-84;

Maslev, *Studia*, 108-109; Mullett, 'Classical Tradition,' 92-93; Obolensky, *Portraits*, 47; Solarino,'Un intellettuale,' 74.
Discussed above: 18, 28, 81, 83, 89-91, 98, 107, 122, 124, 125, 128, 154, 171, 201.

G76, to Mermentoulos

Correspondent: NICHOLAS MERMENTOULOS (5); see also G25, G29, G33, G47, G76

Date: ?July-August? after or with poem 10   **Editions:** Gautier, II, 403-405; Meurs
Place: ?Ochrid to ?CP   20, 393-6
Incipit: Τὸν βραχύν μοι τοῦτον χρόνον   **Desinit:** ἀρωματοφόρον ἡ εὐωδία
Message: plea for more frequent letters   **Genre:** request for letters
Subject matter: letters; ?Antiochos (120)

Structure: 1) NM's letters are rare like manifestations of the phoenix, and should instead be daily occurrences like the sun; let daylight be extended; 2) with his powers of improvisation he is better equipped than Paion; 3) he does not need time; let him send his zephyrs; 4) NM knows Θ's troubles: a terrible dogstar has burned Θ and he has defended himself with iambics; 5) urges NM never to stop attending to Θ's *psychagogia* with his unfailing zephyrs.

Tone: heady   **Bearer:** ?
Length: 274   **Sent with:** ?poem 10 to monk Neilos (67)
Bibliography: Simeon, *Pismata*, 70-71; Gautier, 'L'épiscopat,' 170.
Discussed above: 28, 97, 99, 101, 103, 123-124, 160, 170, 243-244.

G77, to the metropolitan of Kerkyra

Correspondent: NICHOLAS, metropolitan of KERKYRA (8); see also G75

Date: before the synod of 1094-95   **Editions:** Gautier, II, 407-413; Meursius
Place: Ochrid to Kerkyra   22, 395-396
Incipit: Καὶ πάλιν ἡμῖν ἐξ ὕψους   **Desinit:** ἐκ τῆς ὁδοῦ διαρρίπτοντος
Message: communication   **Genre:** *schetliastike*
Subject matter: a troublesome official, a difficult bishop; Θ's journey; his health

Structure: 1) Θ's happy reaction to N's letter; 2) distance and letters; 3) Senachereim the Assyrian (86) and his imitator (87) who persecutes the faithful; 4) all that remains is Jesus and his words of victory; 5) an episcopal missile in the shape of the bishop of a certain city (N complained this was a riddle [in G75]) had almost brought about his death; he explains why he had written so obscurely; 6) because of this the emperor has to be consulted, so Θ is going to make a terrible journey to see him in camp; 7) with his cobweb-like physique this will make him even weaker, 8) if N prays for him all will go well.

Tone: intimate, decorative, but not hectic   **Bearer:**?
Length: 937   **Sent with:**?
Bibliography: Gautier, 'Le synode,' 269; '*Chartophylax* Nicéphore,' 163; Maslev, 'Melissenos,' 182; Simeon, *Pismata*, xxviii, xxxii, 73-79; Nikolaev, *Feodalni*, 57, 99; Maslev, *Studia*, 70-72, 111-112; Polemes, 'Paratereseis,' 381; Solarino, 'Un intellettuale,' 74; Angold, *Church and Society*, 167.
Discussed above: 29, 55, 83, 84, 89-91, 97, 118, 127, 130, 149, 154, 160, 171, 265.

G78, from the same

Correspondent: GREGORY TARONITES (48); see also G65, G81, G92

Date: early May 1103 (or possibly1102)   **Editions:** Gautier, II, 415-417; Meurs
Place: from Prespa to Pontos   23, 401-402

Incipit: οὐδὲν ἐμοὶ λοιπὸν δυσχερές
Message: good wishes for war
Subject matter: arrival of GT in Pontos; *panegyris* at Hagios Achilleios
Structure: 1) Θ is fortunate to have received a letter fom GT and has been rejuvenated by reading of his successes; 2) describes receipt; 3) exhorts GT to defeat the Turks; 4) may God give him strength to destroy the followers of Mohammed (with quotations from the psalms); 5) Θ is confident: GT will win the crown of victory with God's help; 6) ends with usual prayer.
Tone: panegyric
Length: 474
Desinit: ἀνώτερον καὶ κακώσεως
Genre: *profectio bellica*

Bearer: ?
Sent with:?

Bibliography: Simeon, *Pismata*, 79-81; Leroy-Molinghen, 'Grégoire Taronite,' 589-592; Adontz, 'L'archevêque,' 577-588; Maslev, *Studia*, 26-27; Solarino, 'Un intellettuale,' 74; Mullett, 'Madness of Genre,' 240-243; 'Bishop-List.'
Discussed above: 28, 84, 87, 91, 97, **234-235**, 237-239.

G79, to the Grand Domestic kyr Adrian

Correspondent: ADRIAN KOMNENOS, the grand domestic; (41); see also G5, G85, G89, G98
Date: ?after G68, G67, G80
Place: ?from Ochrid to ?CP
Incipit: ἐγὼ δὲ καὶ νεκρὸς ἤδη γενόμενος
Message: to ask for continued help in Bulgaria
Subject matter: the departure of Gregory Pakourianos, a good governor, from Bulgaria
Editions: Gautier, II, 419-423; Meurs 24, 403-408
Desinit: κακύνσεως καὶ κακώσεως
Genre: *parakletike*

Structure: 1) Θ who had been a corpse has been brought back to life by AK: does he wish him to draw back the curtain of *asapheia*? 2) the activities of the *demosion* had reduced Θ to hopelessness but when AK's *gambros* was put in charge of matters nearby hope returned; Θ thanks AK for the change 5) But Gregory is to leave and who will defend the weak (and the rich against the wicked poor and informers) and the church? who will enforce restraint on the grumbling of the Bulgarians? 6) being good he had to flee Kedar; those who enjoyed his goodness wiill grieve, but will pray for AK and his own; 7) ends with usual prayer.
Tone: desperate; ceremonial
Length: 749
Bearer: ?
Sent with: ?

Bibliography: Simeon, *Pismata*, 81-84; Obolensky, *Bogomils,* 171; Polemis, *Doukai*, 55, n.10; Hussey, *Church and Learning*, 129; Zlatarsky, 'Stellvertretende Verwalter,' 150, 156; Nikolaev, *Feodalni*, 215-216; Xanalatos, *Beiträge*, 31, 59; Maslev, *Studia*, 23-25, 112; Papayanni, 'Phorologikes plerophories,' 392; Mullett, 'Patronage,' 132; Polemes, 'Paratereseis,' 380-381; Solarino, 'Un intellettuale,' 79.
Discussed above: 81, 94, 101, 124-125, **130-131**, 149-150, 154, 169, 173, 220, 274.

G80, to the *sebastos* Pakourianos

Correspondent: GREGORY PAKOURIANOS (15), though Vat. gr. 509 has Nicholas; see also G55, G68.
Date: ? after G68, G67, before G79
Place: within Bulgaria
Incipit: καὶ Κύριος παρεβίβασε τὸ ἁμάρτημά σου
Message: to reply to a letter of apology from GP
Subject matter: GP and his faults
Editions: Gautier, II, 425; Meurs 25, 409-410
Desinit: ἀνώτερος καὶ κακώσεως
Genre: *syngnomonike*

Structure: 1) begins with comforting quotation (2 Kings 12.13); 2) Θ does not think GP's a great sin anyway; 3) what he likes about GP is that unlike the Pharisee he regards little sins as large and the mote in his own eye as a great beam; if the beginning of salvation is self-accusation he has a good foundation for virtue; 4) nature, law and sin; 5) GP must on behalf of all wish for good things and preserve the unity of faith in the bond of charity, thus drawing on himself the graces of God; 6) ends with usual prayer.

Tone: pastoral; warm   **Bearer:** ?
Length: 247   **Sent with:** ?
Bibliography: Simeon, *Pismata*, 84-86; Katičić, 'Pros Pakourianous,' 396; Tivčev and Cankova-Petkova, 'Relations féodales,' 108; Maslev, *Studia*, 32-34.
Discussed above: 169, 173, 215, 220.

G81, to kyr Gregory Taronites

Correspondent: GREGORY TARONITES (48); see also G65, G78, G92
Date: May to Sept 1103   **Editions:** Gautier, II, 433; Meurs 26, 409-411

Place: ?Ochrid to Pontos
Incipit: καὶ πόθεν ἂν καὶ ποίας ἀποτίσαιμι   **Desinit:** κακοῖο μήτε κακύνοιο
Message: praise for his young patron's success **Genre:** panegyric
Subject matter: Byzantine gains in the Black Sea; the ransoming of Bohemond
Structure: 1) GT has justified Θ's praises; he has defeated Frank and Turk; Danishmend would wish to have children like him; 2) soon he will liberate Neokaisareia; 3) Bohemond the hard-necked has become softer than wax; 4) Θ shares in the common benefits GT has conferred on Christians and those who guide the empire; 5) this letter is long but not long enough; 6) his exploits spring from divine grace; let him be grateful to God; 7) ends with prayer that GT be delivered from all evil.

Tone: triumphant   **Bearer:** ?
Length: 920   **Sent with:** ?
Bibliography: Simeon, *Pismata*, 87-90; Adontz, 'L'archevêque,' 577-588; Leroy-Molinghen, 'Grégoire Taronite,' 589-591; 'Deux Jean Taronites,' 150-151; Shepard, 'New England,' 18-19; Buckler, *Anna Comnena*, 254; Melikoff, *Danismendname*, 118-119; Cahen, *Pre-Ottoman Turkey,* 90; Vasiliev, *The Goths in the Crimea*, 154-155; Chalandon, *Les Comnène*, I, 241; Uspenskii, *Obrazobranie*, 14; Maslev, *Studia*, 26-27; Mullett, 'Madness of Genre,' 240-243; Polemes, 'Paratereseis,' 381.
Discussed above: 81, 84, 87, 99, 149-150, 169, 173, 175, **234-235**, 261.

G82, to kyr Michael *ho tou Chalkedonos*

Correspondent: MICHAEL *ho tou Chalkedonos* (52); an ecclesiastical archon, nephew of Leo of Chalcedon or his successor.
Date: 1094+ (from succession of *chartophylakes*)   **Editions:** Gautier, II, 435-437; Meurs
Place: ?Ochrid to ?CP   27, 415-418
Incipit: ἕως μὲν μόνα τὰ χρηματικά   **Desinit:** σαῖς εὐχαῖς, πανίερε δέσποτα
Message: to ask M to have a word with the   **Genre:** *parakletike*
chartophylax, in support of a letter of Θ   **Subject matter:** the Kittaba case
Structure: 1) spiritual as well as material goods of the church have been attacked (appropriate); hence Θ informs M of an infringement of canons; 2) explains the specific case, apologising for the barbaric name, of an *eukterion* founded without archiepiscopal, but with patriarchal, permission; 3) Θ has written about the matter to Peter *chartophylax*; asks M to speak to him; 4) canonical relationship between church of Ochrid and patriarchate of CP: statement by Θ; 5) practical difficulties of present arrangement; 6) if this letter and M's words are successful, let God and M's charity be thanked 6) may his prayers bring peace, ending with his title.

Tone: disturbed

Length: 526

Bibliography: Katičić, 'Biographika,' 378; Simeon, *Pismata*, xviii-xix, xxvii, 90-93; Uspenskii, *Obrazobanie*, 18; Xanalatos, *Beiträge*, 30; Panov, *Teofilakt*, 92, 268; Maslev, *Studia*, 18-19, 112-113; Obolensky, 'Byzantine Impact,' 158; *Portraits*, 50; Papayanni, 'Boulgaroi,' 64-65; Angold, *Church and Society*, 168; Mullett, 'Slavs.'

Bearer: ?

Sent with: Lost 8 to *chartophylax* Peter (25)

Discussed above: 125, 129, 149, 173, 205, 212, 269, 275.

G83, to the *chartophylax kyr* Niketas

Correspondent: NIKETAS *chartophylax* (24); Gautier doubts and would give to Nikephoros.

Date: either before 1094 or 1106-11

Place: ?Ochrid to Constantinople

Incipit: διαπτᾶσά τις φήμη περὶ ὑμῶν

Message: to verify a rumour

Subject matter: ??about quarrel over precedence of metropolitans

Editions: Gautier, II, 439; Meurs 28, 417-420

Desinit: ὅπερ ἕκαστος χρῄζομεν

Genre: *erotematike*

Structure: (simple): 1) Θ tells of a rumour he has heard about N which has upset him greatly and which has reached the emperors; 2) he wishes to know if it is true, for N is a healer and comforter; 3) may God set aright those who hate N; 4) may he be guarded like salt, light and leaven.

Tone: concerned

Length: 223

Bibliography: Simeon, *Pismata*, 93; Gautier, 'Le synode,' 274-275; 'L'obituaire,' 163-165; Polemes, 'Paratereseis,' 381.

Bearer: ?

Sent with: ?

Discussed above: 170, 173.

G84, to his pupil Niketas, deacon, *ho tou Chalkedonos*

Correspondent: NIKETAS *ho tou Chalkedonos* deacon (53)

Date: ? before 1108-1110

Place: ?

Incipit: τὸν Ἀντίλοχον οἶσθα

Message: to ask N to carry two letters for him, one to the *protovestiaria* Maria (51), and one for her to give to *protostrator*.

Editions: Gautier, II, 441-443; Meurs 29, 419-422.

Desinit: μήθ' ὑμῖν ἐνοχλοίημεν

Genre: *parakletike*

Subject matter: canon-breaking by the *protostrator*; mother-power.

Structure: 1) begins with the story of Antilochos, who risked danger for his father Nestor; N is not to risk danger for Θ but is to carry out a service without danger; 2) he is to deliver to the lady who is the mother of the empress letter in support of the canons which her son the *protostrator* is oppressing; 3) Θ has written to the *protostrator* himself and that letter is to be shown to her so that she can give it to him; 4) this easy service will earn N the cancellation of his debt (of teaching); may N be capable of greater things and may Θ escape even apparently small trials so that he doesn't bother N or anyone else.

Tone: hortatory rather than suppliant

Length: 293

Bibliography: Simeon, *Pismata*, 94-95; Gautier, L'obituaire,' 248; Litavrin, *Bolg. i Viz.*, 335; Panov, *Teofilakt*, 237; Maslev, *Studia*, 79, 113; Angold, *Church and Society*, 163.

Bearer: ?

Sent with: Lost 14 and Lost 15

Discussed above: 99, 175, 212, 263.

G85, to the Grand Domestic *kyr* Adrian, brother of the emperor

Correspondent: ADRIAN KOMNENOS (41), the Grand Domestic; see also G5, G79, G89, G98

Date: before 1104; Gautier: 1097-1104

Place: ?Ochrid to ?CP

Incipit: τίς εἰμι ἐγώ, κύριέ μου κύριε

Message: AK is to counteract calumnies against Θ and secure the emperor's support

Subject matter: the 'village of the church in Ochrid'

Editions: Gautier, II, 445-451; Meurs 30, 421-428

Desinit: κακύνσεως καὶ κακώσεως

Genre: *parakletike*

Structure: 1) who is Θ that AK should love him, as God loved David? 2) AK has asked Θ to tell him 'in clear' what he coded in his 'prophetic' letter; 3) how to dissipate the clouds of calumny which the emperor is making denser? the unjust witnesses, dismissed by the emperor as such have returned to the attack and gained ground; his imperial judgement is like Penelope's web, woven by truth during the day, unpicked at night by falsehood; 4) the case of the *anagrapheus* and the village; 5) Θ's problems with calumny, which undermines his position; 6) his enemies are like the Hydra; Iolaos is needed; 7) Θ has placed the problem in God's hands, the emperor's and AK's; may AK support his weakness!; 8) and be (usual prayer).

Tone: disturbed

Length: 1034

Bearer: ?

Sent with: ?

Bibliography: Simeon, *Pismata*, 96-109; Leroy-Molinghen, 'Trois mots slaves,' 336, 382; Nikolaev, *Feodalik*, 74; Xanalatos, *Beiträge*, 32, 54, 60, 70; Litavrin, *Bolg. i Viz.*, 87, 324; Panov, *Teofilakt*, 107, 158; Maslev, *Studia*, 23-25, 113-115; Mullett, 'Classical Tradition,' 92-93; 'Patronage,' 125-127; Papayanni, 'Boulgaroi,' 71; Harvey, 'The Land,' 145; Angold, *Church and Society*, 161.

Discussed above: 96, 101, 124-125, 132, 149-150, 154, 169, 171, 213, 215.

G86, to Bryennios, *sympentheros* of the emperor

Correspondent: JOHN BRYENNIOS (34), *doux* of Dyrrachion, the father of Nikephoros; see also G105

Date: 1096/97-1105

Place: ?Ochrid to ?Dyrrachion

Incipit: ἀφ'οὗ πρώτως ἐγευσάμην

Message: welcome to Bulgaria

Subject matter: arrival at Dyrrachion

Editions: Gautier, II, 453-455; Meurs 31, 427-428; Gautier, *Nicéphore Bryennios*, 316-318

Desinit: κακύνσεως καὶ κακώσεως

Genre: adventus/*prosphonetike*

Structure: 1) Θ's long-standing admiration for JB; 2) he is unable to see him, so sends this letter; 3) wishes him health in body and soul and good fortune in his task as liberating saviour; 4) Θ's bitter situation will be described by the bearer; 5) punished by the Father, Θ awaits his consolation; if JB makes God his refuge, no evil will befall him; 6) ends with usual prayer for JB.

Tone: ceremonial

Length: 294

Bearer: lives with Θ and knows all

Sent with: ?

Bibliography: Simeon, *Pismata*, 109-112; Gautier, *Nicéphore Bryennios*, passim; Maslev, *Studia*, 41-43; Obolensky, *Portraits*, 78.

Discussed above: 35, 106, 123, **146-147**.

G87, to the bishop of Triaditsa

Correspondent: N.N., bishop of TRIADITSA (59); see also G58, G59, G60

Date: 1093-94

Place: Ochrid to Triaditsa

Editions: Gautier, II, 457-459; Meurs 32, 429-432

Incipit: ἐδεξάμεθά σοι τὴν γραφὴν

Desinit: καὶ μὴ καταρᾶσθαι βούλεται

Message: responding to a conciliatory letter from the bishop and acceding to his request

Subject matter: excommunication; calumny

Genre: draws on *parangelmatike* and *synkatathetike*

Structure: 1) thanks bishop for his letter, which he summarises; 2) he is angered by his pretence of benevolence; the bishop on his visit to CP used the opportunity to spread calumny against Θ; 3) reply to letter: agrees to lift the suspension because of the bishop's serious illness; but other bishops weere involved hand he has written to the bishops en route and will write to all other bishops; 4) let the bishop pray for Θ and blush for having broken the precept which tells us to bless even our persecutors.

Tone: cool, sparse, critical

Length: 445

Bearer: ὑπηρέτης of bishop

Sent with: Lost 10 to bishop of Pelagonia, Lost 11 to bishop of Stroumitsa, Lost 12 to bishop of Malesova

Bibliography: Zlatarsky, *Istoriia*, II, 337-346; Simeon, *Pismata*, 112-114; Nikolaev, *Feodalni*, 76; Panov, *Teofilakt*, 272-274; Maslev, *Studia*, 72, 115-117; Mullett, 'Classical Tradition,' 92-93; 'Bishop-List;' Obolensky, *Portraits*, 51; Spadaro, 'Archontes,' 109-110; Angold, *Church and Society*, 168. **Discussed above:** 17, 35, **89-90**, 101, 127, 132, 160, 170, 173, 174, 215, **265-266**.

G88, to *kyr* John the *grammatikos* of Palaiologos

Correspondent: JOHN, *grammatikos* of Palaiologos (**54**)

Date: = G127, before G118 (Gautier: 1096-1104/05)

Place: ?Ochrid to ?CP

Incipit: ἄρα καὶ αὐτὸς τὸ τῶν πολλῶν πείσῃ

Message: request to show this letter to George Palaiologos; to prevent an *anagraphe*

Editions: Gautier, II, 461-463; Meurs 33, 431-434

Desinit: ἀνώτερον καὶ κακώσεως

Genre: *parakletike*

Subject matter: Vardar village case; appointment of Constantine Doukas (**36**) to Boleron-Strymon-Thessalonike

Structure: 1) this letter has been written in time of need; 2) a village on the Vardar has been over-taxed by Iasites (**76**); 2) Θ has heard that Michael Doukas's son has been appointed to the Vardar; 3) Θ has written to Michael Doukas (**39**) to ask him to advise his son not to send assessors in; 4) J is to show 'our' letter to ?George Palaiologos (**45**) (?with Lost 17) 5) he must be Herakles, killer of bandits, for that is what *anagrapheis* are; 6) usual prayer.

Tone: business-like

Length: 362

Bearer: ?

Sent with: Lost 17 to George Palaiologos ? Lost 18 to Michael Doukas

Bibliography: Gautier, 'Le synode,' 235, 251; Laurent, La généalogie,' 140-146; Simeon, *Pismata*, xxviii, 115-117; Litavrin, *Bolg. i Viz.*, 80, 296-299; Panov, *Teofilakt*, 249, 272-274; Maslev, *Studia*, 64-65, 116; Mullett, 'Patronage,' 125-127; Harvey, 'The Land,' 148; Angold, *Church and Society*, 161. **Discussed above:** 19, 57, 66, 83, 84, 93, 95-96, 125, 173, **212-213**, 220.

G89, to the brother of the emperor, *kyr* Adrian

Correspondent: ADRIAN KOMNENOS (**41**), the Grand Domestic; see also G5, G79, G85, G98

Date: after G85? (Gautier: 1097-1104)

Place: ?Ochrid to ?CP

Incipit: ἅγιέ μου αὐθέντα

Editions: Gautier, II, 465-467; Meurs 34, 433-436

Desinit: κακύνσεως καὶ κακώσεως

Message: request for AK to mediate with the emperor **Genre:** *parakletike*
Subject matter: Theophylact's troubles with two Bulgars
Structure: 1) in last ep [?G85], Θ wrote tragically, now he does not know how adequately to lament his misfortune; 2) Θ is the plaything of two Bulgars; the situation is like a dead dogs show disdain for a live lion or Samson, shorn by the razor of calumny, handed over to foreigners for blinding; 4) if the justice of the emperor, thanks to AK's talk with him, controls those who torment him, perhaps his hair will grow again and he will destroy their house of *hybris*; 5) ends with usual prayer.
Tone: mournful; elegant   **Bearer:** ?
Length: 204   **Sent with** ? (Gautier: the large postbag)
Bibliography: Gautier, *Nicéphore Bryennios*, 322, n.3; Katičić, 'Biographika,' 374; Simeon, *Pismata*, xvii, xxiii, 117-119; Litavrin, *Bolg. i Viz.*, 241; Maslev, *Studia*, 23-25, 116; Harvey, 'The Land,' 145.
Discussed above: 17, 96, 101, 169, 171, 174, 213, 270-271.

G90, to the *chartophylax*
Correspondent: ?PETER *chartophylax* (25)
Date: winter; 1095-1106 if Peter (Gautier: 1097-1104)   **Editions:** Gautier, I, 469; Meurs 35,
Place: ?Ochrid to CP   435-436
Incipit: Αὐτὸ τοῦτο τὸ τὸν ἀδελφόν μου   **Desinit:** συντριβησωνταί σου τὰ κύματα
Message: request for the *chartophylax* to pray for him **Genre:** *parakletike*
and counteract rumours   **Subject matter:** Ekklesiai case
Structure: 1) that Θ sends his brother in middle of winter is a sign of great need; 2) Θ is closely and painfully involved with a demon; 3) he is being forced to abandon the village Ekklesiai; 4) asks the *chartophylax*'s assistance; 5) P must show the harbour that is close by, i.e. the Logos, to those who think they are drowning and he must teach him who stirs up waves against Θ that it is in vain because he has the help of God, who says, 'Peace; be still;' 6) may the *chartophylax*'s waves be broken down within him.
Tone: disturbed   **Bearer:** brother [Demetrios]
Length: 184   **Sent with:** G91 and G93
Bibliography: Gautier, 'Le synode,' 273; Simeon, *Pismata*, 120-121; Maslev, *Studia*, 34-35, 116; Papayanni, 'Boulgaroi,' 64-65.
Discussed above: 36, 57, 66, 84, 95-96, 124, 170, 173, 246, 269.

G91, to the didaskalos of the Great Church (but see below)
Correspondent: ?NIKETAS *ho tou Serron, didaskalos* of the Great Church (22) (teacher of Θ's brother—but addressed as a 'son'); see also G7, G70
Date: ?=G90   **Editions:** Gautier, II, 471; Meurs 36,
Place: ?Ochrid to ?CP   437-438
Incipit: εἴ με φλεγόμενον ἑώρας, τιμιώτατέ μοι   **Desinit:** ἡμετέρας ἀσθενείας κηδόμενος
Message: request for the *didaskalos*'s prayers and **Genre:** *parakletike*
efforts on Θ's behalf.
Subject matter: alluded to darkly: calumny crisis?
Structure: 1) if N saw Θ on fire and had a jug of water would he not put out the flames? 2) Is not Θ's present position worse than this—and N does live beside the springs; 3) if Θ speaks darkly, N is equipped to interpret; 4) or if he finds his words difficult he should ask Θ's brother, N's pupil about Θ's troubles; 5) may God scatter them through N's prayers and efforts.
Tone: ingenious plea   **Bearer:** my brother, your pupil

Length: 114   **Sent with:** G90, G93
Bibliography: Simeon, *Pismata*, 121-122; Katičić, 'Biographika,' 367; Maslev, *Studia*, 35-36.
Discussed above: 84, 122, 151, 153, 170, 173, 174, 246.

G92, to kyr Gregory Taronites

Correspondent: GREGORY TARONITES (48); see also G65, G78, G81, G92
Date: June-Sept 1103   **Editions:** Gautier, II, 473-475; Meurs 37
Place: from Bulgaria to CP   437-440
Incipit: ἐν μέσῳ δυεῖν εἰλημμένος παθῶν οὐκ ἔχω   **Desinit:** ἀνώτερον καὶ κακώσεως.
Message: greeting for Taronites on return   **Genre:** panegyric *prosphonetikon*
Subject matter: not the 'rebellion' of GT but his triumphant return
Structure: 1) Θ is torn between two reactions; 2) he is glad that GT has returned, bringing spring in place of winter and participating in the emperor's schemes; 2) he is sorry to hear that Danishmend will sleep easy and the cities of Pontos will experience storms after GT's calm; 3) Who could replace GT? Θ's grief has almost made him a tragedian; GT will be with those who love him; he must write frequently to Θ; 4) Θ is enjoying the presence of Theodosios; 5) prayer.
Tone: celebratory   **Bearer:** Theodosios (98)
Length: 517   **Sent with:** ?
Bibliography: as for G78 and Simeon, *Pismata*, 122-123; Xanalatos, *Beiträge*, 58; Panov, *Teofilakt*, 76, 227;
Discussed above: 84, 87, 122, 173, 175, **234-235.**

G93, to the *archiatros* kyr Nicholas Kallikles

Correspondent: NICHOLAS KALLIKLES (3); see also G94, G111, G112
Date: ?winter: ἐν τοιούτῳ καιρῷ; ?=G90, G91   **Editions:** Gautier, II, 477; Meurs 38,
Place: ?Ochrid to ?CP   439-440; Romano, *Nicola Callicle*, 57.
Incipit: Μισούμεθ' οὕτως ὥστε μὴ προσεννέπειν   **Desinit:** δυνήσεσθαι συνευξώμεθα
Message: request for help for Demetrios's mission   **Genre:** *systatike*
Subject matter: Ekklesiai crisis
Structure: 1) 'Am I hated so much that no-one speaks to me?' (Eur. *Or.*, 428) but Θ is speaking because he does not hate; 2) wishes NK good health and enjoyment of the court; 3) asks him to share his good fortune with his friends, particularly by helping Θ's brother, whose winter mission shows the seriousness of his business; 5) let NK display his power; then Θ will pray that it may be increased.
Tone: friendly, fairly light   **Bearer:** Θ's brother
Length: 102   **Sent with:** (probably) G90, G91
Bibliography: Simeon, *Pismata*, 123; Maslev, *Studia*, 37-38, 117-119; Kazhdan, 'Medical Doctor,' 44.
Discussed above: 84, 136, 174, 215, 246.

G94, to the same

Correspondent: NICHOLAS KALLIKLES (3); see also G93, G111; G112; Gautier: 'sans doute' Michael Pantechnes, but no need
Date: ?1097-1104; after G90-93; before G96, G98   **Editions:** Gautier, II, 479; Meurs 39,
Place: fom Pelagonia to ?CP   441-442; Romano, *Nicola Callicle*, 58
Incipit: σὺ δέ, σύ καὶ τὸν 'Αλκμαίωνα εἶδες   **Desinit:** τὸν ἰατρὸν τὸν Παιήονα

Message: plea for help   **Genre:** *parakletike*
Subject matter: ?Lazaros affair?
Structure: 1) Θ compares himself to Alkmaion since he has been driven out from Ochrid to Pelagonia by the fisc; a taxman is an executioner (pun); 2) why tell NK? so that he can end Θ's wanderings by being as helpful as Acheloos was to Alkmaion; 3) his brother will tell him how; 4) be my Paieon!
Tone: intimate   **Bearer:** Θ's brother
Length: 139   **Sent with ?**
Bibliography: Gautier, *Nicéphore Bryennios*, 325; *Michel Italikos*, 46; Simeon, *Pismata*, xvi, xxix, 124; Maslev, *Studia*, 37-38; Leroy-Molinghen, 'Une phrase,' 423-424.
Discussed above: 55, 84, 93, 118, 131, 159, 174, 215.

G95, to the *hypatos ton philosophon*, Smyrnaios
Correspondent: THEODORE SMYRNAIOS (20); see also G6, G28
Date: ? (Gautier: winter 1105)   **Editions:** Gautier, II, 481; Meurs
Place: ? (Gautier: Pelagonia)   40, 441-442
Incipit: εἰ μὲν τραγῳδιῶν ἀκούειν ποθεῖς   **Desinit:** τὴν οἰκείαν χρηστότητα
Message: Θ is not happy   **Genre:** *schetliastike*; tragedies recalled
Subject matter: Θ's troubles
Structure: 1) if TS wishes to hear tragedies he should ask Θ for letters—which are full of lamentations about his situation; 2) he cannot write anything else; 3) may TS escape such disasters; 4) prayer for deliverance from his weakness.
Tone: light, despite subject matter   **Bearer:** ?
Length: 123   **Sent with:** ?
Bibliography: Simeon, *Pismata*, 124-125; Leroy-Molinghen, 'Destinataire,' 435; Katičić, 'Biographika,' 371; Maslev, *Studia*, 38.
Discussed above: 21, 84, 159-161, 261.

G96, to the *panhypersebastos* Bryennios, the *gambros* of the emperor
Correspondent: NIKEPHOROS BRYENNIOS (11), later caesar, husband of Anna, historian; see also poem 1 with Lost 20
Date: 1097-1104   **Editions:** Gautier, II, 483-493; Meurs 41,
Place: ?Ochrid to ?CP   434-451; Gautier, *Nicéphore Bryennios*, 320-337
Incipit: δεῦτε, ἀκούσατε καὶ διηγήσομαι ὑμῖν   **Desinit:** παρανομήσας ὅλως, ὡς οἶμαι
Message: to get a *prostaxis* for the village   **Genre** *parakletike*
Subject matter: Lazaros affair
Structure: 1) NB has taken Θ from the darkness of hell, made the emperor be for him a life-giving sun and checked Θ's enemies who have embittered the emperor and destroyed Θ's church; 2) the cause is the praktors who have told lies to the emperor, made Θ out to be a monster and set up Lazaros, *paroikos* of the church (97); 3) Lazaros makes common cause with Θ's enemies all over Bulgaria; 4) charge of arson in Ochrid; Θ was in Pelagonia; Lazaros, who has been working on the emperor, claims that Θ is dripping with wealth; 5) specific fiscal grievances; 6) case of the *chorion*; 7) begs for a *prostaxis*; 8) wishes he had died before his time for he has done no wrong against God or NB.
Tone: angry and hysterical   **Bearer:** ?
Length: 1692   **Sent with** ?G98 (a little later?)

Bibliography: Gautier, *Nicéphore Bryennios*; 317-333; Leroy-Molinghen, 'Trois mots slaves,' 111-115; Simeon, *Pismata*, xxiii, xxix, xxxi, 125-134; Nikolaev, *Feodalni*, 69; 209-211; Snegarov, *Archiepiskopiia*, 220; Xanalatos, *Beiträge*, 42, 62, 70; Litavrin, *Bolg. i Viz.*, 86-89, 211, 316, Panov, *Teofilakt*, 75-76, 82, 88, 117-119, 157, 198-200; 221; Obolensky, 'Byzantine Impact,' 158; Mullett, 'Classical Tradition,' 92-93; Papayanni, *Ta oikonomika*, 266-267; 'Phorologikes plerophories,' 402-404; 'Boulgaroi,' 64-65, 71; Mullett, 'Patronage,' 125-127; Harvey, 'The Land,' 147-148; Solarino, 'Un intellettuale,' 82; Angold, *Church and Society*,162-3; Mullett, 'Slavs.'
Discussed above: 18, 19, 55, 67, 84, 85, 93, 95-96, 101, 124-125, 127, **131-132**, 149-150, 169, 171, 197, 213, 215, 240, 264, 270-271.

G97, to kyr John Peribleptenos
Correspondent: JOHN PERIBLEPTENOS (**17**), monastic doctor? See also G101
Date: ? (Gautier: 1097-1104)   **Editions:** Gautier, II, 495-497; Meurs
Place: ? (Gautier: Ochrid)   42, 451-454
Incipit: τί δὲ μέλλω ἀφεῖναι τῷ οὕτω μέν   **Desinit:** οἵ γε ἀληθῶς ἄξιοι.
Message: to ask for a letter   **Genre:** request for letter
Subject matter: communication
Structure: 1) for a long time there has been no exchange of letters between JP and Θ; JP should not have accused himself; Θ is at fault; 2) JP has not kept his promise to write and Θ needs his friends' talk as much as the very sick need Asklepios (his own medicines are useless) 3) JP must cure the sick Θ by writing often.
Tone: intimate   **Bearer:** ?
Length: 361   **Sent with:** ?
Bibliography: Simeon, *Pismata*, 135; Maslev, *Studia*, 26; Leroy-Molinghen, 'Médecins,' 492; Solarino, 'Un intellettuale,' 74.
Discussed above: 106-108, 132.

G98, to the brother of the emperor, *kyr* Adrian
Correspondent: ADRIAN KOMNENOS, the Grand Domestic(**41**); see also G5, G79, G85, G89
Date: =G96, after G94; 1097-1104   **Editions:** Gautier, I, 499-505; Meurs 43
Place: from ?Ochrid to ?Constantinople   453-460
Incipit: καὶ ἐβοηθήθην παρὰ τῆς σῆς ἀσυγκρίτου   **Desinit:** κακύνσεως καὶ κακώσεως
Message: to ask for A's mediation with the emperor **Genre:** *parakletike*
Subject matter: Lazaros crisis; *chorion*; fire while Θ in Pelagonia
Structure: 1) thanks AK for help with rumours spread by Medenos (**83**), architect of a fortress of incrimination; he has been denounced to the emperor but with the help of *logos* has defended himself successfully; 2) current problems: Lazaros, notorious villain, has discovered Θ's intolerance of calumny and pretends to be the victim of a fire in Ochrid caused by Θ; this gains the emperor's sympathy 3) Lazaros has ganged up with residents of the *chorion* to have the emperor's *prostaxis* declared null; 4) has not AK defended Θ to the emperor, who will not condemn a man unheard? 5) may God give a more perfect reward to AK for Θ's rescue; 6) and (usual prayer).
Tone: complimentary but desperate   **Bearer:** ?
Length: 950   **Sent with:** ?G96
Bibliography: Dölger, *Regesten*, 1285; Gautier, *Nicéphore Bryennios*, 321, 322, 324; Maslev, 'Melissenos;' 179-186; Obolensky, *Bogomils*, 196, n.1; Hohlweg, *Verwaltungsgeschichte*, 21; Simeon, *Pismata*, xxx, 135-138; Nikolaev, *Feodalni*, 67, 225-226; Xanalatos, *Beiträge*, 31, 55; Panov, *Teofilakt*,

160; Maslev, *Studia*, 23-25; 121-122; Obolensky, *Portraits*, 78; Mullett, 'Patronage,' 125-127, 136; Papayanni, 'Boulgaroi,' 64-65; Harvey, 'The Land,' 145.
Discussed above: 19, 84, 85, 93, 96, 101, 125, 127, 149-150, 154, 174, 214, 215.

G99, to the doctor of the emperor Pantechnes
Correspondent: MICHAEL PANTECHNES (7); see also G39, G48, G50, ??94, G102, G128, G129, G130, G131, ??115, ?116

Date: (Gautier: 1097-1104) ?=G100; after G102
Place: from Bulgaria to Constantinople
Incipit: Χάρις πολλὴ τῷ λόγῳ
Message: request to tell the emperor Θ's story

Editions: Gautier, II, 507; Meurs 44, 459-462
Desinit: σοῦ προϊστάμενος Νέστορος
Genre: *parakletike + apologetike + eucharistike*

Subject matter: Θ's problems
Structure: 1) Θ is grateful to reason which engendered MP in these wicked days which usually engender Empedoclean monsters; 2) MP fights on Θ's behalf and repays him for being his teacher; 3) Θ has improvised responses to calumny but it is for God to illumine the emperor's mind; 4) Θ must trust God's justice and *philanthropia* (he is innocent of the charges); 5) MP must use the darts of his eloquence and fight the Ethiopians as Antilochos on behalf of Nestor.

Tone: energetic, persuasive
Length: 222

Bearer: ?
Sent with: ?G100

Bibliography: Simeon, *Pismata*, 138-139; Darrouzès, *Tornikai*, 49, n.31; Maslev, *Studia*, 28-32; Mullett, 'Classical Tradition,' 92-93; 'Patronage,' 129.
Discussed above: 110, 132, 154, 171, 178, 215, 260.

G100, to the philosopher kyr John
Correspondent: JOHN the philosopher (31)

Date: ?
Place: from ?Ochrid to ?
Incipit: Οὐκ ἄρα μάτην ἐγὼ τὸν ἐμόν
Message: plea to continue to combat rumour
Subject matter: calumny crisis?

Editions: Gautier, II, 509-511; Meurs 45, 461-464
Desinit: τοῦ Πνεύματος ἐπιπεπαίνεται
Genre: *parakletike*

Structure: 1) J is different from other philosophers; they hate their brothers (and God); his love for his brethren mirrors his love for God 2) from the time that he saw Θ suffering (and he was suffering himself) he used his influence with those who could stop it. 3) his words of comfort are sweet and convincing and not intended for self-promotion; 4) if he hears the enemies of truth calumniate Θ again, he must not fail to speak; 5) though gentle, he is to use his intelligence and fight; strengthening the emperor's good will may he be rewarded by the Lord; 6) prayer for J.

Tone: warm; hopeful
Length: 350

Bearer: ?
Sent with: ?G99

Bibliography: Simeon, *Pismata*, 139-142; Maslev, *Studia*, 38-39
Discussed above: 132, 215.

G101, to *kyr* John Peribleptenos
Correspondent: JOHN PERIBLEPTENOS (17); see also G97

Date: ?
Place: from ?Ochrid to ?CP

Editions: Gautier, II, 513; Meurs 46, 463-464

Incipit: Τὸ σκαμβὸν ξύλον, ὦ καλὲ Ἰωάννη   **Desinit:** πονηροῦ παγίδας ὑπερπηδῶν
Message: communication   **Genre:** *schetliastike*
Subject matter: Θ's troubles; one enemy in particular
Structure: 1) begins with *Par.Gr.*, II, 208; 683, and applies it to his enemy who is unchanged; he is like a wild beast, a murderous, possessed outcast; 2) Θ must pray to God; no matter if the enemy's Bulgarian subordinates are sent over a cliff (like the Gadarene swine); 3) prays that he follow his own path and be guided by God; 4) may JP be guided to every good, sidestepping the Wicked One's snares.
Tone: cynical   **Bearer:** ?
Length: 131   **Sent with:** ?
Bibliography: Simeon, *Pismata*, xxiii, 143; Snegarov, *Archiepiskopiia*, 220; Maslev, *Studia*, 124; Papayanni, 'Boulgaroi,' 64-65; Mullett, 'Slavs.'
Discussed above: 270-271.

G102, to his pupil Pantechnes, *kyr* Michael, the doctor
Correspondent: MICHAEL PANTECHNES (7); see also G39, G48, G50, ?G94, G99, G128, G129, G130, G131, ??G115, ??G116
Date: before G99   **Editions:** Gautier, II, 515; Meurs 47,
Place: ?from Ochrid to ?CP   463-466
Incipit: οὐκ οἶδα πότερον συνησθήσομαί σοι   **Desinit:** ἀνώτερον καὶ κακώσεως
Message: congratulations on MP's appointment to the   **Genre:** *syncharitike* (inverted)
imperial court   **Subject matter:** promotion
Structure: simple: 1) doesn't know whether to commiserate or rejoice; 2) advice on behaviour; 3) God will glorify MP; let him keep silence; 4) usual prayer.
Tone: benevolent; didactic   **Bearer:** ?
Length: 197   **Sent with:** ?
Bibliography: Simeon, *Pismata*, xvi, 143-145; Gautier, *Michel Italikos*, 46; Darrouzès, *Tornikai*, 49, n.31; Xanalatos, *Beiträge*, 68; Maslev, *Studia*, 28-32; Kazhdan, 'Doctor,' 44; Obolensky, *Portraits*, 55; Polemes, 'Paratereseis,' 382.
Discussed above: 123, 173, 234.

G103, to the Bulgarians taught (or chastised) by him
Correspondent: Bulgar pupils (63); Nothing is otherwise known of these Bulgars, or whether they are taught or chastised. Zlatarsky suggested they were bishops; Simeon tax-collectors.
Date: ?   **Editions:** Gautier, II, 517; Meurs 48,
Place: ?Ochrid   465-466
Incipit: ἐκλείπει μέν μοι ἡ ψυχὴ τῷ πόθῳ   **Desinit:** καὶ πλασθῆναι καὶ πλάττεσθαι
Message: report of his illness   **Genre:** *schetliastike* with *parainetike*
Subject matter: Θ's injured hip
Structure: 1) Θ's soul faints for the tents of God, Ps.83(84).2; he would take wings to reach the object of his desire; 2) his hip speaks saying, 'stay in bed, wretched one' (Eur. *Or.* 258); 3) he is not long for this world so 4) the Bulgars would be ill-advised to try to get rid of him and gain a reputation for malice.
Tone: fanciful   **Bearer:** ?
Length: 116   **Sent with:** ?

Bibliography: Maslev, *Studia*, 80-81, 124; Zlatarsky, *Istoriia*, 348-349; Simeon, *Pismata*, 145-146, Litavrin, *Bolg. i Viz.*, 370; Gautier, II, 44.
Discussed above: 28, 96, 150.

G104, to the *protonotarios* of the *doux* of Attaleia, *kyr* John Attaleiates
Correspondent: JOHN ATTALEIATES, *protonotarios* of the *doux* of Attaleia (33)
Date: ?   Editions: Gautier, II, 519; Meurs 49,
Place: ?   465-466
Incipit: οἶμαί σε χάριτας ὀφείλειν ἐμοί   Desinit: κακώσεως καὶ κακύνσεως
Message: help from JA for the bishop of Side (99)   Genre: ?*systatike*
Subject matter: troubles of the bishop of Side
Structure: 1) reminds JA what Θ has given him; 2) asks in return help for the bishop; 3) may Θ, when he hears from the bishop, be in a position to bless JA with a father's prayers (Sir.3.9); 4) usual prayer.
Tone: pragmatic   Bearer: metropolitan of Side? or in see?
Length: 162   Sent with: ?
Bibliography: Simeon, *Pismata*, 146-148; Gautier, 'Le synode,' 262; Mullett,'Semnea.'
Discussed above: 28, 36, 99, 136, 173, 175, 204.

G105, to the *doux* of Dyrrachion
Correspondent: JOHN BRYENNIOS, *doux* of Dyrrachion (34); see also G86
Date: 1097-1104; after G86   Editions: Gautier, II, 521; Meurs 50,
Place: from Ochrid to Dyrrachion   467-468
Incipit: εἰ καὶ μικρὰν καὶ ὀλίγην τὴν τῶν ἰχθύων   Desinit: ἀνώτερος καὶ κακώσεως
Message: reinforcement   Genre: *prosphonetike*
Subject matter: gift
Structure: 1) symbolism of the gift of fish; 3) wishes that Bryennios may live his life despising the devil and being a benefactor to the clergy; 3) for he will obtain spiritual goods in place of material ones; 4) usual prayer.
Tone: ceremonial   Bearer: ?
Length: 261   Sent with: 100 fish
Bibliography: Simeon, *Pismata*, 148-149; Gautier, *Nicéphore Bryennios*, 318-321; *Acta Albaniae*, no. 64, 19-20; Snegarov, *Archiepiskopiia*, 223.
Discussed above: 33, 169-170.

G106
Correspondent: Recipient of G106 (61): unknown: high ecclesiastic of smart family
Date: ?   Editions: Gautier, II, 523; Meurs 51,
Place: ?Ochrid   467-470
Incipit: μακρότερα γράφειν τῇ σῇ ἀγάπῃ   Desinit: πάσης ἐπηρείας ἀνώτερος
Message: communication   Genre: *pros philon aspastike*
Subject matter: fisc
Structure: 1) Θ does not have time for a long letter; 2) how is the correspondent amid all his responsibilities? 3) Θ's troubles with the praktor, but Christ gives hope; 4) may the correspondent be guarded against the attacks of wolves.

Tone: friendly
Length: 145
Bibliography: Simeon, *Pismata*, 150; Maslev, *Studia*, 43, 124.
Discussed above: 97, 122, 131, 173.

Bearer: ?
Sent with: ?

G107, to the *despoina* who visited him when he was ill

Correspondent: EIRENE DOUKAINA *despoina* (37)? if so could be during one of the imperial stays in Thessalonike? or Maria of Alania (50)? if so during a visit to CP? (Gautier: Maria c. 1094.)

Date: if Eirene 1106-7 (Gautier: c. 1094)
Place: ?
Incipit: ἐγκαινίζεις ἀεὶ τοῖς ἔργοις
Message: thanks and praise for the lady
Subject matter: visit

Editions: Gautier, II, 525; Meurs 52, 469-470
Desinit: κατόρθωμά τε καὶ μίσθωμα
Genre: *eucharistike*

Structure: 1) she never ceases to renew by her actions the benefits of the incarnation; 2) she deigned to visit Θ and revived him; 3) in exchange, prays that she may not cease to show in herself the divine mystery and know the same reward.

Tone: ceremonial
Length: 74
Bibliography: Polemis, *Doukai*, 73, n.29; Simeon, *Pismata*, xiv, xvi, 150-151; Panov, *Teofilakt*, 272-274; Leroy-Molinghen, 'Médecins,' 492; Mullett, 'Patronage,' 139.
Discussed above: 88, 96, 150, 175, 196.

Bearer: ?
Sent with: ?

G108, to Makrembolites the *archon* of Prespa

Correspondent: N. MAKREMBOLITES (14)
Date: ?
Place: from Ochrid to Prespa
Incipit: οὔπω μὲν καθαρῶς τῆς κατακλινησάσης
Message: request for help in organising synod
Subject matter: synod of Prespa

Editions: Gautier, II, 131-142; Meurs 53, 469-470
Desinit: καὶ συμπέφυκε καὶ συνηύξηται.
Genre: *parakletike + ainigmatike*

Structure: 1) Θ's illness: though not completely recovered he is leaving his bed because of the impending synod (miracle of the paralytic); 2) looks forward to embracing M there; 3) warning not to fail to help the ecclesiastical official charged with victualling (image of grasshoppers); 4) may M (as name suggests) be bombarded with the flowers of Θ's eloquence at him (pun on surname).

Tone: light; intricate; ingenious; firm
Length: 149
Bibliography: Pelekanides, *Prespa*, 65; Ahrweiler, *Administration*, 72; Simeon, *Pismata*, xxv, 151-152; Litavrin, *Bolg. i Viz.*, 297; Panov, *Teofilakt*, 272-274; Maslev, *Studia*, 82; Mullett, 'Classical Tradition,' 92-93; 'Patronage,' 131; Angold, *Church and Society*, 168; Mullett, 'Bishop-List.'
Discussed above: 55, 89-91, 96, 131, 153, 159, 173, 237-239, 263, 270.

Bearer: ?
Sent with: ??flowers

G109 to the *epi ton deeseon*

Correspondent: N.N., the *epi ton deeseon* (57); surely, contra Gautier, the secular official
Date: ?
Place: ?
Incipit: σὺ μὲν πρὸς ἡμᾶς ἃ πρὸς Ὀρέστην

Editions: Gautier, II, 529; Meurs 54, 469-470
Desinit: ἀπὸ δόξης εἰς δόξαν ὑψούμενος

Message: request for the release of a Tornikes/ Tornikios (91) from military duty
Genre: *parakletike*
Subject matter: this request
Structure: 1) he behaves to Θ as the Mycenaeans to Orestes (they did not address him), but Θ does address him with oracular brevity; 2) Θ's gibes about his slowness to write burn like a furnace at his expense, and he adds more fuel; 3) if he releases from military service Θ's *gambros ep' adelphide* the Nile will put the fire out; 4) can he solve the riddle? 5) prays that he be guarded from all evils and the monster of slowness and may Θ ever hear of his growing glory.
Tone: light; involved
Bearer: ?
Length: 187
Sent with: ?
Bibliography: Simeon, *Pismata*, 153-154; Darrouzès, *Tornikai*, 25-26; Adontz, 'Taronites, IV,' 30-42.
Discussed above: 28, 122, 152-154, 173, 201, 212.

G110, to the doctor of the emperor, kyr Niketas
Correspondent: NIKETAS, imperial doctor (32); Gautier gives to Nicholas Kallikles (3)
Date: ?Sept 1105 to Jan 1106 or (Strumica) ?March 1106
Editions: Gautier, II, 531-533; Meurs 55, 471-474
Place: from ?Ochrid or ?Ekklesiai
Incipit: Πολλὰ μὲν τὰ βιαζόμενά με
Desinit: κακώσεως καὶ κακύνσεως
Message: apology for not coming to see him
Genre: *systatike+apologetike+ekphrastike*
Subject matter: the Vardar; Θ's illness
Structure: 1) two streams prevent Θ's coming: his streaming head cold and the Vardar, better called Acheron; 4) instead sends his brother (not ill, not afraid of the crossing); 5) his mission is to provide anything of which Θ's absence deprives N and to enjoy his love and wisdom because of which Θ calls him 'Teiresias in Hades' (quotes Hom, *Od.*, 10.405) and Empedocles; 6) ends with the usual prayer.
Tone: grumbling but friendly
Bearer: brother (Gautier: not Demetrios)
Length: 327
Sent with: ?
Bibliography: Simeon, *Pismata*, 154-155; Gautier, 'L'obituaire,' 255; 'L'épiscopat,' 168; Litavrin, *Bolg. i Viz.*, 332; Panov, *Teofilakt*, 97; Maslev, *Studia*, 69-70; Kazhdan, 'Doctor,' 44; Papayanni, 'Boulgaroi,' 64-65; Mullett, 'Patronage,' 125-127; Polemes, 'Paratereseis,' 382; Mullett, 'Slavs.'
Discussed above: 55, 88, 93, 103, 107-108, 131, 174, 246, 269-271..

G111, to *kyr* Nicholas Kallikles
Correspondent: NICHOLAS KALLIKLES (3); see also G93, G94, G112
Date: Sept 1106-Jan 1107
Editions: Gautier, II, 535; Meurs 56, 473-476; Romano, *Nicola Callicle*,59
Place: from ?Ekklesiai to Thessalonike
Incipit: ἀλλὰ σύ μοι δραστικὰς τάς
Desinit: ἐγὼ θεόθεν ἐξαιτῶ πρόσκομμα
Message: request for NK to approach the emperor on Θ's behalf
Genre: *parakletike*
Subject matter: Ekklesiai case; Demetrios; house in Thessalonike
Structure: 1) NK, who is Θ's Asklepios, has the antidotes for Θ's ills, Thessalonike and Ekklesiai; 2) the house in Thessalonike; 3) the village of Ekklesiai; 4) greetings from Θ's brother who is dying; prayer for God's intervention.
Tone: light and fantastic, turning grave
Bearer ?οἱ ἐν τῷ χωρίῳ ἡμέτεροι?
Length: 236
Sent with: ?

Bibliography: Simeon, *Pismata*, 156; Gautier, 'L'épiscopat,' 168; Nikolaev, *Feodalni*, 73; Xanalatos, *Beiträge*, 48; Litavrin, *Bolg. i Viz.*, 81; Panov, *Teofilakt*, 214; Maslev, *Studia*, 37-38, 125; Leroy-Molinghen, 'Médecins,' 490-491; Mullett, 'Patronage,' 125-127; Angold, *Church and Society*, 161.
Discussed above: 55, 57, 84, 88, 92, 95-97, 125, 127, 151, **153-154**, 174, 201, 213, 214, 244.

G112, to the same
Correspondent: NICHOLAS KALLIKLES (3); see also G93, G94, G111

Date: Sept 1106-Jan 1107; before poem 3

Place: Ekklesiai

Incipit: βίαιον ἐγώ σοι χρῆμα, ἀεί τι λαμβάνειν

Message: demand for medical books

Subject matter: book-exchange

Editions: Gautier, II, 537; Meurs 57, 475-6

Desinit: ἄδολόν τε καὶ ἀκαπήλευτον

Genre: indirect *systatike* included in *parakletike*

Structure: 1) apologises for always asking for something; reference to the parable of the sower; 2) asks for copies of Galen, Hippocratic commentaries and a work on the teachings of Hippocrates and Plato; 4) the bearer who will pick up this 'fruit' will be recommended by Theodore Smyrnaios (20); 5) prayer.

Tone: light

Length: 183

Bearer: relative of Theodore Smyrnaios

Sent with: ?G114

Bibliography: see poems written on return of the books, Gautier, I, 350-351; Simeon, *Pismata*, 156-158; Leroy-Molinghen, 'Destinataire,' 435; Katičić, 'Biographika,' 366; Nikolaev, *Feodalni*, 56; Maslev, *Studia*, 37-38, 125; Leroy-Molinghen, 'Médecins,' 485.
Discussed above: 34, 84, 88, 95-96, 108, 118, 136, 153-154, 159, 213, 240.

G113, to the bishop of Kitros
Correspondent: N.N., bishop of KITROS (9); see also G14, G52, G121

Date: ?summer 1107

Place: Ekklesiai

Incipit: οὕτω μοι κρειττόνως σύνεσο

Message: explanation of his movements

Subject matter: illness of Demetrios

Editions: Gautier, II, 539; Meurs 58, 475-478

Desinit: ἄνωθεν καταρράκτας ἄνοιγε

Genre: *apangeltike*

Structure: 1) Θ would have been better to have gone to Constantinople especially with his sick brother; 2) causes of sickness and treatment; 3) asks for the bishop to intercede with God, healing Θ's weakness.

Tone: despairing

Length: 257

Bearer: ?

Sent with: ?

Bibliography: Simeon, *Pismata*, 158-159; Gautier, 'L'épiscopat,' 168-169; Maslev, *Studia*, 76-77; Leroy-Molinghen, 'Médecins,' 489, 491.
Discussed above: 67, 84, 88, 92, 95, 97, 105, 108, 132, 173, 174, 244.

G114, to the *proedros* and *proximos* Pantechnes
Correspondent: MICHAEL PANTECHNES (7)

Date: =G112; 1106-07

Place: ?Ekklesiai

Incipit: σύ μοι αἴτιος ὄχλων· αἰσθόμενοι γάρ τινες

Message: recommendation

Editions: Gautier, II, 541; Meurs 59, 477-478

Desinit: τῷ βουλήματι σύνδρομον

Genre: subverted *systatike*

Subject matter: relative of Smyrnaios
Message: to apologise for not coming to see him
Structure: 1) MP is a cause of bother to Θ; 2) he is under pressure to write to MP from many people with an exaggerated view of his power; 3) the bearer for example: if you can do anything for him (or even if not) glory to God; 4) MP is guiltless, for his wish to help outstrips his power.

Tone: amiable, teasing   **Bearer:** relative of Theodore Smyrnaios
Length: 131   **Sent with:** G112
Bibliography: Simeon, *Pismata*, 159-160; Darrouzès, *Tornikai*, 50; Leroy-Molinghen, 'Destinataire,' 43; Xanalatos, *Beiträge*, 71; Maslev, *Studia*, 126; Polemes, 'Paratereseis,' 381.
Discussed above: 84, 88, 125, **136-138**, 150-151, 170.

G115

Correspondent: either GREGORY KAMATEROS (4) (Gautier) or MICHAEL PANTECHNES(7) (above, xxx).

Date: ?	**Editions:** Gautier, II, 543; Meurs 60, 479-480
Place: ?	
Incipit: ποθοῦμεν μαθεῖν ὡς ἔχετε	**Desinit:** δυσχερείας πραγμάτων ἀνώτερον
Message: demand for a letter	**Genre:** letter request

Subject matter: news
Structure: very simple: 1) Θ wishes to hear how his correspondent is and explains (obscurely) why; 2) offers two rules to help the correspondent judge Θ's own state: it is just like his own; Θ is subject to another's will (quotation from E. *Hec.*1182); 3) prayer (gloomy): may the Lord rescue him and guard the other from all harm.

Tone: cynical; friendly; mannered   **Bearer:** ?
Length: 126   **Sent with:** ?
Bibliography: Simeon, *Pismata*, 160-161; Nikolaev, *Feodalik*, 56; Maslev, *Studia*, 69-72.
Discussed above: 28, 101, 150-151, 172.

G116, to the same

Correspondent: MICHAEL PANTECHNES (7) or GREGORY KAMATEROS (4)

Date: ?before 1107	**Editions:** Gautier, II, 545; Meurs 61, 479-480
Place: ?	
Incipit: ἀρκεῖ πρὸς τὸ γνωρίσαι σοι τὰ καθ' ἡμᾶς	**Desinit:** κακώσεως καὶ κακύνσεως
Message: to accompany the bearer	**Genre:** *systatike*

Subject matter: formal
Structure: 1) Θ's brother can tell how Θ is; 2) his correspondent should tell others about his situation: he may understand the nature but not the extent—but in fact he does understand since his own situation is similar; 3) usual prayer.

Tone: neutral   **Bearer:** brother
Length: 88   **Sent with:** ?
Bibliography: Simeon, *Pismata*, 161; Maslev, *Studia*, 28-32, 126-127, 247.
Discussed above: 93, 101, 150-151, 173, 174, 246.

G117, by the same

Correspondent: ?

Date: ?
Place?
Incipit: μὴ θαυμάζῃς, εἰ λακωνίζω σοι
Message: communication
Subject matter: formal

Editions: Gautier, II, 547; Meurs 62, 479-480
Desinit: τὰ τῆς ἀγάπης ἐξύμνησε
Genre: a 'laconic' letter

Structure: 1) the correspondent must not be surprised that this letter is short; 2) let him ask the bearer; why: it was the bearer himself who eagerly requested the letter; 3) sends good wishes for health and spirits.

Tone: friendly

Length: 60
Bibliography: Simeon, *Pismata*, 161; Maslev, *Studia*, 28-32.
Discussed above: 149.

Bearer: ? Gautier: same as G112 and G114 (Smyrnaios)
Sent with: ?

G118, to the *sebastos kyr* Constantine Doukas

Correspondent: CONSTANTINE DOUKAS, ruler of the Vardar: (36), son of *protostrator* Michael, official of Boleron-Strymon-Thessalonike. See also G119; G127, G88

Date: just after G88 = G127
Place: Vardar village: αὐτόθι = Ekklesiai
Incipit: Εἰ μὲν ἥ τε τοῦ σώματος ἰσχὺς καί
Message: to apologise for not coming
Subject matter: Vardar village

Editions: Gautier, II, 549; Meurs 63, 479-480
Desinit: κακώσεως καὶ κακύνσεως
Genre: adventus

Structure: 1) Θ would have come if he were well and the season were clement; 2) instead his letter offers *proskynesis*; 3) CD will accept it (indeed has done) and is asking what his request is 4) Θ has a problem in a Vardar village; 5) on the wings of prayer CD is asked to deal with his people from the Vardar village as if they were CD's own servants; 6) he must show he has inherited his father's good attitude to Θ so that he may be rewarded; 7) ends with the usual prayer.

Tone: ceremonial
Length: 241
Bibliography: Simeon, *Pismata*, 161-162; Zlatarsky, 'Stellvertretende Verwalter,' 156; Maslev, *Studia*, 127; Gautier, 'Monodie inédite,' 163; Angold, *Church and Society*, 161.
Discussed above: 38, 57, 66, 83, 93, 96, 146-147, 169, 171.

Bearer: ?τῶν αὐτόθι ἡμετέρων
Sent with: ?

G119, to the same

Correspondent: CONSTANTINE DOUKAS (36); see also G118

Date: after G118, G88, G127
Place: from Ochrid to Thessalonike
Incipit: Εἰ καὶ μικράν τινα ἰχθύων ἀποστολήν
Message: to accompany a gift of fish

Editions: Gautier, II, 551; Meurs 64, 481-2
Desinit: κακύνσεως καὶ κακώσεως
Subject matter: fishing rights of church of O

Structure: 1) the gift of fish is not worthy of CD but he imitates his father in *diakrisis* and piety; 2) in virtue of the former he holds that Θ has no right over the lake; in virtue of the latter he will accept the gift as praise of the Theotokos; 3) for CD every act of praise is great, so he will enjoy the present; if not it will be another fault in Θ's tally 4) Believes he will accept the gift in praise of the Virgin; 5) may she protect him in all his life.

Tone: ceremonial   **Bearer:** ?
Length: 141   **Sent with:** fish
Bibliography: Simeon, *Pismata*, 162-164; Maslev, *Studia*, 127; Mullett, 'Patronage,' 125-127.
Discussed above: 33, 169.

G120, to the *magistros kyr* John Pantechnes
Correspondent: JOHN PANTECHNES (16), *magistros,* ?father of Michael
Date: Spring 1108   **Editions:** Gautier, II, 553; Meurs 65,
Place: Thessalonike to CP   483-486
Incipit: καὶ τί ἀνταποδώσω τῷ Κυρίῳ   **Desinit:** μισθωσάμενος, ἤδη ἄπειμι
Message: description of journey and illness   **Genre:** *hodoiporikon*
Subject matter: second Norman war
Structure: 1) 'what shall I return to the Lord?' Ps.115.3 (116.12) and many biblical references; 2) Θ's illness when he boarded the boat; 3) safe arrival at Thessalonike; 4) Ochrid occupied by [Bohemond] the slave and rebel, the lizard who warmed himself in the rays of imperial favour; Michael *protostrator* is recruiting and organising; 5) Θ is leaving on horseback for Ochrid, there being no Daidalos in Thessalonike to make him wings.
Tone: lively, vivid   **Bearer:** ?
Length: 490   **Sent with** ?
Bibliography: Gautier, *Michel Italikos*, 47; 'Manuel Straboromanos,' 170; Polemis, *Doukai*, 55; Gautier, 'L'obituaire,' 254; *Acta Albaniae*, 79; Darrouzès, *Tornikai*, 50; Simeon, *Pismata*, xxiv, xxx, 164-168; xxxii; Uspenskij, *Obrazobanie*, 10; Katičić, 'Korespondencija,' 184; Xanalatos, *Beiträge*, 45; Maslev, *Studia*, 73-74; 127-128; Litavrin, *Bolg. i Viz.*, 335; Leroy-Molinghen, 'Médecins,' 488; Cheynet, *Pouvoir et contestations*, 95; Barišić, 'Manastira i Struga,' 25; Polemes, 'Paratereseis,' 381.
Discussed above: 16, 55, 69, **88**, 93, 97, 125, 127, 131, 262.

G121, to the bishop of Kitros
Correspondent: N.N., bishop of KITROS (9); see also G14, G52, G113
Date: 1107   **Editions:** Gautier, II, 559; Meurs 66,
Place: from Ochrid to Kitros   485-488
Incipit: ἔστι καὶ γράφοντα μὴ ἀγαπᾶν   **Desinit:** βουλομένους ἀπορραπίζοντος.
Message: request for the bishop's prayers   **Genre:** announcement of death
Subject matter: the death of Demetrios
Structure: 1) writing without loving and loving without writing; the bishop must forgive Θ's *agraphia;* 2) the death of Θ's brother has been added to his other troubles; 3) he asks for the bishop's prayers; 6) Θ is ill; may he be guided by God.
Tone: melancholy   **Bearer:** ?
Length: 150   **Sent with:** ?G122
Bibliography: Simeon, *Pismata*, 168-169; Gautier, 'L'épiscopat,' 168-169; Mullett, 'Patronage,' 125-127.
Discussed above: 84, 92, 97, 132, 142, 170, 173, 174, 244.

G122, to the bishop of Debra
Correspondent: N.N., bishop of DEBRA (58)
Date: 1107   **Editions:** Gautier, II, 561; Meurs 67,
Place: fom Ochrid to some place which is not Debra   487-488

Incipit: ὁ μὲν χρηστότατός μοι ἀδελφός
Message: recall to duty
Subject matter: death of Demetrios

Desinit: ἐπισκεψόμενον πρόβατα.
Genre: announcement of death

Structure: 1) in medias res: the death of his brother, who was happy to have been taken; 2) Θ has lamented according to nature and the bounds fixed by God; 3) God will not leave Θ without support; 4) the bishop must make this prayer and also ask God to ensure his own return to his flock.

Tone: collected
Length: 132

Bearer: ?
Sent with: ?G121

Bibliography: *Acta Albaniae*, 78; Simeon, *Pismata*, 169-170.
Discussed above: 84, 92-94, 128, 132, 142, 150, 172, 174, **244-245**, 264.

G123, to the *sebastos* and *doux* of Veroia, *kyr* Constantine, the son of the *sebastokrator*
Correspondent: CONSTANTINE KOMNENOS (12)

Date: before 1107
Place: from ?Ochrid to ?Veroia
Incipit: ὁρῶν μου τὸν ἀδελφὸν διακεχυμένον
Message: expression of affection for CK
Subject matter: brother

Editions: Gautier, II, 563; Meurs 68, 487-490
Desinit: καὶ εὐγενεῖς τρέφοντος
Genre: cf.hagiography topoi

Structure: 1) describes Demetrios's joy as he departed; 2) Θ asked the reason and was told that Demetrios was glad because he would see the *sebastos* [=CK]; 3) Θ's physical reaction and envy of his brother's good fortune; 4) CK draws all men towards him by a golden chain of goodness; he must persist!

Tone: visionary
Length: 163

Bearer: Demetrios? or followed?
Sent with: ?

Bibliography: Simeon, *Pismata*, 170; Ahrweiler, *Administration*, 63; Gautier, 'L'épiscopat,' 168; 'Le synode,' 227, n.9; Adontz, 'L'archevêque,' 585; Maslev, *Studia*, 49-59.
Discussed above: 20, 29, 36, 160, 173, 178, 246.

G124, to the ex-*chartophylax kyr* Nikephoros
Correspondent: NIKEPHOROS, *chartophylax* (23); see also G30, G51, G6, ??G83

Date: late in the episcopate; after 1094
Place: from Ochrid to ?
Incipit: αὐτοῦ μοι τοῦ σώματος
Message: asks for N's prayers
Subject-matter: health

Editions: Gautier, II, 565; Meurs 69, 489-90; Mercati,186 (362).
Desinit: βουλόμενός τε καὶ ἐπευχόμενος.
Genre: *pros filon aspastike*

Structure: very short: Θ is ill and requests N's prayers.

Tone: feeble
Length: 41

Bearer: ?
Sent with: ?

Bibliography: Simeon, *Pismata*, 171; Maslev, *Studia*, 29-32.
Discussed above: 149-150, 170.

G125
Correspondent ?
Date:?
Place: ?

Editions: Gautier, II, 567; Mercati, 186 (362)

Incipit: ἵππον εἰς πεδίον καλῶ
Message: call for help
Subject matter: unknown crisis
Structure: 1) starts with proverb, *Par.Gr.*, I, 191; 2) letter brief and encouraging; 3) correspondent is quick to come to the aid of the just; 4) races him against Achilles' horses, or Hieron's.
Tone: confident; exhilarating
Length: 41
Bibliography: Gautier, II, 566.
Discussed above: 150, 159, 171.

Desinit: εἰ δὲ βούλει τὸν Ἱέρωνος
Genre: *parakletike*

Bearer:?
Sent with:?

G126, to Palaiologos
Correspondent: GEORGE PALAIOLOGOS (45)
Date: after G88 (Gautier: 1096-1104/5)
Place: ?Ochrid to ?CP
Incipit: διὰ τῆς μεγίστης σου ἀντιλήψεως
Message: thanks for efforts on Θ's behalf
Subject matter: case of praktor in Ochrid

Editions: Gautier, II, 569; Meurs 70, 489-490
Desinit: ἀνώτερον καὶ κακύνσεως
Genre: *eucharistike*

Structure: 1) GP's help has given Θ some relief; intervention with the praktor was successful; 2) Θ will contribute what he can, prayers to God and praise before men; 3) GP should not cease to reclaim this desert; Θ would be at the mercy of its serpents without GP; 4) the just Judge will plait more crowns for him on Judgement Day, guarding him 5) usual prayer.
Tone: grateful
Length: 173

Bearer: ?
Sent with: ?

Bibliography: Simeon, *Pismata*, xxix, 171; Panov, *Teofilakt*, 91; Harvey, 'The Land,' 148; Angold, *Church and Society*, 163.
Discussed above: 96, 169, 171, 212.

G127, to the *protasekretes kyr* Gregory Kamateros
Correspondent: GREGORY KAMATEROS (4); see also G27, G31, G38, G67, ?G115, ?G116
Date: =G88=G118; before 1107
Place: within Bulgaria
Incipit: πάντων ἐγὼ μακαριώτατος νῦν
Message: congratulations on appointment
Subject matter: appointment to Vardar; Alexios's campaigns; Demetrios mentioned

Editions: Gautier, II, 571-579; Meurs 127, 489-498
Desinit: καὶ πλείω εὐεργετώμεθα
Genre: included satire and parainesis

Structure: 1) Θ is glad that his brother and his letter (Gautier: G115 or G116, but see also Table II below) have made GK happy; 2) congratulations on promotion to *nobellissimos* and *protaskretes;* 3) has heard that son of *protostrator* has been appointed to the rule of the Vardar; this will benefit Θ and he is accordingly grateful to GK; 4) he will do GK another favour by identifying to GK his 'Cyclops'; satirical picture of the 'Cyclops'; 5) GK has acquired the services of the charming Theodore Chryselios, who had been an official in Θ's area; another satirical picture; 6) this departure from an old man's seriousness has been occasioned by Θ's troubles and GK's frustration at the long expedition; praise of the emperor; 7) urges GK not to complain, since he is doing good work with the emperor.
Tone: lively; gossipy
Length: 1034

Bearer: ?
Sent with: ?G88, ?G118

Bibliography: Simeon, *Pismata*, 172-178; Gautier, 'Monodie inédite,' 163-164; 'Le synode,' 236, n.52; Polemis, *Doukai*, 79, n.5; Darrouzès, *Tornikai*, 129, n.5, 297, n.83; Uspenskii, *Obrazobanie,*

12-13; Nikolaev, *Feodalni*, 130; Panov, *Teofilakt*, 247; Maslev, *Studia*, 65-68; Angold, *Church and Society*, 163; Mullett, 'Bishop-List.'
Discussed above: **19**, 29, 36, 83, 84, 87, 88, 93-94, **100**, 101, 118, 124, 149-150, 160, 171, 178, 212, 213, 215, 234, 246.

G128 to the *proedros* Pantechnes

Correspondent: MICHAEL PANTECHNES (7); see also G39, G48, G50, ?G94, G99, G102, G129, G130, G131

Date: ?

Place: ?

Incipit: τὸν κολοφῶνα ἐπέθηκας

Message: commiseration with MP

Subject matter: unclear

Editions: Gautier, II, 581: Meurs 72, 499-500

Desinit: θειότερον καὶ ἡμέτερον.

Genre: *sympathetike*

Structure: 1) Θ accuses MP of adding to his worries; 2) Θ has a remedy compounded from the herbs of reason, which he cannot extract from its box; he will send it later; 3) for the present he has one thought to contribute: after winter comes spring; 4) and the Phoenix rising from the ashes relates to something more divine.

Tone: fanciful but sympathetic

Length: 101

Bearer: ?

Sent with: ?

Bibliography: Simeon, *Pismata*, 178; Panov, *Teofilakt*, 84; Maslev, *Studia*, 28-32, 131; Leroy-Molinghen, 'Médecins,' 492; Solarino, 'Un intellettuale,' 75.
Discussed above: 170, 173.

G129, to the doctor of the emperor, *kyr* Michael Pantechnes

Correspondent: MICHAEL PANTECHNES (7); see also G39, G48, G50, ?G94, G99, G102, G128, G130, G131, ??G115, ??G116

Date: ?

Place: ?Ochrid to ?

Incipit: ὑμεῖς δὲ ἀεὶ μὲν ἡμᾶς ταῖς ἐλπίσι

Message: invitation to stay

Subject matter: Blachernites (72) and the invisible *paroikoi*

Editions: Gautier, II, 583; Meurs 73, 499-500

Desinit: πάσης κακίας ἀνώτερος

Genre: *kletike*

Structure: 1) MP holds out hopes of visiting Θ but constantly disappoints him; let him drag himself away and be a comfort to Θ; 2) in spite of his reputation Θ is poor and will treat MP like a beggar seeking crusts and satisfied with the little he will get; 3) just let him come; the *paroikoi* 'lost' by Blachernites will enrich MP by giving him a clove of garlic each; 5) ends with the usual prayer.

Tone: light; intimate

Length: 112

Bearer:?

Sent with: poem 2

Bibliography: Simeon, *Pismata*, 178; Xanalatos, *Beiträge*, 64; Maslev, *Studia*, 28-32.
Discussed above: 125, 130, 150-151, 243.

G130, to the same

Correspondent: MICHAEL PANTECHNES (7); see also G39, G48, G50, ?G94, G99, G102, G128, G131, ??G115, ??G116

Date: ?

Place: ?

Incipit: χαίρω μὴ δεχόμενος ἐκ σοῦ γράμματα

Editions: Gautier, II, 585; Meurs 74, 499-500

Desinit: κακομηχανίας φυλάττοιο

Message: request for news   **Genre:** request for letters
Subject matter: MP's career
Structure: 1) a provocative opening: Θ is happy not to hear from MP because he believes he has been profitably busy; 2) if he is right, he takes comfort amid his own troubles; 3) if he is wrong, they are both under two-handed attack from the Evil One, whom only God will withstand; 4) may MP be preserved from the Devil's mischief.
Tone: piqued?   **Bearer:** ?
Length: 63   **Sent with:** ?
Bibliography: Simeon, *Pismata*, 179; Maslev, *Studia*, 28-32.
Discussed above: 28, 118, 150-151, 159.

G131, to the same
Correspondent: MICHAEL PANTECHNES (7); see also G39, G48, 50,??G94, G99, G102, G128, G129, G132, ??G115, ??G116
Date: ?   **Editions:** Gautier, II, 587; Meurs 75, 499
Place: ?
Incipit: διψῶντί μοι μαθεῖν   **Desinit:** τῶν ἐλπίδων αἷς ἐτρεφόμεθα
Message: to ask for fuller, clearer letters   **Genre:** request for letters
Subject matter: communication
Structure: 1) Θ thirsts for a report from MP on how he is; MP sends muddy drops which do not slake Θ's thirst; 2) Θ asks MP to tell more clearly of his situation and whether it accords with Θ's hopes.
Tone: concerned   **Bearer:** ?
Length: 37   **Sent with:** ?
Bibliography: Simeon, *Pismata*, 179.
Discussed above: 28, 122, 150-151, 173.

G132, to the brother of the deceased Psellos: from the archbishop of Bulgaria
Correspondent: N. PSELLOS (46), brother of Michael
Date: ?April-May1078-or 1097+   **Editions:** Gautier, II, 589; *REB* 24
Place: ?   (1966), 169
Incipit: Ὅτι μὲν ἀλγεῖς   **Desinit:** πάντες ἴσμεν οἷος ἦν
Message: consolation Psellos's brother on his death   **Genre:** *paramythetike*
Subject matter: death of Michael Psellos (84)
Structure: 1) Θ knows how hurt P is and is himself distressed not to be able to be with him; 2) by means of this letter he consoles P's spirit, so that he may take consolation from the thought that brother has migrated to God and escaped distress and illness; 3) all know his life, not just P.
Tone: affectionate; sympathetic; delicate   **Bearer:** ?
Length: 126   **Sent with:** ?
Bibliography: Gautier, 'Monodie,' 169-170; Gautier, I, 23.
Discussed above: 84, 139, **143**, 174.

G133
Correspondent: DEMETRIOS (HEPHAISTOS) (1); see also G134
Date: before 1107   **Editions:** Gautier, II, 591;
Place: ?

Incipit: Τὴν ἐπελθοῦάν σοι
Message: to console his brother in illness
Subject matter: illness of D

Desinit: καὶ συγχαρῆναί σοι
Genre: *paramythetike*

Structure: 1) anguished reaction of Θ when he heard D was ill; 2) no-one will rescue him fom the illness that possesses him unless God and the Virgin are his doctors; 3) Θ urges him to write and say how God has helped him; 4) may he give D health and make Θ worthy to be glad with him.

Tone: affectionate
Length: 146
Bibliography: Gautier, I, 19.
Discussed above: 92, 98, 119, 150, 173, 174, 178, **244**.

Bearer: ?
Sent with: ?

G134, to his brother Demetrios who had asked....

Correspondent: DEMETRIOS (HEPHAISTOS) (1); see also G133
Date: ?
Place: from Bulgaria to ?

Editions: Gautier, I, 335-343

Incipit: δελφῖνα ποιεῖς ἀροτῆρα
Message: information as requested
Subject matter: liturgical practices

Desinit: τὸν βοῦν ἀπωλέσαμεν
Genre: really a letter? *didaktike*?

Structure: 1) Θ used to be a useful ox, treading the corn, but has become a useless dolphin in the sea that is Bulgaria; D is asking the wrong person, but his shamelessness deserves respect; 2) kissing the priest on the shoulder during Lent; 3) elevation of the host under a cloth (πέπλον); 4) why this happens only during Lent; 5) if D finds grain in this reply he should thank God, if he finds chaff, a dolphin's husbandry, let D curse the sea which is responsible for Θ ceasing to be an ox.

Tone: didactic
Length: 1196
Bibliography: Gautier, I, 117.
Discussed above: 98, 243.

Bearer: ?
Sent with: ?

G135, by the archbishop of Bulgaria *kyr* Theophylact from the letter to Tibanios the Armenian

Correspondent: TIBANIOS, the Armenian (55) = Tigranes of *Al.*, X.i.4, L, II, 188
Date: ?1114 (*Al.*, XIV.viii, L, III, 177-182)
Place: ?Ochrid to Philippopolis?

Editions: Gautier, II, 595-597; Finetti 20 253-256

Incipit: μεγάλης ἀνοησίας ἐστὶ τὸ μίαν φύσιν
Message: Tigranes is wrong
Subject matter: natures of Christ

Desinit: τό τε πῦρ καὶ ὁ σίδηρος
Genre: polemic; perhaps not a letter

Structure: 1) it is a great folly to think that after union the human and divine natures of Christ are one; 2) the natures remain unchanged like iron in fire; 3) human and divine wills; 4) role of union was only to glorify what was previously without honour because of sin; 5) the union of fire and iron; they keep their own natural differences.

Tone: polemic
Length: 461
Bibliography: Simeon, *Pismata*, 28-30; Maslev, *Studia*, 73; Gautier, II, 129-131.
Discussed above: 88, 98, **241-243**, 262.

Bearer: ?
Sent with: ?

THE NETWORK

Explanation of headings

Number in network. NAME NAME, office
Letters (with Gautier letter-numbers) written to and/or mentioning this person
Prosopography: secondary works in which the person's career is summarised; all appear in full in the short titles bibliography.
Relation: FORMS: *all forms of address in any letter, transliterated Greek.* ROLE: e.g. brother, close friend; whether instrumental or emotional. INTERACTION: simplex or multiplex, symmetrical or asymmetrical. TRANSACTIONAL CONTENT: of the relationship. FLOW: directional content to or from Theophylact. DURATION: of the relationship as seen in the collection. DEVELOPMENT: of the relationship as seen. All these terms are explained above in 4.2.
Intimacy: explanation of why the person has been placed in a particular intimacy zone. See fig. 1 above, 180-181.
Use: how the relationship is used in the correspondence. See above, 4.3.
Connections: other significant relationships of the correspondent; any in Theophylact's network are identified by the network number, bold in brackets.

N.= unknown name; B=Barzos, *Genealogia;* P=Polemis, *Doukai;* S=Skoulatos, *Personnages*

First order zone: nos 1-126
Second order zone: nos 201-240
Third order zone: nos 301—

I. First order zone (nos. 1-126)

i. *Theophylact's personal cell*
1. DEMETRIOS (HEPHAISTOS)
G133, G134. Mentioned in G4, G7, G28, G90, G91, G93, G110, G111, G113, G116, G121, G122, G123, G127.

Prosopography: Gautier, I, 15-22; 'L'épiscopat,' 168-169; I explain above, 93-94, why I prefer to see Demetrios as the only brother of Theophylact in the collection.

Relation: FORMS: *pampothete kai kale mou adelphe; pankale mou adelphe*. ROLES: brother and close friend, emotional and instrumental. INTERACTION: multiplex relation; symmetrical. TRANSACTIONAL CONTENT: love, emotional support, practical assistance, companionship, political assistance. FLOW: to Theophylact. DURATION: through nearly all the collection, 1090-1107.

Intimacy: unparalleled in the collection; poems 14 and 15, Gautier, I, 369-377.

Use: as letter-bearer, in dealings with the fisc, as having entrée to court.

Connections: dear to Alexios I Komnenos (77); client, *syndoulos*, of Maria (50); pupil of Theodore Smyrnaios (20) and possibly Niketas *ho tou Serron* (22); known to bishop of Kitros (9), Nicholas Kallikles (3), Niketas the imperial doctor (32), Gregory Kamateros (4).

---

2. NICHOLAS ANEMAS
G32, G34, G41.

Prosopography: Gautier, II, 39-40, assuming that Nicholas is an Anemas.

Relation: FORMS: *philtate moi kephale; andron emoi potheinotate; andron emoi philtate kai potheinotate*. ROLE: official, friend. INTERACTION: multiplex; symmetrical. TRANSACTIONAL CONTENT: wordplay, advice. FLOW: balanced. DURATION: over a single tour of duty. DEVELOPMENT: G32: adventus letter; G34 advice on *barbarismos*; G41: *propemptikon*.

Intimacy: nature of forms of address; brilliance of tone; called φίλος ἀληθινός (G41).

Use: not in the collection.

Connections: none in the collection; not otherwise known.

---

3. NICHOLAS KALLIKLES
G93, G94, G111, G112. Gautier doubts G94 and gives him G110, unconvincingly.

Prosopography: Skoulatos, *Personnages* (S157), 251-252; Romano, *Callicle*, 13-17; Kazhdan, 'Doctor,' 44; Gautier, II, 69-73; Sternbach, 'Calliclis,' 315-318.

Relation: FORMS: none. ROLE: instrumental and emotional friend. INTERACTION: simplex and symmetrical. TRANSACTIONAL CONTENT: shared interest, books, help; FLOW: to Theophylact. DURATION: late, from about the calumny crisis on. DEVELOPMENT: G93 after *siope*; G94 request for help (Theophylact has fled to Pelagonia); G111 explicit request for help with properties in Thessalonike and Ekklesiai; G112 request for books.

Intimacy: lack of forms of address; booksharing.

Use: to look after Demetrios, general and specific help, G93.

Connections: see diagram of his first order zone from his poems, fig. 3.2, above, 194; doctor of Alexios I Komnenos (77); succeeded as *didaskalos ton iatron* by Michael Italikos (215); at deathbed of Alexios.

---

4. GREGORY KAMATEROS

G27, G38, G31, G67, possibly G115 and 116, G127.

Prosopography: Skoulatos, *Personnages* (S76), 109-111; Polemis, *Doukai*, 78-9; Gautier, II, 73-79 'Monodie inédite,' 163-164; *Michel Italikos*, 39-41; Laurent, 'Sceau du protonotaire,' 261-272; Darrouzès, *Tornikai*, 43-49; Stadtmüller, 'Familie Kamateros,' 354.

Relation: FORMS: *to so lamproteti; panhyperlampre moi en Kurioi huie kai despota; to so agathoteti; hyperlampre; megalepiphaneia; dexiotatos; hyperlampre moi en Kurioi huie*. ROLE: 'son'; instrumental and emotional friend. INTERACTION: multiplex; symmetrical. FLOW: to Theophylact. TRANSACTIONAL CONTENT: favours and fantasy. DURATION: spans various stages of career, and large number of letters. DEVELOPMENT: G27 asks for a job for young Psellos (**85**); G31 and 38 deal with Ekklesiai (Theophylact asking too much); G67 thanks him for a good appointment; G116 and 117 convey good wishes; G127 refers to his recent double promotion as *nobellissimos* and *protasekretes*.

Intimacy: brilliant gossip of G127; number of letters.

Use: to arrange a job, to override a tax-assessment.

Connections: secretary of Alexios I Komnenos (**77**); present at the interrogation of Nikephoros Diogenes (**208**); married a Komnene, Eirene Doukaina (**212**) with son Michael (**216**); death commemorated by both Theodore Prodromos (**225**) and Nicholas Kallikles (**3**).

---

5. NICHOLAS MERMENTOULOS

G25, G29, G33, G47, G76.

Prosopography: Laurent, 'Légendes sigillographiques et familles byzantines,' 437-438; Guilland, *Institutions*, I, 563-587; Gautier, II, 86-88; 'Le synode,' 248.

Relation: FORMS: *o pantas en pasin hyperlampron tois charakterizousin anthropon; o kai logois kai ergois moi hyperlampre; andron apanton ten sophian hypertere; o panton emoi panhyperlampre; o makarie*. ROLE: emotional friend. INTERACTION: simplex; symmetrical. FLOW: from Theophylact. TRANSACTIONAL CONTENT: friendship and learning. DURATION: from before his appointment to the 1090s. DEVELOPMENT: G25 discusses friendship and letters; G29 reading; G33 begs for a letter to console τοὺς νῦν ἱερεῖς; G47 also requests a letter; G76 thanks him for a letter after a long gap.

Intimacy: lightness and brilliance of tone; developed forms; number.

Use: to console.

Connections: none specific known. Succeeded John Thrakesios-Skylitzes (**227**) in post as Grand Droungarios of the Watch. He may have been succeeded by Nicholas Skleros (**226**) or John Zonaras (**228**). May have known Stephen-Symeon the Sanctified (**230**), an ex-Droungarios. At synod of Blachernai.

---

6. JOHN OPHEOMACHOS

G69, G71. Conceivably referred to in G42, G46.

Prosopography: Gautier, 'Le synode,' 261; He also (Gautier, II, 97) suggests his father was the Michael Opheomachos at the synod of Blachernai. John is unknown.

Relation: FORMS: *O kale Ioanne; O thaumasie, andron emoi philtate kai chrestotate*. ROLE: friend and official. INTERACTION: multiplex; symmetrical. FLOW: even. TRANSACTIONAL CONTENT: ceremony and advice. DURATION: only in the course of one tour of duty. DEVELOPMENT: G69 is adventus on arrival in some post in Bulgaria; G71 exhorts him to carry it out with courage.

Intimacy: informal and unusual forms; lightheartedness of the adventus.

Use: not in the collection.

Connections: unknown.

---

7. MICHAEL PANTECHNES

G39, G48, G50, probably G94, G99, G102, G128, G129, G130, G131, poem 2. Gautier attributes G94 to Nicholas Kallikles(3). G50, G99, G128 are not specifically to Michael and could be ascribed to John (16); those who believe he was never *proximos* would wish to do so.

Prosopography: Skoulatos, *Personnages* (S135), 209-210; Gautier, *Michel Italikos*, 46-49; Kazhdan, 'Doctor,' 47; Gautier, II, 104-109.

Relation: FORMS: *moi philtate; teknon mou; hyperlampre; hyperlampre moi en Kyrioi huie.* ROLE: pupil and 'son'. Emotional and instrumental friend; friend of father. INTERACTION: multiplex, symmetrical. TRANSACTIONAL CONTENT: visits, poems, advice, shared interest in medicine. FLOW: from Theophylact; more letters than to anyone else. DURATION: from before the collection to the last datable letter. DEVELOPMENT: two crucial points must be the death (G39) of John Pantechnes (16) (alive in G120) and Michael's appointment (just before G102) as imperial doctor. G48 and G50 precede it; G99, G128, G129, G130, G131 follow. Brief, witty letters informed by their teaching relationship run throughout.

Intimacy: tone, lack of forms, number, multiplexity, φίλτατε.

Use: only in the calumny crisis is he recruited to present Theophylact's case to the emperor.

Connections: few known. Other imperial doctors. Michael Italikos (215) and an anonymous wrote monodies. At deathbed of Alexios.

---

8. NICHOLAS, metropolitan of KERKYRA

G75, G77, poems 4 and 5.

Prosopography: Lampros, *Kerkyraika anekdota*, 23-27; Gautier, 'Le synode,' 268-271; II, 88-90. It is still unclear whether it was at the synod of Blachernai that he resigned; Gautier's argument is weak. Not seal DO 58.106.1965 or Fogg, no. 2096, see Nesbitt and Oikonomides, *DO Seals*, II, 17.

Relation: FORMS: *anthrope tou Theou; timie pater kai despota; timiotate despota; paniere kai hagie despota; timiotate despota; ton hemon despoten kai patera; te hagiosyne sou; tou theou anthrope.* ROLE: trusted colleague and fellow-sufferer. INTERACTION: symmetrical. TRANSACTIONAL CONTENT; books, poems, moans, riddles. FLOW: balanced. DEVELOPMENT AND DURATION: G77 is very shortly after G75 and clarifies the same problems; poems 4 and 5 could be thirty years later.

Intimacy: collegiality; books.

Use: simply to share problems.

Connections: Nicholas Adrianoupolites (201) according to Marc.524, fol. 1r; at Synod of Blachernai.

---

9. N.N., bishop of KITROS

G14, G52, G113, G121.

Prosopography: Laurent V/2, 429; Gautier, II, 57-60; possibly = eunuch (126), I, 115-116.

Relation: FORMS: *sebasmiotate moi despota; hierotate adelphe kai despota; paniere adelphe kai despota; tou theou anthrope; timiotate adelphe kai despota.* ROLE: colleague and friend. INTERACTION: symmetrical. FLOW: balanced. TRANSACTIONAL CONTENT: gifts, emotional confidences. DURATION: certainly from 1097-1107. DEVELOPMENT: G14 thanks him for a gift of incense and cinnamon; G52 is after a period of *sige*; G113 and G121 confide the story of Demetrios's illness and death.

Intimacy: subject matter.
Use: not in the collection.
Connections: the ex-bishop and archimandrite of St George in the Mangana (231); correspondent of Eirene Doukaina (37), cf. Mercati, 'Gli aneddoti,' 126-143 at 138-140.

---

10. N.N., bishop of PELAGONIA

G21, G36, bearer of G64. I suggest G63 is to him.
Prosopography: Gautier, II, 60-61. Seal: just possibly Laurent, *Sceaux*, V/2, no 1506.
Relation: FORMS: *timiotate adelphe; timiotate adelphe kai sylleitourge*. ROLE: suffragan and friend. INTERACTION: asymmetrical, but balanced flow. TRANSACTIONAL CONTENT: visits, advice, briefing. DURATION: at least 1092-1107. DEVELOPMENT: G21 is a hasty briefing on the changeover of governors; G36 encourages him to read the Scriptures; G64 arranges an introduction to the patriarch; G63 advises him not to trust too much in any one protector (particularly a dead one).
Intimacy: proximity of place.
Use: not in the collection.
Connections: not known.

---

ii. *Theophylact's intimate zone*

11. NIKEPHOROS BRYENNIOS

G96, poem 1 with Lost 20.
Prosopography: Skoulatos, *Personnages* (S144), 224-232; Polemis, *Doukai*, 71, 112; S. Wittek-de Jongh, 'Nicéphore Bryennios,' 463; Gautier, II, 40-44, *Nicéphore Bryennios*, 24-31; 'L'obituaire,' 235-262 at 243-244; Carile, 'Nicefore Briennio,' 74-83; 43 (1969), 56-87; Seals: Z&V no. 2717=Konstantopoulos, *Mol. Suppl.*, no. 1233.
Relation: FORM: *ten basileian humon*. ROLE: patron (G96) and friend (poem 1); son of acquaintance. INTERACTION: multiplex, asymmetrical. FLOW: even. TRANSACTIONAL CONTENT: poems and practical assistance. DURATION: difficult when so much evidence is missing. DEVELOPMENT: equally difficult
Intimacy: clear from light tone of poem 1.
Use: to counteract the alliance of Iasites (76) and Lazaros (97).
Connections: friend of Gregory Taronites (48); George Tornikes (235), who was related to Theophylact, wrote his funeral oration; son of John (34); husband of Anna (217); wrote *Hyle Historias* for Eirene Doukaina (37); Theodore Prodromos (225).

---

12. CONSTANTINE KOMNENOS

G123.
Prosopography: Barzos, *Genealogia* (B27), I, 157-9; Stiernon, 'Notes de prosopographie,' *REB* 21 (1961), 192-198; Gautier, II, 48; 'Le synode,' 236, n.52; Hohlweg, *Verwaltungsgeschichte*, 21; Guilland, *Institutions*, I, 541. Seal: Z&V no. 2716.
Relation: no form; in general this is a puzzling letter, in that it is narrative, with direct speech, and is short. A charming compliment to a friendly governor?
Intimacy: not an impersonal official relationship.
Use: not in the collection.

Connections: Demetrios (1); he was the third son of Isaac the *sebastokrator* (78); Grand *droungarios* and/or *droungarios* of the Watch (there is much dispute); married into Antiochos and Euphorbenos families.

---

13. N. MACHETARES
G44.

Prosopography: Gautier, 'Le synode,' 242; Laurent, 'Légendes sigillographiques et familles byzantines,' 348-349; Adontz, 'Notes,' (1934), 368-371. Of the various candidates known from the eleventh to twelfth centuries, Michael, vestarch and eparch of Constantinople in June 1087 (MM, VI, 33) is perhaps the most likely. Seal: Laurent, *Sceaux* ,V/2, no. 1360.

Relation: FORMS: none. ROLE: friend. INTERACTION: difficult to describe from one letter. TRANSACTIONAL CONTENT: developed theory of friendship and letters.

Intimacy: content and lack of forms; tone eloquent, confiding.

Use: not in the collection.

Connections: ?correspondent of Psellos (84); ?succeeded by John Thrakesios (Skylitzes) (227).

---

14. N. MAKREMBOLITES
G108; Gautier says mentioned in G21; ?another Makrembolites mentioned in G23.

Prosopography: Gautier, II, 80-81. On the family in the eleventh century: Oikonomides, 'Le serment,' 101-128. Gautier's suggestion, 80, that he is the Eumathios Makrembolites 'assez bien connu par sa production littéraire' (for *Hysmine and Hysminias?*) does not stand up; nor does his alternative suggestion of Eumathios Philokales for the inspector of G21. The tone of G108 is hardly appropriate for the rapacious official mentioned in G23, nor does that official appear to be a 'son'. A Symeon *kouropalates*, a Romanos, a Theodore *magistros* in the eleventh century and a John and an Eumathios from the twelfth century are known from Dumbarton Oaks seals.

Relation: FORM: *megalepiphanestate moi en Kyrioi huie.* ROLE: 'son'; official. INTERACTION: multiplex but difficult to determine from one letter. TRANSACTIONAL CONTENT: request for official action.

Intimacy: forms; light, fanciful tone.

Use: only official.

Connections: not enough known.

---

15. GREGORY PAKOURIANOS
G68, G55, G80; mentioned in G67 and G79. Gautier considers assigning G43.

Prosopography: Skoulatos, *Personnages* (S78), 111-115; Katičić, 'Pros Pakourianous,' 386-397; Schlumberger, *Sigillographie*, 684; Hohlweg, *Verwaltungsgeschichte*, 96; Zlatarsky, 'Stellvertretende Verwalter,' 139-158, 371-398; Panov, *Teofilakt*, 313, n.334; Lemerle, *Cinq études*, 160; Gautier, II, 98-100. Although the group of letters is remarkably coherent there is a problem in that G80 in manuscripts VRB, all group B manuscripts, is called Nicholas. (In A he is simply the *sebastos* Pakourianos.) Katičić believed all three letters are to Nicholas Pakourianos; Gautier that they are all to Gregory. No-one now believes, as did Petit, 'Bačkovo,' x, that this Gregory is the great Grand Domestic, founder of Bačkovo. A further difficulty arises with the lemma '*gambros* of the Grand Droungarios' to G68 and the description of him as *gambros* of Adrian the Grand Domestic (41) in G79 although he could not strictly be *gambros* of both brothers; but see Stiernon, 'Sébaste et gambros', 243; Binon, 'Theios-gambros,' 388-393.

Relation: FORMS: *tes ses eugeneias; pansebaste; pansebaste moi en Kyrioi huie; pansebaste mou huie.* ROLE: 'son'; Theophylact's favourite local official. INTERACTION: multiplex, asymmetrical with age-difference. FLOW: balanced, or to Theophylact. TRANSACTIONAL CONTENT: praise, fish, favours. DURATION: fairly brief. DEVELOPMENT: G67 thanks Gregory Kamateros (4) for a good appointment; G68 is the adventus; G55 asks for help, describes their relationship as like that of Plato and Dionysios and sends fish; G80 is in reply to an apology; G79 is after his departure, praise to his relative and Theophylact's patron Adrian (Barzos, *Genealogia*, I, 270, believes he is dead at this point).
Intimacy: G55 is a friendship letter; G68 and forms are formal.
Use: general assistance (G55); defence against the fisc (G79).
Connections: unknown.

---

16. JOHN PANTECHNES, *magistros*
G120; mentioned as dead in G39.
Prosopography: Darrouzès, *Tornikai*, 50, 56; Gautier, II, 104-109, *Michel Italikos*, 47. The consolatio G39 names a John; it is reasonable to follow Gautier in seeing a father or close relative. In my *Theophylact*, 249, n.49, I suggested giving G114 to John, but the provocative beginning sits well with for example G102 to Michael.
Relation: FORM: *lamprotate mou authenta.* ROLE: elevated friend. INTERACTION: difficult on the basis of a single letter, but multiplex, asymmetrical. TRANSACTIONAL CONTENT: journey description, sickness description.
Intimacy: elaborate description suggests a valued correspondent; confidence.
Use: none in the collection.
Connections: none known.

---

17. JOHN PERIBLEPTENOS
G97, G101. Conceivably the καλὸς Ἰωάννης of G42 and G46.
Prosopography: Gautier, II, 109-110. Probably a monk of the Peribleptos, on which see Janin, 'Peribleptos,' 1-10; probably not the twelfth-century writer of Marc XI.31, fols 275-280, Lampros, 'Summikta,' 119, or Laur.conv.soppr. 2, fols 206-208, Rostagno and Festa, 'Indice,' 132; Krumbacher, *GBL*, 466-467. The medical connection remains unexplained, unless he was a doctor in the monastery.
Relation: FORM: *o kale Ioanne.* INTERACTION: symmetrical. FLOW: balanced. DEVELOPMENT: G97 accepts apology for *sige*, set in the context of the calumny crisis, and asks John's help; G101 complains, using the Gadarene swine image.
Intimacy: informal form, elaborate medical vocabulary.
Use: to counteract calumny.
Connections: none known.

---

18. NIKETAS POLITES, bishop of N
G40.
Prosopography: Gautier, II, 111-112. Placename suggests Diabolis as see.
Relation: FORMS: *adelphe theotimete; o ta panta kale k'agathe.* ROLE: friend, possibly suffragan, possibly neighbouring bishop. INTERACTION: difficult to establish from one letter.
Intimacy: forms, elaboration of the οἴκοθεν οἴκαδε formula.
Use: to look after the bishop of Glavenitsa (100) and sort out the Koprinistra problem.
Connections: none known.

19. THEOPHYLACT ROMAIOS

G42, G46. Manuscripts also give G43, but Gautier doubts. I suggest this was to Tarchaneiotes (21).
Prosopography: Gautier, II, 116-117. An unknown.
Relation: FORMS: *lamprotate moi en Kyrioi huie; o makarie; o kale k'agathe.* G43: *megalepiphanestae moi authenta* (overgrand). ROLE: 'son'; Gautier suggests an ex-pupil. INTERACTION: symmetrical, but probably age difference. FLOW: from Theophylact. TRANSACTIONAL CONTENT: jokes, classical allusions, advice. DURATION: impossible to judge. DEVELOPMENT: G42 accuses him of not writing; G46 asks for a letter and advises.
Intimacy: classical vocabulary; forms.
Use: not in the collection
Connections: ὁ καλὸς Ἰωάννης. Cf. (17) above.

---

20. THEODORE SMYRNAIOS

G6, G28, G95. Gautier doubts G6, wrongly. Mentioned in G112.
Prosopography: Gautier, II, 118-120; 'Le synode,' 255-256; Laurent, 'Légendes sigillographiques et familles byzantines,' 327-335; Leroy-Molinghen, 'Destinataire,' 431-437; Baldwin, *Timarion*, 30-31 (beware his interpretation of βασιλεῖς); Romano, *Timarione*, 138.
Relation: FORMS: *philosophotate moi anthrope kai chariestate; chariestate; o ton en philosophois christianon e ton en christianois philosophon hypate;* ROLE: ex-colleague and friend; teacher of Theophylact's brother Demetrios and brother of Theophylact's pupil Paul. INTERACTION: multiplex, symmetrical. FLOW: balanced (Theophylact is very conscious of reciprocity in this relationship). TRANSACTIONAL CONTENT: shared learning, shared troubles exchanged students, wordplay. DURATION: from the beginning of the archiepiscopate to at least the calumny crisis. DEVELOPMENT: G6 is a first-letter-on-arrival; G28 commends Demetrios to Theodore; G95 is a veiled account of his troubles.
Intimacy: elaborate play on the form; duration. Not very close.
Use: to look after Demetrios.
Connections: Demetrios (1), brother Paul (88), the son of the *protostrator* Michael (39), the author of the *Timarion*, Peter Grossolano and the other disputants of 1112.

---

21. N. TARCHANEIOTES

G16, G20. I suggest tentatively G43 .
Prosopography: Skoulatos, *Personnages* (S194), 286-287; Polemis, *Doukai*, 183; Gautier, II, 120-121; 'Le synode,' 15; N. Amantos, 'To onoma;' Lemerle, *Koutloumousiou*, 125; Gautier's proposal that this is Katakalon Tarchaneiotes is overstated but not impossible.
Relation: FORMS: *O megalepiphanestate hemon authentes; paneugenestate;* G43: *megalepiphanestate moi authenta.* ROLE: recipient of spiritual advice. INTERACTION: asymmetrical in that T is older, grander. TRANSACTIONAL CONTENT: advice. FLOW: from Theophylact. DURATION and DEVELOPMENT: no evidence.
Intimacy: there is a respectful distance in G16, 20, almost an embarrassment in advising the other, which would not be impossibly inconsistent with G43: ἀεί μοι τὸν πόθον ἀνάπτεις in the context of spiritual progression.
Use: not in the collection.
Connections: not known. If Katakalon, Nikephoros Bryennios (11); at synod of Blachernai.

---

22. NIKETAS *ho tou Serron*, didaskalos of the Great Church

G7, G70, G91, but this last could be queried on forms of address.

Prosopography: Browning, 'Patriarchal School,' (1963), 15-16; Darrouzès, 'Notes,' 179-184; Grumel, *DTC*, XI, 472-473; Gautier, II, 94-96.

Relation: FORMS: *ten sen hieroteta;* (G91) *timiotate moi en Kyrioi huie.* ROLE: ex-colleague, only possibly 'son'. Possibly teacher of Demetrios. INTERACTION: symmetrical. TRANSACTIONAL CONTENT: contact, shared learning, political assistance, praise. FLOW: even. DURATION: from beginning of episcopate to around the time of the calumny crisis. DEVELOPMENT: G7 is a first-letter-on-arrival; G70 a modest response to praise; G91 (if to him) a veiled request for help.

Intimacy: not very warm, except possibly G91.

Use: (G91): general assistance in crisis.

Connections: Demetrios (1), Niketas Stethatos (233), Eustratios of Nicaea (237).

---

23. NIKEPHOROS *chartophylax*

G30, G51, G66, G124 (as ex-*chartophylax*); Gautier proposes G83.

Prosopography: Gautier, II, 92-94; 'Le synode,' 269; 'Chartophylax,' 162.

Relation: FORMS: *tes ses hosiotates, timiotate despota; hemeteran astheneian; timiotate despota kai pater hemon; agie despota kai pater; panagie despota.* ROLE: benevolent official. INTERACTION: asymmetrical. FLOW: balanced. TRANSACTIONAL CONTENT: business, gloom. DURATION: on both sides of the synod of Blachernai. DEVELOPMENT: G30 replies to a query about the Ἁγιοσερρῆται/Ἁγιοσεργῖται; G51 expresses his troubles; G66 asks advice about Gregory the *psaltes* (95); G124 is a short letter written while ill.

Intimacy: affectionate but business-like.

Use: not in the collection beyond duty.

Connections: monk Theodosios, recluse of Corinth, monk Maximos. Succeeded by Peter (25), by the time of the synod of Blachernai.

---

24. NIKETAS *chartophylax*

G83 if not to Nikephoros (23).

Prosopography: as above. There is a late eleventh-century Niketas, Laurent, *Sceaux*, V/1 no 93, not Niketas of Maronea 1132/33. There is just room for him between Peter (25), last attested in 1106, and Symeon, attested in 1111, but Gautier may be right in proposing a scribal error.

Relation: FORMS: *hagie pater kai despota tes ses hagiosynes.* ROLE: acquaintance. INTERACTION: difficult on basis of one dubious letter. TRANSACTIONAL CONTENT: warning of calumny.

Intimacy: Theophylact's attitude is that of a concerned friend.

Use: not in the collection.

Connections: none known.

---

25. PETER *chartophylax*

not named G90, mentioned by name in G82.

Prosopography: as above. Seals: Laurent, *Sceaux*, V/1, 95-96.

Relation. FORMS: *hagie pater kai despota.* ROLE: friend and contact. INTERACTION: difficult on basis of only one letter; asymmetrical. TRANSACTIONAL CONTENT: hospitality, political assistance. FLOW: to Theophylact. DURATION and DEVELOPMENT: no evidence.

Intimacy: sends Demetrios to him on the winter journey.
Use: to prevent the invasion of Ochrid's rights in Kittaba case; to help in the Ekklesiai crisis.
Connections: succeeded (23) and ?was succeeded by (24).

26. N. CHRYSOBERGES, metropolitan of NAUPAKTOS

G35.
Prosopography: on the see, Laurent, *Sceaux*, V, 513-514; on the family, Treu, *Ad Angelos orationes*, 38-39.
Relation: FORMS: *timiotate despota; te hieroteti sou.* ROLE: colleague and friend. INTERACTION: multiplex, symmetrical. FLOW: balanced (Theophylact aware of age differentials). TRANSACTIONAL CONTENT: included (at least projected) visits. DURATION and DEVELOPMENT: no evidence.
Intimacy: concern for his brother Nicholas (74).
Use: not in the collection.
Connections: nothing known.

27. THEODOULOS N., metropolitan of THESSALONIKE

G72.
Prosopography: Gautier, II, 128-129; 'Le synode,' 264; Petit, 'Le synodicon,' 243-244. Possibly a eunuch (126), see *Théophylacte*, I, no. 7, 296, n.14. Seal: Laurent, *Sceaux*, V/1, no. 457.
Relation: FORMS: *paniere adelphe kai despota.* ROLE: colleague and friend. INTERACTION: symmetrical. TRANSACTIONAL CONTENT: shared woes, prayers. FLOW, DURATION, DEVELOPMENT: inadequate evidence.
Intimacy: tone; shared problems.
Use: not seen
Connections: at the Synod of Blachernai.

28. N.N., metropolitan of SEMNEA

G56, G74.
Prosopography: Gautier, II, 61-63; he is otherwise unknown. For his see, Semnea/Semnaia, Ramsay, *Historical Geography*, 416-417; Darrouzès, *Notitiae*, 1-4, 7, 9-10, 13. Gautier however proposes an otherwise unknown suffragan see Semna on the Semnica river. Inventing a diocese seems unnecessary; Theophylact was in touch with the bishop of Side (99) and the government at Attaleia; the bishop might also not have been in see.
Relation: FORMS: *hierotate moi kephale; timiotate adelphe.* ROLE: colleague and friend INTERACTION: symmetrical or Theophylact slightly superior. FLOW: even. TRANSACTIONAL CONTENT: prayers to subvert the fisc. DURATION and DEVELOPMENT: after reconquest? Otherwise no indication.
Intimacy: tone; shared problems.
Use: not seen
Connections: none known.

29. SYMEON, *hegoumenos* of ANAPLOUS
G37
Prosopography: Gautier, II, 119-120; 'Le synode,' 279.
Relation: FORM: *hosiotate pater*. ROLE: friend, not spiritual father. INTERACTION: difficult on one letter. TRANSACTIONAL CONTENT: gossip and news, prayers. Flow: balanced. DURATION: previous contact wth the monastery implied. DEVELOPMENT: no evidence.
Intimacy: affectionate tone.
Use: not seen
Connections: to the monk of G52 (104); to the ex-*hegoumenos* (111) and to the monks of Anaplous (118); ?at Synod of Blachernai.

30. JOHN the *maistor*
G62
Prosopography: Gautier, II, 68-69. The letter is so fragmentary that there is no means of knowing whether he is the same as John the philosopher (31), John Peribleptenos (17) or John *maistor ton rhetoron* at the Italos trial as Gautier suggests.

31. JOHN the philosopher
G100.
Prosopography: Gautier, II, 68-69; Dujčev, 'L'umanesimo,' 432-436; there is no reason to believe this is John Italos.
Relation: FORMS: none. ROLE: friend. INTERACTION: symmetrical. FLOW: to Theophylact. TRANSACTIONAL CONTENT: philosophy, political assistance. DURATION and DEVELOPMENT: no evidence.
Intimacy: Theophylact claims J is his favourite philosopher. No forms of address.
Use: to combat calumny.
Connections: unknown.

32. NIKETAS, imperial doctor
G110.
Prosopography: Gautier, 'L'obituaire,' 255; Kazhdan, 'Doctor,' 44. Gautier, II, 70 regards Niketas as unknown and so the lemma as a scribal error for Nicholas Kallikles (3). In 'L'obituaire,' however, 255, he commented on the ὁ ἰατρὸς Νικήτας ὁ Πρῶτος in the Pantokrator typikon as 'le chef d'école de médecine et vraisemblablement l'archiâtre de la famille impériale'.
Relation: FORMS: none. ROLE: emotional and instrumental friend. INTERACTION: symmetrical. FLOW: to Theophylact. TRANSACTIONAL CONTENT: vivid description of illness, visit (foregone). DURATION and DEVELOPMENT: no evidence.
Intimacy: lack of forms; Demetrios connection.
Use: to look after Demetrios (1).
Connections: none (except Demetrios) known.

iii. *Theophylact's effective zone*

33. JOHN ATTALEIATES, *protonotarios* of the *doux* of Attaleia

G104.
Prosopography: Gautier, 'Le synode,' 262. On the family, Weiss, *Beamte*, 126-127; Tsolakes, 'Michael Attaleiates,' 3-10.
Relation: FORMS: *lamprotate moi en kyrioi huie*. ROLE: 'son'; ex-pupil. INTERACTION: Theophylact calls in the debt of teaching. TRANSACTIONAL CONTENT: teaching; political assistance. FLOW: balanced (Θ is making sure). DURATION: from before enthronement and ?after reconquest? DEVELOPMENT: not seen
Intimacy: rather calculating.
Use: to ask him to go to the help of the metropolitan of Side (99).
Connections: the *doux* of Attaleia, others unknown.

34. JOHN BRYENNIOS, *doux* of Dyrrachion

G86, 105.
Prosopography: Gautier, II, 40-44; *Nicéphore Bryennios*, 20-23; Wittek-de Jongh, 463-468. Seal: Fogg no. 694; Konstantopoulos, *Byz. Mol.*, 158. It seems fairly clear now that this is the son of the rebel Nikephoros Bryennios, and the father of the *panhypersebastos*, Anna's husband (11).
Relation: FORMS: *megalepiphanestate mou authenta; tes ses megaleiotetos*. ROLE: official. INTERACTION: multiplex, asymmetrical. FLOW: from Theophylact. TRANSACTIONAL CONTENT: praise, fish. DURATION: from before 1097 to some time after. DEVELOPMENT: G86 is an adventus letter, but not the first move in their relationship; G105 accompanies a gift.
Intimacy: letters are formal despite the relation with Nikephoros.
Use: general assistance.
Connections: Hosios Meletios (239); note that he is not the John Bryennios of *Al.*, I.v.2, L, I, 20, Skoulatos (S86), 132-135.

35. N. DIABOLOGYRES, bishop of N

G15.
Prosopography: Simeon, *Pismata*, 206-207; Gautier, II, 53-54. For another member of the family, MM, VI, 96.
Relation: FORMS: *adelphe*. ROLE: suffragan. INTERACTION: asymmetrical. TRANSACTIONAL CONTENT: advice. FLOW: from Θ. DURATION and DEVELOPMENT: no evidence.
Intimacy: only through enthusiasm for a common task.
Use: not in the collection.
Connections: unknown.

36. CONSTANTINE DOUKAS, ruler of the Vardar

G118, G119; mentioned in G88, G127, and in Lost 17.
Prosopography: Polemis, *Doukai* (P30), 76; Gautier, II, 54-55. Seal: Laurent, *Bulles métriques*, no. 482. The post is unexplained; he was *doux* and praktor of Boleron-Strymon-Thessalonike in 1118, but is unlikely to have been there ever since the appointment discussed by Theophylact.
Relation: FORMS: *pansebaste mou authenta kai megiste antileptor; tes ses megaleiotetos; pansebaste mou authenta kai megiste antileptor*. ROLE: official of whom much was expected in advance. INTERACTION: asymmetrical. TRANSACTIONAL CONTENT: praise, fish, favours. FLOW: from Θ. DURATION: during tour of duty. DEVELOPMENT: after his arrival was hailed in G88, G127,

and Lost 10, G118 is an adventus, which uncharacteristically asks for specific help; G119 accompanies a gift.
Intimacy: plays on Theophylact's acquaintanceship with CD's father Michael Doukas (39).
Use: help with village on the Vardar.
Connections: Michael Doukas, otherwise none specific.

---

37. EIRENE DOUKAINA, *despoina*

G107. Gautier ascribes to Maria the ex-*basilissa* (50). Mentioned in G84.
Prosopography: Polemis, *Doukai* (P26), 70-74; Skoulatos, *Personnages* (S83), 119-124; Gautier, 'L'obituaire, 245-247. The letter is so brief that it is impossible to tell to whom it is addressed; the later it is dated the more likely it is to Eirene and not to Maria or Anna Dalassene (121).
Relation: FORMS: none. ROLE: patroness. INTERACTION: asymmetrical. TRANSACTIONAL CONTENT: thanks. FLOW: from Theophylact to *despoina*. DURATION and DEVELOPMENT: not seen.
Intimacy: formal but not elaborate.
Use: not in the collection.
Connections: Manuel Straboromanos (234), Theodore Prodromos (225), Michael Italikos (215), Nicholas Kataskepenos; all those mentioned in Kecharitomene *typikon*.

---

38. JOHN DOUKAS, *doux* of Dyrrachion, then *megas doux*

G8, G17, probably G26.
Prosopography: Skoulatos, *Personnages* (S89), 145-150; Polemis, *Doukai* (P25), 66-70; Gautier, II, 55-57, 'Diatribes,' 14-15; 'Défection,' 215-217; 'Évergétis,' 10. The timing of his various expeditions is tricky; also his spell as *doux* at Dyrrachion is hard to reconcile with Anna's claim (*Al.*, VII.viii.9) that he was there for eleven years. G26 refers to the noble family of Doukas, which would be curious if the addressee were in fact John Komnenos (42).
Relation: FORMS: *pansebaste mou antileptor; o pansebaste; to pansebasto panton antileptori; ten megalosynen sou; dia tes agathotetos; tes ses eudokimeseos;* G26: *authenta mou; ten pansebaston hyperochen tou koinou authentou.* ROLE: official recycled as patron. INTERACTION: multiplex, asymmetrical. FLOW: to Theophylact. TRANSACTIONAL CONTENT: praise, favours. DURATION: from very early in the episcopate until after 1092 campaign. DEVELOPMENT: G26 on Mogila case while still *doux*, G17 after he had left and before John Komnenos (42) appointed, but while he was within reach of Euboia; G8 encomiastic letter after first campaign against Tzachas and before expedition to Crete and Cyprus, again within reach of Euboia.
Intimacy: hero-worship; good official relations.
Use: to ensure that Theophylact is not deprived of the *hospition* and the *aule* at Mogila; to look after Theophylact's relatives on Euboia.
Connections: Hosios Meletios (239); Christodoulos; not certainly the Theotokos Evergetis; brother of (37) and (39).

---

39. MICHAEL DOUKAS, *protostrator*

Lost 15, Lost 17; mentioned in G84, G88, G120.
Prosopography: Polemis, *Doukai* (P24), 63-66; Skoulatos (S129), 202-205; Gautier, 'L'obituaire,' 254; Guilland, *Institutions*, I, 480.
Relation: no letter to him survives. FORM: *pansebastos authentes.* ROLE: patron; offender.

Use: (G84) to tell him to stop violating the canons; (G88) to soften up his son just appointed to the rule of the Vardar.

Connections: Manuel Straboromanos (**234**); brother of (**37**) and (**38**).

---

40. GREGORY KAMATEROS, bishop of N
G53

Prosopography: Gautier, II, 79. Vasilievskii, review of Uspenskii, *Obrazovanie* in *Zhurnal ministerstva narodnogo prosveshcheniia*, 204 (1879), 329 first noticed that it was addressed to a bishop not the *protasekretes* Gregory Kamateros (**4**). See also Maslev, 'Melissenos,' 182.

Relation: FORMS: *adelphe timiotate; adelphe hierotate; o tou Logou leitourge kai hemon adelphe*. ROLE: suffragan. INTERACTION: asymmetrical. TRANSACTIONAL CONTENT: advice. FLOW, DURATION and DEVELOPMENT: inadequate evidence.

Intimacy: concern and sympathy, but part of the job.

Use: to do his job.

Connections: none known.

---

41. ADRIAN KOMNENOS, the Grand Domestic
G5, G79, G85, G89, G98.

Prosopography: Skoulatos, *Personnages* (S3), 5-8; Guilland, *Institutions*, 54-55; Polemis, *Doukai*, 54-55; Gautier; II, 44-47; 'L'obituaire,' 235-262; 'Le synode,' 231-233; Kazhdan, *Sots.Sos.*, 229. Seals: Z&V 2708, 2709, 2709bis; Barzos, *Genealogia* (B16), I, 114-117; Magdalino, Manuel I, 120, n.44.

Relation: FORMS: *hagie mou authenta; to son hypsos/tes emes tapeinotetos; pansebaste mou antileptor; ten humeteran makarioteta; kyrie mou, kyrie; te tes humeteras megaleiotetos agathoteti; he se philanthropia; hagie mou authenta; ten megaleiota sou; o ge kai helie*. ROLE: patron. INTERACTION: multiplex, asymmetrical. TRANSACTIONAL CONTENT: officia and beneficia: praise and patronage. FLOW: balanced. DURATION: from the beginning of the collection to close to the end. DEVELOPMENT: G5 is a first letter on arrival in see; G79 praises his *gambros* the paragon Pakourianos; G85 and G89 are concerned with the problems over a village; G98 is the Lazaros crisis.

Intimacy: only in the sense that he is Theophylact's most important patron.

Use: to stop an *anagraphe*; to intercede with the emperor; in the Komnenian family row.

Connections: Nikephoros Diogenes (**208**), Leo of Chalcedon (**238**); the monastery of the Theotokos Pammakaristos.

---

42. JOHN KOMNENOS, *doux* of Dyrrachion
G10, G11, G12, G19, G22, G23, G24, possibly G61.

Prosopography: Barzos, *Genealogia* (B23), 131-134; Skoulatos, *Personnages* (S87), 135-138; Gautier, II, 48-53; 'Le synode,' 221, n. 7; 'Diatribes,' 11, n.33; Seals; Z&V 2713, 2713bis. 2714 presents a problem in that it shows him as *sebastos* and *doux* of Skopje. He could possibly have been there before his posting to Dyrrachion in 1092; or possibly after the last reference to him at Dyrrachion in 1097 and before he succeeded his uncle Adrian (**41**) after his death, 19 April 1105, as Grand Domestic. Zacos and Veglery suggest he could have combined Skopje with Dyrrachion, or that the seal belonged to John Taronites who called himself Komnenos.

Relation: FORMS: *tes humon agathotetos; pansebaste mou antileptor; pansebaste moi authenta kai antileptor; to hupsei sou/tes hemeteras asthenias kai tapeinotetos; ton hagion mou authenten; hagie* *mou authenta kai antileptor; pansebaste moi authenta moi kai antileptor; authenten kai euergeten; o authentes mou; te se chrestoteti; panmegiste mou authenta kai antileptor; ho megas hemon authentes kai antileptor; pansebaste hemon antileptor; tou authentou mou; ho megas hemon authentes kai antileptor; pansebaste mou antileptor; tes ses megaleiotetos.* ROLE: official. INTERACTION: multiplex, asymmetrical. TRANSACTIONAL CONTENT: fish, favours. FLOW: complex. DURATION and FREQUENCY: more than any other official. DEVELOPMENT: curiously shows no sign of what should be a pivotal point in the relationship, Theophylact's denunciation of John to the emperor, which caused the family row of *Al.*, VII.vii.3. Roth thought he saw it in G12, but the tone is very steady throughout; respectful and business-like. G10 is an adventus, G11 asks for help with the immoral hieromonk (107); G12 and G19 deal with the Pologos case; G22 thanks him for refreshing Prespa and Diabolis and asks for help with Diabolis; G23 deals with the lawsuit; G24 concerns recruitment; G61 is more general, thanking him for support and asking for help with the fisc. **Intimacy**: less than with John Doukas (38).

Use: to deal with the immoral hieromonk (107), to stop the praktors harassing the bishop of Diabolis, to uphold the *exkousseia* of the priests of Pologos (114); to stop recruitment in the Ochrid area; to settle a lawsuit in favour of Michael Beses Lampenos (81) ; to give general help with the fisc.

Connections: Manganeios Prodromos, Balsamon, Cyril Phileotes (232), the monastery of Christ Evergetes.

---

43. NICHOLAS KYRDINIATES, patriarch NICHOLAS III GRAMMATIKOS

G45, G54, G64.

Prosopography: Skoulatos (S160), 253-256; Darrouzès, *Offikia*, 36-38; 455-457; Laurent, 'La chronologie des patriarches de Constantinople,' 80-81; E. Boulismas, 'Nikolaos ho Grammatikos', *Attikon Hemerologion*, 1887, 223-36; Gautier, II, 96-97; 'Le synode,' 226. Seal: Laurent, *Sceaux*, V.1, 18-19.

Relation: FORMS: *o tou pneumatos sophon kai katharon oikterion; panagie despota; me despotes monon, alla kai pater kai pateron o oikeiotatos kai philostorgotatos; panagiotate despota; hagie despota; hagie pater kai despota.* ROLE: benevolent interest. INTERACTION: asymmetrical. FLOW: from Theophylact. TRANSACTIONAL CONTENT: complaints, gifts, prayers. DURATION: not clear. DEVELOPMENT: G45 is an unsolicited complaint; G54 thanks the patriarch for a present of incense (not hiking boots) and cinnamon sticks; G64 is a *systatike*. **Intimacy**: the sense of asymmetry is too great.

Use: to make confession, to win moral support, to look after the bishop of Pelagonia (10).

Connections: Neilos of Calabria (??=67), Theodore Blachernites, Mouzalon, Leo of Chalcedon (238), Basil the Bogomil, all episcopate.

---

44. NIKEPHOROS MELISSENOS

G9, G13, G73.

Prosopography: Maslev, 'Melissenos,' 78-95; Kazhdan, *SotsSos*, 91, 107-109; Skoulatos, *Personnages* (S150), 240-245; Papachryssanthou, 'Date,' 250-255; Matthieu, *Guillaume*, 44, 239, 329; Gautier, II, 84-86. Seals: Laurent, *Orghidan,*. no. 196, 196; Z&V nos. 2697 2697bis, 2698, 2699 (I/3, pp. 1480-1481).

Relation: Theophylact is τοῖς ὑπ'αὐτοῖς ἐλεουμένοις. ROLE: visiting dignitary, patron. INTERACTION: asymmetrical. TRANSACTIONAL CONTENT: requests, thanks, fish, praise. FLOW: from Theophylact. DURATION: early 1090s to 1102-04. DEVELOPMENT: G13 is an adventus; G9 thanks and a request; G73 is a consolatio and accompanies a gift.

Intimacy: would be out of keeping with the adulatory tone.
Use: to obtain the *kanonika* of various villages; supports Theophylact in the Komnenian family argument.
Connections: brother-in-law of Adrian Komnenos (**41**).

45. GEORGE PALAIOLOGOS
Lost 18 (mentioned in G88); mentioned in G126.
Prosopography: Gautier, II, 100-104; 'Le synode,' 233-235; on the family Laurent, 'La généalogie,' 125-149. Papadopoulos, *Versuch*, 1-2; Skoulatos, *Personnages* (S69), 99-105; Polemis, *Doukai*, 74, 153-155.
Relation: FORMS: *pansebaste mou authenta; te aparamillo sou agathoteti*. ROLE: patron (seen as Herakles). INTERACTION: asymmetrical. TRANSACTIONAL CONTENT: requests and thanks. FLOW to Theophylact. DURATION: begins late in the collection. DEVELOPMENT: G88 mentions Theophylact's intention to involve him in a manouevre; G126 is thanking him for successful intervention.
Intimacy: out of keeping.
Use: to take action in the Ekklesiai and praktor crisis.
Connections: Cyril Phileotes (**232**), Nicholas Kallikles (**3**), (through a relative) author of *Timarion*, major informant of Anna Komnene (**217**).

46. N. PSELLOS, brother of Michael
G132.
Prosopography: Gautier, II, 113-116; 'Monodie inédite,' 169; 'L'épiscopat,' 165. A problem here is that Psellos is not known to have had a brother.
Relation: FORMS: ROLE: friend, but rather distant. CONTENT: consolatio. Other evidence lacking.
Use: not seen
Intimacy: information lacking.
Connections: to Michael (**84**) and to his great-nephew (**85**).

47. JOHN SERBLIAS
G49.
Prosopography: Gautier, II, 117-118; 'Le synode,' 236, n.52; Lampros, 'Kodix,' 172-173. Adontz, 'L'archevêque;' Leroy-Molinghen, 'Deux Jean Taronite.' Seal: Laurent, *Bulles metriques*, no. 645, *Hellenika* 7 (1934), 291.
Relation: FORMS: *o kale; o makarie*. ROLE: instrumental friend. INTERACTION: symmetrical. TRANSACTIONAL CONTENT: request. FLOW: to Theophylact. DURATION and DEVELOPMENT: not seen.
Intimacy: evidence of the collection suggests none; business-like tone.
Use: to get a *pittakion* from Gregory Taronites (**48**) for the official at Vodena.
Connections: a disciple of John Italos?

48. GREGORY TARONITES

G65, G78, G81, G92; mentioned in G49.

Prosopography: Skoulatos, *Personnages* (S79), 116-118; Adontz, 'L'archevêque,' 577-588; Leroy-Molinghen, 'Grégoire Taronite,' 589-592; Buckler, *Anna Comnena*, 276; Gautier, II, 121-6; Mullett, 'Patronage,' 'Madness of Genre.'

Relation: FORMS: *tes ses megaloprepeias; megalepiphanestate moi en Kyrio huie kai authenta*. ROLE: 'son', patron, see Mullett, 'Madness of Genre.' INTERACTION: multiplex; asymmetrical. FLOW: from Theophylact. TRANSACTIONAL CONTENT: praise. DURATION: around 1103, but depends on dating of G49. DEVELOPMENT: G65 asks how he is; G78 is an encomium during the Pontic campaign; G81 after capture of Bohemond; G92 after return to Constantinople. G49 could be either before the Pontic adventure or after it.

Intimacy: possible but overshadowed by praise in the collection.

Use: give *pittakion*.

Connections: friend of (11); cousin of (49).

---

49. JOHN TARONITES, *doux* of Skopje

G18.

Prosopography: Gautier, II, 126-128; 'Le synode,' 236-237; Leroy-Molinghen, 'Prolégomènes,' 260-261; 'Deux Jean Taronites,' 147-153;. Seal: Z&V no. 2714, 1/3, 1506

Relation: FORMS: *pansebaste moi authenta; ten sen agathoteta; tou authentou mou; to authente mou* (laying it on with trowel). ROLE: official. INTERACTION: the only letter shows Theophylact angry with him for trying to influence the election of a bishop. TRANSACTIONAL CONTENT: pressure, resistance.FLOW: even. DURATION and DEVELOPMENT: no evidence.

Intimacy: chilly.

Use: not seen.

Connections: Loved by the emperor (77), (*Al.* XII.vii.4); Cyril Phileotes (232); John Tzetzes.

---

50. MARIA of Alania, *basilissa*

G4. Gautier believes also G107, but with no conclusive evidence.

Prosopography: Leib, 'Basileus ignoré,' 341-359; Gautier, I, 58-67; II, 81-84; Mullett, 'The "Disgrace".'

Relation: FORMS: *despoina mou hagia; tes theiotates sou dexias; ten sen agathoteta/te eme tapeinoteti; ten sen agathoteta kai antilepsin; basileia sou; ten sen chrestoteta*. ROLE: patroness, personal more than literary, see Mullett, 'The "Disgrace",' 209-211. INTERACTION: multiplex; asymmetrical. TRANSACTIONAL CONTENT: dedications and presentation volumes; visits (failed); support. FLOW: from Theophylact; DURATION: one letter only. DEVELOPMENT: see 'The "Disgrace".'

Intimacy: more than any other patron.

Use: not seen in the collection, but treated as patroness.

Connection: to Eustratios of Nicaea (dedicated work to her) (237).

---

51. MARIA of Bulgaria, *protovestiaria*

Lost 16, mentioned in G84, see Table II.

Prosopography: Skoulatos, *Personnages* (S122), 192-194; Polemis, *Doukai*, 58.

Relation: acquaintance.

Intimacy: evidence insufficient.

Use: to stop her son Michael the *protostrator* (39) from breaking the canons.
Connections: Euthymios Zigabenos (236); Leo of Chalcedon (238). Mother of (37), (38) and (39). Chora.

---

52. MICHAEL *ho tou Chalkedonos*

G82.
Prosopography: Gautier, II, 91-92; 'Le synode,' 273; Janin, *DHGE*, XII (1950-53), col. 275. Not otherwise known.
Relation: FORM: *paniere despota*. ROLE: acquaintance in the right place; brother or cousin of a 'son'. INTERACTION: multiplex; slightly asymmetrical. TRANSACTIONAL CONTENT: political assistance. FLOW to Theophylact. DURATION and DEVELOPMENT: insufficient evidence.
Intimacy: minimal
Use: to stop the patriarch (43) meddling with Kittaba.
Connections: to (53), and to Leo of Chalcedon (238)

---

53. NIKETAS *ho tou Chalkedonos* deacon

G84.
Prosopography: Gautier, II, 91; 'Chartophylax,' 164. Not otherwise known.
Relation: FORMS: *o pai hierotate; ho sos pater*. ROLE: ex-pupil (lemma); 'son'. INTERACTION: multiplex; slightly asymmetrical. TRANSACTIONAL CONTENT: teaching; political assistance. FLOW: sense of calling in the debt of teaching, correcting the direction of flow. DURATION: only letter, but a prehistory is implied. DEVELOPMENT: no evidence.
Intimacy: suggested in order to exploit it.
Use: to act in the case of the *protostrator*'s canon-breaking; to deliver Theophylact's letters to (51) and (39).
Connections: to (52), and to Leo of Chalcedon (238).

---

54. JOHN, *grammatikos* of Palaiologos

G88.
Prosopography: Gautier, II, 103. Not otherwise known. Probably a hieromonk.
Relation: FORMS: *theotimete adelphe kai despota*. ROLE: Become Herakles, killer of brigands! INTERACTION: asymmetrical (or Theophylact wishes to present it as such). FLOW: to Theophylact. TRANSACTIONAL CONTENT: asking a favour. DURATION and DEVELOPMENT: no evidence.
Intimacy: attraction and respect.
Use: to give a letter to Palaiologos and to consult Theophylact's interests in the case of the Vardar village.
Connections: to George Palaiologos (45); possibly the *protostrator* Michael (39).

---

55. TIBANIOS, the Armenian

G135.
Prosopography: Gautier, II, 129-130. Possibly the Tigranes of *Al.*, X.i.4 and/or the Armenian of the disputations at Philippopolis of 1114.
Relation:. FORMS: none. ROLE: theological opponent. No other evidence.
Connections: possibly Neilos of Calabria; Eustratios of Nicaea (237); archbishop of Philippopolis, Nikephoros (11); Alexios I Komnenos (77).

---

56. N.N., Grand *oikonomos*

G3.

Prosopography: Gautier, I, 47. Brother of an unknown patriarch.

Relation: FORMS: *tou theou anthrope; hagie pater kai despota; ho theokinetos anthropos; ho despotes mou.* ROLE: superordinate. INTERACTION: multiplex; asymmetrical. TRANSACTIONAL CONTENT: praise and promotion. FLOW: from Theophylact. DURATION and DEVELOPMENT: no evidence.

Intimacy: elaborateness in keeping with educational roles; nothing personal.

Use: to get Theophylact a pay-rise.

Connections: to the patriarch—but which?

57. N.N., the *epi ton deeseon*

G109. Not, as Gautier suggests, G6.

Prosopography: Gautier, II, 112-113; 'Le synode,' 246. The civil rather than the ecclesiastical office of Darrouzès, *Offikia,* 378-379. Constantine Choirosphaktes (75) held this job in 1088 (MM VI, 45), and John Taronites (not 49) during the synod of Blachernai; by 1107 John had become eparch of the City. Seal: Laurent, *Bulles métriques,* no 519; Schlumberger, 706, no.2.

Relation: FORMS: none. ROLE: instrumental friend. INTERACTION: simplex; symmetrical. TRANSACTIONAL CONTENT: Theophylact claims he has not written in order to put him in the wrong and ask his favour. FLOW: to Theophylact? DURATION and DEVELOPMENT: not enough evidence.

Intimacy: lack of forms is not supported by any evidence of affect.

Use: to have Tornikios (91) released from military service.

Connections: synod of Blachernai, or see (75).

58. N.N., bishop of DEBRA

G122.

Prosopography: Gautier, II, 560. Nothing is known of him.

Relation: FORM: *timiotate synepiskope* (avoids the use of a*delphe* in the context). ROLE: suffragan. INTERACTION: subordinate, some affect? TRANSACTIONAL CONTENT: personal confidences, advice, exhortation. FLOW: from Theophylact. DURATION and DEVELOPMENT: no evidence.

Intimacy: enough to confide the effects of the death of Demetrios (1), but perhaps just to coax him back to his see.

Use: not seen.

Connections: no evidence

59. N.N., bishop of TRIADITSA

G58, G59, G60, G87. ?Mentioned in G75, G77, G18.

Prosopography: Gautier, II, 63-66. Ex-monk. Seal: Laurent, *Sceaux,* V/2, no 1503 or 1504.

Relation: FORMS: *hierotate adelphe; timiotate adelphe; adelphe; monacho kai geronti ede, timiotate adelphe.* ROLE: suffragan, but relations are strained in these letters. INTERACTION: multiplex, asymmetrical, and age-difference. FLOW: from Theophylact; letters all refer to the one crisis. TRANSACTIONAL CONTENT: reproaches. DURATION: we see only the one case. DEVELOPMENT: G58 summons him to synod to sort out his maltreatment of the *geron* and the case of the bishop of Lipenion; G59 and G60 are from the synod and from Theophylact himself when he refused to come and planned to take his Armenian converts to Constantinople instead;

G75 and 77 show Theophylact complaining about this impasse; G87 shows the argument being patched up, but underlining the damage done to Theophylact's reputation by the bishop's calumny.

Intimacy: it is impossible to see normal relations.

Use: not seen.

Connections: to the metropolitan of Kerkyra (8).

---

60. N.N., bishop of VIDIN

G57.

Prosopography: Gautier, II, 67-68. Appointed from clergy of Ochrid after G18.

Relation: FORM: *adelphe timiotate*. ROLE: suffragan in need of encouragement. INTERACTION: asymmetrical. FLOW: from Theophylact. TRANSACTIONAL CONTENT: exhortation. DURATION and DEVELOPMENT: no evidence.

Intimacy: official relationship.

Use: not seen.

Connections: unknown.

---

61. Recipient of G106

G106.

Prosopography: Gautier, II, 130-131. A high ecclesiastic from a smart family?

Relation: FORMS: *te se agape; hyperlampre moi adelphe kai authenta*. ROLE: ?friend INTERACTION: symmetrical. TRANSACTIONAL CONTENT: establishing contact and informing the other of Theophylact's position. DURATION and DEVELOPMENT: no evidence.

Intimacy: apparently affectionate.

Use: not seen.

Connections: unknown.

---

62. (Undisciplined) pupils

G1 and 2.

As Gautier points out, I, 47, these are more like speeches than letters, addressing them as *o syneton moi akroaterion*, which precludes further analysis here.

---

63. Bulgar pupils

G103.

Much discussion has centred on the translation of the lemma's παιδευθεῖσιν. Gautier renders it 'châtiés', which Obolensky, *Portraits*, 79, regards as a mistranslation, but the content does involve reproach, as well as apology for illness. Simeon, *Pismata*, 145-146, connected it with the fisc; Zlatarsky, *Istoriia*, II, 348-349, with Bulgar bishops. Any interpretation should be subject to extreme caution.

From works of Theophylact other than the collection

64. RODOMIR AARON
Poems 11 and 12.
Prosopography: Skoulatos, *Personnages* (S179), 274-275; Lascaris, 'Sceau,' 404-413; Djurić, 'Arona,' 69-91.
Connections: Eirene Doukaina (37), Maria of Bulgaria (51).

---

65. CONSTANTINE DOUKAS
Paideia Basilike is addressed to him.
Prosopography: Leib, 'Basileus ignoré,' 341-359; Skoulatos (S36), 57-60.
Connections: son of Maria (50); fiancé of Anna Komnene (217).

---

66. NICHOLAS, deacon, *kanstresios* of Hagia Sophia
Against the Latins is addressed to him.
Prosopography: Gautier, I, 105.
Connections: later bishop of Malesova, so ? = (102).

---

67. The monk NEILOS
Poem 10.
Prosopography: Gautier, I, 123-124; Skoulatos, *Personnages* (S162), 257-259.
Use: to persuade the *sebastos* to keep Gregory Antiochos away
Connections: none unless he is Neilos of Calabria, in which case he was dangerously well connected; in the poem: the *sebastos* (?42 ?38); Michael Antiochos (120? = 110).

---

68. A libidinous eunuch
Poem 13.

---

69. A grieving person
Poems 6 and 7.

---

70. A 'wicked slave'
Poem 8.

---

71. Someone who condemned consecrated persons
Poem 9.

---

iv. *Theophylact's nominal zone*
72. SYMEON BLACHERNITES
Mentioned in passing in G129 in a joke to Michael Pantechnes (7); he has overlooked some *paroikoi*. It is tempting to see him as a tax official and to connect him with the Symeon Blachernites in the *praxis* of John Taronites, August 1102, Petit, 'Eleousa,' 31, 41, 42.

73. THEODORE CHRYSELIOS
Described in detail, though satirically, in G127, to Gregory Kamateros (4). He is the master of all arts, mathematical, musical, military, and equestrian, and will be joining the emperor and so Gregory shortly. The name looks like a comic coinage, but the family is attested in Dyrrachion in the period, Cheynet, *Pouvoirs et contestations*, 247, 342 on seal IFEB 840 of Theodore Chryselios, *protospatharios, mystographos*, judge of velum and Armeniakon; Ferluga, 'Die Chronik,' 450, n.73.

74. NICHOLAS CHRYSOBERGES
Brother of the bishop of Naupaktos (26) and friend of Theophylact; mentioned in G35. No Nicholas is known, see Laurent, 'Étienne Chrysoberges,' 214-218.

75. CONSTANTINE CHOIROSPHAKTES
Mentioned in G32.
Prosopography: Skoulatos (S34), 52-54; Gautier, 'Le synode,' 251-252; Herrin, 'Realities,' 267 and chart; Armstrong, 181. Seal: Laurent, *Bulles métriques*, 46-47, no. 738.
Relation: mentioned in the adventus to Anemas (2); Theophylact commends C to him as either mentioned before or sent on before, and describes him as ἀφελέστερος and μαλακώτερος, surely a joke; he is a seasoned politician and Anemas a young official.
Connections: Hosios Meletios (239), Cyril Phileotes (232), Romanos Straboromanos (90).

76. N. IASITES, the praktor.
Mentioned in G11 and G96, probably on two different tours of duty.
Prosopography: for members of the family, see Skoulatos (S82), 119 (a disciple of Italos); Gautier, 'Le synode,' 251 (Constantine, *kouropalatios* at the synod of Blachernai); Zonaras, XVIII.22.29, for the disastrous Komnenos-Iasites marriage, Hill, *Patriarchy and Power*, 94.
Relations: bad.
Connections: the immoral hieromonk (107); Lazaros the *paroikos* (97).

77. ALEXIOS I KOMNENOS, emperor
Lost 4; mentioned in poem 14, G127, ?G102.
Relations: need not be assumed to be bad. Theophylact describes him as dangerous, canny, hardworking, powerful and victorious.

78. ISAAC KOMNENOS, the *sebastokrator*

Mentioned in G73 as dead.

Prosopography: Papachryssanthou, 'Date,' 250-255; Skoulatos, *Personnages* (S84), 124-130; Barzos, *Genealogia* (B12), 67-79; Stiernon, *REB* 22 (1964), 184-198; Gautier, 'L'obituaire,' 249; 'Le synode,' 221-226. Seals: Z&V nos 2701, 2701bis, 2702.

Relations: none known.

Connections: father of John Komnenos (42) and Constantine Komnenos (12); brother of Alexios I Komnenos (77) and Adrian Komnenos the Grand Domestic (41); Nikephoros Basilakes; John the Oxite; Basil of Euchaita; Leo of Chalcedon (238). Famed for his φιλαδελφία.

79. DEMETRIOS KRITOPOULOS

Mentioned in G21; unknown. See Gautier, II, 198, n.6 on the family.

Relations: good. With (80) (οἱ δὲ Κριτοπούλοι ἐμοί), he is to be looked after by the bishop of Pelagonia (10); Demetrios has made many enemies in his official role, since he cannot please everyone.

80. N. KRITOPOULOS

See (79).

81. MICHAEL BESES LAMPENOS

Prosopography: mentioned in G23. Unknown, though a member of the family held the see of Ochrid before Theophylact; Gelzer, *Patriarchat*, 6. Here Theophylact upholds his side in a lawsuit against Nicholas *ho tou Boutou* (93).

Relation: client.

82. N. MAKREMBOLITES

Mentioned in G23 as grasping; hardly the 'son' of G108, the *archon* of Prespa (14) above. But the mention here is in passing.

83. N. MEDENOS

Mentioned in G98 as a previous (to the two Bulgars) oppressor in the case of the village of the church in Ochrid.

84. MICHAEL PSELLOS, *hypatos ton philosophon*

Mentioned in G132 as recently dead and recalled in G27.

Prosopography: Kriaras, *RE*, suppl XI (1968), 1124-1182; Liubarskii, *Mikhail Psell*, 22-35. For the date of his death, see Sonny, 'Todesjahr,' 602-603; Grumel, 'Remarques,' 198-211; Polemis, 'Psellos,' 73-75; Gautier, 'Monodie inédite,' 159-164; II, 115-116, sensibly cautious about a later date.

Relation: clearer from G27 than G132, which is very formal and stresses the link of friendship with the recipient not the laudandus. G27 stresses his eloquence, his charm and his influence on

Theophylact. He nowhere says Psellos was his teacher. Since Psellos may have been dead by 1078 I have not attempted to link his first order zone with Theophylact's.

85. N. PSELLOS

Grandson of (84); mentioned in G27 as a young man stricken by misfortune. Theophylact asks Gregory Kamateros (4) to give him a job.
Relations: as well as Michael (84), his great-uncle, brother of Michael (46).

86. N. SENACHEREIM

Mentioned in G77 to Nicholas of Kerkyra(8).
Prosopography: see Gautier, 89-90.
Relations: bad; presumably a praktor. He is imitated by another Senachereim (87), more unbearable and more stupid than himself.

87. The second SENACHEREIM

See (86).

88. PAUL SMYRNAIOS

Mentioned in G28. Otherwise unknown.
Relation: ex-pupil of Theophylact.
Connection: brother of Theodore Smyrnaios (20).

89. N. SMYRNAIOS

Mentioned as bearer of G112 and G114; relative of Theodore Smyrnaios (20) and Paul Smyrnaios (88). Theodore is described as *pankalos, philosophotatos kai pandexios* but his relative is not described at all.

90. ROMANOS STRABOROMANOS

Mentioned in G17, as having exploited and unloosed his rage upon the Church, and been chased out by ?John Doukas (38).
Prosopography: Skoulatos, *Personnages* (S189), 282-283; Gautier, 'Manuel Straboromanos,' 168-204.
Connections: father of Manuel Straboromanos (234); tortured Nikephoritzes; worked with Constantine Choirosphaktes (75).

91. N. TORNIKIOS

Mentioned in G109 as in need of release—by the *epi ton deeseon* (57)—from military camp.
Prosopography: on the family, Adontz, 'Taronites IV,' 30-42; Darrouzès, *Tornikai*, 25-26.
Relation: γαμβρὸς ἐπ᾽ ἀδελφιδῇ. This may make George Tornikes's maternal uncle the son-in-law of Theophylact's sister. Nothing more is known about him.

92. MICHAEL son of Polyeuktos

Mentioned in G21 as the new *strategos* of ?Ochrid. Nothing is known about him.

93. NICHOLAS *ho tou Boutou*

Mentioned in G23 as aggressor in the law-case against Michael Beses Lampenos (81) above. Nothing is known of him; presumably a local inhabitant of Ochrid.

94. EUMATHIOS, *megalepiphanestatos*

Mentioned in G21 as appointed to inspect the record of the outgoing *strategos* (?of Ochrid). His interests are those of the archdiocese and he is to be helped by the bishop of Pelagonia (10). Gautier says he 'doit être Eumathios Makrembolites plutôt qu'Eumathios Philokales', but there is no reason why he should be either.
Prosopography: on Philokales see Skoulatos, *Personnages* (S54), 79-82; Katičić, 'Korespondencija,' 187; Herrin, 'Realities,' chart, n. 6; on Makrembolites, see Kazhdan, *ODB*, II, 1273.

95. GREGORY *psaltes*

Mentioned in G66 as a eunuch monk whom Theophylact would have liked to have kept for the church at Ochrid, if he had had a proper release from his monastery.

96. JOHN ὁ καλός

Mentioned in G42 and 46 as telling Theophylact what Theophylact Romaios (19) would have said if he had bothered to write. Gautier, I, 16, suggests that he is a brother of Theophylact, and then possibly the 'robust brother' of G110. In II, 272, he identifies him with the *maistor* and philosopher John (30) and (31). The vocative form, ῏Ω καλὲ Ἰωάννη, is used both to John Opheomachos (6) in G71 and to John Peribleptenos (17) in G101. Either would seem more likely than an invented brother, and as Opheomachos appears in Bulgaria he has the edge, but there is not enough evidence to make a positive identification.

97. LAZAROS

Mentioned in G96 and 98 as the major cause of Theophylact's troubles at that time. He was a *paroikos* of Ochrid who had cast off the yoke of slavery and associated with praktors, being bribed by them with fine clothes and meals. He then proceeded to put about calumnies about Theophylact including the charge of arson in Ochrid.
Connection: known to Iasites (76).

98. THEODOSIOS

Mentioned in G92 as telling Theophylact about the achievements of Gregory Taronites (48). The praise suggests that he is part of Gregory's entourage, perhaps the bearer of a letter to Theophylact. Nothing is otherwise known of him.

99. N.N., metropolitan of SIDE

Mentioned in G104 as being in need of the care of John Attaleiates (33) and the *doux* of Attaleia. This suggests he may have been in see. He could have been the *hypertimos* John, first minister of

Michael VII Doukas, who was present at the synod of Blachernai. Seal: Laurent V/1, nos 407, 408, 1720. See Gautier, 'Le synode,' 263.
Connections: Michael Psellos (**84**).

---

100. N.N., bishop of GLAVENITSA
Mentioned in G40 as in need of help from Niketas Polites (**18**). Nothing is known of him.

---

101. N.N., bishop of LIPENION
Mentioned in G58 and G59 as the subject of discussion by the synod. Nothing is known of him.

---

102. N.N., bishop of MALESOVA
Lost 13, mentioned in G87, to ask his consent to lift the interdict on the bishop of Triaditsa (**59**). Unless *On the Errors of the Latins* was written around 1090 it is unlikely that he was the ex-pupil, deacon and *kanstresios* (**66**) of Hagia Sophia for whom Theophylact wrote it. Seal: Laurent no. 1505 is second half of the eleventh century but probably belongs to a Theodoulos.

---

103. N.N., bishop of STRUMITSA
Lost 12, mentioned in G87. He might possibly be Manuel, founder of the monastery of the Eleousa, Petit, 'Eleousa,' 1-153, or the Basil of Laurent no. 1508, V/2, 336-337; Fogg no. 487.

---

104. N.N., monk of ANAPLOUS
Expert bearer of G52 and G37, as well as of a letter from Symeon (**29**) to Theophylact.

---

105. N.N., member of Theophylact's household
Bearer of G86, who can tell John Bryennios (**34**) all Theophylact's problems.

---

106. N.N., *ho paron anthropos hemon*
Bearer of G26: nothing is known.

---

107. N.N., immoral hieromonk
Mentioned in G11, as ignoring the habit, living with a woman and associating with the agents of Iasites (**76**).

---

108. N.N., Bulgar *geron*
Bearer of G58 to the bishop of Triaditsa (**59**). The latter had been angry with him the previous July, and he had come to Theophylact, when the bishop was also with him, and reported his woes. Since he had no faith in Theophylact's powers, he got an order from the emperor, but was chased out of the whole region of Triaditsa. Theophylact took up the case with the synod.

---

109. N.N., second Bulgar *geron*

Mentioned in G59 as complaining to the assembly that his brother, the abbot of the monastery of St John in the *kastron* (of Triaditsa), had been expelled by the bishop. Even if this is the same *geron* (107), there must still be two Bulgar *gerontes*, if not, three.

110. N.N., eunuch praktor

Mentioned in G31, to Gregory Kamateros (4), as causing earlier difficulties at Ekklesiai. G76 mentions a praktor whose baleful influence could be exorcised by writing iambics. One thinks of poem 13. Both G76 and poem 10 identify the dog-star with an enemy; in poem 10 he is Michael Antiochos (120).

111. Ex-*hegoumenos* of Anaplous

Mentioned in G37 to the current abbot, Symeon (29).

112. Two bearers

Of G24, prepared to put the case to John Komnenos (42) that Ochrid should not be depopulated any further by recruitment.

113. Relatives in Euripos

On whose behalf he asks favours from John Doukas (38) (in G8 and G17). Theophylact's origins in Euboia are confirmed by the bishop list of Ochrid and the poem in Paris suppl.gr.219, fol. 294 and Laur.gr.6-26, fol. 243.

114. Priests of Pologos

Clients of Theophylact on whose behalf he asks in G12 and G19 for an *exkousseia* and then for its implementation.

115. *Hagioserretai*

Mentioned in G30; Gautier emends to Ἁγιοσεργῖται, but it is still not clear what monastery is meant and why Theophylact has jurisdiction over it.

116. Villagers of Ekklesiai

Mentioned in G111 as coming to put their case to Nicholas Kallikles (3) and in G112 as having been heard.

117. Pupils of Niketas *ho tou Serron*

Mentioned in G70 as 'my brothers', surely by analogy with G37.

118. Monks of Anaplous

Mentioned as 'his brothers' at the end of G37. Both usages, here and in G70, are surely ceremonial and do not indicate actual kinship.

119. All the bishops of Ochrid

They were to receive Lost 14, similar to Lost 11, 12, 13, asking the bishops to lift the interdict on the bishop of Triaditsa (59).

From works of Theophylact other than the collection

120. MICHAEL ANTIOCHOS, *proedros, primikerios*

Poem 10; perhaps the dog-star praktor (110) referred to in G76.

Prosopography: Gautier, 'Le synode,' 250-251, 258-259; Skoulatos, *Personnages* (S16), 25-27.

Connections: a Constantine Antiochos, *kouropalates* and Grand Heteriarch, also present at the synod of Blachernai; Antiochoi were implicated in the Anemas rising; in the poem Neilos (67) and the *sebastos*, αὐτός ἐστιν αὐτοχρηστότης (?38 ?42).

121. ANNA DALASSENE, *despoina*

Mentioned in the *basilikos logos* of 1088 to Alexios.

Prosopography: Skoulatos, *Personnages* (S14), 20-24; Runciman, 'The end'; Adontz, 'Les Dalassènes,' 171-185; Gautier, 'L'obituaire,' 244-245.

Connections: clients include Eustratios Garidas, Christodoulos of Patmos, Cyril Phileotes (232), Pantepoptes

122. JOHN II KOMNENOS

Mentioned in the *basilikos logos* of 1088 to Alexios.

Prosopography: Barzos, *Genealogia* (B34), I, 203-228.

Connections: husband of Eirene Piroska Komnene (218); son of Alexios I Komnenos (77) and Eirene Doukaina (37); brother of Anna Komnene (217), Eudokia Komnene(219), Maria Komnene (220), Theodora Komnene (221), Isaac Komnenos (222), nephew of Adrian Komnenos the Grand Domestic (41) and Isaac Komnenos, *sebastokrator* (78); patron of Nicholas Kallikles (3) and Theodore Prodromos (225); Pantokrator monastery.

123. SYMEON, superior of a monastery of eunuchs on Athos

Mentioned in treatise on eunuchs; ?=Symeon the Sanctified (230)

Prosopography: Gautier, II, 116-117.

124. N.N., bishop of EDESSA

Mentioned in treatise on eunuchs.

Prosopography: Gautier, I, 297.

125. N.N., bishop of PETRA
Mentioned in treatise on eunuchs.
Prosopography: Gautier, I, 297.

126. N.N., bishop of PYDNA (=KITROS)
Mentioned in treatise on eunuchs; may be Theophylact's correspondent (9), especially if the treatise can be dated to the second Norman war.
Prosopography: Gautier, I, 296; Laurent, *Sceaux*, V/1, 467; Nesbitt and Oikonomides, *DO Seals*, no. 24.1 and 24.2, I, 87.

127. N.N., metropolitan of THESSALONIKE
Mentioned in treatise on eunuchs; ?=Theodoulos (27).
Prosopography: Gautier, 296; Laurent, V/1, 457.

v. *Theophylact's extended zone*

II. Second order zone (from personal cell only)

Here to give some indication I record only the most obvious studies and relations:

201. NICHOLAS ADRIANOUPOLITES
Prosopography: Gautier, 'Le synode,' 216, n.2; Lampros, 'Kodix,' 7.
Connections: Leo of Chalcedon (238).

202. LEO ANEMAS
203. MICHAEL ANEMAS
204. N. ANEMAS
205. N. ANEMAS
Prosopography: Skoulatos, *Personnages* (S111, S128), 154-155, 200-202; Gautier, II, 39; Cheynet, *Pouvoir et contestations*, 100-101.
Connections: Isaac the *sebastokrator* (78); Antiochos family; Hexazenos family; N. Doukas, N. Hyaleas, Niketas Kastamonites, Kourtikios, George Basilakios, John Solomon, N. Skleros, N. Xeros ex-eparch.

206. ANNA ARBANTENISSA, wife of
207. JOHN ARBANTENOS
Prosopography: Barzos, *Genealogia* (B86), I, 489-492; Schlumberger, *Sigillographie*, 619; *Pantokrator Typikon*, 270-288, ed. Gautier, 'Pantocrator,' 46-47; Gautier, 'L'obituaire,' 260-261.
Connections: at the 1166 council; patron of Pantokrator; Roger of Salerno.

208. NIKEPHOROS DIOGENES
Prosopography: Skoulatos, *Personnages* (S146), 233-237.
Connections: Adrian Komnenos (41), Maria the ex-*basilissa* (50); Mouzakes; Gregory Kamateros (4); Michael Taronites; Katakalon Kekaumenos; Anna Komnene (217).

209. N. DOKEIANE
Prosopography: Barzos, *Genealogia* (B47), 273-274; Romano, *Callicle*, 178.
Connections: daughter of Michael; sister of Theodore Dokeianos.

210. ANNA DOUKAINA
Prosopography: Polemis, *Doukai* (P27), 74-75; Romano, *Callicle*, 169-170.
Connections: wife of George Palaiologos (45); mother of Andronikos Doukas Palaiologos (224).

211. ANNA DOUKAINA
Prosopography: Polemis, *Doukai* (P217), 190; Romano, *Callicle*, 179.
Connections: wife of the Alexios Palaiologos (P138) who was at the Councils of 1150, 1166.

212. EIRENE DOUKAINA
Prosopography: Polemis, *Doukai* (P32), 78-79.
Connections: wife of Gregory Kamateros (4); mother of Michael (216).

213. ALEXIOS DOUKAS (of Nicholas Kallikles, poem 36)
Prosopography: Barzos identifies with B67, I, 187-188 but Polemis, *Doukai*, 114 says he is 'invariably called Komnenos'.
Connections: ?son of Anna Komnene (217) and Nikephoros Bryennios (11).

214. N. DOUKAS, son of the *protostrator*
Prosopography: ? = (36), Polemis, *Doukai* ?(P30), 66, n.16; Romano, *Callicle*, 184.
Connections: Smyrnaios (20).

215. MICHAEL ITALIKOS
Prosopography: Gautier, *Michel Italikos*, 14-28.
Connections: Theodore Prodromos (225); patriarch Michael Kourkouas; *sebastokrator* Andronikos Komnenos; Eirene Doukaina (37), Anna Komnene (217); Michael Pantechnes (7); *sebastos* Gregory Kamateros (4); caesar Nikephoros Bryennios (11); ephor Theophanes; Stephen Meles; Michael Kamateros; John II Komnenos (122); Lizix (?223); Tziknoglos; doctor Leipsiotes; the *aktouarios*; Adrian Komnenos; Alexios Komnenos; John Axouch; Bapheopoulos; the *sakellarios*.

216. MICHAEL DOUKAS KAMATEROS

Prosopography: Romano, *Callicle*, 175; Polemis, *Doukai*, 78-79.
Connections: son of Gregory Kamateros (4) and Eirene Doukaina (212).

217. ANNA KOMNENE

Prosopography: Barzos, Genealogia (B32), I, 176-197; Buckler, *Anna Comnena, passim*.
Connections: wife of Nikephoros Bryennios (11); George Tornikes (235); Theodore Prodromos (225); Michael Italikos (215); circle of philosophers including Michael of Ephesos and Eustratios of Nicaea (237); Kecharitomene.

218. EIRENE PIROSKA KOMNENE

Prosopography: Moravcsik, *Die Tochter*; Mathieu, 'Irène de Hongrie;' Živojinović, 'Le prologue;' Gautier, 'L'obituaire,' 247-248.
Connections: wife of John II Komnenos (122); Nicholas Kallikles (3); Theodore Prodromos (225); Nikephoros *ho pantimos*; Michael Olynthinos; Pantokrator.

219. EUDOKIA KOMNENE

Prosopography: Barzos, *Genealogia* (B37), I, 254-259; Gautier, 'L'obituaire,' 251.
Connections: include the ill-fated Iasites marriage, see Hill, *Patriarchy and Power*, 94; first superior of Kecharitomene.

220. MARIA KOMNENE

Prosopography: Barzos, *Genealogia* (B33), I, 198-203.
Connections: wife of Gregory Gabras; daughter of Eirene Doukaina (37) and Alexios I Komnenos (77); sister of John II Komnenos (122), Anna Komnene (217), Eudokia Komnene (219), Theodora Komnene(221), Isaac Komnenos (222).

221. THEODORA KOMNENE

Prosopography: Barzos, *Genealogia* (B38), I, 259-264.
Connections: married Constantine Kourtikes; daughter of Eirene Doukaina (37) and Alexios I Komnenos (77); sister of John II Komnenos (122) Anna Komnene (217), Eudokia Komnene (219), Maria Komnene (220), Isaac Komnenos(222).

222. ISAAC KOMNENOS

Prosopography: Barzos, *Genealogia* (B36), I, 238-254.
Connections: son of Eirene Doukaina (37) and Alexios I Komnenos(77); brother of John II Komnenos (122), Anna Komnene (217), Eudokia Komnene (219), Theodora Komnene (221), Maria Komnene (220); nephew of Isaac Komnenos, *sebastokrator* (78) and Adrian Komnenos the Grand Domestic (41); monasteries of Chora and Kecharitomene.

223. MICHAEL (??LIZIX)

Prosopography: Gautier, *Michel Italikos*, 50-52.
Connections: Michael Pantechnes (7); Nicholas Kallikles (3); Michael Italikos (215). It is not certain that the doctor Michael at the deathbed of Alexios was the Lizix who was a correspondent of Michael Italikos or the Michael Lizix of Prodromos's *Iatros e demios?* Magdalino, *Manuel I*, 361, n.156, proposes Michael Italikos (215) as the third doctor.

224. ANDRONIKOS DOUKAS PALAIOLOGOS

Prosopography: Polemis, *Doukai* (P136), 154.
Connections: son of George Palaiologos (45) and Anna; author of *Timarion*.

225. THEODORE PRODROMOS

Prosopography: Hörandner, *Historische Gedichte*, 21-35; Kazhdan, *Studies On*, 87-114; Beaton, 'Poverty,' 1-28.
Connections: Michael Italikos (215); Eirene Doukaina (37); John II Komnenos (122); Manuel I Komnenos and Bertha; the *sebastokratorissa* Eirene; Stephen Kontostephanos; Manuel Anemas; Alexios Aristenos; Andronikos Kamateros; Sergios Botaneiates; the monk Ioannikios; Constantine Alopos; Constantine Kamytzes; Leo Tzikandeles; Michael Palaiologos; Stephen Meles; Theodore Stypeiotes; the patriarch Theodotos; Anastasios Lizix; Mytas; Stephen Skylitzes; ephor Theophanes.

226. NICHOLAS SKLEROS

Prosopography: Seibt, *Die Skleroi* (no. 22), 93-97.
Connections: ?Michael Psellos (84) (three epp.); succeeded by Leo N. as *epi ton deeseon*.

227. JOHN SKYLITZES-THRAKESIOS

Prosopography: Seibt, 'Skylitzes,' 81ff; Laiou, 'Marriages,' 167.
Connections: Alexios I Komnenos (77).

228. JOHN ZONARAS

Prosopography: Kazhdan, *ODB*, III, 2229; Mango, 'Notices,' 221-228; Grigoriades, *Studies*, 4-11.
Connections: Hagia Glykeria.

229. ROGER, *sebastos*

Prosopography: Skoulatos, (S180), 275-278 identifies with the son of Dagobert of the *Alexiad*; and deals well with the objections of Mathieu, 'Cinq poésies.' But there is also the bureaucrat *sebastos* Constantine Roger of *PantokratorTyp*, 248, ed. Gautier, 'Pantocrator,' 44, backed by Romano, *Nicola Callicle*, 175-176. Gautier, 'L'obituaire,' 255 claims he is the brother of caesar John Dalassenos Roger, revealed by Stiernon, 'Famille Rogerios,' *REB* 22 (1964), 185-187 as the father of an Anna Komnene, of Andronikos Roger, the founder of the Chrysokamariotissa monastery, and of the Alexios Roger *sebastos* who attended the 1166 council; but he could be the father. Both candidates are possible; Kallikles's emphasis on Roger's brilliant marriage might

explain Constantine's status as *sebastos* by 1136, but the date-range of Kallikles's poems favours the latter.
Connections: Alexios I Komnenos (77) and other signatories of the treaty of Diabolis—or John II Komnenos (122) and Pantokrator.

230. STEPHEN-SYMEON the Sanctified
Prosopography: may = (123); see Gautier, II, 116-117; Morris, *Monks and Laymen*, 86, 101, 279-280.
Connections: Nicholas Mermentoulos (5), Nicholas Skleros (226), John Skylitzes-Thrakesios (227), John Zonaras (228); spiritual father of Alexios I Komnenos (77); monastery of Xenophontos.

231. ex-bishop, archimandrite of St George in the Mangana
Prosopography: Mercati, 'Gli aneddotti,' 126-143.
Connections: Eirene Doukaina (37).

Connections of Theophylact's second order zone who are also connected to members of his first order zone beyond the personal cell

232. CYRIL PHILEOTES
Prosopography: Sargologos, *Cyrille*, 13-15.
Connections: Nicholas Kataskepenos; Eumathios Philokales (??=94); Constantine Choirosphaktes (75); John Komnenos, son of the *sebastokrator* (42); George Palaiologos (45); Michael Doukas, *protostrator* (39), Alexios I Komnenos (77), Eirene Doukaina (37).

233. NIKETAS STETHATOS
Prosopography: Darrouzès, *Nicétas Stéthatos*, 7-10.
Connections: Symeon the New Theologian (301); Niketas *chartophylax* son of Koronis; Gregory *sophistes*; Niketas deacon of the Great Church; Alexios monk and philosopher; Manuel N.; Athanasios *hegoumenos* of Philotheou.

234. MANUEL STRABOROMANOS
Prosopography: Gautier, 'Manuel Straboromanos,' 168-204.
Connections: Eirene Doukaina (37); Michael the *protostrator* Doukas (39); Romanos Straboromanos (90).

235. GEORGE TORNIKES
Prosopography: Darrouzès, *Tornikai*, 7-32.
Connections: Tornikios (91); Andronikos Komnenos; John Kamateros; John Komnenos; John Pantechnes; Anna Komnene (217), *protos* of Mt Ganos.

236. EUTHYMIOS ZIGABENOS
Prosopography: Jugie, 'Vie,' 215-225.
Connections: Maria the Bulgarian (51); ?John Phournes; Basil the Bogomil; Alexios I Komnenos (77); Pamphilos.

237. EUSTRATIOS of NICAEA
Prosopography: Joannou, 'Trois pièces,' 23-34.
Connections: Maria of Alania (50); Niketas *ho tou Serron* (22); Anna Komnene (217).

238. LEO of CHALCEDON
Prosopography: Stephanou, 'Le procès.'
Connections: ?nephews Michael (52) and Niketas (53); Adrian Komnenos (41); patriarch Nicholas III Grammatikos (43); Isaac Komnenos (78); George Palaiologos (45); Nicholas Adrianoupolites (201); and all at the synod of Blachernai.

239. Hosios MELETIOS
Prosopography: Armstrong, *Meletios*, 18-20.
Connections: Constantine Choirosphaktes (75); John Doukas (38); John Bryennios (34); Epiphanios Kamateros; Bardas Hikatenos; Leon Nikerites; Michael Kastamonites; N. Batatzes; Theophylaktos N.; John Xeros.

240. GREGORY, abbot of OXEIA
Prosopography: Gautier, 'Grégoire, higoumène.'
Connections: Theodore Prodromos (225), caesar Alexios-Bela; Alexios Komnenos Euphorbenos; *hegoumenos* of kyr Philotheou (?=Symeon, 29); Basil Tripsychos; Manuel Anemas; *porphyrogennete* Theodora.

III. Theophylact's third order zone,
which consists of the networks of each member of his second order zone, includes:

301. SYMEON THE NEW THEOLOGIAN
Prosopography: I. Hausherr, *Un grand mystique byzantin. Vie de Syméon le nouveau théologien par Nicétas Stéthatos* (OCA, 12, Rome, 1928), J.A. McGuckin, 'Symeon the New Theologian (d. 1022) and Byzantine Monasticism,' *Mount Athos and Byzantine Monasticism*, ed. A. Bryer and M. Cunningham (SPBS, 4, Aldershot, 1996), 17-35
Connections: patriarchs Nicholas Chrysoberges, Anthony the Studite, Sergios, Sisinnios; Stephen of Nicomedia *synkellos*, Anthes, Anna *hegoumene*, Anthony *hegoumenos* of St Mamas, Arsenios, Basil, Christopher Phagouras, Damianos, Genesios *patrikios*, Ignatios, monk of the Kosmidion, Hierotheos monk of St Mamas, John, *protonotarios* of the drome, John *ho deeseon*, Ioannikios, Kosmas *hegoumenos* of St Stephen on Mt St Auxentios, Leo Xylokodon, Meletios, Methodios monk of Stoudios, Nikephoros (Symeon) monk at Hagia Marina, Orestes, Peter *hegoumenos* of Stoudios, Stephen of Alexina, Symeon of Ephesos, Symeon, Symeon Eulabes, Soterichos, Philotheos *ktetor*, Theodoulos, Theophano (mother).
Further listing would be voluminous and of decreasing usefulness, see above, 4.2, 194.

TABLES

TABLE I

CONCORDANCE OF LETTER-NUMBERS

G, I=Gautier, *Théophylacte*, I; G, *NB*=Gautier, *Nicéphore Bryennios*; M=Mercati, 'Poesie;'
R=Romano, *Nicola Callicle*; L-M=Leroy-Molinghen, 'Prolégomènes;' G(1966)=Gautier,
'Monodie inédite.'

Migne	Gautier	Other	Migne	Gautier	Other
Vat 1=Lami 2b	G6		Meurs 17	G75	
Vat 2=Lami 4	G8		Meurs 18	G29	
Vat 3	G44		Meurs 19=Lami 24	G32	
Vat 4	G45		Meurs 20	G76	
Vat 5	G46		Meurs 21=Lami 26	G34	
Vat 6	G47		Meurs 22	G77	
Vat 7	G48		Meurs 23	G78	
Vat 8	G49		Meurs 24	G79	
Vat 9	G50		Meurs 25	G80	
Vat 10	G51		Meurs 26	G81	
Vat 11	G52		Meurs 27	G82	
Vat 12	G53	L-M1, 255-258	Meurs 28	G83	
Vat 13	G54		Meurs 29	G84	
Vat 14	G55		Meurs 30	G85	
Vat 15	G56		Meurs 31	G86	G, *NB*, 316-319
Vat 16	G57		Meurs 32	G87	
Vat 17	G58		Meurs 33	G88	
Vat 18	G59		Meurs 34	G89	
Vat 19	G60	L-M2, 260-261	Meurs 35	G90	
Vat 20	G135		Meurs 36	G91	
Meurs 1	G61		Meurs 37	G92	
Meurs 2a	G62		Meurs 38	G93	R1, 57
Meurs 2b	G63		Meurs 39	G94	R2, 58
Meurs 3	G64		Meurs 40	G95	
Meurs 4	G65		Meurs 41	G96	G, *NB*, 320-333
Meurs 5	G66		Meurs 42	G97	
Meurs 6	G67		Meurs 43	G98	
Meurs 7	G68		Meurs 44	G99	
Meurs 8	G69		Meurs 45	G100	
Meurs 9	G70		Meurs 46	G101	
Meurs 10	G71		Meurs 47	G102	
Meurs 11	G72		Meurs 48	G103	
Meurs 12	G73		Meurs 49	G104	
Meurs 13	G74		Meurs 50	G105	G, *NB*, 318-321
Meurs 14	G14		Meurs 51	G106	
Meurs 15	G27		Meurs 52	G107	
Meurs 16=Lami 21	G34		Meurs 53	G108	

Migne	Gautier	Other	Migne	Gautier	Other
Meurs 54	G109		Lami 11	G16	
Meurs 55	G110		Lami 12	G17	
Meurs 56	G111	R3, 59-60	Lami 13a	G18	
Meurs 57	G112	R4, 60-61	Lami 13b	G19	
Meurs 58	G113		Lami 14	G20	
Meurs 59	G114		Lami 15	G21	
Meurs 60	G115		Lami 16	G22	
Meurs 61	G116		Lami 17	G23	
Meurs 62	G117		Lami 18	G24	
Meurs 63	G118		Lami 19	G25	
Meurs 64	G119	Lami 13a	Lami 20	G26	
Meurs 65	G120		Lami 21 = Meurs 16	G28	
Meurs 66	G121		Lami 22	G30	
Meurs 67	G122		Lami 23	G31	
Meurs 68	G123		Lami 24 = Meurs 19	G32	
Meurs 69	G124	M1, 186 (362)	Lami 25	G33	
Meurs 70	G126		Lami 26 = Meurs 21	G34	
Meurs 71	G127		Lami 27	G35	
Meurs 72	G128		Lami 28	G36	
Meurs 73	G129		Lami 29	G37	
Meurs 74	G130		Lami 30	G38	
Meurs 75	G131		Lami 31	G39	
Lami 1	G4		Lami 32	G40	
Lami 2a	G5		Lami 33	G41	
Lami 2b = Vat 1	G6		Lami 34	G42	
Lami 3	G7		Lami 35	G43	
Lami 4 = Vat 2	G8			G125	M2, 186 (362)
Lami 5	G9			G1	G, I, 130-143
Lami 6	G10			G2	G, I, 146-155
Lami 7	G11			G3	G, I, 168-175
Lami 8	G12			G132	G(1966), 169
Lami 9	G13			G133	
Lami 10	G15			G134	G, I, 334-342

TABLE II

TABLE OF LOST LETTERS

All references in 'Evidence' column are to Gautier, I-II
Gautier, P = numbers in 'Lettres perdues,' Gautier, II, 599-602
(?) indicates some uncertainty

Letter	Addressee	Date	Place	Content	Evidence
Lost 1 (G believes this = G6, but there is no reason to believe Smyrnaios was *epi ton deeseon)*	to the *epi ton deeseon*	1089-90	Ochrid to CP	'first letter on arrival'	G7, II, 151.8-9: ζητήσας τὴν πρὸς τὸν ἐπὶ τῶν δεήσεων ἐπιστολὴν ἡμῶν
Lost 2	to the caesar Nikephoros Melissenos	?	Ochrid to CP	previous inadequate thanks for services rendered	G9, II, 157.3: πολλάκις ἀντιταλαντ-εύσας τὴν γλῶτταν
Lost 3 = Gautier, P1	to a hieromonk	1090s	Ochrid to somewhere in archdiocese	to abandon his scandalous behaviour	G11, II, 165.32: καὶ δι' ἐπιστολῆς
Lost 4 = Gautier, P2	to Alexios I Komnenos	1093	Ochrid to ?	to denounce John Komnenos	Anna, *Al.*, VIII.vii.3-8, L, II, 147-151
Lost 5	to caesar Melissenos	1091 or 1093	Ochrid to Macedonia	complaints	G13, II, 171.12-13: ἀλλὰ ταῦτα μὲν ἤδη καὶ λέλεκται
Lost 6 (?)	to Nicholas Anemas	?	Ochrid to somewhere in Bulgaria	Constantine Choiro-sphaktes to beg help for little church property	G32, II, 239.26: ὁ δὲ παρ' ἡμῶν προληφθεὶς Κ ὁ Χ

Letter	Addressee	Date	Place	Content	Evidence
Lost 7 (?)	to Gregory Kamateros	?	?Ochrid to ?somewhere close	??asks him to do something GK would rather he had not asked??	G38, II, 259-261
Lost 8 = Gautier, P3	to the bishop of Triaditsa	before 1094-95	Ochrid to Triaditsa	to treat the *geron* of the monastery of St John on the *kastron* well	G58, II, 331.71: γράψαι πάλιν περὶ τούτου
Lost 9	to the *chartophylax* Peter	1094/95-1106	Ochrid to CP	protests about interference of patriarch at Kittaba	G82, II, 435.24: περὶ τούτου ἐγράψαμεν
Lost 10	to Adrian the Grand Domestic	1097-1104 (early)	Ochrid to CP	village of the church in Ochrid	G85, II, 445.7-8: τὰς νεφέλας τοῦ προφητικοῦ γράμματος
Lost 11 = Gautier, P4	to the bishop of Pelagonia	before 1094/95	Ochrid	asks to agree the lifting of interdict on bishop of Triaditsa	G87, II, 459.38-40: ἔγραψα μὲν ταῦτα καὶ πρὸς τὸν Πελαγονίας
Lost 12 = Gautier, P5	to the bishop of Strumitsa	before 1094/95	Ochrid	asks to agree the lifting of interdict on bishop of Triaditsa	G87, II, 459.39: καὶ πρὸς τὸν Στρουβίτζης
Lost 13 = Gautier, P6	to the bishop of Malesova	before 1094/95	Ochrid	asks to agree the lifting of interdict on bishop of Triaditsa	G87, II, 459.39-40: Καὶ πρὸς τὸν Μαλεσόβης
Lost 14 = Gautier, P7	to the bishops	before 1094/5	Ochrid	asks to agree the lifting of interdict on bishop of Triaditsa	G87, II, 459.42-43: γράψομεν δὲ καὶ πρὸς τοὺς λοιπούς

Letter	Addressee	Date	Place	Content	Evidence
Lost 15 =Gautier, P8	*protostrator* Michael Doukas	?	Ochrid	to stop violating canons	G84, II, 441.22: καὶ πρὸς τὸν πανσέβαστον πρωτο-στράτορα
Lost 16 =Gautier, P9	Maria of Bulgaria, *protovestiaria*	?	Ochrid	to intervene with her son and stop him	G84, Gautier, II, 441.12: γράμμα μοι ἐκτέθειται
Lost 17 =Gautier, P10	*protostrator* Michael Doukas	c. 1093-95 (or 1105-08)	Ochrid	to brief his son, appointed to the rule of the Vardar, on Θ's needs	G88, II, 461.19-20: ἐγράψαμεν τῷ κοινῷ αὐθέντῃ ἡμῶν
Lost 18 =Gautier, P11	*sebastos* George Palaiologos	1093-5 (or 1105-8)	Ochrid	asks to intervene to see that Ekklesiai is not surveyed	G88, II, 463.29-30: τοῦτο τὸ ἐμφανίσαι μὲν τῷ πανσεβάστῳ σεβαστῷ τὸ ἡμέτερον γράμμα
Lost 19 (?)	Gregory Kamateros	?	within Bulgaria	carried by Demetrios	G127, II, 571.2-3: καὶ τῆς ἐπιστ-ολῆς
Lost 20 (?)	Bryennios who had requested a letter	1095/1110		carried with poem 1	poem 1, I, 347.tit: αἰτησάμενον
Lost 21 (?)	Nicholas Kallikles	1106-07	within Bulgaria	carried with poem 3 and the books of G112	poem 3, I, 351

TABLE III

PREVIOUS LETTERS REFERRED TO

Letter	Addressee	refers to	Addressee	Evidence
G7	to Niketas *ho tou Serron*	G5	to Adrian the Grand Domestic	II, 151.5: πυθοῦ τοῦ πρὸς τὸν κοινὸν ἡμῶν αὐθέντην τὸν μέγαν δομέστικον γραμματίου
G9	to the caesar	Lost 2	to the caesar	II, 157.2-5: previous inadequate attempts (if written)
G13	to the caesar	Lost 5 (or the oral message with say G9)	to the caesar	II, 171.12-13: ἀλλὰ ταῦτα μὲν ἤδη καὶ λέλεκται
G38	to Gregory Kamateros	Lost 7 (or the personal contact promised in G31)	to Gregory Kamateros	II, 259: asking Gregory to do something against his better judgement/request to have the *praxis* registered
G60	to the bishop of Triaditsa	G58 G59	to the bishop of Triaditsa	II, 343.5: τὸ ἡμέτερον γράμμα; 343.3-4: ἐν ἑτέρῳ ...γράμματι
G77	to the metropolitan of Kerkyra	G75	to the metropolitan of Kerkyra	II, 409.50: καὶ πρότερον γράψας τῇ ἁγιωσύνῃ; ?cf. II, 401.36-37: ἐπεὶ παρὰ συνιερέων καὶ συνεπισκόπων οἳ δοκοῦσι κρίνειν τὸν λαὸν ἐκτέταται τὰ τῶν θλίψεων ἡμῶν δίκτυα
G87	to the bishop of Triaditsa	G59	to the bishop of Triaditsa	II, 459.38-39: καὶ τὸ συνοδικῶς ἐκτεθὲν πρός σε γράμμα ἐδήλου
G89	to Adrian the Grand Domestic	G85	to Adrian the Grand Domestic	II, 465.2-3: διὰ μὲν τοῦ ἔναγχος πρὸς τὴν μεγαλειότητά σου σταλέντος γράμματος ...
G112	to Nicholas Kallikles	G111	to Nicholas Kallikles	II, 537.2-3: χθὲς γοῦν αἰτήσας τὴν πρὸς τοὺς αὐτόθι ἡμετέρους = G111, II, 535.18-20
G127	to Gregory Kamateros	?G115 or G116	?	?

TABLE IV

PREVIOUS LETTER-SILENCE REFERRED TO

Letter	Correspondent	Date	Evidence
G44	to Machetares	?early	Don't accuse me of not writing to you
G45	to the Patriarch	?	so many years' silence
G52	to bishop of Kitros	1097	so long neither has written
G62	to John the maistor	?	lack of σχολή
G65	to Gregory Taronites	?before 1094	silent but will I always be?
G67	to Gregory Kamateros	?late in the collection	rare little letters from Ochrid
G121	to bishop of Kitros	1107	μή μοι τοίνυν τὴν ἀγραφίαν ἔχειν ἐν λόγῳ

TABLE V

COMMUNICATION PROBLEMS

Letter	Correspondent	Date	Problem	Evidence
G18	John Taronites	before 1094	*pittakion* never arrived	II, 191.2-15
G52	bishop of Kitros	1097	no good bearer	II, 303.14-15
G90, (+91, 93)	the *chartophylax*	?	the middle of winter	II, 469.23
G106	?	?	no time for a long letter	II, 523.2-3
G117	?Michael Pantechnes	?	the bearer rushed Θ	II, 547.2-3

TABLE VI

DOCUMENTS REQUESTED

Correspondent	Document	Date/Place	Content	Evidence
John Komnenos	*pittakion*	early 1090s Ochrid to Dyrrachion	to exempt priests of Pologos from services	G12, II, 167.19-169.23
Diabologyres	letter	Easter 1090	tell me how the service goes	G15, II, 179.19: γράψον οὖν ἡμῖν περὶ τούτου αὐτοῦ
John Komnenos	*sigillion*	1090s Diabolis	for bishop	G22, II, 205.29-30: προσκυνητὸν σὸν ἐπιβραβευθῆναι σιγίλλιον
Nicholas Mermentoulos	letters	?Ochrid to CP	χαρίτων ἀληθῶς στέφανος	G25, II, 213
Theodore Smyrnaios	letters	?Ochrid to CP	gout has tied up his tongue	G28, II, 223 (implicitly)
Nicholas Mermentoulos	many-lined letters	?Ochrid to CP	to charm and console him	G33, II, 241
Theophylact Rhomaios	letters	?Ochrid to CP	Pythagorean joke	G42, II, 271-273
Machetares	letters	?Ochrid to CP	Jacob's ladder/golden chain	G44, II, 277-279
Nicholas Mermentoulos	letter	?Ochrid to CP	drop of nectar	G47, II, 293
John Serblias	*pittakion*	??O/CP	from Gregory Taronites for governor of Veroia, instructions for Bodena	G49, II, 297
Gregory Taronites	letter	?Ochrid to ?	asks to be kept informed	G65, II, 363.24-25: εἰ δὲ καὶ γράμματι δηλώσαις, χρυσοῦν ὄντως ἡμῖν ἐπισκευάσεις τὸν ὄροφον

Correspondent	Document	Date/Place	Content	Evidence
chartophylax Nikephoros	written permission	?Ochrid to CP	release in writing from the *hegoumenos* and the *charistikarios*	G66, II, 367.27-29: καὶ παρὰ τῶν κρειττόνων ἀπόλυσιν λαχεῖν ἔγγραφον καὶ παρὰ τοῦ ἡγουμένου τὴν οἷον ἀπολυτικὴν παράθεσιν
Gregory Kamateros	letters	?Ochrid to	letters to fortify good appointee	G67, II, 371.32-33
Nicholas Mermentoulos	letter	Ochrid to CP	silence and phoenix; be more like the sun!	G76, II, 403-405
Gregory Taronites	letter	Ochrid to CP	send torrents not drop by drop	G92, II, 475.37-46
Nicholas Kallikles	letters (or help!)	Ochrid to with the emperor	do we hate one another so much we do not write?	G93, II, 477
Nikephoros Bryennios	*prostaxis*	1097-1104	for village of the church in Ochrid	G96, II, 493.153: δέομαι πρόσταξιν γενέσθαι
John Peribleptenos	letter	?Ochrid to CP	letter as medicine	G97, II, 497.30: γράφων ...θαμινώτερον
John Attaleiates	letter from the bishop of Side	?Ochrid to Attaleia	to testify to John's help	G104, II, 519.13-14: καὶ γένοιτό μοι μαθόντι διὰ γραφῆς αὐτοῦ
epi ton deeseon	letters (or help!)	?O/CP	treat me like Orestes by not writing	G109, II, 529.3: ὥστε μὴ προσεννέπειν
?Michael Pantechnes	letter	?Ochrid to CP	news	G115, II, 543.2: ποθοῦμεν μαθεῖν ὡς ἔχετε
Michael Pantechnes	letter	?Ochrid to CP	glad not to have	G130, II, 585
Michael Pantechnes	letters	?Ochrid to CP	better than the usual muddy drops	G131, II, 587
Demetrios	διὰ γλυκυτέρας γραφῆς	?Ochrid to ?	that God has made you well	G133, II, 591

TABLE VII

LETTERS RECEIVED

L: letter; LL: letters; X: no letters; ?: possibly a letter; ??: less possibly a letter; Θ: Theophylact

Correspondent	Date	Content	Θ's response	Reply to	Replied to by	Evidence
?? Diabologyres	Easter 1090	conversion of Armenians			G15	II, 179.2: Εὖγε ὅτι... Who else would tell Θ?
L Tarchaneiotes	?	request for advice			G16	II, 183.5: περὶ τὴν ἡμετέραν... οὐδαμινότητα τιμήσας γράμματα
L John Taronites	?before 1094	suggests a candidate for a bishopric	denies it ever arrived			G18, II, 191.11:τὸ πιττάκιον τὸ περὶ τῆς ἐπισκοπῆς
? John Taronites	a little later than the above	complains that Θ has not replied to his *pittakion*			G18	
L *chartophylax* Nikephoros	before 1094/95		describes reception and response		G30	II, 229.6 εἰς χεῖρας ἐνέπεσεν
??LL Nicholas Mermentoulos	?		charm and consolation		G33	
L Symeon abbot of Anaplous	?1097	warns Θ not to overlook the bearer of his letter; news of the death of the old abbot-recluse	describes reaction and response of his *kyklos*		G37	II, 253.2 καὶ πῶς ἂν τὸν πάροντα γραμματοκομιστὴν ὑπερβάς;
L Gregory Kamateros	?	accuses Θ of asking him to act illegally	denies vigorously, and claims objecting too late	Lost?	G38	II, 261.32-33 περὶ δὲ οὗ μοι ἔγραψας

Correspondent	Date	Content	Θ's response	Reply to	Replied to by	Evidence
XLL Theophylact Romaios	?	letters to John	asks for his own		G42	
? Machetares	?	request	Θ turns down		G44	II, 277.23-24 Ἐφ' οἷς ἠξίωσας...
XLL Theophylact Romaios	?	letters to John? or John told him?			G46	II, 289
XX Nicholas Mermentoulos			asks for end of *siope*		G47	II, 293, esp. 12-14
? Michael Pantechnes	?	asks how Θ is	tells in grim detail		G48	II, 295.2: Ἐρωτᾷς πῶς ἔχει τὰ ἡμέτερα
X Bishop of Kitros	1097		notes *siope* and gives own reasons		G52	II, 303.2: πολὺν ἐσιγήσαμεν χρόνον
L patriarch	?	encourages Θ; contains gift	describes supportive effect and enjoyment of ears, eyes, tongue	?G45	G54	II, 313.2: τίς ἡμῶν μακαριώτερος νῦν ὅτε δεσποτικῷ κατευλογήθημεν γράμματι
? bishop of Vidin	1094-95	complains about difficulties	Θ caps each one		G57	II, 323.2 τὰ κατὰ σέ
L bishop of Triaditsa	before 1094/95	tells of success in converting Armenians; intends to take them to Constantinople; cannot leave Triaditsa	read by all at the synod	G58	G59 from the synod	II, 337.2 ἀνεγνώσθη...τὸ γράμμα τῆς σῆς ἱερότητος

Correspondent	Date	Content	Θ's response	Reply to	Replied to by	Evidence
L bishop of Triaditsa	?	objects to being condemned in absence; complains of the tone of Θ's letter; refuses to come while Θ is angry	'most wise justification'	G58	G60 from Θ	II, 343.2 τοῦ σοῦ γράμματος
L John Komnenos	early 1090s	Θ has been slandered	Θ is grateful for slander if it brings a letter; description of reception		G61	II, 351.3-4: ... μοι τοῦ δέξασθαι τῆς σῆς μεγαλειότητος γράμμα 351.5 ὡς ἔγωγε τὸ γράμμα ἐπὶ χεῖρας λαβὸν
? (*chartophylax* Nikephoros) ep. from ?abbot of G's monastery?	before 1094/5 synod of Blachernai	no clear permission for Gregory *psaltes* to travel	Θ cannot keep him without permission		G66	II, 367.29-30 διὰ γραφῆς αὐτοῦ
LL, L caesar Melissenos	1102-04	death of *sebastokrator* Isaac	usually dew of consolation; this one made Θ's heart sink		G73	II, 389, 2-6 ἀεί μοι τῶν σῶν γραμμάτων...τὸ ἔναγχος τοῦτο διακομισθέν
L bishop of Kerkyra	?before 1094/95	encouragement and complaint	received with pleasure		G75	II, 399, 2 ἡδέως ἐδεξάμην σου τὴν ἐπιστολήν
LL Mermentoulos	?	gap (feels a century long, so much does he enjoy M's letters)	like phoenix of Heliopolis when does arrive		G76	II, 403.4 τὸ σὸν γράμμα
L bishop of Kerkyra	?before 1094/5	poured out his woes	paragraph of praise	G75	G77	II, 407.2: ὅτι πάλιν ἐκ σοῦ μοι γράμματα
L Gregory Taronites	early May 1103	his exploits in Pontos	describes effect of letter and receipt on the way to Prespa		G78	II, 415.5 γράμματι γὰρ ἐποχούμενον

Correspondent	Date	Content	Θ's response	Reply to	Replied to by	Evidence
? Gregory Pakourianos	?	letter of apology	Θ accepts		G80	II, 425.2-20
? Gregory Taronites	summer 1103	news of victories	Θ celebrates	?G78	G81	II, 427.8 ὅπερ ἤγγέλη μοι
?? not *charto-phylax* Niketas	?1106-11	distressing rumour about him	Θ asks for verification		G83	II, 439.2 τις φήμη περὶ ὑμῶν
? Adrian the Grand Domestic	?1097-1104 early	asks for clarification	Θ complies		G85	II, 445.7-8 Ἐμὲ διασχεῖν κελεύεις τὰς νεφέλας τοῦ προφητικοῦ γράμματος
L bishop of Triaditsa	?before 1094/95	accounts of success with the heretics	Θ has heard that the bishop has slandered him while in CP		G87	II, 457.2 ἐδεξόμεθά σοι τὴν γραφήν
? Gregory Taronites and Theodosios	1103	G has returned from Colchis to Constantinople	Theodosios has told Θ all about it: mixed feelings		G92	II, 473.3 :... σε τῆς Κολχίδος ἀκούσας
L John Peribleptenos	?	blames himself for not writing and promises to	blames himself and asks for letters		G97	II, 495. = Pr. 18.17
?? bishop of Debra	1107	consolatio	explains his loss; orders back to see		G122	II, 561 abrupt beginning
? Michael Pantechnes	?	tells troubles	Θ sorry		G128	II, 581.3: καὶ αὐτός εἰπὼν συνέχεσθαι θλίψεσιν
? Michael Pantechnes	?	promises to come and stay	encourages him		G129	II, 583.2 ὑμεῖς δὲ ἀεί...ἐπισκεψόμενοι
?? Demetrios	before 1107	asks for guidance	responds		G134	II, 593.1 ἐρωτήσαντα

TABLE VIII

BEARERS OF THEOPHYLACT'S LETTERS

Letter	Bearer	Date	Place	Θ's comments	Evidence
G5 to the grand domestic G6, to Theodore Smyrnaios G7, to Niketas *ho tou Serron* Lost1 to the *epi ton deeseon*	(G7) your pupil my brother	1089-90	Ochrid to CP	bearer will show him G5, G6 and Lost1	II, 151.9
G24 to John Komnenos	δύο συμπρεσβευτάς	1093-94	Ochrid to Dyrrachion	his letter will plead like them	II, 209.17
G26 to ?John Doukas	ὁ παρὼν ἄνθρωπος ἡμῶν	1089-92	Ochrid to Dyrrachion		II, 217.19
G27 to Gregory Kamateros	νεανίας; θυγατριδοῦς of Psellos	1078+? 1097+?	Ochrid to CP	*systatike*	II, 219-221
??G32 to Nicholas Anemas	just possibly Constantine Choirosphaktes	?			II, 239.26
G37 to abbot Symeon (?with G52 to the bishop of Kitros)	γραμματοκομιστὴν τὸν παρόντα; ?monk of Anaplous	1097	Ochrid to Anaplous	Θ accused of passing by this bearer	II, 253.2
G40 to Niketas Polites	bishop of Glavenitsa	?	οἴκοθεν οἴκαδε	*systatike*	II, 267
G52 to the bishop of Kitros	monk from Symeon's monastery	1097	Ochrid to Kitros	no good (γνησίων) bearers until now	II, 303.13

Letter	Bearer	Date	Place	Θ's comments	Evidence
G58 to the bishop of Triaditsa	ὁ παρὼν γέρων	before 1094/95	Ochrid to Triaditsa		II, 327.2
G61 to ?John Komnenos	bishop: ὁ συνάδελφός μου	spring 1090s	Ochrid to ?	will tell the others about his doings περὶ τὰ τῆς λίμνης δίκαια	II, 353.25
G64 to the patriarch	bishop of Pelagonia	before 1111	Ochrid to CP	*systatike*	II, 361
Lost 16 to Maria the *protovestiaria* Lost 17 to *protostrator* Michael	Niketas, deacon, *ho tou Chalkedonos*	?	?within CP	G84 is the letter of instructions to the bearer; he is to give both to Maria	II, 441.11-12
G86 to John Bryennios	ὁ τὸ γράμμα διακομίζων lives with Θ and knows all- ἡμέτερος γὰρ ὢν	1097-1107?	Ochrid to Dyrrachion	will expand on Θ's sufferings	II, 453.23-455.27
G87, to the bishop of Triaditsa Lost 11, to the bishop of Pelagonia Lost12, to the bishop of Strumitsa Lost13, to the bishop of Malesoba	ὑπηρέτης of the bishop	synod before 1094/95	Ochrid to Triaditsa via Pelagonia, Strumitsa and Malesoba	will deliver on the way to the bishop	II, 459.38-42
G90, to the *chartophylax* G91, to the *didaskalos* of the Great Church, G93, to Nicholas Kallikles	τὸν ἀδελφόν μου τοῦ μαθητοῦ σου, τοῦ ἐμοῦ ἀδελφοῦ τῷ ἀδελφῷ μου	midwinter ? ἐν τοιούτῳ καιρῷ		proof of Θ's need of his correspondent	II, 469.2 II, 471.10 II, 477.7

Letter	Bearer	Date	Place	Θ's comments	Evidence
G92 to and ep. from Gregory Taronites	Theodosios	1103	Ochrid to CP	or simply bearer of news?	II, 475.46
G94 to Nicholas Kallikles	μαθήση παρὰ τοῦ ἀδελφοῦ μου	?1097-1104 early	Pelagonia to ?CP		II, 479.11-12
??G104 to John Attaleiates	?metropolitan of Side	?		*systatike*, but may be in see	II, 519.6-8
G110 to the doctor of emperor, Niketas	τὸν ἀδελφόν	Sept 1105-March 1106	Ochrid or Ekklesiai to Thessalonike or Strumica	Θ fears the Vardar but D does not; asks hospitality	II, 531.19-20
??G111 to Nicholas Kallikles	οἱ ἐν τῷ χωρίῳ ἡμέτεροι they probably follow	summer 1106? 1107?	Ekklesiai to Thessalonike	asks NK to rally round when they appear	II, 535.18-20
G112 to Nicholas Kallikles and G114 to Michael Pantechnes ?G117 to ?	Smyrnaios, relative of Theodore	summer 1106? 1107?	?Ekklesiai to ?	blames the other's fame for the frequency of such letters	II, 537.16-19 II, 541.8-10 II, 547.3-5
G116 to (Gregory Kamateros or) Michael Pantechnes	ὁ ἀδελφός μοῦ	before 1107		bearer is sufficient	II, 545.2
G117 to ?	ὁ γραμματοκομιστής, see under G112	?		bearer solicited letters, suddenly	II, 547.2-3
??G118 to Constantine Doukas	τῶν αὐτόθι ἡμετέρου	just after G88 and G127	Ekklesiai to Thessalonike		II, 549.18
?G123 to Constantine Komnenos	Demetrios (or followed?)	before 1107	?Ochrid to Veroia		II, 563
Lost 19 to Gregory Kamateros	Demetrios	before 1107	Ochrid to somewhere in Bulgaria	brother and letter made GK happy	II, 571.2-3

TABLE IX

GIFTS IN THE LETTERS OF THEOPHYLACT

Letter	Sender	Recipient	Place	Gift	Comment	Evidence
?G5	Theophylact	Maria of Alania	from ?Ochrid to Princes' Islands	?incense? scented wood?	wordplay	II, 141.64;141.74;141.7
G12	Theophylact	John Komnenos	from Ochrid to Dyrrachium	100 smoked fish	with *presbeutike*; explicit	II, 169.32-33: δέξασθαι ἰχθύας ταρίχους ἑκατόν
G13	Theophylact	Nikephoros Melissenos	from Ochrid to somewhere in Bulgaria	200 salted fish	explicit; 5 senses x 4 virtues x 10 (queen of numbers); Theotokos	II, 171.18-19: ἰχθύδια τεταριχευμένα διακόσια
G14	bishop of Kitros	Theophylact	from Kitros to Ochrid	2 flasks of rosewater and 4 sticks of incense or cinnamon		II, 175.6: Τὸ...ἐκ τοῦ ῥόδου σταγόνων μύρον ἐν δύσιν ἀγγείοις ὑελίνοις; II, 175.14; Τὰ δὲ εὐώδη ξύλα
??G15	Diabologyres	the church (Theophylact)	from ?Diabolis to Ochrid	a horse	literal? a gift?	II, 179.22-23: καίτοι ὃν μόνον εἶχες ὑπολειφθέντα σοι ἵππον τῇ ἐκκλησίᾳ ἀπέστειλας
??G25	Theophylact	Mermentopoulos	from Ochrid to Constantinople	?honey	wordplay only	II, 213.13-18
??G32	Theophylact	Nicholas Anemas	within Bulgaria	?oil	wordplay only	II, 237.7-10
G34	Theophylact	Nicholas Anemas	within Bulgaria	a work of Chrysostom		II, 243.21: ἐπέμψαμεν
Grumel no. 996	Patriarch	Theophylact	from Constantinople to Ochrid	24 phials of incense and 4 sticks of cinnamon or scented wood?	ἄλειπτα: Gautier: hiking boots; surely not?	G54, II, 313.24-25: ἄλειπτοῖς ἰσαρίθμοις οὖσι τῶν πρεσβυτέρων τῆς Ἰοάννου ἀποκαλύψεως; II, 315.35: εὐώδεσι τέτρασι ξύλοις

Letter	Sender	Recipient	Place	Gift	Comment	Evidence
G73	Theophylact	Caesar (Nikephoros Melissenos)	from Ochrid to Constantinople	200/500 fish, some baked into rolls and others smoked	explicit: in consolation for the death of the *sebastokator*	II, 391.48-49: πλὴν ἀλλ' ἐστάλησαν ἰχθύες, οἱ μὲν ἄρτι ταριχευτοί, οἱ δ' ἀρτίδιοι ἑνοπτημένοι
G105	Theophylact	John Bryennios	from Ochrid to Dyrrachion	100 fish	explicit: number symbolism; association with the Theotokos	II, 521.2: εἰ καὶ μικρὰν καὶ ὀλίγην τὴν τῶν ἰχθύων ἀποστολήν
??G108	Theophylact	Makrembolites	from Ochrid to Prespa	?flowers	wordplay only	II, 527.15-17
Lost 21	Theophylact	Nicholas Kallikles	from Ekklesiai to Thessalonike	poem 3	explicit: thanks for the books requested in G112	I, 351: σοὶ μέν, Γαληνέ, τόνδε τῶν πόνων χάρις
G119	Theophylact	Constantine Doukas	from Ochrid to Thessalonike	a little gift of fishes	explicit; disputed right to the fishing; in praise of the Theotokos	II, 551.2: εἰ καὶ μικρὰν τινα ἰχθύων ἀποστολήν
G129	Theophylact	Michael Pantechnes	from Ochrid to ?	poem 2	has asked him to come and stay; he promises but does not come	I, 349-351: τοῖς νηπίοις φόβητρα τὰ φόβητρά σου; cf. II, 583.5-6: τὰ δὲ φόβητρα, ἃ ἡμῖν ἐπανατείνεσθε, μορμολύκια παίδων εἰσίν
Lost 20	Theophylact	Nikephoros Bryennios	from Ochrid to Dyrrachion	poem 1	has asked Θ for a letter	I, 347, tit: αἰτησάμενον γράφειν αὐτῷ

TABLE X

JOURNEYS IN THE LETTERS OF THEOPHYLACT

other than those of letter-bearers

P: past; F: future; XP: not In the past; XF: not in the future; ?F: possibly in the future; CP: Constantinople

Time	Letter	Traveller	Route	Date	Evidence
P	G4	Theophylact	Ochrid to CP to Nicomedia to Princes' Islands to Bithynia to CP to Ochrid	summer 1095	II, 137.4-5: τῇ βασιλίδι τῶν πόλεων Ἀχριδόθεν II, 137.19-20: ὡς ἀπὸ Νικομεδείας ἐπανερχόμενος II, 139.26-27: πρὸς τὴν Ἀπολλωνιάδα II, 139.27-28: μετὰ τὸ πρὸς τὴν μεγαλόπολιν II, 141.56: ἐν τῇ πόλει ταύτῃ
P	G5, 6, 7	Theophylact	CP to Ochrid	1089-90	genre
P	G8	John Doukas	Bulgaria to near Hellas	1092-93	II, 155.31: τοὺς ἐν τῇ Εὐρίπῳ συγγενεῖς ἡμῶν
P	G10	John Komnenos	CP to Dyrrachion	spring 1092	II, 163.2-3: ἐπαπέστειλε τὴν σὴν ἀντίληψιν
P	G11	hieromonk	from monastery to wandering	early 1090s	II, 163-164
P	G13	caesar Melissenos	CP to Bulgaria, recruiting	before April 1091	II, 171.2-3: τῇ βαρβάρῳ καὶ καθ' ἡμᾶς οἰκουμένῃ Θεὸς ἐπιπεμφθεὶς ἐλευθέριος
F	G15	?John Doukas	Dyrrachion to Ochrid	Easter 1090	II, 179.16-18: μετὰ τὸ Πάσχα ὁ αὐθέντης ἡμῶν ὁ σεβαστὸς πρὸς τὰ πλησιάζοντα ἡμῖν μέρη ἢ πρὸς ἡμᾶς αὐτοὺς ἐλεύσεται· οὕτος δὲ αὐτοὺς ἡμεῖς συνειθίσωμεν

Time	Letter	Traveller	Route	Date	Evidence
P	G17	John Doukas	Dyrrachion to south	spring 1092	II, 187.3-4: ἔστρεψας γάρ σου τὸ πρόσωπον 187.17-18: κἂν γάρ ἐκ τῶν βορείων ὁ ἥλιος νοτιώτερος γένηται
F	G21	1. *Strategos* 2. Eumallos, *anagrapheus* 3. Michael, son of Polyeuktos, *strategos*	Bulgarian theme to CP ?CP to Bulgarian theme ?CP to Bulgarian theme	?	II, 199.3-4: τὸν μὲν πρώην στρατηγοῦντα παρασταλῆναι II, 199.4-5: καὶ ἀναγραφέα τῆς τούτου πράξεως ἀποσταλῆναι τὸν κύριν Εὐμάθιον II, 199.5-6: καταστῆναι δὲ νῦν στρατηγὸν τὸν εὐγενῆ καὶ ψυχῇ καὶ πατρόθι δόξῃ κῦριν Μιχαήλ, τὸν τοῦ κυροῦ Πολυεύκτου υἱόν
P	G22	Theophylact	Diabolis	early 1090s	II, 203.6: τὴν ἐπισκοπὴν Διαβόλεως οἰκτειρήσαις II, 203.22: ἐξῆλθον οὖν ἐπισκεψόμενος
P	G30	Theophylact	Ochrid to army camp and back	before 1094/5	II, 229.2.4: Ἐκ τῆς ἐπιπόνου καὶ πολυημέρου μοι πλάνης ἐπαναστρέψαντι...καὶ τὸ στρατόπεδον ἔριψα
F	G31	Theophylact	1. O to Prespa 2. to where Gregory Kamateros is	? spring 1094	II, 235.34-35: παρέσομαι γάρ σοι, Θεοῦ με πορεύοντος, μετὰ τὴν ἐν τῷ ἐν ἁγίοις πατρὶ Ἀχιλλεῖ τελουμένην ἐνταῦθα σύνοδον
P	G32	Nicholas Anemas	CP to Bulgaria	?	II, 237.16: Ἀλλ' εὖγε ὅτι τοῖς καθ' ἡμᾶς ἐπεφάνης μέρεσιν ἀλεξίκακος
F	G35	Chrysoberges, metropolitan of Naupaktos	O to Kanina to Naupaktos	?	II, 245.20-21: Ἐπὶ δὲ τὰ τῶν Κανίνων μέρη ὅταν δῴη ὁ Θεὸς καιρὸν ἀπελθεῖν ἡμᾶς, ἴσως ἐνωθησόμεθα τῇ ἱερότητί σου
F	G41	Nicholas Anemas	O to ?CP	?	II, 269.16: τῇ γλυκείᾳ πατρίδι
P	G52	First Crusade	through Ochrid	1097	II, 303.4: Φραγγικὴ διάβασις ἢ ἐπίβασις

Time	Letter	Traveller	Route	Date	Evidence
P	G58	geron	Triaditsa to Prespa	before 1094/5	II, 327.3: ἐνέτυχε μὲν ἡμῖν ὁ παρὼν γέρων.ἐπὶ τὴν ἐκκλησίαν εἰσιοῦσιν... 327.20-21: παντὸς μὲν ὁρίου Τριαδίτζης αὐτὸν ἐξελαύνουσαν
P	G59	bishop of Triaditsa	Triaditsa to CP	before 1094/5	II, 339.36: ὡς μετὰ τῶν Ἀρμενίων εἰς τὴν πόλιν
P	G66	Gregory, psaltes	? to Ochrid	1089-95	II, 365-367: not explicit
F	G67	a good governor	changeover	?late in collection?	II, 369.13-15: τὸ γὰρ ἐν τῇ προσούσῃ νῦν σοι δυνάμει ἄρχοντα δοῦναι τῷ καθ' ἡμᾶς τούτῳ θέματι
P	G68	Gregory Pakourianos	CP to Bulgaria	?	II, 373-374: not explicit
P	G69	John Opheomachos	CP to Bulgaria	?	II, 377.2-3: καὶ ὁ καλὸς Ἰοάννης παρηνέχθη Λασιτρυγόσι προσπαλαίσων καὶ Κύκλωψιν
F	G71	John Opheomachos	Bulgaria to CP	?	II, 383-384: not explicit
F	G77	Theophylact	Ochrid to emperor's camp	before 1094/95	II, 411.68: Διὰ ταῦτά μοι ἀναγκαῖον τὴν ἐπὶ τὸν βασιλέα στέλλεσθαι... 413.83: τὴν πρὸς τὸ στρατόπεδον ὁδόν
P	G78	1. Gregory Taronites 2. Theophylact	CP to Pontos Ochrid to Prespa	May 1103	II, 415.10-11: διὰ τὴν ἀπολαύουσάν σου νῦν γῆν τῶν Κόλχων II, 415.17-18: ἀπιόντι γὰρ πρὸς τὸν μέγαν Ἀχίλλειον ὡς ἂν τῇ πανηγύρει συνεορτάσαιμι
P	G79	Gregory Pakourianos	Bulgaria to CP	?	II, 421.33: Εἶτα πρὸς τὸν ὑμέτερον ἀέρα διέβη
?F	G85	anagrapheus	to village of church in Ochrid	1097-1104 early	II, 447.30-31: ὁ ἐπαφεθεὶς ἡμῖν ἀναγραφεὺς ἀφελέσθαι τὸ ἐν Ἀχρίδι τῆς ἐκκλησίας χωρίον

Time	Letter	Traveller	Route	Date	Evidence
P	G86	1.John Bryennios	?CP to Dyrrachion	1097-1104?	II, 453.14: ἐπαναγωγὴν ὡς ἐλευθερωτοῦ τοῦ λυτρωτοῦ ἥκοντος... II, 453.6: μὴ ἔχων δέ...
X		2. Theophylact	O to Dyrrachion		
P	G87	bishop of Triaditsa	Triaditsa to CP	before 1094/95	II, 457.12-13: τίς γάρ οὐκ οἶδεν ὅπως εἰς τὴν μεγαλόπολιν ἀνελθοῦσα ἡ τιμιότης σου
F	G88 G127	1. Constantine Doukas	?CP to Vardar	either 1093-95 or 1105-08	II, 461.18-19: τῷ τοῦ πανσεβάστου αὐθέντου ἡμῶν υἱῷ ἡ περὶ τὸν Βαρδάριον ἀρχὴ νῦν ἀνετέθη
XF	G118	2. *anagrapheus*	? Thessalonike to Vardar village		II, 463.23-24: τὸ μὴ ἀναγραφέας ἐπιπέμψαι
P	G92	Gregory Taronites	Pontos to CP	1103	II, 473.3-4: ἐπανιόντα γάρ σε τῆς Κολχίδος ἀκούσας
P	G94	Theophylact	Ochrid to Pelagonia	1097-1104	II, 479.6: εἶτα πρὸς Πελαγονίαν φεύγοντα
P	G96	Lazaros	round Bulgaria	1097-1104	II, 485.36-37: καὶ τὰς ἄλλας τῆς Βουλγαρίας χώρας περινοστεῖ
P	G107	*despoina*	Thessalonike to Ochrid or Ekklesiai?	1106-07?	II, 525, tit.: ἐπισκεψαμένη αὐτὸν ἀρρωστήσαντα
F	G108	Theophylact	Ochrid to Prespa	?	II, 527.6: προσδέχου τοίνυν ἡμᾶς σὺν αὐτῷ γε φάνται ...κατὰ τὴν Πρέσπαν
P	G110	1.Niketas to ?Thessalonike	?CP to Thessalonike	1105-06	II, 531.2-4: πρὸς τὰς ὑμετέρας διαβῆναι σκηνάς, ὃς ὁ νέος Ἰσραὴλ πήγνυσθε ἐν τῇ δι' ἡμᾶς ἐρήμῳ περιφερόμενοι· ἀνακόπτει δέ μοι τὴν διάβασιν δύο ῥεύματα
FX		2. Theophylact	? Ochrid to Thessalonike		
P	G111	1. imperial agents 2. Theophylact 3. Nicholas Kallikles	to Ekklesiai and Thessalonike CP to Thessalonike	1106-07	II, 535.12:Τοῦτο πλὴροῦν ἐπιχειροῦσι... II, 535. 15-16: τὸ χωρίον αἱ Ἐκκλησίαι, εἰ μὴ ἀνεπηρέαστον ἐαθείη II, 535.13: ταύτην σύ μοι τὴν πλήρωσιν προανάστειλον...ὡς ἐπηρεαζόμενοι προσελεύσονται

Time	Letter	Traveller	Route	Date	Evidence
P X	G113	Theophylact	Ochrid to Ekklesiai to CP	1106-07	II, 539.9: τοῦ γὰρ ἐν Ἀχρίδι ἀέρος τὸν ἐνταῦθα ἀλλαξάμενος
X P	G118	1. Theophylact 2. Constantine Doukas	Ekklesiai to Thessalonike CP to Thessalonike	either 1093-95 or 1105-08	II, 549.6: οὐδὲ τὸ ὑπερβῆναι γοῦν τὸν ὁδὸν τοῦμοῦ δωματίου II.549.12-13: εἴ σε τοῦ Βαρδαρίου ἁρμοστὴν ἐπιστάντα πράγμασιν
P P F 	G120	1. Bohemond 2. protostrator Michael 3. Theophylact	to Ochrid CP to Bulgaria CP to Thessalonike Thessalonike to Ochrid	1108	II, 555.29-31: τὰ δὲ κατὰ τὴν Ἀχρίδα πάντα φόβου μεστὰ καὶ τὸ τοῦ Μόκρου μέρος—ὁ δὲ Μόκρος τῆς Ἀχρίδος τμῆμα—παρὰ τοῦ δούλου καὶ ἀποστάτου λελήισται II, 555.36-38: ὁ γάρ τοι πανσέβαστος σεβαστὸς καὶ πρωτοστράτωρ κῦρ Μιχαὴλ παρὰ τοῦ βασιλέως ἐστάλη ἐφ' ᾧ συλλέξαι τε ἄνδρας II, 553.14: ἐμοὶ γάρ...ἐπιβάντι τοῦ πλοίου... 555.24-25: ἀποσέσωσμαί σοι κατὰ τὴν Θεσσαλονίκην II, 557.45-48: Ἐγὼ δὲ ἅμα τῷ τὴν Θεσσαλονίκην καταλαβεῖν...πρὸς τὴν Ἀχρίδα...ἤδη ἄπειμι
F	G122	bishop of Debra	? to Debra	1107	II, 561.13: σε τάχιον ἐπανελθεῖν τὰ τῆς αὐτοῦ ποίμνης ἣν ἐνεχειρίσθης ἐπισκεψόμενον πρόβατα
F	G123	Demetrios	O to Veroia	before 1107	II, 563.3: ὁρῶν μου τὸν ἀδελφῶν διακεχυμένον
P F F	G127	1. Gregory Kamateros 2. Constantine Doukas 3. Theodore Chryselios	CP to Bulgaria on campaign to Vardar to imperial army	either 1093-95 or 1105-08	II, 579.117: διὰ τὴν δυσχερανομένην σοι ἀποδημίαν II, 571.16-17: ἐπιθόμην τοῖς Βαρδαριώταις ἐπαφεθῆναι τόν...υἱὸν τοῦ πρωτοστράτορος II, 573.43: ἀντίδοσις παράκλησιν
F	G129	Michael Pantechnes	? to Ochrid	?	II, 583.2-3: καὶ ἐπισκεψόμενοι

BIBLIOGRAPHY

Primary Sources

I. Works of Theophylact

i. *Editions, translations and commentaries*

Collected works

Θεοφυλάκτου ᾽Αρχιεπισκόπου Βουλγαρίας ἅπαντα, ed. B. Finetti and A. Bongiovanni, *Theophylacti Bulgariae archiepiscopi opera omnia quae hactenus edita sunt sive quae nondum lucem viderunt cum praevia dissertatione Fr. J.Fran. Bernardi Mariae de Rubeis de ipsius Theophyacti gestis et scriptis ac doctrina*, 4 vols (Venice, 1754-63); reprinted in

Theophylacti Bulgariae archiepiscopi opera quae reperiri potuerunt omnia, PG 123-126 (Paris, 1862-64).

Letters

ed. J. Meursius, *Theophylacti archiepiscopi Bulgariae epistolas Joannes Meursius nunc primum e tenebris erutas edidit* (Leiden, 1617).

ed. J. Lamius, *J. Meursii opera omnia, quorum quaedam in hac editione primum parent, J. Lamius recensebat et scholiis illustrabat*, 12 vols (Florence, 1741-63), VIII, 791-932; 937-990.

ed. B. Finetti, *Theophylacti opera omnia*, Finetti et al, III (Venice, 1758), 559-585; 631-740, all reprinted in PG 126, 307-558.

ed. A. Leroy-Molinghen, 'Prolégomènes à une édition critique des lettres de Théophylacte de Bulgarie,' *Byz* 8 (1938), 255-261.

ed. P. Gautier, *Nicéphore Bryennios, Histoire* (CFHB, 9, Brussels, 1975), 317-333.

ed. R. Romano, *Nicola Callicle, Carmi, Testo critico, introduzione, traduzione, commentario e lessico* (ByzetNeohellNeap, 8, Naples, 1980), 57-61.

ed. P. Gautier, *Théophylacte d'Achrida*, II, *Lettres* (CFHB 16/2, Thessalonike, 1986).

tr. V. Marinerius, *Theophylacti archiepiscopi Bulgariae epistolae a Vincentio Marinerio, Valentino, de graecis latinae nunc primum factae* (M. de la Bigne, Magna Bibliotheca Veterum Patrum, 15, Cologne, 1622).

tr. Mitropolit Simeon, *Pismata na Teofilakt Okhridski archiepiskop Bulgarski* (Bulgarskata Akademiia na Naukitie, 15, Sofia, 1931).

comm. S. Maslev, *Fontes graeci historiae Bulgaricae, IX, Theophylacti Achridensis, archiepiscopi Bulgariae. Scripta ad historiam Bulgariae pertinentia*, I (Izvori za bulgarskata istoriia, 19, Sofia, 1974).

Other Works
Poems
ed. E. Miller, *Manuelis Philae, Opera*, I (Paris, 1855), 447.

ed. S. Mercati, 'Poesie di Teofilatto di Bulgaria,' *Studi Bizantini* 1 (1925), 175-194, repr. *Collectanea bizantina* (Bari, 1970), 353-372.

ed. B. Georgiades, 'Mnemeia ekkesiastika anekdota', *EA* 4 (1883-84), 142; 5 (1884-85), 13-14.

ed. P. Gautier, 'L'épiscopat de Théophylacte Héphaistos, archevêque de Bulgarie. Notes chronologiques et biographiques,' *REB* 21 (1963), 170-178.

ed. J. Koder and J. Paramelle, *Syméon le nouveau théologien, Hymnes,* I (SC, 156, Paris, 1969), 64-67.

ed. P. Gautier, *Nicéphore Bryennios, Histoire* (CFHB, 9, Brussels, 1975), 333-337.

ed. P. Gautier, *Théophylacte d'Achrida, I, Discours, traités, poésies* (CFHB, 16/1, Thessalonike, 1980), 345-377.

Biblical Commentaries

On the Epistles (attributed to Athanasios): *Sixto IIII Pontifici Maximo in prima Pauli ad Romanos epistola Athanasii prologus,* tr. Christoforus de Persona (Rome, 1477).

ed. A. Lindsell, *Theophylacti Archiepiscopi Bulgariae in D. Pauli epistolas commentarii* (London, 1636).

PG, 124, 319-1358; PG 125, 9-464.

On the Minor Prophets: ed. J. Lonicerus, *Theophylacti Bulgariae Archiepiscopi in Habacuc, Jonam, Nahum et Osee prophetas enarrationes, iam primum in lucem aeditae interprete Ioanne Lonicero* (Basle, 1534).

PG, 126, 559-1190.

ed. B. Georgiades, 'Mnemeia ekklesiastika anekdota,' *EA* 4 (1883-84), 109-115; 135-138; 141-143; 5 (1884-85), 11-13.

On the Four Gospels: ed. J. Oecolampadius, *Theophylacti in quatuor Euangelia enarrationes, denuo recognitae, Ioanne Oecolampadio interprete* (Basle, 1525).

On Matthew: ed. W(G).G. Humphry, Θεοφυλάκτου ἑρμηνεῖα εἰς τὸ κατὰ Ματθαῖον Εὐαγγέλιον, *Theophylact in evang. S.Matthaei Commentarius, graece et latine* (Cambridge, 1854).

PG 123, 139-488.

On Mark: PG 123, 487-682.

On Luke: PG 123, 683-1126.

On John: PG 123, 1127-1348; PG 124, 9-318.

Hagiography

Vita Clementis (Long Life of Clement of Ochrid): PG 126, 1194-1240.

ed. N.L. Tunickij, *Monumenta ad SS Cyrilli et Methodii successorum vitas resque gestas pertinentia* (Sergiev-Posad, 1918, repr. London, 1972), 66-140.

ed. A. Milev, *Grutskite zhitiia na Kliment Okhridski* (Sofia, 1966), 76-146;

ed. P. Gautier, *Deux oeuvres hagiographiques du pseudo-Théophylacte* (Thèse de doctorat du 3e cycle, Université de Paris, Faculté de lettres et sciences humaines, Paris, 1968), 47-107.

Historia martyrii XV martyrum (XV Martyrs of Tiberioupolis): PG 126, 152-211.

Speeches
To Constantine Doukas (Paideia basilike): ed. P. Possino, *S. patris nostri Theophylacti archiepiscopi Bulgariae Institutio regia. Ad porphyrogenitum Constantinum* (Paris, 1651). PG 126, 249-286.
ed. Gautier, *Théophylacte*, I, 177-211.
tr. E. Barker, *Social and Political Thought in Byzantium from Justinian I to the Last Palaeologus* (Oxford, 1957), 145-149.

To Alexios I Komnenos: PG 126, 287-306.
ed. P. Gautier, 'Le discours de Théophylacte de Bulgarie à l'autocrator Alexis Ier Comnène (6 janvier 1088)' *REB* 20 (1961), 109-120.
ed. P. Gautier, *Théophylacte*, I, 213-243.

Treatises
On the Errors of the Latins: PG 126, 221-250.
ed. Gautier, *Théophylacte*, I, 245-285.

In Defence of Eunuchs: ed. M.D. Spadaro, 'Un inedito di Teofilatto di Achrida sull' eunuchia,' *RSBS*, 1 (1981), 4-38.
ed. P. Gautier, *Théophylacte*, I, 287-331.

On the Liturgy: ed. Gautier, *Théophylacte*, I, 333-343.

Homilies
On the Veneration of the Holy Cross: PG 126, 105-130.

On the Presentation of the Virgin in the Temple: PG 126, 129-144.

II. Other primary sources

Alexander of Nicaea, epp., ed. J. Darrouzès, *Épistoliers byzantins du Xe siècle* (AOC, 6, Paris, 1960), 67-98.
Acta Albaniae: L. Thalloczy, K. Jireček and M. Šufflay, *Acta et diplomata res Albaniae mediae aetatis illustrantia*, 2 vols (Vienna, 1913-1918).
Anna Komnene, *Alexiad*, ed. B. Leib, *Anne Comnène, Alexiade. Règne de l'empereur Alexis I Comnène (1081-1118)*, 3 vols (Collection byzantine, Paris, 1937-1945).
Anon. Londiniensis, epp., ed. R. Browning and B. Laourdas, 'To keimenon ton epistolon kodikos BM 36749,' *EEBS* 27 (1957), 151-212.
Anselm, *AOO*, ed. F.S. Schmitt, *Anselmi opera omnia*, 6 vols (Edinburgh, 1946-61)
Anselm, epp., ed. F.S. Schmitt, *AOO*, III (Edinburgh, 1946), 93-294; IV (Edinburgh, 1951)
Arethas, epp., ed. L.G. Westerink, *Arethae scripta minora*, 2 vols (Leipzig, 1968 and 1972).
Basil, epp., ed. R.J. Deferrari, *Saint Basil, the Letters*, 4 vols (London and Cambridge, Mass., 1961).

Cassian, *Collationes*, ed. M. Petschenig, *Johannis Cassiani Conlationes XXIIII* (CSEL, 13, Vienna, 1886), repr. *Jean Cassien, Conférences*, ed. E. Pichery (SC, 54, Paris, 1958).

Demetrios, *Peri Hermeneias*, ed. R. Roberts, *Demetrius on Style* (Cambridge, 1902).

Demetrios, *Typoi epistolikoi*, ed. V. Weichert, *Demetrii et Libanii qui feruntur typoi epistolikoi et epistolimaioi charakteres* (Leipzig, 1910), 1-12.

F. Dölger, *Regesten der Kaiserurkunden des oströmischen Reiches von 565-1453*, 5 vols (Corpus der griechischen Urkunden des Mittelalters und der neueren Zeit, A, Regesten, 1, Munich and Berlin, 1924-1965).

EleousaTypikon: To ison tes diataxeos tou hosiotatou patros emon Manouel monachou kai ktetoros tes mones tes hyperagias Theotokou tes Eleouses tes en to themati men Stroumitzes en to chorio de Anopalaiokastro legomeno idrumenes, ed. L. Petit, 'Le monastère de Notre-Dame de Pitié en Macédoine,' *IRAIK* 5 (1900), 1-153.

George Tornikes, epp., ed. J. Darrouzès, *Georges et Dèmètrios Tornikès, Lettres et discours* (Le monde byzantin, Paris, 1970).

Gregory of Nazianzos, epp., ed. P. Gallay, *Saint Grégoire de Nazianze, Lettres*, 2 vols (Paris, 1967)

Gregory of Nyssa, epp., ed. Maraval: P. Maraval, *Grégoire de Nysse, Lettres* (SC, 363, Paris, 1990)

Hierotheos, epp., see J. Darrouzes, 'Un receuil épistolaire du XIIe siècle: Académie Roumaine cod.gr. 508,' *REB* 30 (1972), 199-229.

John Chrysostom, epp., PG 52, 529-760; John Chrysostom, *Pros ten makarian Olympiada kai pros pantas tous pistous*, ed. A.M. Malingrey, *Jean Chrysostome, Lettre d'exil* (SC, 103, Paris, 1964); epp. to Olympias, ed. Malingrey, *Lettres à Olympias* (SC, 13, Paris, 1947).

John Mauropous, epp., ed. A. Karpozilos, *The Letters of John Mauropous, Metropolitan of Euchaita* (CFHB, 34, Thessalonike, 1990).

John the Oxite, *Logos eis ton basilea kyr Alexion ton Komnenon*, ed. P. Gautier, 'Diatribes de Jean l'Oxite contre Alexios Ier Comnène,' *REB* 28 (1970), 15-55.

John Skylitzes, *Synopsis historion*, ed. H. Thurn, *Synopsis historiarum, editio princeps* (CFHB, 5, Berlin and New York, 1973).

John Tzetzes, epp., ed. P.A.M. Leone, *Johannis Tzetzae epistolae* (Leipzig, 1972).

John Zonaras, *Epitome Historion*, ed. T. Büttner-Wobst (CSHB, Bonn, 1897)

Julian, epp., ed. W.C. Wright, *The Works of the Emperor Julian*, III (London and Cambridge, Mass., 1923).

Kekaumenos, *Strategikon pros basilea*, ed. B. Wassilewsky and V. Jernstedt, *Cecaumeni strategicon et incerti scriptoris de officiis regiis libellus* (St Petersburg, 1896, repr. Amsterdam, 1965).

KosmosoteiraTypikon (*Typikon emou tou [sebastokratoros] Isaakiou kai huiou tou megalou basileos kyrou Alexiou tou Komnenou epi to kainisthenti par hemon neosystato monasterio kata ten pentekaidekaten indiktiona tou hexakischiliostou exakosiostou exekostou etous, en o kai kathidrutai to tes kosmosoteiras mou kai theometoros kai en pollois euergetidos dia mouseiou eikonisma*), ed. L. Petit, 'Typikon du monastère de la Kosmosoteira près du Aenos (1152),' *IRAIK* 13 (1908) 17-77.

Koutloumousiou, ed. P. Lemerle, *Actes de Kutlumus* (Archives de l'Athos, 2, Paris, 1946).

Lavra, ed. P. Lemerle, A. Guillou, and N. Svoronos, *Actes de Lavra* (Archives de l'Athos, 5, Paris, 1970).

Leo Choirosphaktes, epp., ed. G. Kolias, *Leon Choirosphaktes, magistre, proconsul et patrice, biographie-correspondance. Texte et Traduction* (Texte und Forschungen zur byzantinisch-neugriechischen Philologie, 31, Athens, 1939).

Leo of Synada, epp., ed. M.P. Vinson, *The Correspondence of Leo Metropolitan of Synada and Syncellus, Greek Text, Translation and Commentary* (DOT, 8, CFHB, 23, Washington, DC, 1985).

Libanios-Proklos, *Epistolimaioi charakteres*, ed. V. Weichert, *Demetrii et Libanii qui feruntur typoi epistolikoi et epistolimaioi charakteres* (Leipzig, 1910), 13-34.

Menander, *Peri epideiktikon*, ed. D.A. Russell and N.G. Wilson, *Menander Rhetor* (Oxford, 1981), 76-225.

Michael Italikos, epp., ed. P. Gautier, *Michel Italikos, lettres et discours* (AOC, 14, Paris, 1972).

Michael Psellos, epp., ed. E. Kurtz and F. Drexl, *Scripta minora*, II (Milan, 1941); ed. Sathas: K.N. Sathas, *Mesaionike bibliotheke*, V (Paris, 1876).

Michael Psellos, *Chronographia*, ed. E. Renauld, *Michel Psellos, Chronographie*, 2 vols (Paris, 1967).

Nicholas Kallikles, ed. R. Romano, *Nicola Callicle, Carmi, Testo critico, introduzione e traduzione, commentario e lessico* (ByzetNeohellNeap, 8, 1980).

Nicholas of Kerkyra, *Paraitesis*, ed. S. P. Lampros, *Kerkyraika anekdota ek cheirographon Hagiou Orous, Kantabrigias, Monachou kai Kerkyras, nun to proton demosieuomena* (Athens, 1882), 30-41.

Nicholas Mouzalon, *Stichoi Nikolaou tou Mouzalonos tou gegonotos archiepiskopou Kyprou en te paraitesei autou genomenoi*, ed. S.I. Doanidou, 'He paraitesis Nikolaou tou Mouzalonos apo tes archiepiskopes Kyprou. Anekdoton apologetikon poiema,' *Hellenika* 7 (1934), 109-150.

Nicholas Mystikos, epp., ed. R.J.H. Jenkins and L.G. Westerink, *Nicholas I Patriarch of Constantinople, Letters* (DOT, 2, CFHB, 6, Washington, DC, 1973).

Nikephoros Bryennios, *Hyle Historias*, ed. P. Gautier, *Nicéphore Bryennios, histoire: introduction, texte, traduction et notes* (CFHB, 9, Brussels, 1975).

Nikephoros Ouranos, epp., ed. J. Darrouzès, *Epistoliers byzantins du Xe siècle* (AOC, 6, Paris, 1960), 217-248.

Niketas of Ankyra, *On Ordinations* (*Hos ou dei ton Konstantinoupoleos cheirotonein eis tas heterois hypokeimenas episkopas, k'an metropoleis timethosin*), ed. J. Darrouzès, *Documents inédits d'ecclésiologie byzantine* (AOC, 10, Paris, 1966), 176-207.

Niketas of Ankyra, *On Synods* (*Pros tous legontas hoti ou dei kata tas makarion pateron diataxeis en Konstantinoupolei ginesthai kat'etos synodous, all' en tas exo monon eparchiais*) ed. Darrouzès, *Documents inédits*, 208-237.

Niketas Magistros, epp., ed. L.G. Westerink, *Nicétas Magistros, Lettres d'un exilé (928-946)* (Le monde byzantin, Paris, 1973).

Pakourianos Typikon (*To typikon to ektethen para tou megalou domestikou tes duseos kyrou Gregoriou tou Pakourianou pros ten par'autou ktistheisan monen tes hyperagias Theotokou tes Petritziotisses*), ed. P. Gautier, 'Le typikon du sébaste Grégoire Pakourianos,' *REB* 42 (1984), 5-145.

Pantokrator Typikon (*Typikon tes basilikes mones tou Pantokratoros*), ed. P. Gautier, 'Le typikon du Christ Sauveur Pantokrator,' *REB* 32 (1974), 83-111.

Philetos Synadenos, epp., ed. Darrouzès: *Épistoliers byzantins*, 48-49; 249-259.

Photios, *Bibliotheke*, ed. R. Henry, *Photius, Bibliothèque*, 6 vols (Paris, 1959-), tr. N. Wilson, *The Bibliotheca of Photius* (London, 1994).

Photios, epp., ed. J.M. Baletta, *Photiou epistolai* (London, 1864), Photios, epp., ed. B. Laourdas and L.G. Westerink, *Photii epistolae et Amphilochia*, I (Leipzig, 1983), II (Leipzig, 1984), III (Leipzig, 1985).

Skylitzes Continuatus, ed. E.T. Tsolakes, *He synecheia tes chronographias tou Ioannou Skylitze* (HetMakSp, 105, Thessalonike, 1968).

Symeon Magistros, epp., ed. Darrouzès, *Épistoliers byzantins*, 99-163.

Synesios, epp., ed. A. Garzya, *Synesii Cyrenensis epistolae* (Rome, 1979).

Theodore Daphnopates, epp., ed. J. Darrouzès and L. Westerink, *Theodoros Daphnopates, correspondance* (Le monde byzantin, Paris, 1978).

Theodore of Kyzikos, epp., ed. Darrouzès, *Epistoliers byzantins*, 317-341.

Theodore of Nicaea, epp., ed. Darrouzès, *Epistoliers byzantins*, 261-316.

Theodore of Stoudios, epp., ed. G. Fatouros, *Theodori Studitae epistolae*, 2 vols (CFHB, 31.1-2, Berlin and New York, 1992).

Timarion, ed. R. Romano, *Timarione, Testo critico, introduzione, traduzione, commentario e lessico* (ByzetNeohellNap, 2, Naples, 1974).

VAnselmi: Eadmer, *De vita et conversatione Anselmi Cantuarensis archepiscopi*, ed. R.W. Southern, *The Life of St Anselm, Archbishop of Canterbury by Eadmer, edited with introduction, notes and translations (from the Latin)* (Oxford, 1962).

VCyril: Nicholas Kataskepenos, *Bios kai politeia kai merike thaumaton diegesis tou hosiou patros hemon Kyrillou tou Phileotou*, ed. E. Sargologos, *La vie de saint Cyrille le Philéote, moine byzantin (+1110)* (SubsHag, 39, Brussels, 1964).

VSym: Niketas Stethatos, *Bios kai politeia tou en hagiois patros hemon Symeon tou neou theologou, presbyterou, hegoumenou mones tou hagiou Mamantos tes Xenokerkiou*, ed. I. Hausherr, *Un grand mystique byzantin: vie de Syméon le nouveau théologien* (OC, 12, Rome, 1928).

Secondary Sources

I. Studies on Theophylact

N. Adontz, 'L'archevêque Théophylacte et le Taronite,' *Byz* 11 (1936), 577-588.

R. Anastasi, 'Note critiche: III, Teofilatto di Bulgaria e Simeone il Teologo,' *Siculorum Gymnasium* n.s. 34 (1981), 271-283.

—'Sul logos basilikos di Teofilatto per Alessio Comneno,' *Orpheus* 3 (1982), 358-362.

E. Barker, *Social and Political Thought in Byzantium from Justinian I to the Last Palaeologus* (Oxford, 1957), 145-149.

W. Blum, *Byzantinische Fürstenspiegel: Agapetos, Theophylakt von Ochrid, Thomas Magister* (Bibliothek der griechische Literatur, 14, Stuttgart, 1981), 79-98.

I.A. Božilov, 'Pismata na Teofilakt Ochridski kato istoricheski izvor', *Isvestiya na Durzhavnite Archivi* 14 (1967), 60-100.

D.I. Chrestides, 'Echidnai kai lakideis,' *Hellenika* 41 (1990), 118-120.

D. Ćuklev, 'Okhridski archiepiskop Teofilakt,' *Period. spis. na bulg. knij. druzhestvo* 69 (1908), 161-199.

B.-M. de Rubeis (de Rossi), *Dissertatio de Theophylacti Bulgariae archiepiscopi gestis, scriptis ac doctrina* (Venice, 1754), repr. PG 123, 9-130.

I. Djurić, 'Teofilakt Ohridski pod shatorom Arona,' *ZRVI* 27/28 (1989), 69-91.

J. Draeseke, 'Theophylaktos' Schrift gegen die Lateiner,' *BZ* 10 (1901), 512-523.

N. Dragova, 'Starobulgarskite izvori na zitieto za petnadesette Tiberiupolski muchenitsi ot Teofilakt Okhridski,' *Prouchvaniia po sluchai II kongres po Balkanistika* (Sofia, 1970), 105-131.

N. Dragova, 'Theophylact of Ochrida's Old Bulgarian Sources on Cyril and Methodius,' *Études balkaniques* n.s. 28 (1992), 107-110.

S. Ferrara, *L'unionismo di Teofilatto d'Achrida nell'opusculo 'De iis quorum Latini incusantur'* (Rome, 1951).

P. Gautier, 'Le discours de Théophylacte de Bulgarie a l'autokrator Alexis Ier Comnène (6 janvier 1088),' *REB* 20 (1961), 93-130.

—, 'L'épiscopat de Théophylacte Héphaistos, archevêque de Bulgarie. Notes chronologiques et biographiques,' *REB* 21 (1963), 165-168.

—, *Deux oeuvres hagiographiques du pseudo-Théophylacte* (Diss. Paris, 1968).

—, 'Un second traité contre les Latins attribué à Théophylacte de Bulgarie,' *Theologia* 48 (1977), 546-569.

—, *Théophylacte d'Achrida, I, Discours, traités, poésies* (CFHB, 16/1, Thessalonike, 1980).

—, *Théophylacte d'Achrida, II, Lettres, introduction, texte, traduction et notes* (CFHB, 16/2, Thessalonike, 1986).

A. Harvey, 'The Land and Taxation in the Reign of Alexios I Komnenos: the Evidence of Theophylakt of Ochrid,' *REB* 51 (1993), 139-154.

I.G. Iliev, 'The Manuscript Tradition and the Authorship of the Long Life of St Clement of Ohrid,' *BS* 53 (1982), 68-73.

R. Janin, 'Théophylacte,' *DTC*, 15 (1946), 536-538.

M. Jugie, 'L'auteur de la vie de Clément d'Achrida,' *EO* 23 (1924), 5-8.

R. Katičić, 'Die akzentuierte Prosarhythmus bei Theophyakt von Achrida,' *Živa antika*, 7 (1957), 66-84.

—, 'Hai pros Pakourianous epistolai tou Theophylaktou archiepiskopou Achridos,' *EEBS* 30 (1960-61), 386-397.

—, 'Biographika peri Theophylaktou archiepiskopou Achridos,' *EEBS* 30 (1960-61), 364-385.

—, 'Korespondencija Teofilakta Ohridskog kao izvor za historiju srednjovjekovne Makedonije,' *ZRVI* 8 (1964), 177-189.

J. Kohler, *Der medizinische Inhalt der Briefe des Theophylaktos von Bulgarien* (Diss. Leipzig, 1918).

B. Leib, *Rome, Kiev et Byzance à la fin du XIe siècle* (Paris, 1924).

—, 'La *basilike paideia* de Théophylacte, archévêque de Bulgarie, et sa contribution à l'histoire de la fin du XIe siècle,' *REB* 11 (1953), 197-204.

A. Leroy-Molinghen, 'Les lettres de Théophylacte de Bulgarie à Grégoire Taronite,' *Byz* 11 (1936) 589-592.

—, 'Prolégomènes à une édition critique des lettres de Théophylacte de Bulgarie,' *Byz* 13 (1938), 253-262.

—, 'Trois mots slaves dans les lettres de Théophylacte de Bulgarie,' *Annuaire de l'Institut de Philologie et d' Histoire Orientales et Slaves* 6 (1938), 111-117.

—, 'Les deux Jean Taronites de l'"Alexiade",' *Byz* 14 (1939), 147-153.

—, 'Du destinataire de la lettre Finetti I de Théophylacte de Bulgarie,' *Byz* 36 (1966), 431-437.

—, 'A propos d'une phrase de Théophylacte de Bulgarie,' *Byz* 52 (1982), 423-424.

—, 'Médecins, malades et remèdes dans les lettres de Théophylacte de Bulgarie,' *Byz* 55 (1985), 483-492.

G.G. Litavrin, 'Budapeshtskaia rukopis' pisem Feofilakta Bolgarskogo: codex Budapestinenis 2 fol.Graec.,' *Izvestiia na Instuta za Istoriia* 14-15 (1964), 511-524.

E. Marsenger, *Der Mattäuskommentar des Theophylaktos von Achrida* (Schweidnitz, 1924).

S. Maslev, 'Les lettres de Théophylacte de Bulgarie à Nicéphore Mélissénos,' *REB* 30 (1972), 179-186.

—, 'Zur Quellenfrage der Vita Clementis,' *BZ* 70 (1977), 310-315.

A.I. Milev, *Grutskite Zhitiia na Kliment Okhridski* (Sofia, 1955).

M.E. Mullett, *Theophylact through his Letters: the Two Worlds of an Exile Bishop* (Unpublished PhD, Birmingham, 1981).

—, 'The "Disgrace" of the Ex-basilissa Maria,' *BS*, 45 (1984), 202-210.

—, 'Patronage in Action: the Problems of an Eleventh-century Bishop,' *Byzantine Church and People*, ed. R. Morris (Birmingham, 1990), 125-147.

—, review of Gautier, *Théophylacte*, II, in *BS* 52 (1991), 157-162.

—, 'The Madness of Genre,' *Homo Byzantinus, Papers in Honor of Alexander Kazhdan*, ed. A. Cutler and S. Franklin = *DOP* 46 (1992), 233-243

—, 'Originality in the Byzantine Letter: the Case of Exile,' *Originality and Innovation in Byzantine Literature, Art and Music*, ed. A.R. Littlewood (Oxford, 1995), 39-58.

—, 'The Imperial Vocabulary of Alexios I Komnenos,' *Alexios I Komnenos, I, Papers*, ed. M.E. Mullett and D.C. Smythe (BBTT, 4.1, Belfast, 1996), 359-397.

—, '1098 and All That: Theophylact, the Bishop of Semnea and the Alexian Reconquest of Anatolia,' *Peritia* 10 (1997), 237-252

—, 'Byzantium and the Slavs: the Views of Theophylact of Ochrid,' *Studies in Memory of I. Dujcev*, II, ed. A. Djourova (Sofia, forthcoming).

—, 'The Monumental Bishop-list at Prespa,' *A Mosaic of Cypriot and Byzantine Studies presented to A.H.S. Megaw*, ed. J. Herrin, M.E. Mullett and C. Otten-Froux, forthcoming.

B. Nerantze-Barmaze, 'Ho Theophylactos Achridas kai ho dutikomakedonikos choros,' *Praktika tou 8. Panhelleniou istorikou synedriou* (Thessalonike, 1987).

B.A. Nikolaev, *Feodalni otnosheniia v pokorenata ot Bizantiia Bulgariia otrazeni v Pismata na Teofilakt Okhridski Archiepiskop Bulgarski* (Sofia, 1951).

D. Obolensky, *The Bogomils. A Study in Balkan Neo-Manichaeism* (Cambridge, 1948, repr. London, 1972).

—, 'The Byzantine Impact on Eastern Europe,' *Praktika tes Akademias Athenon* (1980), 148-168.

—, 'Theophylaktos of Ohrid and the Authorship of the Vita Clementis,' *Byzantium. A Tribute to Andreas N. Stratos*, II (Athens, 1986), 601-618.

—, *Six Byzantine Portraits* (Oxford, 1988).

B. Panov, 'Okhrid vo krajot na XI i pocetokot na XII v. vo svetlinata na pismata na Teofilakt Ohridski,' *Mélanges D. Koco* = Arheoloski Muzej na Makedonija, 6/7 (1967-1974), 181-195.

—, *Teofilakt Okhridski kako izvor za srednovekovnata istorija na Makedonskijot narod* (Skopje, 1971).

—, 'Bogomilskoe dvizhenie v Makedonii na osnovanii pisem Feofilakta Okhridskogo,' *XIV IntCong* (Bucharest, 1976), III, 721-727.

—, 'Gradskata samouprava vo Okhrid kon krajotna IX I početot na XII vek,' *Istorija spisna sojna drustv. na istor. na Makedonija* 17 (1981), 87-93.

—, 'Osvoboditel'noe dvizhenie v zapadnoi Makedonii v kontse 11 veka, otrazhennoe v pismakh Feofilakta Okhridskogo,' *JÖB* 32/2 (1982), 195-205.

J. Papaioannou, 'En cheirographon tou hypomnematos tou archiepiskopou Boulgarias Theophylaktou eis ta 4 euangelia,' *Theologia* 3 (1925), 243-255.

E.S. Papayanni, 'Oi Boulgaroi stis epistoles tou Theophylaktou Achridas,' *I' Panellenio Istoriko Synedrio. Praktika* (Thessalonike, 1989), 63-72.

—, 'Phorologikes plerofories apo epistoles tou megalou Basileiou (329/31-379) kai tou Theophylaktou Achridas (1050/1055-1125/26) *Praktika tou A. Diethnous Symposiou: He Kathemerine Zoe sto Byzantio (Athena 15-17 Sept 1980)* (Athens, 1989), 391-407.

G. Podskalsky, 'Théophylacte d'Achrida,' *DS*, 15 (1990), 542-546.

I.D. Polemes, 'Philologikes paratereseis stis epistoles tou Theophylaktou,' *Hellenika* 41 (1990), 376-382.

H.J. Pollitt, *Theophylact of Ochrida. His Commentary on St John's Gospel: Sources, Methods and Characteristics* (MLitt Diss., Birmingham, 1985).

K. Praechter, 'Antike Quellen des Theophylaktos von Bulgarien', *BZ* 1 (1892), 399-414.

G. Prinzing, 'Entstehung und Rezeption der Justiniana-Prima-Theorie im Mittelalter,' *BB* 5 (1978), 269-287.

G. Prinzing, '"Contra Judaeos": ein Phantom im Werkverzeichnis des Theophylaktos Hephaistos,' *BZ* 78 (1985), 350-354.

A. Quacquarelli, 'La lettera di Teofilatto d'Acrida: gli errori dei Latini,' *Rassegna di scienze filosofiche*, 2 (1949), 3-4, 11-40.

J. Reuss, *Matthaus-, Markus-, und Johanneskatenen* (Munster, 1941), 220-237.

R. Romano, 'La metrica di Teofilatto di Bulgaria,' *Atti della Accademia Pontaniana* 32 (1983), 175-186.

K. Roth, *Studie zu den Briefen des Theophylaktos Bulgarus* (Ludwigshafen am Rhein, 1900).

E.W. Saunders, 'Theophylact of Bulgaria as Writer and Biblical Interpreter,' *Biblical Research* 2 (1957), 31-44.

M. Solarino, 'Un intellettuale in provincia: Teofilatto di Achrida,' *Syndesmos: Studi in onore di Rosario Anastasi* (Catania, 1991), 63-82.

M.D. Spadaro, 'Un inedito di Teofilatto di Achrida ed un horismos di Alessio Comneno; problemi di chronologia, *Quaderni del Siculorum Gymnasium*, 8, *Studi di filologia bizantina* 2 (Catania, 1980), 159-181.

—, 'Archontes a confronto nella periferia dell'impero sotto la basileia di Alessio I Comneno,' *Syndesmos, Studi in onore di Rosario Anastasi* (Catania, 1991), 83-114.

K. Staab, *Die Pauluskatenen nach den handschriftlichen Quellen untersucht* (Rome, 1926), 213-245.

P. Stephanou, 'Teofilatto archivescovo di Bulgaria,' *Enc.Catt.* 11 (1953), 1951.

M. Tombacco, *Teofilatto di Bulgaria tra Oriente e Occidente* (Diss., Bari, 1979)

S. Vailhé, 'Bulgarie,' *DTC* 10 (1903), 1189-1194; 'Achrida,' *DHGE* 1 (1912), 321-332.

A. Vaillant, 'Constantin-Cyrille et le pseudo-Théophylacte,' *Slavia* 38 (1969), 517-520.

V.G. Vasilevskii, 'Vizantiia i Pecheniegi, 1084-1094,' *Trudy*, I (St Petersburg, 1908), 1-175, esp. appx III, Feofilakt Bolgarski i ego sochineniia, 134-49.

D. Xanalatos, *Beiträge zur Wirtschafts- und Sozialsgeschichte Makedoniens im Mittelalter, hauptsächlich auf Grund der Briefe Theophylakts von Achrida* (Munich, 1937).

D. Xanalatos, 'Theophylaktos ho Boulgaros kai he drasis autou en Achridi,' *Theologia* 16 (1938), 228-241.

II. Other studies

N. Adontz, 'Notes Arméno-Byzantines, ' *Byz* 9 (1934), 361-382

—, 'Les Taronites en Arménie et à Byzance,' *Byz* 9 (1934), 715-738.

—, 'Notes Arméno-Byzantines: Les Dalassènes,' *Byz* 10 (1935), 171-185.

—, 'Les Taronites à Byzance, IV,' *Byz* 11 (1936), 30-42.

—, 'L'archevêque Théophylacte et le Taronite,' *Byz* 11 (1936), 577-588.

—, 'Observations sur la généalogie ds Taronites: réponse au R.P. V. Laurent,' *Byz* 14 (1939), 407-13.

H. Ahrweiler, 'Recherches sur l'administration de l'empire byzantine à la fin du Xe siècle-début du XIe siècle et la restauration de la domination byzantine dans la peninsule balkanique,' *BCH* 84 (1960), 1-111.

—, 'La société byzantine au XIe siècle: nouvelles hiérarchies et nouvelles solidarités,' *TM* 6 (1976), 99-124.

Alexios I Komnenos, I, *Papers of the Second Belfast Byzantine International Colloquium*, eds. M.E. Mullett and D.C. Smythe (BBTT, 4.1, Belfast, 1996); *Alexios I Komnenos*, II: *Alexios I Komnenos*, II, *Works attributed to Alexios I Komnenos*, ed. M.E. Mullett (BBTT, 4.2, Belfast, forthcoming).

M. Alexiou, *The Ritual Lament in Greek Tradition* (Cambridge, 1974).

N. Amantos, 'To onoma': 'Pothen to onoma Tarchaneiotes,' *Hellenika* 2 (1929), 335-6.

M. Angold, *The Byzantine Empire, 1025-1204: A Political History* (London, 1984).

—, *Church and Society under the Comneni 1081-1261* (Cambridge, 1995).

Altman, *Epistolarity*: J. Altman, *Epistolarity: Approaches to a Form* (Columbus, Ohio, 1982).

The Byzantine Aristocracy, IX-XIII Centuries, ed. M.J. Angold (BAR IntSer, 221, Oxford, 1984).

P. Armstrong, *The Lives of Meletios of Myoupolis. Introduction, translation and commentary* (MA Diss., Belfast, 1988).

B. Baldwin, *Timarion, translated with Introduction and Commentary* (BBT, Detroit, 1984).

N. Banescu, *Les duchés byzantins de Paristrion (Paradounavon) et de Bulgarie* (Bucharest, 1946).

Barišić, 'Manastira i Struga': F. Barišić, 'Dva Gruka Natpisa iz Manastira i Struge ,' *ZRVI* 8.ii (1964), 13-31.

K. Barzos, *He Genealogia ton Komnenon*, 2 vols (Byzantina keimena kai meletai, 20, Thessalonike, 1984).

R. Beaton, 'The Rhetoric of Poverty: the Lives and Opinions of Theodore Prodromos,' *BMGS* 11 (1987), 1-28.

S. Binon, 'A propos d'un prostagma inédit d'Andronic III Paléologue. Le sens de θεῖος et de γαμβρός,' *BZ* 38 (1938), 388-93.

J. Boissevain, *Friends of Friends. Networks, Manipulators and Coalitions* (Oxford, 1974).

P.R.L. Brown, 'The Rise and Function of the Holy Man in Late Antiquity,' *JRS* 61 (1971), 80-101.

R. Browning, 'The Patriarchal School of Constantinople in the Twelfth Century,' *Byz* 32 (1962), 167-202; 33 (1963), 11-40.

G. Buckler, *Anna Comnena: a Study* (Oxford, 1929).

S. Burke, 'Writing the Self', *Authorship from Plato to the Postmodern: a Reader*, ed. S. Burke (Edinburgh, 1995), 301-339.

Byzantium and the Classical Tradition, ed. M. Mullett and R. Scott (Birmingham, 1981).

Byzantine Diplomacy. Papers from the Twenty-fourth Spring Symposium of Byzantine Studies, Cambridge, March 1990, ed. J. Shepard and S. Franklin (SPBS, 1, Aldershot, 1992).

F. Cairns, *Generic Composition in Greek and Roman Poetry* (Edinburgh, 1972).

A. Carile, 'Il problema della identificazione del cesare Niceforo Briennio,' *Aevum* 38 (1964), 74-83; 43 (1969), 56-87.

F. Chalandon, *Les Comnène, I, Essai sur le règne d'Alexis I Comnène* (Paris, 1900).

J.C. Cheynet, 'Manzikiert: un désastre militaire?' *Byz* 50 (1980), 410-438.

—, *Pouvoir et contestations à Byzance 963-1250* (ByzSorb, 9, Paris, 1990).

D.I. Chrestides, 'Echidnai kai lakideis,' *Hellenika* 41 (1990), 118-120.

G. Dagron, 'Minorités ethniques et religieuses dans l'Orient byzantin a la fin du Xe et au XIe siècle: immigration syrienne,' *TM* 6 (1976), 117-216.

J. Darrouzès, *Épistoliers byzantins du Xe siècle* (AOC, 6, Paris, 1960).

—, 'Notes de littérature et de critique,' *REB* 18 (1960), 179-84.

—, *Nicétas Stéthatos, Opuscules et lettres* (SC, 81, Paris, 1961).

—, *Documents inédits d'ecclésiologie byzantine* (AOC, 10, Paris, 1966).

—, *Georges et Dèmètrios Tornikès, Lettres et discours* (Le monde byzantin, Paris, 1970).

—, *Recherches sur les ὀφφίκια de l'église byzantine* (Paris, 1970).

—, 'Un recueil épistolaire du XIIe siècle: Académie Roumaine cod. gr. 508,' *REB* 30 (1972), 199-229.

—, *Notitiae episcopatuum ecclesiae constantinopolitanae. Texte critique, introduction et notes* (Géographie ecclésiastique de l'empire byzantin, 1, Paris, 1981).

G. Dennis, *The Letters of Manuel II Palaeologus* (DOT, 4, CFHB, 8, Washington, DC, 1977).

I. Djurić, 'Teofilakt Okhridski pod šatorom Arona,' *ZRVI* 27/28 (1989), 69-91.

A. Dostál, 'Les relations entre Byzance et les Slaves (en particulier les Bulgares) au XIe et XIIe siècles du point de vue culturel,' *XIII IntCong* (Oxford, 1966), 167-175.

A. Ducellier, *La façade maritime de l'Albanie au moyen âge: Durazzo et Valona du XIe au XVe siècle* (HetMakSp, 177, Thessalonike, 1981).

I. Dujčev, 'L'umanesimo di Giovanni Italo,' *SBN* 5 (1939), 432-436.

E. Fenster, *Laudes Constantinopolitanae* (MiscByzMonac, 9, Munich, 1968).

J. Ferluga, *Byzantium on the Balkans. Studies on the Byzantine Administration and the Southern Slavs from the VIIth to the XIIth Centuries* (Amsterdam, 1976).

J.V.A. Fine, *The Early Medieval Balkans: A Cultural Survey from the Sixth to the Late Twelfth Century* (Ann Arbor, 1960).

S. Fish, *Is there a Text in this Class? The Authority of Interpretive Communities* (Cambridge, Mass. and London, 1980).

M. Foucault, 'What is an Author?' tr. J.V. Harari, *Textual Strategies: Perspectives in Post-structural Criticism* (Cornell, 1979), 141-160, repr. P. Rabinow, *The Foucault Reader* (Harmondsworth, 1984), 101-120.

A. Fowler, *Kinds of Literature: an Introduction to the Theory of Genres and Modes* (Oxford, 1982).

C. Galatariotou, *The Making of a Saint. The Life, Times and Sanctification of Neophytos the Recluse* (Cambridge, 1991).

P. Gautier, 'L'épiscopat de Théophylacte Héphaistos, archevêque de Bulgarie. Notes chronologiques et biographiques,' *REB* 21 (1963), 159-178.

—, 'Le dossier de Manuel Straboromanos,' *REB* 23 (1965), 168-204.

—, 'Monodie inédite de Michel Psellos sur le basileus Andronic Doucas,' *REB* 24 (1966), 153-170.

—, 'Le chartophylax Nicéphore: oeuvre canonique et notice bibliographique,' *REB* 27 (1969), 159-195.

—, 'L'obituaire du typikon du Pantocrator,' DOP 27 (1969), 235-262.

—, 'Diatribes de Jean l'Oxite contre Alexis Ier,' *REB* 28 (1970), 5-55.

—, 'La curieuse ascendance de Jean Tzetzès,' *REB* 28 (1970), 207-220.

—, 'Le synode de Blachernes (fin 1094), Étude prosopographique,' *REB* 29 (1971), 213-284.

—, *Michel Italikos, Lettres et discours* (AOC, 14, Paris, 1972).

—, 'Les lettres de Grégoire, higoumène d'Oxia,' *REB* 31 (1973), 203-227.

—, 'Le typikon du Christ Sauveur Pantocrator,' *REB* 32 (1974), 1-145.

—, 'Défection et soumission de la Crète sous Alexis I Comnène,' *REB* 35 (1977), 215-7.

—, 'Le typikon de la Théotokos Evergétis,' *REB* 40 (1982), 5-101.

H. Gelzer, 'Ungedruckte und wenig bekannte Bistümerverzeichnisse der orientalischen Kirche,' *BZ* 2 (1893), 22-72.

—, *Das Patriarchat von Achrida* (AbhLeip, phil-hist. Kl., 20, Leipzig, 1907).

B. Granić, 'Kirchenrechtische Glossen zu den vom Kaiser Basil II dem autokephalen Erzbistum von Achrida verliehenen Privilegien,' *Byz* 12 (1937), 395-415

C. Graux, *Essai sur les origines du fonds grecs de l'Escurial* (Paris, 1880).

J. Grigoriades, *Studies in the Language and the Literary Style of the Epitome historion of John Zonaras* (PhD Diss., St Andrews, 1996).

E. Grubgeld, *George Moore and the Autogenous Self. The Autobiography and Fiction* (Syracuse, NY, 1994).

V. Grumel, 'Remarques sur le Dioptra de Philippe le Solitaire,' *BZ* 44 (1951), 198-211.

R. Guilland, *Recherches sur les institutions byzantines*, 2 vols (Berlin and Amsterdam, 1967).

R. Hercher, *Epistolographi graeci* (Paris, 1873).

J. Herrin, 'Realities of Byzantine Provincial Government, Hellas and Peloponnesos, 1180-1205,' *DOP* 29(1975), 267.

B.N. Hill, *Patriarchy and Power: Imperial women from Maria of Alania to Maria of Antioch* (PhD Diss., Belfast, 1994).

History as Text: The Writing of Ancient History, ed. Averil Cameron (London, 1989).

W. Hörandner, *Theodoros Prodromos, Historische Gedichte* (WByzSt, 11, Vienna, 1974).

A. Hohlweg, *Beiträge zur Verwaltungsgeschichte des oströmischen Reiches unter den Komnenen* (MiscByzMonac, 1, Munich, 1965).

Homo Byzantinus: Homo Byzantinus. Papers in Honor of Alexander Kazhdan, ed. A. Cutler and S. Franklin=DOP 46 (1992), 37-46.

H. Hunger, 'On the Imitation (MIMHCIC) of Antiquity in Byzantine Literature,' *DOP* 23-24 (1969-1970), 28-29.

Iliada godini od vostanieto na Komitopulite i sozdava njet na Samuilavata drzava, ed. M. Apostolski, S. Antoljak, B. Panov (Skopje, 1971)

R. Janin, 'Le monastère de la Théotocos Peribleptos à Constantinople,' *Bull. de la section historique de l'Acad.Roum.,* 26 (1945), 192-201.

R. Janin, *La géographie ecclésiastique de l'empire byzantin*, I, *La siège de Constantinople et le patriarchat oecuménique*, III, *Les églises et les monastères de l'empire byzantin* (Paris, 1969).

P. Joannou, 'Eustrate de Nicée: trois pièces inédites de son procès (1117),' *BZ* 47 (1954), 358-378.

M. Jugie, 'La vie et les oeuvres d'Euthyme Zigabène,' *EO* 15 (1912), 215-225.

G. Karlsson, *Idéologie et cérémonial dans l'épistolographie byzantine*, 2nd edn. (Uppsala, 1962).

M. Kaplan, *Les hommes et la terre à Byzance du VIe au XIe siècle: propriété et exploitation de sol* (ByzSorb, 10, Paris, 1992).

A. Kazhdan, *Sotsial'nyi sostav gospodstvuiushchego klassa v. Vizantii XI-XII vv* (Moscow, 1974).

— with G. Constable, *People and Power in Byzantium. An Introduction to Modern Byzantine Studies* (Washington, DC, 1982).

—, 'The Image of the Medical Doctor in Byzantine Literature of the Tenth to the Twelfth Centuries,' *DOP* 38 (1984), 44-51.

— and S. Franklin, *Studies on Byzantine Literature of the Eleventh and Twelfth Centuries* (P&PP, Cambridge, 1984).

—, 'The Social Views of Michael Attaleiates,' Kazhdan and Franklin, *Studies On*, 23-86.

— and A. Epstein, *Change in Byzantine Culture in the Eleventh and Twelfth Centuries* (The Transformation of the Classical Heritage, 7, Berkeley and Los Angeles, 1985).

K.M. Konstantopoulos, *Byzantiaka molybdoboulla tou en Athenais Ethnikou Nomismatikou Mouseiou* (Athens, 1917).

V. Kravari, *Villes et villages de Macédoine occidentale* (Realités byzantines, Paris, 1989).

G. Kustas, *Studies in Byzantine Rhetoric* (Analekta Vlatadon, 13, Thessalonike, 1973).

S.P. Kyriakides, 'Byzantinai Meletai, IV, Boleron,' *EEPT* 3.1 (1939), 267-596.

A. Laiou, 'Imperial Marriages and their Critics in the Eleventh Century: the Case of Skylitzes,' *Homo Byzantinus*, 165-176.

S. P. Lampros, *Kerkyraika anekdota ek cheirographon Hagiou Orous, Kantabrigias, Monachou kai Kerkyras, nun to proton demosieuomena* (Athens, 1882).

S. Lampros, 'Ho Markianos Kodix 524,' *NE* 8 (1911), 3-59; 123-192.

—, 'Symmikta,' *NE* 16 (1922), 115-123.

M. Lascaris, 'Sceau de Radomir Aaron,' *BS* 3 (1931), 404-413.

V. Laurent, 'Sceau de protonotaire Basile Kamateros,' *Byz* 6 (1931), 253-272

—, *Les bulles métriques dans la sigillographie byzantine* (AOC, 2, Athens, 1932), repr. from *Hellenika* 4 (1931)-8 (1935).

—, 'Légendes sigillographiques et familles byzantines,' *EO* 31 (1932), 177-187; 327-349; 437-438; 35 (1936); 80-81.

—, 'La généalogie des premiers Paléologues,' *Byz* 8 (1933), 125-149.

—, *La collection Orghidan* (Paris, 1952).

—, 'Étienne Chrysoberges, archevêque de Corinthe,' *REB* 20 (1962), 214-218.

—, *Le corpus des sceaux de l'empire byzantin*, V.2, *L'église* (Paris, 1965).

B. Leib, 'Un basileus ignoré: Constantin Ducas (r. 1074-1094),' *BS* 17 (1956), 341-359.

P. Lemerle, *Cinq études sur le XIe siècle byzantin* (Le monde byzantin, Paris, 1977).

Ia.N. Liubarskii, *Mikhail Psell. Lichost' i tvorchestvo k istoriivizantiiskogo predgumanizma* (Moscow, 1978).

G. Litavrin, *Bolgariia i Vizantiia v XI-XII vv.* (Moscow, 1960).

—, 'Tmutorakan': G. Litavrin, 'A propos de Tmutorakan,' *Byz* 35 (1965), 221-234.

S. MacCormack, *Art and Ceremony in Late Antiquity* (The Transformation of the Classical Heritage, 1, Berkeley, 1981)

R. Macrides, 'Perception of the Past in the Twelfth-Century Canonists,' *To Byzantio kata ton 12 aiona: kanoniko, dikaio, kratos kai koinonia*, ed. N. Oikonomides (Hetaireia Byzantinon kai Metabyzantinon Meleton, 3, Athens, 1991), 589-599.

P. Magdalino, *The Empire of Manuel I Komnenos, 1143-1180* (Cambridge, 1993).

C. Mango, *Byzantine Literature as a Distorting Mirror* (Inaugural Lecture, University of Oxford, 1975).

—, 'The Development of Constantinople as an Urban Centre,' *XVII Int.Cong.* (New York, 1986), 117-136.

—, 'Twelfth-century Notices from Cod.Christ Gr. 53,' *JÖB* 42 (1992), 221-228.

M. Mathieu, 'Irène de Hongrie,' *Byz* 23 (1953), 140-42.

—, 'Cinq poésies byzantines des XIe et XIIe siècles,' *Byz* 23 (1953), 129-142.

—, *Guillaume de Pouille, La geste de Robert Guiscard* (Testi, 4, Palermo, 1961).

Men/Women of Letters, ed. C.A. Porter (Yale French Studies, 71, New Haven, 1986).

G. Mercati, 'Gli aneddoti d'un codice bolognese,' *BZ* 6 (1897), 126-143.

G. Moravcsik, *Die Tochter Ladislaus des Heiligen und das Pantokrator-kloster in Konstantinopel* (Budapest and Constantinople, 1923).

C. Morris, *The Discovery of the Individual 1050-1200* (London, 1972).

R. Morris, *The Byzantine Church and the Land in the Tenth and Eleventh Centuries* (DPhil Diss., Oxford, 1978).

—, 'The Political Saint of the Tenth and Eleventh Centuries,' *The Byzantine Saint*, ed. S. Hackel (Studies Supplementary to Sobornost, 5, London, 1981), 43-50.

—, *Monks and Laymen*: R. Morris, *Monks and Laymen in the Byzantine Empire, 843-1118* (Cambridge, 1995).

A Moustoxidi, *Illustrazionzi corciresi*, II (Milan, 1814).

M.E. Mullett, 'The Classical Tradition in the Byzantine Letter,' *Classical Tradition*, ed. Mullett and Scott, 75-93.

—, 'Aristocracy and Patronage in the Literary Circles of Comnenian Constantinople,' *Aristocracy*, ed. Angold, 173-201.

—, 'Byzantium, a Friendly Society? ' *P&P* 118 (1988), 3-24.

—, 'Writing in Early Mediaeval Byzantium,' *The Uses of Literacy in Early Mediaeval Europe*, ed. R. McKitterick (Cambridge, 1989), 156-185.

—, 'The Language of Diplomacy,' *Byzantine Diplomacy*, ed. J. Shepard and S. Franklin (SPBS, 1, Aldershot, 1992), 203-216.

J. Nesbitt, 'The Rate of March of Crusading Armies in Europe: a Study and Computation,' *Traditio* 19 (1963), 167-181.

— and N. Oikonomides, *Catalogue of Byzantine Seals at Dumbarton Oaks and in the Fogg Museum of Art*, I (Washington, DC, 1991), II (Washington, DC, 1994).

N. Oikonomides, 'Le serment de l'impératrice Eudocie (1067). Un épisode de l'histoire dynastique de Byzance,' *REB* 21 (1963), 101-128.

—, *Les listes de préséance byzantins des IXe et Xe siècles* (Le monde byzantin, Paris, 1972).

D. Papachryssanthou, 'La date de la mort du sébastokrator Isaac Comnène, frère d'Alexis I, et de quelques événements contemporains,' *REB* 21 (1963), 250-255.

A Papadopulos, *Versuch einer Genealogie der Palaiologen, 1261-1453* (Munich, 1938).

E. Papayanni, *Ta oikonomika tou engamou klerou sto Byzantio* (Athens, 1986).

Patronage in Ancient Society, ed. A. Wallace-Hadrill (London, 1989).

Patrons and Clients in Mediterranean Society, ed. E. Gellner and J. Waterbury (London, 1977).

S.M. Pelekanides, *Byzantina kai Metabyzantina Mnemeia tes Prespas* (Thessalonike, 1966).

L. Petit, 'Le synodicon de Thessalonique,' *EO*, 18 (1918), 236-254.

B. Pike, 'Time in Autobiography,' *Comparative Literature* 28 (1978), 326-342.

D. Polemis, 'When did Psellos die?' *BZ* 58 (1965), 73-75.

—, *The Doukai. A Contribution to Byzantine Prosopography* (University of London Historical Studies, 22, London, 1968).

B. Prokić, *Die Zusätze in der Handschrift des Johannes Skylitzes, codex vindobonensis hist. graec. LXXIV. Ein Beitrag zur Geschichte des sogennanten westbulgarischen Reiches* (Munich, 1906)

W.M. Ramsay, *The Historical Geography of Asia Minor* (Royal Geographical Society Supplementary Papers, 4, London, 1890).

R. Romano, *Pseudo-Luciano, Timarione, Testo critico, introduzione e traduzione, commentario e lessico* (Byz et NeohellNeap, 2, 1974).

—, *Nicola Callicle, Carmi, Testo critico, introduzione e traduzione, commentario e lessico* (Byz et NeohellNeap, 8, 1980).

E. Rostagno and N. Festa, 'Indice dei codici greci Laurenziani non compresi nel catalogo del Bandini', *Studi italiani di filologia classica*, 1 (1893), 129-232.

S. Runciman, 'The End of Anna Dalassena,' *AIPHOS* 9 (1949), 207-221.

—, 'The First Crusaders' Journey across the Balkan Peninsula,' *Byz* 19 (1949), 207-221.

E. Sargologos, *La vie de Saint Cyrille le Philéote, moine byzantin (+1110)* (SubsHag, 39, Brussels, 1964).

G. Schlumberger, *Sigillographie de l'empire byzantin* (Paris, 1884).

W. Seibt, *Die Skleroi: eine prosopographisch-sigillographische Studie* (ByzVind, 9, Vienna, 1976).

—, 'Joannes Skylitzes. Zur Person der Chronisten,' *JÖB* 25 (1976), 81-85.

I. Ševčenko, 'Three Paradoxes of the Cyrillo-Methodian Mission,' *Slavic Review*, 23 (1964), 226-236.

J. Shepard, 'Another New England? Anglo-Saxon Settlement on the Black Sea?' *BS-EB* 1 (1974), 18-39.

B. Skoulatos, *Les personnages byzantins de l'Aléxiade. Analyse prosopographique et synthèse* (Louvain, 1980).

I. Snegarov, *Istoriia na Okhridskata arkhiepiskopiia*, I (Sofia, 1924).

A. Sonny, 'Das Todesjahr des Psellos und die Abfassungszeit der Dioptra,' *BZ* 3 (1897), 602-603.

R.W. Southern, *St Anselm and his Biographer. A Study of Monastic Life and Thought, 1059-1130* (Cambridge, 1963).

—, *Medieval Humanism and Other Studies* (Oxford, 1970).

—, *Anselm. A Portrait in a Landscape* (Cambridge, 1990).

J. Spatharakis, *The Portrait in Byzantine Illuminated Manuscripts* (Leiden, 1976).

G. Stadtmüller, 'Zur Geschichte der Familie Kamateros,' *BZ* 34 (1934), 352-358.

P. Stephanou, 'Le procès de Léon de Chalcédoine,' *OCP* 9 (1943), 5-64.

Stephanos. Studia byzantina ac slavica Vladimiro Vavřínek ad annum sexagesimum quintum dedicata= BS 56 (1995).

L. Sternbach, 'Nicolai Calliclis Carmina,' *Rosprawy Academii umijetnosci Wydziat filogiczny* (Cracow, 1904), 315-392.

L. Stiernon, 'Notes de prosopographie et de titulature byzantines, 1-5': 'Constantin Ange,' *REB* 19 (1961), 273-283; 'Adrien (Jean) et Constantin Comnène, sébastes,' 21 (1963), 178-198; 'A propos de trois membres de la famille Rogerios,' 22 (1964), 184-198; 'Sébaste et gambros,' 23 (1965), 222-243; 'Theodora Comnène et Andronic Lapardas, sébastes,' 24 (1966), 89-96.

V. Tiftixoglu, 'Gruppenbildungen innerhalb des konstantinopolitanischen Klerus während der Komnenenzeit,' *BZ* 72 (1969), 25-72.

P. Tivčev and G. Cankova-Petkova, 'Au sujet des relations féodales dans les territoires bulgares sous la domination byzantine à la fin du XIe et durant la première moitié du XII siècle,' *BB* 2 (1966), 107-125.

M. Treu, *Nicephori Chrysobergae ad Angelos orationes tres* (Programm der Königsliche Friedrichsgymnasiums zu Breslau, Breslau, 1892).

E.T. Tsolakes, 'Aus dem Leben des Michael Attaleiates,' *BZ* 58 (1965), 3-10.

F. Uspenskii, *Obrazovanie vtorogo Bolgarskogo tsarstva* (Odessa, 1879).

V.G. Vasilievskii, rev. Uspenskii, *Obrazovanie, Zhurnal ministerstva narodnogo prosveshcheniia*, 204 (1879), 144-217, 318-348.

S. Vryonis, *The Decline of Medieval Hellenism in Asia Minor and the Process of Islamization from the Eleventh through the Fifteenth Century* (Berkeley, Los Angeles and London, 1971).

V. Weichert, *Demetrii et Libanii qui feruntur typoi epistolikoi et epistolimaioi charakteres* (Leipzig, 1910).

G. Weiss, *Oströmische Beamte im Spiegel der Schriften des Michael Psellos* (MiscByzMonac, 16, Munich, 1973).

S. Wittek-de Jongh, 'Le césar Nicéphore Bryennios, l'historien et ses ascendants,' *Byz* 23 (1953), 463-468.

G. Zacos and A. Veglery, *Byzantine Lead Seals*, I (Basel, 1972).

D. Zakythinos, 'Meletai peri tes dioiketikes diareseos kai tes eparchiakes dioikeseos en to byzantino kratei,' *EEBS* 16 (1941), 208-274; 18 (1948), 42-62; 19 (1949), 3-25.

M. Živojinović, 'Le prologue slave de la vie de l'impératrice Irène,' *ZRVI* 8 (1964), 483-492.

V.N. Zlatarsky, *Istoriia na Bulgarskata durzhava prez sriednitie viekove*, 3 vols (Sofia, 1918-40).

—, 'Namestnitsi-upraviteli na Bulgariia prez tsaruvaneto na Aleksiia I Komnin,' *BS* 4 (1932), 139-158; 371-398, with German summary.

INDEX

Numbers in bold and in parentheses refer to the network number in *The Network*, above, 347-381

Discussions of individual letters are indexed into *The Collection*, above, 291-346

Aaron, brother of tsar Samuel, 58
accuser of consecrated persons (71), 194
administration
  civil, 59-63, 129-130
  ecclesiastical, 64-66
  military, 19, 60 n.256
Adrian Komnenos (41), Grand Domestic,
  130, 145, 184, 188, 214, 215
Adriatic, 54, 55
'adventus' letter, see letters, Byzantine, types
  of
Aelfgyva, 19 n.40
agriculture, 44, 66, 67, 131
agroikia and barbarismos, (rusticity),
  complaints of, 118, 256-257, 260, 274-276
Ailred of Rievaulx, 114
akolouthia, 101, 271
aktouarios, 108, 110
Albania, 55, 56, 57
Alberic of Monte Cassino, 134
Alexander of Macedon, 25
Alexander of Nicaea, 104, 250, 252-253
Alexandria, 41
Alexios I Komnenos (77), emperor, 25, 52,
  69-78, 176, 189
  attributed works: Mousai, 78; speech
  against an Armenian, 78, 239-243; prayer,
  78
  opposition to, 52-53
  reconquest expedition (1092), 82, 85-86
  tax-reforms of (1106-09), 221
  travels of, 88 n.43
Alexios III Angelos, emperor
  chrysobull of (1198), 61
Alexios Doukas (213), 377
Alexios Komnenos, doux of Dyrrachion
  (1107), 94
Alexios, protostrator, builder of Manastir-
  Prilep, 67
Altman, Janet, 13, 20, 289 n.50
anametresis, 95, 213
anagraphe, 96, 212
Anaplous, monastery at
  ex-hegoumenos (111) of, 38-39, 143
  monk (104) of, 35, 190
  monks (118) of, 174, 189
Anatolia, 46, 47, 260

Anatolian communities, exile of, 258
Andronikos Doukas (224), 76
Andronikos Kamateros, Hiera Hoplotheke,
  74, 241
Anemas brothers (202-205), 191
Ankyra, 90, 258 and n.176, 259
Anna Arbantenissa (206), 376
Anna Dalassene (120), 40, 51, 88 n.43, 193,
  196
Anna Doukaina (210), 377
Anna Doukaina (211), 377
Anna Komnene (217), 40, 54, 70-71, 110,
  191, 285
  Alexiad, 72-73, 87, 200
Annales-school history, 7
anonymous schoolmaster, 42
Anselm, 41, 108, 113, 114
  letter-collections, 115
  friends, 115-117
  friendship, 119-120
  friendship and the letter, 121-122
Anthony, St, 106
Apollonios of Gaza, 275
archon, 62, 63, 129, 265, 282
Arethas, 158
Aristides, 42
Aristotle, 77
Armenians, 46, 56
  conversion of, 90, 127, 239-243, 263-264,
  265; see Alexios I Komnenos, speech
  against an Armenian
army, 86, 97, 126-127
'arrival letter', see letters, Byzantine, types
  of
ars dictaminis, 134
Artemios, St, 110
astrology, 100
astronomy, 71
Athanasios, patriarch of Constantinople, 12
Athos, Mt, archives of, 61
Attica, 201
augousta, 80 n.43
Augustine, St, 41, 121
author
  birth and death of, 223-227
  implied, 223
  in the text, 225, 284

auctor, 224-225
autobiography, 76, 283-288

Bačkovo, monastery of Theotokos
 Petritziotissa at, 67
Bagora, Mt, 54, 88
barbarismos, see agroikia
Bari, 443
Basil II, emperor
 Sigillia, 64-66
Basil the Bogomil, 73
Basil the Great, St, 10, 14, 15, 16, 17, 25, 33,
 37, 42, 103, 105, 112, 113, 124, 141
Basil Pediadites, metropolitan of Kerkyra,
 252
Basil, metropolitan of Reggio, 252
bearers (112), 189; in general *see* letter,
 Byzantine
Belebousdion, 64 n.268
Belgrade, 57, 58, 65 n.269
 bishop of, 260
Bible, 100, 160, 225, 274
big basilicas, 67 n.281
biography of medieval persons, possibility
 of, 260
bishops
 absenteeism of, 262
 careers of, 255 n.158
 election of, 263-264
 morale of, 264-265
 pastoral care of, 262 n.206
 problems of suffragans, 128
 problems with suffragans, 128-129
 resignation of, 286-287
 transfers (*metathesis* and *epidosis*), 259
 n.182
Blachernai, 51
Bogomils, 56, 59, 127 n.225, 271
 Bogomil trial, 73 n.307
Bohemond of Taranto, 82, 87, 88, 93 n.62,
 264
Boiana, church of SS Nicholas and
 Panteleemon, 68
Boissevain, Jeremy, 166, 172, 186
Boleron-Strymon-Thessalonike,
 theme of, 60, 61, 62 and n.265
 doux of, 62

Bolkan, 59, 93
books, *see* literacy
Boris, tsar of the Bulgars, 236, 237
Bothrotos (diocese of Ochrid), 65 n.270
Breanotes or 'of the Vlachs' (diocese of
 Ochrid), 66 n.272
Bryennios family, 214
Bulgaria,
 alleged hellenisation of, 266-267
 definition of, 54-57
 local administration of, 59-63
 pattern of fortresses in, 61-62
 prosperity of, in eleventh and twelfth
 centuries, 67
 revolts against Byzantine rule, 57-59
 Second Bulgarian Empire, 59
Bulgarians, 58, 127, 130, 150, 233, 261, 267-
 274
 gerontes (108, 109), 265, 271, 275

caesar, 48, 51, 86, 143, 169, 213
calumny, 16-18
 crisis, 214-215
 Theophylact's problems with, 132
Candavian chain, 56
candlelight, in church, 100
Cavafy, Constantine, 1 n.2, 282-283
ceremony, 52 n.215, 133 n.249
chartophylax of the Great Church, 17, 58,
 84, 128, 129, 143, 150, 194, 215
Chimaira (diocese of Ochrid), 64-65 n.269
Choirovachi, 88 n.43
Christodoulos, St, of Patmos, 53 n.220
 Life of, 75
Christopher of Mitylene, 229
Chrysoberges (26), metropolitan of
 Naupaktos, 97, 118, 174, 185
classics, use of in Byzantium, 6, *see*
 Theophylact, letter-collection
client, *see* patronage
communication problems, 84 n.26, 122
 n.201, 132, Table V
communication theory, 31 n.93, 39
consolatio (paramythetike), 33, 125, 138-144,
 220
Constantine IX Monomachos, emperor, 48,
 49

Constantine X Doukas (65), emperor, 44, 174, 194
Constantine Bodin, 58-59
Constantine Choirosphaktes (75), 36, 74, 147, 189
Constantine Doukas (36), 83 n.24, 94-95 n.70, 96, 147, 187, 204, 212
Constantine Komnenos (12), 184-5
Constantine Manasses, *Hodoiporikon*, 45, 227, 254
Constantine Stilbes, 257 n.171
Constantinople, 16
  attraction of, in eleventh century, 45-46, 254, 257-258
  capture by Fourth Crusade (1204), 255
  churches:Theotokos of Blachernai, 51; Theotokos of Chalkoprateia, 50; Theotokos Hodegetria, 76
  monasteries, 50
    Christ Pantokrator, 75; St George in Mangana, 49; archimandrite (231) of, 192; 253; SS Kosmas and Damian (Kosmidion), 49, 283; St Mokios, 49; Theotokos Peribleptos, 49, 108
  patriarchate of, 269
  praises of, 44-45
context, historical, invention of, 226
court doctors, theologians, etc, 74
Crusade, First, 83, 85, 92, 126, 184
Crusaders, 57
Cumans, 56, 59, 126, 264, 270
  invasions (1095), 87
Cyril Phileotes, St (232), 88 n.43, 194
  Life of, 75, 256

Dalmatia, 54, 63
Damascus, 158
Damnastes, 111
Danube, 54, 57
Darrouzès, Jean, 12, 111, 123, 259
death, 139-140
  death genres, 140-141
  death of the author, *see* author
Deabolis, *see* Diabolis
Debra, 66 n.272
  bishop of (58), 92, 128, 186, 264
Demetrios Hephaistos (1), brother of

Theophylact, 20, 36, 119, 173, 174, 177, 182, 184, 185, 196, 197, 200
  death of, 91-94, 119, 182, 243-247
Demetrios Kritopoulos (79), and his brother (80), 19, 190, 204
Demetrios Kydones, 40
Demetrios Tornikes, 256 n.166
demosion (fisc), 99, 130-131, 287
Derrida, Jacques, 4, 5, 224 n.4, 228
despoina, 88 n.43
Devol *see* Diabolis
Diabolis (Deabolis, Devol), 66 n.272, 88 n.43, 237
  administrative centre at, 55, 62
  as forward base in Norman wars, 56
  bishop of, *see* Michael of Diabolis
  church at, 128, 236
  'refreshing' at, 205, 236
  treaty of (September 1108), 88 n.43
  valley of, 56
Diabologyres (35), bishop, 127, 186, 240, 265
didaskalos ton iatron, 108, 110
Digenes Akrites, 47, 51, 76, 255
  Grottaferrata version, 76
Diogenes plot (summer 1094), 87
Diokleia, 58
doctors under Komnenoi, 108-111, *see also* court
Dokeiane (209), 75
Doukas family, 47, 51, 196
doux, 33, 58, 62, 86, 94, 99, 128, 129, 130 n.235, 187, 204, 205, 213
  of Bulgaria at Skopje, 62
Drin valley, 56
Dristra, 33, 65 n.270
Dryinopolis (diocese of Ochrid), 65 n.270
Dyrrachion, 58, 61
  doux of, 33, 94-95, 128, 129, 187, 204, 205; *see also* Alexios Komnenos, John Doukas, John Bryennios (34), John Komnenos
  metropolitan of, 64
  theme of, 62

Eadmer, 115, 116, 121
Edessa, bishop of (124), 197

Eirene Doukaina (**37**), 40, 70, 75, 88 n.43, 96-97, 150, 188, 194

Eirene Doukaina (**212**), 377

Eirene Komnene, *sebastokratorissa*, 40, 70

Eirene Piroska Komnene, *augousta* (**218**), 378

Eirene-Eulogia Choumnaina Palaiologina, 13 n.7, 197

Ekbatana, *see* Susa

Ekklesiai, 55, 57, 92, 97
  case of, 95-96, 212-213 and fig. 6
  villagers (**116**) of, 189

eleventh century, prosperity of, 44
  as time of rapid social change, 221

epi ton deeseon (**57**), 189

epistolary novel, 13, 19

Erasmus, 230 n.33

Euboia, 204, 205
  relatives (**113**) of Theophylact in, 189, 200, 201

Euchaita, 257

Eudokia Komnene (**219**), 75

Eumathios (**94**), 19, 190

eunuchs, 197, 228, 240, 246
  eunuch, libidinous (**68**), 194, 197
  eunuch praktor (**110** ?=**120**), 130, 197, 213

Euripides, *Orestes*, 275-276

Eustathios Boilas, 285

Eustathios of Thessalonike, *De emendanda*, 45

Eustratios of Nicaea (**237**), 71, 73, 88, 241-242

Euthymios Malakes, 260 n.183

Euthymios Tornikes, 14, 16, 255 n.164

Euthymios Zigabenos (**236**), 194
  Panoplia dogmatike, 74, 241-2; manuscripts of, 74

Euthymios, metropolitan of Sardis, 263 n.217

Euthymios, monk of Peribleptos, 241

exkousseia (exemption), 64, 131

extortion, 19, 131

feudalism, Byzantine, 7

fiction, revival of, in eleventh century, 76-77

First Crusade, 83, 85, 92, 126-127, 184

fisc, *see demosion*

fish, 55, 56, *see* letters, Byzantine, gifts with

formalism, Russian, 4

fortifications, 58-59, 87 n.38

Foucault, Michel, 21, 223, 230-231

friendship, 105, 111-123
  ancient ideas of, 112 and n.145
  Anselm and Theophylact, on, 114-123
  and patronage, 177-178
  detecting, 115
  east and west, 113-114, 168-169
  in letters, 111-112
  instrumentality, 177, 188-189, 214-215

frogs, 21, 145-146, 269-270

Gautier, Paul, 10, 24, 30, 172, 235, 239

genre analysis, 20-23
  inclusion, 22
  kind, 20, n.44
  mode, 20, n.44
  objections to, 246-247
  type, 20, n.44

geometry, 100

George Akropolites, 254

George Bardanes, 255 n.164, 257

George Maniakes, 58

George Pachymeres, 227

George Palaiologos (**45**), 96, 188, 212

George of Pisidia, 229

George Tornikes (**235**), 12, 27, 104, 109, 173, 194

George Vojteh, 58

Geranios, 88 n.43

Gerbert of Rheims, 41, 113

Germanos, St, 69, 233

Gerontios of Lampe, 72

gifts, *see* letters, Byzantine, gifts with
  diplomatic, 32, n.98

Glavenitsa, 65 n.269, 275
  bishop (**100**) of, 128, 138, 188, 264-5

Grand Domestic, 96, 124, 145, 169, 188, 214, 270

Grand *droungarios* of the Watch, 83 n.21, 118, 159, 183, 184

Grand *oikonomos* (**56**), 185

grasshoppers, 91 n.57, 153 n.358

Gregory Akyndinos, 12
Gregory Antiochos, 255 n.161
Gregory of Ankyra, 104
Gregory Kamateros (4), 36, 76, 83 n.24, 87,
    89, 94, 97, 100, 118, 136, 138, 150,
    175, 182-183, 213, 214, 215
Gregory Kamateros (40), bishop, 150, 264
Gregory of Nazianzos, 14, 15, 25, 26, 33,
    42, 103, 104, 105, 107, 122, 148-149, 158
Gregory of Nyssa, 15, 26
Gregory, hegoumenos (240) of Oxeia, 194,
    256
Gregory Pakourianos (15), 94, 130, 146,
    175, 186, 215, 276
Gregory Taronites (48), 19, 83 n.23, 84, 87,
    91, 150, 175, 176, 188, 205, 212, 234-235
Gregory, psaltes (95), 100, 190, 197
Grevena, 66 n.271
grieving person (69), 194
Gryke e Ujkut pass, 56

hagioserretai (115), case of, 128-129, 189
Harvey, Alan, 95, 131, 221
Hellas, 54, 260
Hellas-Peloponnese, theme of, 61
Hephaistos family, 173
Herbert de Losinga, 41
heresy, 72-74, 127-128, 240
Hermogenes, 50, 158, 159
Hierotheos monachos, 15, 26, 105
Hilarion, metropolitan of Mesembria, 260
hodoiporikon, 22
holy men, entertainment of, 70
Homer, 25, 159, 160
ho paron anthropos (106), 190
hospitals, 109 n.134
ho tou, indicating episcopal nephew,
    260
Hungarians, 58, 59
hypatos ton philosophon (consul of the philo-
    sophers), 49, 71, 271
hypogrammateuon, 94, 214

Iasites (76), praktor, 19, 127, 130, 188,
    214
Ignatios of Nicaea, 113
immoral hieromonk (107), 127, 189

Ioannina, 54, 65 n.270
Isaac I Komnenos, emperor, 110, 285
Isaac Komnenos (78), sebastokrator, 74, 84
    n.30, 143, 188
Isaac Komnenos (222), 378
Isaac Mesopotamites, 80 and 81-82 n.16
Isidore of Pelousion, 42

Jerome, St, 230-231
John II Komnenos (122), emperor, 45, 194
John VI Kantakouzenos, emperor, 40, 227
John VIII Xiphilinos, patriarch of
    Constantinople, 48
John IV (V) the Oxite, patriarch of
    Antioch, 52, 255, 258
    speeches, 75
John Apokaukos, metropolitan of
    Naupaktos, 255 n.164, 260
John Arbantenos (207), 76
John Attaleiates (33), 175, 189, 214
John Bryennios (34), 33, 34, 95, 147, 187,
    214
John Cassian, 114, 119
John Chortasmenos, 40
John Doukas, caesar, 48
John Doukas (38), 53, 82, 84 n.28, 94, 187,
    201, 204, 234
    and reconquest, 86
John Geometres, 275
John Italos, 49, 52, 71
    trial of, 70, 77
John Kamateros, 257 n.171
John Komnenos (42), son of the
    sebastokrator, 7, 33, 75, 86, 94, 126,
    147, 187, 201, 236
John Mauropous, 14, 15, 17, 36-37, 38, 45,
    254, 257
John Mesarites, 257 n.171
John Opheomachos (6), 118, 119, 147, 148,
    183, 200, 276
John Pantechnes (16), 84 n.28, 185
John Peribleptenos (17), 106, 108, 118, 184,
    186
John Phournes, 71-72 and n.301
John Serblias (47), 188, 205
John Skylitzes (227), 49, 54, 191, 238
    Historiai, 272, see also John Thrakesios

John Taronites (49), *doux* of Skopje, 187-188
John Thrakesios, Grand *droungarios* of the
  watch, 83 n.21, *see also* John Skylitzes
John Tzetzes, 12, 33, 253
John Xiphilinos the younger,
  hagiographical collection, 74
John Zonaras (228), 191
John (54), *grammatikos* of Palaiologos, 83
  n.24, 189, 212
John (30), *maistor*, 118, 182, 186
John (31), philosopher, 118, 182, 186, 215
John (96), the good, 93, 186
jokes, 19, 159 n.388
Joseph Rakendytes, 42
Julian, emperor, 17, 41, 105-106, 275

Kanina, 55, 66 n.272, 97
kanonikon, 131, 204
Kastamon, 45, 52
Kastoria, 55, 64 n.269
  lake of, 55
  churches: Mauriotissa, 67-68
  bishop of, 263
kastroktisia, 131
kastroktistes, 18, 126, 127, 147
katepano, 18, 126, 127, 147
katepano-doux, 59
Kazhdan, Alexander, 109, 129, 167 n.27,
  175, 246, 290
Kekaumenos, 45, 51, 54, 71, 76, 285
Keos, 16
kinship
  non-kin relationships expressed in
    language of kinship, 173: ἀδελφός, 93-94,
    173-4; υἱός, 175-177, 186
  ritual kinship, 165, 176
  spiritual kinship, 176
  structure, 168
Kittaba (Kitsevo), 275
  case of, 95, 205
Kitros, bishop of (9?=126), 33, 85, 92, 108,
  118, 184, 244
klerikos, 64, 131
Komnenos dynasty, rule of, 52
  reconquest, 85-86, 187
  reform, 52
  repression, 71-73

Komnenos family, 51, 195, 213; *see* Adrian,
  Alexios, Anna etc
  dispute among (1093), 83, 86
Koprinista, 265
Koritsa, 56
kouboukleisios, 157
Kozile (diocese of Ochrid), 65 n.270
krites ton Drougoubiton, 63
kyklos, 70

Larissa, 54, 58
  metropolitan of, 64
language, 268-269, *see also* Theophylact,
  language of
Latins, 114
Laud, archbishop, 230 n.33
law, 49
Lazaros (97), *paroikos*, 19, 66, 85 n.34, 127,
  131, 132, 188, 214
  crisis, 150, 214, 270-271
Leo Choirosphaktes, 250-251
Leo, archbishop of Ochrid, 67
Leo, metropolitan (238) of Chalcedon, 52,
  212
Leo, metropolitan of Syn(n)ada, 12, 113
Libanios, 10, 40, 42
letters, ancient, 15, 32-33, 123 n.207, 137
  n.267, 162 n.5
letters, Byzantine
  as birdsong, 26 and n.68
  as consolation, 14 n.12
  as dew, 25, 28, 122
  as feast, 26, 122
  as flowers, 26
  as gift from God, 27, 123
  as golden chain, 29
  as honey, 26, 118, 122
  as icon of the soul, 26, 105-106, 260, 281
  as Jacob's ladder, 29
  as medicine, 25, 28, 106
  as models of style, 42-43
  as music, 25-26
  as pearl, 29
  as phoenix, 28
  as second best, 14 n.12
  as spring, 29
  as wings to a runner, 122

bearer (*komistes*) of, 31, 34-37, 38-39
bilocation, and, 29
calumny and, 17-18, 132
characteristics expected of
  brevity (*syntomia*), 149-151; *metron*, 149,
  151; clarity (*sapheneia*), 151-159;
  obscurity (*asapheia*), 156-159; grace
  (*charis*), 159-161
collections of model letters, 41
confidentiality of, 16-17
discourse, reciprocity of, 85
dispositio of, 134, 159
documents in, 101
epistolarity of, 134
events in, 18-19, 85-98
everyday problems in, 123-133
failure in communication through, 27, 132
forms of address in, 168-172
from and to women, 197 n.139
genre and, 20-22; inclusion of genre in, 22-
  23
gifts with, 32-34: cinnamon, 33; fish, 32-
  33, 56, 97; lettuce, 32 n.98
journeys in, 15-16, 132, Table X
letter-collections and, 19-20, 40-43
letter-writing, 10, 287-288
medical imagery in, 106
obscurity in, 156-159
parables in, 118, 159
physical appearance of, 32
political function of, 17, 18 n.32
proverbs in, 159
quotations in, 100 n.99, 160
riddles in, 159
seasonality of, 97-98
separation and, 13-15, 248
sickness in, 102-108
silence and, 27
structure of, 160-161
subjects of, 148
third persons in, 18-19 and n.37
types of, 148
  Typoi epistolimaioi, 135-148
  'adventus' letter, 94, 125, 144, 146-148,
  199, 210; 'arrival' letter, 88, 125, 144-146,
  211; consolatio, 125, 139-144, 213;
  hodoiporikon, 22; thanks, 212

vacuity (supposed) of, 23-24, 125
visit by, 15
letters, late antique, 14-15, 33, 41, 112-113,
  249
letters, medieval Latin, 13, 41, 108, 114-123,
  134
letters, views of
  Johnson, Dr Samuel, 281
  Moore, George, 283 and n.19
  Newman, Cardinal, 260
  Scott, Sir Walter, 20
letter-writers, Palaiologan, 16 n.24
Lipenion (Lipainion, Lipljan), 62, 65 n.269
  bishop of (101), 89, 128
literacy practices, Byzantine, 101, 118
  active reading, 39, 101-102, 134, 162
  book-exchange, 34, 99, 178 and n.107, 261
  books, recommended by Theophylact,
  101-102, 263
  books, used by Theophylact: medical
  books, 34, 108; Chrysostom, 34, 276;
  Symeon the New Theologian, 34;
  Galen, 99, 160; Hippocrates, 99; *Peri
  Hermeneias*, 99, 111, 148, 149, 275
  documents cited by Theophylact, 101
literature
  change in, 243-244
  evaluation of, 30 n.90, 228, 285
  persona in, 275 n.3
literature, Byzantine
  alleged inferior nature of, 1-2
  as distorting mirror, 3
  as privileged text, 3, 4
  change in, 247-248
  genres of: *epibaterion*, 88, 125, 144-146,
  213; *epitaphios*, 140; *hodoiporikon*, 22;
  monodia, 140; *paramythetikon*, 125, 138-
  144, 220; *prosphonetikon*, 94, 125, 144,
  146-148, 204, 212; *threnos*, 140
  horizon of expectations of readers of, 11
  interpretative communities of, 2-3
  mimesis in, 135
  originating conditions of, 11
  progymnasmata, 135; *ethopoiia*, 43
  social localisation and, 167
  treatment of death, 137-144
  treatment of exile, 248-260

literature, Komnenian
  autobiography, 76-77, 282-288
  basilikos logos, 232-235
  exile discourse, 248-260, 277-280
  fiction, revival of, 47, 76-77, 280-281
  florilegia, 227
  hagiography, 9, 22, 235-239, 281, 285
  kyklos, 68, 70
  letter-collections, 12-13, 41 and n.156
  panoply of heresies, 74
  parainesis, 76, 125, 128, 147-148, 233 n.53
  politikos stichos, 78
  prose and verse, roles of, 281
  religious polemic, 239-243
  romance, revival of, 76-77
  satire boom, 77, 110 n.137, 280 n.8
  schedography, 50
  theatron, 39-40, 53
  vernacular, use of, 78
local governors, 129-130
logariastes tou genikou, 94
logothete of the *sekreta*, 94
Longinos, 134

Macedonia, 55, 58, 126, 204
  estates in, 67
Macedonia-Thrace, theme of, 61
Machetares (13), 118-119
maistor ton rhetoron, 8, 43, 99, 146, 233 and
  n.50, 271
Makrembolites (14), *archon* of Prespa, 89,
  159, 190
Makrembolites (82), 129, 188
Malesova, bishop of (102), 64 n.269, 190,
  263
Manastir-Prilep, church of St Nicholas (now
  Theotokos), 67
Manuel II Palaiologos, emperor, 10, 12, 40,
  227
Manuel Straboromanos (234), speeches of,
  75, 254
manuscripts
  Acad.roum.gr.508, 42
  Coislin.21, 262
  Coislin.79, 228
  Harvard gr. 3, 227
  Ivoires 100, 227

Laur.acquisti 39, 42 n.160
Laur.gr.6.26, 277
Laur.gr.10.13, 79, 81
Laur.gr.59.12, 79, 80, 85
Lavra Ω 136, 42
Lincoln.gr.35, 228
Matrit.gr.vitr.26.2 (Madrid Skylitzes), 17,
  18 n. 32, 31, 34, 37, 39
Monac.gr.442, 227
Mosq.gr.387, 74
Mosq.gr.4443, 241
Paris.gr.74, 228
Paris.gr.1277, 92
Paris.gr.2144, 228
Paris.suppl.gr.103, 70, 99 n.96
Paris.suppl.gr. 219, 277
Paris.suppl.gr.309, 227
Paris.suppl.gr.1200, 80
Patmos 706, 42
Petrop.gr.250, 80
Reginae suecorum, 98
Sinai gr.364, 228
Vat.gr.432, 79, 81
Vat.gr.666, 74, 228
Vat.slav.2, 227
Vind.hist.gr.53, 227
Vind.hist.gr.91, 227
Vind.phil.gr.49, 227
Vind.theol.gr.90, 243
Vind.theol.gr.242, 229
Manzikiert, 44, 47
Maria of Alania (50), *basilissa*, 34, 36, 51, 70,
  88 n.43, 96, 150, 184, 188, 196, 213, 232,
  261, 271
Maria the Bulgarian (51), *protovestiaria*, 74,
  188, 194, 212
Maria Komnene (220), 378
maternity, praise of, 51
Maximos Confessor, St, 70, 286
Medenos (83), 370
medicine, 71, 102-111, 261
Meletios of Myoupolis, St (239), 53 n.220,
  194
  Lives of, 75
Menander rhetor, 21, 45, 135, 233, 285 n.30
Mestos, 88 n.43
Michael IV, Paphlagon, emperor, 50

Michael VII Doukas, emperor, 48
Michael VIII Palaiologos, emperor, 284
Michael *ho tou Anchialou*, 241, 256 n.166
Michael Antiochos (120?=110), 130, 194, 204, 243
Michael Attaleiates, 48, 239
Michael Autoreianos, 257
Michael Beses Lampenos (81), 19, 190, 204
Michael *ho tou Chalkedonos* (52), 189, 205, 275
Michael Choniates, metropolitan of Athens, 14, 229 and n.29, 254, 257, 260 n.183, 266, 274, 276
Michael of Diokleia, 59
Michael Doukas (39), *protostrator*, 75, 88, 96, 188, 212
Michael Doukas (216),
Michael Gabras, 12
Michael Glykas, 256
Michael Italikos (215), 12, 40, 55, 108, 113, 122, 141, 191, 241
Michael ?Lizix (223), 191
Michael Pantechnes (7), 17, 34, 94, 107, 118, 119, 123, 126, 136, 138, 144, 150, 175, 182, 183, 191, 196, 215, 271, 275
Michael son of Polyeuktos (92), 19, 190
Michael Psellos (84), 10, 14, 26, 40, 43, 45, 48, 49, 51, 53, 71, 77, 84 n.28, 88, 99, 105, 110, 111, 113, 136, 138, 158, 167, 176, 189, 228-229, 257, 285
  brother of (46), N, 138, 143
  grandson of (85), N, 136, 138
Michael bishop of Diabolis (Devol), 238-239, 272
Mogila, 63
  archaia aule, possibly *aule* and *hospition* at, 66
  case, 94, 205
Moglena, 55, 56, 64 n.269, 127 n.225
Mokros, 88
  Mokrenoi, 126
monasteries, 128-129, 205
  foundation of, 50
  stauropege, 128-129, 205
Morava-Branitsova (Branicevo), bishop of, 65 n.269, 263
music, in church, 100

Naupaktos, 129
  metropolitan of, 272
Neilos of Calabria, 72, 240 (??=)
Neilos, monk (67), 130, 194, 204, 243
Neophytos the recluse, of Cyprus, 225 n.11, 256
neoplatonism, 78
network analysis, 163
  brokerage, 201, 204
  centrality, 165, 200
  density, 165, 200
  intimacy zones, 179
  transactions, 164, 186
  see also Theophylact, network of
nephew, episcopal, *see ho tou*
New Criticism, 4, 223, 279
New Historicism, 4
Nicaea, 254
Nicholas I Mystikos, patriarch of Constantinople, 12
Nicholas III Grammatikos (43), patriarch of Constantinople, 28, 125, 186, 258 n.173
Nicholas IV Mouzalon, patriarch of Constantinople, 259 n.182
  resignation poem of, 76, 248, 286-287
Nicholas Adrianoupolites (201), 191
Nicholas Anemas (2), 34, 83, 94, 118, 121, 147, 159, 183, 275-276
Nicholas *ho tou Boutou* (93), 19, 190, 204
Nicholas Chrysoberges (74), 174, 200
Nicholas Kallikles (3), 34, 84 n.27, 92, 107, 108, 118, 136, 159, 167, 179, 183, 196, 244, Fig. 3
  poems of, 75
Nicholas Kataskepenos, *Life of Cyril Phileotes*, 75, 256
Nicholas Mermentoulos (5), 83, 101, 103, 118, 121, 183, 271, 275
Nicholas Skleros (226), 191
Nicholas (66), deacon and *kanstresios* of Hagia Sophia, Constantinople, then bishop of Malesova (?=102), 175, 196
Nicholas (8), metropolitan of Kerkyra, 18, 34, 83 n.23, 89 n.48, 90, 99, 118, 182, 191, 196, 243, 254, 265
  resignation, poem of, 76, 89 n.48, 286

Nicomedia, 16, 87, 97
Nikephoritzes, 48
Nikephoros Basilakes, rebel, 59
Nikephoros Blemmydes, 257, 288
Nikephoros Bryennios (11),
    panhypersebastos then caesar, 35, 40, 88,
    184,196, 214, 215, 243
    Hyle Historias, 47, 76
Nikephoros Bryennios, rebel, 59
Nikephoros Diogenes (208), 191
Nikephoros Gregoras, 40
Nikephoros Melissenos (44), caesar, 33, 84
    n.30, 143, 188, 204, 274
    recruiting mission (1091), 86, 126, 204
Nikephoros (23), *chartophylax*, 17, 71, 83
    n.23, 150, 185
Niketas *ho tou Chalkedonos* (53), 175, 189,
    203, 212, 214
Niketas Choniates, 12, 181, 227, 257
    Thesauros tes orthodoxias, 74
Niketas Eugeneianos, 168
Niketas Magistros, 142, 251-252, 282
Niketas Polites (18), 128, 137, 138, 265
Niketas Seides, 71
Niketas *ho tou Serron* (22), 49-50, 71, 117
    n.167, 146, 174, 185, 230, 261
Niketas Stethatos (233), 49, 71, 194
Niketas (24), *chartophylax*, 185, 192
Niketas (32), imperial doctor, 107-108
Niketas, metropolitan of Ankyra, 255
    n.163, 255
Nikopolis, 58, 228
Niš, 56, 58
nobelissimos, 94
Norman war, second, 82, 87, 92, 94, 95, 98,
    126, *see also* Diabolis
number-symbolism, 33 n.105

Ochrid, 16, 53, 54, 56, 92, 126, 129, 130,
    132, 270
    =Prima Justiniana, 272
    archbishops of, 53, 124
    archdiocese of, administration of, 64-69,
    262-266
    archiepiskope of, Hagia Sophia, 68, 268
    arrival of Theophylact in, 145-146
    bishop's palace, not found, 66

    bishops of (119), 189
    citizens of, 127, 270
    cults of, 68-69, 273
    hermit-caves at, 68
    lake of, 55, 56
    privileges of, 269
    rest and recruitment centre in Norman
    wars, 62
    scriptorium of, 69, 269
    theme of ('small fiscal'), ('small
    military'), 63, 94
    'village of church in', case of, 96 and n.79,
    213-214
    wine of (thin), 67
oikonomos, 49, 157, 186, 231
Oraia, 65 n.270
Ovid, 279, 281
oxysacchari, 92

panegyris, 55, 97, 239, 270
Paristrion, 61, 63
paroikos, 64, 66, 67, 95, 128, 131
parresia, 147
past, the, 226 n.13, 272-274 and n.272
patronage, of painting, 67-69
patronage, personal, 145, 176, 177-178
    client, power of in, 222
    maintenance of, 204, 215
    multiple patrons in, 221
    reciprocity in, 221
Paul Smyrnaios (88), 174, 190, 200
Paulicians, 56
Paulinus of Nola, 112
Pechenegs, 56, 59, 235
    war with (1047-50), 58
Pelagonia, 55, 65 n.269, 88 n.43
    bishop of (10), 101-102, 118, 137, 138, 184,
    220, 240, 264, 265
    plain of, 56
    theme of ('small fiscal'), 63
    Theophylact and, 97, 131
Pentegostis (estate of *basilissa* Maria), 96
personal relationships, *see* friendship, kin-
    ship, patronage
personal relationships, analysis of
    affect, 177, 184, 189
    directional flow, 164

interaction, frequency and duration, 164
multiplexity, 179, 182, 188, 200
reciprocity, 185
symmetry, 164, 185, 188, 189, 200, 221
transactional content, 164, 187, 201
Peter of Blois, 114
Peter Deljan, 58
Peter Grossolano, visit of (1112), 73, 239
   and n.76
Peter the Venerable, abbot of Cluny, 108,
   115, 167
Peter (25), *chartophylax*, 185, 215
Petros/Petrai (diocese of Ochrid), 65 n.270
   bishop of (125), 376
Philetos Synadenos, 253, 275
Philip the solitary, *Dioptra*, 76
Philippopolis, disputations at (1114), 73-74,
   88, 127 n.224, 238
   archbishop of, 88
philosophy, 49, 99-100 and n.97
Photios, patriarch of Constantinople, 43
   n.163
   Bibliotheke, 21
Pindos mountains, 54
pittakion, 36, 101, 205
politikos stichos, 78
polo, 100
Pologos, 63
   priests (114) of, 189
   case of priests of, 128, 204
Poloske plain, 56
Pontos
   campaigns of Gregory Taronites in, 87
   exile of John Chrysostom in, 249
praktor(s), 124, 126, 127, 131
Prespa, 55, 58, 63, 94, 205
   archon of, 63, 129, 186
   church of Hagios Achilleios, 27-28, 38, 68,
      89, 128 n.226, 237-240
   cult of Hagios Achilleios, 273
   Megale Prespa, lake of, 56
   Mikre Prespa, lake of, 56, 237
   panegyris of Hagios Achilleios, 91, 97
   'refreshing' of, 205, 236-237
   synod of, 89-91, 234
Princes' islands, 16, 22, 50
Prisdiana, bishop of, 65, 263

Prizren, 58
Procopius of Caesarea, 55
Procopius of Gaza, 40, 107
proedros, 109 n.135
proskynesis, 147
prostagma, 101, 130
prostaxis, 101, 151
protasekretes, 94
protostrator, 67, 69, 75, 76, 88, 95, 173, 189,
   210; and the canons, case of, 212 and fig. 6
protovestiaria, 188
proximos, 110
psaltes, 129
Psellos (46), brother of Michael, 138, 143
Psellos (85), young relative of Michael, 136,
   138, 190
Psyllos, 88 n.43
Ptochoprodromos, 107 n.127, 280
pupils of Niketas *ho tou Serron* (117), 188
pupils of Theophylact (62), 187
   Bulgar (63), 187

Rasos, 65 n.269
Raška, 59
reading, *see* literacy
recipient of G106 (61), 186-187
reform, Komnenian, *see* Komnenos, dynasty
repression, Komnenian, *see* Komnenos,
   dynasty
reconquest, Alexian, *see* Komnenos, dynasty
resignation of bishops, 286-287
rhetoric, 49-50, 77, 133
   under Alexios I Komnenos, 77
Rhodope mountains, 55
Richard of the Principate, 87
riddles, 152 and n.348, 155
roads, 55-57
Robert Guiscard, 59
Rodomir Aaron (64), 194, 243
Roger *sebastos* (229), 379-380
Romanos III, Argyros, emperor, 50
Romanos IV Diogenes, emperor, 77
Romanos Straboromanos (90), 129, 205
Royal road, 56
rusticity, *see agroikia*

sakellarios, 242-243

Samuel, tsar of Bulgarians, 54, 57, 61, 238-239
Šar Planina, 56
schedography, 50-51
schoolmaster, anonymous, 42
schools, 42, 50
sebastokrator, 7, 71, 75, 84, 86, 143, 188,
seal of Theophylact, 37
seasons, 84 nn.27-28, 97
sebastos, 20, 22, 29, 94, 169, 178
Seljuk invasion, 90
Semnea, bishop of (28), 185
Senachereim (86) and emulator (87), 130, 190
Serbs, 59, 91 n.58
Serbo-Dalmatian wars (1093-94), 86, 91 n.58, 204
Servia, 54, 62, 65 n.270
  basilica of, 67
Side, metropolitan of (99), 36, 48, 190, 201-203
Sidonius Apollinaris, 113, 119
sigillia, 101, 236
Silva Bulgarorum, 57
Sirmion-Serbia, 61-62
  diocese of Sirmion, 65 n.269
Skopje, 36, 57, 58, 64 n.269
  doux of, 129
  presence of emperor in 1093 in, 91 n.58
Skopje-Bulgaria, theme of, 61
Skylitzes Continuatus, 238 n.72
Slopimos, 88 n.43, 92 n.61
smells, Bulgarian, 270
Smyrnaios (89), relative of Theodore Smyrnaios, 84 n.27, 136-137, 188
soldier saints (Demetrios, George, Theodore), 51
Souda, 21
Spaneas, 76
Stagoi (Kalambaka), 66 n.271
Stephanites and Ichnelates, 76
Stephen Magnetes, 111
Stephen-Symeon the Sanctified (230 ? = 123), 380
Sthlanitsa, 66 n.272, 275
Štip, *archon* of, 63
strategos, 19, 59, 60, 62, 204

strougai, 131
Strumitsa, 62, 65 n.269, 88 n.43, 92 n.61
  bishop of (103), 190
  cathedral church of St Leontios, *see* Vodoča
  monastery of Theotokos Eleousa at Veljusa, 67, 92 n.61
Strymon, river, 54, 57
Susa and Ekbatana (compared to Theophylact's residence), 66-67, 132
Sykutres, Ioannes, 12
Symeon Blachernites (72), 130, 190
Symeon Magistros, 26, 105, 113, 157
Symeon Metaphrastes, 38
Symeon Seth, 49, 111
  Stephanites and Ichnelates, translation of, 76
Symeon the New Theologian (301), 49, 99 n.96, 184, 194, 243, 285
Symeon the Sanctified (230 ? = 123), *see* Stephen
Symeon (29), *hegoumenos* of Anaplous, 83 n.23, 143, 185, 194
Symeon, *hegoumenos* of a monastery of eunuchs on Athos (123 ? = 230), 375
Symmachus, 23
synekdoche, 246, 289
Synesios, 13, 14, 33, 37, 40, 42
synod of Blachernai (1094), 83, 87, 183, 201, 262, 286
synods, local, 90
  of Prespa, 89-91, 237-239
Synodikon of Orthodoxy, 72
synodos endemousa, 74, 90 n.53, 258-260
Syntipas, translation of, 76

Tarchaneiotes (21), 119, 176, 185, 240
tax(es), 99, 125, 131
taxis, 37
themes
  'large old', 62
  'little fiscal', 61
  'little military', 61
Theodora Komnene (221), 194
Theodore Balsamon, 90, 256 n.166, 259
Theodore Bestes, revision of the *Nomokanon*, 74
Theodore Blachernites, 73

Theodore Chryselios (**73**), 19, 100, 150, 190

Theodore Daphnopates, 12

Theodore of Kyzikos, 107, 253

Theodore Prodromos (**225**), 45, 55, 107 n.127, 122, 191, 194, 254, 256

Theodore Smyrnaios (**20**), 50, 71, 76, 77, 83 n.23, 99, 117, 121, 145-146, 161, 174, 185, 261

Theodore, *hegoumenos* of Stoudios, 113

Theodore, metropolitan of Nicaea, 157

Theodosios (**98**), 190

Theodotos II, patriarch of Constantinople, 104

Theodoulos (**27**), metropolitan of Thessalonike (? = **127**), 185, 197

theologians, incompetence of, 72 n.302, 73 n.309

Theophilos, emperor, 77

Theophylact Hephaistos, archbishop of Ochrid
  as churchman, 114 and n.152, 261-266
  as client, 177, 221-222
  as scholar, 8-9, 43
  as teacher, 8, 43, 49, 186, 233
  birth of, 8, n.53
  education of, 8, n.55, 43
  family of, 189, 200; in Euboia, 200, 201; brother of, *see* Demetrios; spurious brother of, 92 n.60
  friends of, 117-118; doctors as, 87, 107-108, 118; Constantinopolitan in Bulgaria, 117-118;
  household of, 35, 68; member of (**105**), 190
  illnesses of, 96-7, 131 n.240; as hypochondriac, 96, 103; catarrh and cough, 103; fever, 102; pain in side, 97, 102; sciatica, 96; seasickness, 94, 103
  in Constantinople, 262
  journeys, 36, 55 n.233, 127 n.222, 132 and Table X
  language of, 271-272
  Nachleben of, 229-230
  network of, personal cell, 179-184; intimate zone, 177, 184-186; effective zone, 177, 186-189; nominal zone, 177, 189-190; extended zone, 177, 188-195

patris of, 8 n.55

patrons of, maintenance of, 204, 215-220, 222; recycled, 187, 204; when to use, 201, 215

powerlessness, apparent, of, 222 and n.573

Theophylact, letter-collection of, 79-80
  arrangement, 80-82
  biblical personages in: Beliar, 18, 19, 93; Daniel, 124, 132, 160, 260; Job, 160; Jonah, 160; Samson, 124, 160, 261; Solomon, 160
  biblical quotations in, 100, 160
  classical quotations in, 99-100, 113, 122, 145, 146, 147, 159, 160, 248
  dating of, 82-85
  forms of address in, 168-172, 183, 184-185
  mythological personages in, Alkmaion, 118 n.177, 159; Argos, 160; Asklepios, 108; Briareus, 18, 124, 160; Charybdis, 18, 160; Cyclops, 19, 124, 147, 274; Echo, 159; Euroklydon, 124, harpies, 99, 274; Herakles, 124, 145, 146, 189, 265; hydra of Lerna, 124, 130; Kalliope, 272; Laestrygonians, 124, 147, 274, 286; Machaion, 107; Medea, 27; Muses, 160; Nestor, 160, 260; Orestes, 147, 160, 275; Orpheus, 26; Ossa on Pelion, 145; Paieon, 107, 108, 159; Podaleiros, 107; Polyphemos, 19; Sirens, 26; Scylla and Charybdis, 124 n.213, Tantalos, 159; Typhon, 18, 124; Zeus, eagle on sceptre of, 145-146
  not correspondence, 98
  quotation, use of, in, 160
  separation of, in mss, 82

Theophylact, works of, 8-9, 69-70, 231
  bedfellows of, in mss, 80 n.9
  Commentary on the *Acts of the Apostles*, 9
  Commentary on the *Epistles*, 9, 34-35, 43, 229, 231
  Commentary on the *Gospels*, 9, 196, 229, 243
  Commentary on the minor prophets, 9, 196
  Life of St Clement, 235-237
  Martyrion of the fifteen martyrs of

Tiberioupolis, 235-237
In Defence of Eunuchs, 9, 196, 236, 240, 280
On the Errors of the Latins, 8 n.59, 9, 196, 239-240
On the liturgy, 9, 125
poems, 243-246; anacreontics, 245; iambics, 101, 245; dating, 69-70 and n.291
To Alexios (basilikos logos), 53, 232-234
To Constantine (Paideia basilike), 232-234
Theophylact Romaios (19), 175, 186
Theoreianos, 253 n.166
Thessalonike, 16, 62, 96, 103
　emperor on campaign in, 88 n.43, 92
　metropolitan of, 64, 129, 272
　oikidion where Theophylact stayed and stored things, 66, 126
　rest and recruiting centre during Norman wars, 62
Thessaly, 58
Thrace, 58
Tibanios/Tigranes the Armenian (55), 98, 127, 187, 239-243
Timarion, 77, 183, 255
titles of offices and dignities
　aktouarios, 108, 110
　archon, 62, 63, 129, 265, 282
　augousta, 80 n.43
　caesar, 48, 51, 86, 143, 169, 213
　chartophylax of the Great Church, 17, 58, 84, 128, 129, 143, 150, 194, 215
　despoina, 88 n.43
　didaskalos ton iatron, 108, 110
　doux, 33, 58, 62, 86, 94, 99, 128, 129, 130 n.235, 187, 204, 205, 213
　Grand Domestic, 96, 124, 145, 169, 184, 188, 214, 270
　Grand *droungarios* of the Watch, 83 n.21, 118, 159, 183, 184
　Grand *oikonomos*, 185, 231
　hypatos ton philosophon (consul of the philosophers), 49, 71, 271
　hypogrammateuon, 94, 214
　kastroktistes, 18, 126, 127, 147
　katepano, 18, 126, 127, 147
　katepano-doux, 59
　krites, 63

logariastes tou genikou, 94
logothete of *sekreta*, 94
maistor ton rhetoron, 8, 43, 146 and n.50, 99, 233, 271
nobelissimos, 94
oikonomos, 49, 157, 186
proedros, 109 n.135
protonotarios, 99
protostrator, 67, 69, 75, 76, 88, 95, 173, 189, 210, 212
protovestiaria, 188
proximos, 110
protasekretes, 94
sakellarios, 243
sebastokrator, 7, 71, 75, 84, 86, 188, 143
sebastos, 20, 22, 29, 94, 169, 178
strategos, 19, 59, 60, 62, 204
Tornikes crisis (1047), 45
Tornikes family, 12
Tornikios (91), relative of Theophylact, 190
travel, 15-16, 36, 132
Triaditsa, 56, 64 n.269
　bishop of (59), 17, 35, 39, 43, 91, 106, 127, 132, 150, 185, 212, 240, 265; Theophylact's dispute with, 84 n.29, 89-90, 128
　theme ('small fiscal') of, 63
typikon, 3, 228, 284, 285
Tzachas, emir of Smyrna, 234
Tzernikos (diocese of Ochrid), 65 n.270

Vardar, river, 55, 56, 57, 87, 88, 93, 100, 272, 274
village (?=Ekklesiai ?=Asprai Ekklesiai ?=Eccliso), 66, 87
　case of, 95-96, 212-213
　rule of, 94, 129, 204
Veroia, 36, 62, 66 n.272
　basilica of, 67
　doux of, 129, 205
verse, political, 78
Via Egnatia, 56
Vidin, 16, 65 n.269, 128, 275
　bishop of (60), 57, 87, 161, 186, 264
Vlachs, 56, 58,
　bishop of, 66 n.272
Vodena, case of, 205

Vodoča, church of St Leontios, 68
Veljusa, *see* Strumitsa

wars
  campaigns against Serbs and Dalmatians,
    (1093, 1094), 86, 91 n.58
  Cuman invasions (1094-95), 82-83
  Nicomedia campaign (1095), 87
  Pontic campaigns of Gregory Taronites
    (1103), 87
  second Norman war (1105-08), 81, 82, 87-
    88, 92-93, 126
'wicked slave' (70), 194

women,
  in Theophylact's network, 197
  letters from and to, 197 n.537
  mother-power in the 1080s, 51, 212 and
    n.172
  patronage of literature by, 40 n.151

Zacharias, *kouboukleisios* of the *oikonomos*,
  correspondent of Theodore of Nicaea,
  157
zeugarion, 131
Zygon, 54, 59, 87 n.38